CAMBRIDGE LIBRARY COLLECTION

Books of endurin

Hist

The books reissued in this series includ
movements by eye-witnesses and conte
studies that assembled significant source materials or developed new
historiographical methods. The series includes work in social, political and
military history on a wide range of periods and regions, giving modern
scholars ready access to influential publications of the past.

Annals of the Reformation and Establishment of Religion

The English ecclesiastical historian John Strype (1643–1737) published the
second volume of his monumental Elizabethan religious history *Annals
of the Reformation* in 1725. For over two and a half centuries it remained
one of the most important Protestant histories of the period and has been
reprinted in numerous editions. Volume 2 Part 1 covers the years 1570 to
1575. It focuses on the Queen's use of parliament; royal relations with the
episcopate and nobility; various ecclesiastical commissions; threats from
Rome; religious polemics; difficulties with Mary Queen of Scots; diplomacy
with Spain, France, Germany, the Netherlands and Scotland; the pressures on
the Queen to marry and the printing of the Bishop's Bible. Strype's thorough
use of primary sources and the enormous scope and detail of his history has
ensured its place as an outstanding work of eighteenth-century scholarship. It
should be read by every student of Elizabethan religious history.

Cambridge University Press has long been a pioneer in the reissuing of out-of-print titles from its own backlist, producing digital reprints of books that are still sought after by scholars and students but could not be reprinted economically using traditional technology. The Cambridge Library Collection extends this activity to a wider range of books which are still of importance to researchers and professionals, either for the source material they contain, or as landmarks in the history of their academic discipline.

Drawing from the world-renowned collections in the Cambridge University Library, and guided by the advice of experts in each subject area, Cambridge University Press is using state-of-the-art scanning machines in its own Printing House to capture the content of each book selected for inclusion. The files are processed to give a consistently clear, crisp image, and the books finished to the high quality standard for which the Press is recognised around the world. The latest print-on-demand technology ensures that the books will remain available indefinitely, and that orders for single or multiple copies can quickly be supplied.

The Cambridge Library Collection will bring back to life books of enduring scholarly value (including out-of-copyright works originally issued by other publishers) across a wide range of disciplines in the humanities and social sciences and in science and technology.

Annals of the Reformation and Establishment of Religion

*And Other Various Occurrences
in the Church of England, During Queen
Elizabeth's Happy Reign*

VOLUME 2 – PART 1

JOHN STRYPE

CAMBRIDGE UNIVERSITY PRESS

Cambridge, New York, Melbourne, Madrid, Cape Town, Singapore,
São Paolo, Delhi, Dubai, Tokyo, Mexico City

Published in the United States of America by Cambridge University Press, New York

www.cambridge.org
Information on this title: www.cambridge.org/9781108018005

© in this compilation Cambridge University Press 2010

This edition first published 1824
This digitally printed version 2010

ISBN 978-1-108-01800-5 Paperback

ANNALS

OF

THE REFORMATION

AND

ESTABLISHMENT OF RELIGION,

AND OTHER VARIOUS OCCURRENCES

IN THE

CHURCH OF ENGLAND,

DURING

QUEEN ELIZABETH'S HAPPY REIGN:

TOGETHER WITH

AN APPENDIX

OF ORIGINAL PAPERS OF STATE, RECORDS, AND LETTERS.

BY JOHN STRYPE, M.A.

A NEW EDITION.

VOL. II. PART I.

OXFORD,
AT THE CLARENDON PRESS.
MDCCCXXIV.

THE

PREFACE.

I MUST acquaint the reader with some reasons that prevailed with me to set forth another volume of our church's history under queen Elizabeth; and what encouragement I had to take it in hand, and to proceed therein: and then to give some brief account of what I have done.

In the former volume of these Annals was shewn particularly what method was used, and what steps were taken, in that great and happy enterprise of the reformation of this church from the popish errors in doctrine and superstitions in worship, wherein it was deeply plunged in the reign of queen Mary, queen Elizabeth's immediate predecessor; and how from year to year that good work was carried on, and arrived to some joyful settlement by the twelfth year of the said glorious queen's government. But because that volume reached no farther, and so seemed to break off somewhat abruptly in the course of that history, and the reader that had gone so far in the reading of these godly proceedings would probably be willing to know more of the progress thereof, and how it went on, I was moved to prosecute the said purpose: and that this distinguishing favour of God to this land might remain on eternal record; and for posterity to know, how the divine blessing accompanied, from year to year, along that queen's reign, that noble work of delivering prince and people from the usurped tyranny of Rome; and advancing the true knowledge and free profession of the gospel among us: and that, amidst all the opposition, plots, and endeavours, both at home and abroad, from time to time, to overthrow it: which ought to be had in everlasting remem-

brance by all the inhabitants of this happy island of Great
Britain.

I was also willing to comply with the desires of divers
learned men, as well of the clergy as others, studious of
our church's history; who having read the entrance and
beginning of this reformation in the former volume, would
gladly understand farther of its success, and of the events of
it afterwards; and have thought it pity so useful an history should make a final stop so soon, and go no farther.

And indeed I was loath that all my collections, which I
have for many years past been making, (for my own satisfaction,) and digesting from abundance of MSS. and original letters and records in the nation, and discovering
thence so desirable a piece of our ecclesiastical history,
should be lost. Especially also, being encouraged by the
esteem and approbation of these my pains, so publicly
given me (in the proposals for the printing this volume)
by all our pious and learned archbishops and bishops: as
also by the good opinion I have obtained from the prelates,
dignified and learned men in the other kingdom of Ireland:
which I cannot but acknowledge here, in gratitude to them
all.

That which I have done in this volume is, following the
method of the former, to set down the various occurrences
of the church under each year, as I have met with them.
Wherein observations are made of the bishops in each of
their dioceses; and of their businesses, cares, and diligence
among their respective clergy in the discharge of their function; and of the opposition, troubles, and discouragements
they met with; partly by the inconformity of some of their
clergy to the liturgy, and the custom and practice enjoined; partly by the creeping in of popish priests and Jesuits, to draw away the queen's subjects from their obedience, and for the reconciling them to popery; and partly,
by means of the endeavour of many, to rend away the revenues from their respective bishoprics.

Here is related also what was done in parliaments, (chiefly
with respect to religion,) in convocations, ecclesiastical com-

missions, and episcopal visitations; and what occurred from the endeavours of the Romanists, and other disaffected parties and factions, to undermine the church and its constitution; and what courses were taken with them from time to time, for the safety of the queen, and preserving the peace of her people.

There will be found likewise set down here divers other important matters, well worthy knowledge, concerning secular, as well as ecclesiastical affairs, in this juncture of queen Elizabeth's reign; and her concerns and transactions in that busy and dangerous time with foreign princes and states; as Spain, France, Germany, the Netherlands, Scotland; especially where religion was concerned; and being such matters as our historians have slipt over in silence; tending to the praise of that queen and her government, and of the wise counsellors about her.

There will be also met with, in the current of this history, under each year, matters more private, personal and domestic: whereby many particular things of remark will be seen; and notices of some persons of eminence, either for learning or quality, or office of trust, are given: whereby their memories are revived, and that when by this time they are almost sunk into oblivion, though men of figure in their lives-time.

I have also taken the liberty of relating something concerning literature and our universities, and of controversies arising in the colleges, and among the students there; with characters of some of the learned heads and members of the colleges there. Mention also is made of books, especially of more note, which came forth under each year. And some accounts are given of them and their authors also.

I have been wary in this work not to repeat any thing which hath been read before in any other of my writings published; unless I have done it sometimes to improve the history, or to add some enlargements and more particular accounts of what had been more briefly and imperfectly spoken of elsewhere. And where there may be in this work any omissions or defects observed, or matters more lightly touched, they will be supplied to him that will please to consult the Lives and Acts of the two archbishops of Canterbury, Parker and Grindal, contemporary with the times of this history.

In this whole undertaking I have used all faithfulness and impartiality; and set down things according as I found them in the originals, whether letters, records, registers, papers of state, or other MSS. being the imports of them, and often in the same words. So that the reader may the readier depend upon the truth of what I offer. And for the better credit to be given to me, there is an Appendix set at the end of the book: wherein are entered great numbers of useful papers and authentic writings; some taken from the king's Paper-office, others from the Cotton library, more of them from the Bene't college library; in short, many more from the best MS. libraries in the kingdom; exactly thence and carefully exemplified by my own pen from the originals.

Perhaps some of the readers of this book may esteem some matters set down there as trivial, and of little import. But I had other thoughts of them, otherwise I should not have suffered any of them to have taken place there: for oftentimes there be matters of moment depending upon things seemingly of smaller account. And on this occasion I may use the words of Mr. Madox, late of the Augmentation-office; who gave this answer to such a censurer of a book of his; viz. " That the formulas entered into his book " were some of them of little value. He desired such upon " this occasion to call to mind the several monuments of " antiquity: which at the first sight appeared of little va- " lue; but had afterwards been found to serve some not " contemptible uses: and that many things in antiquity " prove of good use to some, which to others may be of " little or no use at all."

Formular.
Anglican.
Pref.

In short, I hope this will prove an useful history. And the greatest and best use of it will be, to observe the wonderful mercy and goodness of God to us in the preservation and continuance of our excellent reformed religion through that queen's reign, against all the spite and opposition, at home and abroad, to undermine and overthrow it. The benefit and comfort whereof we enjoy to this day. For which success we are beholden under God to the said queen Elizabeth, and her watchful and steady government, accompanied with the prayers of the faithful.

JOHN STRYPE.

THE CONTENTS.

CHAP. I.

CHAP. II.

CHAP. III.

CHAP. XXXI.

CHAP. XXXII.

CHAP. XXXVI.

ANNALS

OF THE

REFORMATION OF RELIGION,

AND AFFAIRS OF THE CHURCH IN THIS KINGDOM OF ENGLAND.

FROM THE TWELFTH YEAR OF THE REIGN OF QUEEN ELIZABETH TO THE TWENTY-THIRD.

CHAP. I.

A testimonial from some in the university of Cambridge concerning Cartwright's readings. His letters to sir William Cecil concerning himself. But is discharged the college and university. Richard Greenham. Dr. Geo. Downham: the odd tempers of several of Cartwright's followers; and their affected separation. Anthony Gilbie's letter to Coverdale, &c. Exiles. Dangers from papists. The archbishop of Cassil's discovery. Steukley comes to the king of Spain. The dangerous condition of Ireland from the Spaniard and French. Caution for the Low Countries.

As in the conclusion of the former volume somewhat was Anno 1570. related concerning Cartwright, one of the public readers of divinity in the university of Cambridge, and of his deprivation for certain positions delivered in his lectures; so I shall begin this book with several other notices concerning him; being the head and most learned of that sect of dissenters then called *puritans.*

In this year, 1570, the heads of that university contended with the said Cartwright, B. D. and late lady Margaret professor, for his readings, wherein he vented his dislike of the

Animosities in Cambridge by reason of Cartwright's readings.

established discipline of the church of England, (as deviating from the primitive institution and practice,) and the habits enjoined to be worn by the ministers of it; and in effect, the whole constitution ecclesiastical. What his opinions and assertions were, have been specified in the first volume

Chap. lvii. of the Annals of the Reformation of religion. He had indeed a great party in the university, and some of them men of learning, who stuck close to him, exceedingly admiring him; though some of them, better informed, fell off afterwards. Great differences and animosities by these means were bred among the scholars; which being past the power of the heads to allay, they complained thereof to sir William Cecil, secretary of state, their high chancellor, desiring him to interpose his authority; but chiefly informing him of the unsoundness of Cartwright's late lectures.

Cartwright's favourers, their testimonial of him.
Nor were the favourers and hearers of Cartwright less forward to write their letters to the same; testifying in his behalf how sparing and tender he was in treating of those subjects, for avoiding offence; whose testimonial ran in this tenor:

Pap. office. *Percrebuit tuæ præstantiæ mag. Cartwrightum hoc esse suspectum nomine, quod in theologiæ professionis munere quosdam discordiæ igniculos, qui post in incendium creverunt, sparserit, et in controversiis de ministerio et re vestiaria omnino se immodice jactaverit. Nos vero, quorum nomina subscripta sunt, et qui illis lectionibus interfuimus, ex quibus iste rumor fluxit, testamur nullas quas unquam audire potuimus, unde simultates aut discordias emersisse; de vestibus controversiam ne attigisse quidem: de ministerio proposuisse quædam, quorum ad amussim nostrum hoc formari cupiebat, sed ea et cautione et moderatione, quæ illum debebant, merito tueri, et ab ista quæ circumfertur calumnia vindicare.*

Robertus Tower, Robertus Willan, Christoph. Kirkland, Rob. Soome, Johan. Swone, Thomas Barbar, Simon Bucke, Richard Chamber's, Richard Howland, Laurentius Washington, Thomas Aldrich, Alan Par, Johan. Still, Wilhelm. Tabor, Johan. More.

So that, if this testimony be to be relied upon, Cartwright's CHAP.
reading touched not the contest about the *garments*, but ————
only about the *ministry* ; taking occasion from some part of Anno 1570.
scripture which he read upon, to wish it reformed according to certain rules he then spake of.

Besides this testimonial, Cartwright himself pleaded his Gives ac-
own innocency in an elegant Latin letter to Cecil, (accom- count of his
readings to
panying the testimonial,) written in the month of July ; Cecil.
complaining, "How he was slandered ; troubled especially Pap. office.
" that these his slanders should reach as far as the court
" and him. Then he declared and freely professed to him, 3
" that none was so averse to sedition and the study of con-
" tention : and that he had taught nothing which flowed
" not naturally from the text which he treated of. And
" that when an occasion offered itself of speaking concern-
" ing the *habits*, he waved it. He denied not but that he
" taught, that our ministry declined from the ministry of
" the ancient and apostolical church, which he wished
" might be framed and modelled according to the purity of
" our reformation. But that he did this sedately, that none
" could find fault with it, but some ignorant or malign
" hearers, or such as catched at something to calumniate
" him. That of these things he heard he was accused be-
" fore him, their chancellor. But how false and unjust the
" reports of his reading were, he offered the testimonial
" of a great many sincere persons that were present : as-
" serting further, that he had well nigh gotten the whole
" university for the witness of his innocency ; and had not
" the vice-chancellor denied him a congregation, he doubted
" not he had obtained it. That he had not room in his let-
" ter to relate every little particular of that lecture that
" raised the rumour ; but promised the chancellor, that he
" would deny nothing to him of those things he then pro-
" posed, if he would require it. And as he refused not to
" suffer, if any real guilt were discovered in him, so, as far
" as his cause was just, he implored his patronage : praying
" him, that he would not suffer him nor the truth to be over-
" thrown by some men's hatred ; who, while they privately

CHAP.
I.

Anno 1570.

Number I.
II. III.

Another
letter of his
to Cecil.

Appeals to
him to
judge his
cause.

" hated him, had a mind to set themselves against the ho-
" nourable and glorious name of *peace* and the *church.*"
But it will give better satisfaction to read the whole letter,
as he penned it himself in his own behalf, which I have
therefore put into the Appendix. To which I have added
two letters more, written by several men of the university
to the same, in his behalf.

Cartwright wrote also another letter to Cecil, in the
month following, having been lately suspended from his
reading; which was in answer to the said Cecil, who had
humanely, in the midst of his weighty affairs, spared some
time to give some advice to him by his own hand. He
seemed to have signified to Cartwright, how his adversaries
had charged him with a factious innovating, and that he
brought into suspicion of novelty that most ancient cause
that sprung up with Christ and his apostles. But he answered, " that he was no νεοτεροποιὸς, no such *stirrer of*
" *new things;* and yet that he would not be affrighted, by
" the envy of *novelty,* from the truth. That he hoped, that
" Cecil was not of that number, that charged that proverb,
" τὰ ἀκίνητα κινεῖν, [i. e. to move things that ought not to
" be moved,] upon whosoever innovated in any thing what-
" soever. And that he knew whose words those were;
" παλαιοὺς νόμους λίαν ἁπλοῦς καὶ βαρβαρικοὺς, [i. e. that old
" laws were very weak and rude.] But he added, that he
" needed not at all to plead in the defence of novelty, since
" the cause, being almost 1570 years old, was venerable
" enough for its antiquity."

And whereas the heads had denied him the liberty of his
public reading, he complained of them to Cecil, and accused
them of injustice, since upon some conditions, which he, the
chancellor, had propounded to them, he allowed him to
read, (which conditions, notwithstanding he was willing to
comply with,) yet they would not suffer him to read again.
This was dated Aug. 18. In this letter he was very earnest
with Cecil, to hear and judge of his cause, being very willing to leave it to him. But lest that statesman might say,
that his abilities were not equal to judge in such a cause,

nor yet his leisure did permit, he urged him with this reply; "That if the cause were just, if it were necessary for
" the church, if without it the commonwealth were dis-
" solved, and the parts in danger to fly asunder from one
" another, (which without discipline must needs be,) the
" cause was worthy for him to undertake; and wherein he
" might bring forth that rare light of his own understand-
" ing, and those divine endowments of his own mind. And
" the cause would again, in recompence, embrace him, and
" render him a person, however eminent before, still more
" honourable, and however oppressed with infinite business,
" he dared to promise, would revive and refresh him, and,
" though ready to sink, would uphold him with strong and
" mighty supports." These were the overweening conceits
he had of his discipline.

I do not find any thing more done with Cartwright in the
university, being discharged of his lecture, outed the college, stopped of his degree of doctor, and silenced from
preaching in or near the university. But we shall hear of
him hereafter in his writings and attempts of setting up the
discipline in certain places in the land, which brought him
into further trouble, and restraint of his liberty, from the
ecclesiastical commission; which could not but take notice
of him, making himself the chief preacher and head of the
new form of church government. Only I must give a hint
concerning some of his zealous and well meaning followers in
Cambridge, who upon more mature deliberation afterwards
fell off from him. Two whereof I will mention among others.

One was Rich. Greenham, of Christ's college, Cambridge,
a pious and good man; whose name we see subscribed to
the earnest letters that were sent to Cecil in his commendation and the high character given him. The young men in
the university were diverted by Cartwright's readings from
the more necessary study of the grounds and principles of
divinity, and the substantial doctrines of Christianity, as
rescued from popery, to controversies of the right way and
manner of governing the church. This was afterwards
justly disliked by the said Greenham, who thought fit to

CHAP.
1.

Anno 1570.

Dr. George
Downham,
ep. before
his conse-
cration
serm. of
Montagu,
bishop of
Bath and
Wells,
anno 1608.
reprove it in the pulpit; blaming the young divines, who,
before they had studied the grounds of theology, would
overbusy themselves in matters of discipline: " and (as he
" said) before they had laid the foundation of their studies,
" would be setting up, as it were, the roof." This passage
Dr. George Downham, of the same college, tells us, he heard
himself, when he was a young student in Cambridge: who
himself consorted among the youth there of that faction
that disliked the habits, and other established ceremonies of
the church, and was a hearer of Cartwright's lectures, in
his consideration about this church of England and the dif-
5 ferences in it. Who tells us of himself what course he took;
" That at first, seeing things grew so hot, he thought it the
" best course for himself and the rest to be no meddlers on
" either side. But afterwards I considered with myself,
" said he, that this church of England, wherein I was
" called to be a minister, did hold and profess all substan-
" tial points of divinity, as sound as any church in the
" world, none excepted, neither in this age, nor in the pri-
" mitive times of the church. And, secondly, that it had
" the testimony of all other true churches. And, thirdly,
" that in it the means of salvation are ordinarily and plen-
" tifully to be had. And therefore to make a separation
" from it, I took to be schismatical, and damnable presump-
" tion."

This Greenham was alive many years after, a godly
preacher, living in London. For I find a letter of his dated
anno 1591, from Warwick-lane, London. And when in the
year 1599 his works were published by H. Holland, in his
epistle he gives this character of the pious and peaceable
spirit that was in him, (shewing, that though his judgment
in some points differed from the church established, yet he
was no separatist.) " That in his ministry he was ever care-
" ful to avoid all occasion of offence; desiring in all things
" to approve himself as the minister of Christ. He much
" rejoiced and praised God for the happy government of
" our most gracious queen Elizabeth, and for this blessed
" calm and peace of God's church and people under it.

" And spake often of it, both publicly and privately, as he CHAP.
" was occasioned; and stirred up the hearts of all men,　I.
" what he could, to pray and praise God with him for it Anno 1570.
" continually: yea, this matter so affected him, that the
" day before his departure out of this life, his thoughts
" were much troubled, for that men were so unthankful for
" that strange and most happy deliverance of our most gra-
" cious queen from the dangerous conspiracies and practices
" of that time."

The writer saith further of him, " that he was the special D. Lopez.
" instrument and hand of God in bringing many, both
" godly and learned, to the holy service of Christ in the
" ministry; and to restrain and reduce not a few from
" schism and error; striving always to retain such in obe-
" dience of laws: and thereby to esteem and regard the
" peace of the church and people of God."

To which I may add, that this party of men that thus
divided and distinguished themselves by this schism, were
observed also to divide from the rest in their behaviour, in The man-
their tempers and qualities, and in their strangeness and ner of the
behaviour
aversion from their Christian brethren who adhered to the of these
followers of
established church. For this is their character, that Dr. Cartwright.
Whitgift gave of them about this time; comparing them
unto the pharisees: " That when they walked in the streets,
" they hung down their heads, looked austerely; and in
" company sighed much, and seldom or never laughed:
" their temper was, that they sought the commendation of Brief an-
" the people: they thought it an heinous offence to wear a swer to the
Admoni-
" cap or surplice; but they slandered and backbit their tion in
" brethren, railed on them by libels, contemned superiors, latter end.
quarto, the
" discredited such as were in authority; in short, disquieted 6
" the church and state. And as for their religion, they se-
" parated themselves from the congregation, and would not
" communicate with those that went to church, neither in
" prayer, hearing the word, nor sacraments: they despised
" all those that were not of their own sect, as polluted, and
" not worthy to be saluted, nor kept company with. And
" therefore some of them meeting their old acquaintance,

" being godly preachers, had not only refused to salute
" them, but spit in their faces; wishing the plague of God
" to light upon them; and saying, they were damned, and
" that God had taken his Spirit from them." And all this,
because they did wear a cap; which strange unchristian
speech and behaviour, T. C. in his reply did not deny, but
that they neither defended nor allowed of any such behaviour: and that the fault of one should not be imputed to
so many. No; but it was brought to shew what ill effects
and prejudices Cartwright's doctrines against the present
constitution of this church had occasioned in many.

A. Gilby's
letter to
divers mi-
nisters
against the
habits.
Part of a
register.

This year (if it were not before) did a brother of this
party, Mr. A. G. [Anthony Gilby, I suppose,] write a very
hot and bitter letter to several reverend divines, that had
been exiles for the gospel, and returned upon queen Elizabeth's access to the crown; exciting them with all their
might against the bishops, for imposing the habits to be
worn by ministers in their ministration; and rather to lay
down their ministry than comply. It was directed, *To his
reverend fathers and brethren in Christ, Mr. Coverdale,
Mr. Turner, Mr. Whittingham, Mr. Sampson, Mr. D.
Humfrey, Mr. Leaver, Mr. Crowly, and others, that labour to root out the weeds of popery; grace and peace.*
Where in one place he thus expresseth himself: " I wot
" not by what devilish cup they [the bishops] do make
" such a diversity between Christ's word and his sacra-
" ments; that they cannot think the word of God to be
" safely enough preached and honourably enough handled,
" without cap, cope, or surplice; but that the sacraments,
" the marrying, the burying, the churching of women, and
" other church service, as they call it, must needs be de-
" clared with crossing, with coping, with surplicing, with
" kneeling, with pretty wafer-cakes, and other knacks of
" popery.——Well, by God's power, we have fought with
" the wolves, for these and such like popish chaff, and God
" hath given [us] the victory: we have now to do with the
" foxes, [i. e. the bishops.] Let us not fear."

As for the papists, the other adverse party to the legally

established church, and to the queen, the supreme governor
thereof on earth, the great apprehensions of them were not
yet blown over; though the rebellion in the north was now Anno 1570.
quieted. Cox, bishop of Ely, was an old experienced court-pists. Bi-
divine, and that by long observation knew what a dangerous very sensi-
sort of men they were, and what a mortal hatred they bore ble thereof.
to the gospel, and all those about the queen that sincerely
professed it. He was therefore, in this juncture, very soli-
citous for secretary Cecil, the queen's faithful and able
counsellor, who, for his wisdom and stability to religion,
was hated by them: and in this dangerous and rebellious 7
time, I find him in one of his letters making this prayer for
him: " I heartily wish you from our heavenly Father and
" his dear son Christ, the full strength of his holy Spirit, to
" the confusion of the enemies of God and of the queen's
" majesty, and of us all, God's true servants, and her grace's
" true subjects." But let me open some light into the practices of papists at this time.

And in order to that, I shall begin with an embassy the An embassy
queen despatched into France to the king in the month of from the
queen for
August, by Francis Walsingham, esq. sir Henry Norris, the French
knt. then her resident there. The chief and main of his protestants.
business was for the sake of the reformed religion, and for
an accord between that king and the protestant princes, viz.
the prince of Navarre, the prince of Condé, and the admiral, with the rest being the king's subjects. That it might
be made as favourable, for the reasonable contentation and
surety of the said princes and their party, as might possibly
be: to the maintenance and continuance of them in the liberty of their consciences: there being no small labour
made by some directly to impeach this accord, and by others
(though not openly) to withstand it, yet by double dealing
in the granting of their requests to ruin the said princes and
their party in the end. " Therefore," as it ran in the Her in-
queen's instructions to the said ambassadors, " she found it structions
to her am-
" the more necessary to use all good means to countervail bassadors.
" such contrary labours, and to procure not only a good
" accord, but therewith a continuance thereof; as in a mat-

" ter which in her conscience and honour she thought good
" both for the king and his whole estate."

Anno 1570.

Those protestants'
petitions
and demands.

The petitions and demands those protestant princes made,
were, first, that they might be restored to his grace and favour as humble and faithful subjects; and consequently, to
serve him with their lives, lands, and goods. Next, that
they might be permitted to serve Almighty God by the exercise of Christian religion, according to their profession and
to the quietness of their consciences. And lastly, that they
might have assurance thereof in some better sort than by
former experience they had: which petitions the queen had
herself considered. And the first she esteemed a thing most
meet for a king to grant both readily and bountifully. The
second was, she said, to a king most profitable to embrace
and accept. And the third, a thing in the sight of God
most commendable and needful of all Christian subjects.
And the last, a matter of the most moment to be regarded,
for a full perfection of all the rest. But this peace and
accord between the king and his said subjects was finished
before Walsingham came. So that when he came, he congratulated the king on the said good accord; and offered
on the queen's part all her endeavours to further the good
continuance thereof. And he gave the admiral and his
party to understand the queen's good intentions in sending
of him at that time; and to make it appear how careful
she was of their well doings.

The archbishop of
Cassils discovers to
Walsingham Steukley's coming to the
king of
Spain.

The archbishop of Cassils in Ireland, a papist, was an
exile in Spain; and (whether it were to reconcile himself to
the queen, or upon some personal pique) comes in January
this year 1570 into France; where, at Paris, resided Walsingham, the queen's ambassador: to whom in March following he made a visit. When Walsingham in discourse
asked him concerning the report that went abroad of the
king of Spain's intent of invading Ireland, the archbishop
then brake, and said, that about September last, the last
year, viz. 1569, one Steukley arrived in Spain with a design to address to that king for an army to reduce Ireland

Camd.
Eliz. p. 153
and 180.

to his obedience: who (as Camden writes) took upon him

with 3000 Italians or Spaniards to reduce all Ireland under CHAP.
the subjection of the Spaniard; and with one or two pin- I.
naces to fire the English fleet.   This bravo, soon after his Anno 1570.
coming to Madrid, before he went to the king, came to the
said archbishop, (as he related it himself to Walsingham,)
telling him he came to see him there, whom he knew to be
catholicly bent.   And that his intent in coming into that
country was to deal with the king of Spain about the reducing of the kingdom of Ireland to his government,
whereby heresy might be expelled, and true catholic religion planted.   And that therefore he, by his interest with
the president of the council, would procure him access to
the king.   But upon some pretences, as the archbishop
proceeded in his relation to the ambassador, of loyalty to
the queen and love to his country, not to see it under any
government than that of the queen and her successors, he
declined Steukley's motion.   Whereupon he applied himself to duke Feria, who brought him to the king: and the
king had conference with him; used him honourably; and Steukley
appointed him a very fair house, and gave him 6000 ducats, honourably
and a daily allowance for the maintenance of his table: so that king.
that he spent thirty ducats a day at least.

The archbishop, continuing his speech, added, that within
a day or two after, the king sent for him, and asked him
concerning Steukley.   He said, he never saw him but there Conference
in Spain: but that he had heard of him, that he had been between the
king and
a pirate upon the sea, of life dissolute, in expenses prodi- the archbi-
gal, of no substance, neither a man of any great account in shop concerning
his country; notwithstanding he heard he was a gentleman Steukley;
born, and descended from a good house.   Then the king
told him of the offer he had made touching the business of
Ireland; and that he had assured him, that he had dealt so
before his coming with the Irish nobility, as the king would
find them ready to receive such forces as he should send.
The archbishop wished the king not to be so light of belief: for that Steukley was not a man of that credit with
the Irish nobility, to be able to bring any such matter to
pass; whom they knew to be but a shifter, and one who,

for the maintenance of his prodigality, sought to abuse all men. The king said, that beside his own report, he was recommended unto him by his ambassador, who wished the king to credit whatsoever he reported.

And between duke Feria and the archbishop concerning him.

Duke Feria afterwards meeting the archbishop, asked his opinion of Steukley. To whom he said, he feared he would abuse the king. Then said Feria, the likelihoods that Steukley shewed the king of the enterprise were such, as they gave great cause why the king should embrace the same. For beside the Irish nobility, added he, he had won a great number of the garrison to be at his devotion, as well soldiers as captains. Well, said the duke further, I perceive you are not willing the enterprise should go forward: and therefore you seek to deface the gentleman whom we honour here with the name of *duke of Ireland.* To which the archbishop replied, that that title and calling was more than ever Ireland was acquainted with. The effect of this was, that Steukley came afterwards and challenged the archbishop, and told him, if he were not a man of the church, he would be revenged of him for the report he made of him. And when Walsingham had asked the archbishop, when Steukley was likely to embark, he answered, about the end of April: and now it was March.

Complete Ambassador, p. 59.

All this was the matter of discourse this archbishop had with Walsingham; as he gave the queen's secretary Cecill intelligence in his letter: though he had a suspicion even of this archbishop, notwithstanding all this that he had said. He pretended by all this discovery to shew himself loyal to the queen; and by this means to obtain a pardon from her majesty, in leaving his own country without her leave; and

The archbishop's end in this discovery, viz. to be restored to his archbishopric.

to have liberty to return back again: and that archbishopric being now void, and his successor dead, that he might be restored to it again. This man being put out of his bishopric about two years past, (viz. 1568,) and another substituted in his room, made a great disturbance and outrage: which he confessed to Walsingham: whereby he had justly incurred the lord deputy's displeasure. But in excuse of his departure without the queen's leave, added, that it was of necessity to seek maintenance otherwhere. That the king of Spain relieved him, and honourably entertained him, and gave him yearly 2000 ducats pension. But before he came to Spain he was at Nantes in France.

Certain it is, that what this archbishop of Cassils or Cashel had communicated to Walsingham gave great offence in Spain, and begat great jars between Steukley and him. Which the earl of Leicester observed to Walsingham in a letter he wrote him April 1571, acquainting him, that his brother, sir Henry Sidney, deputy of Ireland, who was then arrived in England, had shewed him the same; and that it had caused such a great dislike of the archbishop in Spain, that it might possibly recover him, and get him into England. This archbishop's name was Maurice Gibbon, alias Reagh: and having the pope's bull for the said arch- bishopric of Cassil or Cashel, by virtue of that demanded possession of the same: which being refused, the other barbarously stabbed him with his skean. But the archbishop escaped with his life, and the other fled abroad.

But to return to Steukley. He came into such favour with the king of Spain, that he knighted him: and he was commonly called there duke of Ireland. This Walsingham took notice of to Olivarez, the king of Spain's ambassador at Paris. To which he answered, the king was willing to entertain a gentleman of countenance that offered him service, and to honour such with the honour of knighthood. Then Walsingham acquainted him with the course of Steukley's life: and also how little he had to take to. And therefore willed him to consider how unworthy he was of any honour or entertainment in respect of himself. But being, said Walsingham, a rebel unto the queen's majesty, with whom the house of Burgundy had had so long amity, this gave her occasion to think that kind of amity not to answer best to such good-will as ordinarily was professed.

Our historian tells us moreover, what honours the pope also conferred upon this dissolute man, viz. the title of marquis of Leinster, earl of Wexford, and viscount and baron of other places in Ireland: and that in a vapour he pro-

CHAP.
I.

Anno 1570.

mised to make the pope's base son king of Ireland. The same historian, under the year 1578, gives an account of his death ; being slain in a battle in Africa with the king of Fez, going thither with Sebastian king of Portugal. For after the king of Spain had bestowed much upon him, he found him at length not worthy of any more. And his practices were abated in Spain, by discovery at last of his looseness and insufficiency: as secretary Cecill wrote to Walsingham about him.

Preparations upon intelligence of invasion of Ireland.

But upon the said English ambassador at Paris, his intelligence in France, and other intelligences from Spain, concerning the invading of Ireland, the queen sent a gentleman out of hand to that king, to understand the Spaniard's intention ; and who should deal plainly and roundly with him in that matter. And in the mean time she gave order, against all events, for the withstanding of any enterprises ; as well by sending of ships to the seacoasts of Ireland, as by other land forces to be sent thither. And ordered her ambassador there in France (if he should have any occasion) to deal with the Spanish ambassador, and to shew him these reports. And that if he should hear of the queen's preparations by sea and land, he should tell him, that it was for her defence: and that in case she should be offended, she would use them not only for *defence*, but to *offend* for her own revenge: as she wrote in her letter to Walsingham her ambassador. Of these affairs now happening concerning Ireland, our historians are silent: and therefore I relate them the more particularly, and proceed therein.

The ill condition of that kingdom at this time.
MSS. Cecilian.

And it appears that that realm was but in an ill condition, consuming the English treasure. Letters, August the 30th, from the council in Dublin the last year, made all things almost desperate ; viz. " That the Butlers, brothers " to the earl of Ormond, increased their rebellion, and " would not cease upon their said brother's motions made " to them. And that the rebels in the north were coming " to invade the English pale. That the power of the pale " was not able to withstand both the north and the But-

" lers. This secretary Cecill wrote in his private letters
" to his friend Nicolas White, seneschal of Wexford. And
" that they, the queen's council, would attend to the north,
" and leave the Butlers." And many such advertisements 11
came daily. But that other news from Ireland came, that
the Butlers now had stooped to the earl their brother; and
that the lord deputy had had good success. Yet the wars
and hostilities went on this year, and peace went rather
backward than forward: insomuch that the secretary called
it, *a loathsome charge to the crown:* adding, *Pæne mihi
nauseam movet ista profusio, et inutilis inanitas fisci re-
gii:* praying God to send some stay.

Some Frenchmen the latter end of this year, underhand, The French
had invaded unhappy Ireland by De la Roche; who dis- make an
covered to a kinsman, that the enterprise in Ireland was to against
have executed a plot of conquest devised by Peter Strozza Ireland.
in king Henry's time: and which, if the match then in hand ters.
between Monsieur and the queen went not forward, he was
promised he should go in hand withal. This was the
queen's secretary's intelligence to Walsingham, ambassador
in France. For notwithstanding the correspondence between the French king and queen Elizabeth at this time,
one De la Roche, of that king's chamber, was the captain
that led a party of French that had lately made an invasion
in Ireland: but, it seems, without success. And of this the
queen was informed from her viceroy in Ireland. The faction of Guise were the great doers in this enterprise. This
when Walsingham had complained of to the French king,
he denied his knowledge of it: though it was thought he
was privy to it.

It was discovered to be the pope's nuncio that laboured By the mo-
to draw Monsieur, the king's brother, into this practice: tion of the
promising for the maintenance thereof, to be paid in Paris pope's nuncio to Mon-
100,000 [crowns] for his encouragement; and made no dif- sieur.
ficulty to bring the same to pass, in respect of the great intelligence that they had both in England and Ireland. And
that the same being won, it would be an easy step to a step
of more consequence; meaning England. But that if Mon-

CHAP.
I.

Anno 1570.

Walsing-
ham's let-
ters.

De la Roche
brings hos-
tages from
Ireland.

sieur would not accept this promise, yet notwithstanding it was resolved to go forward: and that the bill of credit for the said sum of an hundred thousand crowns was already at Paris. All this an intelligencer employed by sir Henry Norris, ambassador before Walsingham, came and informed Walsingham of, Norris being gone home. And about this time Steukley in Spain presented an instrument unto the king there, not only subscribed with the names of the most part of the Irish nobility, but of divers of England of good quality, ready to be at his devotion. But further concerning De la Roche, Walsingham told the French king, that he had been in Ireland, and had left certain soldiers there; for whose safety he, the said De la Roche, had brought to France two sons of one Fitz-Morice to be in place of hostages: who then remained at Brest in Brittany, at a kinsman of La Roche's.

12

Cautiously
to treat
with duke
d'Alva
about trade,
because of
the popish
league and
prince of
Orange.

By the means of duke d'Alva's seizing the effects of the English merchants in the Netherlands the last year, and the queen in reprisal seizing of the Netherlanders' goods and merchandises in her dominions, all the ancient traffic between England and the Low Countries was at a stay: and great damage was done by the English to the Low Country merchants at sea, by taking their ships, and by the trade removed to Hamburgh and other parts. But after some time, about this year, or near it, a motion was made for the renewing of trade and intercourse between the two nations. Concerning this it was now seriously debated, and thought convenient to proceed more cautiously with Spain; both because of the popish league against the state of religion reformed, and of the Spanish malice against the queen and her realms: also withal lest any commodities might be carried from hence to Flanders, that might turn to the disadvantage or inconvenience of the prince of Orange and the reformed in those countries; that were now struggling for their liberty and religion, against that tyranny and oppression then exercised in those countries.

And for the better understanding of these things, and how matters stood between England and Spain at this junc-

ture, one Aldersey, an understanding merchant, thus wrote CHAP.
to Cecill wisely, and to the reputation of his memory.

" Whereas it hath pleased the queen's majesty to agree Anno 1570.
" unto the opening of traffic between this realm and the Aldersey a
" dominion of the king of Spain, I doubt not to her ma- merchant's
letter to
" jesty's honour and the benefit of the common weal; so Cecill
thereupon.
" do I assuredly think the duke of Alva, &c. hath sought MSS. Ce-
" and doth embrace the same, in hope thereby the sooner cilian.
" to supplant and overthrow the prince of Orange, with the
" states of Holland and Zealand. And considering the de-
" termination of the papistical league, and the particular
" malice of the Spaniard, and namely, the duke of Alva, it
" is greatly to be feared, that if God should permit the
" said prince and countries to be overthrown, there would
" small faith be kept towards her majesty, her highness'
" realms and subjects. Wherefore there is great cause to
" proceed in good policy : how by the use of this traffic
" the said prince, &c. may take the least hurt that may be.
" Wherein hoping of your lordship's goodness to take my
" meaning in good part, I am bold to shew my simple
" opinion.

" I hope there is no need by this agreement to permit
" any more liberal trade of her majesty's subjects into the
" Low Countries, but by the merchant adventurers, and of
" the staple, who have privileges in the said Low Countries;
" whereby of right, and by long use, other her majesty's
" subjects might not occupy into the said countries with
" any commodities of this realm more than to buy those
" country commodities.

" If the same and none other may be permitted by her 13
" majesty, there may so good order be taken, that by, &c.
" only those commodities of the realm, &c. to be vented,
" may be shipped into the Low Countries; which can no
" way so much hurt the prince [of Orange,] Holland, and
" Zealand, as may the carrying of corn, wood, hay, coal,
" beef, butter, and other victuals into Flanders and other
" places under the duke of Alva.

" And herein is to be considered, that as most of these

" things be stolen out in creeks, and in the night time, and
" by pretence of going from port to port within the realm
" without paying any custom; so may greedy desire of gain
" (which is like to be great) cause so much to be trans-
" ported, as this realm may thereby find lack.   And as the
" doers thereof be for the most part fishermen, and of other
" occupations, who leave their faculties to follow these
" things, and much more will do if they may be suffered ;
" even so the restraining of them will enforce them to use
" their several sciences, to the benefit of the realm.

    " Where it may be said, the Flemings will send these
" things, and serve the said parties very amply ; it is to be
" answered, that those of Zealand will by no means suffer
" them; but so to keep the coast of Flanders and other
" places, that the Flemings shall not stir : and yet none of
" them restrained by her majesty, &c.

    " And if they of Zealand may without offence restrain
" such Englishmen as shall carry things into those places
" which shall not be free by the said privileges, nor allowed
" by such order as may be taken with them of Zealand,
" they will cause much better order to be kept in that be-
" half than any provision of her majesty will do.

    " And these things well provided for, in my judgment
" the prince and the said countries shall receive small hurt
" by this opening of traffic, they having liberty to use this
" realm as other subjects of the king.   And so craving par-
" don for my boldness, I pray God long to preserve your
" honour in health.

                    " Your lordship's at command,
                            " Tho. Aldersey."

CHAP. II.

A determination of the general assembly of the church of
Scotland, for obedience to the new king. Queen Eliza-
beth in perplexity about restoring of the Scots queen.
Match for the queen with the French king's brother.
The queen how affected towards it. Astrological inquiry
into her nativity about it. The pope's bull against the
queen set up at Paris. A secret popish design against
England. Wrecks upon the coast of Sussex claimed by
the bishop of Chichester. A suit with the lord admiral
about it. Proclamations about pirates. The governor
of the Isle of Wight sends out ships after them.

THE affairs of Scotland and the Scots queen affected Eng- Anno 1570.
land also at this time. And the fear of popery from that In Scot-
quarter disturbed this kingdom : insomuch, that those of queen de-
the court, and the rest of the land that favoured the re- posed.
formed religion, were secretly well-disposed to the action in
that realm, of deposing that queen, and to the succession of
her son. Which was done by the states of parliament there.
And a solemn decree was also made by the Scotch clergy
in their general assembly in the month of July, 1570, and
obedience accordingly enjoined to be given by all the clergy
to the king, and to pray for him. Which I have seen
among the papers of Randolph, the queen's ambassador to
that kingdom : which also was printed, and ran in this
tenor.

" *A determination of the general assembly of the church of*
" *Scotland, halden in Edinburgh, the 7th day of July,*
" *1570, anent the obedience to be given to the king's ma-*
" *jesty his authority, and for praying for his grace's*
" *prosperous reign, &c.*

" It was concluded by the whole assembly convened, as Decree of
" wel superintendents, commissioners to plain churches, the general
" commissioners of towns, universities, provinces, churches, that church
" baronies, and gentlemen, with uthers of Christes congre- dience to
" gation : that as it hath pleased God of his mercy to erect the new
" the authority of the king's majesty over us by publicte king.

c 2

" consent of the estates in parlament, even so the same
" ought and should be universally obeyed throughout this
" realm, without acknowledging any other authority, what-
" soever title be pretended.

" Moreover, al ministers are commanded, in their pub-
" licte sermons, to pray publictly for the preservation of his
" majesties person and authority: assuring them, that al
15 " such as shal be found negligent or inobedient heirinto,
" shal be punished as the church shal think expedient.

" And further pronounceth, that if any subject or sub-
" jects of this realm (of what estate they) shal presumptu-
" ously take upon them to inhibit any minister to obey this
" ordinance of the general church, what cloik or colour so-
" ever he or they shall pretend, or by manasing make im-
" pediment unto them, so that without fear ministers may
" not serve God in their vocation; that in that case such
" troublers shall be summarlie, upon the notoriety of the
" fault, excommunicate; and shal be halden as rotten mem-
" bers, unworthy of the society of Christ's body, &c.

" And last, commandes al superintendents of commis-
" sioners of provinces to cause this determination to be
" published in al parish churches, that none hereafter pre-
" tend ignorance, &c.   Geven in the general assembly of
" the church of Scotland, and third session therof.   Sub-
" scrived by the clerk of the same: day, year, and place
" aforesaid.

" M. J. Gray."

Queen Eli-
zabeth, how
disposed to-
wards the
Scotsqueen,
deposed.
Queen Elizabeth, apprehensive of her danger from the
popish party in Scotland, and queen Mary's friends there,
yet remained unresolved what to do; and whether to consent to what was done in Scotland towards their queen.
However, her own security inclined her on the other hand;
that is, to favour what the protestants had done: of whom
she was better assured that they were on her side.   And
therefore, when commissioners were sent out of Scotland to
the queen in March to adjust the Scots queen's affairs, (viz.
the bishops of Galway and Ross, and lord Leviston, on

that queen's part; and earl Morton, and two more, on the CHAP.
king's,) and both parties were very stiff; one, for the queen II.
to be restored to her government; the other, for the king Anno 1570.
her son to reign: the English court stood variously affected:
which the earl of Leicester, in the said month of March,
gave this account of to Walsingham, then the queen's ambassador in France: "That the queen was scrupulous about The ac-
" it. The unworthiness of their queen to rule she granted: of by the
" but the instances of their cause, to depose her from her earl of Lei-
" dignity, she could hardly be persuaded in. And so she cester.
" remained much perplexed. That on the one side she
" was loath to set her up, or to restore her to her estate
" again: and on the other side, as loath to defend that
" which she was not yet well persuaded to have justice
" with it. Between these, her council sought for these two
" things, viz. that herself might be preserved in surety,
" and the true religion maintained assuredly. For that as
" the state of the world stood, and upon true examination
" of this cause, it appeared, that both the ways were dan-
" gerous touching the queen of Scots. For as there was
" danger in delivering her to her government, so there was
" danger in retaining her in prison: her friends abroad be-
" ginning to speak proudly for her." Thus the earl of 16
Leicester. But it was known, that all that was done in
this conference was sent by special messengers from the
Scotch queen's party to the French king, the king of Spain,
and the pope; and succours conveyed at this very time
from them; as appears by a paper of secretary Cecill, which Annal. Re-
may be read in the Annals of the Reformation. form. ch.
　　　　　　　　　　　　　　　　　　　　　　　　　　57. vol. 1.
　　Religion was also very much concerned this year, in the How the
motions that were made about queen Elizabeth's marriage. queen stood
affected to-
For though her subjects earnestly desired her marriage, to wards
secure a protestant succession, yet they dreaded her match- matching
ing with a popish foreign prince. But even they that were with France.
in the true English interest, out of a fear of the Scots
queen's succession, could have been glad to see her married with whomsoever it were, equal in dignity with herself.
This appeared, and also how the queen herself pretended,
　　　　　　　　　　　c 3

CHAP.
II.

Anno 1570.

The secre-
tary's in-
structions
to Walsing-
ham in that
affair.
Compl.
Amb.

for the good of her people, to be affected that way, by expressions in secretary Cecill's correspondence (in a letter dated March the 3d) with Walsingham, ambassador in France; instructing him from the queen, "That if any "should deal with him to understand his mind, in the case "of her marriage, he might say, that at his coming from "England, upon some common bruit of such a matter con"cerning her majesty and monsieur d'Anjou, the French "king's brother, he [Walsingham] was assured, that her "majesty, upon consideration of the benefit of her realm, "and to content her subjects, resolved to marry, if she "could find a person in estate and condition fit for her to "match withal. And that she meant not to marry but "with a person of the family of a prince." And that Walsingham should say, that he could not by any means perceive, that her majesty was altered from that disposition. So as that he might conclude, that if any such matter should be moved to him by any meet person to deal therein, he would advertise her majesty thereof. And that her majesty would have him so to do. And then that wise counsellor added his own judgment; "That if God should "permit this marriage, or any other, to take place, he "[Walsingham] might well judge, that no time was to be "wasted, otherwise than honour might require. That he "was not able to discern what was best: but that he saw "no continuance of her quietness without a marriage. And "that therefore he remitted the success to Almighty God." But this, he said, he writ privately to him, as he trusted it should remain to himself. How matters proceeded in duke d'Anjou's courtship of the queen will be shewn under the next year.

The queen's
nativity in-
quired into
for her mar-
riage.

And because the welfare of the nation did so much depend upon the queen's marriage, it seems some were employed secretly, by calculating her nativity, to inquire into her marriage. For which art even secretary Cecill himself had some opinion. I have met among his papers with such a judgment made, written all with his own hand. Which 17 judgment I am apt to believe (if not done secretly by him-

self) he had either from one Bomelius, a Dutchman, and CHAP.
famous for physic and this art, and resiant in England ___ II.
about this time; or perhaps from sir Thomas Smith: who Anno 1570.
studied astrology much; and by this scheme he found that
the queen had not much inclination to marriage: yet that
her wedlock would be very happy to her: that she should
be somewhat elder when she entered into matrimony: and
that then she would have a young man that was never before married [a]: that she then should be in the 31st year ª And so
of her age: that she should have but one husband. Then the duke of
for the *quality* of the man, that he should be a foreigner. Anjou was.
That (especially towards the middle of her age) she should
not much delight in wedlock: that she should obey and
reverence her husband, and have him in great respect.
That she should arrive at a prosperous married estate; but
slowly, and after much counsel taken, and the common rumour of it everywhere, and after very great disputes and
arguings concerning it for many years, by divers persons,
before it should be effected. And then she should become
a bride without any impediment. That her husband should
die first: and yet she should live long with her husband;
and should possess much of his estate. For *children*, but
few, yet very great hope of one son, that should be strong,
famous, and happy in his mature age: and one daughter.
The calculation of all this, by judgment and aspects of the
planets, is set down in the Appendix. It was drawn up, Numb. IV.
no doubt, privately, for Cecill's own instruction, to judge
the better of so weighty an affair, by what might be gathered from astrology; the good estate of the whole realm
so much depending on the queen's marriage.

The bull of pope Pius V. against queen Elizabeth was The pope's
set up in Paris at Pont St. Estienne, containing the self- bull against
same matter, and on the same day (March the 2d) that zabeth set
Felton set it up at St. Paul's, London: putting her under up in Paris.
a curse, and all that adhered to her; and absolving her
subjects from their oath of allegiance: and those that should
obey her to be involved under the said curse. This inso-
lent bull may be read at length in our histories; and par-

ticularly in Camden's Elizabeth.   The people of Paris
flocked mightily together about it.   The queen's ambas-

sadors then in France were the lord Buckhurst and Mr.
Walsingham. Whose servant went boldly and tore it down,
and brought it to his master. Who with the lord Buckhurst,
after some conference, repaired to the king; and immediately broke with him in that behalf. He calling Walsingham unto him, asked him the contents of the said bull.
Whereof being advertised, and Walsingham presenting to
him so much of the said bull as was given him by his servant, the king shewed himself very much moved thereat, in
such sort as that both might very well see he was unfeigned.

Compl.
Amb. p. 49.
And forthwith he called Lansac unto him, to take order
with the judge criminal, for the searching out of the setter
18 up of the same. And assured the ambassadors, if by any
means he could be found, he should receive such punishment as such a presumption required ; considering the good
amity between him and his good sister. Walsingham then
shewed the king, that if he did not take order in this, the
like measure might be measured to himself. To which he
answered, that he did perceive that very well ; and that
whosoever he were, that should seem to touch in honour
any of his confederates, he would make account of him accordingly. After Walsingham departed from the king,
Lansac told him in his ear, that he had great cause to
guess, that this was done by some Spanish practice.

An Italian
practice a-
gainst Eng-
land in
hand.
Compl.
Ambass.
It may open a door to the dangerous practices that followed the next year, by reason of the Scots queen and the
duke of Norfolk, what was told to Walsingham the latter
end of this. Which was, that one who desired his name to
be in cipher, gave him to understand, that a friend of his,
in talk with an Italian bishop, (who came lately to Paris
from the pope to congratulate the marriage of the French
king,) had learned of him, that he had a practice in hand
for England ; which would not be long before it brake
forth : and further shewed, that one merchant in that town
had 14,000 crowns to be employed in that behalf.

Bishop of
Chichester's
Dr. Curteis was this year consecrated bishop of Chiches-

ter, in the room of Barlow, deceased. This bishop had CHAP.
some controversy with the lord admiral for sea-wrecks; II.
which he claimed, as bishop of Chichester: not only such Anno 1570.
as were within his lands and manors, but also some miles right to sea-
wrecks upon
out at sea, on the coast of Chichester. Whereupon a suit the coasts of
was commenced. Several writings whereof remain in the Chichester.
Paper-
Paper-office. There it appears, that information was brought office.
against the bishop, that a hull of a ship was brought by A process
upon it.
one Walkaden, and seized by the lord admiral's deputy, in
the haven's mouth of Chichester: which was sold by the
bishop of Chichester, or his officers, to a servant of his:
and was afterwards broken up by one John Bulke, his servant. For the which there was process served upon the
said John Bulke, out of the court of admiralty. There it
was pleaded, that the said bishop had nine or ten slyages of
iron, pieces of cables, sails, and divers other things, fetched
from a ship sunk at the shoals, twelve miles from the land,
about a year and half past. And that there was no process
against the said fetchers of the same, because they were
poor men; and that it was thought his lordship would take
order for it without suit. That although the said bishop
had by charter *wrakea maris*, within his lordship's manors,
lands, tenements, fees, and possessions; yet he might not
meddle with the hull of the said ship, considering it was a
pirate's, and possessed and seized by the lord admiral before it came near the place where the bishop did claim
that privilege. The other goods were fet from the sea,
twelve miles from the land. That the charter which the
bishop shewed for the jurisdiction of admiralty, made in 19
Harry the Sixth's time, was resumed by the statute of re-
sumption in the twenty-eighth year of his reign. And besides, that the queen's majesty had now the lands where he
did now so challenge the admiral's jurisdiction, so that unless he had reserved the said jurisdiction when he departed
with his lands to the queen, his said jurisdiction did pass
away with the lands. This was the plea on the side of the
lord admiral: what that on the bishop's was, I find not.
But the charter of Henry VI. before mentioned, granting

CHAP.
II. the privilege of wrecks to this see, may be read in the Appendix.

Anno 1570.
Numb. V.
Lord admi-
ral Lisle,
under king
Henry VIII.
yields this
right to the
bishop. This, it seems, had been a cause tried before, in king
Henry the Eighth's time, between a bishop of Chichester
that then was, and sir Arthur Lisle, lord admiral: who
was laying hands upon a wreck in the coast of Sussex.
Whereupon the bishop of Chichester claimed it as his right:
and withal, to satisfy him therein, produced to him a copy
of the foresaid patent from the said king Henry, granting
to Adam the bishop all such privileges: who was bishop of
Chichester anno 1445, 24 Hen. VI. Whereupon the said
lord Lisle sent this letter to the said bishop.

" My lord,

His letter
to the bi-
shop.
Paper-
office. " In my hertiest wise, I commend me unto you, plesyth
" yt you t'understond, that I have perused your graunt of
" your libertyes; which is sure and good, as I am informed
" by lerned men. Wherfore I am very wel contented that
" you sell this late wrack, as yours; for I wyll not, in no
" wyse, be against you nor your church, to break any such
" your liberties or franchises, which by your graunt I per-
" ceive you have: and also of old tyme, accordingly to the
" tenour hereof, have occupied and used. And thus fare
" your good lordship hartily well. From London, this vii
" of March.

" Your own Arthur Lysley."

The wreck, about which the suit above mentioned was
commenced, was, it seems, of a pirate's ship: which the admiral made his plea for claiming it from the bishop. I find,
indeed, the pirates were now very stirring upon our seas.
Proclama-
tion against
pirates, and
receiving
their spoils. Which gave occasion of the queen's issuing out a proclamation, dated in June this year from Hampton-court, against
them; who made good spoils of the goods of the king of
Spain's subjects, as well as of others. These seemed to be
chiefly Flemings. She therefore minding to give as little
offence as possible to that great and proud king, and that
he might have no real cause of quarrelling with her, (as he

sought occasion,) as she had therefore restrained sea-rovers
by a strict proclamation the last year, so now by another
she forbade any of her subjects on the coast of the sea to
receive the commodities such pirates should bring to sell.
It set forth, "how that by a special proclamation last year
" given at Oteland, she had directed sundry good orders to
" her ports, for the removing and expelling of all pirates
" out of the narrow seas upon the coast of her realms. And 20
" that thereupon several evil persons were apprehended in
" her ports; and were, as it was notorious, executed of late
" times as pirates. But that though no manifest pirates
" were then known to resort to any her majesty's ports;
" yet it was supposed, that, by the fraud and greediness of
" some negligent officers in some small ports or creeks of
" the realm, certain goods and merchandises were secretly
" brought into those ports, as was said, from some ships of
" war of other countries; being upon the high seas, and
" out of the danger of her majesty's castles or bulwarks
" to be stayed; and were thought to be by her ma-
" jesty———

" For remedy, she eftsoons commanded all manner of
" persons to have a more earnest regard to the observation
" of all things contained in the foresaid proclamation, upon
" several pains therein contained, and the same proclama-
" tion now publish and observe." And her majesty presently addeth, "that if any officer in any port or creek
" should have any knowledge or information given of any
" person that should buy, or any ways attain to any man-
" ner goods or merchandises, brought in otherwise than or-
" dinarily and publicly by merchants' ships, as lawfully
" trading merchandise; the said officers, for not appre-
" hending the offender, and for not withstanding such
" frauds, to be deprived of their offices, and committed to
" prison without bail, if their offices be of her majesty's
" gift: and if by grant of any corporation, the whole li-
" berty of the corporation, for such misuses, shall be se-
" cured into her majesty's hands, and be extinguished, &c.

" Given at Hampton-court, the 6 of June, 1570, the xii of
" her reign."

Anno 1570.   Notwithstanding, complaint was made, about the latter
The go-
vernor of
the Isle of
Wight
sends ships
after pirates
in those
seas.
Compl.
Ambass.
end of the year, by the Spanish ambassador in Paris, to the
English ambassador there, of pirates, haunting the narrow
seas, (especially about the Isle of Wight,) that robbed the
king's ships. It was true; but the crimes were committed
by some belonging to the prince of Orange: as Cecil wrote
to Walsingham: a thing the English could not help. But
Mr. Horsey, governor of the Isle of Wight, was despatched
with authority to set forth certain ships, either to take them,
or to drive them from the coasts. For he confessed to Walsingham privately, that they were too much favoured *lucri
causa*. But, however, he might avow truly, as he added,
that the queen did not favour them.

21   CHAP. III.

*Orders and injunctions for preventing frays and fightings
in London. Constables to carry staves. The queen's daily
learned studies. Secretary Cecil created lord Burghley.
His troubles. Sir Tho. Smith becomes secretary in his
place. Walsingham ambassador in France, his complaint. Sir Nicolas Throgmorton; his death; disease
and character. Earl of Sussex. Mr. Thomas Cecil's letter to him: who had recommended him to the queen. Sir
Francis Englefield's presumptuous letter. Bishop Sandys
nominated for London: his excuse; and acceptance: his
first visitation. The Italian church in London. Fox's
second edition of his Martyrology.*

Disorders
and frays
in London.
NOW for more domestic affairs, and observations of divers
persons of character or quality. This year, or near it, a
notable proclamation was set forth by the lord mayor of
London, for the regulation and good order of that great
metropolitical city, not only upon the queen's charge to
him to preserve peace in that her chief city, but also be-

cause lately there had been great frays and fightings, and
murders too, committed in and about the said city, by
cudgels, called *bastinadoes*, and other weapons. The latter
forbidden to be drawn, and the former to be carried, by a
very strict and well-penned proclamation published in print.
Which all constables, for their better direction and remembrance, were to have in their houses: and they enjoined to
carry a white staff. It was entitled, *For the suppressing
of frays, and fray-makers, and disturbers of the queen's
peace.*

" It began with the mention of a law of king Edward I.
" in the third of his reign; wherein he did enact, that the
" peace of the holy church and of the land should be well
" guarded, kept, and maintained in all points; and that
" egal justice should be done, as well to the rich as to the
" poor, without respect of persons. And that king Ri-
" chard II. in his parliament the first of his reign, did in
" like manner well and straitly command, that peace in his
" realm should be surely observed and kept: so that all
" his lawful subjects might from thenceforth safely and
" peaceably go, come, and dwell, according to the law and
" usage of the realm; and that justice and right should be
" indifferently ministered. It set forth likewise, that the
" queen's most excellent majesty, as well by her own mouth,
" as by her honourable council, had sundry times given
" strait charge and commandment to the lord mayor and
" his brethren the aldermen, and to their predecessors, that
" they should well and diligently conserve and keep the
" peace of our sovereign lady within the city and suburbs.
" And forsomuch as a far greater confluence, as well of the
" lords, great men, prelates, knights, and gentlemen of this
" land, and other the common people, was made to this
" honourable city of London than to any other part of the
" realm, as well for their suits in the queen's highness'
" courts, as for other their negociations; and for these
" causes there was required a far greater and more diligent
" care, within the city especially, for the conservation of
" her majesty's peace; and chiefly for that this city is the

The lord
mayor's
proclama-
tion for
preventing
the same.

22

CHAP.
III.

Anno 1570.
The mayor
the queen's
lieutenant.

Desperate
affrays in
the city.

Reforma-
tion there-
of.

No drawing
weapon.

" principal city and spectacle of the whole realm; by the
" government whereof all other cities and places do take
" example: and also, whereas the lord mayor is the queen's
" highness' lieutenant in the same city; and by the char-
" ters, liberties, franchises, and customs thereof, hath the
" full execution of the queen's prerogative royal for the
" conservation of the peace and defence of bearing armour
" within all parts of this city and the suburbs thereof:

" And forasmuch as of late times, within this honourable
" city, and the liberties and suburbs, upon quarrels begun,
" as well in other parts of the realm, as within this city,
" and in other places near adjacent, great and desperate
" affrays have been foughten within the said city: where-
" upon hath ensued horrible murder and desperate man-
" slaughters; to the great displeasure of Almighty God,
" and to the manifest contempt of the queen's most excel-
" lent majesty, her crown and dignity:

" For reformation whereof the lord mayor, by the good
" and grave advice of his brethren the aldermen, did in the
" queen's name most straitly charge, will, and command,
" that as well all her majesty's subjects, as all other per-
" sons, resorting, dwelling, or abiding within the said city,
" or the liberties and suburbs of the same, shall from hence-
" forth firmly keep, guard, and maintain in all points the
" peace of our said sovereign lady. And that no person
" presume to draw or use any weapon to fight, upon pain
" of forfeiture of the same, and to have prisonment of his
" body during her majesty's pleasure, and to make fine
" and ransom for the same offence.

" And for the better repressing of such as be common
" disturbers and breakers of her majesty's peace, he com-
" manded all her majesty's good subjects diligently to assist
" the constables, and other her majesty's officers, in pacify-
" ing of affrays, and apprehending of such as were breakers
" and disturbers of her majesty's peace, as often as they
" shall be called upon by the said constables, upon pain of
" imprisonment, and further punishment. And that the
" constables within the said city and liberties may at the

" time of such affrays be the better known, the lord mayor CHAP.
" did hereby charge and command, that every constable III.
" should have a white staff, or rod, of the length of one ell Anno 1570.
" and an half, and of the bigness of a standard shaft. 23
" Which staff, or rod, he or his deputy shall bear in his Constable's white staff.
" hand at all such times as he shall go to the appeasing of
" such affrays. And that no persons but constables only,
" or their deputies, do use the like staves, upon pain of
" imprisonment.

" Herewithal charging all the constables, as often as Raise the
" need shall require, to raise the inhabitants of their several inhabitants.
" precincts, and to take and apprehend all such as shall
" draw or use any weapon to fight, or make an affray, or
" otherwise break her highness' peace. And all such affray-
" makers and peacebreakers to carry forthwith to one of
" the counters, there to remain, until such further order be
" taken with him or them, as may be to the terror and
" example of others.

" And further, he did straitly command and charge, that No cudgel
" no person presume to bear or carry in their hands, or to be borne.
" otherwise, within the city of London, and liberties thereof,
" any manner of ragged or smooth cudgel, commonly called
" a *bastinado*, either with a pike of iron or without. And
" such as now offended therein, to be attached by the con-
" stables, or their deputies, and brought before the lord
" mayor or the recorder, or before some other justice of
" peace of the same city ; there to receive such punishment
" for the same as shall be thought expedient. And to the
" intent that the constables may not excuse themselves by
" ignorance, the lord mayor commanded every constable of
" the same city to have one of these proclamations fixed
" upon a wall within his dwelling-house, in a place meet
" and convenient for the same.

" Imprinted at London, by John Day."

If we turn our eyes from the city to the court: the queen The queen
was now at Windsor; where, besides the public and weighty employs
herself daily
affairs of the state, she customarily set apart some hours in study.
every day in her privy chamber in learned studies; as in

CHAP.
III.

Anno 1570.
Roger
Ascham.
reading Greek, in conversing with ancient authors of philo-
sophy and divinity, and in fair writing, and indicting letters and discourses in divers languages.   Wherein she used
the conduct of the learned and ingenious Roger Ascham:
which he looked upon as one of the greatest felicities of his
life.   And reproached the young gentry of the nation, nay,
and many of the elderly divines, by her example.   And
with what words he addressed himself to them upon occasion of the queen's studies, to excite them to learning, is set
down elsewhere.

Annals,
vol. i.
p. 392.
Secretary
Cecil cre-
ated lord
Burghley.
One of this learned queen's wise counsellors was sir William Cecil, her secretary of state, learned himself, and also
a chief patron of learning and religion: whom this year she
worthily advanced to the honour of a baron of this kingdom, by the title of *baron of Burghley*, the name of his
noble house in Northamptonshire; and still giving title to
his eldest son's issue, the earls of Exeter: not advanced for
24 his wealth, but for his worth.   But he remained secretary
for some time after: though it was thought then, (as the
earl of Leicester wrote to Walsingham,) that ere long he
should have the office of privy seal.   If we will take his
title from his own pen, thus he wrote to Nicolas White, his
friend in Ireland; " My style is *lord of Burghley*, if you
" mean to know it for your writing, and if you list to
" write, truly the poorest lord in England.   *Yours*, not
" changed in friendship though in name, *William Burgh-*
" *ley*."   And about this time he wrote to Walsingham in
France, March the 1st, 1570, subscribing his letter, *By
your assured, as I was wont,* Wil. Cecil; *and as I am
now ordered to write,* William Burghley.   And in his own
Cecil's
Journal.
Journal he wrote, " that he was created baron the 25th of
" February, being Shrove Sunday; yet called lord Burgh-
" ley some time before."

The bishop
of Ross's
congratula-
tion thereof
to him.
The bishop of Ross, the Scottish queen's ambassador,
(but for his pragmatical and seditious spirit committed to
the Tower,) thought fit, in a letter to this lord, to give him
this compliment upon his new honour: " When I was
" going to wreit your lordship's accustomed style of honour

" upon my letter, I was warned of your late honourable C H A P.
" promotion. Wherof I am most heartily glad. For your ___ III.
" vertue, wisdom, and experience hath mereit that, and Anno 1570.
" much more. And happy is that commonwealth whair
" the magistrates are so elected: *et quum aut sapientes*
" *gubernant, aut gubernantes philosophantur.*"

If this wise and good man took any delight in titles of His troubles
honour, it was some recompence to him for the severe trou- and dangers
bles and dangers he was oppressed with, for his public and and reflec-
faithful services. For the last year he had certainly sunk on.
under the malicious combinations of the great men at the
court against him, had not the queen seasonably interposed;
knowing well the worth of the man, and, on that account,
the zeal she had, and must have, for such a man, obliged
her on his side. And this present year, 1570, also, he had
his share of trouble; and the court itself was full of changes.
And how it stood with him now, take his own words, in a
letter to his dear friend in Ireland. " I cannot well re- Letter to
" solve what to write, such are the varieties and changes of Nic. White.
" time, that may alter my advertisements between my writ-
" ing and your receipt. Therefore I will write of things
" not subject to change by me while I live. I do continue,
" nor will desist, to love heartily the honest virtues which
" I am persuaded are settled and rooted in you. For which
" I love you, and so will, [however mutable he found the
" love of others to him,] except you make the change. I
" am, as you have known me, (if not more,) tormented
" with the blasts of the world: willing to live in calm
" places; but it pleaseth God otherwise to exercise me, in
" sort as I cannot shun the rages thereof; though his good-
" ness preserveth me, as it were with the target of his pro-
" vidence, from the dangers that are gaping upon me. *Vita*
" *hominis est militia super terram.* I use no armour of
" proof against the dart and pellet, but confidence in God 25
" by a clear conscience." He was a man that affected me-
ditation and retirement, but could not be spared from the
public. For to repeat one expression more, dropped in the
same letter: "God send me some intermission from busi-

BOOK I.

Anno 1570.

Is made lord treasurer, anno 1572.

" ness, to meditate privately upon his marvellous works, " and to exercise my thankfulness for his mercies and bene- " fits." This was writ in May. But, instead of a recess from business, the queen laid more weighty employment upon him not long afterwards. For upon the death of the lord marquis of Winchester, lord treasurer, in the year 1572, she advanced him to that place. But yet the drawing up of most of the state writings, as instructions to ambassadors, and declarations, and letters, lay upon him even then, and long after.

Sir Tho. Smith succeeds secretary of state.

He was succeeded in the office of secretary of state by sir Tho. Smith, knt. another very faithful, wise, and learned counsellor of the queen's: but not before June 24, 1571; who had late been the queen's ambassador with the French king. He was first called to assist the said new baron in the office of secretary; and was, in order to that, admitted to the council, March the 4th, as the earl of Leicester; but the day before wrote to Walsingham, that the said sir Thomas should be admitted to the council to-morrow; and shortly after to be secretary.

And Walsingham.

His necessity now in France.

Happy was the queen in her secretaries; who were both faithful, able, and diligent. Such was Mr. Walsingham, afterwards secretary, viz. in January 1573, being then admitted joint-secretary with sir Thomas Smith. Which Walsingham, by serving her majesty faithfully in his embassy, to his great cost, in housekeeping and intelligence, ran himself deep in debt: insomuch that, in a letter he wrote this year from France to the earl of Leicester, he shewed him, that his charges grew to be so great, through the excessive dearness of the place, (the like to which was never known,)

Compl. Amb.

that necessity forced him at that present to make his moan unto his lordship, and to desire his aid, that he might not be, as he was, overburdened: whereby his care how to live might not hinder the only care he ought to have, how to serve. And that though his service could not deserve so much as he was allowed, yet his place and his state required, he said, consideration to be had of the present time; otherwise he should not be able to do that which should be

for her majesty's honour and service: adding, that always CHAP.
change of time brought change of allowance. III.

This year, February 12, died sir Nicolas Throgmorton, Anno 1570.
knt. who had been the queen's ambassador jointly with sir Sir Nicolas
Thomas Smith; and employed in other embassies and mat- ton dies.
ters of state: and a great creature of the earl of Leicester's.
He died *ex pleurisi et peripneumonia*, as Cecil, in a diary Cecil's
of his, expressed it. The loss of whom Leicester signified diary.
in a letter two days after (viz. February 14) to Walsingham, in these words: " We have lost, on Monday, our good His disease,
" friend, sir Nic. Throgmorton: who died at my house, of him to
" being there taken suddenly in great extremity on the the public.
" Tuesday before. His lungs were perished. But a sud- Amb.
" den cold he had taken was the cause of his speedy death.
" God hath his soul: and we his friends great loss of his
" body." Some apprehended his sudden death came by
poison: but whether by Leicester's means, being in his 26
house when he died, it is uncertain. He was a busy, intriguing man. Cecil also wrote the same news of his death
to the same correspondent, viz. " That he had been sick,
" and past six or seven days, of a pleurisy, joined with a
" disease called *peripneumonia:*" adding piously, " *he doth*
" *but lead the way to us.*" Walsingham, in his letter back
to Leicester, taking notice of the said sir Nicolas's death,
(whom he called a *dear friend* to him,) gave this judgment
of him; " That by the lack of him, if it were private to his
" friends, the loss were great: but if weighed generally in
" respect to her majesty and the country, the want of him
" would appear greater. For be it spoken, said he, with-
" out offence to any, for counsel in peace, and for conduct
" in war, he hath not left of like sufficiency his successor,
" that I know: concluding, that he would no more insist
" upon that matter, unpleasant for his lordship to read, as
" for him to write." He was buried in the church of St.
Katharine, Creechurch, London; where he hath a fair monument, with his figure in stone.

In the month of October the earl of Sussex was admitted Earl of Sus-
into the privy council: who had merited well. He was into the
privy coun-
cil.

BOOK
I.

Anno 1570.

Mr. Tho.
Cecil, that
served un-
der him in
the rebel-
lion, re-
commended
by him to
the queen.
lord president of the council in the north . and the last
year, being the queen's lord lieutenant in the north, he had
great success against the rebels in the north: and was accompanied with a great many English gentlemen, volun-
teers. And, among the rest, by Mr. Thomas Cecill, secretary Cecill's eldest son: who, for his signal service, and
some promise, expected some reward with others. And
having been particularly recommended unto the queen by
the said earl, he wrote this handsome letter in acknowledg-
ment to him; expressive also of his modesty and virtue,
agreeable to the spirit of his worthy father.

Cecil's let-
ter to him
thereupon.
Titus, B. 2.
" That it might please his good lordship :

" Understanding that such as served under his lordship
" in the late rebellion of the north did generally look at
" this time, by his recommendation, for some recompence
" of their service; among whom, accounting himself one,
" and his suit already being most favourably recommended
" unto the queen's majesty by his lordship's special favour
" unto him, more than any desert of his part; he was the
" bolder to remember himself unto his lordship by these
" his letters: not as one, in respect of his particular gain,
" meaning to be importunate with him; but as he, who
" neither meant to attempt other men's credits in this be-
" half, neither to be bound or thankful unto any, but unto
" his lordship only. And should think himself happy, if
" at any time it might be in him, by any service, to ac-
" knowledge that duty and good-will which he remained in-
" debted unto his lordship. In the mean time he remained
" as his most bounden ; and wishing his lordship his heart's
" desire." It was dated from Burghleigh, the 26th of December, 1570; subscribing,

" Your lordship's at commaunment,

" Tho. Cecill."

Sir Francis
Englefield's
presumptu-
ous letter.
Cecil's
diary.
November the 18th, sir Francis Englefield wrote a presumptuous letter to the earl of Leicester, against the queen's
majesty's authority. It is only so briefly set down by Ce-

cill in his diary: grounding it, as it seems, upon the pope's CHAP.
late excommunication of her, and discharging her subjects III.
from their allegiance, and giving her kingdoms to the king Anno 1570.
of Spain. He was a great popish zealot; and had been a 27
privy counsellor to the late queen Mary, and master of her
wards and liveries: but now living abroad upon pretence
of his religion, and a pensioner to the king of Spain, held a
correspondence with the queen's enemies. Though the queen
deserved better at his hands, as hath been related at large
elsewhere. For she allowed him the revenues of his estate Annals of
here in England; and retained only a small part of it for Reform.
the necessary maintenance of his wife; who was an heiress, ch.36. vol.i.
and brought a considerable fortune to him. And whereas
he pretended his conscience for refusing, at the queen's command, to return to his own country, because he might not
enjoy his religion here; she ordered her ambassador, then
in Spain, to inform that king, (who had by his ambassador
interceded for him,) that none of her subjects were disturbed for their religion, if they were quiet in the state;
nor should sir Francis. But his seditious spirit and animo-
sity against the queen and her authority still remained, as
appears by writing after this manner to one of her chief
statesmen.

Grindal being the beginning of this year translated from Sandys, bi-
the see of London to that of York, Sandys, bishop of Wor- shop of Wi-
cester, was concluded upon by the queen to be the fittest pointed for
person to be removed into that room; a man dear to the bishop of
London.
citizens, and earnestly desired by them to be their pastor.
Secretary Cecil, who was the great instrument of this intended remove, despatched a message to him, to acquaint
him with the queen's resolution: and therefore prayed him
to hasten to London for that end. But the good bishop,
conscious to himself of his own inability for so great a
charge, and not caring, perhaps, to be placed so much in
view of the court and the whole realm, pleading withal his
want of health, and bodily infirmity, laboured to decline it
as much as he could. And thereupon sent up his chancellor to lay before the secretary his unwillingness on those

accounts to remove from that see, where he hoped he did
God service. But the chancellor did his message after that

manner, as though the bishop were not in earnest, and as
though it were but a faint excuse, and that he required
only some further solicitation to accept it. Which caused
a gentle reprimand of him from Cecil; shewing him, how
the queen was not disposed to think of any one else for that
place; and likewise, that the citizens began to be much displeased with him for his denial. This troubled him; and
concluding this a call from God to this bishopric, he sent
up a pious and modest letter to the secretary, importing
his no longer standing out; and that upon the queen's and
council's summons he would obey and come up. Which
letter, deserving to be inserted, as affording some character
of this godly prelate, was as followeth: viz.

" Sir,

His excuse: " I shall humbly pray you not to be offended, that thus
and accept-
ance of the   " often with my letters I molest your honour. My former
preferment.   " and whole suit was simple, my meaning plain; saying of
Letter to
Cecil.   " myself as I thought of myself: [i. e. declining to be
          28 " translated, because of his mean opinion of himself and
              " his abilities.] If my chancellor hath otherwise insinuated,
              " he did it without commission or knowledge of me. The
              " wants in mind, and the infirmities in body, were the chief
MSS. Ceci-   " causes of my refusal. Yet hearing by my chancellor that
lian.
              " you were offended with me, and understanding that the
              " queen's majesty misliked to alter her highness' determina-
              " tion; and being sundry ways advertised of the clamour
              " of London against me for my refusal, and how that with
              " universal joyfulness the people desired me; this touched
              " my conscience very near, and made me write to your ho-
              " nour in such sort as I did.

              " Sir, your answer unto my man was such as hath won-
              " derfully troubled me. I looked for comfort and good
              " advice, but I fear to reap grief and displeasure. I have
              " given no just cause of offence: my conscience standeth
              " clear. I have ever honoured and loved you, before all

" other men. I have been and will be very ready at your CHAP.
" commaunment in what I can. Wherein I cannot other-   III.
" wise pleasure you, I daily in my prayers commend you Anno 1570.
" unto Him, who can in all things benefit you. This to be
" simple and true, I call the true God to record. My de-
" serving being not to the contrary, I hope to find your
" old wonted favour. You will not in honour and good
" nature cast away your poor friend without all cause. If
" you glome upon me, I shall serve Christ's church with
" less comforth, and to less profit. The world understand-
" eth that you are my good friend, and that I may do
" somewhat with you. If the papists may learn misliking,
" they will easily over-crow me; and it will much weaken
" my work in God's church. I have, as it were, already
" lost the earl of Leicester, because I wrote privately to
" you, and not to him. He told my chancellor, that there-
" with he was much offended. If you shall mislike of me
" also, evil is my hap.
      " Sir, if the queen's majesty and the privy council be not
" otherwise resolved, if you bid me come up, I will, and
" take that office upon me, whatsoever become of me; and
" stand to your favour and courtesy. For in that matter
" you shall wholly dispose of me. The full consent and
" calling of the people of London doth not a little touch
" me. If a meeter be already chosen, I shall be most glad
" of it: so that I may live here, and wheresoever, with
" your favour and wonted friendship. Which I humbly
" crave at your hands; more esteeming the same, than the
" best bishopric in the realm. Good master secretary, stand
" my good friend. Commaund me, and I will obey. Bid
" me, and I will do. Your advice will I follow fully. The
" calling of the prince and of the privy council, the calling
" and consent of the whole people, and my private friends
" earnestly requiring the same, hath narrowly touched my
" conscience; and moveth me to think that this calling is
" of God. I pray you write me three lines, that I may cer-
" tainly know what to do, and whether I be fully dis-
" charged, or no. Thus commending me wholly unto your

"friendship, I commend you to the grace of God. In haste,
"at Hartilbury, this 26th of April, 1570.

"Your honour's in Christ, Ed. Wigorn."

29   Thus the good bishop, partly to recover himself from the
displeasure taken at him, and especially being now touched
in conscience, that this universal appointment of him to
the charge of London was a calling from God, was fain,
with much submission, to comply, and revoke his former
refusal.

Holds his
primary vi-
sitation.

Earl's
Journ. in-
ter MSS. D.
Joh. nuper
episc.
Elien. Ar-
ticles for
the clergy.

He visited his diocese this first year of his translation.
And January the 10th he held his visitation in London.
Some Articles and Injunctions of the bishop then given the
clergy, I learn from a journal of one of these London ministers. "We are straitly charged, I. To keep strictly the
"Book of Common Prayer. II. No man to preach without
"a licence. III. To observe the appointed apparel: that
"is, to wear the square cap, the scholar's gown, &c. And
"in all divine service to wear the surplice. IV. None to re-
"ceive strangers; that is, any of other parishes, to their
"communion. V. All clerks' tolerations to be called in."
This will be better understood, when we are informed, that
there had been divers ministers, who had private meetings
in houses: where they preached, baptized, administered the
communion after a new way, different from the public liturgy, and also condemned it, and the established government of the church. For which, some of them were imprisoned. But such was the clemency of the government,
that the former bishop, by permission and order of the
privy council, granted them, after about a year's restraint,
their liberty; and upon promise of their peaceable behaviour, and a certain subscription, allowed them some toleration. But they misbehaved themselves; among whom the
chief were Crane and Bonham. Which was the cause of
this article of calling in all tolerations. "VI. That pa-
"rish clerks intrude not into the priests' duty, as before
"they had sometimes done." That is, they had taken
upon them, on some occasions, to say common prayer, and

use some of the offices. This was presumption not to be
suffered; and thought fit therefore to be taken notice of
by the bishop in his visitation, and to be made one of his
articles to the clergy, no longer to suffer it.

The Italian church in London, which first began in the
time of king Edward VI. was continued under queen Elizabeth, and had the favour of the state, for the liberty of
religious worship for such Italians as embraced the reformed religion. Whereof there were many residing in
that city, both merchants and others, that had fled thither
from some parts of Italy, where the gospel had been
preached, but now persecuted. Which church was thought
profitable also for the use of such English gentlemen as
had travelled abroad in Italy. That by their resorting thither, they might both serve God, and keep their knowledge
of the Italian language: which by disuse they might otherwise have soon forgotten. But it was an observation now
made, of the evil consequence of young men's travelling
from hence into those parts, viz. that they lost all the good
and sober principles they carried out of England with
them, and became negligent of religion, and little better
than atheists. Which caused Mr. Ascham about this time
to say, " These men thus Italianated abroad, cannot abide
" our godly Italian church at home. They be not of that
" parish, (they say,) they be not of that fellowship. They
" like not the preacher: they hear not his sermons; except 30
" sometime for company, they come thither to hear the
" Italian tongue naturally spoken; not to hear God's doc-
" trine truly preached."

This year John Fox set forth the second time his laborious book of confessors and martyrs. Which bore this title;
The Ecclesiastical History, containing the Acts and Monu-
ments of things passed in every king's time in this realm;
especially in the church of England, principally to be noted.
With a full discourse of such persecutions, horrible troubles,
and sufferings of martyrs; and other things incident,
touching as well the said church of England, as also Scot-

land, and all other foreign nations, from the primitive
times, till the reign of king Henry VIII. Newly recog-
nised and enlarged by the author John Fox. This was the
first volume.

The prole-
gomena be-
fore the
work. The prolegomena before the work consisted of divers
tracts, viz. these that follow. The first is, " To the true
" and faithful congregation of Christ's universal church,
" with all and singular the members thereof, wheresoever
" congregated or dispersed through the realm of England,
" a protestation or petition of the author, wishing to the
" same abundance of all peace and tranquillity, with speedy
" coming of Christ the spouse, to make an end of all mor-
" tal misery." The running title is, *A protestation to the*
whole church of England. The second is the epistle dedicatory, entitled, " To the right virtuous, most excellent,
" and noble princess, queen Elizabeth, our dread lady, by
" the grace of God, queen of England and Ireland, de-
" fender of Christ's faith and gospel, and principal go-
" vernor both of the realm, as also over the said church
" of England and Ireland, under Christ the supreme head
" of the same, John Fox, her humble subject, wisheth
" daily increase of God's holy Spirit and grace, with long
" reign, perfect health, and joyful peace, to govern his
" flock committed to her charge ; to the example of all good
" princes, the comfort of his church, and glory of his blessed
" name."

The book
clamoured
against, In which epistle, near the beginning, are these words,
expressing what high displeasure the papalins conceived
against him, only for exposing, by way of historical relation, the barbarous usages expressed by them towards such
as professed the gospel. " That when he first presented
" those Acts and Monuments unto her majesty, &c. which
" her rare clemency received in such gentle part, he well
" hoped that those his travels in that kind of writing had
" been well at an end : whereby he might have returned to
" his studies again, to other purposes, after his own desire
" more fit, than to write histories, especially in the English

" tongue. But that certain evil disposed persons, of intem-
" perate tongues, adversaries to good proceedings, would
" not suffer him to rest; fuming and fretting, and raising Anno 1570.
" up such miserable exclamations against the first appear-
" ance of the book, as was wonderful to hear. A man (as
" he expressed himself) would have thought Christ to have
" been new born again, and that Herod and all the city of
" Jerusalem had been in an uproar; such blustering and
" stirring was there against that poor book, through all
" quarters of England, to the gates of Lovain. So that no To the
" English papist almost in all the realm thought himself gates of
Lovain.
" a perfect catholic, unless he had cast out some word or
" other, to give that book a blow...... They clamoured 31
" against it, to be full of lies, &c. As though there were no The various slan-
" histories else in all the world corrupt, but only this story ders cast
" of Acts and Monuments. That with tragical voices they upon it.
" exclaimed and wondered upon it: sparing no cost (said
" he) of hyperbolical phrases, to make it appear as full of
" lies as lines..... And this only for three or four escapes
" in that book committed. And yet some of them were in
" the same book amended: they neither reading the whole,
" nor rightly understanding that they read, inveighed and
" maligned so perversely the setting out thereof, as though
" neither any word in all that story were true, nor any
" other story false in all the world." But then concerning
such matters related by him that were errors indeed, he
added, (for the satisfaction of all sober, unprejudiced readers,
if not for the silencing of those calumniators,) " That ne- His pains
to stop cla-
" vertheless, in accusing these his accusers, he did not so mours, in
" excuse himself, nor defend his book, as though nothing reviewing
the book
" in it were to be spunged or amended, therefore he had again.
" taken pains to reiterate his labours, in travelling out the
" story again: doing herein as Penelope did with her web,
" untwisting that she had done before: or as builders do
" sometimes; take down again their buildings, either to
" transpose the fashion, or to make the foundation larger:
" so he in recognising this history had employed a little

BOOK I.

Anno 1570.

" more labour, partly to enlarge the argument he took in
" hand, partly also to assay, whether by any pains-taking
" he might pacify the stomachs or satisfy the judgments of
" these importune quarrellers."

Other prefatory tracts in this book.

A third prefatory tract to this book is addressed to the
true Christian reader, on this subject, *What utility is to be
taken by reading of these histories.* A fourth is written, *To
all the professed friends and followers of the pope's proceedings; four questions propounded to them.* Then follow the names of the authors alleged in this book: and of
the martyrs that suffered. Then are set down *corrections*
of sundry faults, defects, and oversights in both volumes of
this history: and next, certain *cautions* of the author to
the reader, of things to be considered in reading this story.
What these *cautions* are, I refer the reader to the Appendix, to inform him in. Where we may observe the dispositions of many to find fault with Mr. Fox's pains, by the
frivolous exceptions that were taken at several things, and
at very minute mistakes or omissions.

Numb. VI.

Lambard sends his Perambulation of Kent to Mr. Wotton.

This year did William Lambard of Lincoln's Inn send
in writing the antiquities of Kent to Tho. Wotton, esq.
a worthy and learned gentleman of the same county: a
book abounding with variety of ancient and curious historical collections of places and matters of that county; entitled, *A perambulation of Kent,* containing the description,
history, and customs of that shire. Which Mr. Wotton
five or six years after published, with his own recommendatory epistle before it, to the gentlemen of the county.

His study of the antiquities of this island.

Mr. Lambard's genius led him to gather, out of all ancient
as well as modern histories of this island, sundry notes of
such quality, as might serve for the description and story
of the most famous places throughout this whole realm;
which he called, *A topographical dictionary,* because it was
digested into titles by order of alphabet, and concerned the
32 description of places. Out of which he meant in time (if
God granted him life, ability, and leisure) to draw, as from
a certain storehouse, fit matter for each particular shire

and county. And resolved first to begin with Kent; as he
wrote in his epistle to Mr. Wotton, when he sent him the
said MS.

This year Dr. Thomas Wylson, a learned civilian, master
of St. Katharine's, near the Tower of London, set forth certain orations of Demosthenes, the famous orator of Athens,
translated by him into elegant English, being a man of po-
lite learning in Latin and Greek; which I took some notice of in the former volume. He set about this translation
with the greatest care and exactness, that it might be
looked upon in that age as a perfect piece of eloquent
English language; and that it might answer the tongue
and oratory of the first and chiefest orator of Athens; as
he writes in his preface. And in this his translation he
made use of the Latin translation made by that singular
learned man sir John Cheeke, sometime the king's Greek
professor in Cambridge; who had read some of these orations formerly to this Wylson and other English scholars
in Padua; whither they were retired for their safety in the
persecuting times of queen Mary. The interpretation whereof Wylson had from his own mouth, who kindly took
care over all the Englishmen there. And the very argument of those causes that orator handled, so agreeing to
those times of queen Elizabeth, made him the rather to enter upon this work of translating into our own tongue; for
the people of this nation to read these orations against king
Philip of Macedon: that king Philip, and Philip king of
Spain, equally ambitious to overrun other countries more
than their own. And that England might stand upon her
guard against one Philip, as Athens was counselled to do
against another.

Thus we have that orator addressing himself to his Athe-
nian auditors with respect to king Philip: " Counselling
" them to take heed of him, as a justly suspected enemy;
" and no ways to trust his forged peace: under shadow
" whereof he doth, saith he, all the mischief he can. And
" therefore willed them to look well to their business,
" and to trust to themselves, making ready against all as-

" says; because that Philip did nothing else but lie in wait
" for them, and all Greece besides, to conquer them, and
" to become a tyrant over them, &c. making it plain, that
" king Philip did hate them deadly; and warning them for
" that cause not to trust his fair promises: for that he had
" most cruelly abused other cities and countries with like
" craft and subtilty. The orator then inveighed against
" those traitors that were king Philip's hirelings: and
" shewed, that their promises and king Philip's doings
" agreed not together, and declared him to be their mortal
" enemy. And therefore advised them to take up arms, and
" proclaim open war, for the better safeguard and defence
" of their whole estate and country." It is easy to see how
parallel the case of England now was with that of Athens
then, in divers particulars: which the publisher of these
orations, no doubt, had his eye upon.

It partly also gave him occasion, (as he tells us,) to set
about this work, whilst once, being solitary among his
books, he recollected his former felicity under the teaching
and instruction of that foresaid learned man, while they
33 conversed at that university in Italy. Of whom he could
not refrain to speak with much honour and respect. And of
him, and such other incomparable men for piety, learning,
and usefulness in that age, I take all opportunities to retrieve the precious memory. Take then Dr. Wylson's words
of him; " That he deeply thought, and often, of that
" learned man and singular ornament of this land. And as
" the remembrance of him was dear unto him, for his ma-
" nifold great gifts and wonderful virtues, so he thought of
" his most gentle nature and godly disposed mind, to help
" all those with his knowledge and understanding, that any
" way made means unto him, and sought his favour. And
" to say for myself, as he proceeded, among others, I found
" him such a friend to me, in communicating his skill, and
" the gifts of his mind, as I cannot, but during my life,
" speak reverendly of so worthy a man, and honour in my
" heart the heavenly remembrance of him."

He mentioned a saying of this Cheek concerning De-

mosthenes; viz. " That none ever was more fit to make an
" Englishman tell his tale praiseworthily in any open hear-
" ing, either in parliament, pulpit, or otherwise, than this
" orator alone was."   His saying
of Demos-
But his main motive for his translating and printing these thenes.
orations may be worth our hearing more at large; namely,
" That he could not suffer so noble an orator, and so ne- The benefit
" cessary a writer for all those that loved their country's of reading
Demosthe-
" liberty and welfare, to lie hid and unknown, especially in nes.
" such a dangerous world as this was." Other reasons moving him lie in these words of his: " He that loveth his
" country, and desireth to procure the welfare of it, let him
" read Demosthenes, and he shall not want matter to do
" himself good. For he that seeketh common quietness, De-
" mosthenes can teach him his lesson. He that would gladly
" prevent evil to come, Demosthenes is for his purpose. He
" that desireth to serve his country abroad, let him read
" Demosthenes day and night: for this is he that is able to
" make him fit to do any service for his country's welfare.
" For never did glass so truly represent a man's face, as
" Demosthenes doth shew the world to us. And as it was
" then, so it is now; and will be so still, till the consumma-
" tion and end of all things. The Devil never ceaseth from
" the beginning of the world to make division, and contrive
" to stir civil wars; to embolden the commons against their
" superiors; to put evil thoughts into counsellors' head;
" to make people ambitious and covetous, and corrupt the
" hearts even of the messengers and preachers of God's
" word: continuing his practice still in all places, with all
" men. And therefore, seeing Demosthenes is so good a
" schoolmaster for men, to decipher the Devil and his mini-
" sters, for the advancement of uprightness in all things, I
" would wish that all men would become his scholars."
To the title of this book, *The Orations of Demosthenes,*
chief orator among the Grecians, &c. was added, *Most*
needful to be redde in these daungerous dayes, of al them
that love their countryes libertie, and desire to take warning
for their better avayle, by example of others. He dedicated

BOOK
I.

Anno 1570.

34

[Number
VI.]

this his translation in a large epistle to sir William Cecil, knight, to whom he had sent the copy for his judgment before he would publish it; and a private letter in Latin accompanying it: which I have transcribed from his own pen, and put into the Appendix; as a remembrance of one who was, besides his great learning, sometime the queen's ambassador, and afterwards one of her principal secretaries.

CHAP. IV.

Motions and letters concerning the queen's marrying with duke d'Anjou. The matter of religion the great article. The queen will not allow him the exercise of the mass. Ambassadors from France move for that article. The queen's resolution. The treaty put off. Renewed again: but to no purpose. Fears and apprehensions hereupon. Amity however endeavoured with France. Motion of the match revived. Discourse about it between the French ambassador and the queen. She hath no inclination that way. Practice of Spain. Sir Thomas Smith sent into France for cultivating amity. Promotes the marriage between the prince of Navar and the French king's sister.

Anno 1571.

Motion of
marriage
between
the queen
and duke
d'Anjou.

THE queen's matching with Henry duke d'Anjou, the French king's brother, as it was moved the last year, so it was earnestly pursued this. A matter that had its conveniencies, it being the best means of securing queen Elizabeth against the Scotch queen's pretences; and its dangers to the state of religion established. I shall therefore collect what I find in letters of ambassadors, and papers of state, concerning this important affair; avoiding what our historians have already written of it. The embassy of Mr. Walsingham was chiefly for this end. And the great aim was, to bring about the changing of duke d'Anjou's religion. And then it was in all fair probability to take effect. As for monsieur, he declared a mighty affection for the queen to Walsingham: and that though he was but young, yet that any time these five years there had been overtures of

marriage made to him; and that he found in himself no CHAP.
inclination unto this present time to yield to any. But that ___IV.___
he must confess, that through the great commendations Anno 1571.
that was made of the queen his mistress, for her rare gifts Anjou's
as well of mind as of body; being, as even her enemies queen.
said, the rarest creature that had been in Europe these five
hundred years; his affections, grounded upon so good respects, had now made him yield to be wholly hers. This
was the noble lover's protestation to the English ambassador.

And of the amendment of his religion, the said ambassador had hope. Which when Cecil the secretary (now newly March 25.
created lord of Burghley) understood by the lord Buckhurst, late ambassador also in France, he thus expressed
himself in a letter to Walsingham, " That if monsieur 35
" were not rooted in opinion of evil religion, as by reason The secre-
" of his young years it was likely such a change might by concerning
" argument be brought about; then by his marrying within that duke's
" England, and becoming a professor of the gospel, (con- his religion.
" sidering his towardness to be a martial prince,) he might
" prove a noble conqueror of all popery in Christendom,
" with such aids as might join with him in the empire and
" otherwhere. And of such a design the secretary wished
" he might be capable." But this, which he wrote from the
court at Greenwich, he enjoined him to keep secret within
his own breast; saying, " The more he writ, the more open
" he was; considering the trust he had in his secrecy, and
" trusting notwithstanding, that nothing thereof should
" have light, to do him any hurt."

Therefore it was privily resolved in the English court, Instruc-
that monsieur, if he married the queen, must not use any ambassador
religion different from that of the queen. For so it ran in about the
the instructions given to sir Thomas Smith, (who was am- religion.
bassador in France immediately before Walsingham,) in
these terms; " That although it may be sufferable to have
" an outward exercise of Christian religion in divers sorts
" among the subjects of one realm; yet to have a diversity,
" or rather a contrariety in outward exercise of religion be-

" tween us, (being queen of the realm, and so the head of
" the people,) and him that should be her husband, seemeth
" not only dangerous, but also absurd, yea, almost impossi-
" ble. This must be for a principal argument."

The private
exercise of
monsieur's
religion not
allowed.
And why.
Cotton li-
brary, Ju-
lius, F. 6.

And when it was required on the French part, that monsieur might have only the private exercise of the popish religion, the counsellors would not admit of it; " Forasmuch
" as the granting unto him the exercise of his religion, be-
" ing contrary unto the laws of the land, might, by an ex-
" ample, breed such an offence as was likely to breed much
" trouble." Walsingham discoursed with the queen-mother
on this argument. When she insisted much upon it, and
used the argument of her son's honour, to obtain this liberty, he beseeched her to consider as well the queen his
mistress's danger as her son's honour; shewing her, that of
this permission great danger would ensue: as, I. The violating of her laws. II. The offence of her good and faithful subjects. And lastly, The encouragement of the evil-
affected. Which three mischiefs, if she would but weigh
with her son's honour, she would find them to be of great
moment. This discourse Walsingham had with this French
queen, upon command from queen Elizabeth's letters
brought by Cavalcant, the French ambassador, lately returned to Paris. Who acquainted Walsingham that it was
the queen-mother's pleasure, that he should come to her at

Discourse
thereof be-
tween the
queen-
mother.
and Wal-
singham.

St. Cloud's about four miles from Paris. Then he desired to
know of her, how she was satisfied with an answer the
queen had sent her by Cavalcant, unto certain articles propounded by the king and her, to the end that he might
advertise her majesty. She then told him, among other
things, that the second article, which was concerning religion, was very hard, and narrowly touched the honour of
her son. Insomuch that should he yield thereto, the queen
herself would receive also some part of the blemish, by ac-
36 cepting for an husband such an one, as by sudden change
of religion might be thought drawn by worldly respects,
and void of all conscience and religion. To which Walsingham replied, that he was willed to say to her, that

monsieur, she doubted not, but that by her good persua- CHAP.
sions, would accept in good part the said answer. And that IV.
she meant not such change of a sudden, as that he and his Anno 1571.
household should be compelled to use the rites of the English church, contrary to his or their consciences. And so
the ambassador proceeded in his discourse as is above mentioned. This I have extracted from Walsingham's original
letter to the lord Burghley, in the Paper-office, endorsed Numb. VII.
thus by that lord's own hand : *April 28, 1571, Mr. Walsingham to me, after the return of Cavalcant into France:*
and by another hand, *Upon the permission or toleration of
popery, what mischief will ensue?* The whole letter containing this more fully, with other matters, I have transcribed
into the Appendix.

De Foix, employed by the French in this business, made Discourse
answer to this; viz. That to live without exercise of reli- with the
French am-
gion, was as much as to be of no religion. And he knew bassador
concerning
the queen's majesty in honour would not have him touched monsieur's
with so great a spot, as to be thought an atheist. To this it religion.
was replied, that if it were true, that he, the ambassador,
had heard, monsieur was not so far from our religion, having had some introduction therein by Carnvallet, his governor, lately deceased. And therefore, if it pleased him to
water those seeds which he had already received, by some
conference, he should be able easily to discern, that the
change of his religion would breed unto him no dishonour.

The queen stood well affected to proceed in the marriage, Great hopes
of proceed-
in case reason might take place in the conditions, as the ing in the
earl of Leicester told Walsingham in his letter. And how match.
Compl.
likely this article of religion was to succeed, the ambassa- Amb.
dor informed the said earl : " That he conceived great hopes
" thereof, by certain speeches lately passed between the
" French king, monsieur's brother, and Teligny ; viz. that
" religion should not be the let, which was the chiefest thing
" respected in this match." For that the king entering into
discourse with that French gentleman, who had said, that
it seemed strange to the world, that monsieur grew every
day more suspicious than other, appearing much bent to

his religion; the king replied, that his brother, if there
fell out no other lets but religion, would be ruled by him.
" And because," said the king, " that I may bring the mat-
" ter the better to pass, I will have my brother with me out
" of this town, and deliver him from certain superstitious
" friars, that seem to nourish this new holiness in him.
" And that he doubted not, within a few days, so to work
" upon his brother, as he would yield to any thing he
" should require." And two days after, the king called Teligny again unto him, and asked him, whether he had lately
any talk with his brother. Teligny then shewed the king,
that the same day at dinner monsieur called him unto
him; and that his whole course of talk was only in commendation of the queen's majesty, and of the great desire
he had to have so happy and so honourable a match.
Whereby, said he, I see him so far, as I hope he will not
make any difficulty at religion; which will be the chief
matter the queen will stick at. To which the king said, No;
observe my brother well; and you shall see him every day
less superstitious than other. By this speech it appeared
what great hope Walsingham conceived of the king's revolt
also from papistry: using these words to Leicester; Surely
I am of opinion, that if this match go forward, it will set
the triple crown quite aside. But our good ambassador
was not yet sufficiently acquainted with that king's dissimulation.

37

Monsieur
studies to
oblige the
queen and
Leicester.
In the mean time, that monsieur might the more oblige
the queen, the queen-mother told the English ambassador,
that her son would send over marshal Montmorancy, [a
person very acceptable unto this court,] because the queen
her sister desired it. And that he desired again, that she
would send thither, into France, the earl of Leicester, [her
favourite.] Whom he desired to see and honour, for the
good affection that he bore to the amity between the two
realms, and to requite him for the presents which he had at
divers times sent unto him. And then she doubted not all
things should be done as her majesty desired.

This business therefore, about the article of religion, was

earnestly transacted here at the English court: whereof the CHAP.
queen made a relation to her ambassador in France. The IV.
French ambassador and Cavalcant, an Italian gentleman Anno 1571.
there, (but one that had long lived in England, and was Ambassa-dors from
well affected towards it,) were come hither from the French France
king about this affair. And the earl of Leicester and the come about this matter.
lord Burghley were appointed by the queen to be her commissioners to treat with them. The ambassador began with
the article concerning the celebration of the matrimony by
the English book. And here he said, he doubted that the
usage of matrimony by the order of this church might
contain matter repugnant to the duke's conscience. And
namely, that he should be urged at that time to receive the
sacrament according to the institution of this church. The The duke's
queen, as to this point, directed Walsingham to tell mon- scruple of being mar-
sieur de Foix, that that was the very order of the book, viz. ried by the
that " it was convenient the married couple should receive English book.
" the communion." But however, that being not of necessity, he might give them some hope, that it might, for
reasonable respects, be forborne. But for the other and
main article, that the duke d'Anjou should have no liberty
for himself and his domestics, to use his own religion, the
French ambassador urged to have it permitted, with these
cautions and conditions; " That he should use his religion Cautions
" in secret place and manner, and with such circumspection, and condi-tions of-
" as thereby no manner of public offence should grow to fered for his religion.
" the queen's subjects."

But to this the queen would not yield : being answered, The queen
that she doubted not, but that monsieur d'Anjou would, by will not permit his
the advice of the queen-mother, be contented with the queen's exercise of
answer, being well weighed ; in that she will be contented, his reli-gion ; nor
that by no means neither he nor his domestics should be compel him
compelled to use the rites of our religion, otherwise than to hers.
should be agreeable with his conscience. But as for the
exercise of his own religion, being especially forbidden by
our laws, she could not, without manifest offence and peril
to her state, accord thereto. And having acquainted Wal-

singham with all this, she told him, that he should use all good persuasions to induce them to be content with her answer in that behalf. And that for the better maintaining thereof, he should require that it might be considered, what peril it might be to the quietness of her state, to have one that should be her husband, (by his example in her house,) to give comfort to her subjects to break her laws, that presently were devoted to obey them. Which might so fall out in process of time, as it might repent her that ever she had been so illy advised, &c. And in any wise, she bade her ambassador give them no other comfort in this behalf. And she thought meet, that before any other things were treated of, this matter concerning the point of religion were first on both parties determined. And this being accorded, there would be no great difficulty in the rest. And that considering this matter for religion seemed of such substance, as none of the rest were, she thought it best to have this first treated of; and so enter to proceed or forbear.

Other mat-
ters about
religion re-
quired on
the queen's
part.
Other articles relating to religion were, that the duke should accompany the queen at the usual times to her chapel and oratory; and there remain in some convenient place, until the queen returned back. And that the duke neither by himself nor any other should procure that a change or alteration be made or attempted of the evangelical laws of religion set forth in the realm of England; nor afford favour to any subject of the queen's; whereby in any part to violate these ecclesiastical laws; but should rather endeavour that such a violator of them be brought to punishment.

Resolution
on the
French
part.
When Walsingham had treated at large, according to these instructions, with the queen-mother about this great article, she said, it was generally feared by the catholics, that this match would breed a change of religion throughout all Europe. And then concluded, that neither monsieur her son, nor the king, nor herself could ever yield to any such sudden change for any respect whatsoever. Add-

ing, that her son would soon be overcome by the queen's
persuasions, he being more zealous than able to defend his
religion.

This put some stop to proceedings. Afterwards De Foix Further
treaty.
writ letters, that this matter might be continued; as though
there would be other offers made by them. But the queen
handled the matter exceeding well with the ambassador, and
gave him no hope, without yielding on their part. And
this the earl of Leicester signified to Walsingham; and
that, as far as he could perceive, they would rather yield
than break off. Walsingham observed, how the French
protestants did earnestly desire this match; and the papists,
on the other side, did seem earnestly to impeach the same:
which made him the more diligent and eager to further it.
And that upon wise considerations, observing how her ma- Walsing-
ham's ap-
prehen-
sions.
jesty's estate, both at home and abroad, stood, as he in his
poor eyesight, as he said, could discern; and how she was
beset with foreign perils; the execution whereof stayed only
upon the event of this match; he saw not how she could
stand, if this matter brake off. These were that statesman's
apprehensions; and this was the reason he laboured to promote this affair, and wrote so earnestly for it, upon no other
particular respect, as God, he said, was his witness, but 39
only the regard he had to God's glory and her majesty's
safety.

It was now the month of May, when the queen wrote her- The queen
writes her
resolution
to Walsing-
ham, her
ambassador.
Compl.
Amb.
self a letter to him, treating of this matter at large; bidding
him tell the queen-mother, or the king, that she found more
great and urgent causes to move her to persist in her former
answer in that article of religion, both for her conscience,
safety, honour, and quietness, than could be alleged or imagined for the conscience and honour of monsieur d'Anjou.
She spake here about our public prayers; that duke d'Anjou Her argu-
ments for
monsieur's
compliance
in religion.
might very well be present at them: for that in them there
was no part that had not been, yea, that was not at that day
used in the church of Rome; and that if any thing more
were in ours, the same was part of the holy scripture. That
if it were said ours was in English, we had them translated

in other languages, as in Latin or French : either of which his own ministers might use in places convenient. That

whereas it might be objected, that hereby he would make a change of his faith in matters of religion, the queen meant not to prescribe this to him, or any person, that they would at her motion, or in respect of her, change their religion in matters of faith. Neither did the usage of the divine service of England properly compel any to alter his religion, in controversies in the church, only the usage thereof did direct men daily to read and hear the scripture, to pray to Almighty God by the daily use of the psalter of David : and the ancient prayers, anthems, and collects of the church were even the same which the universal church had used, and yet did use.

Our liturgy
favourably
represented
to him by
the lord
Burghley. This favourable representation of our reformed service, or liturgy, to monsieur and these Romanists, the French king and queen-mother, was used also by the lord Burghley. For when the French ambassador had asserted to the earl of Leicester and him, that monsieur would never sustain that dishonour, to come hither with that account to be made of him, that he had no religion, if he should not be allowed to have mass ; then Burghley answered, as it was contained before in the queen's letters, setting out the nearness of our divine service to such things as were good and sound in the Roman : adding, that we in our book wanted nothing but such things as were either impious, or doubtful to be against the scriptures. And that this that had been said of our liturgy might be the better known and read in France, Walsingham desired, that by the next, a Common Prayer translated into French might be sent unto him, to present it unto monsieur, saying, that he had seen of them printed at Guernsey, [for the use of the churches there.] And accordingly, in June, a French Common Prayer Book was sent over. But all these endeavours succeeded not.

This treaty
put off upon
the account
of religion
by the
queen : For it was about July the queen put off the match, on the account of religion, she refusing absolutely to permit the use of the mass, which was so stiffly insisted on in that article, viz. that the duke of Anjou should not be molested,

propter usurpationem aliquorum divinorum rituum et cere-
moniarum. Whereupon great were the fears and disturbances of the minds of the best men. " I have done my
" utmost," said the lord Burghley, " and so have other
" counsellors. The lord keeper hath earnestly endeavoured 40
" it. The earls of Sussex and Leicester have joined vigor-
" ously in it." And he knew none directly against it. From
Spain likewise came no good answer; and therefore that Which
great and good statesman concluded that amity to be need- created great ap-
ful for them. " But God," said he, " hath determined to prehensions
" plague us. The hour is at hand. His will be done with and fears.
" mercy." Such dreadful apprehensions had the wisest on
this emergence.

If we would know what the earl of Leicester's thoughts
were of this matter, who knew best the queen's mind, he
signified it in July, to this purpose, in his letter to Walsingham : " That for his opinion in this great matter, he would Leicester's
" deal plainly with him, even as he found her majesty's dis- account of the queen's
" position. That as for her desire of marriage, he per- disposition;
" ceived it continued still as it was; which was very cold. and his thoughts
" That nevertheless she saw it so necessary, as he believed thereof. July 8.
" she yielded rather to think it fit to have an husband, than
" willing indeed to have any found for her. And he feared
" so it would appear in this matter of monsieur. And so it
" might be perceived by the articles passed already, that there
" was among them all, but one that made that difficulty;
" namely, this demand to have the private exercise of his
" religion : which as they all [of the privy council] liked of,
" that is, her majesty's denial to allow of the papistical reli-
" gion, so it did appear, that if he would omit that demand,
" and put it in silence, yet would her majesty straitly capi-
" tulate with him, that he should in no wise demand it here-
" after at her hand : which scruple, he believed, would ut-
" terly break off the matter." And then the earl brake his
own apprehensions; praying God some other amity might be
accepted, as concluding (as the lord Burghley did) a breach
with France. Albeit, as he added, he distrusted not the
goodness of God : but that, whatsoever shall fall out, it was

God's providence for the best, or at least for our just scourge
for our deservings towards him.   And no more could he
say, but that Almighty God would strengthen her majesty's
true zeal for religion; and that, not favouring this match,
she would ally herself with some princes abroad, as would
earnestly join with her therein.

The people of England we now see at their prayers, having a dismal prospect of two powerful neighbouring nations,
their enemies, Spain and France, besides no good understanding with other states and countries : for they looked
upon this refusal of monsieur to be nothing but the opening
a door to hostility with France.   Leicester expressed this in
his correspondence with the English ambassador there, after
this manner : " In Spain we have no cause to look for any
" friendship. What terms we stand in to other places is easily
" known.   Thus we are with our neighbours in all places
" without friendship.   God protect and defend us ; who is
" only able, and must do it, for any policy used."   The
strength and safety of England now depending wholly, in
all human appearance, on the friendship of France, whereof
there was now little hope.

But notwithstanding all these fears and jealousies in the
wisest heads, by Walsingham's means, and God's good providence overruling and concurring, though the match with
41 France went off, a league was concluded with the French
king.   For to this import the said ambassador's next despatch to Leicester tended : " That he was put in hopes, that
" though the matter so much laboured succeeded not, yet
" that the king's intention was to send some person of good
" quality, as well to thank her majesty for her honourable
" proceedings in this cause, as also to desire continuance of
" good amity."   And he advised, that it behoved her majesty to look about her, being environed with so many practices, the execution whereof had stayed, as he said, upon the
event of the match.   And that he did what he could to procure continuance, or rather increase of amity.   And that the
king himself, as he learned, was very well inclined thereto,
and the rather through a mislike he had to Spain.

And this must be looked upon in this extremity as a sin- CHAP.
gular point of God's gracious providence to this state and ___IV.___
church at this dangerous juncture, in turning that king's Anno 1571.
heart towards the queen.   For he willed her ambassador to A gracious
tell her majesty, " That whatsoever became of the cause, in an ex-
" that in respect of her honourable and sincere dealing in tremity.
" the same, and the confidence she shewed to repose in him, ham's letter
" she might assure herself as much of his friendship as of to lord
" any others in the world; and that she had full power to July ult.
" dispose of him and of his realms, to the benefit of herself
" and of her subjects.   And that his sword should be always
" ready to defend her against any that should attempt any
" thing against her.   And he joined, as this letter added,
" his words and countenance so together, as great demon-
" stration outwardly, of his inward good will : which could
" not but be seen thereby."   Such were the king's obliging
terms, unless there were a mixture of deceit and fraud
therein.   For he was indeed the greatest and most artificial
dissembler in the world.

Yet still the match was not in such despair, but the mo- Motion of
tion about it soon began to revive again ; listened to on the the match
part of the English, for the preserving France fast to England ; and on the part of the French, on account of the
greatness and honourableness of wedding with such a mighty
princess, as well as for other ends of their own.   The hinderers of the good proceedings therein in France appeared
now to Walsingham ; who were the pope's nuncio, together Impedi-
with Spain and Portugal, who daily laboured in dissuading its proceed-
the match ; and the clergy also, who had offered to monsieur ing.
a great pension to stay from further proceeding in it.   And
in conclusion, nothing was left undone that might be thought
fit to put impediment to it ; and there were some enemies of
the queen within her dominions that had wrote into France,
that the queen had nothing less than intention to marry,
whatever she pretended.   And hereof he who sent this news
was well assured by those that were about her : and therefore willed them there to be of good comfort, and never to
doubt of the matter.   This person was the Scottish am-

bassador, then at London, as Walsingham afterwards understood; who pretended to know all secrets of state. Whence
the ambassador judged there was bred in them there, in
France, on this occasion, some doubt of late of her majesty's
disposition to marry, so as they knew not how to proceed.
42 Which doubt was now made an advertisement from the said
Scottish ambassador, who was the busy bishop of Rosse.

The protes-
tants in
France,
their con-
cern about
it.   But the protestants in France hung all their peace and
happiness upon either this match, or at least amity with
France. So that if neither amity nor marriage might take
place, (writeth Walsingham,) the poor protestants here do
think then their case desperate. And so they told him with
tears.

French am-
bassador
comes over.
Aug. 3.   Monsieur de Foix was now sent over on purpose to com-
promise (if possible) the matter, to mollify the article of
religion, so much controverted. There was a phrase added in
this article, which was, that " the duke should not be molested
" for using any rite not repugnant unto the word of God."
Which words being delivered unto them in the month
of August, they disliked the expression, viz. *the word of
God.* So that by their importunity it was altered from
verbo Dei to *ecclesiæ Dei;* which in the queen's judgment
was all one. But with that, though they were better contented than with the other, yet they insisted upon changing
that to *catholicæ ecclesiæ.* Whereunto she did not assent.
But that there should be no mistake, the queen by speech
The queen
declares
her mind
to him about
the point of
religion. declared to De Foix, " That as she would be well contented
" that her answer might satisfy monsieur d'Anjou for his
" *honour,* [which was the great pretence,] for that she had
" in sort yielded unto him, to use other ceremonies than
" those of her religion, so that they were not repugnant to
" the word of God; so her meaning was to be declared
" plainly to him, that she could not permit him at his com-
" ing to have the use of any private mass. That so there
" might be no misconceiving gathered from her answer;
" whereby the duke might hope for any sufferance : for that
" she could not find it without peril of her estate and quiet-
" ness to yield thereto." The ambassador had good enter-

tainment in all external offices of respect, well used by her
majesty, defrayed for his diet, while he was at court.

And it being now September, and the queen in her progress at Audley End, near Saffron Walden, he was attended The lord
Burghley
very courteously and honourably by the lord Buckhurst, hearty for
during his being there, in going and returning. And the the marriage.
lord Burghley, for the more honour, caused the earl of Oxford, his son-in-law, to attend on him in divers places: and
in the way from London to Walden the said lord entertained
him at his house at Theobalds. And there De Foix and the
other ambassador resident saw his hearty devotion to the
marriage. And this he did to shew how confirmed his judgment was for it, (as he wrote to Walsingham,) and that he
was not ashamed to utter himself, however it might be perilous to him, if it should not take place. For he reckoned,
(as he, now full of concern for the public, expressed his
thoughts,) " that blessing or vengeance was now to be ex-
" pected at God's hand.   And in the mean time his behold-
" ing of this cloud, and the time to creep nearer, called upon
" him and all good Englishmen to implore God's mercy,
" and to beseech him to direct her majesty's heart to choose
" that which might be most for his glory."

After seven or eight special conferences with her majesty The last resolution
and her council, (wherein several there were that secretly about the
obstructed this great affair, and threw in on purpose hard marriage, in
council. In
terms, and answers given to the ambassador in words were favour of it.
altered in writing, as to the point of religion,) yet it was at 43
last resolved ; " and so the queen pronounced to her coun-
" cil, whom she saw earnestly bent by all means to further
" this marriage, for her own surety, and for avoiding the in-
" evitable ruin of this monarchy, (I do but repeat the words
" of that great and honest counsellor,) that surely, so as
" monsieur will forbear the mass, she will assent to the Lord
Burghley's
" marriage. And this she confirmed with all good speeches letter to
" to give credit. But yet all her counsellors (whereof that Walsingham.
" lord was one) were not so persuaded ; not as doubting her
" assertions, (which surely were agreeable to her mind,
" when she uttered them,) but for doubt that other mis-

" liking the same, might indirectly draw her from her de-
" termination."

The three chief articles required on the French part, concerning monsieur, which were, that he should be crowned
king of these realms, and that he should be joined with the
queen in the administration and government of the kingdom, and for the toleration of the exercise of his religion,
with the cautious answers thereunto, may be found in the
Complete Ambassador.

De Foix was now gone home with the resolutions taken in
England, and the queen and her statesmen were in expectation of the result thereof in France. The queen was persuaded, that they would yield in the matter of religion for
monsieur. And if they did so, she seemed to her council
that she would, according to her word, proceed. But the
earl of Leicester, who knew her temper best, said, that to
speak his conscience, he thought she had rather he [the
ambassador] had increased some hard points than yielded
to them. And therefore the hopes of the court were small,
that ever the match should take place. And Leicester declared, in his correspondence with the English ambassador
in France, " that he was persuaded her majesty's heart
" was not inclined to marry at all, since the matter was ever
" brought to as many points as could be devised: and she
" was always bent to hold with the difficultest. And it
" grieved (as he said) his very heart to think of it, seeing
" no way he could think of might serve how she could re-
" main quiet and safe, without such a strong alliance as
" marriage must be. For the amities of others (as he
" added) might serve for a time; but no account was to be
" made of them longer than to serve the turn of each party.
" And her majesty's years running away so fast, caused him
" to despair of long quietness."

It fell out so indeed. It was now October; and the treaty
about the match was laid aside. Walsingham's great business now was to cultivate a good amity between the French
and our queen Elizabeth; which that king seemed very
much inclined to. And a new embassy from England was

preparing for that purpose. Now towards the declining of the year sir Thomas Smith goes again to France, to make a firm treaty, offensive and defensive, between that nation and the queen; and withal to speak with that king secretly concerning the marriage. He was appointed to go in December, though he came not there till towards February following. Of whom the lord Burghley gives this character; that he was one, he thought, of such dexterity in his actions, and of such dutiful good-will towards England, that no advice or direction could be given to our prejudice.

But Spain all this while had a jealous eye upon these transactions between France and England, and endeavoured all she could to obstruct the friendship now laboured between the two crowns, and particularly to hinder the match in concert between the queen and monsieur; which was so much desired by the English, as tending to strengthen them against the attempts of Spain. In order to which perhaps it was, that in December this year comes a Spaniard, in quality of some secret messenger, as from queen Elizabeth, to the elector of Saxony, pretending himself to be one of her chamber, to signify to him, that the queen being now minded to marry, had sent him to treat thereof with him concerning the prince his son. It looked strange to the elector, especially since he had brought no letters of credence with him. But that was omitted, as he said, for the more privacy. But to be better informed, the elector thought fit to inquire of Christopher Mount, the queen's agent at Strasburgh, concerning this matter. The account of this whole matter take from the agent's own pen, in a letter or two to this purport.

" That a certain Spaniard, calling himself Jacomo, An-
" tonio, Gromo, alias Pacheco, in the end of December last,
" came alone to Heidelberg, and requiring a secret audi-
" ence, was admitted to the elector himself. There he ex-
" pounded, that he was sent out of England by the queen,
" to note and see the person and form of the son of the
" elector, Christophero: for that the queen had altogether
" brought her mind to marry. And that he was sent with-

Marginal notes:

CHAP. IV.

Anno 1571.

Sir Tho. Smith sent ambassador into France concerning amity.

Letter to Walsingham.

44

A Spaniard pretends to be sent from the queen to the elector of Saxony.

The queen's agent's letter to Burghley concerning him.

MSS. Burgh.

" out the knowledge of her counsellors, that so she might
" conceal and hide this her deliberation.   That the elector
" asking, whether he had brought any letters to him from
" the queen, he answered, that to keep this matter in the
" deepest silence, and by reason of the various dangers of
" journeys, and especially through the Dutch quarters, he
" durst not bring letters; but he was in good hope that he
" should within a little while be present again before him
" with commands and letters.   That to make the elector
" more apt to believe him, he said, that seven years before
" he studied in the university of Heidelberg, and had fami-
" liar conversation with certain noblemen, whom he named.
" And that they might give a testimony of his former life.

" That the elector, having received his message courte-
" ously, graciously dismissed him.   That the elector after-
" wards called for those noblemen whom he named, and
" asked them whether they knew this Spaniard : who affirm-
" ed, that a certain Italian some years ago did study at
" Heidelberg; but they knew not whether he were the same.
" Upon this, Mount adds, that the said elector, by a pro-
" per messenger, sent for him, in the middle of the cold
" winter, viz. on the 7th of January.   Being come, he
" asked Mount, whether he knew a certain noble Spaniard,
" named Jacomo, Antonio, Gromo, alias Pacheco, servant
" to the queen, and one of the gentlemen of her majesty's
" chamber.   Mount answered, he knew none such.   Where-
" upon the elector told him the story.   To which the other
45 " answered, that he thought it a fable; and that these things
" were invented by fraud, that he might allure the noble
" youth with hope, and bring him in a snare, if he could."

All this the said agent wrote to the lord Burghley, March
the 25th, by some English merchants at Frankford mart.
The further event of this business was this.   On the 26th
of March a letter was brought to the agent, by the command of the elector's chancellor, that the Spaniard with four
names was returned to Heydelberg, without any letters of
credit, sounding to the same song.   And that prince's counsellors, being offended with this impostor's fraud, as presum-

ing to abuse a very excellent prince, had taken him into cus- CHAP.
tody, till he should discover the authors of this rashness, IV.
and open the causes of this dissimulation. That then he re- Anno 1571.
ferred himself to one Baptist, whom he gave out to be the
fourth man of the number of the queen's chief chamber-
lains, and asserting that he had now written letters to him.
Mount added, that the said chancellor then called upon him,
that he would be instant with Walsingham, the queen's ambassador, (to whom he wrote what is before related,) that
he, with secretary Smith and Killigrew, (the queen's joint
ambassadors at Paris,) would take notice of this matter,
and examine whether there were such a *mandatarius* in the
queen's court. And since that Spaniard had dared to speak
contumeliously of that most worthy and just lord Burghley,
(which they looked upon as a great argument of his fraud,)
that his excellency would do a deed worthy of his pains, to
certify the elector of this device; inasmuch as it concerned
the public, that evil deeds should not go unpunished. And
that to deceive a prince was a great crime; as it is proved,
they said, in the last law of the code, *De his qui a non do-*
mino manumitt.

But whatsoever lay under the practice of this deceitful Spain's
Spaniard, it is certain, Spain was now playing her private against
game with the French against the queen. In the latter end England,
of the year, March the 23d, Standen, an English fugitive, Higgens,
lately come out of Spain, arrived secretly at Blois, where Ratcliff,
the English ambassadors were: who gave out some speech &c. in
unto a Frenchman, whom he trusted, of some hope there France.
should be in England, or ever summer ended. And after
he had stayed one night, went to Paris, (whither the English ambassador writ, to have his doings observed.) Who
coming there, repaired to the Scottish ambassador; where
they had their conferences, together with Higgins, who was
concerned about the duke of Norfolk's business. Which
Higgins had lately come to Paris from Rome. And at his
departure from Paris, protested secretly to a friend of his,
that he would not return thither [i. e. to Paris] in one or two
years; saying, he saw no way with his master [the duke,

perhaps] but one. His sudden return shewed there was
somewhat a brewing.   There was then also at Paris Egre-
mond Ratcliff, a busy man, (who came to an untimely end,
by the sentence of duke d'Alva against him,) and Genny,
who came out of Spain, and also one Chamberlain; who conferred there with the king of Spain's secretary, and repaired
thence to duke d'Alva.   Steukley also, another of the
queen's traitorous subjects, (of whom mention was made the
last year,) was there also; and now returned to Spain, in
company of J. Doria.   He had received great honour from

46 that king, and was put in hopes shortly to be employed by

Steukley's
character.

him in some traitorous attempts against the queen. A great
boaster he was, and promised great matters to that king. But
after he had bestowed much money upon him, he found him
at length not worthy of any more; the opinion of him being greatly abated in Spain, by discovery of his lewdness
and insufficiency, as Burghley afterwards wrote to Walsingham concerning him.   The coming and going of these
traitors of England, and creatures and pensioners of Spain,
evidently bespeak the ill offices they were doing the queen in
France.

A Spanish
marquis
comes to
Paris: and
why.

It was also signified to secretary Smith from Walsingham, (that I may lay these Spanish matters together,) that
a Spanish marquis, that was come to Paris to congratulate
the French queen's delivery, under colour of the same, as
he learned, had commission secretly to treat of three points.
First, for the French king to enter into a league, [called the
holy league.]   Secondly, for a marriage between monsieur
and his master's sister.   Thirdly, to propound some way
for the Scottish queen's deliverance; being procured thereto
by the house of Guise, in recompence of the execution done
upon them of the religion.   Whereby the king of Spain
acknowledged to have saved the Low Countries.   And it
was observed by the said Walsingham, some time before
the arrival of the said marquis, that upon a courier arrived
at Paris, out of Spain, from the French ambassador there,
that though there had been some unkindness grown before,
between those two crowns, upon some complaint made, now

it was thought there was never so great amity between them CHAP.
as at that present was like to be. And these were the IV.
doings and endeavours of Spain, all along this and the next Anno 1571.
year.

Our ambassadors now in France (who were three, viz. The English
Walsingham, Killigrew, and Smith) stirred as much as ambassador
they could in a matter which they reckoned would tend the match
much to the interest of the protestant religion, and the with the
greater liberty and peace of the French protestants particu- Navar.
larly; and that was, the marriage in hand with the prince of
Navarr, a protestant, and the lady Margaret, the French
king's sister. That by this conjunction with a protestant
prince, those of the religion in France might have the
greater countenance: though it proved all wicked hypocrisy
in the end. The great difficulty in accomplishing this marriage was in the form to be used in the solemnization of it:
which the queen of Navarr would not be brought to condescend to be done after popish manner. Here Smith,
Walsingham, and Killigrew took the liberty to interpose.
And that neither the popish office, nor the marriage office
used in the protestant churches in France, might be used, it
was devised by them, that instead thereof, the office of the
church of England might be admitted: the like case happening formerly in England, upon a treaty of marriage between king Edward VI. and the late queen of Spain, the
present French king's sister; wherein it was agreed that she
should be married according to the form of our church.
This treaty the English ambassadors sent a copy of to the
queen of Navarr. This she liked well. And sending to
speak with them, she told them, that it had stood her in
good stead, and declared to them how the marriage stood
between their majesties of France and her; and that there
was no difference between them, but only in the manner of 47
the solemnization. And that she had mentioned the said
treaty to them, but that they had pretended it was no true
copy. She therefore now desired to know of sir Thomas
Smith, (he having been a dealer in the same,) whether he
would justify it to be true. He answered, that knowing the

BOOK I.

Anno 1571.

great good-will that queen Elizabeth did bear her, and how much she desired the good success of that marriage, as a thing that tended to the advancement of religion, and the repose of the French realm, he did avow it to be the same, and would further be ready to do any office that might advance the said marriage.

CHAP. V.

Scottish affairs. Dangers by means of the queen of Scots. Walsingham's intelligence thereof; and advertisement. Money brought over from the pope for her service. The French king moves for her liberty. What passed between him and the English ambassadors. The Scottish queen practiseth with Spain. Monies sent into Scotland for her use from France; intercepted. Letters of hers intercepted, of her depending upon Spain; and taking that king for her and her son's and kingdom's protector. The Spanish ambassador dismissed by the council. And why. Lord Burghley to the earl of Shrewsbury, keeper of the Scottish queen. Bishop of Rosse's book concerning her title to this crown. Answered by Glover, Somerset herald. Rosse in the Tower. His letter thence to the lord treasurer.

The danger of the realm by means of the Scottish queen.

THE Scottish affairs, that touched the English state and religion, were interwoven with those of France. Mary the queen of Scots, a zealous papist, and related to the Guisian bigots, was now in custody in England, whither she had fled from her own subjects. And now all the foreign princes, obedient to the see of Rome, were mightily concerned for her deliverance, and the English nation at the same time as much afraid of her liberty. And what danger accrued by her appeared by a letter of Walsingham, writ in the beginning of March, being still ambassador in France, viz. that the English there were labouring by all means to stir up foreign states to set the Scottish queen free; and their next

Letter of Walsingham, ambassador.

step, to dethrone queen Elizabeth, and set the crown upon CHAP.
Mary's head. And that however some of their attempts <u> V. </u>
had failed, yet more were in hand. And that there were Anno 1571.
great numbers, even in the English dominions, heretics as
well as catholics, that had a sincere kindness and concern for
her. And when in discourse between an English Jesuit in
France, named Darbishire, and another that pretended him- 48
self a catholic, (but was a spy,) he told the Jesuit, that for
his part he could never hope to see her at liberty, nor long
to see her keep her head upon her shoulders: and therefore
could receive no great comfort that way. " Well," replied A saying of
the Jesuit, " I tell you truly, that I dare assure you, that Darbishire
" she shall have no harm: for she lacketh no friends in the concerning
" English court. And as for her liberty," added he, " it her.
" standeth all good catholics in hānd so much to seek it,
" either by hook or by crook, as no doubt but there were
" some good men that would venture a joint to bring it to
" pass. And that if she were once possessed of the crown of
" England, it would be the only way and means to reform
" all Christendom, in reducing them to the catholic faith.
" And therefore you must think," said he, " that there are
" more heads occupied in that matter than English heads;
" and that there are more ways to the wood than one, [mean-
" ing the heads of foreign princes.] And therefore he bade
" him be of good courage; and ere ever one year were at an
" end, he should hear more."

The conclusion Walsingham made of this was, the great Walsing-
danger England was in by reason of that queen. That his ham's ad-
conferring and weighing this with the former intended prac- to the
tices, made him think it worth his advertisement, that the queen on
queen should see how much they built upon the possibility gence.
of that dangerous woman's coming to the crown of England:
whose life was a step to her majesty's death. For that they
reputed her an undoubted heir, or rather (which was a
greater danger) for a right inheritor. And though he knew,
as he proceeded, her mischievous intentions were limited,
that they could reach no further to her majesty's harm or
prejudice than should seem good to God's providence, yet

F 3

her majesty, he said, was bound, for her own safety, and
that of her subjects, to add to the same, his good providence, her policy, so far as might stand with justice.

In March, the lord Seton, a great instrument for the said
Scottish queen, came to Scotland, having escaped privately
through this realm, with a rebel, one of the countess of
Northumberland's men; the ship that brought them over
being forced into an haven in Essex. Which ship was forth
coming, and some of the servants, and such secret writings
and devices of his, and of the queen's rebels, as were left in
the ship, to have been conveyed after him by sea into Scotland; bringing to light such things as contained dangerous
practices against the queen and state of the realm; as the
queen by letter informed Mr. Randolph, her agent now in
Scotland, dated March the 19th. In this expedition, this
lord Seton had received in Flanders from the pope 20,000
crowns, being now ready to repair into Scotland. This
money, whether it was seized in the ship, or carried with
him, it doth not appear: but no mention being made of it
when ship and papers were seized, he seems to have got it
safe with him into Scotland.

Conference
between the
French
king and
Smith con-
cerning the
queen of
Scots.
But the French made earnest interest for her. For a
league being now in hand between the queen and that
crown, and Walsingham there resident, and sir Tho. Smith
late come over ambassador [viz. in February] for that purpose, the king told them, " That he must have his request
" put into the treaty for the queen of Scots, and said, she
" was his kinswoman and his sister-in-law, and was once his
" sovereign; and you know, said he, the league between
" that realm and my realm. I can do no less than have the
" same inserted into the league." To which sir Tho. Smith
said, that they had no commission or authority to treat of
any such matter. And that as touching the late queen of
Scots, that she was his sovereign once, thanks be to God,
said Smith, she is not now, [since that queen's husband was
dead, and he advanced to be king.] Whereat the king
laughed. " And that it was thought," added Smith, "that
" when she was queen there in France, she deserved not

49

" very well of your realm nor of your house. And where CHAP.
" the king had said, she was his kinswoman ; so she is also, V.
" said Smith, to the queen my mistress. But if she were Anno 1571.
" your daughter, or your son, if he or she would procure
" your death, or to have your crown from you, would you
" not see justice done on him or her that should attempt it,
" rather than to be still in danger ?"

To which I add, that Smith had it in his instructions con- The queen's inclination towards the Scottish queen. Julius, F. 6.
cerning that queen's delivery, that before the time of her
malicious attempts against the queen's majesty were discovered, she did never refuse to yield to reasonable conditions, and an end to be made between both princesses, and
between her and her subjects of Scotland ; and that this intention took no effect, there was no default in the queen of
England. But since she had dangerously concluded a bargain to the ruin of the queen's majesty, there was just cause
to detain her, until her majesty's surety should be better
provided.

Mr. Henry Killigrew, who was also the queen's ambassa- Words of Killigrew to the king, concerning taking her into the league.
dor, and present at this conference with the French king,
added to what Smith had said, " That fire and water could
" not be together. That one was contrary to the other.
" That the league was made for a perpetual and strait
" amity between him and the queen's majesty ; and that he
" would not treat for the queen's most mortal and dangerous
" enemy. That this could not stand together. That he
" must take her now for dead ; and that he [the king] could
" not tell whether she were dead or alive. And why,
" said he, should you then require her to be put into the
" league ?" For indeed the parliament had intended to
call that queen into question, upon the discovery of a plot
against queen Elizabeth, wherein she was concerned, as we
shall hear by and by.

We meet with the French's tampering for the Scottish The queen offended with the French ambassador for meddling in that queen's matters.
queen some months past, viz. in September, when the secre-
tary of the French ambassador comes to the court (the queen
now either at Audley End, or Mark Hall in Essex) for relief of the queen of Scots, considering that she had her

BOOK
I.

Anno 1571.

Lord
Burghley
delivers the
queen's
mind to
him.

number [of attendants] now lessened. Whereat the queen
was offended, that he should meddle with that queen's matters; and bade the lord Burghley tell him, that she could
not like his manner of intermeddling with the queen of
Scots' matters; considering her majesty found her doings
[that is, by the discovery of the duke of Norfolk's treason;
of which by and by] not only dangerous to her quietness,
but bent also to depend upon other than the French king,
[meaning Spain, and other popish powers.] And therefore
50 she required him to forbear, and give her leave to consider
in her own realm what was meet for her surety. And when
it should seem meet, it should well appear that she had done
nothing towards the queen of Scots, but in reason and honour she might have done more. And so she deferred the
French ambassador's coming to her, [being now in her progress,] till she should be at Richmond.

The French
move for
that queen
to pass
into France.

About the latter end of this year the French king interceded again for the said queen, that she might be permitted
to go over to France. And when, in March, Malvesire had
insisted much, by the desire of the French queen, that queen
Elizabeth would send her into France, Smith and Walsingham shewed him how by her letters, lately seized, she had
practised with the duke of Alva, to convey the young king
out of Scotland into Spain: and that the original letters
thereof were shewn in England to the king's ambassadors
there. And hereupon they told him how she shewed what

She prac-
tiseth with
Spain.

good favour she bore to Spain, to make a perpetual broil, if
she could, between England, Scotland, and France: for she
had practised by letters since the duke [of Norfolk's] troubles. And then they asked that ambassador, what would
she do there in France, and at liberty, when being straitly
kept, and the matter so plainly known how busy she had
been? And so they desired Malvesire to acquaint the king
with what they had told him. And when he came again,
he brought word to Smith and Walsingham, that it was
true which they told him; and that De la Motte had written
the same from England to the king. And the king acknowledged to him, that it was true; and added, " *Ah! poor*

"*fool, she will never cease till she lose her head.*   In faith,
" they will put her to death.   I see it is her own fault and
" folly.   I see no remedy for it.   I meant to help; but if she
" will not be helped, I cannot help it."

The French ambassador Viracque was this summer in Money sent
secretly by
the French,
for the Scot-
tish queen,
intercepted. Scotland, acting secretly for that queen.   And a great sum of money was remitted privately from France to that ambassador, to be managed for her; but by intelligence it being understood, was seized by the English.   The French ambassador laboureth to have his money again.   The lord Burghley answereth the ambassador's secretary, who came to him with that message, that it must be demanded of them to whom he delivered it.   He came again, and desired he might have the French king's money lately intercepted, sent to Viracque.   The duke of Norfolk had a chief hand in the conveyance of this money; and some that he employed in it, out of fear, discovered it.

There was nothing as yet done towards that queen, not- She is re-
strained
upon this,
but honour-
ably used. withstanding the discoveries against her, but that she was restrained from having such free conference and intelligence as of late she had with the queen's subjects; otherwise right honourably entertained and well used, and so the lord Burghley bade Walsingham inform the French king.   I am the larger and more particular in this relation of matters concerning Mary queen of Scots, to shew what just apprehensions the English court and nation had of imminent dangers by means of her; especially Camden being sparing of shewing her faults, and representing her as fair as might be; publishing his history in the reign of her son.

As we have therefore seen what concern France had for 51
She solicits
Spain to in-
vade Eng-
land. this queen, so I shall proceed to relate the great jealousy queen Elizabeth had of Spain; being very zealous to deliver her, and (more than barely that came to) to invade the realm, and dethrone the queen herself.   For letters of that queen to the king of Spain had been intercepted; and so much found out, viz. of her soliciting that formidable enemy of the queen's to invade England.   And so in a letter dated Lord
Burghley's
letter to in September, writ from the lord Burghley to Walsingham,

BOOK
I.

Anno 1571.
Walsing-
ham.
Compl.
Amb.
then in France, he told him, that he might boldly affirm, that her majesty was able to prove, that the queen of Scots had, by advice of the duke of Alva, resolved to depend upon the king of Spain, and to match herself with Don John of Austria, and her son with the king of Spain's daughter. And this the queen required her ambassador to acquaint the French king with. And therefore that the queen had just cause to proceed otherwise than hitherto she had done, to restrain the practice intended towards her by that queen. And that he, the ambassador, should further say to the French king, that she trusted that he would honourably think of her actions on this account.

Letters of
the Scot-
tish queen
seized. The
import of
them.
But what violences Spain intended upon the realm may be taken knowledge of from sir Tho. Smith's mouth, in his relation made to the queen-mother of France, in the month of March, when things came to be fully known ; viz. that Harwich was to have been the port appointed for the Spaniards and Flemings to arrive at, from the duke of Alva, if the treason had gone forward in behalf of the Scottish queen. That the lord Seton [one of the chief of the Scottish noblemen on the queen's party] did arrive there, and from thence, with two of the earl of Northumberland's men, went into Scotland, and were at that present in the castle of Edinburgh. That that being understood, the lord that brought them was seized ; and among other things found, there were

Compl.
Amb.
p. 196.
the Scottish queen's letters, importing, that she gave herself, and her son, now king of Scotland, into the hands of the king of Spain, to be governed and ruled only by him ; and to assure him, that if he would send any power, the young king should be delivered into his hands. For, by a paper of instructions left in the ship, it did appear, that the lord Seton was named the Scottish queen's ambassador towards the duke of Alva. And there in the ambassage he offered the young king to be delivered into his hands, to be conveyed into Spain. And to animate him more to set up the Scottish queen again, and take the protection of her, he shewed that she had right, both by God's laws and man's laws, to be queen of England, and also of Scotland. And

further, that she had not only all those that were in trouble,
[viz. papists, and such as were concerned in the late rebellion,] but a great sort more in England, on her part. So
that the king [of Spain] in setting her up, would not only
govern both these realms, but should also set up, in both, the
catholic religion again.

All this was told by Smith to the queen-mother: to which
she answered, as owning, and perhaps privy to the business,
" Alas! that head of hers shall never be quiet." Smith
added, how that in the same ship where Seton's instructions,
as aforesaid, were taken, among other papers, a letter was 52
found of the countess of Northumberland, who was one of
the chief stirrers in the last rebellion, to her husband, the
earl, now a prisoner in Scotland for the same cause. In
which letter she writ to the said earl, that the duke of Guise,
disguised, had of late been with the duke of Alva; and affirmed for a certainty, that the duke of Guise, and that faction,
would follow in all points the direction of the king of Spain.

This correspondence with Spain was aggravated on that
queen's part by the circumstance of time when it happened,
namely, when De Crocque, the French ambassador, arrived
in England with commission to help Scotland to a quietness
within herself, and to confer with one whom queen Elizabeth
should send for that purpose. Even at the same time these
letters of that queen to the duke of Alva were intercepted;
whereby she gave herself, her realm, and her son, to be in
the protection and government of the king of Spain.

All this was brought to light by God's providence, the
ship, wherein the lord Seton, with his papers and credentials,
was, being driven by a tempest into the English haven aforesaid; which was the very port appointed, when the Spaniards
and Flemings should arrive in England; Seton himself
escaping, being disguised in the habit of a mariner; and so
went thence, and came to the castle of Edinburgh in Scotland. But a paper of instructions being found aboard the
same ship, declared, that in the name of her majesty [the
Scottish queen] he had assured the duke of Alva, that with
a small party they might bring into their hands the young

king of Scotland, and so carry him into Spain. All this, when Walsingham had related at large to the queen-mother of France, it spoiled De Crocque's message with the king's letters, that required the Scottish queen to be set at liberty, and to be sent into France.

The Spanish ambassador sent away.

And why.

But upon this the queen and her council would no longer suffer the ambassador of Spain to abide in her dominions, having carried things so deceitfully and treacherously against her majesty; so that he was in December sent for to the council, and in the queen's name commanded to depart. The same thing had been often intended before, but never put in execution before this present; when the state was provoked by the intelligence of certain new practices within this realm, to persuade the subjects that the king, his master, would aid them with power this spring, and such like promises. He was dismissed, and Mr. Knolles appointed to attend on him at his house. This was December the 13th: and he was to depart by Dover to the Low Countries. But he could not be got out of town till the 24th, when he went to Greenwich; and on St. Stephen's day to Gravesend. A few days after, he removed to Canterbury. And captain Hawkins, one of the queen's great sea officers, was appointed to pass him over in a ship of the queen's. After a dangerous passage he came to Calais in February. And coming to Graveling, to shew his displeasure against the English nation, he turned out all the English that he found there, notwithstanding that he knew that here in England remained monsieur Sweringham, at the request of the duke of Alva. This ambassador, according as some letters of 53 the lord Burghley relate, had used himself crookedly, perniciously, and maliciously against the state, and the chiefest of the queen's counsellors, and openly against that lord.

The queen orders the earl of Shrewsbury to expostulate with the queen of Scots, now under his custody.

All this came out about August and September, viz. how the Scottish queen practised both with France and Spain, and the pope, and also with the duke of Norfolk, unhappily brought into this business, and several other of the queen's own English subjects; not only to procure her own escape, but to embroil her majesty's kingdom in a war, and in an endeavour to dethrone her. Therefore the queen consulted for the keeping that queen more straitly, and more confined in Tutbury castle. And the charge of her being com- mitted to the earl of Shrewsbury, her majesty, provoked by these practices, gave order to the said earl to expostulate with her freely and plainly, to urge her to speak what she could for herself; giving the lord Burghley commission to write to him to that intent. Whose letter accordingly ran to this tenor.

" That after he had closed up his letters, her majesty Lord
" willed him to let his lordship understand, that she would Burghley's letter to him
" have him use some round speech to the queen of Scots in for that pur-
" this sort; that it was now fully discovered to her majesty pose. Int. epist.
" what practices that queen hath had in hand, both with the com. Salop,
" duke of Norfolk and others, upon the sending away of in offic. ar-mor.
" Ridolphi [the pope's secret agent here, under the show of
" an Italian merchant] into Spain. And though it were
" known to her majesty by writings extant, in deliberation,
" what were best for her to do for her escape out of this
" realm, and thereof caused the duke of Norfolk to be con-
" ferred withal, and that she chose rather to go into Spain
" than into Scotland or France; yet her majesty thought it
" now just cause to be offended with these devices, tending
" to her liberty : neither was she offended with her purpose
" to offer her son in marriage to the king of Spain's daughter.
" In which matter the late queen of Spain had solicited her ;
" neither that she sought to make the king of Spain believe
" that she would give ear to the offer of Don John de
" Austria. But the very matter of offence was, that her
" majesty understood certainly her labours and devices to
" stir up a new rebellion in this realm, and to have the king
" of Spain to assist it. And that finding the said queen so
" bent, she must not think but that her majesty had cause to
" alter her courteous dealing with her.

" And so in this sort (continued that lord) her majesty
" would have you tempt her patience to provoke her to an-
" swer somewhat. For of all these premises her majesty is
" certainly assured, and of much more." He adds, " Her

"majesty told me a while ago, that a gentleman of my lord
"of a—— coming to your house, was by your lordship
"asked, whether he had seen the queen of Scots, or no.
"And he said, No. Then, quoth your lordship, you shall
"see her anon. Which offer her majesty misliking, I said,
"that I durst say it was not true in this manner. I per-
"ceive her majesty would have the queen kept very straitly
"from all conference: insomuch, that it is more like that
"she shall be committed to ward, rather than have more
"liberty." And then he advised the earl to send up the
names of those servants that should remain about her, and
of such as should depart. This was writ in September.

54
Bishop of
Ross in cus-
tody, the
queen of
Scots' a-
gent.
The bishop of Ross, the Scottish queen's agent, being a
very busy man, and being privy to all these dangers to the
realm, was, August the 17th, carried to Ely, to be there
with the bishop. And in October he was brought from
Ely to London, and the next month committed to the
Tower: and there, upon examination, he uttered many
things very plainly; but concerning the queen of Scots her
application to Spain, and the expected assistance thence,
and concerning the duke of Norfolk's treason, nothing. This
bishop of Ross (that I may mention it here) wrote a book
in Latin for the Scottish queen's title to this crown: which
Glover, Somerset herald, a learned man, answered in a
large discourse, never, I think, printed, about the year

His defence
of that
queen's title
to this
crown; an-
swered by
Glover, So-
merset.
Offic. He-
rald. Sheld.
press.
1580. It beginneth thus: "A few years past the bishop
"of Ross, being agent for the queen his mistress, to our
"sovereign lady, the queen's majesty, wrested his wits (with
"the assistance of certain lawyers of this land) to write a
"discourse in defence of the queen of Scots' title to the
"crown of this realm. Which his discourse being then
"hatched in a dangerous time of practices and rebellions,
"and with a malicious intent against her majesty and her
"estate, is now, after many years mewing, let fly abroad
"into the world, in the like time, and with like intent. For
"what other cause than malice to her majesty can be ima-
"gined to move this man, after so many years suppression,
"to publish his discourse at this present, and that in the

" Latin tongue, and to all the estates of Europe? May it
" be thought so long to have stayed in his hands, because he
" could never, until now, find in his heart to advance his
" mistress's title to the eye of the world? It were no reason
" to charge him with so careless a mind of her prosperity
" and happiness, &c.

" I must needs be of opinion, that the present publica-
" tion proceedeth hereof: that he being persuaded that this
" year, 1580, some great attempt should be made by the
" pope and his adherents, against her majesty and her
" estate; and no whit doubting but that his mistress's
" cause should by that greatest colour thereof appear;
" thought good (that the pope's and his adherents enter-
" prise might seem the juster) to publish at this present
" her title to the crown of this realm; meaning not only to
" prove her heir apparent to the crown, after her majesty's
" death, but presently queen *de jure*, by a popish conse-
" quent, even in her majesty's life. For that the Anti-
" christ of Rome hath deposed her, and pronounced her no
" queen," &c.

And as this was the author's exordium to his MS. tract,
so I will subjoin his conclusion: " Thus have I plainly
" proved the title of the crown of England to be examin-
" able by the common laws of the realm, and none other.
" And by the same laws all strangers to be barred from
" claiming any interest therein: and further, the queen of
" Scots to be a mere stranger; and therefore her title to be
" of no account. I have further answered all Ross's vain
" objections. I have confuted his examples; and, I trust,
" satisfied the world, that if any man have been heretofore
" persuaded his mistress's title to be any thing, he will now
" alter his mind, and condemn it as nothing." Whether
there were any things in this book that made it advisable
not to publish it, let others inquire. 55

This bishop of Ross I find lying in the Tower till July
the next year; and then, by means of the mild lord treasurer, he seems to have his liberty granted. In which month
he wrote to that lord a letter to this tenor: " That he had

" put his lordship in remembrance, a fortnight past, by a
" letter, of his cause, committing the same to his lordship's
" hands, having none of his own to suit for him at this time.
" And thinketh me debt bound grietly for your gentle and
" gud aunswer sent unto me. And although I have not
" heard of the resolution taken thairin, yet I abstained to
" trouble your lordship, being persuade with me, that as
" time and occasion should serve, to have gud expedition
" thairof; chiefly be the queen's princely nature and gud-
" ness, with your lordship's labours and patience. And now,
" my gud lord, I trust the tyme is fullie comin to put an end
" thairto, &c. I pray theternal God to preserve your lord-
" ship. At the Tour, the 17th day of July, 1572.

" Your lordship's affectionat to command with service,

" Jo. Rossen."

CHAP. VI.

*Amity judged more advisable with France than Spain.
Treaty with France. Aid required in case of invasion
for religion. The Low Countries, in conference between
count Lodowic and Walsingham at Paris, move for the
queen's assistance. Spain plays the tyrant. Arguments
used to move the queen on their behalf. Archbishop of
Cassils, a pensioner of Spain, comes to Walsingham at
Paris. False. A rebellion in Ireland, hatching in
France. The French king and queen-mother privy to
it. Deny it to the English ambassadors.*

Delibera-
tion about
Spain and
France.
NOW it came to be maturely deliberated, whether of the
two nations, Spain or France, it were more advisable, and
for the profit of England, to enter into alliance with. This
consultation was consequent upon the going off of the match
with France: and, it seems, the potency of Spain made the
queen somewhat dubious to which prince to offer her amity.
Walsingham, the queen's ambassador in France, was uneasy
at these counsels, and thus shewed his thoughts in this mat-

ter unto the earl of Leicester : " That if the dangerous CHAP.
" greatness of the house of Austria were well considered,   VI.
" the miscontentments they had in respect of the injuries Anno 1571.
" received, [i. e. from England,] their natural inclination to Walsing-
" revenge, and the unseen traffic of our merchants at pre- thoughts
" sent, [he seems to mean the small traffic they had then in of it.
" Flanders.]   These considerations well weighed, the cause
" may seem somewhat altered, [from what it was before-
" time, in the benefit of the ancient leagues between Eng- 56
" land and Burgundy.]   And that though France could
" not yield like profit that Flanders did, yet might it yield
" some profit, with less hazard and more safety.   That in
" this cause he considered two things chiefly : first, that the
" house of Austria was become the pope's champion, and Austria the
" the professed enemy unto the gospel, and daily practised pope's
                                                                   champion.
" the rooting out of the same : and therefore that we, that
" were protestants, ought to oppose ourselves against it.
" The other, that the entrance into the league with France
" would not only be an advancement of the gospel there,
" but elsewhere."   [So good Mr. Walsingham then conceived, and so did every protestant beside : so closely and
treacherously were the cruel designs of that French king
carried.]   And therefore he concluded, " That though it
" yielded not so much temporal profit, yet in respect of
" the spiritual fruit that thereby might ensue, he thought it
" worthy the embracing.   Or rather to say better, I think,
" saith he, we have cause to thank God that offereth us so
" good occasion both to advance his glory, and also to pro-
" vide for her majesty's safety."

    A sure amity therefore with France was now transacting A league
by our ambassadors there, in the midst of these fears at between
home.   And among the articles drawn up for the league be- England
tween France and England, queen Elizabeth propounded and France.
one that was very strange at this juncture, namely, in favour
of the king of Spain, to make provision for his safety.   This
was much disgusted by the French ; who shewed, that the
end of this treaty was only to bridle his greatness.   And
therefore to provide for his safety, who sought both their

BOOK
I.

Anno 1571.

Walsing-
ham's letter
to lord
Burghley.

destructions, they could not tell what it meant; especially
since of late he had no way deserved any such favour at the
queen's hands. " Therefore, (as Walsingham in his corre-
" spondence did write,) if her majesty thought that prince
" [viz. the French king] was of any value, who was towards
" all men sincere, [so he now appeared,] toward her ma-
" jesty well affected, towards religion *pius inimicus*, she
" should not balance him in one balance with Spain : who
" was of words insincere, in affection towards her majesty
" maliciously bent, and the common enemy to our religion.
" That if her majesty meant to take profit of Spain's friend-
" ship, the next way should be to strengthen herself with
" the amity of others, in such sort as she should have no
" need of it. For that was the nature," said he, " of a proud
" man, to make best account of him that least esteems him :
" for whosoever yieldeth to him increaseth his pride. Which
" thing those that dealt with the Spanish nation found to be
" most true."

Catholic
league.

He added, " That so long as the late catholic league did
" remain in force, neither her majesty, nor any other princes
" of the religion, could promise themselves any thing at
" Spain's hands, but as much mischief as he could do them.
" Which thing her majesty, with the rest, should find to be
" true by too dear an experience, if the same were not holpen
" by some counter-league."

An article
in the
treaty, in
case of in-
vasion for
religion.

This treaty with France was for a mutual assistance of
each other in case of invasion, chiefly feared from king
Philip. And in that article the queen required it to be
thus expressed; *Etiamsi fuerit* [*invasio*] *religionis causa*
57 *prætextu aut colore*. Which clause stuck. The queen, in
her instructions to Smith, would very earnestly that he
should press this; and to cause those of the religion there
to understand the demand, and to help to further it. But
that if he could not obtain these words to be inserted, then
to run in more general words, *Sub quocunque prætextu, vel
colore et quavis de causa :* and in some secret manner to
move, that some special promise might be made in a secret
writing betwixt the king and the queen, signed mutually

with both their hands, for that purpose expressly, if any in- CHAP.
vasion should be made. And without this the queen would VI.
not have her ambassador to accord.

Anno 1571.

But this the king would not comply with; as likewise to The French
sign any private assurance about it between the queen and king will
not comply
him. But he said he would write a private letter to her, with that
assuring her of it. This, Walsingham (who was deceived article.
with this dissembling prince, and was apt to think well of
him) thought the queen might be contented with, for the
great benefit of a league, offensive and defensive; as he
wrote to the earl of Leicester. " We can," writeth Wal- Walsing-
singham, " by no means draw the king to any other inter- vice.
" pretation of the meaning, touching the point of religion,
" than by private letter. That for his own private opinion,
" seeing this league was to endure but during the life of the
" two princes, and that the substance of all leagues con-
" sisted chiefly in the sincerity of the matters, and that this
" prince had given great show to the world of great sin-
" cerity, [the greater hypocrite,] he thought that private
" letter did bind as much in honour, as any other instru-
" ment or contract that passed between them could do in
" law. For if they should break, the matter was not to be
" tried in the chamber emperial by way of pleading of
" what value the instruments were. God and the sword
" must be judges. That if her majesty could content her-
" self with this private interpretation of the king's meaning,
" then if she would please to use some words of assurance
" towards the ambassador at her court, of the great good
" opinion she had of the king's sincerity, and that she built
" more upon his word than upon contracts, he knew nothing
" could more content him. For he desired, he said, to be a
" prince that esteemed his word and honour above his life.
" Besides, he wished himself to be in her majesty's good
" opinion, before all other princes. And had often taken The king's
" occasion to say, that he hoped there would be no less ear- words in
esteem of
" nest good-will and strait amity between him and her, than the queen.
" was between her grandfather and his grandfather."

To nourish this opinion of amity between them, Walsing-

ham took it, as he said, to be the office of all those who
truly loved their majesties; " as that league that tended
" greatly to both their sureties, being knit together in per-
" fect amity: which, beside their particular safety, would
" breed a great repose in all Europe, especially for the cause
" of religion."

About this time, while Walsingham was in Paris, the
queen was solicited by those of the Low Countries, grievously oppressed by Spain, to protect them. Count Lodowic, of Nassau, (brother to the prince of Orange,) who
came with a message to the French king, having agreed
with Walsingham upon a private conference, came to him
in the month of August, to discourse some secret points, for
58 setting those countries free of that tyranny. With which
that English gentleman was so taken, that he called him in
one of his letters, *the rarest gentleman* with whom he had
Count Lo-
dowic of
Nassau's
conference
with Wal-
singham
about the
tyranny of
Spain. talked since he came into France. The count shewed him
at large how the king of Spain was setting up violently the
inquisition against papists and protestants; who all disliked
it. And that they saw him establishing an arbitrary power
over them, who were a free people. He offered the queen
Zealand, in case she would come to their assistance. He
shewed our ambassador, that the cause in the Low Countries proceeded only upon that the king of Spain sought to
plant there, by inquisition, the foundation of a most horrible tyranny, the overthrow of all freedom and liberty; a
thing which his father Charles V. went about to have established there. But seeing the same so much impugned by
the inhabitants of the said countries, and that without consent it could not be received, unless he would violently, by
tyranny, seek the establishment of the same, contrary both
to his oath and their privileges, he forbore to proceed in that
behalf. They saw it would overthrow all foreign traffic, by
which that country was chiefly maintained. And this they
urged to the cardinal of Arras, who by sundry ways practised to plant the said inquisition, and by persuasion would
have induced the people to like thereof. And when persuasions would not do, he endeavoured to do it by violence:

for the emperor had given but a cold ear to them at the as- CHAP.
sembly at Spires, where they related their grievances. VI.

Thus when they saw themselves (as the count proceeded Anno 1571.
in his relation) void of all help, their natural prince being The cause
explained
carried away by corruption of counsel, from the due consider- of their
ation that belonged to a good prince to have of good sub- taking arms.
jects, as he neither regarded his oath, nor maintenance of
such privileges as were confirmed by his predecessors, nor
the dutiful manner of the proceeding of the nobility, in
seeking by way of humble petition to redress their griefs,
they thought their consciences discharged from all duty of
obedience. And on this occasion the people took arms.

Count Lodowic had first applied himself to the French Propositions
to be made
king this year, to take this people into his protection, and to to the
procure their deliverance from the present tyranny. To queen from
count Lo-
which he seemed inclinable, on condition the queen of Eng- dowic.
land might be brought to be a party, and to join with him
and the princes of Germany in the same enterprise. And
this he privately acquainted Walsingham withal; and that
he should move it to her as from himself. And then to
propound to her majesty, on his behalf, these particulars
following. I. Whether she could be content to join with
him and the prince of Orange in the enterprise. II. Whether upon former assurance offered, she could be content to
lend unto them the sum they required. III. That it would
please her majesty to suffer captain Hawkins underhand to
serve them with certain ships; and also to license them to
furnish them with certain victuals to be transported from
thence, whereof they had present need.

He further backed his request with these arguments; Arguments
for the
that it would be no less honour for her to unite Zealand queen's as-
[which had been offered her] to the crown of England, than sistance of
them.
it was dishonour to her sister to lose Calais. And that by 59
having Zealand, she would have the key of the Low Countries, and a place always for her ships to enter in unto; to
avoid thereby the danger of the enemy, as also of any tempests; and other considerations. And that this enterprise
being done by protestants, the receiving the honour thereof,

should be better able, by increase of credit with the French king, to continue his good devotion towards the queen, in respect of the rare favours they had received at her hands, which they did and would always acknowledge. And further, that the queen would consider how ill affected Spain was towards her; how naturally they inclined to revenge, though outwardly, till convenient time served, they could dissemble their malice; how that king entertained rebellious subjects of her majesty, at his great cost, and how he was become a protector of the queen of Scots, the queen's dangerous enemy.

This was all communicated in the month of August by Walsingham, as advantageously as he could, both to Burghley and Leicester: who extremely approved of it, and resolved to move it to the queen as effectually as they could. But the queen could not be persuaded to meddle any further in this matter, unless to be a mediator, till several years after.

Concerning the archbishop of Cassil, or Cashell, (whose repair to Walsingham we spake of under the last year,) he had instructions sent him to use his interest to get him into the queen's dominions; which that archbishop seemed to be very desirous of, in case he might have the queen's pardon, and his bishopric restored to him again. The earl of Leicester had directed the ambassador to labour to deal so with him as to bring him into England: for they suspected the man as a practiser with Spain, notwithstanding his pretences. And he received instructions from the queen about him, viz. that she did not so much disallow of his request of her pardon, and for the restitution of his bishopric, as of the slender manner of his suit; as he had signified it to Walsingham. And that if he would not humbly desire pardon of his offences, and shew himself repentant, and disposed to live hereafter in Ireland, like a faithful subject, she meant not to bestow upon him either pardon or bishopric. And this Walsingham was to let him know, and to express the same to him in such sort as he should see cause. Otherwise there was no great account to be made of him; nor

was he of kin to the earl of Desmond, as he alleged, nor of CHAP.
any credit in England. And yet that she was content to ___VI.___
draw him home by means not dishonourable.   Anno 1571.

The lord Burghley gave him no better a style than *the* The charac-
lewd lozel of Ireland. And this not without reason: for archbishop,
there were no small grounds to suspect this archbishop to and his
be, notwithstanding all his pretences, false to the queen; for treachery.
he had a great interest with the queen's professed enemies,
and had large allowances from the king of Spain. For when
one captain Thomas, an Irishman, (but a spy for Walsingham,) upon that bishop's desire, got him access to the
cardinal of Loraine, [who was of the house of the Guises,]
they talked together for the space of two hours. And when
he departed, he told not the said captain what their discourse
was, but only that there might be some occasion afterwards 60
to employ him [the captain] in some good service; [that is,
in some insurrection in Ireland, which was now a hatching.]
And that therefore he should do well to make such report
of him, [the archbishop,] that he might grow into credit in
that court. And that he should say, that the archbishop
was a man of a noble family, and of great reputation in that
country: and that Ireland of itself was but weak, and easy
to be gotten by the enemy. All this the captain afterwards
made Walsingham privy to; who appointed the said captain to attend upon him. This archbishop also had told
that ambassador's servant, that the king of Spain had entertained him honourably; having had, during the time of A pensioner
his abode there, besides 2000 ducats for an annual pension, to Spain.
sometimes 100, sometimes 200, sometimes 300 ducats, when
the court did remove. And he related moreover, that D'Alva
had offered 36,000 ducats for the earl of Northumberland,
(the queen's rebel,) who was then a prisoner in Scotland.
So well was this archbishop acquainted with the Spanish
affairs.

The queen also, in another letter of instructions to the Encouraged
said ambassador, signified to him, that considering that into Eng-
party, and the profit that might ensue by his discovering of land by the
the practices, wherewith he was so truly acquainted, she was queen.

G 4

content, that if he meant dutifully to ask pardon, as he pretended by his speech, then the ambassador should give him comfort to continue the same dutifulness and loyal meaning, and provoke him to make repair into England, and to assure him that he should not find lack of grace, if he humbly desired it, and by his truth hereafter deserved it. And to add, that he the ambassador had power from the queen (to whom he had written about him) to warrant him to come into her realm safely, and to make his means unto the queen for her favour. And that if he would shew himself penitent for his former fault, and be disposed hereafter to live dutifully, he should be provided of as good a living as heretofore he had. And that if he obtained not of the queen at his coming according to his liking, the ambassador would give him his warrant under his hand to return safely out of the realm. Which manner of usage the ambassador should tell him was very rare in the queen. But that upon his instance she had yielded thereunto. And so accordingly the ambassador was ordered to give him such a warrant under his hand. But that if he [the ambassador] found that the other had sought but to abuse him, as by his letters there was some reason to doubt, then to forbear to deal with him in the former sort. But yet to procure as much intelligence as he might from him, and to discover his continuance in falsehood and practice there, as he could see occasion for it, and could gather matter against him, to deal with the king there, that he might be delivered as an open known rebel and traitor, especially in those practices used by him in Spain. And that there was the more cause to doubt his lewdness, because Rogers, that brought the ambassador's last letters, met with an Irishman about St. Deny's, who told him that the archbishop had been secretly at the court, and was ready to be despatched away into Spain by the means of the cardinal of Lorain.

61   This was afterwards [viz. in the month of February] spoken of by sir Tho. Smith and Mr. Walsingham to the French king: to whom they related an endeavour of a rebellion in Ireland, by the said cardinal's means, as appeared

A rebellion in Ireland plotted by the cardinal of Lorain.

by the confession of one Stackbold, then a prisoner in Ire- CHAP.
land; who confessed, that the cardinal set him on to stir up ___VI.___
a rebellion there, to the maintenance of James Fitz Morrice, Anno 1571.
a traitor and rebel to the queen; who was to have the counties of Ormond and Ossory. And that he promised them
men and munition to rebel against the queen. And withal,
that the French king and the queen-mother were privy to it. TheFrench
It was true enough, notwithstanding their great protesta- king privy
tions of mighty friendship with her majesty; as appeared
by their behaviour, when Smith, by the queen's commandment, acquainted them both with it. To the king he thus
harangued it freely: " That that cardinal had not done
" enough to raise up trouble to her majesty in your realms,
" and to trouble England and Scotland, but he could not
" let the poor realm of Ireland alone, by encouraging Fitz
" Morrice the queen's rebel there. *And that in your ma-*
" *jesty's name.*"

Whereat the king laughing heartily, said, *In my name?* Denies it
And professed, he never so much as heard of it: and that he to the ambassador
could never think any trouble or hurt to his good sister. Smith.
Upon which, Smith shewed him the articles of Stackbold's
confession, who affirmed it. And when the same day, by
the like order from the queen, he acquainted the queen- And so does
mother with the same matter of the cardinal's evil endea- the queen-
mother.
vours in Ireland, and her knowledge of it, she also turned
it off with a question, whether he dared to say this? And
moreover the said ambassador told her, that the cardinal
said, he did it in the king's name and hers; and that the
queen his mistress ordered him to declare this unto her.
But withal, that she knew it well enough not to be true, for
the good-will that they bare to her. Smith added, that
Walsingham could tell her more.

Who then declared the case unto her; and that he had The ambassadors urge
moved her in it almost a year ago. She said, she remem- this matter
bered that there was such a thing about to be done by the to the
queen.
stirring of a bishop that came from Spain. [That was the
archbishop of Cassils, of whom before.] To this, Smith
also mentioned De la Roche's attempt upon Ireland; who

BOOK I.

Anno 1571.

was a knight of the order, and gentleman of the king's chamber; and the conductor of that expedition, and could tell the whole proceeding. And so prayed that order might be taken in it. She replied, that the king disavowed it; and that he had stayed De la Roche, that he should not go to Ireland, and revoked all his power. But Walsingham then told her, that there were then twenty harquebussiers there, or thereabouts, remaining still, and had remained ever since in a castle. Whereupon the queen promised they should be recalled, if any were there. Thus did the French falsehood begin to appear, by the industry of the queen's ambassadors, and the secret intelligence procured by Walsingham, to his great expense and impoverishing.

62

CHAP. VII.

A parliament. The succession; and matters of religion, transacted there. The bill for reformation. The queen displeased at it, as encroaching on her prerogative. Debates about it. Divers bills for religion brought in. Motion for a new confession of faith. Reformatio legum ecclesiasticarum *produced in parliament. Bills about religion and the state of the church that passed. Acts against papists. Act for subscribing and reading the Thirty-nine Articles. Many are deprived upon this act.*

Succession to the crown moved in parliament.

NOW let us look at home. In the parliament that began to sit April 2, anno 13 Elizab. a motion was made for the succession. And many of the members had but little kindness to the Scottish queen. Insomuch that they laboured to put by her pretended right of succession; and to fix upon the line of the lady Mary, that married to Brandon duke of Suffolk, king Henry VIII. his younger sister; as that queen sprang of his elder. And the ground they went upon was king Henry VIII. his last will Wherein he expressly put the heirs of the lady Frances first, and next the heirs of the lady Eleonor, daughters of his said sister Mary, in remainder and reversion, to succeed to the crown, in case

of failure of issue in his children, Edward, Mary, and Eli- CHAP.
zabeth. And this by virtue of certain statutes made the 28th   VII.
and 35th of Henry VIII. whereby such power was granted Anno 1571.
to that king, to appoint the succession, " according to such
" estate, and after such manner, form, and fashion, order,
" or condition, as should be expressed and limited in his
" letters patents, or by his last will in writing, signed with
" his hand." Now for the making this of none effect, and
that the line of king Henry's elder sister might take place,
it was urged in those times by some, that that king made
no will at all; and by others, that if he did make any, it was
not according to the statute, nor signed by his hand.

Now for the clearing of these things, there was a mem- A speech in
ber who made a notable speech, and of good length; to parliament,
prove that there was a true will made by the king. And king Hen-
therefore, if there were no records remaining then in ry's will, in
chancery of any letters patents, nor original will to be the lady
found; it must have been defaced and destroyed in queen
Mary's reign. That there was a real will was evident, because of the performing of the legacies of it; which were
made to many, both of lands and money, after his decease:
and divers indentures tripartite were made between king
Edward VI., his immediate successor, and the executors of
king Henry's will, and others. And divers letters patents
passed under the great seal, in consideration of the accomplishment of the said king's will. And that there was a will
in the name of king Henry, enrolled in the chancery, and
divers *constats* thereof made under the great seal. All 63
which, as he urged, were arguments that king Henry died
not intestate. And then, that it was without all doubt, that
as the subjects of England had taken them for king and
queens of England, that were expressed in the statute by
name, so they were bound to accept them that were declared by the will in remainder, or reversion; viz. the heirs
of the lady Frances and lady Eleonor.

But then further, in case of no will, he proceeded to And for an-
enervate the Scottish queen's title to this crown; as not be- nulling the
ing inheritable by her, according to the laws of this realm, queen's
title.

BOOK
I.

Anno 1571.

N°. VIII.

Act for se-
curity of
the queen's
person and
govern-
ment; and
succession.

Bill in par-
liament for
coming to
church, de-
bated.
Journal of
Parliament.

proving only such inheritable, as were born in the king's allegiance of father and mother English ; or out of the king's
legiance, one parent English, and in the king's legiance.
But I had rather leave the reader to the whole speech of
this member of parliament, carefully transcribed by me from
a MS. in the Cotton library, as it is set in the Appendix.
But though this bold step in parliament, from a disgust of
the Scottish queen, succeeded not; yet a notable act or acts
were made this session, for the security of the queen's person and government, and for the succession. Especially the
statute 13 Eliz. cap. 1, wherein, among other things of that
nature, it enacts to be treason, " for any to hold or affirm,
" that the common law of the realm (not altered by par-
" liament) ought not to direct the right of the crown of Eng-
" land; or that the queen, by the authority of the parlia-
" ment, might not make laws and statutes of sufficient force
" and validity, to limit and bind the crown of this realm,
" and the descent, limitation, and government thereof:" as
we shall hear more, before we conclude this chapter.

Now let us see what was done, or endeavoured to be
done, in this session, in matter of religion. The first bill
that was read, which was April the 4th, was for coming to
church, and receiving the holy communion. April the 6th,
read the second time. When sir Thomas Smith spake, and
argued for the observance and maintenance thereof. And
in part wished the bishops to have consideration thereof.
Fleetwood, recorder of London, moved, that the penalties
of the statute should not go to promoters; a device but
lately brought in, in the time of king Henry VIII. And he
shewed the evils and inconveniences that grew thereby :
wherein no reformation was sought, but private gain. And
as for the matter of going to church, or for the service of
God, he urged, that it did directly appertain to that court;
[i. e. the court of parliament.] And that they had as well
learnt, that there was a God to be served, as had the bishops. And then he proved by old laws, that princes in
their parliaments had made ecclesiastical constitutions. And
so this bill was referred to committees. This bill, among

others, with additions and provisos, was brought down from CHAP.
the lords May the 19th. But I do not find it passed into ___VII.___
an act this parliament, though there was great pains taken Anno 1571.
about it.

There was a strong party in the house, that resolved to Further re-
press, as vigorously as might be, a further reformation of formation of religion
religion ; namely, by altering several things in the Common urged.
Prayer, and the ceremonies established. Mr. Strickland, an
ancient gentleman, of hot zeal, offered a bill for reformation. Who ushered it in with a long speech, for some re-64
formation of several things in the Book of Common Prayer, Book of
though he acknowledged it was drawn up very near to the Common Prayer,
sincerity of the truth. But yet that there were some superstitious things in it, as, in the Office of Baptism, the sign of
the cross, and some other ceremonies and errors, as he
called them : which might be changed, without note of
changing of religion ; whereby the enemy might slander us.
He further spake of the abuses of the church of England, and church-
and of churchmen : as, that known papists had ecclesiastical ed for cer-
government and great livings: that boys were dispensed tain things.
with, to have spiritual promotions: that, by faculties, unable men were allowed: and some other men allowed to
hold too many livings. In the mean time, godly, honest,
and learned protestant ministers, had little or nothing.
April the 14th, the bill for reformation, preferred by Strickland aforesaid, was read the first time. Upon which ensued
divers arguments. Mr. Treasurer of the queen's household
was one that spake against it to this purport ; " That if Bill for re-
" the matters mentioned to be reformed were heretical, then formation.
" they were presently to be condemned. But if they were
" matters of ceremonies, then it behoved them to refer the
" same to her majesty ; who had authority, as chief of the
" church, to deal therein. And for them to meddle with
" matters of her prerogative, he said, were not convenient."
Mr. Comptroller of the household argued to the same effect.
Another, whose name was Snagg, entered into discourse of
some of the articles, which Strickland had laid down before.
Whereof one was, not to kneel at the receiving of the holy

BOOK I.

Anno 1571.

The queen displeased at it. And one forbidden the house.

The house wants their member.

Debate it.

sacrament; but to lie prostrate, (to shun the old supersti-tion,) or to sit, every man at his own liberty. And the di-rections were also thought fit to be left out of the book [of the Office of Communion] for that posture. Which should be a law; and every man to do according to his con-science.

But the queen liked not at all of these proceedings; reckoning it struck at her prerogative, (as was hinted be-fore by her treasurer,) as though she might not appoint ce-remonies to be used in the worship of God. So that during the time of Easter, (the parliament being adjourned,) in the holydays, Strickland, for his exhibiting a bill for the re-formation of ceremonies, and his speech thereupon, was sent for before the lords of the privy council; and required to attend upon them; and in the mean season to make stay from entering into the house.

But this caused no small disturbance. For on Friday, April 19, in Easter week, being the next day after the par-liament sat again, the house wanted their member. And one of them signified, "How a member of the house was " demanded from them. By whose commandment, or for " what cause, he knew not. And that forasmuch as he was " not now a private man, but to supply the room, person, " and place of a multitude, especially chosen, and there-" fore sent; he thought that neither in regard of the coun-" try, which was not to be wronged, nor for the liberty of " the house, which was not to be infringed, they should " not permit him to be demanded from them." To this a courtier, namely Mr. Treasurer, spake mildly, as the point was tender: " That the man that was meant, was neither " demanded nor misused; but on consideration was re-65 " quired, to expect the queen's pleasure upon certain spe-" cial points. And that he durst to assure, that the gentle-" man should have neither cause to dislike or complain, &c. " That he was in no sort stayed for any word or speech by " him in that place offered; but for exhibiting a bill to the " house against the prerogative of the queen; which was " not to be tolerated. And that oft it had been seen, that

" speeches [in parliament] had been examined and con-
" sidered of." Others were for sending for him. Yelver-
ton urged, " That the precedent was perilous. And that
" though, in this happy time of lenity, under so gracious a
" princess, nothing of extremity or injury was to be feared ;
" yet the times might be altered ; and what was now per-
" mitted, might hereafter be construed as a duty, and en-
" forced even on the ground of the present permission.
" That all matters, not treason, or too much to the deroga-
" tion of the crown, were tolerable there ; [i. e. in the par-
" liament house ;] where all things came to be considered
" of ; and where there was such fulness of power, as even
" the right of the crown was to be determined: that to
" say, the parliament had no power to determine of the
" crown was high treason. He remembered them, how that
" men are not there for themselves, but for their country.
" That it was fit for princes to have their prerogative ; but
" yet the same to be straitened within reasonable limits.
" That the prince could not of herself make laws: neither
" might she, for the same reason, break laws, &c. That
" the speech that had been uttered in that place, and the
" offer made of the bill, was not to be condemned as evil.
" But that if there were any thing in the Book of Common
" Prayer, either Jewish, Turkish, or Popish, the same
" might be reformed. He said also, that among the Papists
" it was bruited, that by the judgment of the council
" Strickland was taken for an heretic :" [meaning, that being so misrepresented, the house had the more reason to
stand by him.]

Another said, that care was to be had for the privileges
of the house. Fleetwood, recorder of London, a wise man,
advised, that they should be humble suitors to the queen ;
and neither send for him nor demand him of right. Those
of the queen's council, while this speech was making, [fear-
ing undoubtedly the consequence,] whispered together.
And then the speaker moved, that the house should make
stay of any further consultation thereupon. And on the
next day, being Saturday, Strickland came to the house ;

CHAP.
VII.

Anno 1571.

D'Ewes'
Journal,
p. 176.

The mem-
ber for-
bidden,
comes to
the house.

BOOK I.

Anno 1571.

upon an advertisement, as it seems, from her majesty's council; and coming just upon the time, when the bill for coming to church and receiving the communion was in referring to committees, the house did, in witness of their joy for his restitution, presently nominate him one of those committees.

Some committees for religion attend upon the archbishop.

I find no more of this bill for the reformation of the Common Prayer and for the ceremonies, but that April the 25th, several of the committees, viz. sir Robert Lane, sir Henry Gate, Mr. Henry Knowles, sen. Mr. Astley, master of the jewel house, Mr. Sandes, Mr. Wentworth, were appointed to attend the lord of Canterbury his grace; for answer touching matters of religion. I suppose this was in pursuance of a former act, whereby the queen, with her metropolitan, was to appoint, and regulate, and reform matters in religion.

66

Seven bills for regulation and reformation in the church. D'Ewes' Journal, p. 184. b.

The bills for religion, and regulation of church affairs, began in the parliament 8 Eliz. and agitated and prosecuted in this parliament 13 Eliz. were seven. But some of them in the issue, dashed by her majesty, saith D'Ewes, persuaded unto it, as it should seem, by some sinister counsel. I. For the articles printed anno 1562, for sound religion. First read on the 5th of Dec. 8 Eliz. All the rest of them that follow had their first reading Dec. the 6th, in the said session; viz. II. The bill for the order of ministers. III. For the residence of pastors. IV. For the avoiding of corrupt presentations. V. For leases of benefices. VI. For pensions out of benefices. VII. Touching commutation of penance by the ecclesiastical judge. Which last was first preferred in this parliament. These were read several times in the house, and countenanced; and some of them came to effect.

Moved, that a confession of faith be made for the use of this church.

The first of these, offered in the beginning of this session, and introduced by Mr. Strickland in a long speech before mentioned, (which was for a new confession of faith, to be made and used in this church,) may be better understood, if we relate some further passages of that speech; viz. " That " he thought it worth the while for the parliament to be

" occupied for some time; that all reproachful speeches CHAP.
VII.
" of slanderers might be stopped; drawbacks in religion
" brought forward; and overrunners, that exceeded the Anno 1571.
" rules of the law, reduced: that a confession of faith
" should be made, and published, and confirmed; as was
" among other professors of religion in foreign parts. As
" those of Strasburge and Frankford: and as learned
" men also formerly in this land travelled in; as Peter
" Martyr, Paulus Fagius, and others. And that an offer
" thereof, that had been formerly made in parliament,
" might be approved." He added, that the book [which
was the Reformation of the Ecclesiastical Laws, effected
chiefly by archbishop Cranmer, by the command of king
Henry VIII. and Edward VI.] rested still in the custody
of Mr. Norton, a member of the house. And thereupon
requested, that the said Norton might be required to produce the same. Which he after did. And shewed that it The book
was the book drawn up [under king Edward] by thirty-two of the Re-
formation
persons, i. e. eight bishops, eight divines, eight civilians, of the Ec-
clesiastical
and eight temporal lawyers: who had in charge to make Laws pro-
ecclesiastical constitutions, and took the same in hand: and duced in
this parlia-
that Mr. Fox [the martyrologist] took some pains about the ment.
said book, and had newly printed it: which the said Norton then and there shewed. I add, that Fox also set a
large preface before it, *ad doctum et candidum lectorem;*
and concludeth with his wish, " That what, by the prema-
" ture death of that king, was then denied to the church's
" happiness, might be supplied in the more happy times of
" queen Elizabeth, by the authority of that present parlia-
" ment, [viz. this, as it seems, of the 13th of the queen,]
" and by the consent and favour of learned men." This
book was printed again in Latin, in the year 1640, at London.

I have this further to add concerning this book. It was And in a
former par-
said, that Dr. Haddon, that learned civilian, and master of liament
brought in
the requests to the queen, had in a former parliament de- by Dr. Had-
livered this book, which had with so much pains, labour, don. Re-
form no
and learning, been prepared and finished in king Edward's Enemy, &c.
By Penry.

67

days: and wherein Haddon himself, having an excellent Latin style, was concerned in drawing up. And that then in that parliament, it was ordered to be translated into English for their better considering it. For this, I make no doubt, was that *book of discipline* which Penry (that was executed for sedition about 1591) hinted at in one of his books, (called, *Reformation no enemy to her majesty and state*, printed anno 1590,) where, after his preface, he makes this request to the reader: " Mr. D. Haddon delivered in " parliament a Latin book concerning *church discipline*,. " written in the days of king Edward VI. by M. Cranmer " and sir John Cheeke, &c. This book (saith he) was com- " mitted by the house to be translated, unto the said M. " D. Haddon, M. George Bromley, M. Norton, &c." His request follows: " If thou canst, good reader, help me, or " any other, that labour in the cause, unto the said book, I' " hope, though I never saw it, that in so doing, thou shalt " do good service to the Lord and his church." So he, sup- posing it had much favoured his admired discipline. But if he had been helped to a sight of it, he would have found it would not have served his purpose.

A motion
for a con-
ference
with the
bishops in
order to a
further re-
formation.

The said Mr. Strickland, in his speech aforesaid, made several motions, " That they should not, for any cause of " policy, permit any errors in matters of doctrine to con- " tinue longer among them. And that the reformation he " urged should not by this be called a chopping and " changing of our religion, [as some had objected,] but " pursuant to our profession; that is, to have all doctrines " brought to the purity of the primitive church. And at " last he moved, that certain of them might be assigned, to " have conference with the lords of the spirituality, for con- " sideration and reformation of these matters." But what stop these earnest motions had, we have shewed before.

The success
of the com-
mittee's at-
tendance
upon the
archbishop.

Only let me add what happened to the said committee for religion, when, according as it was appointed, they attended the archbishop of Canterbury with their model for reforma- tion; wherein, as some articles of religion were allowed by them, so others, already received into the church, were left

out. The archbishop, taking a view of this draught, asked CHAP.
them, why they put out of the book the article for homi- VII.
lies, and for the consecrating of bishops, and some others. Anno 1571.
Mr. Peter Wentworth, (who was one of that committee,) a D'Ewes'
hot man, answered, (as he gave an account of it himself in Journal, p. 239.
his speech the next parliament,) because they were so occupied in other matters, that they had no time to examine
them, how they agreed with the word of God. Whereat the
archbishop replied, that surely they mistook the matter:
saying further, You will refer yourselves wholly to us [the
bishops] therein. To which Wentworth, in some heat, and Went-
somewhat rudely, answered; " No, by the faith I bear to worth's words to
" God, we will pass nothing before we understand what the arch-
" it is. For that were but to make you popes. Make you bishop.
" popes, who list; for we will make you none." But this
gentleman taking the like freedom to talk concerning the
queen in the next parliament, 18 Eliz. and using several
bold expressions concerning her, (as, how rumours ran
in the house, " Take heed what you do; for the queen
" liketh not such a matter,") he was sequestered the house,
and committed to the sergeant as a prisoner for some time.

But what bills about religion and the state of the church 68
took place in this parliament, I shall proceed now to relate. Some were brought in against papists; who at that Bills against
time endeavoured to deprive and depose the queen in fa- papists.
vour of the Scottish queen Mary. This became enacted. For security
" Where it was made high treason to compass, imagine, in- against the Scotch
" vent, &c. the queen's death, or any bodily harm, tend- queen.
" ing to death, maiming, or wounding her royal person;
" or to deprive or depose her from the style, honour, or
" kingly name of the imperial crown of this realm; or to
" levy war against her; or to move any foreigners or stran- Statute
" gers with force to invade this realm or that of Ireland; 13 Eliz. cap. 1.
" or to utter or declare, by any printing, writing, cipher-
" ing, speech, or words, that the queen is not or ought not
" to be queen of this realm, and of the realms of France
" and Ireland; or that any other person ought by right to

" be king or queen of the same realms; or that should
" by writing, printing, preaching, speech, &c. publish, set
" forth and affirm, that queen Elizabeth is an heretic, schis-
" matic, tyrant, infidel, or usurper of the crown of the said
" realms. And further, such to be utterly disabled, during
" their natural lives, to have or enjoy the crown of Eng-
" land, or any style or title thereof, [this was aimed at the
" queen of Scots,] at any time in succession, of whatever
" degree, condition, place, &c. they be, that in any wise
" claimed or pretended themselves to have a right or title
" to the crown of England in the life of queen Elizabeth;
" or should usurp the royal style, title, or dignity of this
" crown; or should hold and affirm, that the queen had not
" right to hold or enjoy the said crown and realm: or after
" any demand should not acknowledge her to be, in right,
" true and lawful queen of these realms.

" And he was adjudged a high traitor by this act, that
" during the queen's life should affirm or maintain any
" right, title, &c. in succession or inheritance in or to the
" crown of England after queen Elizabeth, to be right-
" fully in, or lawfully due unto any such claimer, pre-
" tender, &c. or not acknowledger. And he also to be
" judged an high traitor, that shall not affirm that the com-
" mon laws of this realm, not altered by parliament, ought
" to direct the right of the crown of England: or that the
" queen's majesty, by and with the authority of the parlia-
" ment, is not able to make laws and statutes, of sufficient
" force to limit and bind the crown of this realm, and
" the descent, limitation, and inheritance, and government
" thereof: or that this present statute, or any other sta-
" tute, to be made by authority of the parliament, with the
" royal assent of the queen, for limiting of the crown, or
" any statute for recognising the right of the said crown
" and realm to be rightly and lawfully in the person of
" our sovereign lady and queen, are not or ought not to be
" for ever of good and sufficient force and validity to bind,
" limit, restrain, and govern all persons, their rights and

" titles, that any wise might claim any interest or possi-
" bility in or to the crown of England, in possession, re-
" mainder, inheritance, succession, or otherwise."

By the same act provision was made against contentious
and seditious spreading abroad of titles to the succession of
the crown; and against books or works printed and written,
that did directly or expressly declare and affirm, before 69
any act of parliament were made, to establish and confirm
the same, that any one particular person is or ought to be
the right heir and successor to the queen's majesty, except
the same be the natural issue of her majesty's body; or
shall publish or set abroad any book or scrolls to that effect:
or the abettors and counsellors of such: upon the pain of
imprisonment, and forfeiture of half his goods, for the first
time. The second time, the pains and forfeitures in the statutes of Provision and Premunire.

There was another act made this parliament against bring- Act against
ing in of popes' bulls, or putting them in execution; and bringing in popes'
against bringing in writings, or instruments, or other su- bulls; and
perstitious things from the see of Rome. This was made
on purpose against such as had procured and obtained from
the bishop of Rome divers bulls and writings, to absolve
and reconcile all those that would be contented to forsake
their obedience to the queen, and to yield themselves to the
foreign, unlawful, and usurped authority of the see of
Rome: and by colour of the said bulls, wicked persons secretly, in such parts of the realm where the people were
most weak and simple and ignorant, [as it ran in that statute,] had, by their lewd and subtile practices and persuasions, so far wrought, that sundry such weak and ignorant
persons had been contented to be reconciled to the said
usurped authority; and to take absolution at the hands of
such naughty and subtile practisers. Whereby had grown
great disobedience and boldness in many, not only to withdraw and absent themselves from all divine service, now
most godly set forth in the realm; but also thought themselves discharged of and from all obedience, duty, and allegiance to the queen. Whereby most wicked and unnatural

BOOK rebellion had ensued. All such bringing in of such bulls,
I.
————— and such reconcilers to the see of Rome, were made guilty
Anno 1571. of high treason to the queen and the realm.

Agnus   By the same act they incurred the statute of Premu-
Dei's,
crosses, pic- nire and Provision, made 16 Rich. II. that brought into the
tures,   realm any token or tokens, thing or things, called *Agnus*
beads, &c.
Cap. 2.   *Dei's,* or any crosses, pictures, beads, or such like vain and
superstitious things, from the bishop or see of Rome: the
former of which were said to be hallowed or consecrate by
the bishop of Rome in his own person. And the crosses,
pictures, beads, either by the same bishop, or by others
having power, or pretending to have power for the same,
by or from him or his said see: divers pardons, immunities,
and exemptions pretended, being to be conferred upon such
as should receive and use the same.

Act against   Another act for papists was against fugitives over the
such as fled
beyond sea   seas. This was against such persons, who as (though they
without li- were sovereign rulers themselves, and not under rule) cast-
cence. Cap.
3.   ing away most wilfully and obstinately the service, obedience, and defence of their prince and country, secretly, in
great numbers, without licence of the queen, departed the
realm into foreign parts and dominions of other princes:
under whose obeisance and protection they submitted
themselves, and became their subjects. And there did un-
naturally discover the secrets of this realm, and their native country. And conveyed with them great sums of mo-
70 ney; being naturally a part of the common treasure of the
realm: spending the same to the profit and commodity of
strangers: and in sundry places to the relief of rebels, and
fugitives, and traitors. And not so satisfied, did practise in
those parts traitorous and rebellious seditions, and slanderous things, as well by writing as otherwise; as the expressions of that statute were. The penalty laid upon all such
was the loss and forfeiture of all their manors, lands, tenements, &c. to the queen, during their lives, unless they returned home within six months; and yielded their bodies
to the high sheriff of the county, or some of the queen's
council. And that all benefices, prebends, and other eccle-

siastical promotions, belonging to spiritual and ecclesiastical CHAP.
VII.
persons, so offending in departing the realm, and not returning, should be utterly void to all intents and purposes. Anno 1571.
There was also a bill brought in (though I think passed not
into an act) against priests disguising themselves in serving-
men's apparel.

Another act made this session of parliament with respect Act against
to religion and the good of the church, was against frauds; frauds for
dilapida-
defeating remedies for dilapidations of ecclesiastical livings; tions; and
and for leases to be granted for collegiate churches. The about leases
for collegi-
reason of this statute was for the stopping the practice of ate church-
es. Cap. 10.
some bishops and dignitaries, or other ecclesiastical per-
sons; who had ancient palaces and mansion-houses, and
other buildings and edifices, belonging to their preferments:
and suffered the same, for want of repairs, to run into great
ruins, and some parts utterly to fall down to the ground.
And had converted the timber, lead, and stones, to their
own benefit and commodity, and made deeds of gift, and co-
lourable alienations, and other conveyances of like effect, of
their goods and chattels in their lifetimes; to the intent
after their death to defraud their successors of such just
actions and remedies, as they might or should have had
for the same by the laws ecclesiastical, against their executors; to the great defacing the state ecclesiastical, and intolerable charges of their successors. This act did empower
the successor of him or them that should make such deeds,
to commence suit, and have such remedy in any court ecclesiastical against him or them, to whom such deeds should
be made, for the amendment and reparation of so much of
the said dilapidations and decays, as happened by his fact
or default.

Also, this act provided against colleges, deans and chapters, parsons, vicars, &c. who made long and unreasonable
leases, which were the great causes of dilapidations and decays of all spiritual living and hospitality, and the utter impoverishing of all successors, incumbent in the same: that
henceforth no leases should be made longer than one and

H 4

BOOK
1. twenty years, or three lives. All other leases, grants, &c. to be utterly void and of none effect.

Anno 1571.
Act touch-
ing leases
of benefices,
not to in-
jure hospi-
tality. Cap.
20. Another act was made this session touching leases of be-nefices. The intent of this act was, that livings appointed for ecclesiastical ministers might not, by corrupt and indi-rect dealings, be transferred to other uses. No lease after the 15th day of May, to be made of any benefice, or eccle-siastical promotion with cure, not being impropried, to en-

71 dure any longer than while the lessor shall be ordinarily re-sident, and serving the cure of such benefice, without ab-sence above fourscore days in any one year. But that every such lease, so soon as it or any part thereof shall come to any possession or use above forbidden, or immediately upon such absence, shall cease and be void. And the incumbent so offending, to lose one year's profit of his benefice; to be distributed by the ordinary among the poor of the parish. All chargings of such benefices with any pension, or with any profit out of the same, hereafter to be made, other than rents to be reserved upon leases hereafter to be made, to be utterly void.

In the same act, it was allowed such persons as had two benefices, to demise one of them, upon which he shall not be most ordinarily resident; but only to the curate that shall then serve the cure. The reason whereof seems to be, that hospitality might be the better preserved from the re-venues of the church. But this was but temporary.

An act to
reform cer-
tain disor-
ders in mi-
nisters.
Cap. 12. There was yet another act made touching religion. Which was to reform certain *disorders touching ministers of the church.* This act was intended to keep out from mi-nistering in the church such as would not comply with the doctrine established in this church of England in the be-ginning of the queen's reign; and that the queen's domi-nions might be served with pastors of sound religion, as the preamble ran. It concerned all such persons as pretended to be priests and ministers of God's word and sacraments under the degree of a bishop, by reason of any other form of institution, consecration, or ordering, than the form set

forth in the late king Edward's time, and now used in the CHAP.
reign of the queen. [Meaning undoubtedly to comprehend VII.
papists, and likewise such as received their orders in some of Anno 1571.
the foreign reformed churches, when they were in exile under queen Mary.] The act enjoined all such and all others,
having any ecclesiastical living, to declare their assent, before the bishop of the diocese, to all the articles of religion,
(which only concern the confession [a] of the true Christian ᵃThis clause
faith, and the doctrine of the sacraments,) comprised in the inserted to
book imprinted, entitled, *Articles, whereupon it was agreed* meet with
by the archbishops and bishops, &c. being the thirty-nine house that
articles, framed in the synod anno 1562. And to subscribe moved for
them. Which was to be testified by the bishop of the dio- fession of
cese, under his seal. Which testimonial he [the priest or made;
minister] was openly, on some Sunday, in time of public which need-
service before noon, in the church where he ought to at- those ar-
tend, to read, together with the said articles, [as his con- ticles of re-
fession of faith.] Otherwise to be *ipso facto* deprived; and the church
all his ecclesiastical promotions to be void. of Eng-
land's suffi-
And no ecclesiastical person advisedly to maintain or af- cient confirm any doctrine, directly contrary or repugnant to any of the true
the said articles; and being convented before the bishop, or Christian
ordinary, or queen's commissioners ecclesiastical, shall per- faith.
sist therein, or not revoke his error; or after such revocation, again affirm such untrue doctrines; in such case it
was made lawful for the bishop or ordinary, or the said
commissioners, to deprive such person. And upon such
sentence of deprivation to be actually deprived.

None to be admitted hereafter to any benefice with cure, 72
except he be of the age of three and twenty years at the Qualifica-
least, and a deacon; and first have subscribed the said ar- ministers.
ticles, in presence of the ordinary, and publicly read the
same in the parish church of that benefice; with declaration of his unfeigned assent to the same. And every person
after the end of that session of parliament, to be admitted
to a benefice with cure, within two months after his induc-
tion publicly to read the said articles in his parish church;

and to do all as aforesaid. Otherwise to incur deprivation immediately *ipso facto.*

Also it was enacted in the same statute, that none should be made minister, or admitted to preach, or minister the sacraments, being under the age of four and twenty years; nor unless he should first bring to the bishop of the diocese from men known to the bishop, a testimonial both of his honest life, and of his professing the doctrine expressed in the said articles; nor unless he be able to answer, and to render to the ordinary an account of his faith in Latin, according to the said articles; or have special gift and ability to be a preacher.

None to be admitted to the order of a deacon or minister, unless he shall first subscribe the Articles. None to be admitted to a living of or above the value of 30*l.* a year in the queen's books, without he be bachelor of divinity, or a preacher lawfully allowed by some bishop of this realm, or by one of the universities.

All admissions to benefices, institutions, and inductions, contrary to the form of any provision in this act; and all tolerations, dispensations, qualifications, and licences whatsoever, that shall be made to the contrary, to be merely void in law.

Provided, no title to confer, or present by lapse, to accrue upon any deprivation *ipso facto;* but after six months after notice of such deprivation given by the ordinary to the patron.

By force of this act many that held benefices and ecclesiastical preferments were deprived in this and the following year. I find these two among others in the diocese of Bath
and Wells. Henry Thorn, A. B. was presented by Geo. Speke, knight, to the church of East Dolish, Jan. 28, 1571, by the obstinacy and disobedience of Thomas Elyot, refusing, or at least neglecting to subscribe in his proper person to the articles set forth anno 1562. And so was deprived. Again, June, 1572, Edward Bremel, alias Cable, was presented to the church of Wayford, by the deprivation of

John Haunce, by virtue of a statute, (as it runs in the re- CHAP.
gister,) 13 Eliz. entitled, *An act to reform certain disorders* ____ VII.
touching ministers of the church.   Anno 1571.

<hr/>

CHAP. VIII.

A convocation.   Matters done there.   An act made, very 73
beneficial for employment of multitudes of poor.   The
queen's concernments with Scotland.   Endeavours a re-
concilement of the two parties there.   Her resolution
against the restoring of the Scottish queen: and why.
Articles of pacification propounded by the queen to the
two parties in Scotland.   The queen's agent's notable
letter to Graunge and Liddington.   Sends a challenge
to the French ambassador.   His letters to the lord regent
of Scotland, duke of Lenox, and to earl Morton, inter-
cepted.   A book writ in favour of the queen of Scots.

THERE was now also a convocation; and what was done A convoca-
there is related at large in the Life of Archbishop Parker. tion.
Only we may take notice of some things observed as done in Archbishop
this synod, set down in the dedication of bishop Jewel's Parker.
works to king James; namely, that the synod 1571 did B. 4. ch. 5.
then set forth this canon among others, for the direction of
those that were preachers and pastors, " That they should
" never teach any thing, as matter of faith, religiously, but
" that which was agreeable to the doctrine of the Old and
" New Testament; or collected out of the same doctrine by
" the ancient fathers and catholic bishops of the church."

I find a treatise among the MSS. of William Petyt, esq. Orders in
of Dr. Thomas Wylson's own hand, (who was master of ecclesiasti-
St. Katharine's near the Tower, and afterwards secretary tion. MSS.
of state, a very learned civilian,) being *Orders in eccle-* Guil. Petyt,
siastical jurisdiction.   Which seems to have been drawn up, C.
to be confirmed in this synod.   There is a title, *For pu-*
nishment of persons convicted.   Another, *What order is to*
be taken with false writings, &c.

BOOK
I.

Anno 1571.
Act for
making of
caps, for
the employ-
ment of
multitudes
of poor
people.

To the bills passed into acts this parliament, there is one more, (besides those mentioned above,) which I judge not amiss to be taken notice of, though it have no other relation to religion than charity, which comes very near it. It concerned the queen's care of *employment* for her poorer sort of subjects. It was for continuance of making and wearing woollen caps, in behalf of the trade of cappers; providing, that all above the age of six years (except the nobility and some others) should, on sabbath-days and holydays, wear caps of wool knit, thicked, and dressed in England, upon penalty of ten groats. But notwithstanding this statute, these caps went very much out of fashion, and the wearing of hats prevailed. Which caused the queen, two or three years after, to take such notice of it, as to set forth a strict proclamation for the enforcing of the wearing of caps, the benefit whereof being of more public good than at present was perceived; namely, the employment of such vast numbers of idle, poor, and impotent people throughout the whole nation, that otherwise must either have starved, begged, or robbed. Which thus that proclamation expressed, (mentioning the said act made in the parliament the 13th of her reign,) " That it was for the relief of divers poor towns,
" and of great multitudes of her poor subjects, who other-
" wise were like to perish, or to become unprofitable or
" dangerous unto the commonweal: and that by means of
" this statute, great numbers of idle, poor, and impotent
" persons were set on work, while the awe of the said sta-
" tute, and fear of due execution thereof continued, to the
" marvellous great commodity of this realm, and help of the
" needy, and redress of evil occupied persons; as by experi-
" ence thereof had been notably proved."

The queen's
proclama-
tion for
wearing
them. And
why.

But these caps, it seems, not long after went out of fashion; and so the trade decayed: which caused the queen to set forth the said proclamation. It set forth further,
" How that by little and little the disobedience and wanton
" disorder of evil-disposed and light persons, more regard-
" ing private fantasies and vanity, than public commodity
" or respect of duty, had increased by want of execution of

74

" the said law. Whereby those good and honest subjects, CHAP.
" that had by means of the said statute set to work a great ___VIII.___
" number of poor people, were like to be driven to give over Anno 1571.
" their said trades, and to send abroad again into idleness
" and misery those multitudes that had been by them re-
" lieved. Whereby was like to grow great enormity and in-
" convenience, if speedy remedy were not provided. There-
" fore she charged and commanded all justices of assize,
" justices of peace, mayors, sheriffs, &c. that every of them,
" according to their office, place, and calling, should do
" their uttermost, for the due execution of the said statute.
" And that bailiffs, constables, churchwardens, &c. every
" Sunday and festival day, make diligent view and search,
" in all churches, chapels, and all other places, within the
" circuits and compasses of their offices, for all and singular
" breakers and offenders of the said statute; and without
" delay cause the names of such offenders, and of their pa-
" rents, guardians, governors, and masters of every child,
" servant, and ward so offending, together with the day
" and place of the offence committed, to be then written,
" and lawfully ordered and presented," &c.

The great importance of this manufacture, for the sup- The benefit
port of the lower rank of the queen's people, was more fully of this ma-
declared in that act aforesaid, in these words, worthy of to the na-
note: " That the company of cappers, by means only of tion, set
" their trade and science of capping, not only maintained act. Cap.19.
" their wives, children, and families, in good and conve-
" nient state and degree, but set on work a great number
" and multitude of other poor persons, men, women, and
" children; and also such as were halt, and decrepid, and
" lame; using them in sundry exercises belonging to that
" occupation, as carders, spinners, knitters, parters of wool,
" forcers, thickers, dressers, walkers, dyers, battelers, shear-
" ers, pressers, edgers, liners, bandmakers, and other exer-
" cises: who had in manner thereby maintained and re-
" lieved themselves and their families. And by reason of
" their labour and exercise therein, had eschewed and
" avoided not only the great annoyance of the towns they

" dwelt in, who for lack of exercise must have been forced
" to beg, but also had kept them from ranging and gadding
" through the realm, in practising sundry kinds of lewd-
" ness, as too many of them now did.   And also, by the
" means of this good exercise and occupation, a great many
" of personable men had at all times been ready, and well
" able, when they were called, to serve the queen, or her
" most noble progenitors, in time of war, or elsewhere;
" until of late days, that most, or in manner all men had
" forborne and left off the using and wearing of caps. This
" tended also to the great impoverishing and utter undoing
" of the company of cappers ; and to the decay, ruin, and
" desolation of divers ancient cities and boroughs, which
" had been the nourishers and bringers up in that faculty of
" great numbers of people ; as London, which by good re-
" port maintained eight thousand persons, exercised in this
" faculty : also Exeter, Bristow, Monmouth, Hereford,
" Rosse, Bridgnorth, Bewdley, Gloucester, Worcester,
" Chester, Nantwich, and many more."

Affairs abroad affected the nation, and the state of religion here at home, especially the intrigues of the Scottish
queen, and the match with the duke d'Anjou.

The queen
concerned
in Scotch
matters.   The queen was so certainly informed of the Scottish
queen's and her friends' intrigues against her, that she
found it necessary to keep her strait ; suffering none (but
persons of her own) of all sorts to be about that queen's
person.   Now she pretended a great fear of her life, and
craved a ghostly father, being catholic, to be with her : for
in truth many of her servants had been discharged, having
been found to be dangerous practisers.   And queen Elizabeth, upon this experience, plainly noted to the states of
Scotland, that she would never suffer that queen to have
her government in Scotland restored to her.   Her business
now was to further the young king of Scots his affairs, (who
The two
parties
there. was set up by the protestant party in that kingdom,) and
his friends, against the Scottish queen's party.   The lord
Hunsdon at Berwick had a commission in October, to set
a good face upon the matter, to bring Graunge (who held

out the castle of Edinburgh for that queen) to the king's
devotion: but if he could not, they of the queen's council
were of opinion that he should force them. And the queen
was now in hand (as the lord Burghley writ in certain of his Burghley's
letters) to make an accord between Liddington and Graunge letter to Walsing-
in the castle, and the regent, two considerable parties, the ham.
difficulty between them being rather particular than public. They in the castle looked to have their offices and
lands restored ; and first, surety to be given, that Graunge
might remain captain of the castle. The other party [for
the king, who were protestants] were to keep what they
had catched, as bishoprics and abbeys. Wherein the lord
Burghley's judgment was, that he thought the next avoiding [of these bishoprics and abbeys] might help. But that
greediness and mistrust kept them asunder : and he feared
more the wilfulness of the king's party, than the conforma-
tion of the adverse.

The account queen Elizabeth gave the French ambassa- The queen
dor, of her concern in this Scotch quarrel, was, that she had declares her intention
no other intention in the matter of Scotland, but to have the therein to
hostility and civil wars there to cease, and the government the French ambassador.
of the realm to be established to the contentation of the na- 76
tion. For which purpose she had sent to both parties at difference, to accord an abstinence from war ; so as they might
the better treat and act among themselves.

And for this good end and purpose she propounded to Articles of
them articles of pacification, containing the queen's ma- pacification recom-
jesty's intention for reducing the realm of Scotland to an mended by
inward peace, (as the preface to the articles ran,) and so to the queen to the Scots.
continue free from civil wars and dissensions, [which now MSS. Ran-
were between the lords on the Scottish queen's side, and dolph.
the protestants, who had set up her son to be king.] The
first article was, " That the whole state of Scotland, in all
" degrees of subjection, may submit themselves to the au-
" thority of the king, and do, give, acknowledge, and yield
" full obedience to him. And that the principal states of
" the land, that is, the nobility, prelatie, and the cities and
" boroughs, do acknowledge the same by oath, and sub-

" scription in writing. And that all the same be confirmed
" by a general consent in parliament. And in the same
" parliament to reestablish, as cause shall require, all things
" concluded in the late parliament, for the cause of reli-
" gion." [Which was mentioned under the last year.]
There was also an addition to these articles, of more secrecy, with some enlargements to some other shorter and
general articles; according to the instructions given to Randolph, her agent.

She will
not permit
the Scottish
queen to be
restored.
And why.

As, " To the first, the adverse party to the king must
" directly understand, that the queen of Scots (whose per-
" son is now in England) hath of late attempted such and
" so many enterprises against her majesty, both by stirring
" of rebellion in her majesty's realm, and by provoking of
" foreign power to enter into the realm; all which had
" been enterprised indeed, if God had not this last August
" given to her majesty cause to stay it, by committing the
" duke of Norfolk to the Tower of London; as none can
" trust, that her majesty will ever of herself suffer the said
" queen of Scots to have liberty with power to attempt the
" like again. And therefore, without any further question,
" for the queen to rule alone by restitution, or jointly with
" her son, it must be answered, that the expectation thereof
" is in vain. And to imagine any other government of such
" a realm as Scotland is, but by the king, who is the native
" prince in blood, and in possession invested, is a mere fan-
" tastical device, and not to be heard of. So as this article
" must be clearly answered for the king, or else the rest are
" in vain to be treated."

The queen's
agent's let-
ter to
Grange and
Liddington,
to bring
them off
from her.

Now to bring over the abovesaid Graunge and Liddington from the Scottish queen, Mr. Randolph wrote them a
notable eloquent letter in March, after divers communica-
tions with them together, to little effect. His letter was
pursuant to the queen's command, to deal with them to
obey the king, and to acknowledge the regent. Against
which they alleged for themselves conscience, honour, and
safety. For the satisfying them in the first, he urged,
" that that queen was not worthy to live, whose cause they

" defended, that had committed such horrible offences. And
" that there was therefore no matter of *conscience* in put-
" ting her down, and less in obeying her. That this they
" knew themselves; this they had spoken of themselves; 77
" and that they had wrote against her, fought against her,
" and were the chiefest cause of her apprehension and im-
" prisonment, and dimission of the crown: if at that time
" there was nothing done against conscience, he asked, what
" moved them to make it a matter of conscience now to leave
" her, and to allege conscience for setting up her that had
" been the overthrow of their country?

" Neither should the point of *honour* move them, in which
" the world was chiefly respected: that might be solved,
" and themselves by all honest and godly men better al-
" lowed of. That in respect of their country's weal, they
" should yield somewhat of their own, yea, though to their
" disadvantage, than to see daily so much blood shed. That
" honour was to be respected, where justice proceeded. That
" if the cause they defended were unjust, what honour
" could there be to maintain it? But rather shame to stand
" so long by it as they had done."

And as to the third, viz. their *safety*, he applied himself
first to Liddington. " They [the queen and state of Eng-
" land] were with him in care of mind, had compassion of
" his present hard state and extremities apparent to ensue;
" as friends, they lamented it. Thus far therefore they pro-
" mised, that his state by composition should be no worse
" than theirs presently was, that had been of their part and
" mind with them. Safety to their lives they dared to pro-
" mise; restitution to their lands and livings they dared
" assure them of; for the recovery of their losses, there
" should be as much done as lay in them. That if they
" doubted of the regent, they seemed to know less now
" than beforetime they had done; whose honesty towards
" the world they had allowed of in time past; and whose
" particular good-will towards them was well reported and
" thought of. Of his zeal and love towards the word of
" God, and love to his country, no man ever doubted. And

" that such a reverence he bore to queen Elizabeth, to fol-
" low her advice, that neither should his promise be broken
" unto them, nor any thing be left undone by him, that
" was in his power to perform. If they doubted the lord
" Morton, they should have the like security of him. Fur-
" ther, they should have the queen and England their
" friends, &c. faithful, and indifferent any way that they
" could to do them good. But if nothing would do, he
" bade them trust him upon his word, they stayed to their
" destruction." But the whole letter, as opening the transactions at that time between England and Scotland, and
the infamy the Scottish queen then lay under, I have put
into the Appendix.

N°. IX.

He comes in
favour of
the king's
party.
Writes as
much to the
bishop of
Durham.

This Randolph had been lately sent to bring the Scottish
queen's party over to the king. And on the 25th of March
(which was hard at hand) the assembly of the friends of
either party was to be at Leith, where Randolph was. And
being to make a judgment of this affair, he was not long to
continue there after, as he wrote to the bishop of Durham:
" And that they of the castle attended La Croke, a French-
" man, that was coming; thinking to find more comfort
" and assistance at his hands, than England could or would
" give them, except they would acknowledge their obedi-
" ence to the king and regent; which hitherto they refused
78 " to do. But England without that could do nothing for
" them ;" as he added in his letter to that bishop.

He chal-
lengeth the
French am-
bassador.

MSS. Ran-
dolph.

While Randolph was here, Viracque, the French ambassador, was also in Scotland, transacting the contrary
part. But he had, it seems, falsely reported of the said
Randolph, in some private intelligence, and likewise of the
queen: which coming to the ears of that English gentleman, he shewed an English courage by a challenge he sent
Viracque, in these words, as I find it in Randolph's own
MSS. " Monsieur Virac, I have seen, as I am informed,
" some writings of yours in cipher, containing these words,
" &c.: which toucheth me greatly in honour, and I doubt
" to the queen my mistress, as to have trafficked with Mr.
" Ar. D. for the conveyance of the French ambassador's

" letters in England to you. Wherefore this I write, and
" signify unto you by these presents, that if you have writ-
" ten the words above mentioned, you have not done the
" part of an honest man ; and that in so writing, you have
" lied falsely in your throat : which I will maintain with my
" body against him, you, or any man living, of my quality,
" or under the same, my charge at this time set apart. For
" that I never had any such talk with him, or he with me.
" Answer hereunto, if you think good."

Randolph soon returned back to London. And from
thence, on the 10th of April, he despatched a letter to the
earl of Lenox, [Matthew Stuart,] lord regent of Scotland,
(grandfather to the king, and his governor, and slain this
year by the adverse party, that held for the queen,) and on
the next day to earl Morton. Both letters had respect unto
a conference at queen Elizabeth's court, for compromising
matters between Mary the Scottish queen, and those that
had the government of the king's person, (who was now but
five or six years old,) by certain commissioners on both sides.
Which brake up without any peaceable issue ; especially
those of the Scottish queen's side, who required absolutely
her liberty. But both these letters were seized ; the post-
boy delivering them to the bishop of Galloway, one of that
queen's commissioners, and was gone from London unto
her. Which letters should have been delivered to earl
Morton, being a commissioner on the king's side, that was
also going to Scotland. The said intercepted letters were
brought to the Scottish queen ; and by her sent to queen
Elizabeth, with heavy complaints of Mr. Randolph, by the
French minister, notwithstanding the letters were written by
her majesty's commandment. These letters, to aggravate
some passages in them, (having lines drawn under them,)
had postils or notes set in the margin, which were the Scottish queen's, or made by some about her, to aggravate the
matter the more against him. This complaint was written
in a paper that wrapped up these letters. Both these letters
and the notes I shall exhibit, taken from the very originals,
late in my hands and possession.

" To my lord regent's grace of Scotland.

" Your grace shal hear so much of the state of al things " here [at the English court] by my lord Morton, and other " lords in his company, that I need not trouble your grace " with any long letters; only testifying my good-wil, and " desire to have al matters succeeded to your grace's con- " tentment.   But seeing that cannot be, I trust your grace " wil ᵃ *take the next best, having in the mean time this* " *cause* to rejoyce, that your grace's enemies have had " ᵇ *mich less of their wills than they looked for:* and by " my lord of Morton's grave and wise dealings, gotten unto " your grace mo friends in your actions than ever you " had.   *In whose wil, if al things were,* your grace should " find *a short end to al these cumbers* now your grace is in. " I am hartily glad of the good success your grace hath " had in taking of Dunbriton; a happy turn to your grace's " country, no smal benefit to yourself, and ᶜ *such a dis-* " *pleasure to your grace's adversaries, as none can be* " *greater, except God should deliver you of her that is the* " *cause of your whole troubles.*   I doubt not but your good " grace wil see to the keeping of it.   And as God in this " hath shewed a great good beginning of his favour towards " your grace and country, so I doubt not but he shal re- " ceive the worthy honour due unto him for so great a be- " nefit.   God have your grace in his keeping.   At London " the x. of April, 1571.

" Your grace's humble at commaundment,

" Tho. Randolph."

ᵃ Here he
meddleth
with the
queen's
affairs.

ᵇ Herein he
promiseth
the queen
our mis-
tress's de-
struction,
be the help
of her un-
friends in
this country.

ᶜ Imagins
heir [here]
the queen
our mis-
tress's
death: put-
tis others in
hope there-
of, and
wishes the
same him-
self.

That to earl Morton, dated the day following, was to this tenor.

" Since your lordship departed hence, we have had no news " of any great importance, trusting and looking hartily to " hear from the lord regent some confirmation of that which " was written to your lordship touching Dumbriton; which " the bishops of Rosse and Galloway in no case wil admit " to be true, but give out that it is Dumbar, and not Dum- " briton.   And immediately after they heard the novels,

" they sent a post to their mistress, not to believe any re-
" port until they came themselves.

" The bishop of Galloway hath been among many of our
" bishops, laying out his learning to defend his mistress's
" honour with great eloquence. As also his son hath writ-
" ten a book in Latin, approving her authority, excusing the
" murther, blaming the disobedience of *her rebellious sub-*
" *jects*, that deposed her from the crown. ^d *Treat him ill* ^d Persuad-
" *when he* comes home, and if it be possible, let a copy of ing the queen's ma-
" it be gotten. This day they depart out of this town jesty our mistresses
" [London] towards their queen; and then ^e *what becomes* gud sub-
" *of them I know not.* Now I must pray your lordship to jects to be evil han-
" take al our doings here in good part. I trust that there delid.
" is better meant than doth yet appear. I pray you, cast ^e Be this my ladies
" not the cools with us over hastily. You see how God commis-
" blessed al your actions unlooked for; and so wil from sioners feiris sum evil
" time to time prosper them, so long as they are guided practices in their way.
" under his fear. With my very harty commendations to
" both my other good lords with you, I pray God send you
" a happy journey, and safe to return to your country. At
" London, the xi. of April, 1571.
   " Your honourable lordships at commaundment,
                              " Tho. Randolph."

CHAP. IX.   80

The duke of Norfolk unhappily engaged with the Scottish
   queen. The discovery thereof; by French money inter-
   cepted, sent to the Duke, for her use in Scotland. A let-
   ter in cipher to him from that queen. The duke's con-
   fession; and of his servants. The duke's words at his
   condemnation: the execution put off by the queen. And
   why. One Rolph, a concealer, executed. And why. Ma-
   ther and Verney, hired to kill the lord Burghley; exe-
   cuted. Dr. Story executed. Some particular accounts of
   his death; and of his cruelty. His last will. Darbi-
   shire the Jesuit; his discourse about the English affairs.

THOMAS duke of Norfolk, a protestant, and one of the Transac-
                    I 3   tions be-

BOOK
I.

Anno 1571.
tween the
duke of
Norfolk and
the Scottish
queen dis-
covered.

LordBurgh-
ley's letter
to Walsing-
ham.
prime nobility of England, and beloved of the people, was
unhappily engaged with the Scottish queen, that gave the
nation so much disquiet, and the queen so much jealousy, as
we have heard. But engaged he was in that queen's cause,
out of hope of marrying her. The first discovery of the renewing of that matter was in August or September. Of
which the lord Burghley informed Walsingham, the ambassador in France, viz. " That some matter was dis-
" covered, that my lord of Norfolk should still mind the
" matter of the Scottish queen. For that there was inter-
" cepted a good portion of money, that was by letter in
" cipher, directed to the lord Herris, (which, as appeared
" afterwards, was French money, and delivered to the duke
" by the French ambassador,) for help of the Scottish
" queen's party in Scotland." And that the same was sent
by one Higford, the duke's secretary; who was by order
from Audley-inn (where the court now was) taken and
committed at London. And September 2, was examined
by sir Tho. Smith, who the day before went from Audley-
inn thither for that purpose. The lord Burghley subjoined,
that he was sorry that duke should be found undutiful; but
if it were so, he was glad it should be known : which caused
him to inquire of Walsingham after another servant of the
duke's, viz. one Liggons, that had long been about Paris
and the court there.

Vehement
suspicions
of him.
Earl of
Leicester
to Walsing-
ham.
Of the same matter, about the same time, did the earl of
Leicester give Walsingham these hints : " That the cause
" went hard against the duke, even by his own confession :
" and that vehement suspicions were of more evil than he
" ever thought could fall out in him. And he believed the
" queen would proceed according to equity and justice; and
" added, that she had cause to use but small mercy."

The duke's
crimes.
Compl.
Amb.
After a little while this matter came more fully to light.
Which the lord Burghley declared, in his correspondence
with Walsingham, to this tenor : " That De Foix, the
" French ambassador, delivered money to the duke or his
" order : and that so Walsingham might aver the truth of
81 " it. That the money was taken, being by the duke's com-

" mandment (as he averred and confessed) received by
" Barker his man, from the French ambassador ; and was
" to have been sent to Banister, the duke's man, dwelling at
" Shrewsbury, and so to one Lowther and others of the
" duke's servants, secretly kept upon the west borders. And
" by him should have been sent to the lord Harris, and by
" him to Liddington.   That there was also in the bag let-
" ters in ciphers from the French ambassador to Virac, the
" French agent in Scotland.   That hereof Monsieur de Foix
" (who was now gone) made mention before his departure,
" and thought there was no other matter against the duke,
" which I would, added the lord that wrote this letter,
" there were not.   But it appeared there was much more of
" great danger ; and that God was to be thanked that it
" was discovered ; as now it was.   For there was found a
" long discourse about the duke, sent from the queen of
" Scots in cipher to him the 7th of February last.   By
" which the said queen layeth before the duke, how she was
" counselled from Spain to fly thither ; misliking utterly of
" the French, by reason of the doubt of the queen's mar-
" riage with Anjou : that she used hard words against the
" queen-mother, that she did in this discourse conclude, that
" she would make a semblance to the Spaniard of her liking
" of Don John of Austria, although she assured the duke
" of her countenance.   That she moved, that Ridolph [an
" Italian merchant here in London, and privy to these con-
" cerns,] might be sent to Rome ; and to be directed wholly
" by the duke of Norfolk."   With many other things of
like sort in that letter.

The lord Burghley added, that the duke confessed the The duke's
receipt of this from the queen of Scots : but denied that he plea for himself.
was privy to Ridolph's going, otherwise than that he was
earnestly desired of the bishop of Ross to instruct him, and
to write by him to the duke of Alva, to require aid of men
and money for the queen's party in Scotland.   But that in
it he refused to deal, because of the peril thereof.   He confessed four letters he had received from the Scottish queen
within these twelve months, and did answer them by writing,

and all in cipher : but that they were all of thanks, and to
move the queen to depend only upon the queen's majesty.
But herein the duke could make none of them [of the
queen's council] credit him.   The duke said also, that before the sending of this money, he helped the French ambassador to send his packet to Virac in July.   They had
also found his cipher between the Scottish queen and him;
but that all the writings were conveyed away; which he said
were by him burnt.   That now they had great cause to
think that he was privy to the dangerous practice, in which
they found Ridolph to have been with the duke of Alva; in
offering him that a rebellion should be moved here this summer, if that duke would assist it.   But of this the duke of
Norfolk would not be known.

The duke's
servants
confess the
treason.
      The duke's servants soon confessed all.   Barker, one of
them, being arraigned, (as the lord Burghley writ about the
beginning of February,) confessed the treason, and said, that
the beginning of the offence was, in that he regarded more
the love and pleasing of the duke his master, than of his
prince and his country; and so freely confirmed the duke's
82 guiltiness.   The next, Higford, his secretary, did also confess, terming it a concealment of his master's treasons; and
added, that he did oftentimes dissuade the duke from the
same.   These open acts fortified the duke's condemnation.

The French
ambassador
demands his
money seiz-
ed.
      In the midst of these discoveries, so much to the shame of
the French ambassador, (and his master too,) he had the
confidence to send his secretary to the court, requiring to
have his money again.   To whom the lord Burghley answered, that it must be demanded of them to whom he delivered it.   And notwithstanding this answer, he came again,
desiring he might have his majesty's money intercepted,
sent towards Virac to Scotland.

First pro-
ceedings
with the
duke. Ce-
cil's Jour-
nal.
      From a journal of Cecill's, I have these particulars of the
duke of Norfolk's business, set down by Cecill's own hand.
" July the 1st, the duke was prisoner in his own house,
" called *Howard-house.*   August 2, Higford, the Duke's
" secretary, deciphered the two tickets, taken in the bag,
" wherein was the money, viz. 1606*l.* that was to have been

" sent into Scotland.   September the 4th, sir Ralph Sad- CHAP.
" leir was sent to guard the duke of Norfolk at Howard- IX.
" house; [now called Charter-house.]   September the Anno 1571.
" 5th, the duke, examined at Howard-house, denied all
" that Higford confessed.   The 7th, the duke committed
" to the Tower by sir Ralph Sadleir, sir Tho. Smith, sir
" Henry Nevil, and Dr. Wylson.   The 8th, the duke con-
" fessed many things denied before.   The 10th, the duke
" made means to have the lord Burghley come to the Tower
" to him : who did so.   October — the duke of Norfolk in
" the Tower confesseth the receipt of a message from the
" earl of Arundel and lord Lumley.   October — the lord
" Cobham kept as prisoner in the lord Burghley's house at
" Westminster."   These particulars may not be unworthy
the relating, taken out of such an authentic paper.   The
whole trial of this nobleman, and his condemnation and execution, I shall omit, our historian relating them at large. Camd. Eliz.
Only let me note, that among the peers mentioned by Camden, at the duke's trial, the earl of Worcester is omitted,
who was present, according to a MS. in the Cotton library, Julius, F. 6.
where William earl of Worcester stands immediately after
Reginald Grey, earl of Kent.   And the speech in another
volume of the said library, as spoken by him at his execu- Titus, B. 2.
tion, (which happened not till the next year,) doth somewhat vary.

The relation of the words spoken by the duke after his Words at
condemnation do somewhat vary also ; unless perhaps Cam- his con-
demnation.
den would not set down all that was spoken by him at that Julius, F. 6.
time.   The Cotton MS. relates it thus.   That after his condemnation he used these words : " I have been found by
" my peers worthy of death; whereof I do acquit them.
" For I come not hither to justify myself, nor to charge
" them with injustice.   In dealing in matters temporal to-
" wards the queen of Scots, I dealt not as a good subject,
" for that I made not the queen privy thereunto.   For this
" offence I was committed to the Tower: but upon my
" humble submission, I was delivered ; promising the queen
" to deal no more in those matters.   But contrary to my

" submission and promise, I dealt therein: for saving my
" life, and other causes, I took my oath upon that matter.
" But I never received the communion, as it hath been
" bruited. I had conference with none but only with Ro-
" dolpho, and that but once ; and that not against her ma-
" jesty. For it was known, I had to do with him by reason
" I was bound unto him by a recognisance for a great sum
" of money. I saw two letters which came from the pope ;
" but I never consented unto them, neither to the rebellion
" in the north. I thank God I was never a papist, since I
" knew what religion meant. But I did always detest pa-
" pistry in all the vain toys thereof ; embracing ever, from
" the bottom of my heart, the true religion of Jesus Christ ;
" trusting the full assurance of my faith in his blood,
" that is only my Redeemer and Saviour. Indeed I must
" confess I had servants and friends that were papists :
" but if thereby I have offended God's church, or any pro-
" testant, I do desire God and them to forgive me." Yet
perhaps these were only some short collections of the duke's
speech at his execution, (where Camden placeth them,) rather than what was said by him at his condemnation.

The queen
defers his
execution.
Her states-
men's
thoughts
thereof.

    The queen put off the execution of the duke for some
months, out of compassion to this unhappy nobleman and
her kinsman ; and, out of respect to his high quality, was
not easily brought to pass her warrant. Of this her mercy
in delaying his execution, her statesmen did not much approve. The lord treasurer Burghley's expressions, suggest-
ing his thoughts, were : " The queen's majesty hath always
" been a merciful lady. And by mercy she hath taken more
" harm than by justice ; and yet she thinketh she is more
" beloved in doing herself harm. God save her to his ho-
" nour long among us." So he writ in one of his letters,
apprehensive of the queen's danger. And Thomas Randolph, the queen's agent now in Scotland, liked as little the
deferring of the duke's execution. Who in a letter to the
bishop of Durham, from Leith, dated March the 21st, (that
is, two months after his condemnation,) writ thus : " Out
" of London we hear yet no other, but that he remaineth

" yet alive [meaning the duke] that is to be wished, that CHAP.
IX.
" long since he had been despatched. I fear, added he, the
" bishop of Lincoln's words, in his sermon before her ma- Anno 1571.
" jesty, grow true, alleged out of Augustine, that there was
" *misericordia puniens,* and *crudelitas parcens.* In con-
" sideration whereof in government great evil did ensue."

In another of the lord Burghley's letters to Walsingham, She hesi-
dated February 11, he shewed him how the queen's majesty it. Lord
was diversly disposed. Sometime, when she spake of her Burghley's
danger, she concluded, that justice must be done. Another Walsing-
time, when she spake of the nearness of blood, of his supe- ham.
riority in honour, and such like, she stayed. On Saturday
she signed a warrant to the sheriffs of London for his execution on Monday. And so all preparations were made,
with the expectation of all London and concourse of many
thousands. But their coming was answered not with his,
but another extraordinary execution of Mather and Berney,
[of whom by and by,] for conspiring the queen's death, [and
his own death, he might have added,] and of one Rolph, Rolph.
for counterfeiting the queen's hand twice, to get concealed
lands. The cause of this disappointment was, that suddenly
on the Sunday before, late in the night, the queen sent for
him, [the lord Burghley,] and entered into a great misliking, that the duke should die the next day, and said, she 84
was and should be disquieted; and would have a new warrant made that night to the sheriffs, to forbear till they
should hear further. And accordingly they did so. After
that lord had made this relation of this sudden stop, he only
added his fears in this ejaculation, " God's will be fulfilled,
" and aid her majesty to do herself good," [which he thought
this mild course tended not to.] But though this execution
were deferred for some months longer, yet in the beginning
of June, 1572, he was beheaded at Tower-hill, as we shall
hear in due place.

The said lord Burghley, that wise statesman and sound Mather and
counsellor of the queen's in this dangerous juncture, was so their pur-
hated by her enemies, but especially the Spaniard, that Bor- kill lord
gest, that ambassador's secretary, had hired two desperate Burghley;
executed.

BOOK I. Anno 1571.

men, viz. Mather and Berny, [alias Verny,] to murder him; nay, and the queen too. For they at last confessed, that they intended to kill him; and afterwards plainly confessed also their intention and desire to have been rid of the queen: (as the said lord wrote in his correspondence with the queen's ambassador in France:) and added, " But I think she may " by justice be rid of them." And accordingly they underwent the just pains of death in February, (as was hinted before,) being drawn, hanged, and quartered. It is remarkable, that when Mather had, in the presence of Leicester, Mr. Secretary, and Mildmay, charged that ambassador's secretary, that both his master and he had enticed him to kill the lord Burghley, that secretary denied it: upon which, Mather offered to try it *con la spada,* i. e. by the sword.

Dr. Story suffers for treason.

Another execution, in the month of June, before, was done upon John Story, LL. D. who suffered at Tyburn on Friday; and there refused to give allegiance to the queen's majesty, (as the lord Burghley wrote to Walsingham,) and professed to die as the king of Spain's subject, [being indeed a pensioner of Spain.] And so having been arraigned on the Tuesday before at the king's bench, he would not answer to the indictment; alleging, that he was not a subject of this realm. Whereupon, without further trial, he was condemned as guilty of treason, contained in his indictment. For his treason, inveterate hatred to the queen, and cruelty exercised towards the protestants, I refer the reader to other histories. But some particular passages of him, omitted by our historians, I shall here relate. In his execution he is thus described by Dr. Fulk, (in his Retentive, and in his book against Gregory Martin, at the end of it, where he writ a confutation of the papists' quarrels against his writings:) " Story, for all his glorious tale, in the time of his most " deserved execution by quartering, was so impatient, that " he did not only roar and cry like an hell-hound, but also " strake the executioner doing his office, and resisted as long " as strength did serve him, being kept down by three or " four men, until he was dead. He used," saith the same writer, (that lived at that very time,) " no voice of prayer in

Retent. p. 59.

" all the time of his crying, as I heard of the very execu-   CHAP.
" tioner himself, besides them that stood by, but only roared ___ IX.
" and cried, as one overcome with the sharpness of the pain; Anno 1571.
" as no martyr, as the papists did mightily boast of him.
" God, added he, for his cruelty shewed against the patient
" saints, [in queen Mary's days,] had not only given him a 85
" taste of such torments as he procured to others, but also
" made him an open spectacle of the impatient and uncom-
" fortable state of them that suffer, not in a good cause, nor
" with a good conscience." This Fulk said, to vindicate
himself against a popish writer, that had writ, that upon a
little groaning [of the said Story at his execution] Fulk had
gathered that he was no true martyr.

Now, what a sort of man this Story was, and how addicted Some pas-
to cruelty towards the professors of the gospel under queen sages of his
Mary, that short epitome of him, drawn up by Mr. Fox's Foxii MSS.
own hand, and perhaps upon this occasion, will shew; which Annals, ch.
I have inserted in my Annals, under the year 1569.   53.

I cannot omit here the reciting of some old rhymes concerning this Story and his fellow bigots; which I meet with
written by one Lawrence Ramsey, a poet, near about this
time, in a book, entitled, *The Practice of the Devil;* wherein the Devil is brought in, speaking thus to them :—

> Stand to it, Stapleton, Dorman, and Harding,   A rhyme of
> And Rastal, that Rakehell, to maintain my order.   Dr. Story.
> Boner and Gardiner are worth the regarding,   Pract. of the
> For keeping articles so long in this border.   Dev.
> O Story, Story, thou art worthy of recorder ;
> Thou stoodst to it stoutly against God and the king ;
> And at Tyburn desperately gav'st me an off'ring.

I have met with this man's last will, made by him divers
years before his death, viz. 1552, while he was at Lovain;
fled thither in the time of king Edward VI. out of ill will
to the religion then professed in the nation: wherein are
some passages that may be remarked.   " He gave laud and Dr. Story's
" praise to God, for leading him out of his native country, MSS. Guil.
" that was swarved out of the sure ship of our salvation, Petyt, ar-
                                                             mig.

" our mother, the catholic church; and that he had belief
" and full trust in all and every article, clause, or sentence,
" that his said mother, holy church, from the time of the
" apostles, hath or shall decree, set forth, and deliver to be
" kept and observed by her children.   That for the break-
" ing any command, set forth by the authority of the same
" church, and for the non-observing of any of her decrees,
" and especially for his offence in forsaking the unity of it,
" by the acknowledging of any other supreme head than
" Christ's deputy here in earth, St. Peter, and his succes-
" sors, bishops of the see of Rome, he did most humbly and
" penitently cry God mercy, and desired all Christian people
" remaining in the unity of the said mother catholic church
" to pray for him.   Then he gave to his daughter Elen, six
" hundred and threescore florins.   But if by God's good
" motion she entered into religion, then he gave and be-
" queathed to the house and company where she should be
" professed, 120 florins; desiring them of their good cha-
" rity to pray for the souls of his father and mother, and for
" his soul, and all Christian souls.   His body to be buried
" in the Grey Friars in Lovain.   And to the same covent,
" for the exequies done and solemnized for the wealth of
86 " his soul, twenty florins; and forty florins more, that of
" their charity, in their daily celebration of mass, they
" would pray for the soul of Nicolas and Joan, his parents,
" and for his soul, and all Christian souls : and to appoint
" one devout person of their company, by the space of three
" years next after his burial, daily to make a special me-
" mory to God for his soul, and for all Christian souls."   I

refer the reader to the Appendix, for his other superstitious
bequests; and to observe what sort of wills and testaments
were framed by popish zealots, acted by the craft of monks
and friars, to draw treasure to themselves.   And lastly, he
charged his wife Joan not to set foot on the land of England, or carry his daughter thither, (according to a promise
she had made to God and him,) until it were restored to the
unity of the church.

Darbishire, a Jesuit, may be mentioned next to this zea-

lous, hot civilian; who was such another persecutor in this CHAP.
church under queen Mary; having been canon of St. Paul's, IX.
London, archdeacon of Essex, and chancellor to bishop Boner, Anno 1571.
who was his uncle by his sister. Walsingham, understand- hopes. Walsingh. Let.
ing this man was in Paris, found a means to feel the man Mar. 2.
and his principles. He caused one, under colour of a catholic, to repair unto him there; knowing that there was a
concurrence of intelligence between him and those English
papists of Lovain, and also with those of the Scottish queen's
faction. The party sent did seem very much to bewail the
ill success of the late practices in Scotland; and now he
feared that their case would grow desperate: especially, for
that Mather's enterprise was also discovered. To this the
Jesuit answered, " That the ill handling of matters was the
" cause that they took no better effect. But bade him not-
" withstanding to be of good comfort; and assure himself
" that there were more Mathers in England than one: which
" would not scruple, when time should conveniently serve,
" to adventure their lives in seeking to acquit us of that
" lewd woman, (meaning her highness.) For, said he, if
" she were gone, then would the hedge lie open; whereby
" the good queen, that is now the prisoner, in whom rested,
" he said, the present right of this crown, should easily en-
" joy the same. For besides that all the catholics in the
" realm of England were at her devotion, there were, said
" he, (and thanked God,) divers heretics that were well af-
" fected towards her. Which was no small miracle, that
" God had so blinded their eyes, as that they should be so
" inclined to her, that in the end would yield unto them
" their just deserts, unless they returned to the catholic
" faith." And so went on in further discourse, assuring the
other, that that queen would have no harm. For that she
lacked for no friends in the English court: and what assistance she was like to have to deliver her, though they ventured their lives for her, as others had done before; and
that there were divers ways to bring it to pass. And that
chiefly considering how this matter would tend to the good
of the catholic cause, and utter ruin and extirpation of he-

BOOK   resy. And that this should be brought to pass ere a year
  I.   were at an end. And besides his villainous and undutiful
Anno 1571. language of her majesty, he used very lewd bitter speeches
against the earl of Léicester and the lord Burghley. This,
as that ambassador concluded, was the sum of their talk.

87 By the way, one might hence make an observation upon
what a prejudiced person the chief evidence of the *Nagg's
Head ordination* doth depend. For the popish writers do
allege this Darbishire's evidence with the greatest confidence.

I add only one thing more of Darbishire. That in his
conference with Hawks, (afterwards burnt for the profession of the gospel,) he called the Bible, in contempt, *his
little pretty God's book.*

CHAP. X.

*The present concerns of the nation for the queen's safety.
Her marriage thought necessary. She falleth sick. Her
verses upon the Scottish queen and her favourites. She
requires liberty of religion for her merchants in France.
Orders and exercises of religion in Northampton; with
their confession of faith. The ecclesiastical commissioners sit at Lambeth. Christopher Goodman cited before
them: his protestation of allegiance.*

IF we now turn our eyes to the queen, about the month of
March her people had two extraordinary concernments for
her; whence they apprehended the kingdom to be in great
danger.

The queen's   The one was for her marrying; which the wisest of her
marriage
judged the   statesmen saw to be the only way for safety, as things then
only way of stood. I allege the judgment of some of them. Walsing-
safety.
ham, in December last, was in pursuit of some ways to establish her majesty's state; which was threatened, as he observed, with two lacks, viz. the want of friendship abroad,
and our doubtful state at home. Whom the earl of Lei-

cester seconded in their correspondence, by acknowledging, CHAP.
that it fell out too manifest daily; and that without some ___ X.
remedy it would prove a danger irrecoverable. But the Anno 1571.
means, as he added, were easily seen and perceived; [mean-
ing the marriage with monsieur, and peace with France;]
and which he supposed not yet without hope to be obtained.
But now two or three months were past, and little or no
hope appeared thereof.

For though sir Thomas Smith was lately despatched to Sir Thomas
France, to renew the treaty about it, yet the queen herself Smith's ap-
seemed to have little or no inclination that way, as was well of the
perceived. Whereat Smith, in a letter from Blois, thus queen's
writ: " That all the world saw that they [her people] wished ness.
" her majesty's surety and long condition. That her mar-
" riage, and issue of her highness' body, should be the most
" assurance of her highness, and of the wealth of the realm,
" &c. What, doth her majesty mean to maintain still her
" danger, and not proceed for her surety? I assure your
" lordship I can see no reason. God preserve her majesty
" long to reign over us, by some unlooked for miracle. For
" I cannot see by natural reason that her highness goeth 88
" about to provide for it." And again, soon after, in another letter, thus he expresseth his thoughts: " There is
" nothing whereof we are more sorry, and do lament in our
" hearts, than to see such uncertain, so negligent, and irre-
" solute provision for the safety of the queen's majesty's
" person, and of her reign over us. God of his almighty
" and miraculous power preserve her long to reign over us."
These expressions shewed the dismal apprehensions the best
of men, and most concerned, had for the good of the queen,
the state, and the religion of the land. But the good hand
of God preserved all safe and well, though this marriage,
so much desired and depended upon, took not place. For
a good understanding with the French king was thought
then sufficient to balance the mischievous purposes of Spain:
but the French king's heart being disposed to a league with
the queen, that way the English security was provided for;

BOOK
I.
The queen
falls sick.
The fears
thereupon.

as shall be shewn in the following year, when the league was made.

The other terror upon the nation now was the queen's falling sick. In the month of December, her subjects took great satisfaction, that notwithstanding their danger in other respects, she enjoyed perfect good health. So Leicester, in his correspondence, writes to Walsingham : " That they had " no news, but of her majesty's good state of health ; which " was such as he had not known to have been these many " years ;" [as though she were none of the healthfulest constitutions.] And this he the rather informed the ambassador of, because that in October before, she was taken very ill. Of which malady, thus did the lord Burghley write to the said ambassador : " That a sudden alarm was given him " by her majesty's being suddenly sick in her stomach ; but " that she was relieved by a vomit. You must think, said " he, (speaking not only his own sense, but of all that loved " the present state of the nation,) such a matter would drive " me to the end of my wits. But God [as he comforted " himself] is the stay of all that put their trust in him." But now, in March, the queen fell sick again ; yet in a few days recovered, to the great joy of all. Of this sickness of the queen, (sweetening it also with the news of her restoration to perfect health,) the same lord writ to the two ambassadors then in France. They both read the letter in a marvellous agony, (as Smith expressed their concern in his answer.) But having the medicine ready, that her majesty was within an hour recovered, it did in part heal them again. And when the said lord had wrote, that the care had not ceased in him, Smith replied, " That he might be sure it " did as little cease in them ; calling to their remembrance, " and laying before their eyes, the trouble, the uncertainty, " the disorder, the peril, and danger, which had been like " to follow, if at that time God had taken from them the " stay of the commonwealth, and hope of their repose ; that " lanthorn of their light, next to God ; whom to follow, nor " certainly where to light another candle [they knew not.]

But, added he, as to their present negotiation, " if her ma- CHAP.
" jesty still continued in extremity to promise, and in reco-   X.
" very to forget, what shall we say, but as the Italians do, Anno 1571.
" *Passato il pericolo, gabbato il faute ?*"

    Queen Elizabeth would sometimes, in the midst of her 89
cares, divert herself by study and reading; and sometimes Queen Eli-
versifying, as she did in composing a copy of verses upon zabeth's
verses upon
the queen of Scots, and those of her friends here in England the Scottish
near this time: which Dr. Wylson hath preserved to us in queen.
Wylson's
his English Logic. For she, to declare that she was nothing Logic.
ignorant of those secret practices among her people, and
many of her nobility inclining too far to the Scottish queen's
party, though she had long with great wisdom and patience
dissembled it, (as the said Dr. Wylson prefaceth her verses,)
wrote this ditty most sweet and sententious; not hiding
from all such aspiring minds the danger of their ambition
and disloyalty. Which afterwards fell out most truly, by
the exemplary chastisement of sundry persons, who in favour of the said Scottish queen, declining from her majesty,
sought to interrupt the quiet of the realm, by many evil and
undutiful practices. Her verses were as follow:

That doubt of future foes exiles my present joy;
And wit me warns to shun such snares as threaten mine annoy.
For falsehood now doth flow, and subjects' faith doth ebb:
Which would not be, if reason rul'd, or wisdom weav'd the web.
But clouds of toys untry'd do cloak aspiring minds,
Which turn to rain of late repent, by course of changed winds.
The top of hope suppos'd the root of ruth will be,
And fruitless all their graffed guiles, as shortly ye shall see.
Those dazzled eyes with pride, which great ambition [a] blinds,   [a] That of
Shall be unseal'd by worthy wights, whom foresight falsehood finds. the duke of
Norfolk.
The daughter of debate, that eke discord doth sow,
Shall reap no gain, where former rule hath taught still peace to grow.
No foreign banished wight [b] shall anchor in this port: [b] The Scot-
tish queen.
Our realm it brooks no strangers' [c] force: let them elsewhere resort. [c] France
and Spain.
Our rusty sword with rest shall first the edge employ,
To poll their tops that seek such change, and gape for joy.

BOOK
I.

Anno 1571.

Her care of
religion for
her mer-
chants a-
broad.

Another thing deservedly to be related of the queen was her care she took to preserve her subjects in that true religion which was established by law in her kingdom. And that her subjects not only at home but abroad might have the free exercise of it; and not incur danger in popish countries for it. In her treaty with France now, she made that one of the articles, namely, a liberty of religion for English merchants in that king's dominions. Sir Thomas Smith, with Walsingham and Killegrew, put the queen-mother in mind thereof, for the said merchants in the Staple or Haunce; that they might have the exercise of religion after the manner of the English church, and which the queen their mis-

Particularly
in France.

tress also professed. The said queen-mother had promised them that they might have it in their house with the doors shut, and in the English tongue; but the king's deputies appointed to treat with the queen's ambassadors would not admit it. And both the king and his mother (neither of them meaning sincerely) would not have it put as an article in the treaty, but that it should be allowed some other way. As namely, by a letter missive from the king to queen Eli-

90 zabeth, wherein he should promise it. Which when Smith and the others objected against; and since they could not too much insist upon it, to please the king, and to go as far as they could, they were content, if he would, by another article, or treaty declarative, made apart between his majesty and the queen of England, under the great seals of England and France, declare that in general words he did mean also, in the matter of religion, to give her merchants their liberty. But the queen-mother, upon this, asked the ambassadors, whether they thought that the king her son would deceive them? [But whether they then thought so or no, it appeared afterwards that he went upon nothing but deceit and dissimulation.] And she would have persuaded the ambassadors, the queen their mistress would be contented with such a private letter from the king. But Smith told her he could not believe it of her majesty for his part: and that they, her ministers, must do wisely, surely,

and substantially in such affairs for her majesty, as she did
put in their credit. But when the queen-mother still shifted
this off, Smith said at last, " That except there were suffi-
" cient assurance for the matter of religion, they could not
" nor durst subscribe the treaty ; until they were better cer-
" tified that the queen would be so content with such a let-
" ter. For his conscience was against it, to leave so great a
" point upon so little a hold."

Prophesyings, or *exercises*, were much used now throughout most of the dioceses. Wherein the incumbents in livings, and men in orders, were employed in explaining certain places of holy scripture, in certain parish churches appointed by the bishop of the diocese for that purpose. Which
were very acceptable to those of the people that favoured
the protestant religion: and had also their good use, both
for the improving of the clergy in their studies of the word
of God, and for the instruction of the laity in the right knowledge of religion.

These exercises were used in the church of Northampton,
by the consent of the bishop of Peterburgh, Scambler, the
mayor of the town and his brethren, and other the queen's
majesty's justices of the peace within the county and town :
who appointed these orders for religious worship, to be set
up and established therein.

I. The singing and playing of organs, beforetime accustomed in the quire, is put down, and the common prayer
there accustomed to be said, brought down into the body of
the church among the people, before whom the same is used
according to the queen's book, with singing psalms before
and after the sermon.

II. There is in the chief church every Tuesday and
Thursday, from nine of the clock until ten in the morning,
read a lecture of the scripture, beginning with the confession in the Book of Common Prayer, and ending with prayer
and confession of the faith.

III. There is in the same church, every Sunday and
holyday, after morning prayer, a sermon, the people singing
the psalm before and after.

IV. The service be ended in every parish church by nine of the clock in the morning, every Sunday and holyday ; to the end the people may resort to the sermon in the same church. And that every minister give warning to the parishioners in the time of common prayer, to repair to the sermon there; except they have a sermon in their own parish church.

V. That after prayers done, in the time of sermon or catechising, none sit in the streets, or walk up and down abroad, or otherwise occupy themselves vainly, upon such penalties as shall be appointed.

VI. The youth, at the end of evening prayer, every Sunday and holyday, (before all the elder people,) are examined in a portion of Calvin's catechism, which by the reader is expounded unto them ; and holdeth an hour.

VII. There is a general communion once every quarter, in every parish church, with a sermon; which is by the minister at common prayer warned four several Sundays before every communion, with exhortation to the people to prepare for that day.

VIII. One fortnight before each communion, the minister with the churchwardens maketh a circuit from house to house, to take the names of the communicants, and to examine the state of their lives. Among whom if any discord be found, the parties are brought before the mayor and his brethren, being assisted by the preacher and other gentlemen. Before whom there is reconcilement made, or else correction, or putting the party from the communion, which will not live in charity.

IX. Immediately after the communion, the minister, &c. returneth to every house, to understand who have not received the communion, according to the common order taken; and certifieth it to the mayor, &c. who, with the minister, examineth the matter, and useth means of persuasion to induce them to their duties.

X. Every communion day each parish hath two communions; the one for servants and officers, to begin at five of the clock in the morning, with a sermon of an hour, and to end at eight: the other for masters and dames, &c. to begin at nine the same day, with like sermon, and to end at twelve.

XI. The manner of this communion is, besides the sermon, according to the order of the queen's book; saving, the people being in their confession upon their knees, for the despatch of many, do orderly arise from their pews, and so pass to the communion table, where they receive the sacrament: and from thence in like order to their place; having all this time a minister in the pulpit, reading unto them comfortable scriptures of the passion, or other like, pertaining to the matter in hand.

XII. There is on every other Saturday, and now every Saturday, from nine to eleven of the clock in the morning, an exercise of the ministers both of town and country, about the interpretation of scriptures. The ministers speaking one after another, do handle some text; and the same openly among the people. That done, the ministers do withdraw themselves into a privy place, there to confer among themselves, as well touching doctrine as good life, manners, and other orders meet for them. There is also a weekly assembly every Thursday, after the lecture, by the mayor 92 and his brethren, assisted with the preacher, minister, and other gentlemen, appointed to them by the bishop, for the correction of discord made in the town: as for notorious blasphemy, whoredom, drunkenness, railing against religion, or preachers thereof; scolds, ribalds, or such like. Which faults are each Thursday presented unto them in writing by certain sworn men, appointed for that service in each parish. So by the bishop's authority and the mayor's joined together, being assisted with certain other gentlemen in the commission of the peace, evil life is corrected, God's glory set forth, and the people brought in good obedience.

XIV. The communion table standeth in the body of the church, according to the book, at the over end of the middle aisle, having three ministers: one in the middle to deliver the bread; the other two at each end, for the cup. The ministers often do call on the people to remember the poor, which is there plentifully done.   And thus the communion being ended, the people do sing a psalm.

XV. The excessive ringing of bells at forbidden times by injunction, (whereby the people grow in discord, to the slaughter of some, and the unquieting of others, given to hear sermons,) is inhibited ; allowing notwithstanding such orderly ringing, as may serve to the calling of the people to church, and giving warning of the passing and burying of every person.

XVI. The carrying of the bell before corpses in the streets, and bidding prayers for the dead, (which was there used until within these two years,) is restrained.

XVII. There is hereafter to take place, order that all ministers of the shire, once every quarter of the year, upon one month's warning given, repair to the said town ; and there, after a sermon in the church heard, to withdraw themselves into a place appointed within the said church ; and there privately to confer among themselves of their manners and lives. Among whom if any be found in fault, for the first time, exhortation is made to him among all the brethren to amend. And so likewise the second and third time, by complaint from all the brethren, he is committed unto the bishop for his correction.

The order of the exercise of the ministers, with a confession of the faith.

Orders for the exer-cises.   First, Every one at his first allowance to be of this exercise, shall, by subscription of his own hand, declare his consent in Christ's true religion with his brethren, and submit himself to the discipline and orders of the same.

Secondly, The names of every man that shall speak in this exercise shall be written in a table. For it shall be unlawful for any man to speak in this exercise, until he be admitted by the same, and his name, by his own consent, registered in the said table. Neither shall it be lawful for any man to occupy the room of the second speaker, except he have spoken in the first place, unless he be desired by the moderators.

Thirdly, The first speaker beginning and ending with prayer, ought to explain the text that he readeth. Then he may confute any false or untrue expositions, if he know that the place have been abused by any sinister interpretation. Then he may give the comfort to the audience as the place ministereth just occasion. But he shall not digress, dilate, nor amplify that place of scripture whereof he treateth to any common place, further than the meaning of the said scripture.

Fourthly, Whatsoever is left of the first speaker, either in explaining the text, either in confuting, &c. he or they that speak afterwards have liberty to touch, so as they observe the order prescribed to the first speaker. And that without repeating the selfsame words which have been spoken before, or impugning the same, except any have spoken contrary to the scriptures.

Fifthly, The exercise shall begin immediately after nine of the clock, and not exceed the space of two hours. The first speaker shall fully finish whatsoever he hath to say within the space of three quarters of an hour: the second and third shall not exceed (each one of them) one quarter of an hour. One of the moderators shall always make the conclusion.

Sixthly, After the exercise is ended, the president for the time being shall call the learned brethren unto him, and shall ask for their judgment concerning the exposition of the text of scripture then expounded: and if any matter be then untouched, it shall be there declared. Also, if any of the speakers in this exercise be infamed, or convinced of any grievous crime, he shall be there and then reprehended.

Seventhly, After this consultation it shall be lawful for any of the brethren of this exercise to propound their doubts or questions, justly collected out of the place of the scripture that day expounded, and signify the same unto the president for the time being, and the other brethren, and deliver the same in writing unto the first speaker. And order shall be taken by common consent for the satisfying of the said questions against the next exercise. No speaker shall move

BOOK I.

Anno 1571.

publicly any question extempore; but which he shall satisfy himself presently.   And this consultation shall be ended with some short exhortation, to move each one to go forward in his office, to apply his study, and to increase in godliness of manners and newness of life.

Eighthly, When this exercise is finished, the next speaker shall be appointed and named publicly; and the text which he shall expound shall be read.

Ninthly, When the last man, whose name is written in the tables, hath kept his turn in this exercise, then the first man written shall be required to keep the next exercise.   If that man be absent, so as he cannot keep that day and time, the next written in the table shall be required to satisfy the place of the other, when his turn is, so as the exercise decay not for any one man's absence.

Tenthly, If any man take upon him to break these orders and rules, or seem to be contentious, let the president of the exercise presently command him, in the name of the eternal God, to silence.   And after the exercise, let that 94 unadvised person be judged before the brethren there gathered for the said exercise; that he, and others by his example, may learn modesty thereafter.

Then followed a *confession*, which these exercisers were to subscribe; which was to stand to the scriptures alone, and not to any human authority, for doctrine, in opposition to papistry; and was as followeth:

The confession in the exercises.

A confession to be subscribed.

We whose names are hereunder written, as well to declare unto the world, according to the commandment of the Lord, the confession of that faith which in our consciences we hold, as also to cut off all occasion of quarrelling and slanderous reports of our dissenting among ourselves in matters of faith and religion, to the wounding and hurt of the simple; do shew our judgments and consent in sum, as followeth: being ready further and more particularly to explain the same, to the satisfying of our brethren, when and as occasion shall be thereunto offered:

First, We believe and hold, that the word of God, written in the canonical scriptures of the Old and New Testament, (which books contain in them sound, perfect, and sufficient doctrine, as well for the trade of all men's lives, as also for their faith,) are and ought to be open, to be read and known of all sorts of men, both learned and unlearned. And we esteem this written word as the infallible truth of God, full of majesty; and the authority thereof far to exceed all authority, not of the pope of Rome only, (who is very Antichrist, and therefore is to be detested of all Christians,) but of the church also, of councils, fathers, or others whosoever, either men or angels.

Then, we condemn as a tyrannous yoke (wherewith poor souls have been oppressed) whatsoever men have set up of their own inventions, to make articles of our faith, or to bind men's conscience by their laws and institutes. In sum, all those manners and fashions to serve God, which men have brought in without the authority of the word, for the warrant thereof; commended either by custom, by the title of unwritten verities, traditions, or other names whatsoever. Of which sort are, the doctrines of the supremacy of the see of Rome, purgatory, the mass, transubstantiation, the corporeal presence of Christ's body in the sacrament, adoration thereof; man's merits; free will; justification by works; praying in an unknown tongue, to saints departed, for the dead, upon beads; extolling of images, pardons, pilgrimages, auricular confession; taking from the lay-people the cup in the administration of the sacrament; prohibition of marriage; distinction of meats, apparel, and days; briefly, all the ceremonies and whole order of papistry: which they call the *hierarchy;* indeed, a devilish confusion, established as it were in despite of God, and to the mockery and reproach of all Christian religion. These, I say, with such like, we abjure, renounce, and utterly condemn.

And we content ourselves with the simplicity of this pure word of God, and doctrine thereof. A summary abridgment of the which, we acknowledge to be contained in the confession of faith, used of all Christians, which is com-95 monly called, *The creed of the apostles:* holding fast, as the apostle warneth, that faithful word, which serveth to doctrine and instruction: and that both to edify our own consciences withal unto salvation in Christ Jesus, as the alone foundation, whereon Christ's true church is built, he himself being the chief corner-stone; as the same apostle witnesseth in another place: and also, to exhort others with the same sound and wholesome doctrine; and to convince the gainsayers: finally, to try and examine, and also to judge thereby, as by a certain rule and perfect touchstone, all other doctrines whatsoever.

And therefore to this word of God we humbly submit ourselves and all our doings; willing and ready to be judged, reformed, or further instructed thereby, in all points of religion.

This method of devotion, agreed upon and used for the public practice of religion in this town, and for the better improving both clergy and laity in Christian knowledge and godliness, had such notice taken of it, that it seemed not to escape without the censure of men of looser principles. And this being a year wherein the archbishop and several other bishops sat in an ecclesiastical commission; and they by a special letter from the queen commanded to look narrowly into any novelties introduced into the church, and to set an effectual stop thereunto; this scheme might have been sent up from Northampton to them: it being said in the title to it, *To have been taken and found* [as by some inquisition] *the 5th of June,* 1571, *anno* xiii°. *reg. regin. Elizab.* But I do not find this well-minded and religiously disposed combination of both bishop, magistrates, and people, received any check from that commission.

Before these commissioners sitting at Lambeth were several puritans, that were preachers, cited; as hath been elsewhere shewn. And among these was Chr. Goodman, the preacher, a man famous for his book written against the government of women, in hatred to queen Mary, the great persecutor of her protestant subjects, and for the lawfulness of resisting princes in some cases. This gave great disgust to the queen, and to the governors of this church; CHAP. insomuch that he was brought to a revocation of that book, X. as hath been also shewn. Now he is required to make a Anno 1571. protestation of his obedience to the queen's majesty. Which Annals of Reforma·· at length he did, with the subscription of his own hand to tion, chap. the same. The original whereof is still extant; and bears ix. p. 126. this title, *A copy of the protestation willingly made by* Goodman's protestation *Christopher Goodman, preacher of God's word, the 23d day* of his obe- dience to *of April,* 1571, *at Lambhith, before the reverend fathers in* the queen. *God, my lords of Canterbury, Ely, Salisbury, Worcester,* Paper-office. *Lincoln, and Bangor; concerning his dutiful obedience to the queen's majesty's person, and her lawful government, being thereof demanded by the said lords; as also requested to put the same in writing, as followeth:*

" I Christopher Goodman, preacher of God's word in
" this realm of England, have protested, the day and year
" above written, before the reverend fathers aforesaid, and
" in this present writing do unfeignedly protest and confess
" before all men, that I have esteemed and taken Eliza-
" beth, by the grace of God queen of England, France,
" and Ireland, defender of the faith, &c. evermore sithence 96
" her coronation, as now, and shall during life and her
" grace's government, for my only liege lady and most
" lawful queen and sovereign. Whom I truly reverence in
" my heart, love, fear, and obey, as becometh an obedient
" subject, in all things lawful; and as I have at sundry
" times in open pulpit, willingly and of mine accord, (never
" constrained by any, otherwise than occasion of time and
" matter have offered,) declared in great audience. Who can
" and will bear me sufficient record. Exhorting and per-
" suading all men, so far forth as in me did lie, to the
" like obedience to her majesty. For whose preservation
" and prosperous government I have earnestly and daily
" prayed to God, and will, being assisted by his holy Spirit,
" during my life. In witness whereof, I the said Christo-
" pher have subscribed this protestation with mine own
" hand, the 26th day of April, 1571.

" Per me Christopherum Goodmanum."

BOOK I.

Anno 1571.

His perverseness noted.

Letter of archbishop Whitgift.

I find him in Cheshire, anno 1584, a refuser of subscription to the Articles, and a dissuader of others thereto. Of whom archbishop Whitgift complained unto the lord treasurer, that it was Mr. Goodman, a man that for his perverseness was sufficiently known, and some other evil disposed persons, that instilled these things into men's heads; that is, objections against subscribing to all the articles of religion, and to the Book of Common Prayer.

CHAP. XI.

Zanchy writes to the queen concerning the habits. And to bishop Jewel. His advice. Blackal, a pretended minister, does penance. Popish priests officiate in the church. Bishop Jewel's death. His answer to Harding. His Apology. Friendship between him and bishop Parkhurst. William Kethe. Loans. Walsingham's diligence: earl of Rutland. Sir Tho. Smith, ambassador. Victory over the Turks.

Zanchy writes to the queen against imposing the habits.

ZANCHY, the learned Italian, public professor of divinity in the university of Heidelbergh, this year interposed with the queen, in the behalf of the puritan ministers; that she would not enjoin wearing of the surplice. In his letter to her he said, "There were many bishops then alive in the " kingdom, greatly renowned for all kind of learning, that " chose rather to leave their offices and places in the church, " than against their own consciences to admit of such gar- " ments, the relics of popish idolatry and superstition, or at " least signs and tokens of it; and so to defile themselves, " and give offence to the weak by their example. And that " by these means the seed of dissension was cast among the " bishops. He added, that this letter he wrote by command 97 " of the most noble prince, one of her majesty's most spe- " cial friends, the prince elector palatine." The letter be-

Lib. epist. i. p. 242. tom. viii.

ing very long, is extant in print among Zanchy's epistles, and was translated into English in a late book, called, *A fresh suite against humane ceremonies.* The letter was sent

to bishop Grindal, by his hand to be presented to the CHAP.
queen. But upon serious deliberation, and consultation with XI.
other learned and wise men, he declined to deliver it; and Anno 1571.
gave his reasons to Zanchy in a letter, mentioned elsewhere.
But Zanchy was misinformed, as appeared by his letter to Life of
the queen, in the true state of the controversy; and parti- Archbishop Grindal.
cularly concerning the bishops; who were not upon the Book i.
point of leaving their bishoprics, rather than to wear their ch. 11.
habits, but did all unanimously comply with the ecclesiastical order, as bishop Grindal assured him.

But to relate the occasion of Zanchy's letter. Mount, (a By Mount's instigation.
German by birth, but much employed formerly in messages
out of England to the German princes and states,) coming
into Germany in June this year, 1571, shewed unto Zanchy and others how the contest about the apparel was revived in England; and that the queen required the bishops
and ministers duly to wear the habits enjoined, in the administration of the word and sacraments. And withal, he
added, that there were not a few, even of the bishops themselves, that were minded rather to resign their office, and
depart from their places, than yield to wear the garments.
He begged Zanchy, therefore, that he would address a letter to the queen, and admonish her of her duty. And that
in case she would not be brought to relent, and revoke her
orders, that then he and the brethren at Heidelberg should
write to some of the chiefest and prudentest bishops, howsoever not to forsake their function. The foresaid reverend
man, after denial and excuse of himself, in regard of his
own inability for such a work, being overpersuaded by
friends, and at last by the counsel of the prince elector himself, composed a letter to the queen, as was touched before.
Wherein he beseeched her, that she would not hearken to
such counsels as certainly repugned the office of a good
prince; which he made to consist in three things. I. To
take care that true religion and the worship of God be restored; and being restored, to be preserved pure. II. That
all her people live honestly and godly. III. That public
peace and friendship be kept. And then he fell upon the

BOOK I.

Anno 1571.

The substance of his letter to Jewel.

habits at large, marshalling up all his arguments against them. And another letter he also wrote to bishop Jewel; and yet another to bishop Grindal.

The bearers of these letters were Ralph Gualter, junior, and Ralph Zuinglius, grandchild to Zuinglius the great reformer of Helvetia. The substance of that to bishop Jewel was;

" That having heard from Mount, lately returned from Eng-
" land, that many godly bishops were determined to lay down
" their offices, and leave their places, rather than to wear the
" habits; he was earnestly called upon by the brethren there,
" to persuade the said bishops not so to do. And that he
" wrote to him, being a person of so great learning and
" sway in the church, to use his interest with them to con-
" tinue in their places; seeing that Satan sought nothing
" more than to dissipate the church, by scattering away the

98 " true bishops. For there seemed to be no reason, why a
" pastor should leave his flock, so long as he might freely
" teach and administer the sacraments according to the
" word of God, although he be compelled to do something
" which is not wholly approved of, so it be of the nature of
" things which of themselves and in their own nature are
" not evil, but indifferent, being commanded of the queen:
" and when one of these two must happen, either to depart
" his place, or obey such a command, he should rather
" obey; but with a lawful protestation; and the people to
" be by him taught, why, and upon what account, he

Nunquam enim prop- ter res sua natura adi- aphoras de- serenda est vocatio le- gitima et necessaria. Zanch. ep. tom. viii. p. 391.

" obeyed that command. And that this opinion was so plain
" and clear, both by scriptures, the fathers, and ecclesiastical
" historians, that it would be needless to bring any proof to
" them which were any thing exercised therein. For a law-
" ful and necessary vocation is never to be forsaken by rea-
" son of things in their own nature indifferent."

Blackal, a scandalous churchman, does pe- nance.

As for the papists, many of the popish priests still kept their parishes, and their old inclination to superstition too. But among the scandalous churchmen in these days, the greatest surely was one Blackal, born at Exeter, who did penance at St. Paul's Cross, Aug. 6, and then and there, before all the congregation, cried and breathed out against

Northbroke many foul and slanderous reports, to the grief of the godly, and joy of the wicked. For this Northbroke had detected his horrible vices, and manifested them to cer- tain of his friends, to the end he might be the better reclaimed. Upon this slander, the queen's commissioners sent for Northbroke to come before them. But when he appeared, Blackal stole away from his keeper, to the prisoners then in the Marshalsea; knowing that he had falsely accused him. So that he could not have him face to face before the commissioners. The crimes which brought him to this penance were, that he had four wives alive: and also that he had intruded himself into the ministry for the space of twelve years, and yet was never lawfully called, nor made minister by any bishop. Four days after his penance at the Cross, he was set in the pillory in Cheapside, with papers on his head, for taking the archbishop of Canterbury's seal from one writing, and setting it to a counterfeit commission. He was a chopper and changer of benefices, little passing by what ways or means, so he might but get money from any man. He would run from country to country, and from town to town, leading about with him naughty women. As in Gloucestershire he led a naughty strumpet about the country, named Green Apron. He altered his name wheresoever he went; going by these several surnames, Blackal, Barthal, Dorrel, Barkly, Baker.

And what sort of popishly affected priests still officiated in the church, the forementioned Northbroke will tell us, in his epistle to a book entitled, *A brief and pithy sum of the* *Christian faith.* Therein he spake. " of certain men, then " ministers of the church, who were papists, and so gave out " themselves to be in their discourses. Who subscribed and " observed the order of service, wore a side gown, a square " cap, a cope and surplice. They would run into corners, " and say to the people, Believe not this new doctrine; it is " naught; it will not long endure: although I use order " among them outwardly, my heart and profession is from " them, agreeing with the mother church of Rome. No, no, " we do not preach, nor yet teach openly. We read their

L

99

"new devised homilies for a colour, to satisfy the time for a
"season.

"Several nowadays of the popish priests, he said, were
"thieves, perjurers, murderers, buggerers, [I blush to re-
"peat the rest,] and some of them were arraigned at the
"bar for it in Exeter, and elsewhere."

This Northbroke was minister of Redcliff in Bristol, and
was one of the first persons that Gilbert, bishop of Bath and
Wells, ordained.

Bishop
Jewel dies.
His last
words and
prayer.
Preface to a
View of a
seditious
Bull.

This year put a period to the life of the singularly learned
and most eminent bishop, John Jewel. His discourse and
prayer on his deathbed, a little before his death, was very
devout and edifying; and therefore worthy recording to
posterity: as it was taken from his mouth by John Garbrand, who was always about him, and then present, (as
well as divers others,) and set down by him. The day and
night before his [the bishop's] departure out of this world,
he expounded the Lord's Prayer, and gave short notes
upon the seventy-first Psalm [the suitable Psalm appointed
to be read in the Office of Visitation of the Sick] to such as
were by him. He thought good to say somewhat at that

time of the books written by him, and set forth in print;
and also of his preaching. In both which services done by
him to the glory of God, he made protestation of his good
conscience; which even then, he declared, witnessed, and
should witness with him before God, that he dealt simply
and plainly, having God only before his eyes, and seeking
the defence of the gospel of Christ, and that the truth
thereof might be opened and maintained. And further, he
gave thanks to God, that made him his servant in so great
a work. And then visited him by this messenger of death,
whilst he was doing the message of God in visiting his diocese. That then he called him to rest from his labours,
when his weak body was spent and worn out in setting
forth the glory of God. For which he many times prayed,
it would please God to let him be offered in sacrifice.

He was at that time very fervent in prayer, which he
poured out before the Lord abundantly, and in great faith;

crying often, " *Lord, let thy servant now depart in peace:* CHAP.
" *Lord, let thy servant now come to thee.*   I have not so   XI.
" lived, that I am ashamed to live: neither am I afraid to Anno 1571.
" die: for we have a gracious Lord.   There is laid up for
" me a crown of righteousness.   Christ is my righteousness:
" thy will be done, O Lord; for mine is frail:" with many
other such godly speeches.   In the extremity of his disease
he shewed great patience; and when his voice failed, that
he lay speechless, he lifted up his hands and eyes, in witness of his consent to those prayers which were made.   Thus
being virtuously occupied, and wholly resting himself upon
the mercies of God through Jesus Christ our Saviour, he
rendered up his soul to God.

This John Garbrand, who gave the foregoing account of MSS. of
bishop Jewel's holy end, had a legacy in the said bishop's $\substack{\text{bishop}\\ \text{Jewel be-}}$
last will, of all his papers, writings, and notes of his travails queathed.
in God's vineyard, and other his devices of learning whatsoever.   And from this rich stock of manuscripts, he set
forth the bishop's answer to the pope's bull against queen 100
Elizabeth, called, *A view of a seditious bull:* with Garbrand's preface: wherein the former relation of his death is
mentioned.   Published anno 1582.   He was master of arts
of Oxford, and a prebendary of Sarum.   Dr. Tho. Wylson,
master of St. Katharine's, (whom we have occasion to mention sometimes,) had writ a learned book against usury:
which this bishop having perused, sent the writer a letter,
signifying his judgment and allowance thereof.   Which excellent letter Wylson now sent to Garbrand; that he might
treasure it up among the rest of those valuable papers in his
possession.

Concerning his book against Harding, three great princes His book
successively, viz. queen Elizabeth, king James, and king $\substack{\text{against}\\ \text{Harding.}}$
Charles, and four archbishops, were so satisfied with the
truth and learning contained in it, that they enjoined it to
be chained up and read in all parish churches throughout
England and Wales.   Which the author of the book, called
^{a} *The holy table, name, and thing*, had noted in honour of $\substack{\text{a Holy}\\ \text{Table,}}$
that prelate's works, upon occasion of the dissatisfaction that $\substack{\text{Name, and}\\ \text{Thing,}}$

his antagonist had expressed concerning something written
therein, concerning the ancient standing of the altar or com-

munion-table.

And this year of the said bishop's death, the second impression of his Apology of the Church of England came
forth, dedicated by him to the queen. And was again reprinted with the rest of this excellent bishop's works, anno
1611, dedicated to king James I. In the said dedication to
the queen, I cannot but insert here, *ob rei memoriam*, what
What was
done in the
reforma-
tion.
Ep. dedic.
to the
queen. is there told to have been done in the reformation. " Nei-
" ther have we, (said he,) in the public reformation of our
" church, doctrine, and service, changed or purged out any
" thing taught and approved by the fathers; but only
" such errors, superstitions, and abuses, as beside and con-
" trary to this rule or sense crept into the church, by add-
" ing of things that formerly were not, or detracting of
" them that were, or otherwise altering or perverting them
" from the right sense, meaning, and use, wherein they
" were instituted, taken, and used by the said godly fa-
" thers: as also through the foolish imitation of Jews or
" Gentiles, wanton curiosity of men's inventions, blindness
" of devotion, emulation for the continuance and increase of
" such vanities once begun: but chiefly through the envy
" and malice of that wicked one; who while the husband-
" man slept, sowed tares in the Lord's field, to the corrupt-
" ing and choking of that good corn sown by our Saviour
" Jesus Christ's holy apostles. Which lawful reformation
" of our church, and necessary repurgation of such enormi-
" ties, is so far from taking from us the name or nature of
" true catholics and Christians, or depriving us of the com-
" munion and fellowship of the apostolic church, or from
" overthrowing, endangering, or any whit impairing the
" right faith, religion, sacraments, priesthood, and govern-
" ment of the catholic church, [as the papists then charged
" the reformers with,] that it hath cleared and better settled
" them unto us; and made us a readier and surer way to the
" true knowledge, right use, and happy fruit of them."
This Apology he set forth in the name of all the bishops,

as a book containing their professed judgment and doctrine. CHAP.
So Parkhurst, bishop of Norwich, one of those bishops, XI.
wrote to Johannes Wolphius, one of his correspondents in Anno 1571.
Helvetia, *Is* [*Juellus*] *omnium nostrorum nomine edidit.* Sets out
And so well approved of was this work of his, not only the name
here at home, but by the reformed divines abroad, that the of the bi-
said Wolphius, a learned divine of Zuric, translated it into 101
the German language; which the said bishop took notice of,
and commended him for doing. And not his Apology
alone, but all the rest of his labours in vindication of the
reformed church, had been put into the learned language
by himself probably, had he lived. For the said bishop had
earnestly excited him so to do, for the public good, and for
the exposing of the errors and superstitions superinduced
upon the Christian religion. For so in one of his letters he
relateth; that though at first he refused upon his motion
to set upon that work, yet afterwards he made no doubt,
had he lived, he should (for the great interest he had with
him) have persuaded him to have done it. But however, he
resolved to put some one of his learned friends to undertake
it. And at length William Whitaker, D. D. performed it
well.

There was a dear affection between the said bishop Park- Jewel's let-
hurst and him, which began in the university; where Park- ter from
hurst was his tutor as well as his friend. Some marks of Parkhurst,
this intimacy appear in a letter (still extant) written by MSS. R.
Jewel from Oxford to him, now shifting for himself in ob- Joh. Ep.
scure places, and deprived of his rich benefice of Cleves, Eliensis.
soon after the access of queen Mary to the crown; in these
words: *Parkhurste mi, mi Parkhurste, quid ego te nunc
putem agere? Morine, an vivere; in fletione esse, an in
Fleta?* &c. " My Parkhurst, mine own Parkhurst, what
" may I think you now do? Are you dead or alive? Are
" you a weeping, or are you in the Fleet? [in which pri-
" son many of the professors of religion were now commit-
" ted.] Certainly such ever was the equity of your mind,
" that you take all these afflictions (whatsoever they are) in
" good part.......News with us there is none. We have

BOOK I.

Anno 1571.

" old things enough, and too much ;" [meaning the old superstitions brought in again among them at Oxford.] And
then he prayed Parkhurst to write to him, what was become of Harley ; [late made bishop of Hereford ;] and in
what condition his own affairs were, and what were his
hopes, what his fears.

And in another letter wrote a few days after to him, he
hath these expressions: *Quid ego nunc ad te, Parkhurste,
scribam, vel quid potius taceam ?* &c. " What shall I now,
" Parkhurst, write to you ? or rather, what shall I be silent
" in ? It is now a great while that I have desired to hear
" how you do, how you have done, and where you are.
" And although Cleves [your living] be taken from you,
" and all things be changed with you, I hope that mind of
" yours can neither be taken away from you nor changed."
But I refer the reader to the letters themselves, exemplified
in the Appendix.

Numb. XI.

Bishop
Parkhurst
sends the
news of his
death to
Zuric.
MSS. Jo-
han. nuper
epis. Elien.
102

The divines of the church of Zuric in Switzerland had
a very great veneration for bishop Jewel ; who had sometime sojourned with them there. And therefore of his
death, his friend, bishop Parkhurst, sent the news to Rodolphus Gualter, after this manner : " My Jewel, my trea-
" sure, yea, the treasure of all England, died September
" 23." And so to Lavater, another learned man there:
" Jewel, the learnedest of all the bishops in England, is
" dead." He also writ, that Lawrence Humphrey, president of Magdalen college, Oxon, (whom they also knew
well,) was commanded to write his life. And that he had accordingly wrote two letters to him, the said Parkhurst, beseeching him, (Jewel having been his scholar, and always
most dear to him, to furnish him with what he knew concerning him. And that accordingly he had prepared and
sent Dr. Humphrey several notices concerning him, *ut justa
persolvam* (as he wrote) *amicissimi Juelli.* For indeed,
as he added, he could relate more of bishop Jewel, than all
England beside.

A sermon
preached by
Wil. Kethe,
against pro-

I will make a short mention here of another divine, and
an exile, as Jewel was, but by nation a Scot ; namely, Wil-

liam Kethe. He was with Coverdale, Whittington, Gilby,
one of the chief exiles at Geneva, noted for his learning,
and one of those that were employed there in translating
the Bible into English; which Bible was thereupon com- faning the
monly called the Geneva Bible; and who put some of the sabbath.
Psalms into metre; viz. those noted with the two capital let- Lambith
ters *W. K.* This year, or the last, was printed a sermon libr. vol.
preached by him at the sessions holden at Blandford Forum, xxv. 8. 13.
in the county of Dorset: which he dedicated to Ambrose
earl of Warwick. In this sermon he inveighed against such
as profaned the sabbath. The earl he acknowledged his
special good master and lord, and, under God and the
queen, one of his chief protectors and defenders against
such as would offer him injury. He was with that lord at
Newhaven, (which the queen held against the French, anno·
1563,) to discharge the office of a minister and preacher
there: which he also spake of in his said epistle : and was
with him likewise the last year [viz. 1570] in the north
parts, one of the preachers unto the queen's army there
against the rebels; saying also, that he practised there a
kind of discipline, even upon those that by birth and parentage were far above him: meaning, as it seems, the Geneva discipline, that he had learned at Geneva. This letter
was dated from Childokford, the 29th of January, 1570.

I add one notice more of this man. There be at the
end of Goodman's book, entitled, *How superior powers
ought to be obeyed by their subjects,* some verses of his to
the reader, (for he was poetical,) on the subject of wicked
princes; viz.

> Whose fury long fost'red by suff'rance and awe,
> Have right rule subverted, and made will their law.
> Whose pride how to temper this truth will thee tell ;
> So as thou resist may'st, and yet not rebell, &c.

It is worth observing the substance of a proclamation, set Loans re-
forth by the queen, November 24, to keep up an assured paid by the
credit with her subjects, that had lent her money. For as queen.
she sent privy seals for loans to them sometimes in her

BOOK I.

Anno 1571.

103

need, so she was most exact in the just and easy repayment of them again. The purport therefore of this proclamation was, to declare, how she had caused knowledge to be given to the parties that lent her money the last summer, at what time the same should be certainly repaid to every of them, having respect to the time of their first payment made to the collectors. And now she notified by this proclamation, (meaning to observe the said determination,) that the payment should be made in this sort: to every person, that should in respect of the time of their payment made, receive any sums of money in the month of November, should have the same freely and fully paid before the end of the present month of November. And whosoever should have payment according to the aforesaid signification in the next month of December, should have the same also freely and fully paid immediately after the 20th of the same month. And so consequently every person every month afterward. So punctual was the queen to keep up her credit with her people, whereby she obtained such a degree in their love, and readiness to serve her with their estates.

In the same proclamation she took notice of some abuses heretofore in some of her ministers, who had charge to make payment of like sums lent to her majesty, contrary to her meaning: and that in some parts of her realm, some of her good subjects had been, by sinister dealings, induced to make payment of parcel of the money demanded by privy seals: which sums had been returned, and not paid over to her use. And some also had been paid, or lent by way of reward, to procure a forbearance to lend any to her majesty. These abuses, she declared, she meant to cause to be searched, tried, and punished. And for more surety, that none of her subjects, that had lent to her upon her privy seal any sum of money, should be delayed or misused in the payment, she gave commission to the lord keeper of her great seal, the earl of Leicester, the lord Burghley, and sir Walter Mildmay, knight, to direct the repayment thereof.

Abuses of some of her ministers in the loans.

So that whosoever should bring her majesty's letters of her privy seal, with the subscription, or bill of the collector,

testifying the receipt of any money, demanded or con- CHAP.
tained in the said privy seal, and shew the same to the lord XI.
keeper, &c. should have order immediately to receive the Anno 1571.
whole sum due to him at Westminster, without paying any
manner reward to any officer or person for the payment, or
any manner colour for expedition therein.

And if any such person were not able, or should not be
disposed to come personally, by some letter of attorney, or
other assignation, authorizing another party to receive the
money, he should have present free and full payment, without delay or reward, in any sort or manner. For such was
her majesty's intent, that her loving subjects should be
thankfully and freely paid. Which also should have been to
their proper hands in the countries, but for more delays
and uncertainties, that thereof many ways might follow, to
the hinderance of her subjects.

Finally, her majesty most earnestly desired, that if any
person had been misused, by pretence of demanding any
money upon any such privy seal, to give any thing in reward, or lend any portion to be spared from lending to her
majesty; that the same persons would speedily notify the
same, either to the sheriff of the shire, or to any such person as had charge in these last years to be lieutenants of the
shires, or to, &c. whom her majesty chargeth to make certificate to the said lord keeper. That upon the certainty
thereof known, the parties should have full repayment 104
thereof. Given at her manor of Greenwich, the 24th of November, 1571, in the fourteenth year of her reign.

Walsingham was still in France, the queen's active and Walsing-
most useful ambassador at that court: so faithful and dili- ham ambassador in
gent, that he stuck at no pains or charge in her service. He France, his
diligence.
had intelligencers of all sorts: so that his news and informations sent into England were large and important. One
of these was an Irishman, named captain Thomas; who
seemed to be his spy for Irish affairs. And another a Spaniard. Of whom he gave secretary Cecil this character,
(which was somewhat extraordinary for men in this kind of
employment,) that he was " wise and religious, honest and Comp. Am-
bas. p. 184.

"learned." This gentleman he sent over from Paris to the secretary with news. He knew well the office of an ambassador: which made him use these words in one of his private letters, written this year to Cecil, (having writ something to him contrary to what the queen was doing; and saying, that nothing could be more fit in his *poor opinion*, added;) This I am bold to write as a private man, in a private letter, having *no opinion*, as an ambassador, [i. e. no opinion of his own,] but according to the will of his prince. But in this public service he ran himself much in debt; and had done injury to his own patrimony. Of this with no little concern he acquainted the earl of Leicester and sir Walter Mildmay, his friends; and likewise the secretary; shewing him more particularly his case; viz. " That her majesty's allowance did not by 10*l.* in a week defray his ordinary charges of household. And yet neither his diet was like " to any of his predecessors, nor yet the number of his ser- " vants so many as they had heretofore kept. And that of " 800*l.* that he brought in his purse into that country, he " had not left in money and provision much above 300*l.* " Far contrary to that account he made: who thought to " have had 500*l.* always aforehand, to have made his pro- " visions. So that, as he concluded, unless there were, by " his lordship's good means, some consideration had of him, " he could not but sink under the burden." And in another he repeats the same complaint; desiring that he might have some consideration from the queen, that he might with the better courage employ himself in her service. And that he craved no recompence, only required to return home in no worse state than he went forth. The secretary acquainted the queen with this condition and suit of his. And she well knowing his merits, meant to do somewhat for his relief.

The noble earl of Rutland, Edward Manners, in the month of January travelled into France. Whom the said secretary desired our said ambassador to present as soon as he might to the French king. And that in expressing of his lineage, he might boldly affirm him to be akin to the

queen's majesty, both by king Henry VIII. her father, and
also by the queen's mother.   And that he was of the blood
royal in the same degree that the earl of Huntingdon was;
the difference being only, that the lord Huntingdon was of
a brother of king Edward IV. and the lord Rutland of a
sister of the same king, [viz. Anne duchess of Exeter, and
so bears on a chief quarterly two flowers de luce of France,
and a lion of England.]   And thereby was indeed as near 105
in blood, though further in danger of fortune's wheel, (as
the said secretary writ,) which was busy with carriage of
kings' crowns to and fro.   This lord, besides his own quality,
had many good parts to recommend him.

Great matters being now in hand with France, in the beginning of the month of December sir Tho. Smith was appointed to go into France, in quality of the queen's ambassador; but went not before February following, in order to
the making of a firm treaty, offensive and defensive, between
that king and her majesty: and to speak with the king secretly concerning the marriage between the queen and the
duke.   The instructions are preserved in the Complete Ambassador.   Secretary Cecil (by this time created lord of
Burghley) writ hereof to Walsingham, and gave this character of Smith; that he was one whom they thought of such
dexterity in his actions, and of such dutiful good-will hitherto, as no advice or direction should be given by him to
the prejudice of her majesty and her state.   The particular
transactions of Smith and Walsingham with the French king
in this embassy have been shewn before.

The Christians in the Levant had the latter end of this
year given a notable defeat to the Turks, and destroyed
abundance of their ships.   Of this the duke of Alva gave
the queen intelligence: which being of such public concern
to Christendom, she ordered public acknowledgments to be
made thereof to Almighty God, in the churches of her metropolitan city, and all tokens of joy.   Whereby she might
also, taking this occasion, wipe off those slanderous popish
aspersions cast upon her, as though she held friendship and
correspondence with the infidels.   A letter to that end was

CHAP.
XI.

Anno 1571.

Smith goes
ambassador
to France.

Comp. Am-
has. p. 154.

His charac-
ter.

Chap. vi.

Thanksgiv-
ing appoint-
ed for vic-
tory over
the Turks.

despatched from the privy council to the bishop of London
in the month of November, to cause common prayers,
praises, and thanksgiving, to be solemnly used, for a victory gotten against the Turks; and notice to be taken of it
in the Paul's Cross sermon.   The minutes whereof were as
follow :

The queen's
command
to the bi-
shop of
London for
that pur-
pose.
MSS. Whit-
gift.

" After our hearty commendation to your good lordship.
" The queen's majesty, having intelligence given her from
" the duke of Alva, of a great victory lately given by God's
" goodness to the Christian army, serving in the Levant
" seas, against the Turk, to the destruction and ruin of many
" of their galleys, and great numbers of their people; and
" being thankful and joyful therefore, as for a singular
" great blessing sent by Almighty God, to the benefit of
" the universal state of Christendom, hath thought it neces-
" sary, as well by common prayers, as otherwise, to have a
" public demonstration within her highness's household, or
" the comfort that her majesty conceiveth of so general a
" good turn.   And having commanded to the lord mayor
" of London a like joyful signification, to be expressed
" throughout the city by common bonfires, and other to-
" kens of joy and thanksgiving to Almighty God to-morrow
" at night, being Friday ; her majesty hath likewise thought
" convenient, and so her pleasure is, that we should signify
" unto you, that you give order, not only within your ca-
" thedral church, but also throughout all the other churches
106 " throughout the city, and near abouts, that the people may
" be solemnly assembled at some common prayer of praise
" and thanksgiving at some convenient time to-morrow in
" the forenoon.   And for that so great and beneficial favour
" of Almighty God ought to be deeply impressed in the
" hearts of the people, to provoke their thankfulness the
" more, to the continuance of God's great goodness towards
" us, and the state of Christendom, it shall be very neces-
" sary that he, who shall preach at the Cross on Sunday
" next, be prepared to say something on this behalf.   And
" the same also being no less than her majesty's plea-
" sure, that we should signify unto you, we doubt not

" but your lordship will be careful that every part thereof CHAP.
" shall be effectually performed, according to her majesty's   XI.
" godly intention.   And so we bid your lordship right Anno 1571.
" heartily farewell.   From Greenwich, the 8th day of No-
" vember, 1571."

And these also were minutes (corrected and enlarged by
the pen of secretary Cecil) of the council's letter, by the
queen's command, as above said, to the lord mayor of London, for the giving all public demonstrations of joy at this
good success, by making bonfires, and the like, viz.

" That the queen's majesty being lately advertised of a The council
" most happy and glorious victory given by God's goodness to the lord mayor for
" to the Christian army, in a conflict by sea against our bonfires.
" common enemy, the Turk, to the destruction of a great MSS. Whit-gift.
" number, both of their galleys and armies, in the sea, to
" the benefit and comfort of all Christendom; like as the
" same is to be acknowledged to have proceeded of God
" Almighty's power and omnipotent hand, who is therefore
" to be thanked, praised, and magnified accordingly; so
" her highness, to make demonstration of her own house-
" hold, how joyfully her majesty received the news of so
" general a benefit, hath commanded, that order be given,
" that to-morrow at night, being Friday, there may be a ge-
" neral signification of like to be given throughout her city
" of London by such solemn manner of bonfires in every
" ward; and such other joy and thankfulness to God, as
" hath been in such cases accustomed upon a victory, or any
" other benefit received.

" And for that purpose we require you earnestly, in her
" majesty's name, that you do forthwith appoint, that the
" same may be performed accordingly throughout the city
" and suburbs of the same.   And that also you give pre-
" sently notice to all franchises, and places exempted, within
" or near the city, that the like order may be used there at
" the same time, as is in your jurisdiction.   And that while
" the same fires are, there may be a good watch to continue
" the greater part of the same night used."

CHAP. XII.

Campion, the Jesuit, persuades the bishop of Gloucester to renounce his religion. Many now leave off coming to church. Of this sort were some gentlemen in Norwich diocese. The bishop's letters thereupon, moved by orders from the privy council. The said bishop's sermon for satisfaction of puritans. Their exceptions to it in divers articles. A case of matrimony. The earl of Sussex to the bishop of Norwich, about buying and selling an advowson. The Dutch church in Norwich.

Campion writes to the bishop of Gloucester, to return to the Roman church.

To complete my relation of affairs falling out this year, especially with reference to religion, I shall first make a remark upon Edmund Campion, the Jesuit; who wrote a very earnest letter this year in the beginning of November, to Cheny, bishop of Gloucester, to return to the Roman church; superscribed, *Ornatissimo viro Ricardo Cheneo episcopo Glocestriensi, Edmundus Campion, S. P. D.* (not

Printed at Antw.1631.

as it is now abusively printed in his *Opuscula, pseudoepiscopo Glocestriensi.*) That bishop had entertained and been kind to Campion when he was an Oxford scholar, and afterwards at Gloucester. And upon the occasion of that cloud

Life of Archbishop Parker.
B. iv. ch. 5.

the bishop now lay under, viz. that of excommunication, (as may be seen elsewhere,) the Jesuit, (being now turned a zealot for popery,) presuming upon his old acquaintance with the bishop, directed his epistle to him. And to make him the more disaffected to the reformed church, whereof he was at present cut off from being a member, he put him in mind of a former accusation of him, brought by certain learned men of Oxford, viz. Cooper, Humphrey, and Sampson: who had sometime charged him with false doctrines, and

His arguments to the bishop.

made complaints of him on that account. Against whom he still justified himself by appealing to antiquity, and the ancient fathers and councils. In this epistle he took the advantage of the bishop's years and constitution of body, being aged threescore years and upwards, and but weakly. He also took the advantage of the state in which he stood at

that present, being neither esteemed by the reformed nor
the catholics; calling him, *hæreticorum odium, catholico-*
rum pudor, vulgi·fabula, tuorum luctus, inimicorum ludi-
brium; i. e. the hatred of heretics, the shame of catholics,
the talk of the people, the grief of his friends, and the sport
of his enemies.   He urged moreover to him his own judgment, that he was an enemy to Calvin and Zuinglius; that
he did not approve of this pestilent sect, [as he styled the
reformation,] and yet by holding his peace, he did in effect
recommend it.

Further, he reminded him how he used to advise with
him, when he was young, being with him privately in his
study at Gloucester, that he should go plainly and uprightly
as it were in the beaten road, and follow the steps of the 108
church, of councils, and fathers.   And that he should believe there could be no spot of falsehood laid to the charge of
these.   He remembered him, how being to dine with Mr.
Tho. Dutton, at Shirburn, about three years past, and meeting with a Cyprian, he [Campion] took occasion to object to
the bishop the synod of Carthage, which erred about the
baptism of heretics: and that therefore it seemed, that councils were not always to be relied on.   Which he said on purpose to get out the bishop's answer: which was, that the
Holy Ghost was not promised to one single province, but
to the church, [meaning, the œcumenical councils were only Councils.
to be regarded, and that they only could not err.]   And
that the universal church was represented in a full council;
and that it could not be shewed how such a general council
was ever deceived in any doctrine.   And that it was upon
this ground that he believed the real, corporeal presence in
the sacrament, and the freedom of the will.   And finally, he
urged to the bishop his opinion, that the ancient bishops
were to be the interpreters to us of the scriptures: those
who were *custodes depositi,* i. e. those that were the keepers
of the ancient faith.

He took this handle to make a great flourish with the Council of
most famous fathers (as he styled them) and patriarchs, and ed by Cam-
apostolical men of the late council of Trent, who strove pion.

BOOK
I.

Anno 1571.

together for the faith of the ancient fathers. There were legates, prelates, cardinals, bishops, ambassadors, doctors of most nations, all men of great age and singular wisdom, princes for dignity, for learning admired ; gathered together from all countries, Italians, French, Spaniards, Portuguese, Greeks, Poles, Hungarians, Flemings, Illyrians ; many from Germany, some from Ireland, Croatia, Moravia, and one from England.

His threat-
enings.

And being so near to the catholic truth, Campion thought to have persuaded him by this and the foregoing plausible arguments to have fallen quite off from the reformed church of England. And then, lest all that he had said before might not serve to reclaim him, he proceeded to threatenings : that he had now one foot in the grave ; and perhaps presently might be hurried away by death, be set before the dreadful tribunal, to hear that word, *Give an account of thy stewardship.* Then those hands of his, which had admitted so many miserable young men into spurious orders, should beat and pierce his sulphurous body with anguish : then that impure mouth of his, defiled with perjuries and schism, should be filled with fire and worms, and the spirit of whirlwinds : then that ambitious pomp of his flesh, his episcopal chair, his yearly revenues, his spacious house, his honourable salutations, his retinue of servants, his plenty and abundance, (wherein the foolish common people reckoned him a happy man,) should all end in horrible weeping and gnashing of teeth, in stench and filth, and prisons : where the ghosts of Calvin and Zuinglius, with whom he then contended, should continually vex him, together with the rest of those heretics, Arius, Sabellius, Nestorius, Wickliff, and 109 Luther ; in a word, with the Devil and his angels of darkness. That there with them he should be tormented, and belch out blasphemies.

But yet he could not but commend him, that he put out no Roman catholics in his diocese, but was favourable to those of that persuasion ; that he kept good hospitality, entertained the citizens of Gloucester and other honest men ; and that he did not, as some other bishops in his time, di-

minish and wrong his bishopric, his palace, nor his farms. CHAP.
I have set down this matter the more largely, because both XII.
the bishop and the Jesuit were of note about these times. Anno 1571.

This is the sum of a Latin epistle written by Campion to
that bishop; printed at Ingolstadt; with other letters and
orations of the said Campion, published anno 1602, by Robert Turner, a Jesuit, his scholar.

And indeed by this instance, as well as by the defection Many leave
off coming
from the established church, since the late rebellion in the to church
north, the diligence of the Roman missionaries appeared. in the diocese of Nor-
For many now were wholly departed from the communion wich.
of the church, and came no more to hear divine service in
their parish churches, nor received the holy sacrament, according to the laws of the realm. This was especially taken
notice of in the diocese of Norwich. Whereupon letters
were directed from above to that bishop, shewing their dislike thereof, and requiring him to make a reformation
therein, by putting in execution those rigours as by his authority he might. The bishop had, before this came to his
hands, endeavoured to set a stay to this disorder. And
thereupon had wrote to his ten commissaries, who were his
eyes (as he said) in his bishopric, to view and take notice of
the behaviour of such in his diocese, and to inform the bishop of them that did amiss. But ever since the rebellion
they gave him no answer. Whereupon, and upon the receiving of this order from the court, he despatched his letters to all his said commissaries; which ran to this tenor:

" After our hearty commendations. I have received The bishop
of Norwich
" letters from them in authority; wherein it is much mis- to his com-
" liked, that in this diocese there are divers, which neither missaries.
MSS. Joh.
" come to their parish church to hear divine service, or to nuper episc.
" receive the communion, as by the laws of God and the Elien.
" realm they are straitly bounden. The fault whereof
" resteth in you, as the eye of the bishop within your cir-
" cuit; unto whom I have written ere this, that I might
" be certified who they were that did not perform their duty
" in that behalf. But thereof was I not answered, since the
" rebellion in the north. These are to require and charge

BOOK I.

Anno 1571.

" you, that you use all lawful means to understand of such
" persons so disobedient within your circuit. And the same
" to call before you; and either to reform them, or to use
" such punishment towards them, as in law and right is due
" to their offence, without respect of persons. And if any
" shall shew himself more wilful, or obstinately disposed,
" than that you can by your authority reform them, I would
" you should advertise me thereof, that I may take order,
110 " as shall appertain. Herein requiring you to use all dili-
" gence and fidelity, I leave you to God. At Ludham, this
" 27th of December.

" Joh. Norwich."

Townsend
and Hare,
in the said
diocese, pa-
pists.

There followed now a diligent search for papists throughout the kingdom: and many were taken up. For the nation was awakened not only by the insurrection in the north,
but also more lately by the practices of the Scottish queen
and her friends. In the diocese of Norwich there were two
persons of eminence taken notice of, viz. Mr. Townsend and
Mr. Hare. The former with his wife had before come to
church, and partook of the prayers and sacrament; but
more lately absented, and forbore both. But upon admonition he did again resort to the church; but his lady would
not. This caused the bishop to write this careful letter to
him:

The bishop
of Nor-
wich's let-
ter to Mr.
Townsend.
Epist. Joh.
ep. Norw.

" After my hearty commendations. I have been often
" advertised, that you, and my lady your wife, do absent
" yourselves from church, and hearing divine service, and
" the receiving of the sacrament. I have hoped still that
" my favourable forbearing, together with your duties in
" this behalf, would have moved you to have conformed
" yourselves. And yet I hear, and thank God for it, that for
" your own part you come on very well, and shall by God's
" grace increase daily. But touching my lady, I hear she
" is wilfully bent, and little hope as yet of her reformation,
" to the displeasure of Almighty God, the breach of the
" queen's majesty's laws, my danger and peril to suffer so
" long, and an evil example and encouragement to many

" others. And because I am sharply called upon by some
" in authority to see speedy reformation of such abuses,
" either else to certify such disobedience, that it may be re-
" formed elsewhere, I have thought good at this time by
" my friendly letters to admonish you and your wife; that
" for her own part chiefly, she be more diligent from hence-
" forth to come to the church, to hear the word of God,
" and receive the sacrament according to the right institu-
" tion of the gospel of Christ, to her comfort; as she hath
" done beforetime, as I have heard, in the time of king
" Edward, and since, in the days of queen Mary in popery
" and blindness, where that sacrament was abused, and yet
" the half thereof taken away from the people; and where
" prayers were made in a strange tongue ; neither edifying
" to the hearer, nor to the utterer for the most part.

" St. Austin saith, ' Set apart the understanding of the
" mind, and no man hath fruit or profit of the thing he per-
" ceiveth not.' And again ; ' What profit is there in speech,
" be it never so perfect, if the understanding of the hearers
" cannot attain to it ?' St. John saith, *This is the con-*
" *demnation of the world, that light is come into the world,*
" *and men love darkness more than light.* I could use
" many authorities and ensamples ; but at this time I for-
" bear to be tedious. The fault is great in a subject to
" disobey the laws established, and to give example of dis-
" obedience to others, in keeping a form in honouring God
" to his dishonour, under a vain colour of zeal, but con-
" trary to knowledge.

" My duty and place of calling, together with my con- 111
" science to Godward, cannot suffer me to know such dis-
" order, and to suffer the same any longer. And therefore
" I desire you both from henceforth to frequent the church,
" and the receiving of the sacrament, as becometh Chris-
" tians: so as I may be certified forthwith both of the one
" and the other ; which I look for. Otherwise, this is most
" assured, I will not fail to complain of you both to her ma-
" jesty's council. Wherewith neither of you shall have just
" cause to be offended, since you are so friendly admonished

" of your faults, and have so long a time to amend. And
" thus I bid you heartily farewell. At Ludham, this 12th
" of February, 1571.

" *To Mr. Townesend of Braken Ashe.*"

Sir Tho.
Cornwallis
comes to
church.
Mr. Hare
cited to
appear.

Sir Thomas Cornwallis, another backslider or recusant,
upon this method now on foot against them, complied. But
Mr. Hare before-mentioned was more stubborn. Whereupon he was cited in the month of February to appear before the bishop's chancellor. But it being such an unseasonable time of the year for taking a journey, (or at least on
that pretence,) endeavoured rather to come to the bishop.
And so the said sir Tho. Cornwallis (who was his relation)
signified to him, and entreated it as a favour from him. But
the bishop thought convenient not to yield thereto: but advised rather, that he should do as sir Thomas had done;
and then all further trouble would be at an end. Otherwise
he was determined to certify up to the council his disobedience, since he had himself been severely checked for his
negligence in this behalf. These were the contents of his
letter to the said Cornwallis; which was to this purport:

The bishop
of Norwich
his advice
concerning
him. MSS.
Joh. episc.
nuper Elien.

" That touching his request for his kinsman, Mr. Hare,
" as the same was not altogether unreasonable, the weather
" considered, so could he be persuaded for a week or twain
" to defer his repair to Mr. Chancellor. That as for his
" coming before him, it was but so much the more travail,
" and no whit the more favour to be found. For that since
" he and such other, after so long a time to conform them-
" selves, [had refused,] why should any such, said he, look
" for favour from henceforth? That his conscience toward
" God, his duty to the queen's majesty, and the sharp re-
" buking letters which he had received from men in autho-
" rity, all these bound him to be more diligent herein.

" And that therefore he might be advertised, that Mr.
" Hare and all others did frequent the church and com-
" mon prayers, with the receiving of the sacrament, as they
" were most dutifully bounden, then might such spare to
" take any journey to him. Otherwise, that they must be

"contented to feel of justice, without all further favour or CHAP.
"forbearing. And surely," added he, "this is the conclu- XII.
"sion, that he would not fail to complain of all such disobe- Anno 1571.
"dient ones unto the queen's most honourable council, and
"that without further deferring of time. And that it was
"high time, or rather more than time; the examples of
"the late rebellion and traitorous conspiracies of papistry,
"even against her majesty's most royal person, were most
"apparent witnesses. Subjoining, that his [sir Tho. Corn- 112
"wallis's] kinsman should do better to follow his good ex-
"ample, in resorting to the church, hearing of sermons, and
"otherwise conforming himself. So should he procure to
"himself the favour of God, and all that be godly, and
"avoid the danger provided for all that be so wilfully ob-
"stinate. And so he heartily left him to the keeping of
"the Almighty. At Ludham, the 25th of February, 1571.
"Subscribing,

"Your assured loving friend,

"Joh. Norwich."

From the papists let us turn to the other party disaffected Offence
to the church of England, and the practice and worship used puritans
in it. About this time, or thereabout, Parkhurst, the said against the
bishop of Norwich, had preached a sermon; (whether at his Norwich's
cathedral, or at St. Edmund's Bury, or elsewhere in his dio- sermon.
cese, is to me uncertain;) wherein he endeavoured to satisfy
and bring over to conformity to the church established those
of the *discipline*. But instead of having that good effect,
many of that party that heard him were offended; and
taking exceptions at divers passages in that sermon, digested
their scruples and objections under certain heads and arti- In several
cles, and sent them unto him by way of letter. One was, MSS. Joh.
that he having quoted a passage out of the prophecy of Je- nuper episc.
remiah, (viz. *What is the chaff to the wheat? saith the Lord,* Elien.
Jer. xxiii. 28.) persuaded them to be content with the chaff,
as long as they had the wheat with it. And that seeing they
had the wheat, they should not strive about the chaff. And
that those that were not content therewith, were wanton and

M 3

full, and had not the Spirit of God.   That it was therefore the obligation of the people to submit peaceably to them; and added examples of Paul, circumcising Timothy, and of shaving his head.

Another passage they excepted against was, that alleging several places of scripture for his purpose, to shew, as it seems, the indifferency of the things prescribed, he had said, he came not to defend those things, neither would he deceive one child of God for all the good in the world.   But they took hold of this, and charged him with great *deceit*, in alleging scriptures and examples, which seemed to make for him, and to omit such as were directly against him.   Again, that whereas he said in his sermon, that some had been offended, because in giving orders he used to say, *Receive the Holy Ghost: whose sins ye forgive*, &c. he proved it by the words used in baptism, and by the words which our Saviour spake to his disciples concerning absolution; that the minister might say in baptism, *I baptize thee in the name of the Father, Son, and Holy Ghost.*   Therefore they [the bishops] might say in giving orders, *Receive the Holy Ghost:* and perceiving a man to be truly penitent for his sins, the minister may certify him, that his iniquities are before the face of God in Jesus Christ forgiven him.   Therefore bishops, in ordering ministers, may say, *Whose sins ye remit, they are remitted.*   Which they said were slender proofs.

113   Again, he wished, that if he were the cause of this rent in the church, he might with Jonas be cast into the sea.   But they, in their animadversions, wished not so, but wished that God would stir him up from his slackness in doing his duty, as he did Jonas; and that he would move him and the rest of the bishops from their offensive states, pompous livings, and lordly titles.

Again, they carped at that passage of the bishop, where from 1 Cor. iii. *I am of Paul, and I am of Apollos*, &c. he made it applicable to such who refused to follow the prescriptions of the church.   They said, St. Paul there only blamed those that preferred one with the dispraise of another; they all teaching one sincere truth, without any

pharisaical mixture: and not fitly applied to them, who CHAP.
would not follow those that coupled their own devices and __XII.__
Antichristian remnants with the gospel of Christ.   Another Anno 1571.
expression excepted against by them was, that the bishop
had said, *As meat was for the belly, and the belly for meats,*
yet God would destroy both; even so (as he went on) the
back was for apparel, and apparel for the back, but God
would destroy both.   But they said, apparel was for warm-
ness, and not for pride and superfluity; as woollen upon
linen, and linen upon woollen, and silk upon silk, &c.   The
bishop had said, that *meat commendeth us not to God: and*
that if we eat, we were not the worse ; nor if we eat not, were
we the better.   And this the bishop also applied to apparel.
But they replied, that excess or pride in apparel, or delight
to wear *strange apparel,* as was the habit of Antichrist, men
did wear the same to the hurt of their brother, and so offend
the weak, grieve the strong, encourage the obstinate, confirm the hypocrite, and by defending the same, make glad
the heart of God's enemies, &c.   And then further, they
added, apparel so used made a man worse.

   And whereas he had said, What is white ? What is black ?
What is square ? What is round ? They said to this, that
if he had but a spark of that love that St. Paul had, he
would have said with him, he would never wear white, black,
round, nor square, as long as the world stood, that he might
not offend his brother.   He said, these were trifles, and of
small importance.   They asked him then, what should move
him to maintain them so stoutly.   Neither ought he, if they
were of no more moment, to have deprived so many from
their livings, thrust them into prisons, and stopped the
mouths of so many learned and godly preachers, as he had
done.   And whereas, lastly, he had said, that white, black,
round, square, were all but the good creatures of God ; they
said, that these, as they then wore them, were not God's
creatures, as he created them, but as Antichrist had formed
them.   From thence they received both fashion and form ;
and so the creatures of Antichrist.   But I refer the reader
to the Appendix, for the whole entire answer. Whether the N°. XII.

                     M 4

BOOK I.

Anno 1571.

bishop thought fit to make reply to all this, I cannot tell. Perhaps he thought it needed not.

I shall here subjoin two or three other things relating to this bishop, and this diocese of Norwich.

A case of matrimony brought before the bishop of Norwich.

A notable case of matrimony happened this year. One Mr. Minn had married a young gentlewoman, widow to Mr. Gray, a child scarcely twelve years old, and dying within a few days after his marriage with her. The question was,

114 whether she should by right have a dowry, as widow to the said Gray. This case was referred from the court of Common Pleas at Westminster to the bishop of Norwich, in whose diocese the parties lived. He was earnestly solicited by Dr. Wylson, one of the masters of requests, and his great friend, to give it in favour of Minns. But he, resolving to be swayed by truth and right only, sent to the Arches, to Dr. Gibbon, Dr. Dale, and Dr. Huick, three of the learnedest civilians there, for their judgment in this matter; writing to them March 4, to this tenor:

The bishop writes to certain civilians for their judgment. MSS. Joh. nuper ep. Elien.

" After my hearty commendations. These are to let " you understand, that I, being troubled with a matter of " your skill, am desirous, and by reason of an old acquaint- " ance, am bold therein to request your judgment. There " was in my diocese a face of matrimony solemnized between " a couple; the man (being not fully twelve years of age, " and departing this life within three or four days after) " to the woman now claiming in common law a dowry, by " reason of the said marriage. It is replied, that none is " due; *quia nunquam fuerunt legitimo matrimonio copu-* " *lati.* And her party affirming the contrary, hath pro- " cured a writ, to me directed; whereby I am willed to call " such as are in this case to be called, to search the truth, " and to certify, *utrum legitimo matrimonio sint copulati,* " *necne.* I am persuaded by some learned both in the com- " mon and civil laws, that this writ, the nature whereof you " know better than I, may be satisfied to the benefit of the " woman; and that certificate may be made according to " the ecclesiastical laws, *partes prædictas legitimo matri-* " *monio copulatas fuisse.* My chancellor persuading me

" otherwise. For that the matter is of some weight, and I CHAP.
" am willing to pleasure the gentlewoman in this case, law   XII.
" and conscience not offended. I earnestly pray you to Anno 1571.
" write unto me your learned and conscionable opinion,
" what I may or ought to do, for the satisfying of this writ,
" and the laws spiritual in that behalf provided. For the
" which I shall remain to you beholden."

The answer the civilians gave to the bishop's letter was as
follows :

" After our humble commendations. It may please your Their an-
" lordship to be advertised, that immediately upon the re-swer.
" ceipt of your letters of the 4th of March, we have con-
" ference together, how you might with safety of conscience
" and estimation make your certificate in the case pro-
" pounded. And to the intent we might deal the more
" substantially in the matter, we have gotten into our hands
" a copy of the writ unto you directed; where it doth ap-
" pear of certain faults and imperfections noted to be in
" your former certificate. And considering the same to
" stand in two points, upon the word *circiter*, and upon the
" word *procuraverunt*, we think that your lordship may
" well certify as you did before; leaving out, for supplying
" of the said fault or imperfection, the word *circiter*, making
" the age certain. And for *procuraverunt*, to say, *inter se* 115
" *solemnizaverunt*: and to declare the fact as it was in
" truth; leaving the judgment upon this declaration of the
" fact to the court: which we take to be most agreeable to
" law, equity, and conscience. For it may be, (and so we
" have been informed,) that the determination of the com-
" mon law differeth in this special case from the law eccle-
" siastical.

" For by the law ecclesiastical there was not properly
" *matrimonium* between the parties named in the writ; yet
" it hath been given us to understand, that by the common
" law, in allowance of dowry, it is otherwise. Therefore,
" to certify in form as aforesaid, it seemeth meetest: for
" thereby no party shall be prejudiced. And the words of
" the latter writ seems to direct thereunto. And thus being

BOOK I.

Anno 1571.

" ever at your lordship's commandment, we wish to the
" same long life, with the increase of felicity, to God's ho-
" nour. From London, the 18th of March, 1571.
" John Gibbon. Valen. Dale. T. Huick."

Then followed the form of the certificate to be sent from
the bishop to the Common Pleas court: viz. *Venerabilibus
et egregiis viris, Jacobo Dyer, militi, &c. comperimus, &c.
ex dict. testimoniis, quod prædict. Tho. Gray, ætatis duo-
decim annorum, et prædict. Elizabetha, ætatis sexdecim, ab
omni contractu matrimoniali, sive sponsalitio liberi et im-
munes, respective existen. nec ullo alio impedimento ecclesiastico subsisten. matrimonium per verba de presenti con-
traxerunt. Ac illud in facie ecclesiæ apud Baconthorp. in
comit. Norf. legitime inter se solempnizarunt.*

Other civi-
lians to the
bishop a-
bout the
same cause.

But this certificate was objected against, as insufficient,
by four other learned civilians, (who were engaged in the
cause,) because it was the bishop's part to declare, not so
much the matter of fact, as whether the matrimony were
lawful or not: which they asserted was not, because one of
those years could not legally give consent. And of this
those civilians explained their opinion in another letter to
the said bishop the month after: which take also as I found
it among that bishop's papers, with this title;

*A letter to the bishop of Norwich, from Dr. Yale, Dr. Jones,
Dr. Harvey, and Dr. Hammond, concerning the controversy between Mr. Nicolas Mynne and Mr. Gray.*

Their letter,
importing
the mar-
riage not
lawful.

" Our duties unto your lordship premised. Where our
" opinions are required in the case before you, between
" Mynne and Gray, both touching the lawfulness or vali-
" dity of the marriage therein alleged, and also of the na-
" ture and form used by the ordinaries, in certifying in the
" like cases: wherein, God willing, without respect, we will
" lay down that we think to be true, discharging thereby
" our consciences towards God, our fidelity towards our
" client, our credit towards the world, and our duty towards
" your lordship; of the marriage between Thomas Gray

" and Elizabeth Drury; the said Thomas being at the time
" of his marriage not past twelve years of age, and depart-
" ing this world within six days after the same; we say,
" that we take the law to be plain in this point, that the 116
" said marriage can no ways be called *legitimum matrimo-*
" *nium ;* because it had not *legitimum consensum* on the
" behalf of the said Thomas Gray, being not of lawful age
" to consent. Which *legitimus consensus* can never be
" given but of him that is *legitimæ ætatis* for marriage.
" And your lordship knoweth, that *ætas legitima*, in that
" case, is in a man fourteen years complete, and not under.
" And if the said Thomas Gray had lived until his lawful
" age, yet without some other special ratification, either by
" express declaration of his consent, or some fact amplify-
" ing the same, the marriage could not have been accounted
" lawful.

    " What certificate the ordinary should make in this case
" to the queen's writ, thus for our skill and experience we
" take it : that the ordinary must answer the writ and the
" court, only to that which is commanded to do by the writ;
" and not other matter, or other terms. For in this case
" the ordinary hath only to answer to the law, and not the
" fact. For the fact were triable by the country, and not
" by the ordinary. So that the ordinary must say, that the
" marriage is *legitimum* or not *legitimum*. Other kind or
" manner of certificate, in the like case, we never learned,
" nor never heard of. And if your lordship should make
" other certificate, by declaration of any fact or circum-
" stance, leaving to express the lawfulness or unlawfulness
" of the marriage by direct words, the court may, at their
" discretion, amerce your lordship from time to time, until
" you have answered the writ directly by yea or no.

    " And forasmuch as a copy of a certificate sent unto your
" lordship by learned counsel, as to be made by you in
" this case, is shewed unto us by our client, we cannot in
" conscience and duty but discover to your lordship certain
" words, as we take them, not well nor plainly placed in
" the said certificate, but covertly, to make white black, and

BOOK " black white.   As to say, *nullum aliud impedimentum ec-*
I.   " *clesiasticum subsistebat,* when the said certificate declareth

Anno 1571. " the age of Thomas Gray to be not above twelve years,
    " which is *impedimentum ecclesiasticum,* utterly avoiding
    " the marriage ; and then colourably to knit it up at the
    " end with *legitimum inter se solempnizarunt.* Which words
    " are *multiplices,* and rather a sophism than a plain report
    " of a truth.   For if *legitimum* referred to the matrimony,
    " then it was untrue ; if it be referred to the act of solem-
    " nization, or to the ceremony, then it is impertinent, and
    " answereth not the writ, as we have afore said.

    " Thus, as we trust, we neither abuse our duty towards
    " your lordship, our client, nor ourselves ; as knoweth the
    " Almighty ; who ever preserve your lordship.   From Lon-
    " don, the 13th of April, 1572.
            " Your lordship's to command,
                    " Tho. Yale.   Henry Harvey.
                    " Henry Johns.   John Hammond."

    I do not find the proceedings consequent hereupon.

117   This bishop shewed his care of his diocese in respect of a
The bishop living, called Wetherden, in Suffolk, now vacant for near
of Norwich
informeth six months.   The fault whereof he had learned lay in a
concerning
a simoniacal corrupt patron ; who kept it so long in his hand, to make
patron.   the better bargain for himself with him who should get the
    presentation from him ; that is, who should bid most : he,
    and such like patrons, never considering the greatness of
    that trust reposed in them, viz. to provide an able, godly
    person for the guidance of a whole parish committed to his
    charge ; nor regarding the people's want of divine service,
    preaching, and administration of the sacraments, for some
    months together.   Such a matter happened this year in the
    benefice aforesaid remaining void from Easter last to the
    latter end of October ; the next advowson being granted
    from sir Nicolas Bacon, lord keeper, to Mr. John Bacon,
    his kinsman.   The bishop upon this wrote to the said lord
Epist. Joh. keeper, to this purport ; shewing him, " How the people of
ep. Norvic. " that parish were destitute of service : and that he upon

" whom the said benefice should be bestowed was like to CHAP.
" fall into the danger of perjury. [That is, be guilty of ___XII.___
" simony.] Of which he knew (as he writ to that lord) his Anno 1571.
" honour had special care ; as might appear by such articles
" as he had appointed to be ministered to such as entered
" any cure." This was dated from Ludham, the 25th of
October, 1571. This was the bishop's seasonable monition
to prevent this abuse.

Simony was too common in this diocese, occasioned often The earl of
by buying and selling advowsons. Near about this time Sussex to
the bishop was concerned again about such a matter. An of Norwich
advowson of the earl of Sussex's patronage was passed to ing an ad-
and fro, from one person to another. This the earl hearing vowson.
of, and it looking like buying and selling, thought it reflected upon him. Which put him upon writing to the
bishop, declaring his mislike thereof; and requiring him to
deal and provide in that matter, as that neither earl nor
bishop might be blotted with allowing of simony.

To this the said bishop : " That although he did utterly His endea-
" disallow all such corruption, too commonly used in eccle- vours to
" siastical matters, and did put in use for the avoiding His answer.
" thereof such provisions as he could devise, and more in-
" deed than his predecessor had done ; yet having used
" some conference herein with such as were doctors of the
" civil laws, and other well learned, he understood, that the
" old civil laws allowed not that buying and selling of ad-
" vowsons. But that took no place in the laws of this
" realm. By the which all controversies about the title of
" right of patronage were ruled and decided, making pa-
" tronages merely temporal ; and by common use were
" bought and sold. That it was not therefore in his juris-
" diction, as he supposed, to examine every man's right
" that presenteth to a benefice. But the presented per-
" forms an oath, that he hath not procured his presentation
" by any pact simoniacal, or other means unlawful. So as
" his conveyance must be very cunning, and his conscience
" large, (as the bishop added,) except simony touch him, if
" he have committed any."

BOOK I.

Anno 1571.

118

Contest among the ministers of the Dutch church in Norwich.

The bishop interposes.

There was a church allowed in the city of Norwich for strangers that fled thither for religion from the parts of Flanders: which church was supplied with three ministers, named Anthonius, Theophilus, and Isbrandus. These, falling in their sermons upon particular doctrines controverted among themselves, preached so earnestly in answers and confutations one of another, that the congregation was all in confusion, and the peace of the church broken. Whereupon the bishop interposed, and enjoined them to forbear that manner of preaching one against another. But they would not obey; looking upon it as an infringement of the privileges of their church, for any but the members thereof, with the ministers, to make any orders for them. So that at length the business was brought up to the commission ecclesiastical at Lambeth; and the three ministers were all silenced, and others put into their rooms. And since they were excluded, there was great peace and concord in that church. This was some of the news that the said bishop wrote to Bullinger, at Zuric, concerning the affairs of religion here. See more of this matter in the Life of Archbishop Parker. The said bishop related in his letter concerning some members of the same church, that there were seventeen of them, November 1, expelled the city for drunkenness.

Life of Archbishop Parker. B. iv. ch. 7.

CHAP. XIII.

The queen's progress this year. Treaty with France about the match renewed. Sylva, an Italian physician, in London. The lord Burghley's troubles, by means of the Spanish ambassador. Who charges him before the council. Falls sick. Marries his daughter to the earl of Oxford. Whose behaviour creates great trouble to the lord Burghley. An adulterer brought before the commission ecclesiastical in York. Does penance at Bury in Suffolk.

Now let us turn to the court. We shall find the queen this summer in her progress into Essex. The gests whereof were as followeth:

Aug. the 7. At Hatfield.   Sept. At Hunsdon.   CHAP.
Sept. the 2. At Audley Inne. Sept. At Theobald's.   XIII.
Sept. the 14—17. At Markhal.   At S. James's. Anno 1571.
Sept. the 18. At Lees.   Oct. At Richmond. The queen's progress.

Which last place finished her progress. Soon after her return to this place, she was, October 19, taken suddenly sick at her stomach, and as suddenly relieved by a vomit. And from thenceforth, and so in December, continued in as good a state of health as she had been for many years; as the letters from the court reported. *The queen suddenly sick.*

There were now, in the beginning of October, endeavours used of bringing on again the match between the queen and monsieur, the French king's brother; the wisest then in the court concluding it the best (nay the only) course for the peace and safety of her majesty and her dominions, to enter into a strict amity with France: and some able man was thought most necessary now to go thither in quality of ambassador for that purpose: and none was judged more sufficient than the lord Burghley. And he was the man nominated (October) for this great business of a treaty with France. But he declined it all he could possibly; disabling himself, there being many impediments why he could not go thither; but the principal was, as he modestly said, because he was far unmeet to treat of any thing out of England, being, as he was known, only meet to speak as his mother taught him; as he signified to Walsingham, still in France, but in very ill state of body, and retiring from that court for his cure. And so he procured that his brother-in-law, Henry Killigrew, should go in that quality, and supply Walsingham's absence, while he was seeking remedy for his malady. *Treaty about the match with France renewed again.* **119** *Lord Burghley nominated to go, declines it.*

For whom the said lord shewed his great concern, knowing how useful a man Walsingham was. There was now in London one Sylva, an Italian physician of great note, and thought to be more experimented in surgery than physic. The lord Grey of Wilton was his patient at this time; who was afflicted with the like disease with Walsingham, that required chirurgical skill rather than medicinal; and seemed *Sylva, an Italian physician, in London.*

to have been cured or eased this summer by Sylva's industry and ability. The lord Burghley advised Walsingham
of this: and desired him to send him some note or description of his distemper, and therewith the method there taken
in curing him; and then he would confer with Sylva, and
advertise Walsingham of his opinion.

The queen
depends
upon the
friendship
of the
French ad-
miral in her
treaty with
France. The queen was full of thought about the weighty affair
now taking in hand with the French; and deliberated whom
she might depend upon as her sincere friends there, by
whose advice and assistance she might proceed. And she
concluded it to be those of the religion there. This was the
cause that she gave secret instructions to her ambassadors
to confer first with the admiral Coligni, a pious and wise
man of the religion, and not to proceed without making him
acquainted with their message. And that in case the admiral were not at the French court when they came, they
should appoint some trusty messenger, fully intrusted with
all the proceedings already past in the matter, to be sent to
him, and to impart the same to him, with demonstration of
the queen's trust and affiance in him; and to give her the
best and friendliest advice: and to let him know upon what
points they stuck, [which was the granting monsieur the exercise of the mass.] And that if upon this they should perceive that he seemed to be earnest, and to allow of the matter, and to have it go forward, that it should be told him,
that it was the queen's desire that he should be at that court
when sir Thomas Smith was there, that he might the better, from time to time, be privy to their dealings, and her
determinations also. For that she did mean freely and frankly to impart all things to him that should concern her therein; not doubting but he would have regard to her majesty's
honour, and especially to see that she were not abused or ill
120 handled by sinister practices of some that were great enemies to this matter. She also opened this her mind to another nobleman of France, count Montgomery, a protestant,
then at the English court.

The queen's chief counsellor, the lord Burghley, was,
about the month of December, in great danger of his life by

some of the Spanish faction; who had procured an Englishman to kill him, nay, and to kill the queen too.   But the
horrible treachery was discovered, as hath been shewn before.   Other troubles of this prime minister from that faction were, that the Spanish ambassador, in the month of
December, as he had used himself very crookedly, perniciously, and maliciously against the state, so openly against
him; and not forbearing, but in open council he directed
his speech to him, and said, that he had been and was the
cause of all the unkindness that had chanced between the
king his master and the queen's majesty.   Whereunto, as it
became him for truth's sake, [as that lord related the matter himself in his letter to Walsingham,] he answered with
more modest terms than he deserved, and referred himself
to all the lords in council, to report of him, whether any
thing had been said or done of him from the beginning of
these broils, concerning him or his master, or the arrest, that
had not been ordered and directed by her majesty in council.   All which all the lords did then affirm.   And the earl
of Sussex, in the Italian tongue, did very plainly and very
earnestly confirm it.   But yet that Spaniard's choler would
not be so tempered: and so he was dismissed.   And Mr.
Knolls was appointed to attend on him at his house, [as
though under some restraint;] and so he departed the kingdom, being (as it seems) sent away.

Of this matter, thus did Parkhurst, bishop of Norwich,
write to Bullinger, by way of news, about the middle of
December.   " A Spanish ambassador carried himself so pe-
" remptorily and indiscreetly, and was such a spy, instead
" of ambassador, that he was commanded within three days
" to depart the realm, upon pain to have his head cut off.
" But whether this were true or no, he could not tell, as he
" added.   But true it was that he was gone."

Besides these troubles from without, the lord Burghley
was in the next month oppressed with several fits of a fever.
But yet, such was his concern for the public, that he said,
that fear occupied him more in the queen's cause, [that is,
about her marriage with monsieur,] seeing God had suffered

her to lose so much time, than for the next fit. And yet (as he added) that he had more cause than beforetime. For that it came of a great cold, and a rheum fallen into his lungs; where it was lodged, and so remained without moving. But in respect of other things, which I see and suffer, (said he, as anxiously careful for the public,) I weigh not with mine own carcass.

This lord, in the Christmas holydays, married his beloved daughter, Anne Cecil, to Edward earl of Oxford; to his present (but not future) joy, and made great feastings with his friends. The queen honoured the marriage with her presence and great favour. She was a most virtuous lady, bred up at court, and instructed in good literature by one Lewin, afterwards a learned doctor of the civil law; who, 121 in a letter to the lord her father, speaks of her *ingenii et naturæ bonitas;* i. e. *goodness of wit and nature, derived from him her father.* She had been desired in marriage before this by sir Henry Sidney, for his only son, that most accomplished man, sir Philip Sidney; and afterwards by the earl of Shrewsbury, for his son: which, for some reasons shewed before, was declined. The earl of Oxford was bred up in Burghley's family; but proved an humourist, and unkind, and a great embeciller of his estate. And not long after his marriage, absented himself from his wife, and went over to Calais, and so to Flanders, without leave or knowledge of the queen.

But the queen, displeased at his absence, and doubting whether his purpose was to join himself with her rebels, sent for him forthwith into England: to which he sent word he would obey. Upon which the queen was graciously inclined towards him; whose peace, by the lord Burghley's means, was the more easily and speedily made. For that she conceived that his obedience in his return had fully satisfied the contempt of his departure: and the rather, through his honourable and dutiful carriage of himself in respect of those rebels and other undutiful subjects in that country. Which was an argument of his approved loyalty: as the lord Burghley himself related to a friend of his.

It is necessary here to vindicate the lord Burghley from an imputation given out in some of our later historians concerning him; viz. that the reason of the extravagances of this earl, and his squandering away of his patrimony, was a distaste taken against his father-in-law, for refusing, when it lay in his power, to save the life of his beloved and entire friend, the duke of Norfolk, condemned for dealings with the Scottish queen. And this story is taken up in a book not long ago printed; and from thence in the book called *The Baronage of England.* Whereas this is a surmise and imagination, borrowed from the papists; as smelling of their malice to blur the memory of that excellent wise statesman. They that know any thing of those matters, know that that lord did whatever he could to bring that duke into favour: and did it; till again imprudently meddling in that affair, the treason being so apparent, he was condemned by his peers. And the queen would not pardon, since her own crown and life was in such hazard thereby.

The earl's disobliging carriage, and his wild way of living, was a great affliction to the lord Burghley, his father-in-law, who had deserved so very well of him. On which occasion, sir Thomas Smith, the secretary, his friend, in the year 1576, wrote thus to him: " That he was sorry to hear " of the undutiful and unkind dealing of the earl of Oxford " towards his lordship, which he was sure must very much " grieve his honour, since he had such a love towards him " from his childhood, being brought up in his house. That " his lordship's benefits towards him, and great care for him, " deserved a far other recompence of duty and kindness." And he charged this evil upon his counsellors and persuaders, whosoever they were. And concluded with this sound advice; *sed hæ sunt procellæ domesticæ sola prudentia sustinendæ.*

To which I will add, what the said lord Burghley, divers years afterwards, (the earl still following his old prodigal courses, and discontented for want of places and preferment, the fault whereof he laid upon his father-in-law,) told him, in his own vindication, (when the earl, in a letter, had used

CHAP.
XIII.

Anno 1571.
A surmised cause of that earl's prodigality; falsely attributed to lord Burghley.

Athen. Oxon. Fasti. p. 727.

Afflicted for the earl's behaviour. Smith's letter thereupon.

122
Lord Burghley's vindication of himself to the earl.

these plain words to him, *That he found himself but little strengthened in estate by him, and nothing in friendship,*) that he took it very ill at his hand, being unjustly charged by him, as having (as he replied) often propounded ways to prefer him to services, though his motions took not place, but were hindered. And for this he appealed to the queen's counsellors to bear him witness. Though, as he added, he thought not fit to name the hinderers, or to offend him, in shewing the allegations to impeach his lordship of those preferments. And then further, he avowed of his faith before God, that at all times, when occasion served, he had him in remembrance to be used in honourable service. And to clear himself from a report that one Wotton had made of him, as though he had used speeches in council to the earl's disgrace, he was so stirred at this, that he tells the earl that he affirmed, that *he lied* that so reported ; and that he was sorry that his lordship should put him in a balance of credit against him.

Two living in adultery brought before the commission ecclesiastical.

I meet this year with an exemplary piece of justice executed by the ecclesiastical commissioners at York, upon a wicked adulterer and adulteress: he, one Ambrose Stone, of St. Edmund's-Bury, in Suffolk, and she, the wife of one Page, of Horninger; Grindal being then archbishop, and Dr. Hutton dean of the cathedral. It was plotted between these two sinners, that she should get leave to go away for some time from her husband, and to repair to her friends at London, or elsewhere, upon pretence to gather money among them, to answer a loss of 10*l.* that her husband had sustained by some default of hers ; which it is likely she had embezzled or stolen ; and then, to pacify him, offered to go abroad to her friends, to beg of them to make it up. And that she might pass up and down where she pleased with the more liberty, it was so contrived, that she should get a certificate or testimonial under her husband's hand, of leave and consent to depart from him ; which ran to this tenor :

By a deceit she gets her husband's consent to depart.

" All men shall know by these presents, that John Page, " of Horninger, in the county of Suffolk, yeoman, one of " the queen's majesty's servants, for divers and sundry

" causes especially me moving, have licensed one Katharine CHAP.
" Page, my wife, to repair over to her friends in London, ___ XIII.
" or elsewhere, for so long a time as she shall think good, Anno 1571.
" and to demand their gentle good wills for a certain loss of
" 10l. which the said Katharine did negligently lose; and
" with her friends there to remain as long as she shall think
" good. And for that no man shall hinder her in her jour-
" ney and travail, I have caused this bill of testimonial to
" be made; and do all men to understand that she departed
" with my good will; and this bill of testimonial to be her
" discharge : willing all justices, mayors, bailiffs, and con-
" stables, that she may quietly pass. And also I have
" given her in purse 40s. and a gelding, to travail withal.
" In witness of this truth, I have caused this bill to be 123
" made, August 27, in the 13th year of the reign of our so-
" vereign lady the queen," &c.

And so by this deceitful trick invented by Stone, Page The com-
allowed his wife to depart, and supplied her to bear her mission
charges. Then did these two wander about, even as far as to appear
York. Where after some months they were taken up, and before his
bishop.
brought before the archbishop and the commission, and imprisoned. And at length he gave bond to appear before his
diocesan, the bishop of Norwich, there to bear due punishment to be inflicted on him for his crime, and obtained one
in those parts to be his bail for appearance.

The condition of which bond was, " That if the above
" bounden Ambrose Stone do present himself, and person-
" ally appear, as well before the reverend father in God,
" the bishop of Norwich, as also before two or three at least
" of the justices of peace of the said county of Suffolk ; and
" before them do confess and acknowledge his fault, in using
" unlawful company with Katharine Page, the wife of John
" Page ; submitting himself to their order and correction,
" and well and truly in every behalf perform, do, fulfil, and
" keep such punishment and order, as they or any of them
" shall enjoin or assign unto him ; if also he doth from hence-
" forth utterly abstain from the company of the said Ka-

" tharine, with whom he hath lived in adultery in all places,
" wheresoever, except in church and market, and other open
" and used places, in the daytime, between sun and sun,
" and that in the presence of other honest persons without
" all suspicion : and if he do bring true certificate under
" the hands and seals of the bishop of Norwich, and two of
" the justices of the peace aforesaid, to the city of York,
" the 3d day of March next coming, of his appearance be-
" fore the said bishop and justices, and of their full pro-
" ceedings or orders taken with him ; and that day exhibit
" the same certificate to the most reverend father in God,
" Edmond, by the permission of God, archbishop of York,
" primate of England, and metropolitan, and other his asso-
" ciates, the queen's majesty's commissioners for causes ec-
" clesiastical within the province of York, or three of them ;
" and also content, pay, or cause to be contented and paid
" unto John Mudd, servant to Mr. John Eynns, esq. to the
" use of the said John Page, the sum of 3*l.* of lawful Eng-
" lish money, in full payment of 5*l.* due to the said John
" Page, on this side and before the feast of the Epiphany
" of our Lord next coming ; that then," &c.

> *Capta et recognita coram venerabilibus viris, magist.*
> *Matt. Hutton, D. D. dean of the cathedral church of*
> *York, Tho. Eynns, and Tho. Bomton, esqrs. com-*
> *missioners for causes ecclesiastical, within the pro-*
> *vince of York.*

He does
penance.

Stone did accordingly deliver this writing to the bishop
of Norwich, November 28, 1571.   And penance was accordingly enjoined him for his sin by the bishop's commissary, Mr. Brome : which was, to do his penance in Bury
church, and also at Horninger.   And also on the 10th of
February following, he was adjudged by the said commissary to stand in the market the whole time of the market.

124 For some remission of this, Mr. Ambrose Jermyn, a gentleman in those parts, and probably related to this Stone,
bearing his name, wrote to the commissary, that since he
had so gently used himself as he had done, his trust was,

that he would remit a great part of that penance for that CHAP.
XIII.
day.   After all this, Page intended to have the good abearing against him. Anno 1571.

-------◆-------

CHAP. XIV.

A new parliament.   The lord keeper's directions to them Anno 1572.
from the queen ; particularly relating to the doctrine and
discipline of the church.   Bills for rites and ceremonies
brought in ; which gives the queen offence.   Her message.
thereupon.   Severely reflected upon by one of the mem-
bers, viz. Peter Wentworth: for which he is sequestered.
The parliament earnest upon a bill against the Scottish
queen.   Dashed by the queen.   Duke of Norfolk : his
virtues : his fall.   The practices of the Scottish queen.
The parliament's proceedings against her.   The queen's
directions to them in that matter.

A NEW parliament the next year (viz. 1572, 13 Eliz. A parlia-
May the 8th) began.   And herein the lord keeper made a ment.
long speech by the queen's commandment, directing the keeper's
houses with affairs to enter upon.   And they were of two the houses.
sorts, viz. matters of religion and matters of policy.   Under
the matters of religion (which he called *God's cause*) he recommended to them both *doctrine* and *discipline*.   Under the
head of *doctrine*, he directed them to have an inspection on Concerning
the ministry ; namely, for the providing that the ministers doctrine.
of God's law and doctrine should preach and teach, as
purely and reverently, so with diligence and application;
and that all officers, having spiritual as well as temporal
government, should be preserved in credit and estimation :
because many of the laity did not give that esteem and
countenance unto the ministers of God's doctrine, as they
ought of right to have.   And further, that in respect of the
want of ministers at that time, and the insufficiency of many
of them, he exhorted that bishops should do in this scarcity
of fit men what could possibly be done in that behalf; and

that with what diligence and speed and care they could. And further, that ministers that shewed any strange doctrines contrary, or varying from that which by common consent of the realm was published, be sharply and speedily reformed. Thus much said the lord keeper for *doctrine*. But not a word, suggested to the parliament, to examine and look into or determine any particular matters of faith and the doctrines of religion.

125   Then he proceeded to *discipline*, directing them to take

care of that; namely, that where laws were imperfect for the countenance of religion, and sundry ordinances made for that purpose were disused, or otherwise had not their force, or where the laws remained, but for their softness few made account of, that the parliament would consider well for the regulation of both. And likewise in regard of the slothfulness and corruption, or fearfulness of ecclesiastical ministers and officers, in the due execution of those laws that were good, to provide for the due execution of them: that so men might not live dissolutely and licentiously, as they listed. Another point of discipline to be regulated by the parliament was, the better keeping and better esteeming of the laudable rites and ceremonies of the church, or pertaining to the ministers of the same, agreed upon by common consent; the very *ornaments* of our religion, as the said lord keeper called them: mentioning also under this head the great neglect in the country, universally, of coming to common prayer and divine service.

Now for the remedying of this, besides the good examples of the chief personages both in town and country, he particularly left it to the bishops, that they should divide their dioceses into deaneries, [meaning, I suppose, those called *rural deaneries*,] and committing these deaneries to men well chosen, and the keeping of certain ordinary courts at prescript times, for the well executing the said laws of discipline.

And because the proceeding in matters of discipline and doctrine chiefly concerned the lords the bishops, both for their understanding and ecclesiastical function; therefore he

added, that the queen looked, that they, being called toge- CHAP.
ther in parliament, should take the chief care to confer and ___XIV.___
consult of these matters.   And that if in their conference Anno 1572.
they found it behooveful to have any temporal acts made for
the amending or reforming of any of these lacks, then they
should exhibit them in parliament to be considered upon.
And so *gladius gladium juvabit*, as beforetime had been
used.

May the 19th, a bill for *rites* and *ceremonies* was read Bill for rites
the second time, and on the next day read the third time, and ceremo-
                                                            nies.
and referred (with another of the same nature) to be con- D'Ewes'
sidered by Mr. Treasurer, sir Tho. Scot, Mr. Attorney of Journal,
                                                         p. 207.
the Duchy, and others, saith the Journal. [Mr. Peter
Wentworth, I think, one of them, of whom more by and
by.] This seemed to be a bill for calling into examination
such rites and ceremonies as were established in this church,
and used in the public service of God.   This bill gave such
offence to the queen, that two days after, [viz. May 22,] the The queen's
speaker declared from her majesty unto the house, that her message to
                                                            the house
pleasure was, that from henceforth no bills concerning reli- hereupon.
gion should be preferred or received into the house, unless
the same should be first considered and liked by the clergy,
[i. e. in convocation.]   And further, that it was her majesty's pleasure to see the two last bills read in the house,
touching rites and ceremonies. Whereupon it was ordered
by the house, that the same bills should be delivered unto
her by all the privy council that were in the house, viz. Mr.
Heneage, Dr. Wylson, &c. or by any four of them.

The next day, being May the 23d, Mr. Treasurer re- 126
ported to the house the delivery of the said two bills to her Reported.
majesty; together with the humble request of that house,
most humbly to beseech her highness not to conceive ill opinion of that house, if it so happened that her majesty should
not like well of those bills, or of the parties that preferred
them.   He reported further, that her majesty seemed utterly to dislike of the first bill, and of him that brought the
same into the house.   And that her express will and pleasure

BOOK
I.

Anno 1572.

was, that no preacher or minister should be impeached or indicted, or otherwise molested or troubled, as the preamble of the said bill did purport; yet adding these comfortable words further, " that she, as the defender of the faith, would " aid and maintain all good protestants, to the discouraging " of all papists."

Wentworth's undutiful speech; he is sequestered the house.

The next sessions, after divers prorogations, was on Wednesday the 8th of February, 1575; begun 18 Eliz. (that I may bring these matters together;) when Peter Wentworth, esq. one of the burgesses of Tregony, in Cornwall, for irreverent and undutiful words uttered by him in the house concerning the queen, was sequestered, that the house might proceed to conference and consideration of his speech.

D'Ewes' Journ. p. 236.

The speech is set down by D'Ewes, transcribed by him out of a copy he had by him. Towards the beginning whereof he saith expressly, that he was never of any parliament before the last, and the last sessions of it: which must be this of the 13th of the queen; wherein she checked those that brought in the bills about the rites and ceremonies, as was

The sum of his speech.

shewn before. In his speech he spake of the liberty of free speech, that was so many ways infringed, and of the many abuses offered to that honourable council, [reflecting upon what the queen had done the last sessions, viz. this in 1572,] as it grieved him, he said, of very conscience and love to his prince and country. And (to manifest what he drove at in his dissatisfaction about the liberty of speech, and that it was indeed the message she sent by the speaker, for no bills of religion to be preferred or received in the house, unless they were first considered and approved by the clergy,) thus he spake; " That two things did great hurt in that place: " the one, a rumour which ran about the house; and this it " was, Take heed what you do; the queen liketh not such " a matter: whosoever preferreth it, she will be offended " with him. And the other, that sometime a message was " brought to the house of commons, either commanding or " inhibiting, &c. And he told Mr. Speaker, that he would " to God both these were buried in hell. He meant, as he

" explained himself, rumours and messages: for wicked un-
" doubtedly they were, and the Devil the first author of
" them."

And by what followed, it evidently appeared it was his
offence taken at the queen for stopping the bill for rites and
ceremonies, which the hot puritans were the great managers
of, for the overthrowing of the established constitution of
the church, viz. the liturgy and orders of it; and also such
of 'the Thirty-nine Articles which they thought most touched
them.   For in the process of his discourse he gave his reasons to prove these rumours and messages wicked.   " Be-
" cause (said he) if they of the house were in hand with any
" thing for the advancement of God's glory, [as the puritans 127
" usually called their labours, to overthrow the matters ec-
" clesiastical which they disliked,] were it not wicked, said
" he, to say, The queen liketh not of it; or commandeth
" that we should not deal in it? Greatly were these speeches
" to her majesty's dishonour.   Much more wicked and un-
" natural were it, that her majesty should like or command
" any thing against God, or hurt to herself and the state.
" That it was dangerous always to follow a prince's mind.
" Many times it might fall out, that a prince might favour
" a cause perilous to himself and the whole state."

Then after, to put all out of doubt that he referred to
the session in the year 1572, he makes mention of the message that Mr. Speaker brought that last sessions into the
house, viz. that they should not deal in any matter of religion, but first to receive it from the bishops.   On which he
makes this severe reflection; " Surely this was a doleful Charges the
" message.   For it was as much as to say, Sirs, ye shall not queen to
                                                            hinder
" deal in God's causes; no, ye shall in no wise seek to ad- God's glory.
" vance his glory.   [This was freedom of speech indeed.]
" I assure you, Mr. Speaker, there were divers of this house
" that said with grieved hearts, immediately upon the mes-
" sage, that God of his mercy could not prosper the session.
" Well, God, even the great and mighty God, &c. was the
" last session shut out of doors.   But what fell out of it?
" Forsooth, his great indignation was therefore poured out

" upon this house: for he put into the queen's majesty's
" heart to refuse good and wholesome laws for her own pre-
" servation. Which caused many faithful hearts for grief to
" burst out with sorrowful tears; and moved all papist
" traitors, &c. who envy good Christian princes, to laugh
" (in their sleeves) all the whole parliament house to scorn."
      He proceeded in this manner; " So certain it was, that
" none was without fault; no, not our noble queen: sith
" then her majesty had committed great fault, yea, danger-
" ous faults to herself." That fault was, that she would
not yield to the trial, much less execution of Mary queen of
Scots, her prisoner; which in this same session they were
very busy about. He went on freely and confidently charging the queen of dealing unkindly, and abusing her nobility
and people, and opposing and bending herself against them
in the last parliament. And by divers questions making
and representing the queen as not as good as her word to
them, and leaving them open to their enemies. Then he
asketh, " Is this a just recompence in our Christian queen,
" for our faithful dealings? The heathen do require good
" for good; how much more then is it to be expected in a
" Christian prince? And will not this her majesty's han-
" dling, think you, Mr. Speaker, make cold dealing in any of
" her majesty's subjects towards her again, &c. And prayed
" God to send her majesty a melting, yielding heart unto
" sound counsel; that will might not stand for a reason."
      And then, as a further proof of God's judgment upon
that session of parliament, [viz. this in 1572,] he brought in
the bishops; whom, he asserted, God's Spirit did not descend
upon all that session, because, as it appeared, they were not
for the bill about ceremonies, drawn up by the innovators.
" But was this all?" proceeded he; " No, for God would
128 " not vouchsafe that the Holy Spirit should all that session
" descend upon our bishops. So that in that session nothing
" was done to the advantage of his glory."
      Then he proceeded with much show of bitterness and dis-
affection to that holy order, to disparage them as spiritual
men, that did no good in the church, but rather harm. " I

" have heard," said he, " of old parliament men, that the _{CHAP.}
" banishment of the pope and popery, and the reforming of _{XIV.}
" true religion, had their beginning from this house, and not _{Anno 1572.}
" from the bishops. And I have heard, that few laws for _{Reflects on the bishops,}
" religion had their foundation from them. And I do surely _{as back-}
" think, (before God I speak it,) that the bishops were the _{ward in re-formation.}
" cause of that doleful message, [which the treasurer, sir
" Francis Knowles, brought from the queen."] And then
gave his reason for his conjecture, viz. because in the last
parliament, when he, and other members appointed, repaired
to the archbishop of Canterbury, some words had passed
between him and the archbishop. Wherein the archbishop
expecting that such matter relating to religion should be
left to them, the bishops, to reform and regulate, he roundly
replied, " That that would be to make them popes: and that
" for his part, he would make them none, whoever would;
" as it hath been related before. And he feared, as he _{Chap. vii.}
" added, lest the bishops attributed that of the pope's canon
" to themselves, *Papa non potest errare.* For otherwise
" they would reform things amiss." And so with a great
deal more spite against them, blamed them particularly for
spurning against God's people, that writ for reforming of
things amiss in the church. All which shewed him to be a
zealous follower of those innovators, Cartwright and others,
who then were in the midst of their writing *The admonition
to the parliament.* And then he flings at the queen's message again; saying, " That the acceptance of such messages,
" and taking them in good part, offended God highly, and
" was the acceptation of the breach of the liberties of that
" honourable council."

This speech of Mr. Wentworth's was so illy taken of the _{He is se-}
house, out of the reverend regard they had of her majesty, _{questered for his}
that they stopped him before he had finished his speech. _{speech.}
And first they sequestered him; and after sundry motions
and disputations had, it was agreed that he should be committed to the sergeant's ward, as prisoner; and so remaining, to be examined upon his speech by all the privy coun-
cil, being of the house, and many others. The report is set _{D'Ewes' Journ. p. 241.}

BOOK
I.

Anno 1572.

Examined
by a com-
mittee of
the house.

The queen
of Scots the
cause of the
duke of
Norfolk's
ruin.

down of what was done with him, related by himself: for which I refer the reader to the Journal of this parliament.

On Thursday, February the 9th, Mr. Treasurer, in the name of all the committees appointed for the examination of Wentworth, declared, that they all met yesterday afternoon in the Star-chamber, according to their commission ; and there examined him touching the *virulent* and *wicked words* (as they are called) the same day, pronounced by him in the house touching the queen's majesty ; and made a collection of the same words. And he could say nothing for his extenuating of his said fault and offence ; and took all the burden thereof upon himself. Then the said Mr. Treasurer moved for a punishment and imprisonment in the Tower, as the house should think good. Whereupon, after sundry speeches and debates, it was ordered, that he should be committed close prisoner to the Tower for his offence. And immediately he was brought to the bar by the sergeant, and received the said judgment accordingly by the said speaker. And so the lieutenant of the Tower was presently charged with the custody of him. But by the queen's special favour he was restored to his liberty and place in the house March the 12th, that is, three days before the prorogation of that parliament ; namely, the parliament sitting 1575.

One of the particulars wherein Mr. Wentworth was so sharp upon the queen, (as was hinted before,) was her favour to the Scottish queen, after all the endeavour of this parliament to secure the realm against her. For about June they had indeed, with full consent, brought a bill to full perfection, to make that queen unable and unworthy of succession to this crown. But to this the queen neither consented, neither rejected ; but thought fit to put it off. This disappointment all her parliament took very heavily.

And what just cause the parliament had to be jealous of the Scottish queen, appeared by many things that now came to light.

For to give some fuller relation of this business. The apprehension of the nation from the queen of Scots was one of the great matters that took up the cares of the queen and

parliament this year, after the business of the duke of Nor- CHAP.
folk with her had so opened their eyes.   That queen was ___XIV.___
the cause of bringing to his end that very worthy, useful, Anno 1572.
and beloved peer of this realm.   I shall not rehearse his
trial, condemnation, or execution, our historians having set
those things down at length.   Only I shall recommend to
the reader a true report of the words and confession of that
duke at his death, taken by me from a MS. in the Cotton Nº. XIII.
library, Camden having but a short account thereof, as
much as he could carry away in his memory, being present; and Holinshed's report thereof being larger, but
not so exact.

   It was now five months since he was condemned, the queen His execu-
hitherto, out of her love to him, being loath to give her necessary
warrant for his execution.   May 16, the house joined to by the par-
signify to her, that it was their general resolution that exe- and so pro-
cution was necessary to be done upon the duke, and that it pounded to
should be propounded unto her, not by way of petition to the queen.
move her thereunto, but as their common opinion.   This
Leicester, in his correspondence with Walsingham, mentioneth ; and that great suit was made by the nether house
to her for the execution : but he addeth, as knowing her inclinations, that he saw no likelihood thereof.   Yet, though
she stayed for some time, she yielded to it at last: and
June 2, the duke was executed, in compliance with her
parliament and the necessity of affairs, to her great grief.
And when but a day after, (the execution being on Monday,) letters on Tuesday from her ambassador in France
were brought to her by the lord Burghley ; and he telling her, that he thought his purpose in those letters was
only to shew her the opinion of wise men, and her majesty's well wishers in France, both for the queen of Scots
and the duke of Norfolk ; she bade him open the letters.
And so he did in her presence.   And in his reading them,
observing the queen somewhat sad, and discomposed at the
duke's death, he took occasion to cut off the reading thereof,
and so entered into speech concerning the queen of Scots :
which she did not mislike, and commended her said am- 130

bassador's care and diligence in what he had writ concerning her.

This fatal stroke was of the more public import to England, seasonably to prevent greater dangers to the kingdom,
in that " he was (as a wise man, and well known in the pub-
" lic affairs of those times, wrote in his Memoirs,) one of
" the greatest subjects in Europe, not being a free prince:
" for he ruled the queen, and all that were most familiar
" with her. He also ruled (saith he) the council, and ruled
" also the two factions in England, both protestant and pa-
" pist, with the city of London, and whole land. The great
" men, who were papists, were all his near kinsmen; whom
" he entertained with great wisdom and discretion. And
" the protestants had such proof of his godly life and con-
" versation, that they loved him entirely. So that he was
" taken and secured when he thought all England was at
" his devotion." This author tells us further of the duke's
plain language in behalf of the Scottish queen; boasting
and speaking out, " that he would serve and honour the
" queen his mistress so long as she lived. But after her
" decease he would set the crown of England upon the
" queen of Scotland's head, as lawful heir." And this he
avowed to secretary Cecil, bidding him to go and prattle
that language again to the queen. The secretary answered,
that he would be no taleteller to the queen of him, but would
concur with him in any course, and serve him in any honourable thing wherein he would employ him.

The duke's
ambitious
designs.   Further, that he told earl Murray, regent of Scotland,
that he was resolved to marry the queen [of Scots.] And
that he would never permit her to come to Scotland; nor
yet that he would ever rebel against the queen of England
during her time. Also, that he had a daughter, who would
be better for the king than any other, for many reasons.

The duke
religious.   Upon the death of men of rank and figure, we commonly
are inquisitive into their character. This duke, among his
other qualifications, was himself endued with religion, and
had a care for the education of his children therein. And
as that part of it which consisteth in devotion and prayer is

proper to keep up a sense and awe of God, so he provided CHAP.
that they might be conversant therein.   And for that pur- XIV.
pose, in the year 1569, he recommended to one or two of Anno 1572.
his chaplains, namely, Dering and Hansby, to instruct them
in this duty of prayer, and, in order thereunto, to draw up
some proper forms for their use.   Which they did, suiting
them to divers occasions, according to our various needs and
wants, to be supplied from Almighty God.   And when they
had finished this book of prayers, they presented it to the
duke fairly written, all of Mr. Dering's own writing, with an
epistle in Latin before it, signed with both their hands.
Wherein they observe and commend his good inclinations
to religion, and exhort and stir him up with much good advice to increase and make more and more progress therein.
And according to their duty, being most bound to him and
his merits in the service of his religion, they beseeched the
God of all grace and father of mercy, that he who first put
those counsels in his mind, (those true tokens of his piety,)
would confirm and cherish the same; and that from those 131
holy roots of immortality might spring up in time ripe fruits,
which would grow unto eternal life.   They put him in mind
of those mighty benefits and blessings God had adorned him
with; in what place he had set him, with what great grace,
and in how great benevolence God had furnished his mind:
that he had all things bestowed on him above his age, above
custom, nay, above mortality.   And so they went on, expa-
tiating upon God's goodness to him; and therefore, what
returns of gratitude he was to make to him.   And further,
they added their Christian counsel, that whensoever God,
or prayer, or piety, virtue, religion, or mortality, came into
his mind, that they should not be cursory thoughts, but that
he should more accurately and closely apply them, and not
be drawn from such purposes and meditations, until he
found and knew himself better.   And so at length to shew
himself in mind and will most thankful to God, the author
of his salvation, that had so exceedingly well deserved of
him.   And then these good thoughts of his would not be
indeed sure testimonies of the honours of this world, that

are but the mockeries of a short day, but of his eternal felicity; to the great and wonderful peace of his mind here,
and after his departure hence would assure to him immortality.   Much more such pious advice and admonition did
these his chaplains, both fellows (I think) of Christ's college
in Cambridge, give to this noble duke; which may well de-

serve therefore a place in our Appendix.

Sir Roger
Mannours,
intimate
with the
duke, sus-
pected.
The excellent qualities of this unhappy duke rendered
him dear to all the honest nobility and gentry.   Among the
rest to sir Roger Mannours, of the right noble family of
the earls of Rutland: whom I mention, because the queen,
though he had been her servant ever since she came to the
crown, did suspect to be too familiar with him; and (as a
consequent of that) not so well affected to religion nor to
her.   Which when he came to understand, by some mention
thereof after, from the mouth of the lord Burghley, he,
under a great concern, conscious of his sound religion and

His letter
to the lord
Burghley,
in vindica-
tion of him-
self.
MSS. Burg.
unspotted loyalty, protested his mind thus unto that lord;
requesting him to make it known to her majesty: " That
" he had gathered by his lordship's speech, that he should
" seem to stand somewhat suspected both in religion, and
" for the good will he bore to the late duke.   For the one
" it behoved him, he said, not to dissemble; and for the
" other, he would say truth.   He protested to him, that he
" abhorred all superstition and popish idolatry, as much as
" any man living.   And that he judged little better of these
" bull-papists [meaning those that sided with the late pope's
" bull against queen Elizabeth] than he did of rebels to her
" majesty: for that he thought they carried the same mind.
" And not much otherwise did he account of those new
" fond puritans.   Neither could he judge why any man
" should mistrust him in religion, but one of them.

" Touching the said duke, he confessed he loved him
" while he was good; yet was he never beholden to him for
" any benefit: but that he honoured him for those virtues
" which he thought to be in him; and for that he believed
" he was a true and faithful subject to her majesty, and as
" it were a very pillar of her realm.   And that herein he

" deceived not him only, but the wisest and the most part
" of this realm; who then, he was sure, so believed of him.
" But that after he had been at his arraignment, and heard
" how he was charged, and what his answers were, if I (as
" the said sir Roger Mannours added) said not to your
" lordship, I am sure I said to some others of great calling,
" that then asked me what I thought, that if his peers had
" acquitted him, or that the queen's majesty afterwards
" should pardon him, I would never keep him company:
" and since that time, I am sure no man heard me any ways
" excuse any part of his faults. For surely, my lord, I never
" meant to love any man longer than I thought he loved
" the queen's majesty; whom God preserve ever, as our
" only safety. How desirous I have been to understand
" matters of state, or intermingle in that which appertained
" not unto me, I appeal, my lord, to your own conscience:
" for you can best judge of me in that cause, my lord. I
" have served her in the office which I now hold full four-
" teen years, and, I trust, hitherunto undetected of any dis-
" honest dealing towards any man. Blame me not, if now
" it grieveth me to be suspected in that wherein I did only
" glory, my truth to her majesty, in which, if I once fail in
" deed or thought, I crave extremity of justice. In all other
" things I desire her mercy, but not in that," &c. In these
lines, and many more, did that noble person and courtier labour to vindicate his own steady loyalty to his royal mistress, and unshaken adherence to the true religion, however
he had loved the noble duke, as most of the nobility had
done.

Now as to the *great cause*, as the business of the Scottish
queen was called, that justly created so much apprehension
to the queen, and the state of religion in this kingdom, I
shall rehearse some things that our records, letters, and advices, and manuscript papers do inform us of it. When sir
Robert Melvil returned home from his first ambassage in
England, he brought the handwriting of twenty-five earls
and lords in England, that were ready to set the crown of
this realm upon that queen's head. The captains in the par-

Twenty-five
of the nobi-
lity ready to
make Mary
queen of
England.

BOOK
1.

Anno 1572.
Melvil's Me-
moirs, p.
112.

ticular shires were named, and by those lords set down in that paper; only they wanted that queen's opportunity and her advertisement, when to stir. And upon this intelligence that queen presently writ to France, to her uncle, the cardinal of Lorain. Who, upon her desire, sent her his secretary. To whom the Melvils, sir James and sir Robert, by her command, declared the state of England, and the great party she had there, to espouse her interest; desiring her uncle to send his advice, when it would be the fittest time for her to stir; and to send what help he and his friends could procure. When the cardinal understood this, he acquainted the queen-mother of France with it; and how prejudicial to the crown of France the union of this isle of Great Britain would be. That therefore it was her interest to oppose it. And advised her therefore to advertise the queen of England concerning the said intended plot, as the only and most effectual way to prevent it.

The queen
informed
thereof:
how she
took it.

But whatsoever the queen of England's thoughts were thereof, she appeared to give no credit thereunto; as though she looked upon it as an Italian fetch, [that French queen was an Italian,] to put her in suspicion with her nobility. This account Melvil writes he had from the queen herself.

133

The parlia-
ment re-
solve to
touch that
queen as
well in life
as title.

This was then the cause of the parliament's meeting; namely, the Scottish queen's practices with the said duke, and also with other the queen's enemies abroad; intended for the invasion and destruction of the realm. Therefore, a few days after the parliament met, the lord keeper sent for the lower house, and declared to them, that it was the queen's pleasure, that a certain number of the upper house, and of the lower, should the next morning meet together in the Star-chamber, to consult and debate upon the queen of Scots' matters. A committee accordingly was appointed of commoners, to meet with the lords, to consider how to proceed in that great cause. And after the conference, Mr. Attorney of the court of wards made report of that conference. And at length it was resolved, for the better safety and preservation of the queen, and the present state, to proceed against the Scottish queen in the highest degree of

treason. And therein to touch her, as well in life, as in title
and dignity; and that of necessity, with all possible speed,
by the voice of the house.

There be *reasons* set down in the journal of the house of
commons, (which the publisher of that journal met with in
some of his papers; and concluded that they were presented
to the queen, May the 28th,) to prove the queen's majesty
bound in conscience to proceed in severity in this cause
of the Scottish queen, as being guilty in two the highest
crimes; both concerning God's religion, and the disinherit-
ing and destruction of their prince. Shewing, how she was
the only hope of all the adversaries of God, throughout all
Europe, and the instrument whereby they trusted to overthrow the gospel of Christ in all countries, &c. That she
had heaped up together all the sins of the licentious sons of
David, adulteries, murders, conspiracies, treasons, and blasphemies against God also, &c. And that she, with her allies,
by the pretended title, and other like devilish and traitorous
devices and workings, was like to bring confusion to this
realm of England and the people thereof. Then another
reason was offered, persuading, that the queen ought to
have, in conscience, a great care of the safety of her own
person.

On the 28th of May abovesaid, it was signified to the Which the
queen dis-
likes. Her
directions
to them
how to
proceed. house by the speaker, that it was the queen's pleasure, that
the committees for the *great cause* should attend her.
When they were come, they presented their humble petition to her; and (besides the reasons aforesaid) reasons gathered out of the civil law by certain appointed by authority in parliament, to prove, that it standeth not only with
justice, but also with the queen's majesty's honour and
safety, to proceed criminally against the pretended Scottish queen. But the queen, though she liked not of these
proceedings to be taken with the Scottish queen, yet received their message very graciously, and said, she thought
the course chosen by the house, and wherein the lords had
joined with that house, to be the best and surest way for
her preservation and safety; yet for certain respects by her-

BOOK I.

Anno 1572.

134

self conceived, she thought good for this time to defer, but not to reject that course of proceeding. And that in the mean time they should go forward in the great matter against that queen; but that her majesty therein would not have that queen, by any implication or drawing of words, to be either enabled or disabled, to or from any manner of title to the crown of this realm, nor touched at all. And therefore that the bill should be first drawn by her learned council, and by them penned, before it were treated of, or dealt with in the house.

The queen then further declared her judgment to the house, that she, the Scottish queen, should be disabled from enjoying any preeminence or dignity in this land : and that, not seeking to deal with her according to her deserts, she was contented only to have her made incapable of princely dignity. But the committee answered, that as to the disabling of that queen for any clause or title to the crown, they took it for a known truth, that by the laws and statutes of the land, then in force, she was already disabled.

Their answer.

The bill of treason against the Scottish queen.

But notwithstanding, the house finished a bill, and sent it up to the lords, June 26, wherein that queen was declared guilty of treason; and they solicited earnestly with the queen that she might be executed. But the queen not intending to proceed after that rigorous manner, the next day adjourned that sessions. And the parliament met not again until three years after ; viz. anno 1575, 18 Eliz. after divers prorogations,

CHAP. XV.

The thoughts of the wisest men concerning the state, by rea-
son of the Scottish queen. Her crimes under five articles.
The queen's instructions to her ambassador going to
France, concerning that queen. Walsingham's fears of a
Bartholomew breakfast. Talk of putting the Scottish
queen to death. Account given of her by the earl of
Shrewsbury, her keeper. Linen sent to her, with secret
writing on it.

NOW while these things were thus earnestly transacting Anno 1572.
in parliament, I will subjoin the judgments and opinions of
the wisest and gravest men, and the observations that were
then made by them.

" The parliament now assembled, both nobility and peo- The judg-
" ple had considered, that the queen's majesty's surety divers no-
" could not be preserved, without some severe proceeding blemen
" against the queen of Scots. Whereunto her majesty had the pro-
" not yielded in such extremity. And so that queen had ceedings
" more favour indeed, than either she deserved, or than Scottish
" was thought meet by the whole realm." So the English queen.
commissioners delivered themselves to the French commissioners, who required she might have some favour upon the
conclusion of a treaty. These commissioners were, the lord 135
keeper, the earls of Sussex and Leicester, the lord chamberlain, lord treasurer Burghley, master comptroller, sir Ralph
Sadlier, and sir Walter Mildmay.

That the queen was so dilatory in this great concern The lord
with her parliament mightily troubled the lord Burghley ; judgment,
opening his mind thus to Walsingham, the ambassador in and discou-
France : " That the parliament was earnest ; and that there
" could not be found more soundness in the commons'
" house, and no lack in the higher house ; but in the
" highest person such slowness, in the offers of surety, [i. e.
" the surety of the queen and realm offered by the parlia-
" ment in securing both against the Scottish queen's prac-
" tices,] and such stay in resolution, that it seemed God was

" not pleased that the surety should proceed. That he
" could not forbear to lament this secretly. And that
" thereby with it, and such like events, he was overthrown
" in heart, so as he had no spark almost of good spirit (he
" said) left in him, to nourish health in his body; being
" every third day thrown down 'to the ground, so as he was
" forced to be carried into the parliament-house, and to her
" majesty's presence. And to lament it openly, was (as he
" added) to give more comfort to the adversaries.

" These (as he proceeded) are our miseries, and such as
" I see no end thereof. And among other, shame doth as
" much trouble me as the rest; that all persons shall be-
" hold our follies, as they may think ; imputing these lacks
" and errors to some of us that are accounted inward coun-
" sellors; where indeed the fault is not. And yet they
" must be so suffered, and so to be imputed, for saving of
" the honour of the highest."

Lord
Burghley to
Walsing-
ham.

Again, in another letter the same lord thus expressed his
trouble about this emergence, soon after the parliament
broke up. " For the parliament I cannot write patiently.
" All that we laboured for, and had with full consent
" brought to fashion, I mean, a law to make the Scottish
" queen unable and unworthy of succession to the crown,
" was by her majesty neither assented to nor rejected, but
" deferred until the feast of All Saints. But what all other
" wise and good men may think of it, you may guess." He
added, that some, as it seemed, abused their favour about
her majesty, to make herself her most enemy ; [viz. by dissuading her to countenance these proceedings in parliament
for her safety.] He prayed God to amend them. But he
would not write who these were that were suspected: he
was sorry for them ; and so would you also, (writing to
Walsingham,) if you thought the suspicion to be true:
meaning probably the earl of Leicester.

Earl of
Leicester's
thoughts at
this junc-
ture.

Yet that great courtier and favourite used these words
to the said ambassador in the month of May, when this
weighty matter was earnestly debating in the news: " Our

"news is, we are presently in hand to attaint the Scottish CHAP.
"queen of treason. And yet we fear our queen will scant   XV.
"agree to it."   Anno 1572.
    The thoughts of that grave statesman, Walsingham, shall Walsing-
take up the next place; who, upon consideration hereof, Letter to
used these words: "That when he considered, how things Leicester.
"of moment, tending to safety, proceeded at home, he knew
"not what to judge necessary, unless it were for every man
"to provide for the cross." And again, upon the solicita- 136
tions made in France about this time for that queen, and for
her reestablishment in her government, he brake out into
these words: "That he feared, that as long as that woman
"lived, there would never grow good accord to Scotland,
"nor continuance of repose in England; nor perfect and
"sound amity between her majesty and the crown of
"France."
    And when all that had been endeavoured in parliament Walsing-
was not only ineffectual, but soon after she was enlarged, T. Smith.
and had more liberty granted, the same Walsingham thus
discovered his mind to a friend in England, in the month of
August: "That if her majesty had accepted the provision
"for her safety by her subjects in parliament, and not so
"soon have yielded to any enlargement, those Scottish mat-
"ters (then in debate) had been ere this accorded; [viz. the
"civil wars among the Scots, occasioned by that queen.]
"But we use (said he) to build with one hand, and over-
"throw with another: concluding, that he could rather la-
"ment it, than hope after a remedy. And therefore to God
"he committed it."
    It was the quick apprehension of the imminent danger
that still hung over both the queen and people of England's heads at this time, that so pressed the necessity of removing the *fomes* of contention round about. Which caused
the same wise man to utter himself and his fears thus to the
same friend a little after, in the month of October: "That
"until such time as the root of the evil [meaning that
"queen] were removed, it was rather to dream of remedies,
"than to apply such as the disease required." And there

BOOK
I.

Anno 1572.

being now some hopes of matters growing to an accord in Scotland, by the means of queen Elizabeth, he added, " That if the postern gate were shut up, [meaning Scotland,] " and other inward medicines applied, she [the queen] " would be more esteemed and feared." And again, " That " the tempest that hung over our heads was to man's judg- " ment so apparent, as, if she overslipped any remedy that " might be used, she must not long look to keep the state " that she then enjoyed. And that if England and Scot- " land were united, and such unsound members cut off as " had been the cause of inward corruption, both her ene- " mies should have less will to attempt any thing against " her safety, and she remain in less peril of such mischiefs as " otherwise were like to fall upon her: adding, that violent " diseases must have violent remedies."

Queen of
Scots ac-
cused under
five articles.
Cotton
librar.

I find that queen's crimes reduced to five articles, of dangerous import to her majesty and to the state of England; which by certain commissioners sent to that queen by queen Elizabeth were charged upon her. First, her claim to the crown of England. Secondly, seeking a marriage with the duke of Norfolk. Thirdly, the procurement of the late rebellion in the north. Fourthly, the relief of the rebels after they fled. Fifthly, the practising of an invasion of the realm by strangers. This paper at length transcribed from a Cotton MS. I have reposited in the Appendix.

N°. XIV.

But further, to enlighten this singular piece of history, wherein not only England, but the other neighbouring kingdoms had their shares; especially since our historians, and chiefly Camden, have so briefly slipt it over. The reasons of the Scottish queen's restraint and troubles queen Elizabeth gave in her instructions to the lord admiral, going ambassador into France, to declare the same to that king; who had interceded for her restoration: " That it " was well known that she [the queen] was often well " disposed to have obtained an accord betwixt her and her " subjects of Scotland. And that always, when she was " most earnest to have done her pleasure therein, she was " most ready to practise against her, [the queen,] as it

137

The prac-
tice of the
Scottish
queen
against
queen Eli-
zabeth.

" seemed, not satisfied with the recovery of her own coun- CHAP.
" try, without the practice to have also this of England, as   XV.
" by manifest proof they, the lord admiral and sir Thomas Anno 1572.
" Smith, could avow, to be ready to be shewed. And that
" thereupon she was forced, both for her own safety and
" the weal of her realm, to take another course : that is, to
" continue her favour towards the king, [the Scottish
" queen's son, now king of Scotland,] having been accepted
" by the three estates in full parliament.

" That she [the Scottish queen] had of late, by sundry Her mes-
" her own letters to the duke of Alva, and by her ministers sage to
" to the king of Spain, laboured to oblige that king to at- Spain.
" tempt to break the amity between the French king and
" the realm of Scotland, with plain assurance, that she
" would not in any wise depend upon the French king.
" But had wholly given herself, her son, and realm, so far
" forth as she could, to the said king of Spain. And to
" that end had done her utmost to move the same king
" to send forces into England, to join such as she promised
" should be aiding thereunto, to surprise her son, and to
" carry him into Spain by sea. And according thereunto,
" the duke of Alva had sent several men to peruse the ports
" in Scotland for that enterprise.

" That as for the Scottish queen, she was well treated The Scot-
" for her diet, and other things meet for her health, how- tish queen,
" ever the contrary seemed to be reported. She might at her tained in
" pleasure take the air on horseback ; so she did it in com- her confine-
" pany with the earl of Shrewsbury [her keeper.] For her ment.
" diet, it was such as her own ministers did and would
" prepare without respect of charge. Only it was prohi-
" bited, that no stranger should come to her, to practise
" with them, as she had long time used. And yet it was
" found daily that she did not cease, by letters and mes-
" sages, to solicit all manner of things for her purpose ; as by
" interception now and then of letters and messages was to
" be seen. Among which were found her continual labours
" to procure her son to be stolen, and taken away into

BOOK
I.

The parlia-
ment solicit
the queen
against her
in vain.

" Spain ; besides her attempts against the queen herself
" and her realms."

The estates then (assembled in parliament) did solicit, as
before they had done, her majesty, both in respect of herself and whole realm, to proceed against the Scottish queen
by order of justice. Wherein her majesty was so perplexed
with incessant clamour, and request of her people in that
behalf, as she was marvellously therewith troubled. As of
her own nature she had been found (even in her most private causes, and where her person had been in danger) not
given to shew any vehemency or to pursue revenge ; so to
refuse the universal motion, the general advice and exhortation of her states, she thought it no small hazard of their
love.

How she
had dis-
obliged
queen Eli-
zabeth.

138

And in these things moreover did this queen disoblige
queen Elizabeth. First, her secret seeking of marriage with
the duke of Norfolk, without her majesty's knowledge, even
at that time that her majesty was travailing to compound
her causes with her subjects. And after that her majesty
had imprisoned the said duke for that attempt, and that
her practices in the same were discovered ; and therewith it
was not unknown to the queen what comfort she had given
to her majesty's subjects to enter into rebellion, as they did,
[viz. anno 1569 ;] but being subdued and forced to fly, they
were openly maintained in Scotland by the Scottish queen's
means. Moreover, it was notorious how the queen, by sundry solicitations, partly of herself, and partly of the French
king and his ministers, was content as it were to bury the
former notable injuries ; and did newly enter most earnestly
to treat with her subjects for restitution ; and left no good
turn unessayed, neither by request nor threatenings, to
move them to accept her majesty's earnestness then with the
nobility of Scotland, professing obedience to the king her
son : that her majesty plainly charged them, that if they
would not condescend to her motions for her, she would utterly abandon them ; and rather be a party against them.
Whereupon they were entered into such hard terms, as

they answered, that they would so persist in their obedience to their king, as they would venture their lives in the quarrel.

And yet finally, by some persuasions, they were induced to accord with her majesty, that a parliament should be holden with as much speed as might be. And there these her majesty's motions were propounded. And certain persons should have authority to treat thereof with her majesty's counsellors. Whereupon her majesty did look for some good success. But before it could be granted thereunto to proceed, her majesty discovered daily most dangerous attempts of treason, both against her person and realm, wholly and only set forth by the said Scottish queen. And she found these new treasons intended, and almost brought to their mischievous perfection; by not only renewing the former message with the duke of Norfolk, but by giving order for a rebellion and invasion of this realm. All which was by her devised, set forth, and delivered to be executed, even in the very same time that her majesty did deal so earnestly for her with her subjects; and was in hope to have obtained some reasonable end for her.

So also had she now discovered the truth of her former practices, in stirring of the first rebellion, only to have by force obtained the marriage, and with the same force sought the crown. This will give a true light into the displeasure of the queen and this parliament against queen Mary, and open the just reasons thereof; being the contents of the instructions given to the earl of Lincoln, lord admiral, to shew the French king and his mother; who had fervently solicited the queen to be favourable to her. The said admiral, together with these declarations concerning that queen's practices, shewed the French king a letter in cipher, which she [the Scottish queen] wrote to the duke of Alva, of the matters before mentioned.

And yet notwithstanding, soon after the Paris massacre, that happened but some months after, they began to talk in France, that it would be a deed of charity for the princes catholic, not only to set the queen of Scots at liberty, but

139

BOOK
I.

Anno 1572.

Fears of a massacre.

A talk that the Scottish queen must suffer.

Earl of Shrewsbury, the Scottish queen's keeper, gives intelligence of her to court.
Epist. Com. Salop. in Offic. Armor.

also to restore her to her right: whereupon Walsingham, the ambassador there, wrote to secretary Smith, that her majesty was not ignorant what he had written, touching the opinion of wise men, what was to be done in that behalf for her own safety. "If the sore be not salved, I fear, " (said he,) we shall have a Bartholomew breakfast, or a Flo- " rence banquet;" that is, that such a bloody massacre was like to ensue in England as those were.

And so, indeed, in the month of December, there was much talk that this queen must die, the nation, both queen and subjects, having been terrified with the late barbarity in Paris against the protestants, and she continuing her practices. And so De la Mot, the French ambassador in England, advertised, that her majesty's meaning was, that that queen should suffer; and that the matters found against her were so great, that it was generally talked of, and thought that she should have been executed. Which when the report thereof was brought to France, they, her friends there, discoursed among themselves, that it were good to stay the noblemen that should be sent thither by her majesty to christen that king's son, to stand proxies for her, (as that king had desired of the queen,) as a pledge for that queen's safety: for so Walsingham hinted to the lord treasurer, December 28. For now, after the massacre in France, and the queen of Scots holding correspondence with the pope and France, and the secret false dealing of the French, more severe thoughts were taken up against that queen; and she was very diligently watched by the earl of Shrewsbury, to whom was committed the keeping of her.

This nobleman was very trusty and faithful; and took diligent notice of letters sent her, and many other correspondencies from abroad; and had also frequent discourses with her; of which he gave intelligence to the lord treasurer Burghley from time to time. In one of his letters he writ; "That she seemed much discontented, that having "sundry times written to the queen's majesty, she was "neither answered, nor suffered to receive money out of

" France, nor things needful for her use. So that she could
" not with good patience write to her majesty at this time.
" That within a few days she was become more melancholic
" than of long time before, and complained of her wrongs
" and dishonour: and for remedy thereof seemed not to
" trust her majesty, but altogether hoped of foreign power.
" That by her talk she would make appear, that both Spain
" and France stood her and her son's friends: and that
" to keep them both her friends alike, forbore to write to
" any of them. That she would persuade, that Spain in
" Ireland, and France in Scotland, intended some attempts.
" For to Ireland, she said, the pope long since gave licence
" for the king of Spain as his right. He added, that this
" speech of hers was not without her accustomed threaten-
" ing; nor that she shewed less enmity than of old."

He proceeded: " My lord, this sudden disposition to
" talk so fairly of these matters, whereof she a long time
" had scarcely seemed to think, (no occasion thereof being
" given by me,) presumeth some intended practice of hers
" lately overthrown. For sure I am, her melancholy and
" grief is greater than she in words uttereth. And yet ra- 140
" ther than continue this imprisonment, she sticks not to
" say, she will give her body, son, and country, for liberty.
" And here she infers, that . . . . This she gives out, to
" move some fear. God preserve the queen's majesty long
" in health."

And in another letter by the same earl, written in February this year, upon a letter from the French ambassador
to her, (which the lord treasurer had sent the earl to deliver to her,) and which she read in his sight, he writes,
that she said thereupon, " How she perceived, that am-
" bassador was informed of great sums of money re-
" ceived out of France into this realm to her use, as forty
" thousand crowns, known by some means of the duke.
" Truly, said she, I received not so much. But if the duke
" said so, quoth she, I will not deny it. Then she made a
" long discourse of the money she spent by the bishop of
" Rosse, termed her ambassador, and the bishop of Gall-

" way, with other her commissioners, and gifts also to her
" servants: which by her long tale amounted, I dare say,
" (writeth the earl,) to double the said sum. He [the earl]
" told her then plainly, that he had heard by sundry reports
" of divers sums of money to be secretly conveyed from time
" to time into this realm, to be employed for practices, to
" her use. Which being found true, or any part thereof, he
" said, she was of good reason to blame her own self for
" her wants, and none other. Nay, said she then, let them
" never be afraid (which she repeated divers times) of any
" money that I will have come into England. For I have
" given sure order, that all which I can make shall be em-
" ployed in my service in Scotland; which shall not be de-
" feated for ought they can do.

" The earl said again, that he spake not for any fear that
" was any way to be had in the matter: and that if she
" thought so, she was much deceived. But his speaking of
" those reports was, to move her the better to consider with
" herself where the fault was, if she wanted. Whereunto
" she replied not. But entered then into her wonted con-
" jectures, and said, I see now they go about some exploit,
" to be done in Scotland against me. And therefore would
" find means to hinder the coming of money to me, as out
" of France. But, said she, I have taken sure order for
" their relief in Scotland. And that the same may be the
" more large unto them, I will spend on myself here as little
" as I can.

" The earl asked her if she knew of any such intention
" or act in doing in Scotland against her. But he could
" not perceive by her answer that she understood any
" thing either of the present sieges, or otherwise of weight;
" but only occupied herself with suspicion, according to her
" old customs.

" As concerning her sending into France, or the coming
" of any from thence unto her, he could not but think
" much danger in either of them. For that certainly what-
" soever she pleaded of wants for herself and hers, her very
" meaning and desire is of intelligence and practice for her

" purpose, not tolerable. Albeit, if her majesty, of her plea-
" sure, will needs grant licence for one of these two ways,
" his opinion was, that the sending thither of some such
" her servants were most meet for providing her apparel
" and receipt of money necessary; so that they be not
" .... For sometimes discourses were of less danger
" than the coming of some expert persons from thence, that 141
" could not upon the sudden be judged of as well known
" here. But seeing such dangers to be, either in sending or
" coming, he must, he said, of good reason conclude with
" his lordship, the best way to be, that she might be li-
" censed to have some money brought from France to her,
" to serve for her necessaries. And that her majesty was
" now the more inclined to be suspicious of her doings, he
" could not but think she had great cause so to do, not
" only remembering that which is past, but also expecting
" the return of the cardinal of Lorain, with the rest of that
" house, and herself also principally; with the cruel inten-
" tions of every of them, well known to be toward her ma-
" jesty, and the state of this realm, if they had power and
" liberty to serve to their wills. This was dated from Shef-
" field castle the 20th of February, 1572."

And by way of postscript, he writes, that when he was
about to seal up this letter, she sent for him, and at his
coming brast out with complaints of her estate; especially,
how she was not well used in France, by such as she had
put in trust touching her living there; saying, that her
uncle, the cardinal, who chiefly pretended good-will unto
her, did so dispose her profits and casualties there, at his
own liberty, as nothing thereof came to her necessary use.
Wherefore she desired, that her new officer, whom she had
lately put in trust about her living, might have licence to
come and declare her state unto her. The name of this her
new officer, she said, was monsieur de Verge. This seems
to have been her device, to let in some intelligence from
France unto her.

And good reason there was for these suspicions of messengers from France, since the state had experience before

BOOK
I.

Anno 1572.

Linen sent
to the
queen;
with secret
writing in
it.

this, of the dangers of messages brought to her from thence. One whereof was in the month of December, when information was given by Walsingham, ambassador then in France, that there was linen to be sent to her from thence: and that he had discovered one that carried the box wherein it was put; which within three or four days departed thence. And communicating this to the lord treasurer he told him, that he thought they would see somewhat written in some of the linen, contained in the same box, that should be worth the reading; and cunningly advising, that her majesty, under colour of seeing the fashion of the ruffs, might cause the several pieces of linen to be holden before a fire, whereby the writing might appear. For that he judged there would be some matter discovered; which made him the more willing, as he said, to grant the passport.

142

CHAP. XVI.

*A league offensive and defensive with France. Delibera-
tion about the assistance of the prince of Orange. Duke
Montmorancy comes over ambassador. His reception.
Sir Philip Sydney goes into France with the English
ambassador. A motion made by the French ambassador
for duke d'Alençon's matching with the queen. His qualities. Lord Burghley's thoughts and advice concerning
it. The queen irresolute. Sir Philip Sydney's letter to
her against the match with France. Cases of conscience
in respect of marrying with a papist; and suffering
mass to be said. Answered favourably.*

W E will now return a little backward towards the beginning of this year, to take a view of the weighty affairs between France and England.

Sir Thomas Smith and Mr. Walsingham were both now in France, soliciting a good league between the two king-doms; and in the month of April effected it. Which was looked upon as an happy effect for this land. Smith certi-fied the lord treasurer, that at last they had concluded the league. In this league the French obliged themselves not to assist the Scottish queen; being content to make no mention of her, or of being her friend and ally; but gave her over to the queen's majesty, whatsoever demands they had made for her before. And in all things they relented to her majesty's desire; as Smith wrote; so that they might have colour to save the king their master's honour. And hereupon the said ambassador added, he hoped and trusted, it was the best league that ever was made with France, or any other nation, for her majesty's surety. And within a day or two after, they hoped to sign the treaty. This was writ April 17; and April 20, Smith writeth the same from Blois to the queen.

The French king's commissaries at this treaty were, The terms Francis duke of Montmorancy, Renatus Byragus, Sebastian and conditions of it. de Laubespine, episcop. Lemovicensis, and Paulus de Foix. Cott. libr. The queen's were, the said Smith and Walsingham. This Julius, F. 6. was a confederacy, league, and union, for mutual defence, against all persons of what order soever; who under any pretence whatsoever, and any cause, none excepted, do invade or shall invade, the persons, or territories by them possessed. And this league to remain firm, not only between the said princes, while they live, but also between their successors; if the successor shall signify to the survivor within a year, by ambassadors and letters, that he receiveth the same conditions. Otherwise the survivor shall be understood to be free of the observation of this league. And that the French should innovate nothing in Scotland.

In the next month, May the 7th, the said ambassador, 143 Smith, reflecting upon the benefit of this league, used these The benefit of this words; " That now it could not be said, her majesty was al- league. " together alone, having so good a defence, of so noble and " courageous a prince, and so faithful of his word, and so " near a neighbour, provided for, and bespoken beforehand " against any need, partly that [of the Scottish queen] and " partly the troubles in Flanders. Which God, he said, " had provided to deliver his poor servants there from the

Delibera-
tion for as-
sistance of
the prince
of Orange.

Walsing-
ham moves
it to the
lord Burgh-
ley, in order
to the safety
of England.

That it
concerned
France and
England to
join in aid-
ing the
prince.

"Antichristian tyranny." But our ambassador, however wary enough, and suspicious of that court, saw not yet the dissimulation of that French potentate.

But as this supposed good understanding with France was now effected for England, so it wanted defence from another implacable and more formidable enemy, the powerful monarch of Spain. In order to which, another great matter was now in hand, and under consultation; namely, concerning assisting the prince of Orange; who headed the free people of the Low Countries, intolerably oppressed and tyrannized over by duke d'Alva, the king's great officer there. And because France, equally with England, was in danger from that insulting prince, it was laboured, that both kingdoms should assist the said prince of Orange.

Walsingham is (now in May) persuading the lord Burghley to join with them in their resistance of that oppressive duke, and for aiding them of the Low Countries. He sent a messenger that month, throughly instructed touching the state of that country, and the proceedings in Flanders; and that he hoped, after that he had throughly debated the matter with him, it would manifestly appear unto him, that upon the good or evil success of this common cause of religion, and without the same well proceeded, her majesty could not promise to herself any great safety, having so dangerous a neighbour; whose greatness should receive no small increase, if he overcame this brunt. And in another letter he writ, that he perceived, that if there were no assistance given underhand by her majesty, they should be driven to such inconveniences as should be laid upon them by the nation of France: and further, that they should be forced to consent to have Strozzi [a sea-commander belonging to the French] in Zealand; unless they might have some supplies elsewhere.

And in July he acquainted the same lord, that one of great credit, (sent thither, [i. e. to Paris,] as it seems, from the prince of Orange,) told him, that it behoved the queen and the French king to consult jointly, in maintaining of that prince's enterprise. For that otherwise he saw many

reasons to induce him to think, that it would be dangerous
to them both; especially to her majesty, considering the
practices that reigned in her own country.   Anno 1572.

Walsingham shewing his zeal in this cause, wrote also in Walsing-
this aforesaid month to the great earl of Leicester, to the cester, to
like purpose: " That to suffer that prince to miscarry, the same
" knowing our own danger, were to lack both policy and July 26.
" magnanimity. That we could not deny, but upon that
" that lately was discovered, if God had not raised up that
" prince of Orange to entertain Spain, a dangerous [flame]
" ere this time had been kindled in her own home. To as- 144
" sist him therefore, added he, was to assist ourselves. For
" that we were to run one fortune with him. The difference
" was, that by miscarriage the mischief should first touch
" him, and then, consequently, as many of us as profess
" one religion with him. For the supply that was given
" by the pope, Florence, and divers catholic princes in
" Germany, shewed, that the quarrel was mixed, and con-
" sisted as well of religion as of state. That they failed
" not to make distinction thereof. And therein, said he,
" they shewed their courage and zeal. But contrariwise,
" we [i. e. of the English court] do nothing underhand;
" and thereby we did discover both lack of zeal and cou-
" rage." And here he made an observation ; " that no coun-
" sellor's enterprise accompanied with fear had ever good
" success. For there could be no greater enemy to sound
" counsel than fear." And then, speaking of the endeavours
of those of Flanders made to the French king, to assist
that prince, and about the queen's joining with that king
therein; " Surely, said he, though it import that king
" very much to look to it, yet that it more imported her
" majesty, and to look for nothing else (Spain overcoming
" this brunt) than the extremity of such mischief as he could
" work her." And so he excites the earl of Leicester to forward this cause.

And that these apprehensions of Walsingham were not The pope's
groundless, in the month of May, he sent over from against
France to the lord Burghley a gentleman, and with him England.

BOOK I.

Anno 1572.

certain advices out of Germany and Switzerland, which he had received, and that gentleman was privy to. Whereby his lordship might perceive, that the holy father's intention was, not only to trouble England, but all other places that professed the gospel. But now to return to this laboured friendship with France.

The commissioners sent for the signing of it.

This league was afterwards confirmed and signed by very honourable ambassadors sent over on both sides; viz. Montmorancy from France, and the lord admiral from England. There were other commissioners appointed to go with Montmorancy. One whereof was monsieur de Battaile, who died before he went. Of whom, this may *en passant* be mentioned: that having dissembled his religion, either for fear or interest, before his death he much lamented the same; and gave his advice to those about him, to resort to the reformed churches, and to bring up their children in the religion professed by the same; as Walsingham thought fit to impart in one of his letters from France.

Mon. Battaile.

The reception of Montmorancy here.

Great expectation there was of the coming of these ambassadors; the queen being determined to receive them very splendidly. At Dover were her officers of the household; and provisions there made for them. The earl of Pembroke, lord Windsor, lord Buckhurst, were there also with great and mighty trains. And the delay of the French (who made some stay in their coming) put the queen to vast charges. To court also at this time came flocking such levies of ladies to attend, as their husbands cursed the delay, as the lord Burghley said between jest and earnest. Duke Montmorancy, with all his train, to the number of forty, was received with great honour, being entertained for meat and drink, each in their degrees; as it was to be af-

145 firmed, (as the lord Burghley writ), the like had not been seen in any man's memory. That honour also done to him was such as her majesty could not do more, namely, in her courteous using of him, and by appointing sundry sorts of the nobility to attend him. The earl of Leicester feasted him. And at midsummer the lord treasurer also feasted him and all his gentlemen, with a collation of all things

that he could procure, being not flesh; to observe their
manner.

His reward (though not so great as the lord treasurer
could have wished) was a cupboard of plate gilt; a great
cup of gold, of one hundred and eleven ounces; and monsieur de Foix's was a cupboard of plate.

The admiral that now went to France was accompanied
with many young English gentlemen; and among the rest,
sir Philip Sidney, then but young, about eighteen. The
earl of Leicester his uncle writ to Walsingham at his going, tenderly, concerning him, to this tenor: " That foras-
" much as his nephew, Philip Sidney, was licensed to tra-
" vel, and did presently repair unto those parts with the
" lord admiral, he had thought good to commend him by
" those his letters friendly unto him, as unto one he was
" well assured would have a special care of him during his
" abode there. That he was young and raw, and no doubt
" should find those countries and the demeanour of the
" people somewhat strange to him. And that therefore his
" [Walsingham's] good advice and counsel should greatly
" behove him for his best directions. Which he [the earl]
" did most heartily pray him to vouchsafe him, with any
" friendly assistance he should see needful for him. That
" his father and he [the earl] did intend his further travel,
" if the world were quiet, and he [Walsingham] should
" think it convenient for him. Otherwise they prayed him,
" that they might be advertised thereof; to the end the
" same (his travels) might be thereupon directed accord-
" ingly." What experience this young gentleman learned
in France, and the small esteem he had for that court, we
shall hear by and by.

While Montmorancy was here, transacting and confirming
the treaty, another very weighty matter was in hand; namely, an earnest motion made by him for the queen's matching with duke d'Alençon, the French king's younger brother; (who was now but seventeen years of age.) A matter very acceptable to many of the queen's subjects; and
of the wisest and carefulest sort. Of those were the lord

Burghley and Walsingham. By the latter of these he was described advantageously, the better to recommend him to the English court. That for his stature and proportion, he left it to be expressed by word of mouth by sir Thomas Smith, Mr. Killigrew, and others, who had been lately in France and seen him. That as for his conditions, generally, this opinion was conceived of him, that he was of as good and tractable a disposition as any, either prince or gentleman, in France; and withal, both wise and stout, and subject to the French lightness. So that they did apply to him the French proverb, *Qu'il a de plume en son cerceau.* That he was confirmed in it (beside the general opinon) by the admiral [Coligni,] count Rochefoucault, Tilligny, and 146 others of the best judgment of the religion, with their earnest protestation: so that he could not but credit the same.

His qualities and conditions.

146

The admiral debated with Walsingham (as he farther related to the lord Burghley) in this matter; and protested sundry times to him, calling God to witness, that he would not advise the queen unto it, if he thought it would not prove both honourable, profitable, and comfortable, and for her safety. And for his religion, they had great hope, grounded upon good conjecture, that he was easy to be reduced to the knowledge of the truth. Walsingham added, that for his part he had many great reasons to induce him to think, that if there were no other impediments than the use of his mass, that he would be easily induced to embrace the same.

Admiral Coligni is earnest for it.

His religion.

And touching his affection towards the queen, Walsingham was informed, that where it had been objected to him, that he would be glad to have the title of a king; he protested, that if he were not moved with a great and honourable report of her majesty's rare virtues, more than at any desires he had to a kingdom, he would never have desired the king, nor the queen his mother, to have made any mention thereof.

His affection towards the queen.

Touching the devotions of his followers and servants towards the propounded match, Walsingham tells, how he

The inclinableness of his servants.

was informed, that they also earnestly desired the same;
especially those whose advice he chiefly used. Who though
they were not of the religion, yet were not enemies to the
same; and rather inclined that way than otherwise. Of the
which a dozen of them were discharged of his brother's service in respect thereof.

All this was in answer to what the lord treasurer Burgh- Lord Burghley had writ to Walsingham; being willed by the greatest ley's inquiries; and
to require the said ambassador to use all good means pos- thoughts of
this match.
sible to understand what he could of that duke, viz. of his
age, his stature, his conditions, his inclination to religion,
his devotion this way, the devotion of his followers and ser-
vitors. And hereof her majesty sought speedily to be advertised. That she might resolve within a month. For the
ambassadors, upon their going home, did what they could
in that matter. Whereunto they had neither yea nor nay,
but delay only for a month. That wise lord's present
thoughts were, (as he signified in his correspondence to that
English ambassador,) that he could not see in her majesty
at that time any lack towards this, but in opinion for the
age. Which defect, if it might be supplied with some recompence, it were meet to be thought of. He wished we
might have Calais to the issue of their bodies : and he to be
governor thereof during his life : so as the English might
have security for their staple there. He wished also, that
secretly the queen's majesty might be assured, that (although there be no contract therefore,) he would hear no
mass after his marriage.

But however this lord and that ambassador laboured to The differ-
bring this marriage about, the queen, it appeared now by ence of age
disliked by
the month of July, had little inclination unto it. The dif- the queen.
ference of age undoubtedly might be one cause. And thus
did that lord express his mind in this matter to that ambassador in the month aforesaid : " That the queen found the 147
" marriage to be necessary for her; and yet the opinion of
" others misliking of that party, for the *person*, did more
" hinder her purpose than her own conceit. And that he
" saw such difficulties on both sides, that he could make no

" choice for no marriage.   That all evils must be looked
" for; and for marriage without liking, no good could be
" hoped thence.   Therefore to God he left it.   He saw, as
" he added, his negotiations there full of perplexities ; and
" prayed God to direct him : for he found the queen very
" irresolute."

Surely all this present negotiation about marriage was
rather to blind the queen's and every Englishman's eyes,
against the bloody massacre that was now hatching, and the
next month executed.   And further to blind her eyes, a
messenger was sent this month to the queen, to tell her of
the intended marriage of the lady Margaret with the king of
Navarr, as though it was going now to be fair weather with
the protestants.

These amours were continued both this year and the
next.   I will draw what I find more of it into this place.   In
the midst of this wooing happened the barbarous and inhuman massacre in France, which justly put a stop to it:
the English nation abhorring the action, and all those that
Sir Philip
Sydney to
the queen,
dissuading
her from
marriage.
were concerned in it.   Among the rest, young Philip Sydney, that was at Paris at the execution, took the freedom to
express his mind to the queen not long after, in a private
letter, shewing his dissuasion from matching there, though
with all humble and dutiful address.   The contents whereof,
and some remarkable sentences, I have met with among
some papers of sir Michael Hicks, sometime secretary to the
lord Burghley ; which I shall here set down, (in the want of
MSS. Mich.
Hicks, eq.
the complete letter,) both to give a light into this matter,
and to preserve any remainders of that incomparable man.

" To arm an excuse with reasons, were to acknowledge
" that I did willingly amiss.   It were folly to lay on fair
" colours, where judgment is so ready to discern of the
" thing itself, &c.   Therefore bearing no other olive branch
" of intercessions than my unfeigned good-will, nor using
" any other information, &c.   A matter of great import-
" ance, importing both the continuance of your safety, and
" the joys of my life; shallow words, springing from the
" deep well of affection.   Having travailed long time in

" thought do now declare; not able to suppress it any
" longer, it striveth so vehemently to discover itself......
" Nothing can be added to your estate, being already an
" absolute born, and accordingly reputed princess.   As the
" Irish are wont to say, *What need have they to do any*
" *thing, that are rich and fair ?* So, what need have you
" to change the course of your estate, settled in such a
" calm...... To so healthful a body to apply so unsavoury
" a medicine...... What hope to recompense so hazard-
" ous an adventure, as to alter so well a maintained and
" approved trade?...... Sudden change in bodies na-
" tural, dangerous; much more in politic.   Hazard, then
" meetest to be regarded, when the nature of the agent
" and patient fitly composed to occasion them...... The
" realm patient, majesty agent...... A true inward strength
" resisteth outward accidents.   An inward weakness doth
" not lightly subvert itself without foreign force...... The 148
" treasure, the sinews of the crown; the league, the love of
" the subject.

" Two factions [the papist and the protestant] irrecon-
" cileable...... By your dealings at home and abroad,
" against our adverse party, you are so enwrapt to the
" other, that you cannot pull yourself out.   As a ship, al-
" though it be beaten with waves and tempests, yet there
" is no safety but within it...... The protestant the chief,
" if not your sole strength.   They cannot be, nor look for
" better estate than that they be...... Their hearts galled,
" if not aliened, when you marry a Frenchman and a pa-
" pist: the son of the very Jezebel of our age; although
" fine wits excuse it. His brother [the French king Charles]
" made oblation of his sister's marriage, [with the protestant
" king of Navarr,] that he might massacre of all sexes......
" Himself, contrary to his promise and gratefulness, having
" his [dependence] and chiefest estate by the Hugonots,
" sacked *la charité.* This maketh all true religious to abhor
" such a master, and to diminish that love they have long
" time borne you.

" The papist spirits full of anguish, forced to [take] oaths

" [of allegiance, &c.] they counted damnable. . . . . . Ambi-
" tion stopt. . . . . . [Laid] in prison, disgrace, banishment
" of their best friends. . . . . . Some think you an usurper.
" Some think the king [your father] is rightly disallowed
" by the pope. . . . . . Burdened with the weight of their
" consciences. . . . . . [They consist of] greater numbers, and
" riches, because they have not offices laid upon them. . . . . .
[They have] united minds, as all oppressed are.

 " Joined to these discontented persons, either for want;
" *quibus opus est bello civili,* as Cæsar said; or such as
" have high minds, and are not advanced. These men most
" dangerous. They embrace all estates, and stay but ad-
" vantage of time.

 " I am glad, I may say, they did not prevail. For if
" they had, it had been no time now to deliberate. . . . . .
" These people want but a head, and such a head [as mon-
" sieur] wanteth but a few of their instructions. . . . . . That
" occasion, with a small show of title, [i. e. king of Eng-
" land,] will do for a turn. Remember Warbeck; and
" Lewis the French king's son, in Henry the Third's time.
" That monsieur is to be judged by his will and power. His
" will is as full of high ambition as is possible. French dis-
" position. His education is in constant attempts against
" his brother. His thrusting into the Low Countries. . . . . .
" Sometimes suitor to the king of Spain's daughter; some-
" times to you. . . . . . Carried away with every wind of
" hope. . . . . . Taught to love greatness any way gotten. . . . . .
" The motioners and ministers of his mind only young men,
" that have seen no commonwealth. Defiled with odious
" murder; apt to rebellion.

 " How will he be content to be the second person in Eng-
" land, that cannot be in France, and heir apparent? His
" power great. . . . . . The way will be made for him. Who
" needs nought, but an head to draw evil humours. . . . . . Of
" great revenues. . . . . . A populous nation of the world;
" especially of soldiers, that have learnt to serve without
" pay, where their hope is the spoil. . . . . . His brother ready
" to help for old revenges; as also to keep him occupied

" from troubling France ; and also to carry naughty fellows
" out of his country.

" King Philip and queen Mary, all of one religion. The
" house of France ready to impeach any his attempts. And 149
" yet, what might have been the event of that marriage,
" your gracious reign hath made void...... Your realm
" ready to receive hurt. M. [monsieur] ready to [take
" hold of] the occasion to hurt [us in our] peace, and the
" fruits of peace.

" There cannot happen any thing more full of evident
" danger to your estate royal...... Your person the scale
" of our happiness. What good can come to balance with
" the loss of so honourable constancy ? ..... I will not shew
" so much malice, as to object the doubts of the unhealth-
" fulness of the whole race...... His proceedings in his suit
" agree like hot and cold...... I will temper my speeches
" from any particular disgrace, though never so true......
" If he come, either [he must] have the keys of your king-
" dom, or live in lower reputation than his mind will bear ;
" or depart far off, displeased more than before...... If it
" be unprofitable for your kingdom, and unpleasant for
" you, [it is] too dear a purchase for repentance...... You
" can have by him no bliss but children...... He cannot
" enrich you ; for he hath not ; or else to bestow other-
" wise...... To ease you of the cares of government, is as
" much as to ease you of being queen. This may hurt ; if
" not, at the best, it cannot help.

" The mention of charges, [viz. from] foreign fears, and
" the Low Countries. Those buildings most firm that stand
" upon their own foundation...... A true Masinissa......
" It were not fit to contrary the enterprises of mighty Car-
" thage. And if it were, how can this be applied to M.
" [monsieur.] ..... Strongest leagues are made between
" such as are joined by a vehement desire of a third thing :
" ours a vehement fear...... Parallels can never join truly,
" because they maintain different ends...... Contrary prin-
" ciples cannot beget one doctrine...... He a papist ; and
" if he be a man, must needs have that manlike proportion,

" to desire all to be of his mind.   He desirous to make
" France great.   Your majesty meaneth nothing less than
" that it should grow so, especially by England. . . . . . He
" by his own fancy, and youthful governors, embraceth all
" ambitious hopes; having Alexander's image in his hall,
" ill painted.

  " Your majesty [taught] by virtue, if you should hope;
" by wisdom, what you may hope. . . . . . Your council re-
" nowned over all Christendom for their tempers and minds,
" having set the uttermost of their ambition in your favour,
" and the study of their souls in your safety. . . . . . No ex-
" ample in the world fit to blazon you by. . . . . . No men
" ever weary of a good prince.   For either men never saw
" other [than you,] or are too old to have joy, to seek
" other. . . . . . Abuse in government ruineth of itself.   Our
" neighbour's fire giveth us light to see our own quiet-
" ness. . . . . . Examples of good princes [shew] the longer
" they reign, the deeper they sink in the subjects' hearts.
" The subjects willingly grant and dutifully pay subsidies,
" and all impositions demanded.   Less troublesome to you
" now, in making request [for them] than in the beginning
" of your reign.

150   " For *succession*, albeit I have cast the uttermost anchor
" of my hope ;   yet for England's sake I will not say ought
" against any such determination. . . . . . That uncertain good
" shall bring contest to [obtain] good, beyond all reach of
" reason. . . . . . The *rising sun* first used by Scylla to Pom-
" pey.   *Rising* and *falling* dependeth upon a popular
" choice. . . . . . In a lineal monarchy, when the infants suck,
" where there is the love of their rightful prince, who would
" leave the beams of so fair a sun, for the dreadful expe-
" rience of a divided company of stars ? . . . . . Virtue and
" justice [are] the bands only of love. . . . . . By your loss
" all blindness light upon him that seeth not our misery.
" [It is time] to look after the ship brought, after we see
" we cannot be safe in the ship [wherein we are.] . . . . . The
" best rule is to do so, as they may not justly speak evil of
" you.   Augustus the emperor [said,] *But let them speak*

" *evil, since they cannot do much hurt.* Charles V. when
" one said, *Hollandois portent mal,* answered, *Mais ils pai-*
" *ent bien.*...... Care not for the barking of curs, being
" carried upon the wings of innocence.

" I durst with blood avow, never prince was had in more
" precious account of her subjects. Some loose wretch may
" defile such a name, but cannot raze out the impression of
" love you have made in such a multitude of hearts. Their
" love cannot fade, if you keep in your own likeness, and
" alter not yourself in other colours. *Metus in authorem*
" *redit.*

" He can bring no more good than any body else ; evil he
" may, [i. e. monsieur.] ..... Either fear of that which can-
" not happen, or by him cannot be prevented...... You
" have stood alone a great while. Take it for a singular
" honour God hath done you, to be the only protector of
" his church. And so may continue for worldly respects,
" if you continue, and make religion your strength. And
" those whom you find trusty, to be employed in the affairs,
" to be held up in the eyes of your subjects.

" This man, as long as he is but monsieur, in might can-
" not stead you ; and being a papist, he will not. And if
" he be king of France, his defence will be like Ajax's
" shield, that rather weighed down those that bear it, than
" defended them."

For besides the disproportion of age, which was one of
the queen's great objections, another obstacle to the current
proceeding of this marriage was the matter of religion, it
being looked upon as a matter of conscience. Which was
reduced to two cases. The one was, whether it were lawful
for a protestant to marry with a papist. And the other,
whether the queen might permit to have mass said in her
kingdom. For the better informing of the lord Burghley in
both these, being the queen's greatest counsellor, and in
whose advice she chiefly reposed herself, some learned divines were employed to write their judgments according to
the word of God. There are several tracts I have met with
among that lord's papers, written in resolution of both these

Two cases
of consci-
ence con-
cerning this
marriage.

BOOK I.

Anno 1572.

151

Nº. XV. XVI. XVII. XVIII.

questions, some negatively, and some affirmatively. Wherein objections were answered that made it unlawful: and a book writ to that purpose confuted, in favour of the match. These tracts I look upon as valuable, consisting of the arguments then made use of among the learned, in the points of difference between the church of Rome and the protestants. They that are minded to consult them may read some of them in the Appendix. But by assailing of the arguments and objections made against the marriage, it appears how inclinable and desirous the chief men generally were for the accomplishing thereof.

Lord Burghley's cares for the public in respect of this match. Compl. Amb.

I add to the rest what the lord treasurer wrote in March to Walsingham in France, as the result of his serious thoughts of this weighty matter: " That he saw the immi-" nent perils to this state; and namely, how long soever " she should by course of nature live and reign, the success " of this crown so manifestly uncertain, or rather too mani-" festly prejudicious for the state of religion, that he could " not but still persist in seeking for marriage for her ma-" jesty. And finding no way that was liking to her but " this with the duke, he did force himself to pursue it with " desire; and did flatter himself with imaginations, that if " he [the duke d'Alençon] should come hither, her majesty " would not refuse him. And for his religion, methinks," added that lord, " if he were otherwise liked, he would not " lose a queen with a kingdom, for a priest's blessing of a " chalice."

CHAP. XVII.

The massacre at Paris. Many nobles and others of the
English nation preserved in Walsingham's house there.
Among the rest, Mr. Philip Sydney. Walsingham about
departing home. The king relates to him the reason he
took this course. Walsingham writes of these matters
into England. The French ambassador comes to the
queen. Her excellent speech to him of the admiral's mur-
der ; and her advice to the king. Some account of the
massacre. Nothing but extremity towards those of the
religion. England now upon its guard. Roulard, a
catholic, murdered.

BUT that hideous inhuman massacre of the king's pro- Anno 1572.
testant subjects in France, in this very juncture, broke off The massa-
that pretendedly good understanding and friendship with cre at Paris happens
him, that the queen and her court were too credulous to be- about this
lieve and to take a satisfaction in. For by this horrible act time of treaty with
they might plainly see, how abhorred all those that pro- France.
fessed the true religion were to France.

Walsingham, the queen's ambassador, was at this time in The Eng-
Paris. And it was a wonderful escape he had, that in that lish fly to the ambas-
hot zeal for popery, he was not murdered, undistinguished, sador, and
with the rest. For whether it were by some order from the escape the massacre.
king, or otherwise, not only himself, but those of the Eng-
lish nation that could escape to his house, were preserved.
And among the rest was one Tim. Bright, doctor of physic ; 152
who divers years after, viz. anno 1589, published an abridg- Abridgment of John Fox's Book of Martyrs : and in his dedica- ment of the Book of
tion, which he made to sir Francis Walsingham, he remem- Martyrs by
bered that great benefit that both he and many others, Eng- T. Bright, quarto.
lish, and of other nations too, strangers then in Paris, received ; being preserved in his house from being massacred.
" And so the benefit was common to many. And that his
" lordship's house at that time was a very sanctuary, not
" only to all of our nation, but even to many strangers then
" in Paris, that were virtuously disposed to true religion.

" So was it therefore the most memorable deliverance, and
" far more honourable, and bound him, as he said, with
" great obligations of thankfulness; who thereby had cause
" to rejoice, not only for his own safety, but for so many of
" his countrymen, partly of his acquaintance, and partly of
" noble houses of this realm; who had all tasted of the
" rage of that furious tragedy, had not his honour shrouded
" them."

Among the
rest Mr.
Philip Syd-
ney.
Several of the privy council declared themselves beholden
to Walsingham for the harbouring these gentlemen: many
whereof were related to them; as they did wisely in retiring
thither. And in this emergence they desired the ambassador to advise those gentlemen to return home, as their safest
course, having seen enough of France. And particularly
for the lord Wharton, (whose schoolmaster was slain,) and
Mr. Philip Sydney, to procure the king's licence and conduct to come thence. And further advised him, that if he
could get leave from the king, to come home too, till matters were better settled there; (and that so was the queen's
mind;) leaving a secretary there. But the queen afterwards
was unwilling yet to send for him. The lord treasurer and
secretary Smith (knowing the worth of the man, and the
danger he was in) had been suitors to her majesty, more
than once, for his return: which she at length granted, and
then strait revoked, the letters being written, and immediately called back. So that in a letter to him, dated September the 12th, the secretary told him, he saw he must endure
there for a time, which he trusted would not be long.

The queen
upon send-
ing for her
ambassador
home.

Walsing-
ham's dan-
ger told by
some come
from
thence.
About this very time came to the court three gentlemen,
viz. Fawnte, Argol, and South, from France; who did amplify the cruel disorders there; and thereupon Walsingham's
danger, that was talked of in every man's ears. Whereof his
friends made relation to the queen. The effect was, finally,
that she was content to write her letter for his return to the
French king, dated from Woodstock. Which letter, when
the said ambassador-had delivered to the king, he would
not yield to the revocation; saying, that he must then recall
his ambassador at the English court, which would look as

if the amity were broke: and therefore prayed Walsingham to speak no more of it. And so he continued there still.

But to look a little upon this massacre, and the behaviour of the king after it was done, and the consequences and effects of it with respect to the English court. But a day or two after, (viz. August 26,) Walsingham sent his secretary to the queen-mother, willing him, in his name, to thank her and the king for the great care it pleased them to have of his safety, and for the preservation of the English nation in this last tumult: and that he would not fail to make honourable report of it unto the queen's majesty, his mistress. And the secretary was to add, that since there were divers reports made of the late execution there, and that he [the ambassador] would be very loath to credit reports; that it would please their majesties to send him the very truth; to the end he might accordingly advertise the queen's majesty. The answer of the queen-mother was, that the king and she gave special command, that good regard were had of him, and all the English, as a thing that tended to the preservation of good amity between the king and the queen's majesty. And that if he could devise any better means for his greater safeguard, he would give them understanding thereof. To the second message, she said, that monsieur La Mot, the French ambassador, had, she doubted not, advertised the queen's majesty of the late accidents there. Nevertheless, to gratify him, she would cause secretary Pinart to send him an abstract of that which the king before had sent to his ambassador there resident. This abstract Walsingham received, and sent it to Smith enclosed in this letter, wherein he informed him of all this. And added, that the duke of Nevers had shewed himself much affected to the English nation; who spared not to come and visit Walsingham in his own person, with offer of all kind courtesy, not only to him, but to divers other English gentlemen. And besides, entertained three English gentlemen, that otherwise had been in great jeopardy of their lives.

Soon after, viz. the 1st of September, the king (whose business now was to excuse his barbarity as well as he could)

Anno 1572.
His message to the king upon the massacre. With the answer.

153

sent for the English ambassador, and withal sent two persons of eminency, and a dozen other gentlemen, to conduct him safely. Being come into his presence, he told him, he sent for him to satisfy him of the late execution, whereof, he said, men might judge diversely; and that he had, for the satisfying of the world, caused the process to be made of the admiral, [Coligni murdered in his bed,] and the rest of the conspirators. And that as soon as it should be finished, he would not fail to send it unto her majesty, his good sister; who, he did assure himself, would interpret in good part his doings. He being constrained, to his great grief, to do that which he did for his own safety sake; and which if he had not done, both he himself, his mother, and brethren, had been in danger of their lives. And that he desired nothing more than to continue, or rather increase, amity with her majesty. And therefore hoped, that she would not take occasion, upon this late proceeding, to suspect the contrary. To which Walsingham gave a prudent and agreeable answer to the king. And then he made the king acquainted, that three of this nation were slain, and that divers were spoiled. For which, when the king shewed himself to be very sorry, and said, that if the offenders of that party could be produced, there should be exemplary justice used, Walsingham said, it would be hard to produce them, the disorder being so general, and the sword being committed to the common people.

Afterwards the queen-mother, to disguise the matter, sent a writing to him, to be sent to the queen, expressing the summary of this fact: which seemed to be described in a disguised method, to cover the execrable manner thereof. And being in her presence, she shewed him, that the king's meaning was, that the heads of the conspirators being now taken away, to continue the edicts, and that every man should live in repose and liberty of his conscience. But this was only still to blind the poor protestants, that they being now secure, might in greater numbers fall into the hands of the butchers, and not stand upon their own guard, nor to revenge themselves.

The queen-
mother's
dissimula-
tion con-
cerning the
protestants.

For Walsingham, in his correspondence with secretary
Smith, let him understand, in a letter dated September 13,
that albeit it was shewn him, that the heads being taken
away, the meaner sort should enjoy, by virtue of the edicts, *That they should have*
both lives and goods, and liberty of their consciences; which *the liberty*
notwithstanding also was assured by print, [which print he *of their con-*
enclosed in his letter,] yet nothing thereof was performed; *sciences.*
but all extremity used. Which manner of proceeding was
by the catholics themselves utterly condemned, as he added.
And that they desired to depart thence out of such a country, to quit themselves of this strange kind of government;
for that they saw none could here assure themselves either
of goods or life.

He further gave him intelligence: That even still at *The cruel-*
Lions, Bourdeaux, and Orleans, great and most barbarous *ties in Lyons,*
cruelties had been executed. And that at Orleans divers of *Bourdeaux,*
the Almains had been slain and spoiled. The most part of *and Or-*
them put to the ransom. For that since justice took not place *leans.*
there, they forbore to require redress, but departed thence
with great desire of revenge. And further, that they were
preparing the Bastile for some persons of quality: and it
was thought it was for the prince of Condé and his brethren.
Marshal Montmorancy was commanded, as it was said, to
keep his house, and to forbear to make any assembly.

The news of this cruelty was soon brought to England *News brought*
by several first, that escaped from Diep; bringing the news *hither of*
of the admiral's murder, with a great multitude of the reli- *the massa-*
gion, on the 24th of August, in a most cruel sort: as upon *cre.*
the first intelligence thereof the lord treasurer, the earl of
Leicester, and others of the privy council, wrote, September
9, unto Walsingham; and that it gave to her majesty no
small cause of grief: and so much the more, in that she
could hear no manner of certainty thereof from him. Of
whose person also in such a horrid time, her majesty was
very careful. And notwithstanding the French ambassador *The queen's*
affirmed to her, that he was in safety, she was not quiet in *care for Walsing-*
mind for him, until his own servant came, who had stayed *ham.*
long in Bulloin for a wind.

BOOK I.

Anno 1572.

La Mot's account to the queen of the cause of this execution.

In the mean time the king, as soon as might be, ordered La Mot to represent this bloody fact of his, as fair as might be; namely, that he was of necessity, for safeguard of his life, forced to cause such execution to be done upon the admiral and his accomplices: for that he and they had conspired his death. Of which matter the king was very well able to make a verification. And that her majesty should shortly see, by the process of the admiral then in making. And that nothing was meant by the king against the cause of religion.

155

To prevent a desperate conspiracy to seize the king.

For thus he related the matter to the queen and council, when he came to the court; that when his master the king heard that the admiral was wounded, (which he was two days before, being shot out of a window,) he was greatly grieved thereat, and that he determined to have done due justice upon the authors of it. In which mind he continued until Saturday, [two days after,] late at night. At which time advertisement was given him, that the admiral and his friends had concluded not to expect the order of the king for the punishment of the fact, but would avenge themselves; and that they would certainly seize the person of the king, queen-mother, and his brethren: and so his person and theirs should be in danger, and a new war should thereby be begun. And to make this to be true in the king's sight, it was also informed, that some such as were of this confederacy with the admiral had for conscience sake disclosed the same; and that it was made the more probable to the king, by reason of certain bold speeches used by Teligny [the admiral's son-in-law] to the king. Whereupon, said the ambassador, the king was so daunted with the present fear of his own person, and his mother, and his brethren, and of the imminent danger of a new civil war; and being thus overcome with this extremity, and having no time long to deliberate thereupon, (scarce the space of an hour,) he was in this manner forced to yield to another extremity; which was, to suffer the parties that were enemies to the admiral to proceed to the execution of him, although not with such a general fury as was used.

After the ambassador had made this fair story, he prayed CHAP.
the queen to shew her compassion of the king, rather than XVII.
to condemn him, making great assurance of the king's in- Anno 1572.
nocency herein; for the intention of his own part being only
for his defence and safety, against the perils discovered to
him by the informers. And that the king might find comfort of her, in condoling with him for this so miserable and
lamentable an accident.

But all this was but a second invention to palliate this
crime, and a purpose of committing more. For the king's
first report of it to the queen, by his own letters, was quite
different; whereby the English court concluded all to be but
fable, with intent to put a false covering over that horrible
fact. For thus did the lord Burghley declare the matter in
his correspondence with Walsingham.

" The French ambassador, in his negotiation, did seek to A fable in-
" persuade us, that the king was forced, for safety of his vented to cover the
" own life, to cause that execution to be done as it was; and murder of
" that thereof we should see the proofs by the admiral's the admiral.
" process. And then added, You may imagine how hard a
" thing it is for us to be persuaded against our natural
" senses. And how they will accord these two jars, we
" know not: for the king's letters first written after the ad-
" miral's death did declare it to be done in manner of sedi-
" tion, and privately, by the house of Guise; who were
" afraid that the admiral and his friends would pursue
" against them the avenge for his hurt, [by shooting him.]
" And that the king's own guard [which he sent to be]
" about the admiral, was forced; and the king himself 156
" driven to hold the guards about him in the Louvre for
" his defence. And now yet it must needs be notified, that
" the king did, for his own security, cause the execution to
" be done."

But this latter pretence the aforesaid privy counsellors, in The queen's
their letter, soon acquainted Walsingham with; namely, prudent an- swer to the
how that ambassador disguised the black business, and made French am-
a fair tale of the admiral's intention to seize the king, the bassador.
queen-mother, and his brethren. The said counsellors did

then shew him, how very wisely and princely the queen answered the ambassador, viz. to this effect: " That although
" upon the first report of the general murder of so many,
" being all under his protection in the principal city, it was
" very hard to conceive well of the king, yet it had been
" her former opinion of the singular integrity of his actions ;
" and namely, of his many outward favours that he had,
" since the time of the admiral's coming to his presence,
" shewed him, and his friends, that howsoever this fact of
" itself, with the circumstances of so many horrible murders,
" did outwardly charge the king with all manner of dis-
" honour that might touch a prince ; yet she, particularly
" for reverence of his princely state, for her love she bare
" him ; and finally, for that she had not yet received the in-
" formation from him, did determine with herself not to
" pronounce any evil judgment of the king, nor yet to con-
" ceive that which the most part of all others did conceive
" of him.

" But now that she had heard (as she proceeded) by him,
" the ambassador, in what sort the king had willed him to
" declare the process thereof, she did much desire the con-
" sideration of the king's honour, and the continuance of
" the amity with him. And that she most heartily willed
" that he might so use the matter in time, as the world
" might find him excusable in one of these two sorts ; that
" is, that either it might be made manifest to indifferent
" persons, (that is, to such as were not known to have borne
" deadly malice to the admiral and his party, now mur-
" dered,) that if the confirmation that was given to the king,
" of the admiral's evil intention and conspiracy against him,
" were grounded upon truth, and not upon malice or pre-
" text, and if the information might be verified, then might
" the king be excused in some part, both towards God and

Her dis-
course with
him about
the murder
of the ad-
miral, &c.

" the world, in permitting the admiral's enemies by force to
" prevent his enterprises. Although, indeed, the same in-
" formations had been true, yet the manner of the cruelty
" used (as she went on well) could not be allowed in any
" kingdom or government ; and least in that place where

" the king might, by order of justice, have done due execu- CHAP.
" tion, both to the admiral and all others that should have   XVII.
" proved offenders. For (as she said) it could not be de-Anno 1572.
" nied, but the same force that murdered so many mul-
" titudes, might more easily have attached them all, or the
" principals ; and brought them to answer to justice, when
" the king would. And of all other the admiral, being on
" his bed, lamed both on his right hand and left arm, lying
" in danger under the care of chirurgeons ; being also
" guarded about his private house with a number of the
" king's guards, and so might have been, by a word of the
" king's mouth, brought to any place, to have answered,
" when and how the king should have thought meet.

    " But the fault thereof, (as she continued,) as to the dis-157
" order of proceeding, however the information had been
" true, she forbore to impute to the king ; but left the same
" to the burden of others about him, whose age and know-
" ledge ought in such a case to have foreseen how offenders
" ought to be punished with the sword of the prince, and not
" with the bloody swords of murderers, being also the mortal
" enemies of the party murdered. The information whereof,
" for the recovery of the king's honour, (which was by the
" facts of others herein greatly touched,) she left to the king
" to be considered, and willed him opportunity to do what
" should be to God's honour and to his own praise.

    " But on the other side, (as the queen more closely sug-Her serious
" gested,) if such information, so suddenly given to the advice to
                                                          the king on
" king against the admiral, should not be duly and mani-this emer-
" festly, without subornation, proved true, (as therein surely gence.
" the manner of the circumstances did lead all indifferent
" persons to think the same not only falsely forged, of pri-
" vate deadly malice to the admiral and his party, but also
" perilously devised, to weaken the king's estate, and to de-
" prive him of the great honour and surety that daily was
" growing unto him by counsels or services of the said ad-
" miral, and his friends, now murdered,) her majesty then
" found the cause of so great importance to be pitied ; wish-
" ing him to have grace to use his power, by faithful coun-

" sellors and servants, to make an example to the world of
" the same manner of punishment on such detestable traitor-
" ous attempts: whereby his honour, which was then much
" blemished, might be saved; but principally himself and
" his person and surety be in good time provided for. And
" further, she added, that if it should please him therein
" to require the use of her advice, and of her assistance,
" she should not fail but to shew herself in this time a per-
" fect friend to him, by all good means that were in her
" power."

The queen's
thoughts of
the protes-
tants' tak-
ing up of
arms.

Then particularly, as to the admiral, she subjoined,
" That she was very sorry for his death, as for one whom
" she thought a very good minister to continue amity be-
" tween them two. And for the rest of the noblemen, she
" had reason to bewail them for the like cause. And that
" as he, the French ambassador, could well tell, she could
" never allow of the taking up of arms contrary to the king's
" commandment. But now perceiving of the king's receiv-
" ing them to grace, and taking them to his protection, and
" that it was by consequence of things manifest, that the
" taking of arms was not against the king's state or person,
" but to defend themselves in the profession of their reli-
" gion, according to the king's own edicts and grants, she
" did greatly lament their deaths; and that she did surely
" persuade herself, that if the king should not use his power
" to make some amends for so much blood, so horridly shed,
" God, who saw the hearts of all, as well princes as others,
" would shew his justice in time and place; when his honour
" should therein be glorified, as the author of all justice, and
" the revenger of all bloodshedding of the innocent."

I could not abridge this noble and admirable admonition
of the queen, to that king's ambassador, shewing both her
wisdom and piety, and intimating this treachery to be too
158 broad to be covered from her by any pretences; and fore-
warning that king of divine justice and revenge; which, indeed, as a prophecy, fell upon him most remarkably but the
next year.

The process
against the

It may be observed here, by the way, that when the queen

had desired for her satisfaction that she might understand CHAP.
particularly the conspiracy of the admiral, which was made XVII.
the ground of the massacre; and which both the queen- Anno 1572.
mother and the king had promised, viz. that the process admiral not
against him should be transmitted to her, as was related be- the queen.
fore; it was not done October 8, pretending it was not yet
ready. And then Brulart, that came from the king to Walsingham, told him, it should be sent to the queen as soon as
it was finished; though, he added, the king had hoped, that
without further suspense she would have given credit to
him, as he would have done in the like case to her.

It would be too tedious to relate all the particulars of this
massacre. Only that this age may have some *idea* of such
a never-to-be-forgotten wickedness, brought about by popish
zealots, take it from a French historian, that writ the history
of France, from the reign of Henry II. to Henry IV. French
kings, translated into English. The beginning of it was
thus: " The palace clock struck. Then a noise was heard An account
" about the streets of Paris, that the Hugonots were in arms, sacre.
" (they being in their beds,) and meant to kill the king, History of
" &c. The gentlemen, officers of the chamber, governors, chap. ix.
" tutors, and household servants of the king of Navarr and p. 256.
" prince of Condé, were driven out of their chambers, where
" they slept, in the Louvre; and being in the court, mas-
" sacred in the king's presence. The like was done to the
" lords and gentlemen that lay about the admiral's lodgings;
" and then throughout the town, in such sort, that the num-
" ber slain that Sunday night, and the two days ensuing,
" within the city of Paris and the suburbs, was esteemed to
" be about 10,000 persons; lords, gentlemen, pages, ser- The num-
" vants, and of all sorts; justices, scholars, lawyers, physi- sacred.
" cians, merchants, artificers, women, maids, boys; not
" sparing little children in the cradles, or in their mothers'
" bellies."

The courtiers of the king's guard, and strangers, that
massacred the gentlemen belonging to the king of Navarr
and prince of Condé, said, that in one day, by weapons,
they had ended those processes, which pen, paper, sentences

BOOK I.

Anno 1572.

Accused slanderous-ly of con-spiracy against the king.

of justice, and open war, could not find the means to execute in twelve years' space. These honourable lords and gentlemen protestants, slanderously accused of conspiracy and practice against the king, being stark naked, thinking only upon their rest, scarce awakened, unarmed, in the hands of infinite cruel, crafty, and treacherous enemies, not having so much leisure as to breathe, were slain, some in their beds, others upon the roofs of houses, and in whatever other place they might be found.

The admiral's head sent to Rome.

The admiral's head was carried and presented to the king and to the queen-mother; and then embalmed, and sent to Rome, to the pope, and the cardinal of Lorain. The common people cut off his hands and his privy members, and drew his body for the space of three days about the city. Which done, it was borne to the gibbet of Montfaucon, and there hanged by the feet.

159

The num-ber and cruelty of the cut-throats.

" Let the reader herein consider, (saith that French au-
" thor,) how strange and horrible a thing it was in a great
" town, to see at least 60,000 men, with pistols, pikes,
" courtlasses, poniards, knives, and other such bloody in-
" struments, run, swearing, and blaspheming the sacred ma-
" jesty of God, through the streets, and into the houses;
" where most cruelly they massacred all whosoever they
" met, without regard of estate, condition, sex, or age. The
" streets paved with bodies cut and hewed in pieces; the
" gates and entries of houses, palaces, and public places,
" dyed with blood; shoutings and hallooings of the mur-
" derers, mixed with continual noises of pistols and calivers
" discharged; the pitiful cries and shrieks of those that
" were murdered; slain bodies cast out at windows upon
" the stones, drawn through the dirt, with strange noises
" and whistlings; breaking of doors and windows with bills
" and stones, and other furies; the spoiling and sacking of
" houses; carts, some carrying away the spoils, and others
" the dead bodies, which were thrown into the river of Seine,
" all now red with blood, which ran out of the town, and
" from the king's own palace."

The ven-geance of

And hence the aforesaid writer makes this observation:

" Since that time, by that which happened to that French CHAP.
" king, Charles IX. his brother and successor, his mother, XVII.
" his bastard-brother, the house of Guise, the town of Paris, Anno 1572.
" and all the realm of France, in the space of twenty years God for this
" after this massacre, it sufficiently appeared, that God re- markable.
" vengeth the blood of innocents, and that their death is
" precious in his sight."

But this slaughter of those of the religion ended not so ; Nothing
for there was nothing meant but extremity towards them. but extremity meant
On the 14th of September, as the ambassador there wrote towards
to secretary Smith, the young princess of Condé was con- religion.
strained to go to mass, being threatened otherwise to go to
prison ; and so consequently to be made away with. The
prince of Condé yielded also to hear mass upon Sunday ensuing, being otherwise threatened to go to the Bastile ;
where he would be not like long to abide. And yet the
Friday before, the queen-mother told him, [Walsingham,]
nobody's conscience————[so writ undoubtedly to be filled
up in words at length, after this manner,] *should be constrained or forced.* For, said she, here is the king of Navarr,
the prince of Condé, and divers others in this court, that
live with liberty of conscience, and so shall continue. And
then, after some ciphers, Walsingham adds, " And there-
" fore I hope her majesty will stand upon her guard, and
" strengthen herself with the amity of the protestant princes The pro-
" of Germany : who, as he heard, were awakened, and mar- testant
princes of
" vellously stomached this late cruelty ; and thought that Germany
" the danger thereof would reach to themselves, if they did awakened.
" not seek to prevent it." And then by some other ciphers
he seems to reflect upon the queen of Scots, and the queen's
danger by means of her. And advises, that she would not Walsing-
suffer herself to be abused by her fair speech, having so late vice.
experience of her faithless dealing ; and that when once the
king was possessed of Rochel, which he hoped to have
shortly, Strozzi was then to go directly for Scotland.

And indeed this warning the English court took ; and 160
upon this news immediately put itself into a posture of de- England
provides for
fence, reckoning that this practice looked over hither. Thus itself upon

BOOK I.

Anno 1572.

these popish practices.

Lord treasurer's letter, Sept. 19.

the lord treasurer piously and providently spake to his correspondent in France : " I see the Devil is suffered by Almighty God for our sins to be strong in following the persecution of Christ's members. We are vigilant in our own defence against such treacherous attempts as have lately been put in use there, in France. And also call ourselves to repentance. A national fast being appointed on this occasion. All the seacoast was put in defence, and the queen's navy sent to sea with speed : which was so to continue, until they saw further whereunto to trust." And this was to secure themselves against a fleet preparing by Strozzi, (as Walsingham had informed.) Although the French ambassador told the court, that the king willed him to assure her majesty, that his navy should not any ways endanger her. On which that wise lord said, We have great cause in these times to doubt all fair speeches.

All the Hugonots' lands to be sold.

To shew further the extremity used towards the Hugonots, Walsingham gave intelligence, that all their lands (amounting to many millions) were to be sold, and employed in the conquests of countries. But he added, that he hoped in God it would prove an account without the host ; if God do not blind the eyes of the princes of the world : who, joining together, should be able to make their parts good against any of those that had will to do them harm.

One Roulart, a catholic, murdered in prison.

Nay, one Roulart, a catholic, canon of Notre Dame, and also a counsellor in the parliament, uttering certain speeches in mislike of these lawless kind of proceedings without justice, was apprehended, and committed to prison ; and in prison murdered, as disorderly as any of the rest : wherewith divers of the catholics themselves were offended. On which occasion Walsingham reported, that this manner of proceeding bred general mistrust in them of the nobility, and every man feared God's vengeance.

CHAP. XVIII.   161

The motion renewed for the marriage. Walsingham de-
clares his scruples to that court. An interview desired
between the queen-mother and queen Elizabeth. The jea-
lousy conceived thereof. Declined. The French's dissimu-
lation. Walsingham's letter thereupon. The resentments
of the English court. Still more bloodshed. The king
hurt. Two put to death as conspirators: unjustly. The
French king sends to the queen to christen his daughter.
Her excellent answer. England a harbour for the per-
secuted French protestants. The queen protects them.

BUT notwithstanding this cruel execution, the king and Anno 1572.
the queen-mother were soon after for putting forward the The match
marriage between duke d'Alençon and the queen; and queen
called upon the English ambassador to further it; and in moved
order to that, for an interview. But he shewed what little again.
stomach he had now thereunto. And the queen-mother
asking him the reason, he replied, that this last strange accident had bred in men discourses, opinions, and mistrusts;
among the which he was not free from his doubts and suspicions. And that touching the scruples he had of the king's
and her sincere meaning in respect of the marriage, he had
three reasons, as he frankly told them, that moved him
thereunto.

First, the violating of the late edict, [whereby the king
granted the Hugonots the free use of their religion,] and
the present severity used against those of the religion. Secondly, the strange dealing in the first match propounded
[with his other brother, the duke d'Anjou.] And thirdly,
certain discourses then given out concerning conquering
England and Ireland.

Touching the first, he shewed the queen-mother, that the The scru-
chiefest cause that moved the queen, his mistress, to make ples now
account of the amity of that crown was, that the king suf- by the am-
fered certain of his subjects to enjoy, by virtue of his edict, bassador.
the exercise of the same religion her majesty professed.
Which was, he said, the chiefest ground of the league.

BOOK
I.

Anno 1572.

Which being taken away, that amity could not but grow doubtful. And that the matter of an *interview* was suspected but to serve for an entertainment. To the second, he shewed how this late accident gave vehement suspicions, that the first match propounded was but a kind of entertainment, to abuse those of the religion. And that the *discourses*, though they did but move mean personages, (and he hoped their majesties were free from any such intention,) yet the strangeness of the late accident could not altogether rest free from it.

162

His fears of war from protestant princes.

After she had made him some reply, he added, that he feared this late severity executed there, in Paris, would make all princes of the religion to repute the same a general denunciation of war against them; and which he feared would prove as bloody as ever war that happened; whereof he thought the benefit would chiefly grow to the Turk.

What the queen directed to be said to the French king.

And further, the queen instructed him to declare her mind now to that king on this juncture; that for the king to destroy and utterly root out of his realm all those of that religion that she professed, and to desire her in marriage for his brother [at this time,] must needs seem to her at the first a thing very repugnant in itself; especially, having before confirmed that liberty to them of that religion, by an edict of his, perpetual and irrevocable.

The queen-mother moves for an interview.

But to look a little more upon the *interview* before mentioned. Notwithstanding the late bloody business, the queen-mother had the confidence, but the next month, viz. in September, and almost in the midst of the tragedies in France, to propound this interview between queen Elizabeth and herself; hoping that by speeches with her to do more in forwarding this match with her younger son, than by any other way of ambassage; and to make a quicker despatch. And for that end, the cunning and intriguing queen offered to come with her son as far as Calais or Bulloign; and queen Elizabeth to come to Dover. But she began now justly to be more wary and suspicious of the French. And so in her instruction, wrote this month to her ambassador, she signified; directing him to tell the king,

that she must needs deal plainly, that this murdering of
the admiral, and of so general slaughter of them of the religion, had made such alteration in her majesty, and moved
such doubts in her mind, that she knew not how to interpret
of the offers of this marriage and of this interview; especially, since the king also had said nothing concerning it.
The queen-mother's motion was, that they might have a
communication upon the sea between Dover and Calais, or
Bulloign; a matter that seemed strange to the queen;
and the more, since the French ambassador had moved the
queen, that the queen-mother, with her son, was willing to
come into the realm at such place, and with such numbers,
as her majesty should allow. And that the queen had said,
she would be better advised by her own ambassador; who
should have charge afterwards to understand her mind and
the king's. And that upon knowledge thereof, she herself
would come to a further resolution.

In short, the queen suspected treachery herein. For the The French
king at this time kept a great navy and army near Bur- king hath
deaux and Rochel, under the command of Strozzi. Where- a navy
by her majesty's merchants, who were wont all the year, abroad,
and especially about this time [of vintage,] to traffic that and spoiled
way for wines and other commodities, divers of them had some Eng-
been of late spoiled thereabouts by Strozzi's band, not only lish mer-
of victuals and munition, but of money and merchandises, chants'
and some of them also of their lives. And therefore the ships.
queen bade her ambassador to require the king to let her
understand what the meaning might be of that navy.

In the next month, viz. October, a motion was made again 163
by the queen-mother of France, for an interview to be before A motion
the twentieth of that month; and the place to be the isle of again for
Jersey. Which the lord Burghley, by word of mouth, told an inter-
the ambassador, seemed to her majesty to be so strange, view; de-
both for time and place, as that if the ambassador had not clined.
shewed the letters from the queen there and the queen-
mother to that effect, she should either not have believed it,
or concluded that the ambassador had mistaken the same.

BOOK
1.

Anno 1572.

Suspicion of treachery against the queen.

French dissimulation.

Thus plainly did she shew her disgust and just jealousy of these invitations.

" For," as the said lord by the queen's order proceeded with that ambassador, " the 20th of October was not fourteen days off from the time of the motion, nor one month from the date of the king's letter to that purpose. And Jersey was a place so far distant, as never king of this land would venture to sail unto, for many causes; nor yet any merchant would take upon him to pass thither almost in that time. Besides, that the late proceedings in France, to the destruction of all sorts of her majesty's religion, (which also was not ceased, as the queen understood,) could not but argue this manner of motion very absurd: and besides would engender in the subjects of this realm such conceits, as it were a dangerous thing for counsellors to be so careless of their prince as to give ear to such motions. And that it was stranger, now to make this motion, when the French ambassador did say at Reading to the queen's majesty there, that the queen-mother was content to come into any place of this realm: which was now strangely changed, that the queen's majesty should come over her own seas to the coast of France."
All this looked as if the French, could they have got the queen upon the sea, had intended to entrap her.

For indeed, by this time, the French dissimulation became more and more discovered. This Walsingham, that then was among them, shewed in his letters sent over; that the more he observed their doings there, the more his jealousy increased of their evil meaning. And that they never spake more fair to the admiral than a few days before he died. Nothing was demanded by him that was not granted. Insomuch, that Tiligni said to a gentleman, a friend of his, a few days before the execution, that their liberal granting of requests without any denial, did make him to suspect some unsound and hollow meaning; and thereupon to allege an Italian proverb to that purpose. He added, that the French never used fairer words than now they did, nor

greater protestation of amity. And that because it was more CHAP.
than was accustomed, and being now at such a time as the XVIII.
English had cause to suspect the contrary, he could not Anno 1572.
but be jealous of her majesty's safety.

The same ambassador (who had been very apt to think The ambas-
the best of the French court, and the benefit accruing to sador to the queen's
England by friendship with it) speaks his judgment now in council
another strain, in a letter to the queen's council. " He con- hereupon. Walsing-
" fessed he was deceived by the dissimulation of that court. ham's let-
" That he was sorry he could not yield that assurance of ter, Sept. 24.
" amity that heretofore he had done; wherein he might
" seem to have dealt over confidently. But he knew their
" honours would consider, that his error in that behalf was 164
" common in a great many wiser than himself. And that
" now there was there [at the court] neither regard either
" to word, writing, or edict, were it never so solemnly pub-
" lished; nor to any protestation made heretofore to fo-
" reign princes for the performance of the same; seeing the
" king prosecuted that religion with all extremity that her
" majesty professed; and was now like to be an instrument
" to execute any thing by that people offered unto him, to
" the prejudice of her majesty; seeing that they now that
" possessed his ears were sworn enemies to her majesty;
" and that the nourishers of the late amity were separated
" from him; seeing that the king's own conscience (so com-
" mon a companion is fear with tyranny) made him to re-
" pute all those of the religion, as well at home as abroad,
" his enemies; and so, consequently, not to wish one of
" them alive: he left it to their honours now to judge what
" account they might make of the amity with that crown.
" And that, if he might without presumption or offence
" say his opinion, considering how things presently stood,
" he thought it less peril to live with them as enemies than
" as friends."

Again: " The cruelty here executed is void of all just Bloody hy-
" defence," writeth the same to the lord Burghley; " and pocrisy. Letter to
" therefore in God's just judgment is like to receive just pu- lord Burgh-
" nishment. And if the same doth not happen so soon as ley, Oct. 8.

BOOK
I.

Anno 1572.

"we desire, our sins are the let...... They here are so far
"imbrued in blood, as there is no end of their cruelty. For
"no town escapeth, where any of the religion is found,
"without general murdering and sacking of them. And yet
"they protest all this to be done against their wills, though
"it is evident it is done by their commandment."

Again, how much in danger the queen was by this hypocrisy, which was not before discovered, thus he subjoined;

The ambas-
sador now
undeceived
in the
French pro-
testations.

"That he had not heretofore been so ready to commend
"their sincerity as he was forced now to set down their in-
"fidelity. Surely I cannot see, that all their fair speeches
"and friendly offers tend to any other end but to abuse
"....... Adding, that it was the opinion there of all men
"of judgment, that her majesty was to look for any mis-
"chief, that either Spain or that country [i. e. France]
"could yield. And therefore, that if she should now seek
"to quiet herself, [by not preparing for her own defence,
"but sitting still,] they did not see any reason for her to
"hope to keep the crown upon her head."

The resent-
ment of
these
French
matters in
the English
court.

But now at length let us see the resentment of our court,
and of the wise men about the queen. Secretary Smith expressed his thoughts in this manner: "If the admiral, and
"all those murdered on the bloody Bartholomew-day, were
"guilty, why were they not apprehended, imprisoned, in-
"terrogated, and judged? Is this the manner to handle
"men, either culpable or suspected? But grant they were
"guilty that dreamt treason that night in their sleep, what
"did the innocent men, women, and children at Lyons?
"What did the sucking children and their mothers at
"Roan deserve? at Caen? at Rochel? Will God, think
"you, still sleep? Will not their blood ask vengeance?
"Shall not the earth be accursed, that hath sucked up the
"innocent blood poured out like water upon it?.....I am
"glad," added he, "you shall come home; and would wish
165 "you out of that country, so contaminate with innocent
"blood, that the sun cannot look upon it but to prognos-
"ticate the wrath and vengeance of God."

The earl of
Leicester
writes to

The earl of Leicester related the news of this massacre in

a letter to the earl of Shrewsbury, dated September 6, with his detestation of it, to this tenor: " That he doubted not " but his lordship had been advertised at large of the tra- " gical news out of France; which had been used with that " cruelty, that he thought no Christian, since the heathen " time, had heard of the like. And that it was the more " horrible, for that it seemed it was done with the consent " of that prince, who had given his faith, and laid his ho- " nour in pledge for the contrary before. But the same " God, proceeded he, that had suffered this punishment to " fall upon his people for their own sins, would find time to " revenge it upon his enemies for his own cause sake. God " defend our mistress from the hidden practices laid for " her, among these open facts committed, so nearly to " touch her. For she, as he added, is the fountain and the " well-spring of the griefs that procure this malice. And " though others smart, yet she is the mark they shoot at. " And so must she think; and accordingly must she pro- " vide. Or else all will be naught. But his trust was, that " the same Lord that had all this while preserved her, would " also put into her heart to do that which should be best for " her own and her people's safety, &c. Dated from Wood- " stock."

CHAP.
XVIII.

Anno 1572.
the earl of Shrews-
bury this
news out of
France.
MSS. in Of-
fic. Armor.

These fearful slaughters of the king's subjects continued from one city and town to another. Near a month after that at Paris, report came to court, that there was a general effusion of blood at Roan, of all that could be imagined protestants; so that the channels of the streets ran down with blood. And this happened there when the English court thought all the bloody work was done. The same letters certified, that Diep (where many Englishmen and merchants were) was kept close; and the same execution of the true Christians (as Smith writ to Walsingham) expected there. Notwithstanding Sigoigne [the governor of that place] did warrant all the English to be out of danger, and encouraged them not to be afraid. " But," said Smith, " what warrant can " the French make, now seals and words of princes are but " traps to catch innocents, and bring them to the butchery?"

Massacre
at Roan,
and Diep
kept close.

And indeed the king was now grown so bloody-minded,
as they that advised him at first to these bloody courses did

Anno 1572.
The king
grown
bloody. He
is hurt by a
sword.
repent, (as Walsingham wrote,) and did fear, that the old
saying would prove true in respect of themselves, *Malum
consilium consultori pessimum.* And every body looked
out for some dreadful accident to happen to him; and
reckoned it some plague of what would follow, that in the
month of December the king was hurt by another man's
sword; receiving a little hurt in his left arm. Which was
not great; but that every small hurt is great to a prince;
as Walsingham said: and he might have added, a token of
more of his blood to be shed.

And this passage is worthy to be added to that king's
horrible guilt of iniquity and bloodshed, related also by the
English ambassador. That to make the pretended plot seem

166 the truer, they added the blood of two innocent persons,

Two upon
the pre-
tended con-
spiracy.
tried in
form of
justice, and
executed.
protestants, named Bricquemont and Cavannes; who, in the
month of October, underwent a formal trial of justice; as
persons that had been concerned in the late conspiracy.
And were executed on the 22d day of that month, being
the same day that the queen of France was brought to bed
of a daughter. Whose nativity, as that ambassador observed, was consecrated with blood. The former (who was
one of the king's eldest soldiers) was asked by the under-
provost, who was sent to him, to know if he could say any
thing touching the late conjuration; which if he would confess, he should save his life: whereunto he said, that the
king had never a more faithful nor truer subject. But this
I know, added he, proceedeth not of himself, but of evil
counsellors about him. And so lifting up his eyes to heaven, he said, " O my God! at whose tribunal seat I stand,
" and whose face I hope shortly to see, thou-knowest well,
" that I know nothing; nor did not so much as once think
" of any conjuration against the king, nor against the estate.
" Though contrariwise they have untruly put the same in
" my process. But I beseech my God, that he will pardon
" the king, and all those that have been the cause of this
" my unjust death, even as I desire pardon at thy hand for

"my sins and offences." He would have spoken to the CHAP.
king, (who was present at this spectacle,) and said he had XVIII.
somewhat to utter unto him. But he said, he saw he might Anno 1572.
not use any further speeches. And so shrunk up his shoulders. He was a gentleman, and yet was hanged: a thing
very rare in France; especially, he being reputed of his
enemies to be innocent of the thing that had been laid to his
charge.

His death was bewailed of many of the catholics that The king
were beholders of the same. As were also the king, the and queen-
mother, &c.
queen-mother, the king of Navarr, with the king's brethren, present at
and prince of Condé. Which was generally misliked; as a these men's
deaths.
thing unworthy of the heads of justice to be at the execution of justice. They were hanged about five or six in the
evening by torchlight.

It is remarkable also what Walsingham writ into Eng-They made
land concerning this matter unto the lord Burghley, that them sign
blanks, to
they caused these two, a little before their deaths, to sub-acknow-
ledge a con-
scribe certain blanks. Which they filled up with such mat-spiracy.
ter as might best prove that there was such a pretended Letters to
Burgh.
conspiracy. Which blanks so filled up, they sent by two Dec. 5.
messengers into Germany, to shew unto some princes there,
for the better justifying of the late execution.

Another piece of French courtship of the queen, at this The queen
sent to, to
wretched time, was their invitation of her to christen the christen the
French king's daughter. It was the beginning of Novem-French
king's
ber, that the French ambassador sent word to the lord child.
Burghley, that the French queen was brought to bed of a
daughter; and to know whether her majesty would christen
it with her own name; and to send either the earl of Leicester thither or the lord Burghley, for that purpose, as
her proxy. Perhaps it was to catch one of those chief counsellors of the queen's. But the prudent answer the queen
gave was, that she would not desire to christen it; nor
would she send either of those lords. But that if the queen
would desire her to be godmother, she would not refuse it;
and would send some person qualified. The king afterwards 167
sent an agent to invite her to be gossip with the empress

and the duke of Savoy. But the ceremony was not performed before the month of January.

Anno 1572.
The queen's
excellent
answer
upon the
French
king's am-
bassage to
her. The king, for the greater pretended honour to the queen,
sendeth in December, Mauvesire, ambassador to her, first,
for continuance of amity; secondly, to be godmother to the
infant, his daughter; and lastly, to pursue the request of
marriage with the duke d'Alençon. The answer she then
made by her ambassador there (to round him in the ear
again by a second message, for his cruelty, and the many ag-
gravations of it) was to this tenor : " That she was sorry to
" hear what she had heard of her good brother, (the which
" sprung from her good-will to that amity.) First, that
" great slaughter made in France, of noblemen and gentle-
" men, unconvicted, and untried, so suddenly, as it was
" said, at his command, seemed so much to touch the ho-
" nour of her good brother, as she could not but with la-
" mentation, and with tears of her heart, hear it of a prince
" so near allied unto her, and in a chain of indissoluble
" love knit unto her by league and oath. That being after
" exposed by a conspiracy and treason wrought against her
" good brother's person, (which whether it were true or
" false, being in another prince's kingdom and jurisdiction,
" where she had nothing to do, she minded not to be curi-
" ous, yet that,) they were not brought to answer to law
" and judgment, before they were executed, she heard it
" marvellously ill taken; as a thing of a terrible and dan-
" gerous example. And was sorry that her good brother
" was so ready to condescend to any such counsel, whose
" nature she took to be more humane and noble. But that
" when more was added unto it; that when women, chil-
" dren, maids, young infants, and sucking babes, were at the
" same time murdered, and cast into the river; and that li-
" berty of execution was given to the vilest and basest sort
" of the populace, without punishment or revenge of such
" cruelty, done afterwards by law upon such cruel mur-
" derers of such : this increased her grief and sorrow in her
" good brother's behalf; that he should suffer himself to be
" led by such inhuman counsellors.

" And now, sithence it did appear by all doings, both by
" the edicts and otherwise, that the rigour was used only
" against them of the religion reformed, whether they were
" of any conspiracy or no; and that, contrary to the edict
" of pacification so often repeated, they of the reformed re-
" ligion were either driven to fly, or die, or to recant, or
" lose their offices; whereby it did appear by all accords
" now used by her good brother, that his scope and intent
" did tend only to subvert that religion that she did pro-
" fess, and to root it out of the realm. At the least, all the
" strangers of all nations and religions did so interpret it.
" As might appear by the triumphs and rejoicings, set out,
" as well in the realm of France as in others. Which
" made, that it must needs seem strange, both to her and
" to all others, that her good brother should require her to
" be godmother to his dear child, she being of that religion
" which he did now persecute, and could not abide within
" his realm. And that if she should believe the persuasion
" of others, and the opinion of all strangers her friends,
" who were not her subjects, she should in no case conde- 168
" scend to any association in that or any other matter.

" But as she had always hitherto, as she concluded, had
" a special love to her good brother in his younger age, and
" a desire to the continuation of his good estate and quiet-
" ness, which she had indeed manifestly shewed, never
" seeking any advantage of trouble against him, &c." [And
so going on with much *douceur*, she endeth:] " That
" notwithstanding that doubt and impediment before men-
" tioned, she intended to send a worthy personage, a noble-
" man of her realm, to repair to his court, to visit the king,
" her good brother, and the queen-mother; and to do that
" office which was required. Wishing that these spiritual
" alliances might be to their comfort, and to the conserva-
" tion of the amity begun between them."

England was now very hospitable to such of the religion England a
as could escape, and had got over hither. And among the harbour for
rest one was a great nobleman of France; viz. the vidame such as
of Chartres. For whom the queen had a great sense of The queen
receives the

BOOK I.

Anno 1572.

vidame, fled hither.

And writes in his behalf to the French king.

pity. Insomuch that secretary Smith uttered his tenderness also, by acquainting the queen's ambassador there, that it did him good to see the princely compassion that was in her majesty towards the poor vidame, who was escaped by good fortune into England. For whom the queen had, at his humble and lamentable suit, written to the king in his favour. Which he bade her ambassador deliver with as good words as he might; and to require his answer.

The king's answer to the queen.

To which letter the king gave this answer, sending the message by her said ambassador, that as he was glad any way to gratify her majesty, so he could not grant this her request, without touch of his honour, to suffer any of his subjects to live in a foreign country, without a kind of defiance of his sincerity, &c. Yet he could, for gratifying her majesty, be content that the vidame should return home, and enjoy his livings there, with such surety as he should not have occasion to doubt his safety.

The king's demand of her.

But the vidame dared not to trust himself there, notwithstanding this protestation; his hypocrisy by this time being well seen through. And the French protestants fly still to England on all opportunities. Which occasioned the French king to demand, that the queen should admonish, or rather command them to avoid the realm, as rebels to the French king.

Her free answer in behalf of those that fled into her dominions.

Upon which the queen gave the earl of Worcester (who was then her ambassador there) these instructions, to return to that king in answer: "That she did not understand "of any rebellion they were ever privy to; and that she "could perceive nothing but that they were well affected to "their prince. But when such common murdering and "slaughter was made throughout France, of those who "professed the same religion, that it was natural for every "man to flee for his own defence, and for the safety of his "life. And that it was the privilege of all realms, to re-"ceive such woful and miserable persons as did flee to it "only for defence of their lives. And that as for their re-"turn, she instructed him to say, that the chiefest of them "had been spoken unto; and they made their answer, that

" the same rage of their enemies, which made them first to CHAP.
" flee hither, did still continue the cause of their tarrying XVIII.
" here. For as they did then kill with fury, as it might Anno 1572.
" appear, the greatest number of those that were killed, 169
" without the commandment or avow of the king; so it
" was most like they would execute still their malice, if the
" persons were there. Against whom it was then, and yet
" was inflamed, notwithstanding any letters declaratory, or
" other prohibition by the king. As it was manifest and
" notorious, that very many had been publicly, and were
" almost daily slain and murdered in France, that were of
" their religion, sith these contrary edicts were published
" and cried by sound of trumpet.

    " And that therefore, until they might see, that the
" quiet of the realm were better established, the fury of the
" people, and the bloody murderers appeased; they would
" live here, and obey the king's edicts. That they thought
" themselves unsure there, and had prayed the queen of
" her mercy to have compassion on their misery. And if
" so be the king would suffer them to enjoy their revenues,
" whether they remained here, or went into any other coun-
" try, the earl was instructed to say, that she supposed
" they would be as faithful subjects to him as any other in
" the realm. For others, she espoused none of them. And
" that if she could perceive at any time, that they were
" otherwise minded, or should attempt any thing for the
" disquietment of his person or realm, she would not suffer
" them to remain within her realm."

    The better sort of the queen's subjects were very kind Pitied by
unto these poor protestants; and glad to see them retired the better sort of the
unto more safety in this country. But another sort (divers of English,
the common people and rabble, too many of them) behaved grutched at by others.
themselves otherwise towards these afflicted strangers, men
and women, who grudged at their coming hither, and would
call them by no other denomination than *French dogs.*
This a French author sometime afterward took notice of
in print; to the disparagement of the English nation, and
their insensibleness of the misery of others that suffered for

BOOK I.

Anno 1572.

Lectures upon Jonah, by Dr. G. Abbot. Printed 1600.

righteousness' sake. But George Abbot, D. D. afterwards archbishop of Canterbury, could not let this reflection pass, without taking notice of it in one of his morning lectures preached at Oxford; vindicating our kingdom from a charge that lay only upon some of the meaner and worst sort. Speaking thus upon this occasion; " How that it " grieved his soul at the unkindness of our nation, (those " of the common sort,) that had, by occasion of the han- " dling of their last great massacre, noted it to posterity, " that by a most inhospitable kind of phrase, our English " used to term them no better than *French dogs*, that fled " hither for religion, and their conscience sake. To which " the preacher joined also the many conspiracies, which by " some of the meaner people in one city of this land, [i. e. " London,] had been oftentimes intended against out- " landish folks, [in risings and insurrections against them.] " But those, said he, that were wise and godly, used those " aliens as brethren: considering their distresses with a " lively fellow-feeling; holding it an unspeakable blessed- " ness, that this little island of ours should not only be a " temple to serve God in for ourselves, but an harbour for

170 " the weatherbeaten, a sanctuary to the stranger, wherein " he might truly honour the Lord; remembering the pre-

Levit. xix. 33.

" cise charge which God gave to the Israelites, to *deal well* " *with all strangers;* because the time once was, when " themselves were strangers in that cruel land of Egypt: " and not forgetting, that other nations, to their immortal " praise, were a refuge to the English in their last bloody " persecution in queen Mary's days: and in brief, recount- " ing, that by a mutual vicissitude of God's chastisements, " their case might be our case. Which day, he prayed, the " Lord might long keep from us."

It was near this time, that another of our authors could not refrain his pen from reproaching those of this nation (or at least many of them) for this inhospitable temper; which he called, " the inveterate fierceness and cankered malice" of the English nation against foreigners and strangers. It " is," saith he, " worthy the consideration, to call to me-

" mory what great tragedies have been stirred in this realm,
" by this our natural inhospitality and disdain of strangers,
" both in the time of king John, Henry his son, king Ed- Anno 1572.
" ward II. king Henry VI. and in the days of later me- Lambard's
" mory, &c. wishing, that whatsoever note of infamy we of Kent,
" have heretofore contracted among foreign writers, by this p. 388. edit.
" our ferocity against aliens, that now at the last, having
" the light of the gospel before our eyes, and the perse-
" cuted parts of the afflicted church as guests and strangers
" in our country, we so behave ourselves towards them, as
" we may both utterly rub out the old blemish, and from
" henceforth stay the heavy hand of just *Jupiter hospitalis*.
" Which otherwise must needs light upon such stubborn
" and uncharitable churlishness."

CHAP. XIX.   171

The earl of Worcester goes into France to assist at the
christening of the French king's daughter. The earl a
Roman catholic ; but loyal. The protestants fly to Ro-
chel ; and hold it against the French army. The new
star in Cassiopeia. Divers of the murderers slain before
Rochel. Rochel still holds out. Some others of the mur-
derers slain. Some English offer to raise an army to go
to Rochel. Books set forth to palliate the massacre. How
the Scots resent the massacre. Now more inclinable to an
amity with England. France false to England in Scot-
tish affairs ; and to the religion. That king and Spain
privately conspire. A plot hatching to invade England.
The pope's legate in France practising.

THE earl of Worcester was now (in the month of Ja- The queen
nuary) in France, sent thither by the queen, in the quality sends the
of her ambassador, partly to be her proxy, to stand in her cester to
room for godmother to the French king's daughter, as she French
had promised, and partly to concert the matter of duke king's
d'Alençon. Being arrived, he was magnificently entertained child.
at that court. But it is to be noted, that in the queen's in-

structions, she would not suffer the earl to be present at the mass, when the child was to be christened, though he were a papist himself, and a favourer of the queen of Scots, otherwise a good simple gentleman, (as Leicester gave his character to Walsingham.) For thus ran the instructions: "If the emperor's ambassador hold the child himself, you may also do it. But that if you shall perceive, that any device or other sinister means shall be gone about to bring you to their mass, or any other superstitious ceremony, which the order of our realm doth not allow, you shall not consent, nor assist in it; but rather absent yourself. And understanding that before, he should with honourable excuse require the queen-mother, that the queen of Navarr (to whom she had in this case written her special letters) should be her deputy for him. Or in the absence or let of her, any other princess or noblewoman; whom it should please the queen-mother to appoint to it."

The child was named Mary Elizabeth, the empress and the queen's majesty both giving the name; as the earl of Leicester wrote to the earl of Shrewsbury, in his correspondence, among other things. One more whereof was, the accident that befell the said earl of Worcester in his voyage to France. Where, near Bulloign, where he landed,

he was robbed by pirates; who were very numerous at that time upon the seas, and had taken many merchants' ships: which caused the queen to set forth some of her fleet to take and disperse them. The success of which (as the same

172 earl wrote) was, that in the Downs, Mr. Holdstock, that went out for the admiral, and had taken on him that charge, had taken seven great piratical ships; and in them four hundred men: and in the west there were three or four more such ships taken. So that in short he trusted the sea should be scoured; and hoped they that robbed the earl were some of them.

The queen had prudently fixed upon this earl for this honourable ambassage, a person of great honour, and of the Roman catholic religion, as one like to be the more ac-

ceptable to that court: for notwithstanding the slight cha- CHAP.
racter Leicester gave of him, the lord Burghley recom-   XIX.
mending him to Walsingham, in order to his reception of Anno 1572.
him, when he should come to Paris, told him, that he
should find him a nobleman of great gentleness and thankfulness. And that he should see good reason to shew him
all good offices and favours. And adding, that in very
truth, [such was his merits,] that he loved him dearly. And
this passage is remarkable of him, that though he were of
the Romish religion, such was his loyalty and love to the
queen, that being come to Paris, the countess of Northumberland, who was his sister, sent unto him a messenger, signifying her intent to visit him. This he made Walsingham
privy to. And though she were so nearly related to him,
yet in respect of his dutiful carriage towards her majesty,
he did look upon her but as a mere stranger; and so
meant, he said, to do, until such time as her peace was
made. Nor would he so much as vouchsafe to give ear to
any messenger or message from her. And therefore willed
the messenger to forbear to repair unto him. And so did
Charles Somerset [his brother, as I suppose] behave himself in regard of the message brought to him, utterly refusing to speak with the bringer. This Walsingham signified
to the said lord Burghley.

But now to see a little the issue and event of these cruel The pro-
and unjust counsels of France; and what troubles it drew testants fly
upon itself presently; according to accounts of them written and hold it.
in private letters of our own statesmen. Many of the protestants, in the midst of these slaughters, fled away, and got
to Rochel; which they kept, and defended themselves
there; and held out, and raised considerable forces at Languedoc; while the king was troubled to raise men against
them: for at a diet in Switzerland they agreed to allow no
man to be sent as a soldier to France; fearing to be served
as they had served the protestants there. And the Germans
(whence also they used to have their supply of men for the
wars) answered the king's messengers roughly; who were

BOOK I.

Anno 1572.
Some English go thither to assist them.

Several overthrows of the king's side there.

Troubles begin in France. Walsingham portends God's revenge.

173

sent to raise men there; according to Walsingham's intelligence sent hither.

The Rochellers took the isle of Ree in December; whereby they had the haven free, and might receive such succours as came unto them by sea. Divers English also came thither, to give them their assistance. Insomuch as, in January, Mauvesire let the English ambassador at Paris understand, that the king was informed, there should be certain ships (to the number of fourteen) preparing to repair to Rochel. And that though Frenchmen and Flemings bare the name of them, yet they were not unfurnished of some English mariners. And that therefore the king and queen-mother desired the queen would give order for the restraint of them.

In February secretary Smith wrote to the earl of Shrewsbury, that the French king made great preparations for the besieging of Rochel; but made no great haste thither, [for want, as it seems, of men.] And that when they came before it, to besiege it, the Rochellers gave them divers overthrows. And that all kinds of victuals were extremely scarce in France. So that great suit was made for some wheat from hence.

The French court was much aggrieved, as well in this as in other matters: that things framed so untowardly, and went backward with them, as Walsingham made his observation; and the wisest sort sticked not to say, that the greatest troubles were now but a beginning. And if it should prove true that was written out of Germany, that the marquis of Brandenburgh was like to be chosen king of Poland, they might perhaps have just cause to repent their late dealings. But however, added that same ambassador, that it fell out so, that we should see that God would work somewhat, whereby it might appear that the blood of his saints was dear to him. And then added, as it were prophetically; "Perhaps we did build too much upon the "courage and wisdom of them that be dead, [viz. the ad-"miral, &c.] but God can raise up stones to set forth his

" glory. So that we need not doubt to see his revenge, un-
" less our sins be the let." Thus did that good man portend
what indeed came to pass soon after.

And so did another, namely, secretary Smith, (in abhorrence of the thoughts of this enormous act,) express his
mind upon the appearance of a new star, in his letter to
Walsingham, dated December 11, writing, " That he was
" sure he had heard of, and did think he had seen the new
" star comet, but without beard or tail. Which had ap-
" peared these three weeks on the back-side of the star of
" Cassiopeia, and on the edge of the Via Lactea. The big-
" ness whereof was between the bigness of Jupiter and Ve-
" nus; and kept there to his appearance; he having no in-
" strument to observe it; and because of the cold weather
" also was dark. Which also observed the precise order of
" the fixed stars, such an one, he said, he had never ob-
" served, [who yet was a great astronomer,] nor read of.
" And prayed Walsingham to let him know what the wise
" men of Paris judged upon it. He knew, he said, they
" would not think it the admiral's soul; as the Romans did
" of the comet, next appearing after the murder of Julius
" Cæsar, that it was his soul. But it may be, added Smith,
" it may be Astræa, now peeping out afar off in the north,
" to see what revenge shall be done upon so much innocent
" blood shed in France at a marriage banquet, and rere-
" suppers after it."

But upon so wondrous a phenomenon, what further observations the learned Smith made, and what his inquiries
were, may be seen in his Life written by me.

Rochel still in the month of March was held by the protestants, and bravely was maintained of them against all the
forces of the French king hitherto. And two of the chiefest
executors of the late murder in Paris were slain in a skir-
mish happening between the king's camp and those of Rochel, viz. duke d'Aumale and Schaviger. The queen's ambassador sent a messenger on purpose to relate to her the
particularities thereof. And had this passage in his letter

174

BOOK I.

Anno 1572.

Innocent blood revenged.

concerning this remarkable just bloodshed upon the shedders of blood, that God of that good beginning gave them some hopes, that the blood of the innocent should not be unrevenged. The marshal Tavannes, one of the greatest persecutors at the massacre, died the next year, eaten up of lice. And one Besme, who murdered the admiral Coligni, had the same year his thigh shot off with a cannon at this siege: as Dr. Dale, ambassador there at Paris, in the year 1573, wrote to the earl of Sussex.

The queen will not let the English go to Rochel.

Many of the English nation, both noblemen and gentlemen of antiety, and great quality, offered now at their own charge to find an army of 20,000 foot and 2,000 horse, for six months in Gascoine. And so earnest they were, that it was already known to themselves both where the men were to be had, and the money too. And they only desired a permission from the queen. And the queen had much ado to detain them from adventuring themselves thither; shewing herself much offended therewith; and that with great charge under pain of her high indignation. This the lord treasurer signified to Walsingham; and that this was told the French ambassador. Who confessed he had understanding of the same; and was constrained to confess how much his master was bound unto her majesty. This also the said lord treasurer writ to Walsingham, and told him withal, that he might notify it to the king, and amplify it; for that it was true, and meet to be uttered.

Books set forth to cover the late murders.

Thus did these wicked counsels and courses begin to create work and trouble enough for France. And one part of their labour was still to smother the villainy with lies. Books were set forth for that purpose. A lewd letter was written by one Carpenter, an apostate, in defence of the late doings, (which Walsingham sent to the lord treasurer;) written originally in Latin, and then translated into French. Divers of them in Latin were spread studiously into Germany. But the author's lewdness was so well known, as it would but little help their cause. They were also sent into Poland; labour being now made for monsieur, the king's brother, to be chosen king there; for the bishop of Valence had writ, that the late accident would be one of the greatest lets to that they were seeking for.

Scotland was now in civil wars; the queen of Scots' party on one hand, and that of the kirk (who had set up her young son for king) on the other, labouring to overpower each other. It was now queen Elizabeth's care to set both parties at peace with each other: which in the month of August she had pretty well effected. Both parties (as secretary Smith informed Walsingham in their correspondence) had subscribed and sealed to it: and both likewise had written letters of thanks to her for the pains taken by the marshal of Berwic, [Drury:] and likewise professed to stand to that order; which was very honourable both to the French king, and the queen, and not dishonourable to the Scotch king, viz. that in his infancy such a noble person should accord to make quietness in that realm. But however, this abstinence from war was not so well kept by the king's party as reason would; the town of Edinburgh being wholly at the direction of the regent; and contrary to 175 the covenant, he kept the men of war there. Whereof they of the castle complained; as the lord treasurer soon after informed the said Walsingham.

The queen pacifies the wars in Scotland.

But now, a little time after, let us look over into Scotland again, and see what effects this French massacre had upon them; otherwise before not very friendly to England. It opened their eyes, and they began to abhor the French, and to abate the good opinion of them, or trust to have any help from them. The lord Levingston, and divers other Scotch gentlemen, were now in France soliciting their cause there. But seeing no way to enjoy the liberty of their conscience, desired passports of the English ambassador there, to return home. Wherein he was less difficult to grant their desire than before he was, since they seemed, as he saw upon the late accident, to desire most perfect amity between the two crowns of England and Scotland in respect of the common cause of religion.

The Scots' affection alienated from France.

And the said ambassador did suppose, that by their pass-

s 2

BOOK
I.
ing by that way, [viz. by England,] and receiving good entertainment at her majesty's hand, they would rather do
Anno 1572. good than harm at home; that is, by making them in their
Inclinable
to a better
understand-
ing with
England.
Walsing-
ham's ad-
vice.
country understand what had passed in France; and the
danger that was like to follow without perfect union between the said crowns. Adding, that some of the wisest
sort that were there, [in France,] and that were before enemies, and now become friends, did wish that her majesty
would seek to make reconciliation between earl Morton and
lord Liddington; and that she, by some pension, make
both him and others assured to her. And that they thought,
that by disbursing 2 or 3000*l.* a year, she might save the
disbursing of many thousands; besides the avoiding of
many dangerous practices that were like to grow that way;
viz. from Scotland. Walsingham backed all this with the
consideration of the circumstances of the present time;
which rendered this device reasonable.

Smith's ap-
probation
thereof.
The Scots
in France
terrified
with those
beacons.
To which advice, I find secretary Smith, in the month of
October, giving this answer from Windsor, in approbation
thereof, that the Scots were awakened by those beacons in
France; and that the lords in Scotland drew nearer and
nearer to accord. So that now it was rather in hope than
in despair, [as it was before.] And that these cruelties in
France had helped not a little; and now continuing, would
much more. And that he [Walsingham] had given good
advice, that all Scotchmen should not be stayed [that were
minded to come home from France, where they were practising.] And lastly, he added, that some of the late commissioners [about Scottish affairs with England] had given the
rest in Scotland a good . . . . . [jog] to make them awake.

France
treacherous
to England
in Scottish
matters.
What little confidence the queen might put in her late
league with France, did before now appear in their underhand dealings in Scottish matters. Messengers, that were
Englishmen, often came to Paris from Spain and Flanders,
to transact matters privately, to blow the coals in Scotland
against the queen of England. Standen, (of whom before,)
in the month of November, arrived at Paris in post out of
Flanders; and stayed there only five days, having daily

conference with the Scottish ambassador; together with
another Englishman of the same strain, one Liggons, who
at his return (which was by post) accompanied him into
Flanders. Whereby a Scottish man there, that wished con- 176
tinuance of quiet in his own country, feared hereby that
there was some dangerous practice in hand. And William
Seers, another Englishman, and servant to the earl of West-
moreland, (that headed the rebellion in the north,) arrived
there, at Paris, likewise, November 24, sent thither by the
said earl. Immediately upon his arrival, Viracque went
with him to the court. And he reported, that in the north
country and York, to the borders, all the whole country
was at the earl's devotion. So that a few men employed
there by the king, [the French king, to whom this message
was brought,] might assure him, that her majesty [queen
Elizabeth] should be kept so occupied, as she should have
no leisure to send any supply to Rochel: which was suspected by France.

And the French also in the mean time laboured to keep The Scot-
up distractions in Scotland; thereby to consult the better tish queen's
ambassa-
for the Scottish queen's advantage, now in hold in Eng- dor's pri-
land. It was observed by Walsingham, in this month of to the
vate access
November, that the Scottish ambassador did daily repair to queen-
the court, and had often conference with the queen-mother mother.
at an extraordinary time in the morning; whenas commonly no ambassador had access but in the afternoon. And
that before, in talk apart with his friends, he said, that if
the troubles of Scotland had not been, his mistress had been
at liberty, and perhaps had enjoyed a better crown than
Scotland was. And said further, that if his mistress had as
many good friends in Scotland as she had in England, she
had not long remained in prison, as she did. And knitting
up all in the end of this relation, he concluded, Thus you
see, said he, what a dangerous guest her majesty har-
boureth. Insomuch that the said Walsingham asserted,
that the French also had a secret understanding with the
Spaniard, in order to the destroying of the religion every

BOOK where; saying, Surely there is a great mischief a brewing.
I.   And that he was assured, that within these eight days ⌐1⌐

Anno 1572. [meaning by that cipher, probably, the French king] protested, that he would never be quiet as long as the exercise of religion continued in any place of Christendom. He
added, that he knew further particularly, that their king
had said, he would never forget Newhaven, until revenge
were made: so that the said Walsingham professed, that he
never knew so deep a dissembler as that king. And that he
was sure, that the murder of the admiral should have been
executed at Blois, [where the league of peace and amity
was made, and the greatest friendship pretended,] but
that they saw him too well accompanied [to be assassinated
there.] Yet his further intelligence was, that it was agreed,
that both he and Spain should, for avoiding of suspicion of
the legate's coming, entertain the ⌐3⌐ [queen Elizabeth's ambassador, as that cipher seems to import] with good words;
and that Spain should make some show, to be glad to come
to some accord.

The queen   That king, by these his practices, received another dis-
dares not   appointment of a desire he made to the queen; by her distrust the   trusting him, and not daring to venture upon his word; a
king.   mortification to him. For when, in October, the French
177 ambassador signified to the queen, that it was his desire
that she would send over either the lord treasurer or the
earl of Leicester, to confirm the league on the queen's side,
that was made between him and her; the answer was,
" That the queen was sorry that there was such an alter-
" ation of occasion of doing such an office: for as her ma-
" jesty before had intention to have sent either one of them,
" or such other as should have been as agreeable to the
" king; so now there was to all the world one great cause,
" that her majesty might not with honour, nor with law of
" nature, send any whom she loved, to be in danger, as it
" seemed they might be, though the king had never so
" good a meaning: for by the death of so many, whom
" the king did not avow, nor yet punished the murderers,

" what could strangers expect; especially, when the king
" pretended, as by his own letters it appeared, that it was
" the fury of the catholics against those of the religion?"
It is very likely these prime counsellors of the queen were
designed to be butchered, could they by this wile have got
them there.

The secret ill designs of France against the queen did A private
now appear more and more. And their favour to the Scot-plot car-
rying on in
tish queen was learned, notwithstanding their hypocritical France
pretences, and concealments of their minds. The vigilant against
England to
Walsingham gave private intelligence, that January 19 invade it.
there was a great secret council, (present only the cardinal of
Lorain and two others,) for delivering that queen: which
was, that they should for the present maintain peace with
those of the religion at Rochel and other places; because,
until such time as England might be kept occupied, there
could grow no thorough redress in France without hazard-
ing the whole state; therefore it was requisite to yield to
them of Rochel. After that was done, the marquis of
Maine should bring a thousand shot into Scotland, in respect that he was the queen of Scots' kinsman; (but this to
be disavowed by the king.) And so to join the queen's
party. And then to repair to Edinburgh; where Liddington and George Kirkaldy had promised to deliver up the
castle to such as the king should appoint; upon recompence
to receive some living there in France. And there a sufficient garrison should fortify other important places, beside
Dundee, and at Haymouth. This done, the duke of Guise
should come over with forces to procure the delivery of the
queen of Scots. And such of that queen's friends that were
in England would incontinent take arms. Who gave out
to them in France, that her party and forces were so great,
that having good leaders and munition, they should be able
to make their party good enough, and to deliver that queen,
in despite of her majesty.

The pope's legate now in France opened the scene still The pope's
legate in
more, it being learned by the industrious English ambassa-France
dor there, that among other articles of his instructions, (as practiseth
with the

the said ambassador wrote over, December 28,) he was commanded earnestly to commend the queen of Scots' case to the king, and to devise with him some means for her deliverance. Whereby it might come to pass, that England might be reduced to the catholic faith. The Scottish ambassador had more often recourse to him than any other ambassador there: which made the English ambassador, as 178 he said, the rather to doubt some practice. And Hamilton, brother to him that killed the regent in Scotland, sent this message to duke Chasteauherault, viz. to do what he might to keep the castle of Edinburgh, and to maintain his party, until Whitsuntide next; assuring him, that by that time they should have assistance, both from the pope, Spain, and that crown [of France.] This intelligence Walsingham had from the messenger himself, who was to carry it: as he wrote to the lord treasurer: that the party himself that was to do this message made him acquainted with it, who was then departed toward Scotland: and had promised to declare no less to Mr. Randolph, [the queen's agent in Scotland,] who knew him. Perhaps this messenger was Steward, a Scot, that Walsingham sometimes mentioned in his letters,

---

CHAP. XX.

A libel printed in France against the state of England. The queen would see duke d'Alençon: who still courted her. Her resolutions. The Scots move for a league with queen Elizabeth. The Papists hope for a golden day. Massmongers practise conjuring. Several of them taken, and sent up. The disciplinarians busy. Admonition to the parliament. Divers deprived upon the act 13. Eliz. Divers disaffected to the government of the church. Chark, of Peter-house, expelled for a clerum at St. Mary's. His appeal to the chancellor of the university. Dering, reader of St. Paul's, writes a reflecting letter to the lord Burghley. His answer to it. And Dering's vindication of what he had writ.

WHAT else, but French ill-will to England, could be

gathered from a most malicious lying book, that was now CHAP.
printed in France, about the month of January; aiming XX.
chiefly against the queen's two great ministers, viz. the lord Anno 1572.
keeper of the great seal, and the lord high treasurer : wrote Libels printed in
by some French rancorous person, having his instructions France a-
from some crafty rebellious papist of England.   Who, gainst the lord treasur-
though he meant it maliciously against the whole state, yet er, &c.
he vented his choler and despite chiefly against those two,
by nicknames.   The good lord Burghley, lord treasurer,
was so moved at his slander, that he uttered these words :
" God amend his spirit, and confound his malice.   And for
" my part, if I have any such malicious or malignant spirit,
" God presently so confound my body to ashes, and my
" soul to perpetual torment in hell."

The subject of this book was concerning the queen of
Scots, and the case of the duke of Norfolk.   Concerning
the former, it would be said by her friends in France, that
it was but reason that answer should be made to such 179
books as were published for the condemning of that queen.
But to have the duke of Norfolk's case brought in question
[a subject of England, and condemned by public justice]
by those that were counsellors to the queen, to be so maliciously and falsely calumniated, might not well stand with
the terms of the amity professed : as that lord wrote to the
English ambassador.   Who had a great mind to understand
who the author was.   And desired him to make his inquiry : Endeavours
adding, that if by means of the printer it might be found to discover the author.
out, he would bestow a reward upon the discovery.   But
that if it could not, then he wished that some means might
be used, as of himself, to the queen-mother, that the print
might be destroyed.   For that otherwise they should think
themselves, considering the places they held in this estate,
not well considered by that estate.   He added, that this
licentiousness, to inveigh against men by name in printed
books, who did not themselves use by books to provoke
any, was in all good estates intolerable.   And then he added, by way of protestation of the integrity and faithfulness
of both their services : " God," said he, " send this estate

" no worse meaning servants, in all respects, than we two
" have been. Who indeed have not spared labour nor care
" to serve our queen and country. And if we had not, we
" might truly avow, neither our queen nor country had
" enjoyed that common repose that it hath done."

The queen's
last resolu-
tions about
D'Alençon.
The courtships of duke d'Alençon still went on notwithstanding; it being now the month of March, when the
queen's resolutions about it, (as the lord treasurer imparted
to her ambassador in France, in order to his acquainting
the king and the queen-mother therewith,) were, that she
could not consent any person to be her husband, that with
her authority and assent should use any manner of religion
in open exercise, that was in her conscience contrary and
repugnant to the direct word of Almighty God: and so consequently prohibited by the laws of the realm. And that
she could not accord to take any person to her husband,
whom she should not first see. That if therefore monsieur
le Duc would obtain her for his wife without sight of him,
her majesty could not so be had. And yet, that she was
very loath, that he should think that she desired his coming,
but as himself should find it meet, by the advice of the king
his brother and the queen-mother. To whom she remitted
the consideration thereof: with this assurance, that she
meant in good faith to marry with him, if upon his sight
the one might like of the other. And that for the cause of
religion, he and she might so accord, as that which he
should demand were assented to, without offence of her
conscience, and without trouble of her estate. And that
that point of religion was thought meetest to be left at
large, to be communed upon between themselves. So as if
it should mishap, that if one of them might not fall in like
of the other, as to a conclusion of marriage, that the refusal, or breaking up, might be imputed to the cause of religion. And so either party might honourably be discharged
to the world, and no occasion grow thereby of unkindness
between them.

180   The business then coming to this issue, the duke's person
D'Alen-
çon's person
was a stay to the match, he being, it seems, no very person-

able man, whereof take this account from the queen's am- CHAP.
bassador himself; who, when the lord Burghley had re- XX.
quested him to shew what his private opinion was of that Anno 1572.
marriage, gave him this answer: " That the great impedi- not like to be accept-
" ment he found was the contentment of the eye. That able to the
" gentleman," he said, " was void of any good favour, be- queen.
" sides the blemish of the small-pox. Adding, that when he
" weighed the same with the delicacy of her majesty's eye;
" and considering also, that there were some about her in
" credit, who (in respect of their particular interests, hav-
" ing neither regard unto her majesty, nor to the preser-
" vation of our country from ruin) would rather increase
" the misliking, by defacing of him, than by dutifully lay-
" ing before her the necessity of her marriage : and that in
" true choice the satisfaction of the ear imported more than
" that of the eye, and so he hardly thought there would
" ever grow any liking."

Now let us look over a little into Scotland : where Ran- Scotland
dolph was the queen's ambassador. The late bloody doings thinks of making a
in France, and the secret *holy league*, (which was now dis- league with
covered,) to extirpate the true religion, wheresoever it had the queen.
taken root, made those that had the government of the
kirk of Scotland to open their eyes. Who, in October, made
and finished certain articles entitled, *Articles of the ministry,*
barons, and commissioners of the reformed kirk in Scot-
land, in their assembly : given at Edinburgh, the 20th day
of October; to be presented to the king's majesty, our sove-
reign lord, by the council, nobility, and states of his high-
ness's realm, when they shall be conveniate. I shall only set
down here the preamble to the said articles, and the conclusion, which do concern entering into a league with queen
Elizabeth, (the rest relating to their government of the state
and church of that kingdom.) It beginneth ;

" Understanding the treasonable cruelty and fearful per- Their rea-
" secution begun, and intended to be executed against the sons for it. MSS. Tho.
" professors of God's true religion over all Christendom, Randolph.
" according to the bloody decrees of the council of Trent ;
" and assembled at command and desire of your highness's

" letters, to consider of the common danger, and advise
" upon the remedies, we have collected certain heads and
" articles, to be presented to your majesty, and to your
" honourable council and estates for this your realm; most
" humbly requiring the same to be considered. And if
" they shall find the same to tend to the advancement of
" God's glory, your majesty's obedience, and the surety of
" your highness, and us, all your good subjects, professors
" of the same true religion; that then the same articles may
" be allowed of, &c.

" Lastly, seeing the enemies of God's truth are conjured
" to suppress the same, and all professors thereof; and that
" all leeful means of defence are allowed; that there may
" be motion made for a league between your highness and
" the queen's majesty of England, your realms and do-
" minions, for resisting of the cruelty and treason of the
" papists. And that her majesty may be also moved to draw
" into the same league other professors of the said true re-
" ligion in other countries. And that there be solempne
181 " bands among the professors of the religion within the
" realm, to join for resisting of the common enemy. And if
" they be found negligent, to be esteemed false friends, and
" excommunication to pass against them therefore."

The papists
expect
their gold-
en day.
For matters more domestic, and to come nearer home,
and within our own territories, I-begin with the papists:
who were now very busy, and entertained great hopes of
the *golden day*, as they called the restoration of the old religion into this nation, and the deprivation of queen Elizabeth, and I know not what. They talked much of a great
revolution about this year, and a turning back to popery
again. And they would usually say, *they hoped for a day:*
There was a piece of poetry (such as it is) that went about
in print near this time, called, *The practice of the Devil.*
Wherein the Devil is brought in speaking thus, concerning
the emissaries of Rome:

Practice of
the Devil.
By Laur.
Ramsey.
But now, alas! their cloyning is so spyed,
That there's no way but fly quite ore the seas.
In England but a few in respect I can hide,

The gospel so bewrayed their obscured knavery,
But yet some do escape by the means of hypocrisy.
And bears it out braglie, and little wil say,
But few words is best: they hope for a *day*.
And those that are fled out of country's soyle,
Have friendship privily to their contentation :
And watch for the vintage to come to some spoile,
Greeting by letters their whole generation,
By subtil ciphering; which is their demonstration.
Alluring the rest to stand to their hope,
That the *day* is coming, to have again their pope.

And a little after, the same foul spirit is personated, giving his counsel to these sworn creatures of the pope, with their golden expectation.

Practise, prate, and conjure, play Sylvester's part,
Or Hildebrand, that hel-hound most execrable :
Poison prince or king, and consume them by art,
As divers have been stirred by the Romish rable :
Flatter, ly, and cogg at every man's table ;
Having blind prophesies, and whisper in their ear,
That ere long they shal have great change of this geare.

Among the rest of the methods made use of by the priests and Jesuits, to amuse their proselytes, as this author mentioneth, one was *conjuring*. A nest of these conjuring massmongers was discovered now in the north parts by the diligence of Gilbert earl of Shrewsbury, lord president of the north, and keeper of the Scotch queen ; amounting to a great number, that is, such massing priests, as commonly used conjuration, to foretell and make the people believe this *golden day*. The said lord president had employed two diligent persons, whose names were Pain and Peg, to find them out. The lords of the council, by letters from secretary Smith, returned him their most hearty thanks. And the queen also, as he wrote, had heard of his careful ordering of those matters, with great contentation to her highness. And that those matters touching the massing, and such disorders, were referred to the archbishop of Canterbury, and the rest of the great commission ecclesiastical. And that which

Massmongers and conjurers taken in the north.

182
Epist. Com.
Salop. in
Offic. Armor.

BOOK I.

Anno 1572.
Kellet, one of them, discovers their practices.

should appear, by examination, to touch the state and the prince, was to be referred again to the lords of the council.

But to know more perfectly who these conjurers were, and to what their conjuration tended, take the earl's letter, dated Feb. 1, from Sheffield castle, sent to the privy council concerning them. Which was to this purport: " That he " had sent up to them one Avery Kellet, servant unto " Rowland Lacon of Willy in Bridgenorth, esq. who had " sent him to the said earl, being thereto required by his " servant, that had searched for him upon his command-" ment. That this Avery, upon his examination of him at " the first, would needs seem to be simply plain, and ut-" terly both innocent and ignorant of any lewd doings or " practice, either by himself or by any other person. But " after sharper imprisonment for one night, he confessed " that he was a dealer with the conjurers; and that he " brought several books of that art unto John Revel, which " the conjuring scholars, called Palmer and Falconer, and " Skinner the priest, did occupy in their practice at the " said Revel's house. And he said further, that they con-" jured for divers causes; viz. for hidden money; for help-" ing the diseased; for knowing some secret place to hide " them; and to have certain knowledge also touching the " state of this realm. And hereby the said earl did gather, " that this Avery could declare some further matter need-" ful to be discovered. That therefore, considering his be-" ing there might do more service by conference with other " examinations, than he could do in those parts, [where he " was taken,] by trying the more speedily those practices; " he thought meet not to stay him any longer, but forth-" with thus to send him to be used there, according to their " lordships' wisdoms.

" He signified also, that he had given order for further " search and apprehension of such others, as he was in-" formed of, suspected to be doers, or privy to the said " practice. Subscribed,

" Yours at commandment to my power,

" G. Shrewsbury."

And no wonder these northern parts were so replenished CHAP.
with such popishly affected people, since the late rebellion, XX.
which sprang hence. They were observed to be so many Anno 1572.
now in Yorkshire, and their numbers still so formidable Papists formidable
there, that one Mr. Wharton of Rippon, a worthy gentle- for their
man, and apprehensive of the danger arising hence, (where- numbers in Yorkshire.
of he had felt the smart before,) thought convenient to
write to the lord treasurer at large concerning it : with his
earnest advice, (the gentlemen in those parts being either
too weak to take them up, or disperse them, or too well affected towards them, or related to them, to do it,) that for 183
the more effectual watching that country, and clearing it of
such false subjects, some active men of the queen's council
in the south should be sent down thither: the same gentleman offering freely his own service therein, and to come up
and give his information. The letter will shew these things,
and the like, more at length ; and is well worth preserving.
It ran to this tenor :

  " That it might please his good lordship to be advertis- Warning
" ed, that when he considered how honourably the estate thereof given in a
" imperial of this most noble region, ever since the begin- letter to the
" ning of the queen's majesty's most gracious reign, (which treasurer by Mr.
" he beseeched God long to continue,) had been most pru- Wharton.
" dently and politicly governed, and also most godly and
" virtuously directed, to the advancement of God's true
" glory, and the singular consolation and comfort of all her
" grace's faithful and obedient subjects, until then of late,
" that in those north parts a wicked company or rabblement
" of notorious, malicious traitors, against all loyalty, and
" their bounden duties and allegiance, and the great annoy-
" ing and disturbance of our common peace, committed and
" stirred up an unnatural, odious, and a most detestable re-
" bellion.   The original whereof was ambition, with im-
" patient poverty, secretly maligning and repining at the
" worthy vocation of others, placed in higher authority.

  " And that albeit God had poured down upon them his
" just vengeance, and had supplanted and overthrown their
" wicked devices and practices, to the perpetual infamy and

BOOK
I.

Anno 1572.

" extinct of blood for ever; and to the terrible example of
" all others, to attempt the like heinous offence; yet was
" there a remnant there, which were vehemently to be sus-
" pected to be singular favourers and privy supporters of
" that naughty seditious company.

" For consanguinity and affinity, with hope for a day,
" bore there such a stir and a sway, that by means thereof
" divers good subjects and well-willers were *pessuntate*, and
" clear out of countenance in these parties : and all and sin-
" gular good and politic orders and directions, set forth by
" proclamation against the maintainers and supporters of
" the rebellious fugitives, little or nothing at all regarded,
" or in any way executed.

Moves for
a commis-
sion of some
of the
queen's
council to
be placed in
those north
parts.

" Wherefore he had thought it his bounden duty, both
" forenempst God, and in discharge of his natural sub-
" jection towards his prince, to signify unto his honour,
" that it would please the queen's majesty, by his lordship's
" accustomed good counsel, and others with whom he might
" best like, to impart the contents of this his letter; to
" place there immediately, by a special commission, some of
" her honourable, most trusty, and dearest friends and
" counsellors, in the south parts : by whose better industry
" and vigilant regard *our crooked natures* (said he) may
" be the more aptly bridled and abandoned: a nest of lurk-
" ing traitors weeded out, and the secret supporters and
" favourites discovered, and brought to light.   That there
" was no doubt, but that their common peace (which then
" stood in great peril) should not only thereby be the more
" firmly established and preserved, but also that the queen's
" majesty, his lordship, and others of her faithful nobility,
184 " with her poor and loving subjects, should reign and live
" together in more quiet and better security.

" My lord, (proceeded he,) remember the effect and
" familiar example of these two old verses following :

" *Principiis obsta ; sero medicina paratur,*
" *Cum mala per longas convaluere moras.*

" And further, that it might please his lordship to under-

" stand, that if his own health were gud ; or that his habi-
" lity were such as it was before that rusty and haulty trai-
" tor, Richard Norton, had brought him to extreme po-
" verty, he would not have made this his letter to have
" been an instrument, or a spokesman unto his honour in
" this behalf : but his assured expectation and trust was,
" that his lordship would vouchsafe to take and receive this
" his advertisement in gud part ; as unfolded out of the
" bosom of a faithful and obedient subject. And that when-
" soever it should be his pleasure to send his command-
" ment for him, to come before his honour, for further in-
" telligence, touching the cankered state of that country,
" infected with the poison of disloyalty, or otherwise, in
" these cases to direct him, to the lord president, or vice-
" president of the queen's majesty's council in those north
" parts, he would prepare himself to the uttermost of his
" power, to give his diligent attendance ; and not to leave
" any person untouched to his knowledge, either with com-
" mendation or reproach, as he or they had justly de-
" served."

He sent to his lordship also herewith enclosed, " certain
" instructions by way of information, against divers persons,
" to be put in execution, as should stand with his pleasure,
" and other his most singular gud lords of the queen's
" grace's most honourable privy council. But he thought
" it very necessary, that the houses [of these] should be di-
" ligently searched by faithful and trusty commissioners,
" and the said persons thoroughly examined. For that there
" was great presumption of their evil practices and behavi-
" ours ; and great possibility to find in their houses divers
" letters directed unto them from divers their friends, now
" beyond the seas."

And then applying to the lord treasurer concerning himself, and the danger he was like to incur by this faithful
intelligence, should it be known, he added ; " My lord, as I
" have made a singular choice to open these matters unto
" your honour before any other, as unto such a worthy ma-
" gistrate, in whom I have reposed my only confidence and

CHAP.
XX.

Anno 1572.

The canker-
ed estate of
the country.

Sends in-
formations
against
some trai-
torous per-
sons.

"trust, so do I likewise most humbly crave your good "lordship, that for my faithful and further just service "hereafter, I may not only enjoy, and have from time to "time, gud countenance, aid, and friendship, by your gud "lordship's means, as that I need not to fear the violent

His danger for this his service.

"hands and privy malicious practices of such evil disposed "persons, as will not forget (for this mine advertisement) "to seek by all means possible to persecute me with secret "extremities: but also, that it please your gud lordship to "write your friendly letters in my behalf unto the lord pre- "sident or vice-president of the queen's highness's council 185 "in these parties. So that I in the mean time enjoy and "have such his good countenance and friendship, as may "be a terror for mine adversaries to attempt any matter "unlawfully against me. For otherwise, as he gave the "reason, he should be either enforced to seek a receptacle "for his poor wife and children in the other country; or "else to remain there with continual fear of bodily harm, "comforting himself with this saying of Horace,

"*Dulce et decorum est pro patria mori.*"

And then concluding his handsome, well-penned, loyal letter with these words: "And thus most humbly craving pardon "for this my bold writing to your gud lordship, I beseech "the Almighty so to prosper all your doings, as may tend "to the continual advancement of your honourable estate. "From my poor house at Ryppon, the 9th day of Decem- "ber, 1572.

"Your gud lordship humbly to use, "and command, during his life, "William Whartone."

The disciplinarians very busy for further reformation.

The *disciplinarians*, another sort of men, friends indeed to the reformed religion in this land, but very ill affected to some of the constitutions and practices of it; these were also now creating trouble and disturbance here; labouring for a still further reformation. The book called *The admonition to the parliament*, that now came forth, and spread abroad still more the next year, shewed their discontents, and what

they would have reformed, or rather what they would have
quite cast away, and abandoned in this church. Which
book, with the answer, hath been at large accounted for, in
the Life of the learned and excellent Dr. Whitgift, arch- Life of
Archbishop
bishop of Canterbury; to which I refer the reader. I shall Whitgift.
add here to all the rest, an extract taken out of the said Ad- The Admonition.
monition, "containing such slanderous and unseemly terms,
" as there, by the authors thereof, against the orders of
" the church of England, and state of the realm that now
" is, are uttered." Those are all drawn and written out fair
by archbishop Parker's secretary, but, as it seems probable,
gathered by the archbishop himself; each folio, page, and
line, where such obnoxious passages are, set down: and
that perhaps for the better direction of Dr. Whitgift, to
take particular notice of in his answer; who was employed
therein by that archbishop. The treatise itself they entitled,
A view of popish abuses yet remaining: which is in two View of
the popish
parts. The notes whereof throughout, in the reflections Abuses.
and charges made therein upon the church and the practice MSS. G.
Petyt, ar-
thereof, are set down in the said MS. For which I refer mig.
the reader to the Appendix, being somewhat too long to in- Nº. XIX.
sert here.

Some of these hot new *discipline-men* were now com- Field and
Wilcox in
mitted to Newgate. Their fault was, that they had offered Newgate.
something to the parliament, earnestly condemning the present settlement of religion in discipline and worship, and 186
exciting to a further reformation; especially reproaching
the calling of bishops, as well as divers other matters in the
religion observed, in very abusive terms. This book, I
make no doubt, was the same with the Admonition aforesaid. Two of these were taken up and imprisoned, namely,
Field and Wilcox, for offering this seditious book to the
parliament. In vindication of themselves, and petitioning
for their liberty, they wrote a well-penned letter in Latin in
the month of September to the lord treasurer Burghley:
but rather vindicating than blaming themselves for what
they had done.

Wherein they write, " That they confided in his singular Their letter
thence to

BOOK
I.

Anno 1572.
the lord
treasurer.

" benevolence, which moved them to write, with a firm
" trust both of obtaining their liberty, and of propagating
" the truth. They were sensible, (how unjustly soever,)
" they were spoken against among the nobility by evil men,
" and how (a thing more horrid) the truth of God was
" slandered by many. But let truth, (as they proceed,)
" that seeks no corners, speak for itself; and commending
" to him their innocency, and the equity of their cause,
" they very earnestly beseeched him to favour it. That
" they had indeed lately writ a book, requiring the reform-
" ation of horrid abuses; with that intent, that sincere re-
" ligion, being freed from popish superstition, might be re-
" stored by the whole parliament, with the queen's appro-
" bation. But by themselves they attempted neither to cor-
" rect nor change any thing; but referred all to their judg-
" ments, according as so great a matter called for. Hoping
" by this means, that the peace of the church, and the re-
" conciliation of brethren at difference, (a thing to be la-
" mented,) might be restored.

The schism
in the
church la-
mented.

" And that by this ecclesiastical hierarchy, not consonant
" to the word of God, they had seen a sad schism in the
" church, disturbances daily stirred up among the godly:
" that most sweet peace, that ought to be among those that
" profess one and the same religion, was destroyed. That
" in the mean time they said nothing of the contempt of
" good learning, the corruption of the more sincere religion,
" the depraving of the ministry, the increase of sin, and the
" like, occasioned hereby. All which they reckoned a suffi-
" cient justification of their writing. They added, that con-
" cerning these abuses, by them mentioned, all the foreign
" churches of the purer reformation, and the writings of
" men most eminent for learning, did unanimously acknow-
" ledge and own to be very foul." For the rest I refer the
[Nº. XIX.] reader to the whole letter in the Appendix, transcribed from
the original.

Depriva-
tions upon
the statute
13 Eliz. c.
12.

Divers of the clergy of this sort, (and perhaps some secret
papists too,) that had benefices and preferments in the
church, were now deprived, for not subscribing to the Ar-

ticles of Religion, according to a statute 13 Elizab. entitled, CHAP.
An act to reform certain disorders touching ministers of XX.
the church. Whereby all such as had livings, or ecclesiasti- Anno 1572.
cal preferments, were to subscribe the Articles of Religion,
agreed upon in the convocation, anno 1562, and confirmed
by the queen's authority: and order therein provided for
their reading the said Articles, and for declaring their assent thereunto, in their parish churches. I find these deprived in the diocese of Bath and Wells. March 21, one 187
Printost, or Printer, was presented to the church of Dun- Reg. Bath
kerton, by deprivation of the incumbent for not subscribing Collectan.
the Articles. And June 7, one John Haunce, incumbent Mat. Hutton, D.D.
of the church of Waysford, was deprived of the same; and
Edward Bremal, alias Cabel, came in his room. October 1,
John Gold was instituted to the vicarage of East Cokes, by
deprivation of the said John Gold, by virtue of the said
act; at the presentation of the dean and chapter of Exon:
the said Gold refusing, as it seems, or neglecting to subscribe in due time: and so undergoing the penalty of deprivation: and afterwards subscribing, admitted again to the
said vicarage.

January 24, William Bele, M. A. was presented to the Reg. Bath
prebend of Schalford, alias Scanford, at the queen's pre- and Wells.
sentation by lapse: because one Alwood, the then pretended
canon and prebendary, was *merè laicus*, as it is set down
in the register: so esteemed perhaps for having no legal orders, or such as were taken at some private congregation at
Antwerp, or elsewhere, as Cartwright and Travers had
done: and so that mere laic needed no formal deprivation.
And one more I find, viz. Nicholas Rogers obtained the
church of Pryston, by the deprivation of Richard Cove,
upon the same statute of 13 Eliz. in the presentation of the
queen by lapse.

There were these deprived in this diocese of Bath and
Wells, for refusal or neglect of subscription to the Articles
of Religion. We may hereby guess at the numbers that were
deprived through the rest of the dioceses for the same cause.
And from thence also, how many there were of the clergy

T 3

BOOK
I.

Anno 1572.
of this land, that were tainted with principles dissonant to those of the church of England, both puritans and favourers of popery, that hitherto had kept their ecclesiastical livings and prebends, till by this statute they were searched out and discovered.

Many in
Cambridge
disaffected
to the con-
stitution of
the church.
And no wonder those principles of the *new discipline* disaffected many ministers to the present constitution of the church, since, in this year and some years before, the universities were so heated with these controversies. In Cambridge were, Cartwright, Browning, Brown of Trinity college, Millain of Christ's, Chark of Peter-house, Dering of Christ's college, and many of St. John's, more than any of the rest; who, being men of some learning, had made a strong impression upon many of the younger students.

Life of
Archbishop
Parker, and
Archbishop
Whitgift.
These I have taken notice of elsewhere. Only of two or three of them, I have some other things to add, besides what I have shewn of them already.

Chark ex-
pelled the
university,
appeals.
Chark, in a *clerum* at St. Mary's before the university, had roundly condemned the hierarchy of this church, and the ecclesiastical officers thereof, as we have related in the Life of Archbishop Whitgift, under the year 1572: laying down these two bold positions;

Isti status episcopatus, archiepiscopatus, metropolitanatus, patriarchatus, denique papatus, a Satana in ecclesiam introducti sunt.

Inter ministros ecclesiæ, non debet alius alio esse superior.

188   But he having so openly impugned the established order of the church, and so broken the statutes of the university, was convented before the vice-chancellor and heads; and in fine, was required to make a public revocation of what he had so publicly asserted, or else to be expelled the university. And accordingly, some reasonable time was allowed him, to consider what he had to do. But when the time came, and he still refused to comply, he was actually expelled in February. Then did he make his appeal from the judgment of the heads unto the lord Burghley, their high chancellor, in a well-penned epistle, in a good Latin style,

and written in a fair hand, desiring by his lordship's means
to be restored. Therein he telleth the reason of his banishment from the university.

Non dissimulo, quin argumentis e scriptura, et externa-
rum ecclesiarum exemplo adductus, aliquid abesse putem,
quo ecclesia nostra, nuper e tenebris vindicata, propius ad
splendorem πρωτοτύπου χαρακτῆρος *possit accedere, &c.*

Upon this letter (which may be read in Archbishop Whit- The chancellor al-
gift's Life) the lord Burghley, in compassion to Chark, lows of
whom he held a good scholar, and in consideration that he their proceedings a-
was somewhat hardly dealt withal, (according to the im- gainst him.
port of Chark's letter,) wrote to the vice-chancellor, and
the rest of the heads in his favour. To whom they gave
him so satisfactory an answer, both in respect of their regular proceedings and Chark's behaviour, that the good
chancellor, in his next message despatched to Dr. Byng, his
vice-chancellor, wrote, " That he was sorry that he was not
" made privy of Chark's *fancies,* as he styled his novel doc-
" trines against the calling of archbishops and bishops, &c.
" and for the equality of ministers. And that only by his
" submission to him, with request of mercy to be shewed,
" he was moved, he said, to wish as he had done. But
" that now he was ready to forbear to entreat otherwise for
" him, than that he publicly revoke his slanderous asser-
" tions. And that without the doing of which, he was not
" worthy of favour. And so he prayed the vice-chancellor
" to impart his meaning to the senate and his collegiates."
Written March the 3d, 1572. Whence it appeared, that
there was in the university a combination of disaffected
scholars to the church, and they a very strong party. For
Chark was, by a consultation of them, appointed to preach
the doctrine he did.

Chark's cause, and the reason of the chancellor's inclina- The chancellor to the
tion to have favour shewn him, may appear in a former let- heads, upon
ter to his vice-chancellor and the heads, upon Chark's per- Chark's re-
presenta-
sonal application to him, and his relation of his pretended tion of his
hard usage. Thus writing, Feb. 20, " That where they had cause.
T. Baker,
" expelled Will. Chark, late fellow of Peter-house, for some S.T.B.

" speeches used by him in a sermon he lately had *ad cle-*
" *rum;* tending to the disturbing of the quietness and peace
" of the church, and manifestly contrary to the orders taken
" for the maintenance of the same peace: that forasmuch as
" the said Chark had been with him, and partly wisely ex-
" tenuating his fault, partly very honestly acknowledging
189 " that he committed the same by overmuch vehemency of
" spirit; and faithfully promising never hereafter to deal
" therein again, or in the like, that might be offensive; and
" had shewed some good parts of nature, and good gifts to
" be in him; the which in his [the high chancellor's] opi-
" nion, it were great charity and good wisdom, by gentle
" usage and persuasion, rather to reduce to be profitable in
" the church of God, than by sudden cutting him off from
" the course of his studies utterly to lose: that therefore
" these were heartily to pray them, the rather for his sake,
" and for proof of him hereafter, to receive him again into
" that university, and his fellowship within the college;
" upon his like promise made to them, not to meddle here-
" after in such kind of doctrine. Wherein if they would
" shew some indulgence for this time, and the rather sup-
" press the memory of his said speech and doctrine, for
" that it was delivered in the Latin tongue, and not popu-
" larly taught, in his judgment they should do well. And
" so praying them to do, he bade them heartily farewell."

Remits him
to the
heads.
T. Baker,
S. T. B.

But afterwards, upon a more particular account of Chark's
behaviour and stiffness before the vice-chancellor and heads,
represented to their chancellor, " he remitted him in an-
" other letter, dated March the 25th, to be ordered as they
" should think expedient. And that he had now less re-
" spect unto him: for that he found not that submission
" and conformity in him, whereof he had conceived some
" opinion at his writing of his letters unto them in his fa-
" vour." But more of Chark's business may be read in the
Life of Archbishop Parker.

Browning
troubled for
a sermon at
St. Mary's.

To whom I subjoin the trouble of one Browning, a fellow of Trinity college in the same university; who underwent the censure of that university also, for a sermon of

his, preached at St. Mary's; being one of these novelists. CHAP.
He was charged for preaching the Novatian heresy. Of   XX.
whose matter some notice hath been taken in the Life of Anno 1572.
Archbishop Parker. To which I add, what concern the uni- Book iv.
versity's chancellor had in this business, as well as in that of
Chark's. He had appealed, it seems, to him, for favour
against the proceedings of the vice-chancellor and heads
against him. But Browning being brought to relent before
the chancellor, had revoked his opinions, and made his submission and confession by word of mouth before him and
others there present; and subscribed the same. Whereupon
the kind chancellor desired the vice-chancellor and the rest
of the heads to receive him. Whose letter to them ran in
this tenor:

" That forasmuch as Browning had, both by his speech The chan-
" before him, and by his confession, subscribed by himself cellor's let-
" before him, Mr. Secretary, and Mr. Chancellor of the Ex- university,
" chequer, did not only affirm, that he was much mistaken him.
" in his sermon, but had promised to give open testimony of
" his conformity in those points, wherein he was mistaken,
" at any occasion that shall be offered unto him. He
" thought good therefore to write unto them in his behalf
" in a former letter: and now he sent unto them his said
" confession subscribed, as they might see; to the intent
" they might make some proof, whether he should con-
" tinue in that conformity and submission that he pretend-
" ed there, with his lordship and the rest. Which if he 190
" should do with effect, then they should do well to receive
" him, and cherish him with all good countenance and usage.
" If not, then he both referred to their discretion the reform-
" ing of him; and very carefully commended to their dili-
" gence and wisdom the conservation of the peace of God's
" church, and the good fame of that university." This person seems to overcome this trouble; but fell divers years
after into another, with the college and university, for taking
his doctor's degree at Oxford: which is shewn in the Life of
Archbishop Parker.

Edward Dering, contemporary with them, was another, Dering the
disciplina-
rian.

and of good learning, who stood thus affected, and made a chief figure in the same university near this time. Of whom some things also have been by me written in another place. This man, by reason of his being a reader in St. Paul's, London, and a preacher of a ready utterance, and of great confidence, did also draw away many proselytes. It was therefore thought convenient to silence him from preaching his lecture any more. And so he was the next year, viz. 1573. This man was a great enemy to the order of bishops. He was known to the lord treasurer; and took often the freedom to write unto him, sometimes earnestly stirring him up to favour Cartwright and his opinions, and such as were his followers; and sometimes accusing him for his faults: endeavouring to make that great lord an instrument for the bringing about their purposes. And in the beginning of this year he sent him a letter so indecently writ, and with such rude reflections and charges upon that most pious and wise nobleman, that it did somewhat stir his mild and good nature, as appears in a letter unto him, dated April 3, wherein is seen as well this lord's modest and Christian deportment, in justifying himself against Dering, as Dering's principles and lofty spirit. It ran to this tenor:

Lord
Burghley's
letter to
him, con-
cerning the
restoring
Cartwright.

"That since he received from him, in a piece of paper, a
"biting letter pretended, as by the beginning of a few of
"his lines appeared, for Mr. Cartwright; whose name he
"[Dering] reiterated, (willing him not to be in heat at the
"mention of his name,) he had been in doubt, he said,
"whether he should, either for wasting of his time, or for
"nourishing Dering's humour, make him any answer by
"letter: but he yielded, as he saw. That for so much as
"concerned Cartwright, he answered *sine excandescentia*,
"(which was Dering's term to him, that he would not be in
"a passion at his request,) that his return [back to the uni-
"versity again, from whence he had lately been expelled]
"would be very grateful to him, and that he, for his part,
"wished him well. But for his return to the reading of
"any public lecture there, (which Dering had, it seems,
"earnestly moved for, to that lord,) he could promise no-

" thing of himself. For he knew no power he had therein:
" though he knew it to be his duty to further all good
" learning and quietness in the university; that indecent
" contentions might be excluded.

  " That all the rest of his pamphlet or letter (for he would
" call it no worse) contained divers ejaculations against
" him : as making him void both of knowledge and godli-
" ness. But if he were such an one, he should be ashamed, 191
" he said, to live in the place where he did ; and might be
" accounted a mere pagan, without sense or knowledge of
" his God. And that, except it pleased God to direct good
" men to think better of him than he [Dering] did, he
" should not be in danger of vainglory.   That though he
" would not flatly deny his pronunciations of him, or say
" that he spake not right; yet that he might be licensed to
" pray him not by recrimination to charge him, and say,
" that he justified himself.   That, contrary to his hard
" speeches, through God's goodness, he affirmed, that he
" had not, to his knowledge, conceived or held *obstinata*
" *consilia*, [as he seems to have been charged by Dering.]
" And that further he would say, that through God's good-
" ness, and through good erudition in his young years, he
" had beheld the gospel of Christ; not *eminus* [i. e. at a
" great distance] now for many years, [as Dering had
" abusively accused him,] but in very deed, with such in-
" ward feeling of God's mercy by Jesus Christ, and con-
" firmed to him by his sacraments, as he trusted he might
" say with the church, *Pater noster, sanctificetur nomen*
" *tuum.* And whereas he had pronounced hardly of him,
" in taxing his religion, [i. e. as it seems, in queen Mary's
" days,] this calumniation, or uncharitable reprehension,
" that it proceeded of any just cause, he utterly denied to
" him, and all his bolsterers, if any he had in this his li-
" centious liberty of writing what he listed. And that he
" must bear it with the rest, since he [Dering] wrote *tan-*
" *quam ex sublimi speculatorio ;* [so magisterially and
" loftily.]"

He continued his letter to a greater length, with much

BOOK piety, modesty, and a great government of himself under
I.   such unjust provocations from an inferior. And in the end,

Anno 1572. the worst he said of him, was, " That he wished to himself
" that which Dering judged he lacked, and to him all that
" which he seemed to have, and more than by his be-
" haviour he seemed to have, and both of them to require
" of God, the knower of hearts, to plant in their hearts the
" true fear of him, and transplant out of their hearts all
" seeds or roots of vainglory." The whole letter of so memorable a man deserves well to be read over and preserved.

Numb. XX. And therefore I have reposited it in the Appendix.

Dering's   To this moderate letter penned by the good lord treasur-
answer.   er, (who had been so severely and undeservedly reflected
on,) Dering in a day or two sends another in answer, so
full of stiffness, and so abounding in his own conceit, that
we cannot but gather a character of that man's temper and
spirit thence. It was writ in Latin, and too long here to repeat. I have therefore only observed briefly divers passages
in it. As where that lord had taken notice of the liberty
and boldness he took in his writing, he affirmed, " That in
" all his letters and business which he ever had with him,
" he diligently took heed of that, that he did not abuse
" mercenary praises, either for his own benefit, or that
" lord's damage. And that this was all that licence of writ-
" ing that he so blamed : by which neither of them were the
" worse. And that his lordship had herein the true cause of
" that holy liberty which he took ; and which he with the
" highest injury called *libidinem et licentiam.* That where
" his lordship conjectured, that his piety seemed so little in
192 " Dering's esteem ; he prayed him, that he might look
" again upon his own letter, and if there were any thing
" therein so unworthy of his honour, or of Dering's func-
" tion, he should be willing to have such rashness of his
" punished, if he did not under his own hand confess it.
" And that to asperse his thoughts and cares to be obsti-
" nate counsels, such as Satan's were, and which God
" would one day destroy, was a greater crime than he ac-
" knowledged to be his.

" His lordship took it ill that he [Dering] should say,
" that his lordship did for a great many years *evange-*
" *lium eminus aspicere, nunc fere diligere,* i. e. had looked
" upon the gospel a great way off, and scarcely had any
" love now to it: he answered, he did not thereby deny
" his lordship's cares above others, to be most ready to
" propagate the gospel. That he knew, (unless he was
" much deceived,) that he had done there at court, and
" how great contest and struggle he had sustained. But,
" added he, take heed how you think you have here done
" any thing, so as you ought to do. Set before your eyes
" your labours, your watchings, your cares, your troubles,
" your anxieties of your mind. And then [as though all
" this his pains was only for the aggrandizing and enriching
" of himself] he asketh him, What at length are the ends
" to which you devoted your so many heavy tasks ? Whe-
" ther it were not for your heaping up of honours to your-
" self, and for the increasing of wealth ? O! misery, gotten
" very dearly! So it is, my lord, so it is, if you deny it to
" eternity.

" Whereas the said lord had writ in his letter, that he
" had dedicated his studies and endeavours to promote the
" gospel: O! said Dering in his answer, I wish you this
" light of the gospel of God, which hath, as you say, en-
" lightened you *cominus,* [i. e. so near,] and inwardly ac-
" cording to the measure of the gift of Christ. And may
" Christ so shed forth upon you his love, that hereafter
" you may not *eminus* [i. e. afar off] look upon it, but also
" be fervent in spirit."

And among other reflecting sayings Dering writ, this was
one, (in respect of something that was like to be done at
the parliament approaching,) *Nescio quid alunt monstri, qui
infulata authoritate subnixi, sic ambulant, ut evangelium
regni e sublimi despiciant;* i. e. I know not what monster
they breed up, who, upheld by the authority of a mitre, so
walk, as looking from on high, in contempt, upon the gospel of the kingdom. For the favourable acceptation of
which expression, he prayed his lordship to take heed, how

BOOK he took his words; and that he should not think he struck
I. at any truly pious man, even though he were a bishop. But
Anno 1572. to make amends for this short and imperfect account of the
former letter, wherein Dering delivered and explained his
mind and sense to the said lord, and with as much affected
learning as he could, I have put the whole into the Ap-
N°. XXI. pendix; especially containing several things of remark in it.

---

193 CHAP. XXI.

*A sermon preached by Cooper, bishop of Lincoln, at Paul's
Cross, in vindication of the church of England and its
liturgy. An answer thereto sent to him by some disaffected person. Observations therein made, of bishops
maintaining an ignorant ministry. Of the Service-
book. Of the titles and honour of the bishops. Of the
government of the church. And the applying of some
places of scripture.*

The bishop AND to shew more of the endeavours of the disaffected to
of Lincoln's the church, and its liturgy and rites, Dr. Cooper, the learned
sermon at
Paul's bishop of Lincoln, having made a sermon at St. Paul's Cross,
Cross: and on Sunday the 27th of June, touching these matters, (oc-
an answer
thereof sent casioned by the book called, *An admonition to the parlia-*
him. *ment,*) an answer was soon penned against it; which I have
seen in MS. And because I think it was never printed, I
shall here exemplify it. Wherein will be seen the anger of
the party against our church's constitution, and with what
arguments they maintained themselves, and what objections
were used against it. It is entitled, *An answer to certain
pieces of a sermon made at Paul's Cross, &c. by Dr. Cooper,
bishop of Lincoln.* Who this answerer was, I cannot tell.
But that it came to the bishop's own hands, appears by the
address at the beginning, and by a marginal note or two, of
the bishop's own hand; which I shall set down as they oc-
cur. It begins thus:

MSS. G. Pe- " Forasmuch, master Cooper, as your sermon, preached
tyt, armig.

" upon Sunday the 27th of June, in anno 1572, did offend
" many, and among the rest, me, I thought myself bound
" in conscience to deal with you touching two or three
" points; leaving other matters to other men, grieved as
" much as I: who, I know assuredly, will, either by word
" of mouth or by writing, or both, talk with you concern-
" ing the same. But the occasions which moved me to
" write are these points following; wherein I dissent not a
" little from you:

" I. In your maintaining of an ignorant and unlearned
" ᵃ ministry.

" II. In your magnifying of the English Service-book.

" III. In your defending of the ungodly titles and un-
" just lordship of bishops.

" IV. In your depraving of that government, which Christ
" hath left to his church.

" V. And last of all, in your wresting and wringing of
" scriptures from their natural sense and meaning."

And then his discourse upon each point was as followeth:

I. Concerning the first. You seemed to allow and like
well of the unlearned company that now is of English ministers; and you seemed in some sort also to dislike them.
By the way, take this with you;

Conveniet nemini, qui secum dissidet ipse.

You took occasion to treat of this matter, as I suppose, by
reason of a little book, entitled, *An admonition to the parliament;* which wisheth, (as you all yourselves then did,)
that every congregation might have a godly, a learned, and
a painful preacher. But this seemed unto you impossible:
for they are not now to be had, said you. Neither were
they at the first to be had, because mutability of religion in
king Henry's days, king Edward's days, queen Mary's days,
&c. caused many towardly wits to refrain the ministry in
the beginning of this queen's reign; and to commit their
studies to physic, to law, to teaching schools, &c. And
therefore the bishops were at that time enforced˙ to admit
into the ministry ignorant and unlearned persons.

This, so far as I remember, was the effect of your words.

ᵃ I did not allow them, nor shew myself to like well of them, but bewailed the cause, and wished the continuance only in respect of necessity. And in comparison of papistical priests, I somewhat diminished the grievousness of the crime. Bishop Cowper's hand.

For the proof whereof it had been good for you to have
shewed, out of the writings of the Old and New Testament,
some plain testimonies or examples, and not to have dealt
so carnally as you did: for both it worketh a suspicion in
the minds of the hearers concerning your grounded knowledge in divinity, and also declareth that you yourself are
but carnal. For the things uttered by you savoured not of
God's spirit, but of the fleshly reason and worldly policy,
one of the greatest enemies that true religion ever had or
can have. He that dealeth in such a public place, for the
stay of the conscience of the auditory, must leave worldly
reason and fleshly policy as very weak grounds, nay, rather
no grounds at all, for Christians to stay their faith upon, and
flee and stick to the holy scriptures only.

But you then saw, and the rest of your fellow-bishops since
understood, that if you should deal that way, your juggling
would be espied. And therefore, like crafty michers and
subtile foxes, you flee into the dark, (*for every one that doeth
evil hateth the light,*) and are afraid, like heathen and ethnic
rhetoricians; to the end that you might bring those good
men out of credit with your auditors, contrary to your own
consciences, to object unto them horrible and wicked un-
truths. (As that they should go about to hinder the course
of the gospel, and to gape for your livings.) Following in
this point your most familiar doctor, father Quintilian, the
orator, who commandeth an adversary to bring and forge of
another whatsoever by any probable means he can, although
he knoweth right well that all is false. It had been plain
dealing for such doughty divines, as yet will seem to be, (if
ye had then the book before named,) to have taken the places
of scripture there quoted, and to have answered them ; and
if they had been wrongly applied, to have shewed it to the
people. But that way was not best for you: for you saw
that they were too plain, and could not be rightly gainsayed.

195 And therefore you not only willingly confessed this to be
true, that every congregation should have a preacher, as is
before specified, but did run out into blind and odd corners ;
to the scouring and sweeping whereof I am enforced to

come, seeing you will not deal with the scriptures in the book cited.

The first reason you made for the bolstering of your learned ministries was this, that oft altering of religion altered men's minds for meddling in the ministry; therefore you could have no learned ministers. What is this else to say, I pray you, but that they and you too, I fear, did rather seek unjust honour and ease in the ministry, than a burden or labour? They forgot, and belike you did not well remember, that death itself should not alter their minds from that whereunto God's Spirit[a], according to his revealed word, had moved them. So that one of these must be granted; either that they were void of God's Spirit, and therefore neither God's children, nor fit men to be ministers of the gospel; or else that worldly preferment and gain, if they would take that charge upon them, did stir them thereto. And therefore should not be received, &c.

[a] I did not defend the thing, but shewed the cause. Bishop Cowper.

As for those unlearned ones, whom you call, neither are they ministers, though you so term them, neither have authority to minister sacraments, though you give them power so to do, except they can minister the word by preaching also. Neither are they called; but they run and seek, and by letters come in. Better it were that some honest parishioners should be appointed to read the scriptures in order, till they might have a preacher, than such reading ministers should be admitted. Yea, and you and your fellow-bishops shall answer for all the parishes in your dioceses, where such insufficient hirelings are. How are such dispensers of the word? How can they divide the scriptures? What manner of watchmen are these? What kind of light shew such forth? What can be seasoned with such salt? How work they in the Lord's harvest?

And you added further concerning this matter, that there were in England 20,000 parish churches, and not 20,000 preachers to furnish them : so that such ministers as were required in so great a number were not to be had. About this matter let me ask you one question. Are you sure, that that which you speak is true? I think, for the safeguard

of your honesty, (as for your honour I let it pass, as smelling too much of Antichrist's stench,) you will answer, Yea.
For if you should answer otherwise, you should doubt of
your doctrine, and make a manifest lie.   Both which are in
a preacher very notorious faults.   And is it sure indeed that
such a number cannot be found? Why then do you, by
urging your gay gear, and enforcing popish abomination,
hinder them that would enter? And for the same, by persecuting, as imprisoning, depriving, banishing, excommuni-
cating, suspending, &c. lessen the number of them that are
entered; and, as so many rods of God's vengeance, stop the
mouths of them that would do good.   Belike, either your
churches are well furnished, and provided for, (which cannot be, both because you have confessed the contrary, and
196 also for that you give by your *bull*-licences, to one man to
enjoy two benefices, to have three, to have more, and as
many as he list, or can get,) or else yourselves have not so
great care for them as you pretend, and would fain seem
to take.

For if the one of them, or both, were not true, you would
deal in another sort than heretofore you have done.   Yea, if
it be true that there want so many ministers, why do not
you, following Christ's and Paul's example, setting aside all
worldly offices, instead of ruffian-like and idle-serving men,
take into your houses as many scholars, and instruct them
(as Christ did his apostles, and Paul those that waited on
him) in divinity and understanding of the word; reading
unto them, and expounding for your own exercise, such
scriptures as you intend afterwards yourselves to entreat of?
This would help to increase the number of good preachers,
si hoc vobis ita curæ esset, ut simulatis ; and make you such
bishops as Paul requireth ; whereas you have not one thing
almost that Paul commandeth to be in a bishop, &c.

Christ doth will his disciples, considering the greatness of
the harvest, to pray to the Lord of the harvest, to send labourers into his harvest ; and not to do as you do, to make
idle shepherds, dumb dogs, sleepy watchmen, blind guides,
unskilful teachers, yea, bare readers.   And St. Paul telleth

us, that *God hath given some, apostles; some, prophets; some,*   CHAP.
evangelists ; and some, pastors and teachers : for the gather-   XXI.
ing together of the saints, for the work of the ministry, &c. Anno 1572.
Not once making mention of any such lewd and loitering
ministers as you both make, and thrust upon the congregations. . . . . . . Justly may your coldness and impiety be reprehended, both for suffering enemies to join with you, I mean
papists, and also for maintaining idle vagabonds and loitering lubbers, who bring not so much as one stone to the building up of the Lord's spiritual temple.

But you add further, that the people should have lived
like heathens, and without a God in the world, if there had
not been such made to read the scripture unto them. Now
surely you shew what a divine you are, (setting aside your
doctorship,) better in physic, or teaching a school, than in
the mysteries and secrets of holy scripture. For neither
doth God allow a reading ministry, because the minister
must be διδακτικὸς, that is, *able to teach ;* neither is it lawful
for you to do evil that good may come thereof, unless you
will have the sequel of the sentence to fall upon your pate.
And what good hath come by your reading ministers, if you
truly examine your diocese, you shall be able easily to judge.
Surely, if you find one in a township able and willing to
render a reason of his faith and hope, you shall find the rest
not unwilling only, but unable too. And yet, if the matter
might be truly sifted, it shall be found, that that one person
hath not so well profited by hearing of the scriptures barely
read, without interpretation, but by frequenting sermons in
other places. But you think you have well mended the
matter, when you have justified the English ministry, in
comparison of the popish priesthood, because, as you say,
they can read their service comely, decently, and distinctly;
whereas the popish priests huddle it up without reverence, 197
and are rascal companions.

To answer this : as you make great account of reading
decently and distinctly, so papists judge it a great glory to
mumble mattins swiftly; and I cannot but affirm, that a
great company of your English ministers behave themselves

as irreverently in saying of the divine service, as the popish priests; which evidently appeareth, by those galloping sir Johns in the country, that have licence from you and other bishops to serve two or three cures. And though, either of ignorance you cannot, or of wilfulness you would not see this, yet some of your fellow-bishops have seen it; and therefore in agony and grief of stomach, out of the same place have both spoken against it, and wished a redress thereof, &c. But, I pray you, how long will it be *impossible* to have preaching ministers? Could you do nothing therein these thirteen years? If it pleased God to open the queen's majesty's heart, and to put her willing hand thereto, I could find means that both the universities and cathedral churches, as the matter might be used, should be able to bring forth so many preaching ministers within the space of ten years, as should serve all England. And no man, that hath reason in his head, would or can deny it, the matter is so plain.

The li-
turgy.
II. The second cause of my writing was, because you commended above the moon the liturgy or form of prayer, and administration of the sacraments, which the English church useth; saying, it is most agreeable to God's word of any since the apostles' time, and least clogged with unprofitable ceremonies. When you uttered this, you had forgotten, belike, that saying of the wise man; *He that justifieth the wicked, and he that condemneth the just, even they both are abomination to the Lord.* Neither did you remember, that *he that speaketh lies shall perish;* and, *The mouth that speaketh lies slayeth the soul.* But it should seem, that you spake of ignorance, not having seen the forms of prayer used in other foreign churches. For if you had cast your eye upon that order which the English church in the time of queen Mary used, both in Geneva and this realm in those days, you should have seen an order not so full of superstitions. If that will not please you, you may view those forms that both the church of Geneva itself, and the reformed churches in France and Germany now use. If those like you not, look into Scotland, and consider that order. If none of those will content you, because you are loath to

go so far, you shall do well to behold even under your nose, CHAP.
here at home, the French, and Dutch, and Italian churches XXI.
in London; and you shall see another manner of form, more Anno 1572.
agreeable to God's word, and not clogged (that I may use
your own terms) with so many idle, unprofitable, ungodly,
and idolatrous ceremonies. For there is among them no
private communion, no private baptism, no service for the
burial of the dead, no churching or purifying of women, no
crossing of infants in baptism, no kneeling at the Lord's
supper, no hindering of preaching, no expounding of scripture by bare reading of psalms, lessons, suffrages, collects,
patches, and pieces of epistles and gospels; no prescript
order of service for saints' days, &c. But all things done 198
in order, according to the apostles' rule, and to edifying.

If I would enter into the dispraise of the book of service, as you did in the commendation thereof, I could
avouch, and that justly, more against it out of God's book,
than you are able to bring for the praise thereof. At this
time I will say no more but this: find me any form of
prayer, and administration of sacraments, set forth since the
apostles' time, more full of corruption than this, except it
be the pope's *portuise*, and a book that one Hermannus,
archbishop of Colen, did make, (out of both which you
have patched yours,) and I will not only willingly yield to
it, but as stoutly defend it as you now do. And as for the
authority of Ignatius, Tertullian, Cyprian, Justin Martyr,
Eusebius, and others, they were very vainly alleged, and
brought rather for an ostentation, and to blind the eyes of
the simple, because you would seem rather to have somewhat to say, than to confirm any truth. And yet the most
of them may be justly laid against yourself; and a man may
with your own weapon easily wound you. If you will
stand so precisely to their judgment in some points, why
not also in some others? You know that in Cyprian's time
young children were admitted to the Lord's supper, contrary
to God's word; and men carried off the bread (when the
sacrament was administered) home to their neighbours, and
delivered it to them; which, in many men's judgments, was

not lawful. Neither were the other, which were before Cyprian, (as Tertullian and Ignatius,) void of their errors. And you know that many works are thrust upon us in both their names; of which the best learned doubt whether they were theirs or no. And for us to stand so much upon men's judgment, seeing that *every man is a liar*, and to ascribe so much unto the time wherein they lived, seeing that the apostle tells us, that the *mystery of iniquity began to work* in his days, I judge it a mere vanity, and a deluding of the simple.

But I would fain deal in a word or two with you about Justin's place, because you seem to make most account thereof: for you guessed that it served well for the maintenance of your bare reading, without interpretation and exhortation. Yet if you view the place well, you shall see that it maketh wholly against you: for he sheweth, that as in his time the writings of the apostles and prophets were read upon the Sunday in the public assembly, so the reading being ended, they were expounded and applied to the hearers, to the end that the people might better understand the mind of the Holy Ghost; and out of the mouth of the minister receive also some comfortable doctrines and instructions. Is it so now? Are no scriptures now read, but interpretation and application follows? If you answer truly, you must needs say, No; and withal confess, that this place serveth no whit for your purpose, though you did bear the world in hand that it made mightily for you.

Now, if you will hereafter deal out of the doctors, you were best look that they serve fitly for your heart, lest you utter them to your shame, as you have done these. You must consider this much. That there resort to that place 199 [i. e. Paul's Cross] such as can *try all things, and prove the spirits, whether they be of God, or no:* and, though they lack your countenance and estimation, are able to deal with you, or the best bishop in this church, in any point of Christian religion. Who come not to sleep, as some, or for a show, with other some, or to tangle you, (as you unjustly report,) but to hear your doctrine, and to search the

scripture daily, whether things be so that you speak. God CHAP.
give you grace to walk before him with a simple heart, ut- XXI.
terly renouncing all these shifts and shows which you use Anno 1572.
for the maintenance of your Antichristian honour, and the
defence of the tale of the beast. For you know that *he that
walketh uprightly walketh boldly and surely; but he that
perverteth his ways shall be known.* And *the Lord will
honour them that honour him; and they that despise him
shall be despised.*

III. For that you went about to prove these Anti- Names and
christian titles, *archbishop, lord bishop, honour, grace, me-* titles of archbishops,
tropolitan, primate, dean, archdeacon, official, &c. in mi- lord bishops,
nisters and preachers of the gospel, lawful, which indeed &c.
are altogether contrary to God's word. And first, your
titles of dignity, as *lord's grace, lord bishop, honour,* &c.
how repugnant they are to the scripture, every one, that is
not willingly blind, seeth. And as for your joining civil
offices to your ecclesiastical functions, how wicked that is,
none that hath any taste or feeling of godliness can, without horror and grief of conscience, consider. You know
that one office requires a whole man ; and he that laboureth
most faithfully in one function, shall never do his duty in
such a strait sort as God requireth at his hands. And what
an absurd thing is this too, to confound those too several
callings, which in all commonwealths, either of Gentiles or
Jews, (unless there hath been a very great disorder among
them,) have been sundered ; and to appropriate them both
to one person, which have been severally allotted to two !
You see that Moses was God's magistrate, appointed to
hear hard matters among the people, and to give sentence
therein. And Aaron was the Lord's priest, and laboured
in that office. So Joshua was the Lord's captain, to go in
and out before the people. And Eleazar executed the
charge and function of a priest. But touching this matter,
I will refer you for this time to the judgment of one of
your own coat ; I mean Mr. Alley, late bishop of Exeter.
And this much be generally spoken at this present, concerning those proud titles and unlawful offices.

Now because you dealt with some spiritual ones, to wit, *archbishops* and *metropolitans*, I mean, with God's assistance, to join with you about them. But first you must give me leave to disclose your subtilty and craftiness, which did on set purpose omit to treat of primates, deans, archdeacons, suffragans, commissaries, officials, chancellors, &c. because you were able in defence of them to say nothing. For if you had been able concerning them to utter any thing to the purpose, yea, though it might have had but only a show of some force, you would not have concealed it, no more than you did that which you unfitly and weakly, God knows, concerning archbishops and metropolitans, then spoke. For what a feeble argument is this, There were 200 archbishops in the first Nicene council, three hundred years after Christ, and perhaps before that time : therefore the office is agreeable to God's word, and may well be used. To speak my mind herein, I judge you will prove this argument *ad Græcas calendas;* so weak, nay, so reasonless a reason, was never heard come out of the mouth of any, that had but the countenance of learning.

It is much like a reason that Harding maketh against bishop Jewel, for the communion in one kind. Melchizedek met Abraham coming from the spoil, and offered him bread and wine : therefore we must have the sacrament delivered under one kind. And this one thing I would have you to note, that this word *arch* is not attributed, throughout the whole New Testament, to any officer or minister of God's church militant here in earth. Indeed St. Peter doth call Christ ἀρχιποίμην, the *chief Shepherd.* By which he teacheth us, that if any man vindicate or claim the same title to himself, or receive it, being by other given unto him, he, as much as in him lieth, spoileth and robbeth Christ Jesus of his glory : because, if he doth not exalt himself thereby above God's Son, yet he maketh himself equal with him ; inasmuch as he taketh to him that name and title, which by right doth only belong to Christ.

And as to *metropolitans,* and their first original, we have little to say besides that which you yourselves confess,

namely, that they were by men devised, for the pacifying CHAP.
of schisms and controversies in the church. But here is a __XXI.__
question, whether the primitive church ever appointed any Anno 1572.
such. I am sure you will answer, No; because you are not
able to shew out of the apostles' writings any such order
was taken among them: for they had another way to end
strifes and contentions. If there were any discords in a
church about any matters and points of religion, there was
no metropolitan then of the same church to decide the
matter. But they sent brethren to the ministers and elders
of another church, who gave their sentence according to
truth; and so contentions ceased. This was the order
then; and in reformed churches, this is, at this day, their
common practice. And so it should be among us; unless you will blasphemously say, you can prescribe better
orders for the ending of schisms and quieting of strifes,
than did the apostles, to whom the Holy Ghost was abundantly given.

This then that hath been declared being true, as it is
the infallible truth of God's word, and therefore shall prevail, what remaineth, but that, if you will be accounted followers and favourers of this truth, you renounce these Antichristian titles and honours, being so directly contrary to
God's word; and content yourselves with that ordinary
function and office, that God in his word hath unto you
allotted: labouring also earnestly to bring in that way and
means of pacifying controversies, that God's word appoint-
eth, and the apostles in their times practised; and not so
stoutly to maintain that which man's brains hath devised.
Because that men's inventions, throughout all the scriptures, are generally condemned; especially being so repugnant to God's word as these are. Bind not therefore two
sins together, by enjoying and defending also these unjust
matters: for the wise man telleth you, that *in one sin you
shall not be unpunished.*

IV. Because you said, that for the external form of go- 201
vernment in the church, for administration of sacraments Form of
church go-
and ceremonies appertaining to order, to have them done vernment,

BOOK
I.

Anno 1572.
administra-
tion of sa-
craments
and cere-
monies.

according to the prescript of God's word, you judged it an error; if this be not blasphemy intolerable, then let all the world judge. Christ saith, that *whosoever shall speak a word against the Son of man, it shall be forgiven him; but blasphemy against the Holy Ghost shall not be forgiven unto men.* Hath not the Holy Ghost in the scripture precisely pointed out the spiritual government of his church, which no mortal creature may alter and change? Yet you in the fulness of iniquity say, we are not bound to that order. What voice more blasphemous could that Romish Antichrist have uttered? Indeed, if you had dealt only in the circumstances of the administration of sacraments and ceremonies, your judgment would have been better liked. Yet Beza writeth, that they are able to prove, that not only the doctrine of the church of Geneva doth agree with God's word, but also, that it should not be hard for them to shew, that the simplicity of the ceremonies of that church, and the whole order of their discipline, are drawn out of the same fountain, &c.

Hereby surely you bewray yourself to be without skill in the holy scriptures, because you make no difference between regiment and ceremonies. For *regiment* we have plain and particular commandment, testimonies, and examples. As for *ceremonies*, we have one general rule for all; *Let all things be done to edify; comely, and according to order:* because God is the God of peace and order, and not of confusion. But because you would seem to make this matter more glorious, and to get greater credit among the hearers, you judged that every godly man in Europe is of your mind, if his judgment were asked in these points. And are you sure thereof? Have you travelled throughout all Europe, to understand what they think? I suppose, No; because I have heard you were yet never out of this realm. Where then have you seen their judgments? Writings, I think not: for you came to be a divine but yesterday in respect; and therefore you could not so soon peruse all their works and writings. How durst you then take upon you thus to deal in so public and so learned an assembly? Cer-

tainly what other men guess at it, I know not; but, in my
judgment, it is great boldness and folly. And this further,
to the overthrow of your assertion, I dare say, that if any
learned man's judgment in all Europe were asked, (excepting atheists, libertines, Lutherans, and papists, who des-
perately cast from them, and of set purpose refuse this
godly kind of government,) especially if either they were
of churches reformed, or had seen them; that then he or
they altogether would answer and confess, that this surely
were not the voice of any one that did preach or profess the
gospel, but of some scullion of Antichrist's kitchen, or of
some other instrument that the Devil useth to deceive the
minds and souls of the simple.

And as this was most blasphemous and false, so most untrue also was that which you, out of the poison of your
venomous stomach, then uttered against many, who, because they desired the reformation of cathedral churches, 202
the dens of all loitering lubbers and thieves, you unjustly
accused, saying, that they wished, and sought in like sort,
the overthrow of colleges and universities. But to prove
you deceived, and to declare the thing never to be thought,
much less to be put in practice, this much, in those persons'
behalf, be truly and faithfully spoken. They have as great
care (in the spirit of humility be it said) for the maintenance of colleges, universities, learning, and learned men,
as you, or any other, possibly can have. And if God had
given them as many means and as great abilities to do
good in that behalf, as he hath to you and others, no doubt
but their love would plainly appear, by their deeds and li-
beralities, to be far greater than yours or others is. Yea,
without boasting be it spoken, some of them enjoying spiritual promotions, as you term them, and some others lack-
ing the same, have done more good, to the relief of poor
scholars, than as yet many of your coat and calling.

Further, you know that it becometh all men, but especially bishops and ministers, to speak the truth: and yet, if
I had not before, according to my duty, reproved you for
lying, I would here have dealt more sharply with you for

BOOK the same. *Attamen quod defertur, non aufertur;* espe-
I. cially if you go on forward as you have begun. *Nam qui*
Anno 1572.*pergit, ea quæ vult dicere, ea quæ non vult, audiet.* In the
mean while, God give you and every one grace to speak the
truth to his neighbour from the bottom of his heart.

Places of   V. Because you wrested and perverted sundry places of
scripture al-
leged by the scripture which you alleged. As first, *Nemo potest venire*
bishop.   *ad me, nisi Pater qui misit me, traxerit eum.* Which you
English twice for failing, after this sort : *No man can come
unto me, unless my Father lead him.* Which interpretation savoureth somewhat of Pelagianism, (though you and
your fellow-bishops unjustly charge others therewith,) because it seemeth to attribute some small unwillingness to be
in man, as coming to God ; whereas the apostle telleth us,
that *God worketh in us both the will and the deed, according to his good pleasure.* And God's Spirit sheweth, that
the *imaginations of man's heart are only evil every day.*
So that we cannot of ourselves think a good thought, much
less do a good and acceptable deed in the sight of God.
To lead, you know, is not so forcible as *to draw.* For
many times we may be led thither, whither we would gladly
and without resisting go, &c. Our Saviour Christ's meaning in these words is, both to set forth our unwillingness to
come unto him, that full fountain and treasure of all goodness, and also to declare the forcible means that God the
Father doth use ; who, will we or nil we, will draw us unto
his Son. If you had considered the nature of the place, or
weighed the drift of our Saviour's talk, or scanned the
Latin or Greek word, you would never have interpreted it
after that fashion, &c. The Greek word ἕλκυσε, which generally throughout the scriptures, especially of the New
Testament, (so far as I have yet read,) signifieth in the
agent, *with violence to draw,* &c.

203   The second place which you abused was this, *Every
plant which my heavenly Father hath not planted shall be
plucked up by the roots.* You understand it of doctrine
only, and not of ceremonies ; as much in this behalf wresting the mind of the Holy Ghost in this second, as in the

former, falsely and corruptly expounding the word. For
if you view the text well, you shall see that the matter betwixt the Scribes and Pharisees, and our Saviour Christ,
was about ceremonies and traditions, as washing of hands,
&c. In observing of which order, he gave them to understand, that they were a great deal more precise and rigorous, than in keeping God's commandments; and therefore
calleth them hypocrites: plainly proving, out of Esaiah
the prophet, that they were deep dissemblers before God.
With which plain kind of speech, as it should appear by
the disciples' words to their Master, the Pharisees were
offended. Whereupon Christ taketh occasion to utter this
sentence, *Every plant which my Father*, &c. referring it
not only to *doctrine*, as you say, because in the next chapter he dealeth with their doctrines in these words, *Take
heed and beware of the leaven of Pharisees;* but also to
ceremonies, ordinances, and traditions, whereupon in the
beginning of the chapter the question was made.

Thirdly, you perverted a place in the prophecy of Ezechiel against such as seek the sincerity of the gospel. That
you were somewhat earnest against papists, is not to be disliked; and would to God you would perform in that behalf as much indeed as you prattle in your words. But
that you joined, as it were in one yoke, papists and zealous
gospellers, wishing severe punishment, belike, to be appointed for them, you were not only misliked, and caused
many to judge, that you spake rather of choler than charity; but also you and others, by such vehement words,
have plainly declared yourselves whose children you be.
To what end, I pray you, should you wish more extreme
laws and penalties to be made against poor protestants?
Certain it is, that unless you took their lives from them, you
cannot more cruelly handle some of them, than heretofore
you have done, and at this present do.

For to let pass your former banishments, imprisonments,
suspensions, excommunications, deprivations, &c. (by which
tyrannous kind of dealing you have taken away the means
by which poor men should live, and so in God's sight are

become murderers; for he that taketh away the bread of the poor, taketh away the life of the poor: which we have even now before our eyes, a notable spectacle of your good heartedness;) do you not keep at this hour as godly ministers in close prison, so that no friends can come to visit them? Do you not separate them and their wives, which in God's sight is a horrible iniquity? Do you not labour, as much as in you lieth, by this your tyrannous dealing, to make their wives widows, and their children fatherless? And yet you would have more extreme punishment. Is it not punishment enough, think you, for refusing your popish apparel, and other relics of the Romish beast, to be thrust from house, living, and all that one hath? Is it not a hard censure, for speaking or writing against your missals and pontifical, to be imprisoned at your pleasure? Is
204 it not cruelty almost unheard of, for seeking a reformation of religion, to be thrown into Newgate? Doth not this savour somewhat of a bloodthirsty heart? It argueth to me, (I know not what it doth to others,) that you are of your father the Devil, who was a liar, and the murderer from the beginning. This I can say for them both, that by your tyranny and forcible dealings, they, their wives, children, and families, are utterly beggared.

Is not this to rule with cruelty and rigour? If Ishmael's mocking of Izhach be counted by God for persecution, what will the Lord account this your cruel handling? And do you think for it, you shall escape unpunished? Assure yourself, that as you persecute them, so shall you be persecuted; and as you bring them and theirs to beggary, so shall you and yours, for all your lordships, unless you repent, be brought to as great necessity. Shall I heap up examples against you? Look upon Adonibezek, as right a pattern for you to behold, as possibly can be, &c.

But, methinks, it is reason, that since you linked them and papists together, to make their cause more odious, (whereas indeed there is no just comparison between them; for papists are traitors to God, and their prince, but these as true to both of them, as you, or all the bishops in this realm, meagre your heads,) they should not be more cruelly handled than papists are. Which of the papists did you ever use after this sort? Had not Bonner, while he lived, his strumpet resorting to him daily? Have not the prisoners, which were removed out of the Tower to the Marshalsea, the liberty of the whole house? And none forbidden to resort unto them? Have not you taken some of them home to your houses? set them at your own tables? and made them good cheer? And is those men's case worse than these? I dare therein appeal to your own consciences. Why do you then miserably misuse them, and handle them more cruelly than papists, traitors, atheists, felons, drunkards, whoremongers, blasphemers? &c. Belike, you think, God seeth it not, and therefore say with the wicked, *Tush, God careth not for this.* Or else you have forgotten that God counteth the injury and villainy done to his children as done to himself. Let the hard sentence pronounced against the careless servant somewhat terrify you. And flatter not yourselves herein: for surely God is a sharp revenger of the injuries done to his saints, &c.

But to return to the place of Ezechiel. You went about, out of these words of the prophet, *But I will destroy the fat and the strong: and I will feed them with judgment,* &c. to prove that sharp laws should be made against the seely poor sheep, that in your judgment were unruly; because they would not be ruled by the laws, ordinances, constitutions, and government of Antichrist. Doubtless you should have done well to have considered of what fat and lusty sheep the prophet there speaketh, before you had pronounced so hard and sharp a sentence against the Lord's lambs. The prophet speaks not there of such as refused to subject their necks to the yoke of idolatrous slavery; for from that they were commanded to flee, &c. But he speaketh in that place of swelling and lofty spirits, who not only exalted themselves above their brethren, but thought also, that they had no need to be ruled and governed of God himself, &c. Whether this may be rightly applied against 205 such as seek for the simplicity and sincerity of the gospel,

BOOK and wish to be subject only to God's will in his word re-

I.   vealed, or to papists and you, which will not have Christ,

Anno 1572. by his word and discipline, to reign over you, let all that
have at all any sight in God's word faithfully judge.

I here link you and papists together, (for which I would
not have you to be grieved,) more justly a great deal than
you before did us; not so much for the likeness of your
garments and attire, (which is evil,) as for your unwillingness to submit yourselves (which is much worse) to the
order and form of regiment which Christ hath left to his
church; and stoutly defending, as it were for life and death,
that corrupt and sinful government, which Antichrist, the
pope, and the Devil, have devised and set abroad for the
establishing of their kingdom, &c.

And thus you plainly see my mind concerning some
parts of your sermon. I would willingly have dealt with
you in some other, but that I think I have been somewhat
long in these, and am certainly persuaded that others will
either write to you, or talk with you about those points
which I have not touched, &c. Thus hoping you will
shortly satisfy them by some retractation or apology, whom
in so open a place you have deluded, I take my leave of
you: promising, if you take no regard hereof, not only to
publish this writing, but also further confutations of other
men's doings, that your poison be not received of more, to
their utter confusion. Fare you well.

Whether the bishop of Lincoln vouchsafed any answer to
this challenge and threatening, and the many severe and unjust reflections made upon all the bishops, and the constitution of the church itself, I cannot tell. But, however, I
have transcribed this long paper, that hence might be seen
the spirit of this sort of men in these times, rude in language
to their superiors, dogmatical, confident in their charges of
popery, persecution, and Antichristianism upon this church,
and the reformed governors of it, and extolling their *new
discipline*.

CHAP. XXII.

Serious deliberation about a reformation of divers things in church and state. Memorials. Lent enjoined. Commissions for concealed lands abused: revoked: but granted again. An act against concealers. Grants for penal statutes checked and regulated. Massmongers at the Portugal ambassador's house. The queen's progress. Earl of Northumberland executed. The queen hath the small-pox. Her letter thereof, and of her recovery, to the earl of Shrewsbury. She hath fainting fits.

BUT that these malecontented men, that pretended them- Anno 1572. selves the great reformers of religion, might have no just Reformation set and reasonable cause to find fault for want of correction of about in things really amiss in the church or churchmen, the wise church and state. and good lord treasurer (while the queen was abroad in her progress this summer, and he with her) took this matter into his serious thoughts, the court being now at Reading, and drew up memorials about it. And when the nation seemed to be in great apprehensions of plots and dangers, the queen herself, in order to her better peace and safety, intended a more careful reformation of whatever might be amiss in her kingdom, in all sorts of people, laity as well as clergy, bishops, ministers of the laws in the several courts of justice, commissioners of the peace; and for prudent providing against national dangers and insurrections. Inspections also were thought expedient to be made into the navy, and into the demeanour of the several lord lieutenants of the counties, and inquiry to be made after such as were in any office, whether temporal or spiritual, that were contemners of the orders of religion established. For this purpose the same lord treasurer, in the month of October the same year, at the same place, (where it seems the queen still was,) drew up other memorials with his own hand for Memorials. her use, entitled,

" *Certain things necessary to be better ordered.*

" *The state of the church and religion.* The bishops and MSS. Burglian. penes me.

BOOK
I.

Anno 1572.

A good visitation for this.

" clergy [to be] reformed for their wastes of their patrimo
" nies: the negligence of teaching, and the abuse of plu-
" ralities and nonresidence by unnecessary dispensations:
" the decays of churches, chancels, and chapels ordained
" for divine service, to be repaired: the lack of parsons,
" vicars, and curates in sundry places.

" *The obstinate contemners of religion.* To be punished
" according to the laws of the realm.

207

The lords of the privy council to reform this in the Star-chamber.

" *The ministers of the law* to be reformed. Justices of
" courts and assizes, sergeants, pleaders, counsellors, advo-
" cates, proctors, and attorneys, in both laws, would be
" sworn to the queen's majesty. The excessive taking of
" fees for counsel, and for all other writings in all courts, to
" be moderated, for the ease of the subjects.

" *The houses of court and chancery* to be visited, and the
" abuses reformed: whereby no such confluence of unmeet
" persons, given to riot, sedition, and such misrule, may be
" permitted.

The lords of the council.

" *The councils in the marches of Wales,* and in the north,
" to be considered; that sufficient number of wise, able,
" and meet persons, for the reverence of the place, and for
" furtherance of justice, to be there placed, and the unmeet
" removed; and the abuses of multitude of attorneys' clerks,
" and their excessive fees, also reformed, to the ease and
" comfort of the subjects.

The lords of the council.

" *The commissions of the peace* in all shires to be viewed;
" and the unmeet persons removed, and the rooms supplied
" with more trusty and able persons.

The che-quer-chamber, and the queen's majesty.

" That good and faithful men be appointed *sheriffs* for
" this year.

" Some consultation to be had how the *vent of the com-*
" *modities* of the realm may be more frequent, as well for
" her majesty's benefit in her customs, as for the weal of
" the owners and workers of the said commodities.

Vice-admi-rals, officers of custom-houses, and the officers of the port towns.

" *The navy of the realm* to be surveyed in every port,
" with the numbers of ships and vessels, and the mariners
" for that purpose.

" That *lieutenants* be appointed in every shire: and

" their power to be limited only to attend to the musters of
" the able people; to the furnishing of them with armour
" and weapon; and to have force in a readiness to suppress
" any rebellion, or to serve as by her majesty they shall be
" commanded; and not to deal in hearing of matters de-
" terminable by the laws. That every county be in readi-
" ness with their captains and leaders: and no musters nor
" assemblies to be made, but where the lieutenants shall
" appoint.

" That the late statute for *rogues* be diligently and ear-
" nestly executed.

" That knowledge be had who they are in every county
" that bear office, either spiritual or temporal, that do not
" resort to their churches; and who they are that, though
" they do resort sometime to their churches, be either con-
" temners or deriders of the orders of religion established
" by act of parliament."

The state now thought it highly needful, upon politic accounts, that Lent, and other yearly fasting times, should be
duly observed, according to the ancient orders for abstinence: but the people were not apt at all to comply therewith, and could very unwillingly be restrained from eating
flesh. The queen therefore did now, somewhat before the
season of Lent, give forth a strict and ample proclamation
for the yearly observance of that fast, and all other fish
days, according to the ancient and laudable order for fasting
those times: " Weighing the great and notable commodities
" growing by the due observation thereof within her ma-
" jesty's dominions. She, by virtue of that proclamation,
" commanded all officers, ecclesiastical and temporal,
" straitly to see the same well and duly observed: willing
" and commanding them, in the name of Almighty God,
" to whom they should answer for their peculiar charges,
" and as they would answer to her for their contempt, that
" they did not, either by their own example, or by lack of
" execution of their authority, permit such licentious and
" carnal disorder, in contempt of God and man, and only

208

" to the satisfaction of devilish and carnal appetite:" as the words of the proclamation ran.

And for the city and borough of London and Westminster, the queen gave charge to the mayor of London, and the steward and principal officers of Westminster, to take care, that no butcher, poulterer, or victualler should hereafter kill, sell, or cause to be killed or sold, any flesh between Shrove-Tuesday and the Tuesday next after Palm-Sunday. And that no table-keeper or inn-holder, &c. should dress, or suffer to be dressed or eaten, any flesh within their houses in Lent time, or upon any fish-days, upon pain of forfeiture of 20*l*.: to the queen one half, and the other to be disposed by the church-wardens to the poor. And if any citizen should offend herein, he was to be disfranchised by the mayor and his brethren; and being a table-keeper or victualler, to be utterly disabled to use the same trade: and if he were not a citizen, then, besides the said forfeiture, to endure ten days' imprisonment. And if the person offending were not able to pay the forfeiture, he was to stand one market-day openly upon the pillory during the space of six hours.

Every alderman in his ward was twice in the Lent to cause an inquiry and presentment to be made by oath of twelve honest and substantial citizens of every ward, (being no butchers, poulterers, common victuallers,) what persons did offend in eating or killing flesh. One inquiry to be the Monday after Midlent-Sunday, the other in the week next before Easter. The mayor with his brethren to cause once every fortnight privy search to be made, by honest and trusty persons, of the houses of butchers, poulterers, victuallers, tavern-keepers, for the better understanding whether they, or any of them, did offend in the premises: and if they found any such, to punish them without favour, affection, or respect of persons. The like order to be kept by the discretion of the steward and head officers of Westminster.

The said mayor and aldermen, and steward, were yearly to certify in the court of chancery, before the first day of

Easter term, upon pain of an 100*l.* what they had done in CHAP.
execution of the premises, under their hands and seals, to XXII.
the intent that her highness might consider what diligence Anno 1572.
or negligence was used in the execution hereof.

But this order was not to punish persons that by the laws
ecclesiastical and temporal, for needful and just considerations, were permitted to sell, kill, or eat flesh. And for the
better intelligence of persons licensed it was ordered, that
every person having licence should yearly, the first Sunday
in Lent, notify the same to the alderman of the ward, and 209
to the curate of his parish, or to one of them at the least,
where he dwelt, or else the dispensation to be void. And
this manner the queen commanded to be observed throughout all places in her realm, as nigh as might be, with like
penalty; and especially in towns corporate. From which
towns corporate, situate within an hundred and forty miles
from London, certificate, in form aforesaid, was to be made
in the chancery, at the furthest before the second return of
Easter term, upon pain of an 100*l.* to be levied to her majesty's use upon the corporation so making default: and
from all other corporations further distant, certificates to be
made before the last day of Easter term.

She charged, by the said proclamation, all bishops, curates, and other ecclesiastical persons, to exhort and persuade the people in their sermons to forbear this carnal licence, and boldness to break common order; and to let
them understand the great danger of the wrath of Almighty
God, that will always light upon rebellious and obstinate
people. And because this proclamation should have continuance, she charged all mayors, sheriffs, and other head
officers, that it should be proclaimed in every place usual,
and yearly to be hereafter proclaimed, upon such market-
days as should next go before the first week of Lent: and
that at every leet, at Easter, inquisition should be made of
the execution hereof.

This year a command from the queen went forth for the Commis-
withdrawing her commissions for *concealments* from all to sions for
whom she had granted them: which gave a great quieting lands a-
bused.

x 3

to her subjects, who were excessively plagued with these
commissioners. When monasteries were dissolved, and the
lands thereof, and afterwards colleges, chantries, and fra-
ternities were all given to the crown, some demeans here
and there pertaining thereunto were still privily retained
and possessed by certain private persons, or corporations, or
churches. This caused the queen, when she understood it,
to grant commissions to some persons to search after these
concealments, and to retrieve them to the crown. But it
was a world to consider what unjust oppressions of the people and the poor this occasioned by some griping men that
were concerned therein : for under the pretence of executing commissions for inquiry to be made for these lands concealed, they, by colour thereof, and without colour of commission, contrary to all right, and to the queen's meaning
and intent, did intermeddle and challenge lands of long
times possessed by church-wardens, and such like, upon the
charitable gifts of predecessors, to the common benefit of the
parishes ; yea, and certain stocks of money, plate, cattle,
and the like. They made pretence to the bells, lead, and
such other like things, belonging to churches and chapels,
used for common prayer. Further, they attempted to make
titles to lands, possessions, plate, and goods belonging to
hospitals, and such like places, used for maintenance of
poor people ; with many such other unlawful attempts and
extortions, to a pernicious example, if the same had been
further used and suffered, by colour hereof.

Proclama-
tion for
calling in
these com-
missions.

210
At length the queen set forth a proclamation, Feb. 13,
at Westminster, to withstand this manner of extortion, and
unlawful practices and troubles of her subjects : and commanded therefore, " That all commissions which were then
" extant, and not expired, for inquisition of any manner of
" concealments, should be, by *supersedeas* out of her court
" of exchequer, revoked. And because the frauds of of-
" fenders in such cases did so abound, as it might be, that
" they which had already begun, by colour of commission,
" to use such extortion and vexation for gain, would them-
" selves so conceal the revocation of their commission, being

" but by process of *supersedeas*, therefore her majesty, to
" notify this her gracious disposition more publicly to her
" subjects, and to procure due punishment of the offenders,
" with restitution of things wrongfully taken, gave to un-
" derstand by these presents, that all manner of commis-
" sions then extant, that had passed from any of her courts,
" to inquire of any lands, tenements, and hereditaments, or
" of any goods or chattels, concealed or supposed to be
" concealed, before the day hereof, should cease, and not
" continue; and that no commissioner should, by virtue of
" any such commission, charge any person to inquire fur-
" ther of the contents of any such commission. And if
" any person should have cause to complain of any other,
" for any manner of extortion or misusage by colour of
" such commission, the same might exhibit their complaint
" to the justices of assize the next circuit, or to any other
" two or three justices in the shire; whom the queen
" charged to cause the truth of the complaint to be ex-
" amined, and the offenders to be severely and speedily
" punished, and to make due and large restitution. Or if
" the causes of the extortion should be great, or that the
" offenders could not be found within the county, then that
" certificate be made thereof by the justices of assize or of
" the peace, either to the privy council or the keeper of the
" great seal, to be further tried and punished in the Star-
" chamber for a further example.

  " But though her majesty meant to relieve her subjects
" from wrongs and vexations in this sort, yet she gave them
" withal to understand, that she intended not to forbear,
" by some better ordinary means, and by persons of known
" honesty and wisdom, to inquire of such lands and other
" things as duly and justly did belong to her crown, and
" were withdrawn and concealed. Wherein such care should
" be had, as hereafter no commission should be granted,
" but to such persons as should be reputed of such trust
" and honesty, as should by no means give cause to offend
" any, but such as of mere wrong would keep and detain
" things belonging to the crown.

" And she would have her justices of assize to have some
" special care, not only to the premises in that their next
" sessions, but also to the reforming of certain covetous
" and injurious attempts of divers that had of late time, by
" other colour than for her majesty's use, taken away the
" lead of churches and chapels, yea, and the bells of the
" steeples, and other common goods belonging to parishes:
" an example not to be suffered unpunished nor unre-
" formed."

Thus were these *harpies* and *helluones*, this *turbidum ho-
minum genus*, these graceless and wicked men, (they are
the lord Coke's expressions bestowed on them,) thus were
211 they for a time laid asleep; but they awake again at times,
and plagued the nation throughout this queen's and the
most of the next king's reign.   And the cathedral of Norwich had like to have lost most of its revenues, under pretence of concealment, towards the latter end of queen Elizabeth.   A patent of *concealment* was granted certain persons, who, under obscure words, endeavoured to swallow up
the greatest part of the possessions of that ancient and famous bishopric : which, by the industry and prosecution of
the then attorney-general, was overthrown.   And yet, for
more surety in a matter of so great weight, a bill was preferred in parliament for the establishing of the bishopric:
which passed as a law, an. 39º. Eliz. cap. 22.   See this case
at large in the fourth part of Coke's Institutes.

The church
of Norwich
in danger
by them.
Lord Coke,
Instit. part
4.

Cap. lii. of
the city of
Norwich.

An act to
put an end
to them.

There was a statute in the 21st of king James I. against
these *concealers*, and all pretences of concealments whatsoever: it was entitled, *An act for the general quiet of the
subject against all pretence of concealment whatsoever.*
Above an hundred lay hospitals, by the benefit of this act,
having had priests within them in former days to pray and
sing for souls, were established against all vexations and
pretences of concealments.   I add only this more concerning
them: that they began in queen Mary's days; she granted
letters patents of concealments; and the first was to sir
George Howard, as the lord Coke writes.

To this I add, that there were now grievous oppressions

every where, and great complaints, by reason of grants of CHAP.
commissions upon penal statutes of forfeitures to the crown XXII.
obtained by some greedy persons. Thus, in this 14th year Anno 1572.
of the queen, (besides her commissions for concealments commissions
for for-
above mentioned,) she granted to two persons to compound feitures.
for all forfeitures upon nine statutes: viz. I. The statute
against usury. II. The statute for preservation of wood.
III. That timber be not felled to make coals. IV. For the
assize of fuel. V. For the true making of leather. VI.
Against transportation of corn, wood, and victual. VII.
For keeping of sheep. VIII. Against extortion of bribes.
IX. Against procuring and committing wilful perjury. And
the queen was to be answered the fourth part of the money
so forfeited and obtained. There was another grant, for
finding of armour, and against unlawful games. And yet
another, to make search at sea for prohibited and uncus-
tomed wares. And, among the rest, there was a grant to
vex the clergy, (which was by commission to George Delves
and Lancelot Bostock, esquires,) to compound for offences
against the statute of *non-residence*, and other offences of
the clergy, and to take the whole commodity to themselves:
and a like grant was made to sir Raulf Bagnal.

But of all these there went such common complaints, and Regulation
so much vexation of the subject by means thereof all the thereof by
the queen's
land over, that the queen graciously revoked these grants command
for the execution of these penal statutes. But the promoters, treasurer.
to the lord
upon this, immediately entered on the prosecutions of such
transgressions as were put in suit before by those to whom
the said grants were passed. This created new vexations.
The queen therefore, that her gracious intentions of reforming so grievous vexations of her subjects might take place,
ordered her secretary to signify to the lord treasurer, that 212
he should give order for the stay of process in that behalf.
And yet that her laws should not be loose, and void of all
execution, she would have his lordship and the rest of the
lords to devise some convenient plot for the execution of the
same. Which the said lord treasurer accordingly did; and
finished it in the next year, viz. 1573.

And the provision that was made for the preventing of these vexations, and yet providing for the execution of the laws, (as the queen commanded,) was this: devised by the wisdom of the said lord, as appears by the hand used in correction of a draught of the same.   It was entitled,

*Articles to be observed by all such persons as have any grants
of forfeitures upon penal laws.*

I. That there shall be no inquiry by commission: to the end that the charges and trouble of the country, and the grudge and murmur that ariseth among the people, may be avoided thereby.   But to try all their causes by information or action in the exchequer or king's bench, according to the ordinary course of the law.   For so the law doth appoint.

II. That they shall make no composition with any offender, without the making privy thereto the court wherein they shall sue, and also the lord treasurer, or chancellor of the exchequer: to the intent, the portion due to the queen's majesty may be known to be answered.

III. That the patentees shall prefer all informations and suits in their own names, or in the names of such their deputies as the courts of the king's bench or exchequer shall allow of.

IV. That they shall have no process before the information or action entered in the king's bench or in the exchequer.

V. That they shall make no deputies, to execute for them in the country, but such as the court of exchequer shall allow of.

VI. That the patentees shall be bound to the queen by recognisance in the exchequer: that if they vex, or cause any to be vexed wrongfully, then to pay such cost as the court shall tax. And that they shall likewise be bound, that they shall make no compositions without the privity of the court as aforesaid.

These articles were very good checks to these greedy men, that laboured to enrich themselves by extorting, on pretence of some statutes, from the poor commons, both of the clergy and laity: being drawn and contrived by the wise head of that great and useful counsellor, and by the direction of the gracious queen to him.

CHAP.
XXII.

Anno 1572.

The Portugal ambassador, under pretence of having mass said privately in his family, by his privilege as ambassador, had now a good while entertained several mass-mongers in his house in Tower-street: which was now discovered, and a warrant was sent forth, to attach those of the queen's subjects that were present there against her laws. The bishop of London understanding that this ambassador had fostered these persons long time in his house, contrary to our laws, he and the rest of the commissioners for ecclesiastical matters required the sheriff of London, Mr. Pipe, to go and apprehend such as he should find there *committing idolatry*, as the bishop of London expressed it in his letter to the lord treasurer: which warrant the said sheriff executed the 1st of March; *and many he saw there ready to worship the calf.* He apprehended (the rest escaping by the ambassador's means) four students at the law, most of them Irish. These the bishops committed to the Fleet, until the lords' further pleasure were known. Francis Gerald (for that was the Portugal ambassador's name) offered to shoot dags, (which we call pistols nowadays,) and to smite with his dagger, and to kill, in his rage. There was found the altar prepared, the chalice of their bread-god, and a great many English hid in the house, that were minded to hear mass. The bishop gave commission to Norris the messenger to apprehend the Portugal and the mass-priest: but the messenger returned answer, that the Portugal was at the court, to complain. He cunningly told the tale first, and made himself plaintiff: so that the queen was somewhat offended with these proceedings against the ambassador. Upon which the bishop, grieved, wrote thus to the lord treasurer:

Mass-mongers taken at the Portugal ambassador's.

213

" Truly, my lord, such an example is not to be suffered. " God will be mighty angry with it. It is too offensive. If " her majesty should grant it, or tolerate it, she can never " answer to God for it. God's cause must be carefully con-

The bishop of London's zeal thereupon.

" sidered of. God willeth that his ministers purge the
" church of idolatry and superstition. To wink at it is to
" be partaker of it. He told the lord treasurer, that he
" would do well to see that idolater and godless man se-
" verely punished. Or, if you will, added he, set him over
" to me, and give me authority, I will handle him *secun-*
" *dum virtutes.*" In another letter upon the same occasion
he said, " That such idolatry was not to be suffered. That
" strangers were to be borne with *usque ad aras.* But
" princes might not be pleasured with the displeasing of the
" Prince of princes. That such toleration would not be
" suffered in Spain. That this ambassador had mass said
" in his house for a twelvemonth, and twenty at least of
" her majesty's subjects used to resort thither. That the
" queen would do well to send home both Francis Gerald
" and Anthony Guarrez; who did but lurk here in the
" realm as spies to practise mischief: and that they might
" serve their god Baal at home."

The queen's
progress.
The summer of this year the queen went her progress,
beginning it in the month of July. In this progress she
went into Essex. Where, from Havering Bowre, an ancient
seat of the kings of England, (and where queen Maud used
to retire,) instead of going to Enfield, she lay at Theobald's
(the lord treasurer Burghley's house) three days. And then
went to Gorambury, (beside St. Alban's,) the lord keeper
Bacon's. Thence to Dunstable. Thence to Woburne. She
was also at Killingworth, the seat of the earl of Leicester,
another of her great peers: where she was most splendidly
entertained, in the month of August. She also took Reading in her way, where she remained some time. And at
Windsor, September 24, she ended her progress: as secretary Smith in his correspondence acquainted Mr. Walsingham in France.

214
Earl of
Northum-
berland ex-
ecuted at
York.
While the court was at Killingworth, the earl of Northumberland (who was the chief head of the rebellion in the
north some years past) was now brought to York, to be executed: and so the earl wrote in a letter to Walsingham,
dated from Killingworth, August 22, that the said earl of

Northumberland suffered death that day. For that the day before it was ordered, that he should be brought thither that day, under the conduct of sir —— Foster, for that purpose. The effect of this just putting to death of a traitor did but increase the malice of the papists; as was found by the diligence of the said Walsingham, the queen's ambassador in France. Who gave intelligence thence to the court here, of a certain popish spy, named Davy Chambers, who was lately returned out of England, and had conference both with the French king and the duke of Guise, and had let fall these words: how that the death of the earl of Northumberland had increased the number of the queen of Scots' friends; and that she was now grown to have such a party in England, as that five or six thousand shot, with some good leaders, would make her strong enough to encounter any forces her majesty could make. He informed further, that it was secretly whispered in corners, that there was some new practice in hand for the said queen's deliverance. This intelligence was sent over in October.

CHAP.
XXII.

Anno 1572.

Upon which the queen of Scots' friends in England increase. Walsingh. Let.

The queen about this time had the small-pox, as her disease was commonly said to be. For the true account whereof I will set down a clause or two of secretary Smith's letter to Walsingham, written October 13th: " That the " [French] ambassador had audience of the lord treasurer, " the earl of Leicester, and some others; the queen at that " time not being perfectly recovered of that distemper, as " the physicians said, although her majesty and a great " many more would not have it so. But it made no matter " then, as the secretary added, what it was: thanking God " that she was then perfectly whole, and no sign thereof " left in her face."

The queen sick, as was supposed, of the small-pox.

But to pacify her people, especially in the north part, where the Scottish queen was kept prisoner by George earl of Shrewsbury at Sheffield, she so far condescended as to write to him, giving a description of her disease, and assurance of her recovery. For the earl, hearing that her majesty was taken ill with the small-pox, was in no small confusion; and (though it were reported she was better) hastily

The queen writes to the earl of Shrewsbury of her sickness and recovery.

sent to the lord treasurer, to learn of him her true state of health: who acquainting her with the earl's letter, and she knowing what a charge she had committed to him, thought fit to take this opportunity to oblige him further with a letter from herself, (part whereof was of her own hand,) which was as followeth:

"By the queen. Right trusty and right well-beloved
" cousin and counsellor, we greet you well. By your letter
" sent to us, we perceive that you had heard of some late
" sickness wherewith we were visited. Whereof, as you had
" cause to be greatly grieved, so, though you heard of our
" amendment, and was thereby recomforted, yet, for a satis-
" faction of your mind, you are desirous to have the state of
215 " our amendment certified by some few words in a letter
" from ourself. True it is, that we were, about fourteen
" days past, distempered, as commonly happeneth in the
" beginning of a fever; but after two or three days, with-
" out any great inward sickness, there began to appear cer-
" tain red spots in some part of our face, likely to prove
" the small-pox: but, thanked be God, contrary to the ex-
" pectation of our physician, and all others about us, the
" same is vanished away, as within four or five days past
" no token almost appeared; and at this day, we thank
" God, we are so free from any token or mark of any such
" disease, that none can conjecture any such thing.

" So as by this you may perceive what was our sickness,
" and in what good estate we be: thanking you, good cou-
" sin, for the care which you had of the one, and of the
" comfort you take of the other. Wherein we do assure
" ourself of as much fidelity, duty, and love that you bear
" us, as of any of any degree within our realm. Given at
" our castle of Windsor, 22d October, 1572, in the four-
" teenth year of our reign."

This following postscript is the queen's own hand:

" My faithful Shrewsbury, let no grief touch your heart
" for fear of my disease: for I assure you, if my credit were

" not greater than my show, there is no beholder would be- CHAP.
" lieve that ever I had been touched with such a malady.   XXII.

" Your faithful loving friend,   Anno 1572.
" Elizabeth."

Upon this letter let me subjoin the contentation and joy
administered unto the good earl: expressed by his own
letter, dated from Sheffield, November 4: " That her ma- The earl's
" jesty's late letters, which he received with his, [the trea- grateful letter.
" surer's,] declaring her highness's good health, were most
" comfortable unto him: and in respect of the word written
" with her own hand therein, far above the rate used to any
" subject; and that he thought himself more happy thereby
" than any of his ancestors. And therefore that he meant,
" for a perpetual memory, to preserve the same safely, as a
" perpetual evidence of his great comfort to his posterity.
" And then beseeched his lordship to yield most humble
" thanks unto her majesty in his name therefore: and also
" for that it pleased her highness to accept his true and
" faithful service; which, by God's grace, (he said,) should
" never be wanting."

But the next month, viz. November, the queen was again The queen
under some disorder in her health, by reason of some faint- hath faint-ing fits.
ing fits: which gave again a mighty disturbance unto her Leicest.
subjects from the news of it; which now was fled abroad, Lett.
as though she were very sick. Wherefore the earl of Leicester, to satisfy Walsingham, the ambassador in France,
did write to him, how this little distemper in the queen
bred strange bruits at home of her danger, and which he
might possibly have heard of there: but that she was at
present in good health. That indeed she had been troubled
with a spice or show of the mother: but indeed not so;
and that the fits she had were not above a quarter of an
hour.

CHAP. XXIII.

*The Great English Bible, called, The Bishops' Bible,
printed. Some account of this edition; and other older
editions. Prophesying set up at Bury by the bishop.
The said bishop's admonition to a contentious clergyman. Stays admitting a clerk into a living: and why.
His advice to his chancellor, upon a disturbance of divine service. His trouble with a fraudulent receiver of
his clergy's tenths. Occasions a statute.*

A new edition and translation of the Bible set forth.

IN this year Parker, archbishop of Canterbury, set forth a
new edition (in large folio) of the holy Bible of the Old and
New Testament in English, new translated, and diligently
compared, by several bishops and other learned divines,
with the former English translations, and the originals. In
the beginning, before the Book of Genesis, was the map of
the land of Canaan placed. On which map were the arms
of Cecil, lord Burghley, engraven, in a void place of it, by
Humfrey Cole, engraver, born in the north, and pertaining
to the mint, 1572. In another void place is the printer's
arms, with this fancy; a bush with a nightingale on one
branch of it, and a label proceeding out of her mouth, with
these words inscribed, *Jug, jug, jug, jug:* Cecil, I suppose,
being at the cost of the engraving the plate for this map.
There was in this new Bible another map of the holy land,
containing the places mentioned in the four evangelists,
with other places and towns in Syria near adjoining.
Wherein may be seen the ways and journeyings of Jesus
and his apostles, going about to preach the gospel in Judea,
Samaria, and Galilee. And this therefore was placed before the New Testament. And moreover, a new chart of
the peregrination of St. Paul was set before the epistle to
the Romans. There were also some coats of arms set in
other places of the book; namely, of such as were chief be-
nefactors to the work, and contributors of sums of money
towards the printing or adorning of it. As, besides the
arms of archbishop Parker and archbishop Cranmer, prefixed to their two prefaces, there be the arms of the earl of

Leicester at the beginning of the second part of the Bible, CHAP.
viz. at Joshua; and the lord treasurer Burghley's before XXIII.
the third part of it, beginning at the Book of Psalms. Anno 1572.
Where are also prints of their persons, viz. Leicester in armour; the other in his gown, as a man of peace. And at
the beginning of the prophecy of Jeremiah stands the coat
of arms of the earl of Bedford.

There be also many explanatory cuts dispersed through- Explana-
out the book. As also divers useful tables for the better un- tory cuts
and tables
derstanding of scripture history. As, I. At the eighteenth in this
chapter of Leviticus are two tables, entitled, *Degrees of* Bible.
kindred which let matrimony; and, *Degrees of affinity or
alliance which let matrimony.* II. Before the book of Ezra 217
is a table for the understanding of the histories of Ezra,
Nehemiah, Esther, Daniel, and of divers other places of
scripture, very dark, by reason of the discord that is among
historiographers, and the expositors of holy scripture, touching the successive order of the kings or monarchies of Ba-
bylon and of Persia: of the years that the said monarchies
lasted, from the transmigration of the Jews under Nebu-
chadnezzar, until the monarchy of the Greeks: and of
the confusion that is in the names of the kings of Persia.
III. Before the books of the Macchabees is a third table, for
the knowledge of the state of Judah, from the beginning of
the monarchy of the Greeks, where the former table ended,
until the death and passion of Jesus Christ. IV. There is
yet another table placed before the New Testament, to
make plain the difficulty that is found in St. Matthew and
St. Luke, touching the generation of Jesus Christ, the Son
of David, and his right successor in the kingdom. Which
description beginneth at David, and no higher; because the
difficulty is only in his posterity. V. There is a fifth table
before the epistle to the Romans, which shews the order of
times from the death of Christ; and a synchronism of the
years of the reigns and governments of the emperors, presi-
dents of Judea, and the Herodians, with Christ and St.
Paul; to his beheading at Rome; beginning with Tiberius,
Pilate, and Herod.

BOOK
I.

Anno 1572.

Besides all this, in this Bible is each chapter divided into verses; which, I think, no English Bible had before, excepting that of the Geneva translation. And also there be many references and marginal notes, to explain difficulties, or for observation of matters remarkable. For further account of this Bible, commonly called, *The Bishops' Bible*, (because the bishops were chiefly concerned in the preparing of it,)

Life of Archbishop Parker, p. 403.

the reader may have recourse to the Life of Archbishop Parker.

It is to be further observed in this Bible, that the Psalms are printed in two columns; viz. in one column the old translation of them, as they were and are in our liturgy; and the new translation of them in the other column. Where, for preventing any displeasure any person might take thereat, as somewhat differing in divers places from the reading in the Common Prayer Book, this note was prefixed, (by archbishop Parker, I suppose,) which follows:

A note concerning the new translation of the Psalms.

" Now let the Christian reader have this consideration with
" himself, that though he findeth the Psalms of this latter
" translation following not to sound so agreeably to his
" ears, in the wonted words and phrases, as he is accus-
" tomed with; yet let him not be too much offended with
" the work, which was wrought for his own commodity and
" comfort. And if he be learned, let him correct the word
" or sentence (which may dislike him) with the better. And
" whether the note riseth either of good-will, or charity, or
" of envy and contention, not purely; yet his reprehension,
" if it may turn to the finding out of truth, shall not be re-
" pelled with grief, but applauded to in gladness. That
" Christ may ever have the praise. To whom, with the Fa-
" ther, and the Holy Ghost, be all glory and praise for
" ever." *Amen.*

It may not be amiss here to enumerate some of the first and oldest editions of the Holy Bible in our vulgar tongue,

218 which, by the peculiar blessing of God, were vouchsafed to

An account of the old editions of the English Bible.

this land, besides the translation and publishing of the New Testament, which was done by Tyndal about the year 1525. In the year 1535 the whole Bible was printed in folio, (and

that, I think, was the first time it was set forth in English,)
in an old, and, as it seemed, outlandish letter. In the end
it is said to be printed in the year of our Lord 1535, and
finished the 4th day of October. This Bible I have seen in
Sion college library, London. It was done by Miles Coverdale, with his dedication thereof to king Henry VIII. entitled, *Unto the most victorious prince, and our most gracious sovereign lord, king Henry VIII. king of England
and of France, and, under Christ, the chief and supreme
head of the church of England.* Therein he set forth the
encroachments of the pope upon princes, and Christian
realms, and especially upon this his majesty's realm ; " By
" getting money by his pardons, and by benefices and bi-
" shoprics, by deceiving the people's souls by devilish doc-
" trines, and sects of his false religion, and by shedding the
" blood of many of the king's people, for books of the scrip-
" ture. And since his imperial majesty was the chief head
" of the church of England, and the true defender and
" maintainer of God's laws, he thought it his duty, and be-
" longing to his allegiance, to dedicate this translation unto
" his highness." But I refer the reader to the Appendix, Nº.XXII.
if he be desirous to peruse that epistle ; wherein some
things may be found acceptable to such as are studious of
the history of those times, and of matters passed in those
times.

What helps Coverdale had in this his labour, especially The helps
for the supply of his want of skill in the original languages, Coverdale
it must be known, that living in Germany, and conversing his transla-
with the Lutheran divines, (many whereof were good Hebri-
cians,) he had the opportunity of perusing several Dutch
translations. This may be better understood by what he
wrote himself in his prologue to this edition. Which began
after this manner :

" Considering how excellent knowledge and learning an His pro-
" interpreter of scripture ought to have in the tongues, and logue.
" pondering also his own insufficiency therein, and how weak
" he was to perform the office of a translator, he was the
" more loath to meddle with this work. Notwithstanding,

" when he considered how great pity it was, that we should
" want it so long, &c. That for to help him herein, he had
" sundry translations, not only in Latin, but also of the Dutch
" interpreters. Whom, because of their singular gifts, and
" special diligence in the Bible, he had been the more glad
" to follow for the most part, according as he was required.
" But to say the truth before God, he added, that it was
" neither his labour nor desire to have this work put into
" his hand. Nevertheless it grieved him, he said, that other
" nations should be more plenteously provided for with the
" scripture in their mother tongue than we. Therefore,
" when he was instantly required, though he could not do
" so well as he would, he thought it yet his duty to do his
" best, and that with a good-will, &c. And that, according
" as he was desired, he took the more upon him, to set
" forth this special translation, not as a checker, not as a re-
219 " prover, or despiser of other men's translations; (for that
" among many, as yet he had found none without occasion
" of great thanksgiving unto God;) but lowly and faith-
" fully he had followed his interpreters; and that under
" correction."

This book hath in divers places little pictures, explanatory of the history; as of the creation, the deluge, &c.
There be no marginal notes, nor any contents before the
chapters; as there were in some after-editions, which gave
offence to some of the churchmen.

Another
English
Bible,
printed
anno 1537.
Another English Bible in folio, with marginal notes, was
printed anno 1537, with an epistle dedicatory also to king
Henry VIII. subscribed *Thomas Matthew*. At the bottom of the title-page it is said to be *set forth with the
king's most gracious licence*. This is truly Tyndal's Bible,
as may be concluded by the two flourished text letters
W. T. standing at the end of the prophecy of Malachi.

Another
printed
anno 1540.
Another large Bible in English came forth anno 1540,
the marginal notes being all struck out, as having given
offence. It was printed by Whitchurch; and had a large
prologue before it, made by archbishop Cranmer. And was
said in the title-page to be *printed for the use of the*

churches. In the said page are sculptures of king Henry CHAP.
VIII., archbishop Cranmer, and the lord Crumwel. And XXIII.
this edition is said to be overseen at the king's command- Anno 1572.
ment by Cutbert, bishop of Durham, and Nicolas, bishop
of Rochester. Concerning these two last editions of the Life of
Bible, see what is more at large related in the Life of Arch- Archbishop
bishop Cranmer. Cranmer,
chap. ix.

Again, another edition of the English Bible came forth Another
the next year, viz. 1541. And so it is said in the title, *The* edition,
whole Bible, &c. finished 1541. These two last Bibles also 1541.
I have seen in Sion college library.

The English Bible was again printed anno 1549. Which Another
was Tyndal's Bible; and the very same with that which edition,
was printed 1537, and was called Matthew's Bible. There 1549.
might have been other editions between these two last; but
I have not seen them.

Now I shall proceed to take notice of some particular Exercise of
occurrences in the church. Towards the latter end of the prophesy-
year, the exercise of *prophesying* was set up at Bury St. Ed- at Bury.
munds, in Suffolk, as was used in some other places of MSS. D.
this and other dioceses, to the profit and edification, in the Elien.
knowledge of the scripture, both of the clergy and laity.
For the exercise was, that certain ministers within a convenient compass in the diocese, assembled in a parish church
(commonly in some market town) together; and there,
one after another, gave their judgments briefly of the sense
and import of some place or places of scripture, propounded
before to be discussed, either by the bishop or the archdeacon's order, or some other of the gravest sort: and then
lastly, it was determined by a moderator. By which means,
the ministers were obliged to study, to prepare for the
better acquitting themselves in these exercises: and their
knowledge in scripture increased; and the people also present were edified, by hearing of a sermon then preached.
But however, these *prophesyings* (as they were called from
1 Corinth. xiv.) were in danger of degenerating into con- 220
troversies and contentious disputings. And the puritans took
their advantage of it by broaching their doctrines. Which

BOOK
I.

Anno 1572.
The bishop
appoints it
by his let-
ters.

N°. XXIII.

The dealing
of the bi-
shop of
Norwich
with two of
his clergy.

His admo-
nition to
one that

was the cause that not long after, the queen absolutely required the bishops to put them down.

But the occasion of setting up this practice at Bury was,
that several of the sober and well learned people in that
neighbourhood sued to the bishop for his licence and appointment; that they might enjoy the benefit thereof, as
well as other places in his diocese did. The bishop hereupon, judging it profitable for the advancement of godly
knowledge, sent his letters to three of the gravest ministers
in Bury, to take care of settling this exercise, as to the
time, place, and persons; and rules for performance of it in
the more orderly manner; and that the respective clergy
should obey their orders herein. Yet warning, that nothing
be done contrary to the orders and laws of the realm; but
all to the furtherance of both laity and clergy in good
Christian knowledge. For the fuller understanding of this
exercise, now to be settled in this town, and the bishop of
Norwich his direction therein, I have put his letter in the
Appendix.

The bishops in these times were careful in their great
charge, and watchful of the manners and behaviour of their
clergy, if we may charitably conjecture at the diligence of
the rest by one of them. It may deserve mentioning, what
a sharp, and withal grave admonition the bishop above-
named gave to one minister of his diocese, that was of a
contentious disposition; and likewise of his conscientious
boldness of staying the admission of another into a benefice,
being unqualified; though he endangered thereby the displeasure of a great nobleman and privy counsellor, viz. the
earl of Sussex. Both which happened within a few days
one of another. For the knowledge and understanding of
both these passages, there needs nothing but the rehearsing
of the said bishop's letters.

To Nesse (the name of the contentious clergyman) thus
he wrote:

" Mr. Nesse,

" I am ashamed to understand of your troublesome and
" disordered behaviour, not only at home, among your

" neighbours, but abroad also, and that before the justices CHAP.
" and worshipful of the shire. Which being come to my XXIII.
" knowledge, it standeth me in hand to see reformation. Anno 1572.
" And therefore, by these my letters, I do advise and was conten-
" straitly charge you, that all former quarrels and matters MSS. D.
" in controversy may be stayed and forgotten; and that ep. Elien.
" you do forthwith seek in charitable manner to reconcile
" yourself towards your neighbours: who for their parts
" promise the like; bearing no manner of displeasure to-
" wards your person, but to your manners, which are out of
" order. And if you shall reply, that you be not in fault, I
" answer you, it may be untrue that one or a few shall re-
" port; but to be accused generally, and of all that have to
" do with you, this cannot proceed without your great de-
" serving.

" If this my friendly motion shall not persuade you to 221
" conformity, I have appointed process to call you before
" my chancellor, where your cause shall be heard, and re-
" formed accordingly. But if these ways shall not help, I
" assure you I will use more sharp means, intending not to
" leave you, until I have either reformed or removed you.
" Putting you also in remembrance, how slanderous you
" are, in frequenting a suspected house, and refusing law-
" ful matrimony. Herein also I wish you forthwith to avoid
" the occasion, for fear of further inconvenience. And so I
" leave you to God. At Ludham, this 25th of February,
" 1572.

" Your friend in well doing,
" John Norwic."

Of the matter the bishop had with the other clergyman,
this was the purport.

The earl of Sussex had presented one Mr. Hilton, his He refuseth
chaplain, to the living of Disse, in his diocese, a good bene- to admit a
fice, above the value of 30*l.* in the king's books; and had clerk, for in-
sent to the bishop to admit him thereunto. But he wanting sufficiency.
certain qualifications, the bishop refused, and gave his reasons for so doing in the following letter to the said earl:

Y 4

telling him, " That since he so well allowed of the man, he
" could be contented to admit him to the benefice: but that
" there was a let that stayed his admission hitherto; which
" was a branch of a statute made in the last parliament, viz.
" that no person, not being a bachelor in divinity, nor suf-
" ficiently licensed by some bishop, or one of the universi-
" ties, should take any benefice with cure, being above the
" value of 30*l.* as this was. Herein he wished to be satisfied
" by such as were learned in the laws. Till which time he
" had persuaded Mr. Hilton to stay his admission. Adding,
" that if he [the bishop] should not be able by authority
" of the statute to admit him, nor he [the said clerk] be
" able to receive the same; then he assured himself, his
" honour would not impute the cause to him, but to his
" own insufficiency. And that, as for his own part, as it
" should not become him to attempt any thing contrary to a
" statute law, so would he be most willing to satisfy his ho-
" nour herein, or any way else, as knew the Almighty; to
" whom most humbly he commended his honour. Dated
" at Ludham, the 4th of March, 1572."

This clerk, the good bishop, as is likely, saw to be ignorant; and of small learning and abilities: and so, to bear
him out to the earl, in refusing him, took the opportunity
of the late prudent act, that none but learned and able men
should possess livings of such considerable value, and to encourage the clergy to take degrees, and study, and become
preachers.

The bi-
shop's or-
ders about
a disturb-
ance in
prayer time
in a church
in Norwich.

Disorders committed in a church in Norwich, (and so
even under the bishop's eye,) while divine service was reading, caused him again to exercise his episcopal authority. It
happened in February this year, in the parish church of St.
Simon, (a parish noted for their disorders,) at evening prayer,
222 after the minister had begun, and proceeded to the midst
of the service, reading the Psalms distinctly to the people;
three or four lewd boys, set on by some lewder persons,
(whether they were papists, or protestants disaffected to the
liturgy,) came into the church, and as the said minister began to read, *My soul doth magnify the Lord,* &c. they

brast out into singing of psalms suddenly and unlooked
for; and being commanded by the minister to cease, they
continued singing, and he reading; so as all was out of order, and the godly, well-disposed auditors there disquieted,
and much grieved. Of this the bishop having notice, sent
word to his chancellor to take cognizance of this great
abuse. Of which nevertheless he had no great marvel, because (as he wrote) he could never understand of any good
order or conformity in that parish; and as persons that
had vowed themselves contrary to God and good ordinances, so it fared with the most part of that parish. He
also informed his chancellor, of one of them, (who were the
great setters on of these boys,) and his character, namely,
one Thomas Lynn; " whose contumelious and disobe-
" dient dealings, especially in matters of religion and the
" church, was, as he admonished, most necessary to be
" looked on; as one that dared to attempt whatsoever he
" listed.

" It ought to trouble us both, added that reverend fa-
" ther, that knowing and being informed often of the mis-
" orders of that parish, there hath nothing been done to this
" day; whereby their lewd liberty had not been restrained,
" but enlarged." And requiring him earnestly to call the
church-wardens and the parson before him, and whom else
of the parish he should think meet; and understanding the
course of these disorderly dealings, he should appoint such
punishment as the fault deserved. The bishop required his
chancellor to regulate another as great a fault in this same
parish also: which was, that where all the churches in
Norwich did forbear to toll a bell to evening prayer, till
the sermon was done; in this parish the bells jangled when
the preacher was in the pulpit. And they were piping (as
the bishop expressed it) when they ought to be at the
preaching.

" And herein, and in such like, (as the good bishop pro-
" ceeded in his letter,) if we shall continue slow and negli-
" gent in reforming, the blemish and discredit will light
" upon us both at the length, and that more heavily than

" will be well borne." [Meaning, that such irregular and scandalous practices in divine worship, and contrary to the decency required in the time when it was celebrated, must needs come at last to the ears of the queen and council, to answer it.] And so slack, it seems, was the exercise of discipline in this civilian, to whom the bishop had committed this office, that he subjoined and informed him, that the godly sort of the parish had determined to seek reformation at the high commissioners' hands: and that forthwith; being weary, as they said, of complaining, and finding no redress. And that for his own part, he washed his hands of it, and laid the fault in him, if any were; to whom he had referred these and such causes in his absence, as he knew. But to stay the complaints above, which was presently intended, he straitly required him to examine the misorder, and to punish it severely; using this reason to 223 enforce it, " That it touched the credit of them both in the " sight of the world. Our place and calling bindeth us, and " God looketh for it at our hands. And so I commit you " to the Almighty, this 3d of February, 1572.

" Your assured in God,

" Joh. Norwic."

A great
debt due to
the exchequer falls
unjustly
upon this
bishop;

I have one thing more to relate of this pious bishop: for I love to revive the memory and actions of these our first protestant bishops and confessors. He had the misfortune to intrust one with the collection of the tenths of his diocese. Who took the sums that he had received of the clergy, and converted them to his own use, instead of paying them into the exchequer. So that at length a heavy debt fell upon the poor bishop, for two or three years' arrears of the tenths, that almost brake his back, and drove him to great necessity. For the revenues of his bishopric were obliged to make good this debt to the queen. Which was the reason he was fain to absent from Norwich, and live more privately at Ludham, a country seat belonging to the see. Whence some letters above rehearsed were written.

This receiver of the bishop's was one George Thymel-

thorp: who being behindhand in his payments of the CHAP.
clergy's tenths, for the twelfth and thirteenth year of the XXIII.
queen, a summons came down from the exchequer to the Anno 1572.
bishop, to pay them. Whereupon the bishop sent to his By means of
clergy to produce and send to him their acquittances given his receiv-
them for their said payments by Thymelthorp; which the er, disco-
bishop accordingly sent up, that the said receiver might be
charged with those sums, and that it might be seen how
he had cheated the bishop. He had made use of this money
to buy land. And these lands, and other his goods, he had
fraudulently made over by deeds unto his brother, one
Rugg, (a clergyman, as it seems,) and others; and himself
absconded. The bishop, in this case, made his condition
known unto the queen by petition, which he desired his old
learned friend Dr. Wylson, master of the requests, to forward and countenance. It so far succeeded, that a commission was sent down to the high sheriff of the county, to
make inquisition of what goods and estate Thymelthorp had,
in order to seize them for the queen's use. Besides this,
there was a letter sent before, to the high sheriff, from the
lord treasurer Burghley, to search for this man; but he
could not be found. But he found in his house to the value
of 218l. 15s. 4d.; his goods, and all his plate and jewels, and
things of most value, being conveyed away before. He
found also his will; whereby it might evidently appear,
that his former deeds of gift, and his feoffment made to
Rugg his brother, and others, were altogether forged and
deceitful; to the defrauding of the queen's majesty of her
due debt, and the utter undoing of the bishop. The sheriff was threatened by Rugg for exceeding his commission; offering him 100 marks, or 100l. in plate, to leave
the will behind him. Which, when the sheriff refused, he
threatened him vehemently. Wherefore the bishop prayed
the lord treasurer, that the sheriff might be further au- 224
thorized with such assistance, and a sufficient warrant for
bringing away the said will.

The lord treasurer soon after, sir Walter Mildmay, chancellor of the exchequer, the lord chief baron, the queen's

BOOK
I.

Anno 1572.
A commis-
sion to the
high she-
riff for an
inquisition
against
him.
solicitor, and others of the exchequer, granted out a commission accordingly from the queen; which somewhat favoured the bishop against his said receiver. Whereupon by
inquisition it was found, as above, that Thymelthorp had
made all his deeds of gift fraudulently. This gave some re-
viving to the afflicted bishop; making this pious reflection
in a letter to a friend of his: " Thus doth God deliver his
" seely poor souls (which meant hurt to nobody) from the
" falsehood and subtil cozening of devilish men, or rather
" monsters of men." Adding, "You would not think into
" what rejoicing and gladness all the country (as I might
" so say) is resolved; excepting a few Thimelthorpians.
" The Lord be praised for ever and ever." This he wrote
from Ludham in January.

Fraudulent
convey-
ances found
by inquisi-
tion.
He informed also sir Walter Mildmay, a little after, that
by authority of the last commission of inquiry, sent from
the exchequer, it was found by inquest of office, that the
deeds of gift, and conveyances, made by that deceitful person, were fraudulently made. And thereupon the sheriff
had extended his lands, and such goods as were found, and
put into inventory; desiring sir Walter, and the rest of the
officers of the exchequer, to take order for the sale of those
lands and goods, or otherwise, that they might be conveyed
to her majesty's best avail; to the answering his debt, and
to the discharge of [the bishop's] poor living, which was
charged therewith, after 400*l.* a year, i. e. 100*l.* payable
each term, and out of which he had paid 400*l.* and was still
liable for more. And so pressed with it, that he was behindhand to the exchequer, for the debt that was stalled, and
could not perform his own offer in payment. So that God-
frey, of that court, had sharp words, because he had not,
for forfeit of payment of 100*l.* in arrears, caused the bishop's lands to be seized and sequestered, out of respect and
concern for the bishop. And so he wrote to him in February.

Thimel-
thorp taken.
His submis-
sion to the
bishop.
Thimelthorp was now in prison; and was sued by the
bishop, to repay all that he had paid into the exchequer.
And now I find him humbly addressing himself to the bi-

shop; acknowledging his fault by letter, and offering all
satisfaction; using these words, *Venio tanquam prodigus
filius.* The good bishop gave a kind answer to him after
so much suffering and extremity brought upon him by
means of the unjust dealings of the other. " That all the
" world might see through his failings to pay the prince, he
" [the bishop] had been and was burdened more than he
" could bear. And therefore, if by all lawful means he
" sought to ease himself, neither he nor his friends could
" justly blame his dealings. That he must pronounce, that
" if his meaning were advisedly to draw him into the mire,
" after such courtesy that he [the bishop] had friendly
" shewed him, and constantly continued, and by so doing
" caused him to sustain great loss of substance, and brought
" also his credit into question; assuredly, said he, all per-
" sons might perceive and deem, that he had given him
" [the bishop] no cause to think his friendship well be-
" stowed. However, the bishop made him this offer, That
" if he would pay him what he had disbursed for that debt
" of his, and would satisfy the prince for the payment
" yearly at every term appointed, and laid upon him, he
" [the bishop] would leave all further proceedings against
" him, and shew him all friendly courtesy as he might per-
" form, or Thimelthorp desire."
Then at length he urged to him, " the great necessities
" he was driven to by his means. That he was forced to
" live in miserable sort, neither able to maintain a family fit
" for his place, neither to build nor repair his houses, nor
" bestow his liberality where he would, neither to keep hos-
" pitality, or relieve the poor, according to his will, and as
" was convenient." Yet humanely and christianly concluding, " Your loving friend, hitherto unfriendly handled, and
" yet your assured friend for ever, if you forthwith perform
" that both duty and conscience bindeth you to." This
dated from Ludham, March the 21st.

The aforesaid matter was the occasion of that statute,
made this 13 Eliz. cap. 4. (which the bishop himself first
moved in parliament: and the bill thereof was by the una-

CHAP.
XXIII.

Anno 1572.
And his
Christian
letter to
him.

225

This deceit
occasions
a statute
made this
parliament.

nimous consent of bishops, peers, and commons, approved
and passed; as he wrote to his friend Gualter. By which,
he said, he hoped in a short time to have his losses made
good;) viz. to make the lands, tenements, goods, and chattels, of tellers, receivers, &c. liable to the payments of their
debts; and, against fraudulent deeds, gifts, grants, alienations, conveyances, bonds, suits, judgments, as well of
lands and tenements, as of goods and chattels; that are
said in that statute to be more commonly used and practised in those days, than had been seen or heard of heretofore. Which feoffments, gifts, grants, &c. were devised and
contrived of malice, fraud, covin, &c. to the end to delay,
hinder, or defraud creditors, and others, of their just and
lawful actions, suits, debts, accounts, &c. the parties to
such feigned and fraudulent feoffments, &c. to incur the
penalty of one year's value of the said lands and tenements, &c. and the whole value of the goods and chattels:
the one moiety to the queen, and the other to the party
grieved by such feigned and fraudulent feoffments, &c.
And also being lawfully convicted, to suffer imprisonment
for one half year without bail or mainprise.

And an-
other for
bishops' un-
der-receiv-
ers of
tenths and
subsidies.
For to meet with under-receivers, (such as Thimelthorp
was,) intrusted by the bishops, there was another statute
made, for the more effectual avoiding and redress of great
deceits done to the queen's highness, and to the prelates and
clergy of the realm, by under-collectors of the tenths and
subsidies of the clergy appointed by and under the archbishops and bishops. The tenor of it was, That the statute
made in the thirteenth year of the queen, to make the
lands, tenements, goods, and chattels, of tellers, receivers, &c. to be liable to the payments of their debts, should,
to all intents and purposes, as amply and largely extend,
and be construed to extend, to all such under-collectors of
tenths and subsidies of the clergy: for satisfying of such
money as they had collected, or should collect, of the said
226 tenths and subsidies, to the use of the queen's majesty.
And that every such under-collector should, upon process
to be awarded out of the court of exchequer, be chargeable

to account for the receipt of such tenths and subsidies.
And every archbishop and bishop, and dean and chapter,
sede vacante, to whose charge the collection of such tenths
or subsidies did appertain, should be discharged of so much
of the same of the said tenths and subsidies, as should be
satisfied to the queen, her heir or heirs, of or by the lands,
tenements, or hereditaments, goods, &c. of such under-collectors. By virtue of this act the lord treasurer (who was
the great instrument thereof) sent his letters, in October, to
the high sheriff of Norfolk, &c. as we related before.

And this seems to have been partly effected by the means The bishop
of the archbishop of Canterbury; to whom the bishop ad- writes to
the archbi-
dressed in a letter, dated April 2, 1573, to use his interest shop about
with the lord treasurer for forbearance; acquainting him, this business.
that Thimelthorp had promised an agreement with him;
but he could not persuade himself to believe him, such had
been his former dealings. And that all that while he remained in miserable state, paying 400*l*. by the year for
his debt. And that it was supposed by some that were
learned, that the last statute against the deceit of collectors
was not sufficient for the sale of this deceiver's lands. So
that he told the archbishop he was like to be smally relieved
thereby. That he had therefore been an humble suitor to
the lord treasurer, that those great payments of his might
be spared till the next parliament; where, by farther authority, the said statute might be enlarged, and he [the bishop]
holpen. For truly (said he) I am not able to continue these
great payments. And prayed his grace, when he saw time
convenient, to use some favourable words to the lord treasurer, that he might the rather be spared for a time, in
hope of further relief.

The bishop's Christian disposition towards this ingrate- Other
ful man may further appear by other his deceitful actions, cheats put
upon the bi-
having played other tricks with him. He had forged a shop by this
man.
writing as it were from the bishop; wherein he gave the
reversion of the archdeaconry of Norwich to him. And he,
upon this writing, presented his brother William Rugg to
it. The bishop, (having indeed the presentation in him-

BOOK I.

Anno 1572.

self,) when it fell, had presented Mr. Roberts, a dear friend of his, to the same. And this occasioned a suit between Rugg and Roberts. Further, he had forged a patent for the receivership of Norwich. And doubting lest it should come to light, threw it into the fire, and burnt it. He had a man, to whom he gave 5*l.* a year, named Ibbots, that graved seals, and such like things, very cunningly, (as the bishop himself writ in a letter to his friend,) who might serve his turn in such cases.

Thimelthorp, a prisoner, begs the bishop's pardon.

This man I find remaining a prisoner the latter end of the next year, and the queen's and bishop's debt not yet paid; when he obtained leave of the council (the bishop being willing also) to go for a while into Norfolk. Where he was twice at Ludham with his lordship: and there, holding up his hands, and falling on his knees, beseeched him that he would pardon him the injury. To whom the bishop christianly answered, that he would pardon the injury done him; but the payment of money due to him and the queen he could not pardon. The conclusion was, that he promised he would do all: and so returned to his prison; and the poor bishop left in as bad a condition as before.

227

Gualter and Zuinglius the younger come to bishop Parkhurst.

Dec. 6.

Rodolphus Gualter and Rodolphus Zuinglius, the sons of those learned Helvetians of the same names, came over into England this year to travel, and to see and study at our universities; and were recommended by Gualter, the father, to the said bishop Parkhurst. With him they were in the beginning of December at Ludham. Where, among the rest of the entertainment, he treated them with oysters: which the young men wondered to see him eat. But however young Gualter *ventured at last upon them:* for so the bishop merrily wrote to his father. But as for Zuinglius, (as the bishop went on,) he dared not *cum vivis animalculis congredi.* Yet the day after, *evaginato gladio, vir se præstitit:* i. e. he drew his sword, and shewed himself a man. From the bishop they took their journey to London with their letters, and waited upon bishop Sandys there: who received them very obligingly, for their relations' and country's sake: and assigned each of them 5*l.* against their

going to Cambridge. They returned again to Ludham the
same month. And in January following, the bishop sent them, and two more, their fellow-travellers, with a servant of his, to that university, the plague being then at Oxford.

The bishop intended wholly to find Gualter with maintenance, while he remained in England: and so he told him. But when Gualter's father had promised in a letter to repay him whatsoever sums the young man should take up of him, and to reimburse him for his expenses, as he was resolved to take that opportunity of shewing his gratitude to Gualter, by bearing all his son's charges; so in no small trouble and concern at it, he thus affectionately expressed his mind to the said learned man.

Iniquo animo fero inhumaniter abs te dictum: nec dum ingratam hanc molestiam bene concoquere queo. Egon' abs te vel hallerum acciperem? Nondum tibi Tiguri satisfactum putas? An omnem humanitatem me exivisse putas? O mi Gualtere, ne quicquam tale in posterum abs te audiam. Nullis tuis impensis vivet in Anglia: nulli tibi erit oneri. Ego enim hinc alam; et liberaliter quidem. Curabitur ut meus filius, ex me genitus, &c. "What you so unkindly said,
" I take not well. Nor can I yet well digest this unkind
" trouble you have given me. Should I receive even a farthing
" from you? Do you think that I have satisfied you, when
" I lived at Zuric with you? Do you think that I have put
" off all humanity? O my dear Gualter, let me hear no
" such thing of you hereafter. Your son shall not live in
" England at your charge: he shall be no burden to you
" here. I will maintain him here, and liberally too. He
" shall be taken care for, as my own son. This I promised
" you often by letters, and, God willing, I will certainly
" perform it."

The bishop, now ready to send young Gualter to Oxford 228 the next summer, out of his care for him, wrote in June both to Dr. Humfrey, head of Magdalen college, and Dr. Cole, concerning his coming thither: and prayed the former to provide him a convenient chamber in his college; and that he might be in fellows commons, and that he would

see all his expenses discharged from time to time.   And to
Gualter himself, being upon his departure to Oxford, he
wrote, " When you come to Oxford, you shall be provided
" with all things.   If any thing be wanting at any time, I
" have written now once again to Dr. Umphrey and Mr.
" Cole, to provide the same for you.   And at one of their
" hands you shall receive what you have need of: and I
" will see the same discharged."   Concluding with his counsel; " If you apply yourself to your studies, and do well,
" you shall want nothing, but shall find me, not a friend
" only, but another father unto you.   God keep you, and
" give you his grace to do that becometh you, to his glory,
" and all your friends' comfort."

CHAP. XXIV.

*Walsingham, the queen's ambassador in France, impover-
ished in his embassy, comes home. Dr. Wylson sets forth
a learned book against usury. Bishop Jewel's letter in
commendation thereof. Epigrams formerly made by bishop Parkhurst, printed. Divers historical matters, both
of himself and others, gathered from them.*

Walsing-
ham, am-
bassador in
France, so-
licits to
come home. WALSINGHAM, the queen's ambassador in France,
after he had done her majesty the best service he could, in
this critical and dangerous year, by his intelligences and
spies, (which, for the public good of religion and the state,
cost him great sums of money, to the impoverishing of himself,) did earnestly solicit all his great friends, to obtain of
the queen the calling of him home.   Thus pleading to one
of his chief friends at court, (viz. sir Thomas Smith,) " That
" if the cause of his stay there grew only in respect of her
" majesty's service, (as he was told by some letters hence,)
" though he had, he said, as much cause to desire his re-
" turn, as any other that was employed in the like service,
" yet he could with more patience digest the same, as one
" that thought both his travail, substance, and life, as well
" employed in her service, as any other subject she had.

" [For indeed both his substance and life were in great de- CHAP.
" cay and danger.] But he hoped, when her majesty should <u>XXIV.</u>
" see his stay there not needful, she would tender his case, Anno 1572.
" and yield to his revocation."

I shall only insert this note concerning the necessitous condition of Walsingham, in this his public service, that the earl of Lincoln, being sent from the queen to Paris, upon his own experience of the intolerable charges there, through 229 the daily increase of dearth, promised Walsingham that he would confer with the lord Burghley, to consult with her majesty for the increase of his diet. For otherwise he should not be able to hold out his monthly charges, now His great 200*l.* a month : notwithstanding his diet was thin; his fa- expenses, mily reduced to as small a proportion as might be ; and his living. horse being twelve only.

But the queen could not be drawn to comply with Wal- Kept there singham's earnest request ; knowing how fit and able a per- still, not-withstand-son he was to serve her with that prince. Insomuch, that ing his mi-at last, for necessity, and want of health, his condition was dition. miserable. He remained in France all the winter, even to February, when he wrote again, that he hoped his stay should not have been so long protracted, and that his miser-able case (as he called it) should have been otherwise weighed, especially since his stay there could breed but an hinderance to himself, and no benefit to her majesty. For that the court then removed from Paris ; and he should be driven to remain there, and not to follow the same, for lack of ability, having neither furniture, money, nor credit. But notwithstanding, his return was put off still. For in the MSS. next month, viz. March, I find sir Walter Mildmay solicit- Burghlian. ing the lord treasurer to take a seasonable opportunity that offered itself then, to help his brother Walsingham home : adding, that without his only help, he feared it would be put off again, with such delay as would be, he said, in-tolerable to him : praying his lordship to bear with his friend that thus pressed him : and that the reasons were so well known to them, that they could do no less. And that he would hereby bind Mr. Walsingham for ever to him.

z 2

BOOK
I.

Anno 1572.
Comes
home.

Made secre-
tary of state.

Dr. Wylson
sets forth
a book
against
usury.

Dedicated
to the earl
of Leicester.

At last, viz. in the month of April, he came home, and Dr. Valentine Dale went ambassador in his room. But he was run so far behindhand in his estate by this embassy, as that, though he lived divers years after, and once more was sent ambassador into France afterwards, yet died in debt. He was recompensed after his return home, and made principal secretary of state, with sir Tho. Smith, in the month of January after.

This year Dr. Wylson, master of St. Katharine's by the Tower, and master of the requests, (afterwards secretary of state,) one of the most learned men of his time, set forth a book against usury : entitled, *A discourse upon usury : by the way of dialogue and oration, for the better variety, and more delight of all that shall read this treatise : by Tho. Wylson, doctor of the civil laws, and one of the masters of her majesty's honourable court of requests.* He dedicated it to the earl of Leicester, the great affected patron of learn-, ing and learned men ; wherein he is styled, *the high and mighty earl.* The occasion of his writing this tract was this, that usury, in the excesses of it, was now so common in the kingdom, that it arose to extreme extortion and oppression. For thus he writes in one place of his book:
" That ugly, detestable, and hurtful sin of usury, which
" being but one in grossness of name, carrieth many a mis-
" chief linked unto it : the same sin being now so rank
" throughout all England, and in London especially, that
" men have altogether forgotten free lending, and have
230 " given themselves wholly to live by foul gaining: making
" the loan of money a kind of merchandise : a thing directly
" against all laws, against nature, and against God. And
" what should this mean, that instead of charitable dealing
" and the use of almose, (for lending is a spice thereof,)
" hardness of heart hath now gotten place, and great gain
" is chiefly followed, and horrible extortion is commonly
" used."

And again : " I am sorry to say it, and know it over
" well ; and therefore I must needs say it ; I do not know
" any place in Christendom so much subject to this foul

" sin of usury, as the whole realm of England is at this CHAP.
" present, and hath been of late years."

The book is the more to be esteemed, in that the copy Anno 1572.
was read over and approved by Jewel, bishop of Salisbury, Bishop
in the year 1569; who wrote and prepared a letter to the judgment
author in commendation thereof. The letter was found in thereof, in
that bishop's study certain months after his death, and sent the author.
by John Garbrand, M. A. in Oxford, and prebendary of Juelli.
Salisbury; to whom the bishop gave all his papers, writings,
and notes of all his travails in God's vineyard, and other
devices of learning. Which letter Dr. Wylson thought fit
to set before his book, and was as followeth :

" I have perused your learned and godly travayl touch-
" ing the matter of usury, Mr. Dr. Wylson, and have no
" doubt, but if it may please you to make it common, very
" much good may grow of it. Such variety of matter, such
" weyght of reasons, such examples of antiquity, such au-
" thoritie of doctors, both Greeks and Latines; such allega-
" tion of lawes, not onely civil and canon, but also provin-
" cial and temporal; such variety of cases, so learnedly and
" so clearly answered ; such learning and eloquence, and so
" evident witness of God's holy wyl, can never possibly
" passe in vayne. I wil not flatter you : I cannot: it be-
" cometh me not. I assure you, I like al notably wel; *si-*
" *quid mei est judicii;* and if my liking be worth the liking.

" But of al other things, this liketh me best. Of the
" three parties, you make eche one to speak naturally, like
" hymself, as if you had been in eche of them, or they in
" you.   What it shal work in other I cannot tel : for mine
" own part, if I were an usurer, never so gredily bent to
" spoyle and ravine, *ut sunt fœneratores;* yet would I think
" myself most unhappy, if such persuasions could not move
" me. But what man would not be afraid, to lyve despe-
" rately in that state of ' life that he seeth manifestly con-
" demned by heathens, by the old fathers, by the auncient
" councelles, by emperours, by bishops, by decrees, by ca-
" nons, by al sects of al regyons, and of al religions, by the
" gospel of Christ, by the mouth of God ? *Ago breviter, ut*

z 3

" *vides. Non enim id mihi sumo, ut damnem large tam*
" *horrendum peccatum. Id tibi relinquo.*

" *Ut vivat liber, usura pereat.*"

" From Salisbury, this 20th of August, 1569,"

The book is written dialogue-wise, (the manner of writing in those times,) between a rich worldly merchant, a 231 godly and zealous preacher, and two lawyers, the one temporal, the other civil: who are all brought in, speaking naturally their sentiments upon this argument of the loan of money for gain, which is his description of usury; some for, and some against it. And this was that which the bishop in his letter declared he had such a liking for.

Some wise sentences of Dr. Wylson.

Dr. Wylson was a very eloquent man; and excellent for the γνῶμαι (i. e. *sentences* of great importance and practical wisdom) his book abounded with : and a taste of them may deserve here to have a place. As, " The Devil, whom " that ancient father of famous memory, Hugh Latimer, " called, *the most vigilant bishop in his vocation.*"

" If there be not as quick weeding hooks, and as sharp " iron forks, ready at hand to cleanse soil from time to " time, as the weeds are and will be ready to spring and " grow up, in the end all will be weeds : and Antichrist " himself will be lord of the harvest."

" Wariness in all things is evermore wisdom ; and of ad- " vised dealings come perfection. Things foreseen, do al- " ways the less harm."

" I do wish, that man were as apt to do right, as he is " ready to speak of right: and to be altogether as he would " seem to be."

" Sweet is that sacrifice to God, when the lives of lewd " men are offered up to suffer pains of death for wicked " doings."

" As good pick straws, as make laws that want a ma- " gistrate to see them well obeyed.——The law itself is a " dumb magistrate to all men : whereas magistrates are a " speaking law to all people.——As one may be a good " magistrate to the people, and yet no good man to him-

" self; so may one be a good man to himself, and prove CHAP.
" no good magistrate to the people." XXIV.

" Diogenes said well, Where neither laws have force, nor Anno 1572.
" water hath course, there should no man willingly seek to
" dwell."

"Plainness of speech, and freedom of tongue, in de-
" ciphering sin, and advancing virtue, are not the best
" ways to thrive by."

I will take my leave of this book, after I shall have men- An usurer
tioned a punishment, which the author shews out of the refused
Christian
civil and canon laws, appointed for usurers convict: viz. burial.
that when they are dead, they shall not have Christian burial. And that if any minister do receive any known or
convicted usurer to the communion, the same priest or
minister shall be straightway suspended from celebrating in
the church. And that whoso burieth an usurer so convicted shall immediately be excommunicated. This Dr. Wylson fitted with a story he had read. A rich usurer being
notorious, and therefore often warned to amend; and yet
amending never the more, departed this world; when and
where he could not tell, (for the book from whence he had
it went not so far for time and place.) But after the man
was dead, his kinsman that succeeded him, (as rich men
want none,) desired to have him buried in his parish church,
before the high altar. The parson being a zealous godly
man, would not bury him at all, no, not in the churchyard;
much less in the church, or at the high altar. His kinsman
hereupon being greatly dismayed, offered largely to have this 232
favour. But all would not serve. At length understanding
that the parson had an ass, which brought his books daily
from his parsonage to the church, being a pretty distance
asunder, they politicly desired to obtain this favour for
him; that as his ass did daily carry his service-books to the
church, so it would please him, that for this time the ass
might take pains to carry this dead ass in a coffin, with this
condition, that wheresoever the ass stayed, there the body
should be buried: persuading themselves, that as the ass,
by an ordinary course, used to go every day from the par-

BOOK
I.

Anno 1572.

sonage to the church, with a burden of books upon his back, so of course he would take the same way with this dead man's corpse, being chested, even straight to the church. The priest, upon their importune suit, was content that his ass should deal in this matter for the usurer, and be his dumb judge. Who, when he had the chested body upon his back, feeling the weight heavier than was wont to be, (as usurers want no weight, being overladen with sin,) or else by some secret motion of God, I think, as Balaam's ass was inspired; so this foresaid beast, being laden and overladen, as it should seem, did fling and take on immediately, as though wildfire had been in his tail: and leaving the ordinary course to the church, took the straight way out of the town; and never left flinging and running, till he came to a pair of gallows at the town's end: and there wallowing himself under the gallows with the corpse upon his back, did never leave tumbling and tossing himself upon the bare ground, till he was clean disburdened of so miserable a carrion: a fit altar undoubtedly for usurers to be sacrificed upon alive, or buried under when they are dead; and a most worthy tabernacle, or shrine, miraculously assigned for all such lewd saints to be shrouded in, either dead or alive. The facetiousness of this story makes me insert it.

Bishop
Parkhurst's
epigrams
printed.

To this book I add another, for the eminency of the author, set forth also this year, by the same Dr. Wylson; being the elegant Latin epigrams of bishop Parkhurst, written in his younger days; (famous for his human as well as divine learning;) the copy thereof being sent by the author as a new year's gift to the said Wylson, his dear friend and old acquaintance. Which he called the bishop's *good, godly, and pleasant epigrams:* and was minded, with the bishop's consent, to put them to the press, as fit to be preserved to posterity, and worthy public view.

His epigrams, historical.

These epigrams (in imitation of Martial) are to be esteemed, not so much because they were pieces of handsome wit and fancy, as chiefly because they are historical. Wherein Parkhurst doth both give us an account of many remarkable passages of the former part of his life, his education,

his learning, his acquaintance, and his exile and sufferings, CHAP.
for adhering to the true religion; but also lets us into much XXIV.
of the knowledge of the latter times of king Henry VIII. Anno 1572.
as also of divers things in the reigns of king Edward VI.
and queen Mary, especially relating to religion, and of persons of both sexes, eminent in both reigns, either for their rank and dignity, their religion or learning, with their characters.

Concerning himself we learn divers things by some of his 233
verses; as that he was born at Guilford in Surry, by his epigram to Dr. H. Polsted, a physician of Guilford, *conterraneum suum.* That he was educated first under the famous grammarian, Mr. Robertson, and after, at the school of Magdalen college, in those verses, *ad Gymnasium Magdalenense:*

> *O præclara domus, musarum candida sedes, &c.*
> *Me quoque nutrieras olim, cum parvulus essem,*
> *Nunc factus juvenis, sum memor usque tui.*

That he was in his younger days but of mean circumstances, as appeared by his relation of certain of his dreams:

> *Somnia me Crœsum fecerunt sæpe superbum,*
> *Et gazis visus sum superare Midam.*
> *Somno experrectus mox sum mendicior Iro.*
> *Irus ita usque fui, desii at esse Midas.*

And that his profession of the gospel, and abhorrence of popery, was the obstacle to his hopes of wealth from one Crisp, his father-in-law; whom, in his verses to Jewel, he denotes to be rich:

> *Possidet ille gazas, ego paupertate laboro.*

And when Jewel had asked him the cause he was no kinder to him, he answered,

> *Impia non possum dogmata ferre papæ.*

That he was not wanting to himself in his diligence of seeking preferment: but had no success. This he expressed to one Estwic, his friend, upon occasion of his inquiring of him what he was doing:

> *Quid faciam, quæris? Venor. Quid? Venor honores.*
> *At frustra: invitis venor adhuc canibus.*

Yet afterwards his *hunting* was more successful. For he became chaplain to persons of the highest dignity. As, to Charles Brandon, duke of Suffolk. On whom he made a funeral epitaph, styling him there, *dom. suus clementissimus.* He was domestic also to the most excellently accomplished woman, for birth and virtue, the lady Katharine, his duchess. (To whom likewise he wrote some epigrams.) To which honour he attained anno 1542, by an address to her in a copy of Sapphics:

Si velis inter numerare servos
Me tuos, o gloria fœminarum, &c.

And which was higher yet, he was domestic chaplain to a greater princess, viz. Katharine Parr, king Henry's last 234 queen: as we find also by some of his verses. Wherein, when a friend of his asked him why he abode so much at court, he gave him the reason, that it was partly the great obligingness, affability, and piety of his mistress, the queen, and partly to enjoy the society and converse of some excellent scholars, that were likewise at court, as Coverdale, Huic, Ælmer, &c.

Quod tam volens, quod tam lubens,
Reginœ in aula mansito,
Facit hujus benignitas,
Pietas, facilis clementia.
Necessitudo addi huc potest,
Coverdali, Huicci, et Ælmeri,
O! dii, viros quos nomino?

After serious deliberation about his entrance into the state of matrimony, at last concluding it the most safe and godly course, he resolved upon it; writing thus to his friend:

Commodius vivit cœlebs, sed tutius ille, et
Sanctius.

And thereupon concludeth,

Ipse brevi castus nempe maritus ero.

Though being a man in holy orders, many severely censured him for it; especially such as favoured popery. To' one he gave this answer:

Conjugium meditor. Tragide obstrepis, atque probro des.
Quid faceres, essent si mihi scorta? Nihil.

John Jewel, afterwards the most learned bishop of Salis- CHAP.
bury, was his scholar in Merton college; signified in those XXIV.
verses writ to him;

Olim discipulus mihi, chare Juelle, fuisti,
Nunc ero discipulus, te renuento, tuus.

That he was incumbent of the rich benefice of Cleve:
but left it upon queen Mary's altering religion, for the sake
and love he had to Jesus Christ: as he expressed in this
pious distich to his friend:

A me cur locuples subito sit Cleva relicta,
    Quæris. Præ Christo sordida Cleva mihi.

The cause of religion was so dear to him, that (besides
the loss of that) he took up a resolution to leave the kingdom, whatever dangers and evils befell him, and piously
commended himself to the protection of God, against hang-
men and against papists; putting them together, as equally
dealing in blood:

Nescio quid mihi mens præsagit adesse malorum;
    Nescio quid sperem; nescio quid metuam.
Quicquid erit, Deus alme, tua me protege dextra;
    Carnifices perdant me, neque pontifices.

And now being departed from his native country, and in 235
his voyage, his heart trembled to think of the cruelties intended against him and the rest of those pious Christians
that would not turn papistical idolaters, and dreaded the
handling of those that remained behind. But especially he
had a great concern for the princess Elizabeth, and his
noble patroness, the good duchess of Suffolk. Praying God
for his protection of them all, against the wolves, lions, and
tigers: meaning those inhuman popish persecutors under
queen Mary, sensible also of the danger the whole kingdom
was in from foreigners. In regard of which matters thus
expressing himself, while he was sailing upon the seas:

Dolos maligne qui struunt,
Nostramque vitam quæritant,
Ne prævaleant nobis, Deus;
Funes eorum rumpito,
Laqueos cruentos scindito.

Ab hostibus civilibus,
Et exteris, Britannicum
Regnum misericors libera.
Prænobiles viros bonos,
Prænobilesque fœminas,
Elizabetham principem,
Suffolciæ, et meam, ducem,
Deum colentes, rictibus
Lupi, leones, tygrides,
Immanibus ne devorant.

He and divers more divines, and learned men of the universities, and of the church of England, under king Edward, thus became voluntary exiles, and settled themselves at Zuric in Switzerland: and in their travel, near to that place, they were to pass over a very high hill, where was a rock, on which he engraved these extemporary verses; (the rest of them having inscribed their names :)

Huic insculpserunt Angli sua nomina saxo,
Charam qui patriam deseruëre suam.
Deseruëre suam patriam pro nomine Christi :
Quos fovet, ut cives urbs Tigurina suos.
Urbs Tigurina piis tutum se præbet asylum.
O! dabitur grates quando referre pares?

He and the other exiles being not only most kindly received at their coming, by Bullinger, Zanchy, Wolphius, Gualter, Lavater, and the other ministers and rulers at Zuric, but also living easily there among them : so much love and hospitality had such an impression upon him, that he thought he could never sufficiently extol it, nor be thankful enough for it : as he expressed it in these verses :

Vivo Tigurinos inter humanissimos :
Quibus velis vix credere, quantum debeam.
O! quando Tigurinis reponam gratiam?

Parkhurst
kindly re-
ceived at
Zuric.
Balei Acta
Romanor.
Pontif. in
Præfat.

How kind the divines of that city shewed themselves (and especially Gualter) to him, John Bale took notice of in the preface to his books of the *Acts of the popes: Vir optimus* (speaking of John Parkhurst) *et meliori fortuna dignior; quot nominibus,* &c. " An excellent man, and

" worthy of better fortune ; upon how many accounts is he CHAP.
" debtor to you, Mr. Gualter, and the whole city [of Zu- XXIV.
" ric?]"

The same writer, an exile also then at Basil, records 236
gratefully the entertainment of the rest of the English there. And the
That they lived together in one house [like a college of stu- English ex-
dents.] That Bullinger took a fatherly care of them, and iles there.
that by the full consent of the citizens. And he adds, that
these that were daily with him at Basil, related those ministers' care, their trouble, and their paternal affection towards them, while they lived under the shadow of that city,
covered against the heat of persecution, with the love of the
whole people. They related also to him the incredible munificence of the magistrates: who most liberally offered by
Bullinger subsistence, by provision of bread-corn and wine,
as much as might suffice to sustain thirteen or fourteen of
them. But the English refusing to be so burdensome to
them, [having relief elsewhere,] they of the city were sorry
that some opportunity of gratifying them was wanting.

While Parkhurst sojourned here in this place, he exercised sometimes his poetical strain. And once, at the motion of Zanchy and Wolphius, knowing his genius towards
poetry, he comprised the Ten Commandments in ten he-
roic verses. And again, at the desire of the said Zanchy, he
composed elegantly in Latin verse the history of the life of
Christ: shewing the occasion thereof in these words: *Cur-
sus vitæ Domini nostri et Servatoris Jesu Christi : rogatus
a D. Hieronymo Zanchio hæc scripsi Tiguri*, 1557. He
began with *Adventus Christi in carnem.* Then his Nativity.
Then his Circumcision. Then the Epiphany. Then his
Disputation with the doctors: and so to the last Judgment,
in several distinct poems.

And being settled in this city, Zuric, this safe harbour
for the poor English exiles, he gave a character of this
place, in the end of a letter which he wrote to Harley, late
bishop of Hereford.

Urbs habet Helveticæ me nunc primaria gentis ;
Urbs plane armipotens, pacis amica tamen.

Urbs facunda piis verbi præconibus, atri
Urbs expers odii, cædis, avaritiæ, &c.

He shewed himself a prophet, as well as a poet: comforting the English exiles by foretelling the restoration of the
gospel to England within a short time:

Numinis ira brevis, bonitas pia gaudia præbet.
Est nox tristis? Erit postera læta dies.

And likewise the death of Gardiner, bishop of Winchester, in a distich to Ponet, who had been deprived of that
bishopric:

Salveto nuper præsul, præsulque futurus.
Namque brevi Stephanus, præsul, puto, desinet esse.

And so in all probability Ponet had been restored, had he
lived to return; but died before.

237   But for the historical characters this epigrammatist giveth
of others of the English nation, both of the nobility and
clergy, whether papists or protestants, I refer the reader to
the Appendix; as containing many things that will be acceptable to such as are studious of those times.

CHAP. XXV.

Remarks upon particular men. Sparks, a suffragan bi-
shop. John Fox. John Cottrel. John Rugg. Justinian
Lancaster. Bartholomew Clark: his testimonial. John
Hales: his epitaph. Cardinal Chastillion: poisoned in
England. The villain that poisoned him confesseth it
two years after. Nowel, dean of St. Paul's, founds a
free-school in Lancashire. His letter to the lord Burgh-
ley about it. One Blosse reports king Edward to be
alive, and that the queen was married to Leicester. Mines
of silver in Cumberland: a corporation for the managery
thereof.

AND as I have thus made mention of several persons of
figure before, so I shall proceed to add some short notices
of divers other eminent men, whose preferments or deaths,

or other accidents, fell within this year, with some remarks CHAP.
concerning them. XXV.

Thomas Sparks, bishop suffragan of Berwick, assistant Anno 1572.
to Cutbert, sometime bishop of Durham, died this year. Bishop suf-
And John Fox, M. A. [the martyrologist, if I mistake not,] fragan of
Berwick
entitled, *Sacri verbi Dei professor*, promoted to a prebend dies.
in that church of Durham, vacant by the natural death of John Fox
hath his
that reverend father, dated Sept. 2, 1572. Which prefer- prebend.
Regist.
ment he resigned the next year, viz. 1573. Durham.

John Cottrel, LL. D. archdeacon and prebendary of John Cot-
Wells, a great civilian in these times, and before, a mem- terel, LL.D.
ber of the famous synod anno 1562, dieth. And August 4,
John Rugg, M. A. was made archdeacon of Wells, and was John Rugg.
presented to the church of Winford, by his death, at the
presentation of Maurice Rodney, of Somersetshire, esq.

Justinian Lancaster, archdeacon of Taunton, (who also, Justinian
if I mistake not, was in the said synod,) was presented this Lancaster.
Matt. Hut-
year, in the month of March, to the prebend of Yatton, in ton.
the church of Wells.

Bartholomew Clerk, fellow of King's college in Cam- Barthol.
bridge, commenced this year doctor of laws. He was much Clerk com-
menceth.
esteemed for his learning and Latin style; and whom arch-
bishop Parker had preferred to the deanery of the Arches,
and had employed sometime in writing against Saunders
his book. But having, notwithstanding, enemies, Byng,
vice-chancellor, and Dr. Whitgift, master of Trinity college, and public professor of divinity, both gave him this
testimonial, under the university seal, in their letter to the 238
lord treasurer:

" Our duties in most humble manner to your honour Testimonial
" premised. Whereas this bearer, Mr. Bartholomew Clarke, of his abi-
lities.
" being now lately admitted a doctor of the civil law in this MSS. Burg.
" university, hath earnestly required our special testimony
" to your honour of that his degree, we could do no less for
" truth's sake, but according to his petition to advertise
" your lordship of the same; adding, moreover, that as
" well in replying as answering, he did so learnedly demean
" himself, that he hath thereby not only much encreased
" the good opinion long sithence conceived of his toward-

" ness, but also obtained a right commendable report of
" those that bear the chief name among us in that faculty.
" Thus, with our prayer to th'Almighty for the long pre-
" servation of your honourable estate, we humbly commend
" your lordship to his most blessed tuition. From Cam-
" bridge, this vi. of December, 1572.

" Your lordship's most humbly at commandment,
" Tho. Byng, vice-chancellor,
" Jhon Whitgyfte."

The death
of John
Hales.

This year put an end to the life of John Hales, a learned
man, and a courtier, under the reigns of king Edward and
this queen.   He made himself known in these times, as for
his good zeal towards religion, so for his writing in favour
of the succession to the crown, of the family of the Grayes;
one of which family was queen Jane, who was beheaded for
that cause in the beginning of queen Mary's reign.   Hales,
for this attempt, underwent much trouble, as the histories
of queen Elizabeth's time do relate.   He was buried in
the church of St. Peter's Poor, London; where, on a brass
plate against the north wall, was this account of him engraven :

*Dom. Joannes Hales, a pueritia literis deditus, excel-
lenti ingenio, docilitate, memoria, studio et industria sin-
gulari; adjuncta, linguarum, disciplinarum, juris, anti-
quitatis, rerum divinarum, et humanarum, magna et mul-
tiplici doctrina, instructissimus, evasit.   Innocentia, inte-
gritate, gravitate, constantia, fide, pietate, religione, gra-
vissima etiam ægrotationis et rerum difficilium diuturna
perpessione, et in patientia, ornatissimus fuit, vitæ hones-
tissime sanctissimeque actæ diem supremam 5to. cal. Ja-
nuar. 1572, clausit.   Anima exeunte, corporis reliquiæ hoc
loco sitæ sunt.*

Expecto resurrectionem mortuorum, et vitam æternam.

Cardinal
Castillion
poisoned in
England.

To these learned men I shall subjoin another churchman,
viz. cardinal Chastillion; who flying hither out of France,
anno 1568, for the safety of his life, with the bishop of
Arles, upon his return was basely, by some unknown hand,

poisoned; but was honourably buried among the metropolitans, in the cathedral at Canterbury, which happened in
the year 1570.   But I choose to mention it here, because
the vile practiser of this murder was not known till the 239
latter end of this present year.   The reason of his coming
was supposed to be for religion: for arriving at Tower-
wharf, Sept. 13, he, with the other bishop, was received
by some eminent citizens there, whereof the chief was sir
Thomas Gresham, and (as it seems) by secret order from
the queen.   They were conducted to his house in Bishops-
gate-street, and there lodged.   And the next day he rode,
attended with the said knight and others, to the French
church, to shew his approbation, as it might be interpreted,
of the protestant religion.   And thence he went with the
same state to the Exchange in Cornhill; and thence to St.
Paul's church; and so back to dinner with the said Gresham.   And on some day after, he went to court, to wait
upon the queen.   His name was Edet, or Odet Colligni, of
a noble family in France: which made the queen shew him
great respect.   He was also noted by Thuanus for a person of great virtue and integrity.   Being at Canterbury, he
died suddenly.

That he was poisoned was not known, nor by whom, till
in the month of January this year, when intelligence came
to the English court from Rochel, that a servant of the
late cardinal Chastillion, put to death there, for going about
and conspiring to betray that town, confessed, as he went
to execution, that it was he poisoned the same cardinal in
England.

I shall also add here a remark of another very worthy
and reverend man, viz. Alexander Nowel, dean of St.
Paul's: who, for the better encouragement of learning and
true Christian religion among the rude inhabitants of Lancashire, he being a native there, was now founding a free-
school at Middleton in that county, and providing for the
maintenance of such scholars as went from thence to Brazen-
nose college in Oxford.   A charter for the founding of the
same from the queen, for the establishing of this Christian

charity, lay now before the lord treasurer. And now, in the month of July, the said dean solicited that lord in behalf thereof; and that for the better maintenance of the master and usher, it might be capable of being well endowed: addressing to him to this tenor; " That in the patent of the " foundation of her majesty's school of Middleton, and of " her thirteen poor scholars of Brazen-nose college in Ox- " ford, the sum of the mortmain was not named. For the " which, by the advice of sir Walter Mildmay, a blank was " left, upon good hope that it would please her majesty to " license a large sum to be purchased to so goodly uses; " and in her majesty's name he humbly prayed his honour " to finish the good work which he had so happily begun; " and to move her majesty to license the sum of 100*l.* or so " many marks at the least, by him and others, to be pur- " chased in mortmain, for the increase of the stipends of " the schoolmaster and usher, and of the number and exhi- " bition of the said scholars, and the better relief of the " great company of that poor college: and all to be done in " her majesty's name. And to cause the said mortmain to " be entered in the blank of the said patent, with a note of " her majesty's consent hereunto; that no doubt may grow " by the diversity of the writing." Adding, " Your ho- " nour shall hereby bind, not only me, but all the inha- " bitants of the rude country of Lancashire, and the scho-
240 " lars of the said college, next after her majesty, to pray for " your honour, &c.

" Your honour's always to command,
" Alex. Nowel."

William Fulk, a member of the university of Cambridge, (afterwards well known for his learned writings and disputations against the Romanists, and head of Pembroke-hall,) had the honour this year to attend, as chaplain, upon the earl of Lincoln, lord high admiral, going to France. And so his absence from the commencement being necessary, when he was to take his degree of doctor, he obtained the queen's letters to the heads, to grant him his degree, not-

withstanding his absence.   And that by virtue of her royal CHAP.
dispensing with a statute to the contrary.   The said letter XXV.
to the university deserves here to be inserted, being copied Anno 1572.
by an exact hand.

    " Elizabetha R.

    " Trustie and welbeloved, wee greet you wel.   Wheras R. T. Baker,
" we are informed, that William Fulk, batchelor of di- B. D.
" vinity of that our university of Cambridge, hath both
" performed al the scholastical acts that are appointed by
" our statutes for the trial of them that are to be admitted
" to the degree of doctors in the same facultie ; and also
" very neer accomplished al that time of study, which is
" required by the same statutes : these are to let you under-
" stand, that in consideration that he is appointed to attend
" upon our right trustie and right welbeloved cosyn and
" counsellor, the earl of Lyncolne, our high admiral of
" England into France, so that he cannot be present at
" your next commencement, wee are wel pleased to dis-
" pense with him ; and by these presents do dispence with
" him.   Requiring ye therefore, that by grace of that our
" said university, he may be admitted to the said degree,
" notwithstanding his absense, in as ample maner as hath
" byn used to be granted there, before that libertie, for sun-
" dry good causes, was restrained by our statute ; the said
" statute, or any thing contained therin in any wise notwith-
" standing.   And these our letters shal be your sufficient
" warrant and discharge in this behalf.   Geven under our
" signet, at our mannor of S. James, this 19th day of May,
" in the fourteenth year of our reign."

    One Blosse, alias Mantel, was in the month of January One Bloss
taken up, for affirming king Edward VI. was yet alive ; and affirms king
that queen Elizabeth was married about the year 1564 to living, &c.
the earl of Leicester, and had four children by him : and he
had confidently told the same many times.   This was such
a piece of impudence, that it could not but be taken notice
of.   The latter report he had received from a popish priest,
as such, making it a great part of their business to slander

and defame the queen to the utmost degree, to make her odious.   And the former lie he had gathered from one in Oxford, in the time of queen Mary.   He was brought before Fleetwood, recorder of London, who examined him: to whom he made a confession of what he had said, but with sorrow and repentance, though perhaps partial only; and the said recorder consulted with the attorney-general, sir Gilbert Gerard, what penalty by law should be laid upon him; and whether the crime could be found treason.   In short, no law then was found to prosecute him.   This matter being somewhat curious, I will relate both the examination of this fellow, as it was taken by the recorder, and sent to the lord treasurer, together with his letter, giving a further account of his dealing with him, and the judgment of both in this case.   For both examination and letter the reader may apply himself to the Appendix.

Anno 1572.

241

N°. XXV.

Let me add, in the conclusion of this year, that certain mines were discovered in Cumberland, wherein was rich ore; whence were extracted copper, lead, and silver: which gave such encouragement, that a society, formed into a corporation of persons of eminent rank, was established, for the carrying on the work thereof.   For in this 14th of the queen she granted letters patents, bearing date the 4th of December, of privilege for making of copper and quicksilver, by way of transmutation, with other commodities growing of that mystery, to sir Tho. Smith, knt. (who was the chief contriver,) Robert earl of Leicester, William lord Burghley, and sir Humfrey Gilbert, knt. who were incorporate by the name of *the governor and society of the new art.*   They took into the said corporation some High Dutchmen, to be joined with them, who better understood the practical and laborious part.   Among those, the chief undertaker was one Daniel Heckstetter, who was termed sometimes Dr. Heckstetter, and sometimes Mr. Daniel.   In these mines the queen had her part, which was the fifteenth share; the rest went among the corporation.   They extracted copper, lead, silver, brimstone, &c.   But these works stood still this year, 1572, for want of money, and by reason

Mines of silver, &c. in Cumberland discovered.

A corporation for the same.

of the disagreement of the Englishmen in company with the CHAP.
Dutch. Upon which, one Richard Dudley, a judicious XXV.
person, (and concerned, as it seems, in this business,) did Anno 1572.
advise, that if they agreed not, and were not willing to consent and agree to all things according to their covenants,
then those wilful persons should lose their portions for a
time, and the queen to have their parts for three years;
and as the quantity or portion required, to pay money after
the rate. Also, he wished some skilful man to be appointed
to join with the Dutchmen, for making the assays of copper,
and for making bargains for wood, seacoal, making char-
coal, &c. And that the queen keeping them in her hand
the space of three years, she should come to know and understand their commodity, and whether they were to be
continued; and, as he supposed, would encourage the
Dutchmen to travail more earnestly, when her majesty
should deal in it.

At length the Englishmen were contented to let the
Dutch have their parts for three years, and to be at all
charges. The chief undertaker in this work, Heckstetter,
at the expiration of those three years, made two petitions to Petition to
the queen. One, for forbearance of her debt lent; so as the queen
her debt might be paid so much yearly, according as the for the bet-
mines might bear, with the favourable consideration of their on these
continuance; and the other, that it might be permitted to mines.
vent and transport over the seas such quantity of coppers
yearly, as the said Daniel should find merchants willing to 242
buy of him; paying her majesty due custom thereof, according to the company's privilege.

In short, by an extract it appeared, the debt and benefit
of these works was, that the queen lent to the works, to the
carrying them on, 2500l. at Christmas, 1575; and was owing
by the mines 4807l. 19s. 4d.; paid, and owing to the mines,
from Christmas 1575, to Christmas 1576, 3547l. 7s. 10d.
How the state of these mines stood about this year, 1576,
will be seen in the Appendix. Nᵒ. XXVI.

Towards the end of the year all things were framed to
quiet, peace abroad and at home. Though (as Dr. Wylson

observed in his correspondence with the bishop of Norwich) that he did not think that princes, being once quiet within their own states, would suffer this state [of England] to be long quiet. And so indeed it proved, as we shall find in the progress of this history.

The parliament being to sit in April next, having been prorogued to that month by the queen, (to take off the eagerness of the house against the Scottish queen,) the bishop of Norwich, now ancient and sickly, began a month or two before to be concerned where he should get lodgings when he came up: and therefore sent up a messenger before him, to provide some convenient place for his reception. The lady Jerningham, of his diocese, had offered him the use of an house of hers in the Black-friars: but he had no great stomach to accept of her kind offer, because she was noted to be a great enemy to religion; sir Henry Jerningham, knt. deceased, her husband, having been captain of the guard to the late queen Mary. But necessity had no law, as the bishop wrote his friend Dr. Wylson; and that therefore, for any thing he knew, he must be contented therewithal.

This is but a slight remark, and yet I cannot but take notice of it; to observe hence how this bishopric was now wholly devoid of any house or inn in London or Westminster, when as his ancestors, the bishops of Norwich, (as well as the rest of the bishops,) had all their inns or houses belonging to their bishoprics, for their harbour, when they had occasion to come up to the court or parliament; a thing so convenient. But now there was scarce one (except the bishop of Ely) had any, but what he borrowed or hired, their houses having been, either by the latter kings and princes, or the importunity of courtiers, obtained from them. Thus the bishops of Norwich had their house in St. Martin's in the Fields; which came in king Henry VIIIth's time to Charles duke of Suffolk. The bishops of Hereford had their inn in the parish of St. Mary Mounthaw; which was alienated to the lord Clinton, under king Edward VI. The bishop of Lincoln's inn was situate in Holborn, beyond the

bars; which came afterwards to the earls of Southampton.
The bishops of Chichester had their house in the same
street, now called Chancery-lane; built by Ralph Nevyl, Anno 1572.
bishop of Chichester, near the office called Cursitor's Office.
Afterwards it came to the earls of Lincoln, and was called
Lincoln's inn; now one of the inns of court. The archbishops of York had their house at Westminster, called
York-place, where Whitehall now standeth, given to his
successors by Walter Grey, archbishop of York: but king
Henry took it from cardinal Wolsey. The bishops of
Exeter, their inn was where Exeter-house now standeth.
The bishop of Bath's inn was likewise in the Strand, which 243
afterwards came to sir Tho. Seymour, knt. admiral of England under king Edward VI. who built much there: and
from him to the earl of Arundel, and had from him the
name of Arundel-house, now built into a street. The bishops of Bath, after they were put from this inn, had their
house in the Minories in Aldgate. Further westward in the
Strand was Chester's inn, belonging to the bishops of Chester; the same with Litchfield and Coventry. Further that
way the bishops of Landaff had their inn, lying near the
church of our lady at Strand. Further still was the inn of
the bishops of Chester. This house was first built by Walter
Langton, bishop of Chester, lord treasurer of England.
Adjoining to it was the bishop of Worcester's inn. All
these were demolished by the duke of Somerset, for building of his own fair palace of Somerset-house. Near the
Savoy was the bishop of Carlisle's inn; now belonging to
the duke of Bedford. Durham-house, belonging to the
bishops of that see, and still bearing their name, was built
by Tho. Hatfield, bishop of Durham. Beyond Durham-
house was the house of the bishop of Norwich; which
Heth, archbishop of York, bought, for him and his successors, of that bishop; but is now also become a street.

I shall only add a letter in French, (intercepted no
doubt,) wrote by a Scotch nobleman to the pope; dated
from Brussels, Jan. 1572. which letter will give further
light into these times, and the busy dealings of the papists.

Je ne desirois riens d'advantage, tres heureux pere, &c.

" I should desire nothing more, blessed father, than that it
" might be permitted me to come before your holiness, to
" kiss your feet, and to render you thanks, as well for the
" benefit and pleasure made to the queen, my sovereign,
" and to all my country, as especially for the singular love
" which your holiness hath well shewn me, to bear to the
" coming of my son to Rome. Who writ me, the 21st of
" October last, of the good reception and favourable treat-
" ment which it pleased your holiness to make him; to
" wit, insomuch as to hold and repute him your *only son :*
" promising him aid of that which shall be possible from
" your holiness, &c. Duke d'Alva, according to whose ex-
" cellence's will I am sent by my sovereign and the nobility
" of Scotland, &c. I have nevertheless, and have conceived
" in my heart, a little joy, to understand, that the reverend
" father, Nicolas Sander, goeth to your holiness, whom of a
" long time I have known, a man of good; whom I much
" love, as he deserveth; and knoweth very well the state of
" the queen, my sovereign, the condition of her country,
" and of mine; and the studies and wills of us all, that live
" in the Low Germany, and that which may be done and
" hoped. He shall fully instruct your holiness of the state
" of all things and persons; and shall suggest counsels,
" which will seem most seasonable for the remedying our
" evils. I have laid open to this so fit a man some secret
" businesses of mine, and my special proceedings, and touch-
" ing the state of my country, for that end and purpose, to
" communicate it to your holiness alone. To whose narra-
" tion, that certain credit may be given, I pray again and
" again. Yet so, that the business itself remain buried and
" entire; and nothing come to light, until it obtains its full
" effect, and be brought to the wished-for issue."

CHAP. XXVI.

Dr. Valentine Dale goes ambassador to France: the condition of Rochel. The ambassador's letter concerning the successes there against the besiegers. Pacification with the protestants. The queen instrumental therein. Occurrences of matters in France, sent hither by Dale. Monsieur elected king of Poland. A safe conduct desired for him from the queen: and also for duke d'Alençon. Liberty granted for the Scottish queen to go to Buxton well. Orders to the earl of Shrewsbury. The queen suspicious of the lord Burghley's favouring the Scottish queen. His caution in that respect. Earl of Leicester esteemed by that queen to be her enemy. How far he was so, as he declared. Queen Elizabeth's real concern for that queen. A plot to deliver her from the custody of the earl of Shrewsbury. His chaplain and another of the clergy accuse him falsely: examined.

CHAP.
XXVI.
───────
Anno 1573.
244

DOCTOR DALE, being now the queen's ambassador in the court of France, gives account into England of the state of affairs there, on which the safety and welfare of the queen and her state did so much depend; especially concerning the religion there, which she laboured, as much as she could, to favour, and provide against the oppression of those that professed it. In May, the said ambassador wrote over to the earl of Sussex, lord chamberlain and a privy counsellor, that Roan still held out. And this was so important an affair, and did so much employ all the counsels and arms of that king, that at court their whole doings depended upon Rochel; and of it they wished to be rid one way or other, that they might mind other matters. The queen-mother herself said, that they were out of hope to bring them to any composition, although they did all they could to bring them thereunto. And therefore they appointed to give them a general assault, as that day, [wherein Dale wrote all this, viz. *ult. Maii.*]

Then he went on to describe the town of Rochel, all men's eyes being upon so famous a siege as that was, and

Dale, ambassador in France, writeth concerning Rochel.

Rochel described.
Titus, B. 2.

especially the English nation; which, on the account of religion, wished well to them. It was in a manner (as he described it) four square. The west side lay upon the sea;
the south side upon the salt marshes, full of pits to make
salt; the north side was overflown with the tide at every
full water; and the east side, which was only accessible, had
at the corner toward the south one bulwark, called the bulwark of the port of Cogne; and at the corner toward the
north, one other mighty bulwark, called St. Angeli: which
two bulwarks did flank on the curtain on the east side.
Monsieur has battered the bulwark St. Angeli, but holds it
245 not himself; and lays in the ditch at the foot of a breach
made into the curtain of the wall. They of the town were
on the rampart, sometimes at the half pike. What trenches
or fosses were within was not known. There were divers
gobions and platforms in that town, that did command the
rampart at the place of that breach. Now the town being
thus, as the ambassador added, and their doings here being,
as he had expressed them in particular advertisements,
which he enclosed, his lordship (he said) would best consider the state of that country: and so humbly took leave of
his lordship, from Moreton, the last of May, 1573. These
advertisements I have laid in the Appendix. Where we
may see the wonderful successes, by the providence of God,
that poor persecuted people had; as well as other occurrences in France in that juncture, with relation to England.

The condition of Rochel.

N°. XXVII.

To which I may subjoin what Dr. George Abbot (afterwards archbishop of Canterbury) delivered in a lecture at
Oxford, concerning a kind of miraculous providence, supplying the besieged Rochellers, in their necessity, with food.
Where shewing divers instances of God's providence in preserving of his church and people, he relates, that after the
massacre of Paris, the whole power of that kingdom of
France were gathered together against the city of Rochel,
and besieged them with extremity, who defended the place.
And that God, in the time of famine and want of bread,
did for some whole months together daily cast up a kind of
fish unto them out of the sea; wherewith so many hun-

The besieg-
ed miracu-
lously sup-
plied with
food.
Exposit.
upon Jon.
lect. xv.

dreds were relieved, without any labour of their own: even
as the Israelites were fed with manna every morning, while
they were in the wilderness.   And as all the while that the
enemy was before them this endured, to their marvellous
comfort; so, to proclaim to the world God's providence the
more, when the enemy's tents were once removed, and the
city was open again, this provision immediately did cease.
And then the preacher concluded, " That it was a good
" testification that the Lord of hosts would leave a remnant,
" even a seed of his faithful, in that land." For this he
quoted *Comment. Religionis et Reip. in Gallia,* lib. ii.

This brave resistance, or rather self-defence, and success Pacification
of the poor Rochellers, had a good effect in the next month, of matters in France.
together with the queen's influence in Scotland, and her
despatching another ambassador, Mr. Horsey, to France.
For Dr. Dale, in a letter dated the last of June, thus related the state of matters in France, to the same earl of
Sussex : " That things were in such a case in that realm,
" that they were contented to bear all things : and that they
" made as though they were not moved with the matters of
" Scotland : [where their ambassador had no success to pro-
" voke the Scots, and to continue the differences among
" them :] nor to be offended with any dilatory answer of
" the queen, nor with the coming of Mr. Horsey, nor with
" any other thing that was past ; but took all in good part
" in outward appearance.   And yet," added the ambassa- Dale the
dor to the earl, " that his lordship did best know how much ambassa- dor's letter
" they might be grieved with those things, and how they concerning
" might be in doubt what carriage they of the religion the same. Titus, B. 2.
" would take, by the coming of Mr. Horsey at this time.
" And therefore they made the more speed to make some 246
" pacification.   That they had accorded with them of Ro-
" chel, Sancerre, Montauban, Nymes, free exercise in reli-
" gion ; and were contented to have no garrison in Rochel,
" but only that De la Nove should be governor for the
" king, of certain bands of the town's appointment, and pay
" for the performance thereof.
   " That the king of Polonia was content to gage his ho-

" nour, which he made much of now, because of his going
" into Poland. And yet they of the town would not trust
" him; so much the less, because he gave an escalade of
" late, during the time of treaty. They found the rampart
" so trenched and flanked within, at their last escalade, that
" it was thought they were past hope to do any good by any
" assault. And now the king of Polonia was so hastened
" away, that he could not tarry; and so was to carry so
" many of the chiefest gentlemen and soldiers, and so much
" of their treasure with him. And besides, that here were
" many in arms in Languedoc, Dauphiné, and Berne, that
" the king was weary of it; and what would be done, he
" knew not himself.

" And so promising to do his diligence, as things fell, to
" give that lord his best advertisement, if he could, he
" prayed God to keep his lordship in good health." Dated
from Paris the last of June.

The queen
instrumen-
tal to the
peace with
Rochel. By another intelligence in the month of July, the same
ambassador sent the earl notice of the peace made between
the French king, and the afflicted, his subjects; being
signed by him on the 2d of July: which was hastened by
occasion of queen Elizabeth's sending Horsey thither very
seasonably, as was suggested before. The capitulation
whereof that gentleman was promised to have along with
him when he returned. But yet the terms were such, that
it was not yet known whether they of Bearn, Languedoc,
and Dauphiné had accepted them, or laid down their arms.
The terms
were ac-
corded for
the exercise
of religion. The king had accorded to the exercise of religion to them
of Rochel, Nymes, and Montauban: but it was with the
misliking of divers of those about him. Dale added, that
he judged that that little munition, that came out of England to Rochel, preserved the town; and the countenance of
Horsey's coming over had done much good. This letter
was dated from Paris, July 17.

Thus, after all that king's murders of his protestant subjects, that thereby he might take the surest course to put
an effectual end to their religion, he was forced, after much
trouble and vexation to himself, and infamy to his name,

to allow under his own hand the continuance and practice CHAP.
of it.   XXVI.

By this yielding of the king to his subjects, professing the Anno 1573.
religion, to suffer them to be at quiet, he, weary of war, Occurrences
in France,
consulted for his own peace and quiet. But yet he obtained sent by the
not his desired end; for (as the same ambassador soon after into Eng-
ambassador
informed) all parties were in misliking, and every man drew land, July
23.
the king into disquietness, as much as they might, for the
maintenance of their faction, [i. e. the bigoted popish faction.] And the better to judge of these matters, he sent
over to the secretary here an extract of an oration of the
cardinal of Loraine. And beside gave a further light into
these turbulent affairs now in France, occasioned by the persecution there; which he had gathered with as much care 247
and diligence as he could.

" That at the time the peace was thoroughly passed at
" Rochel, the king elect of Poland, to avoid the murmuring
" and mutiny of his soldiers, (for that they were unpaid,)
" unaware to the greatest number of the captains them-
" selves, conveyed himself privately away; and took galley
" at Rochel, feigning to go for his pastime on the sea, and
" took his voyage presently to Nantes: and from thence, the
" 20th of this month of July, appointed to arrive at Tours.
" That the duke of Alençon was king of Navar. And the
" duke of Guise came from Rochel by land to meet him."

That neither they of Languedoc and Dauphiné, neither
yet the town of Nismes, did accept the peace. That the
king elect, for performance of his vow, went from Blois to
Notre Dame de Clery, on foot. It was said, that the marshal Tavanes died *ex morbo pediculari:* which was much
noted, because he was one of the greatest persecutors at the
massacre.

There was a very great report spread, that neither the
emperor nor the princes of Germany will assure a passage
unto the king elect through Germany. But that certainly
was not known, until the time that news might come from
monsieur Momory; who went to the emperor for that purpose. That Alasco, one of the chiefest ambassadors that

BOOK I.

came from Polonia, was already arrived at Metz, and the rest were looked for there the 23d of this present.

That it was said, that the Muscovite did make preparation against Polonia. That it was reported, that the navy of the Turk was consumed by fire from heaven. But the ambassador that was come to congratulate from Venice did report, that there should not be above the number of twenty ships of them consumed. It was further said, that the rest of the Turk's navy was withdrawn for this year.

That the peace was not published in the camp nor in the town at the coming away of the king elect; but the publishing thereof was referred to the Rochelois. That the townsmen came to the king elect, at the departure, and used certain speeches touching their submission, duty, and good love towards the king, desiring the king elect to be a means that such articles as were accorded unto them might be performed. That to this the king elect answered, that before this time, for his part, he had never made any promise to the protestants; but now, since he had given his promise for the *accord*, he himself would see it performed. That the king elect being departed from Rochel, it was said, there entered in certain ships, English and British, with victuals. That the ships that were laid to stop the entry of the haven were withdrawn, and the carac burnt, with the forts builded by the king elect.

" That it was said, that the protestants were possessed of " a very strong town in Languedoc, called Lodeve, where " the most part of the riches of that country was bestowed; " because it was taken, by the situation thereof, to be inac- " cessible. That the protestants had gotten the harvest of the " country as far as Tholouse, and had devised to surprise 248 " the town of Tholouse, but were discovered." I have set down the whole intelligence sent by the ambassador, though some matters therein are foreign to our history, that I might not give a defective and imperfect account thereof.

And thus the religion in France appeared in better circumstances through the late dismal clouds upon it, by the influence of queen Elizabeth's counsels, and the blessing of

God upon them, notwithstanding the inveterate malice of CHAP.
the enemies of it.   XXVI:

The next month, viz. August, the French ambassador Anno 1573.
requested two things of her majesty concerning the French Two re-
king's two brothers, while she was at Eridge, the lord Bur- by the
gavenie's house, in Waterdon forest in Sussex. The one French ambassador to
was for a safe conduct for the new king of Polonia, for him-the queen.
self, his ships, and train, (among the which should be 4000
soldiers, Gascoigns,) to be well used in any of her majesty's
ports, if by tempests any of them should be driven into any
her coasts. Which suit, although it were reasonable, where Epist. Com.
good meaning were sure, (as the lord treasurer wrote in a Salop. in
Offic. Ar-
letter to the earl of Shrewsbury, August the 10th,) yet at mor.
this time, for many respects, it was very suspicious : and yet
in the end the same was granted. But when that king
should take his voyage, was then uncertain: for they at
the English court heard from Polonia, that although he
were chosen by one number, yet another number were not
thereto agreeing. And that thereto the Muscovite, the king
of Sweden, and some said the emperor, (who were all com-
petitors at the election,) did give great furtherance to continue the disaccord.

And the said lord treasurer added, that there were some Jealousy of
at court had entered into some jealousy, that at this time the the king
elect of Po-
ambassador had dealt very earnestly for the queen of Scots land coming into our
going to Buxton wells, and withal, for a safe conduct for seas with
the said king's entry into this realm, having such a number his navy.
of soldiers and ships. But (as though himself were one of
those jealous persons) he thanked God, that his lordship
[the earl] was, with his charge, far enough from any ports.
And yet, as the time occasioned, he advised, that his lordship might be more circumspect with secresy, without note
to her or hers.

The second suit of the French ambassador was, for a like A safe conduct desired
safe conduct directly for the duke d'Alençon to come to the for d'Alen-
queen's majesty, ere long to be at Dover. But thereto such çon.
answer was given to discomfort the wooer, [the said duke,]

that the lord treasurer thought that surely he would not come. And that as yet he was sure none was granted.

Anno 1573.

The Scottish queen desires to go to Buxton well.

The French ambassador also solicited for favour to be shewed to the Scottish queen, who now pretended to be indisposed as to her health, or really was so: and therefore desired she might have liberty to go to Buxton wells. This request the earl of Shrewsbury, that had the charge of her, signified to the lord treasurer in the month of August: and though it was not thought safe to permit it, in the midst of such plottings for her escape, and that the French had now a navy and force upon the seas, ready to conduct the French king's brother into Poland; yet it was granted,

Order to the earl of Shrewsbury for the said queen's going thither.

upon caution given to the said earl, to be very watchful of her in her journey thither. For thus did the said treasurer write to him: " That he was now commanded by the queen " to write to him, that she was pleased, that if his lordship

249 " should think he might without peril conduct the queen
" of Scots to the well of Buckston, according to her most
" earnest desire, his lordship should do; using such care
" and respect for her person to continue in his charge, as
" hitherto his lordship had honourably, happily, and ser-
" viceably done. And that when he should determine to re-
" move with the said queen thither, it were good, that as
" little foreknowledge abroad, as might be conveniently,
" were given. And that nevertheless, for the time that she
" should be there, all others, being strangers to his lord-
" ship's company, should be forbid to come thither, during
" the time of the said queen's abode there. This he writ,
" as he added, because her majesty was very unwilling she
" should go thither: imagining, that her desire was, either
" to be more seen of strangers resorting thither, or for the
" achieving of some further enterprise to escape. But on the
" other part the lord treasurer subjoined, that he told the
" queen, that if in very deed her sickness were to be re-
" lieved thereby, her majesty could not in honour deny her
" to have the natural remedy thereof. And that for her
" safety, he knew this earl would have sufficient care and

" regard. And so her majesty commanded him to write to CHAP.
" his lordship, that he might conduct that queen thither;   XXVI.
" and also to have good respect to her. And that, accord- Anno 1573.
" ing to this her majesty's determination, the French am-
" bassador, being with her at the lord Burgavenie's house,
" had received knowledge from her majesty for the earl
" thus to do."

While this queen was here, at Buxton well, the lord Lord trea-
treasurer Burghley went thither also for his health. Which to Buxton
gave occasion to the queen to suspect that otherwise wary well.
nobleman ; (especially happening to be there also a year or jealous of
two after;) as though he came thither on purpose to ingra- him.
tiate himself with that queen. But hereby he incurred his
mistress's great jealousy and displeasure. For some of his
enemies at court took this opportunity to put into the
queen's head, that he came there with some such intent.
Which that good lord had enough to do to remove, and to
persuade the queen otherwise of him a good while after. Insomuch, that he declined an honourable motion that the earl
of Shrewsbury had propounded to him, of a match between
one of his sons and the said treasurer's daughter. Lest, if
he should have listened unto it at that juncture, it might
have increased the queen's suspicion of him. This I find in
a letter of this lord's, to that earl, in the year 1575.

The continual jealousy and fear at court now was, of the The fears at
Scottish queen's being conveyed away out of the earl's cus- Scottish
tody, to whom the queen had committed her, and of that queen's es-
earl's watchfulness and fidelity in this his charge. This will
appear by a secret conference that happened between Dr.
Wylson, master of the requests, and the earl's son, then at
court; occasioned by the remove of that queen to Sheffield.
Which he communicated to his father, in a private letter
written in May, " That two days ago, Dr. Wylson told May 10.
" him, he heard say, that his lordship, with his charge, was
" removed to Sheffield lodge; and that he asked him, whe-
" ther it were so, or no? To whom he answered, that he 250
" heard so, that his lordship, with his charge, was gone
" thither of force, till the castle [Tutbury castle] could be

" cleansed.   And that further, the said Wylson willed to
" know, whether his lordship did so by the consent of the
" council or not?   He answered, he knew not that; but
" that he was certain his lordship did it on good ground."
And then he earnestly desired Wylson of all friendship to
tell him, whether he had heard any thing to the contrary?
Which the other did swear, he never did.   But that the reason he asked was, because he said once, that lady should
have been conveyed from that house.   Then the lord George
told him, what great heed and care the said earl his father
had to her safe keeping, especially being there.   That good
numbers of men, continually armed, watched her day and
night, both under her windows, over her chamber, and on
every side of her.   That unless, said he, she could transform
herself into a flea or a mouse, it was impossible she should
escape.

At this same time, Wylson shewed him some part of the
confession of one; (but who he was, or when he did confess
it, he would in nowise tell him:) that that fellow should
say, he knew the queen of Scots hated the said earl deadly,
because of his religion, being an earnest protestant; and all
the Talbots else in England, being all papists, she esteemed
of them very well.   And that this fellow did believe verily,

The Tal-
bots.
all we Talbots did love her better in our hearts, than the
queen's majesty.   And this Wylson then told the said earl's
son, because he should see, what knavery there was in some
men to accuse.   Then he charged the said lord Gilbert, of
all love, that he should keep this secret: which he promised.   Notwithstanding, considering he would not tell him
who this fellow was, he willed a friend of his, one Mr.
Francis Southwel, (who was very great with Dr. Wylson,)
to know (among other talk) who he had last in examination.   And he understood, that this was the examination of
one at the last sessions of parliament, and not since.   But he
could not yet learn what he was.

Scottish
queen looks.
on Leicester
as her ene-
my.
That unhappy queen, as indeed she confided much in the
interest she had in the hearts of a great many of the English nobility and gentry, so she would point sometimes at

her enemies. In which rank she reckoned chiefly the earl
of Leicester. Of which, in communication by letter between that earl and the earl of Shrewsbury, the former
understood: being advertised thereof from some talk that
happened between that queen and him, concerning her enemies. Leicester, upon this, beseeched his lordship to be-
friend him so much as to gather, as near as he could, the
reason thereof. And withal he confessed, " That he was *Epist. Com.*
" a true and careful servant to his own sovereign, and *Salopien. in Offic. Ar-*
" therein had a respect to none other. Yet that this he *mor.*
" might truly say, that he had been no aggravater of that *His words*
" queen's cause, neither a hinderer of any favourable incli- *on occasion thereof.*
" nation that at any time he had found in the queen's ma-
" jesty towards her. Neither will I rob her majesty (as he
" proceeded) of her due desert, but must confess, that her
" own goodness hath more natural consideration of that
" queen, than all the friends she hath beside are able to
" challenge thanks for. And as I am bound to be most
" careful for the safety and preservation of mine own so- 251
" vereign every way; so neither have I been, nor am I, any
" practiser to do ill offices against any others. And right
" sorry have I been, when any cause hath been given the
" queen's majesty to be moved, or to alter those good and
" princely dispositions, which I have sundry times known
" her framed unto. And before such time as these causes
" have barred me so, as in duty I could not be a dealer, I
" think I was rather thought a friend than an enemy ; and
" of some too much. Though I knew best, I was but as I
" ought; and so mean I to remain." Thus that earl endeavoured to set himself in a better opinion with that queen:
who would soon be acquainted with all this by the earl her
keeper. But in the end, he beseeched the said earl of
Shrewsbury to let him know, what cause was now supposed: being content to take upon him his own fault; but to
have to do with none other.

And whereas the queen had a little before sent certain *The queen's*
special messages to Shrewsbury, concerning a careful look- *message to the earl of*
ing to that queen, by her special order given to Leicester ; *Shrews-*
bury.

BOOK
I.

Anno 1573.

he now assured him, that (to be plain with him) he knew no other grounds, than was delivered him by her own mouth. Nevertheless, as he added, he perceived, that he had need to look well about him: for there were many eyes upon him. Howbeit, one thing his lordship might take comfort in; that he found her majesty continued his assured good and gracious lady, and that she held still her wonted good opinion of him. This was dated from the court, the 10th of December.

A plot to bring the earl of Shrewsbury into disgrace.

Cunning plots seemed the next month to be hatching in the north, by the Scottish queen's favourers, to bring the earl of Shrewsbury into distrust and disgrace with the queen; out of hopes thereby, that he might be discharged from the custody of her. This business was managed chiefly by two persons that went for ministers and divines, viz. Haworth, and one Corker, the earl's chaplain. The charge against the earl seemed to be either matter of treachery or carelessness. The information whereof was brought up to the court, and came unto the queen's ears. This bred a great disturbance to the faithful earl, when he heard of it. And for the clearing of himself, despatched a message, in the month of January, to the earl of Huntington, president of the council at York, and another to the earl of Leicester at the court.

President of the north writes to him thereupon.

Some papers there were in the hands of the earl of Huntington, that might have been of good use to vindicate Shrewsbury, and which he now sent for. But they could not be found by him: and upon recollection, he thought he had torn them, upon account of their secresy, and that by the said earl of Shrewsbury's commandment. But like a friend he advised him, not to let that matter trouble him more than it required; not doubting of his provident foresight in looking to his charge. And then, said he, let the Devil and his instruments do their worst. " For my part," as he added in his letter, " you shall be sure I will have " some care that way also. [That is, of any attempts by pa- " pists made in those parts of the north, for rescuing the " Scottish queen.] And if I hear any thing worthy your

" knowledge, you shall speedily be advertised. And I trust
" ye shall see the papists of the north, a crooked measure,
" reasonably met withal. They seek to deceive all men,
" but I doubt not they shall be first deceived themselves." 252
This he wrote from York, the 18th of January.

The queen, soon suspecting it to be a falsehood, and *The queen*
wicked design against the earl, gave a commandment to the *suspects them, and*
earl of Leicester for the apprehension of those two mi- *orders an*
nisters; who pretended themselves voluntarily to be going *examination of them.*
up with their information. Which Leicester acquainting
Shrewsbury with, and that he should take them up, and
send them to him; Shrewsbury answered, that he verily
thought they were come to London by that time: and that
he thought fit neither to stay them, nor use any extraordinary speech or dealing with them; and to suffer them at
liberty to return up unto the council, unto which, as they
said, they had occasion to make their speedy repair: nothing doubting on his part, but that, upon due examination
of them, they should plainly appear, as they were, vile,
wicked varlets, and shameful slanderers of true religion.
Nevertheless, he told the earl of Leicester, he would cause
diligent search to be made in places in the country where
they were most likely to haunt. And if they, or any of
them, could be found, he would with all diligence take order for the sending them up, according to her majesty's
pleasure. And then, in a great sense of gratitude to the
queen, added, " That he thought himself much bounden
" unto her majesty, for that her highness' pleasure was, to
" have them thoroughly examined and tried: whereby their
" falsehood might be known; and so himself to be esteemed,
" as he doubted not he should be, of her majesty, as he had
" deserved, her true and faithful servant in all parts of his
" duty; and wherein, as he proceeded, he trusted in God to
" end his life, against the wicked practices of all false var-
" lets, with their maintainers."

He concluded this his letter to the earl of Leicester with
these grateful and obliging words; " That he saw his lord-
" ship's dealings in all matters touching him, not only like

BOOK
I.

Anno 1573.

Corker
brought be-
fore Leices-
ter.

His letter.

" a true nobleman unto her majesty, but also as a very
" kinsman towards him. Whereof his lordship should well
" find he would never be unmindful to his power."

 This letter, with another to the queen, the good earl of
Shrewsbury writ the latter end of January. But what was
done further in the discovery of this wickedness, (which it
seemed was cloaked under the profession of religion,) the
earl of Leicester's letter to that nobleman will acquaint us
with : viz. that Corker, Shrewsbury's chaplain, came into
London, and repaired to Dr. Wylson, master of requests,
in order to make his information. Who forthwith brought
him to Leicester's house by Temple-bar. He had skulked
in London for some days, consulting (as it seems) with some
of his complotters for the better management of their enterprise : though he utterly denied it. The earl ordered him
to be kept at Dr. Wylson's, till he were, by her majesty's
appointment, examined. He then made foul and evil reports of Shrewsbury. But Leicester told the earl, that he
was like to prove them, or forswear them, ere he departed :
and withal, that the queen meant to prosecute his doings
by due examination thoroughly; and after that, he should
receive according to his deserts. And then the earl made a
253 reflection upon the credulity of Shrewsbury, and good opinion of the religion of his chaplain, saying, " that his lord-
" ship might see all was not gold that glistered : and that
" many had cloaks for all weathers. And so did this good
" companion make religion his countenance, to utter his
" knavery."

 As for Haworth, he was come to Islington. Whither Leicester had sent to apprehend him. And doubted not, as he
continued his letter, but his lordship should hear much stuff
to come out of these two devilish divines.

 I cannot trace this story further; but by the honourable
correspondences of the two earls, we may see enough of the
intrigues in behalf of the Scottish queen; and how busy the
popish faction then was.

 I do affect (as may here and in other places be perceived)
to take opportunities, as they offer themselves, to revive the

memories of persons of quality and figure, and preserve their CHAP.
characters, and divers memorable passages of their lives, XXVI.
taken from their own authentic writings and letters. A Anno 1573.
thing that may be acceptable to many.

CHAP. XXVII.

*Foreign popish princes conspire to invade England. A
French gentleman at the Spaw gives information thereof. Papists fled abroad, called home. Edward lord
Windsor one of these: his plea. Theses propounded in
Louvain, against the jurisdiction of temporal princes.
Bishop of Durham's judgment of them. A commission in
every county, to punish the breakers of the orders of the
church service: the bishop of Norwich gives order to his
chancellor for information of such. Several ministers
suspended hereupon in the diocese of Norwich: but get
licence to catechise and preach. A letter upon this to
that bishop. He restrains them. The lady Huddleston, a
great papist in Ely diocese, searched for.*

NOTWITHSTANDING all the fair show from abroad Confedera-
towards England, a black cloud hung over it: and the cy of popish
danger the queen and state was now in from papists was gainst the
very great and imminent. For the foreign popish poten- queen.
tates (the chief whereof was Philip king of Spain) had entered into a league to invade this land, and to spoil it by
fire and sword. This was discovered by De la Tour, a
French nobleman, at the Spaw, unto an English gentleman
there, named Bromfield; Bochart, another French gentleman, present. Which relation the said nobleman was moved
to make, out of that high respect and honour he had for 254
queen Elizabeth, and for her particular favour and harbour
which she gave to the poor persecuted people in their own
country, for the religion. A particular relation of this, written by the said De la Tour in Latin, I met with, among
the Burghleian papers, to this purport.

BOOK
I.

Anno 1573.

Discovered
by De la
Tour to an
English
gentleman
at the
Spaw.

"That the lord De la Tour, bound on many accounts to
" the queen of England, in regard of her hospitality shewn
" to all the refugees of France, for the word of God; and
" esteeming the benefits by her majesty bestowed upon all
" the brethren professing the same religion to be common
" to him and all the French exiles in Germany, or in any
" other part of the world; that he being at the Bath near
" Aquisgrane, [Aix la Chapelle,] and holding some dis-
" course with a certain English baron, and having thereby
" come to the knowledge of somewhat that concerned the
" safety of the whole kingdom of England, he would not
" conceal it. But hearing that a certain noble knight, a
" captain of the queen's guards, was in the Spaw, he thought
" it his duty to certify the said officer, being a person very
" devoted to her majesty, of certain matters, which a great
" many princes were contriving, and endeavouring to bring
" to pass against the kingdom of England, and of the man-
" ner by which they thought to invade it on every side.

" And first, among these confederates against her ma-
" jesty it was agreed, that the king of Poland, [the French
" king's brother,] feigning to prepare a fleet for Poland, on
" the maritime parts, should convert his arms against the
" kingdom of England; and on a sudden, if he could, in-
" vade some port of England. And that, as at the same
" time, the Scots, persuaded by the cardinal of Lorain, with
" a very great army, consisting partly of French, partly of
" Scots, should break into England. And on the other
" part, the fleets of the king of Spain and of France, being
" joined, should attempt to seize some port in England. At
" which time, the duke D'Alva, with the aid of the bishop
" of Colein and other bishops, and of the duke of Bavaria,
" with 10,000 foot out of Flanders, resolved to wage war
" with the queen of England. And to the waging of that
" war, the antichrist of Rome, the king of Spain, and
" the above-said bishops, and the antichristian order of all
" France, consisting of all the prelates and papists of that
" kingdom, did combine. And lest the courage of all the
" confederates should quail, the cardinal of Lorain, whose

" hopes have devoured the kingdom of England in favour CHAP.
" of his niece, the queen of Scots, had promised to yield XXVII.
" the pay of 30,000 men, for one year. Which nation he Anno 1573.
" hoped shortly to set at liberty out of the hands of the
" queen's majesty.

" From the premises especially, it was to be conjectured,
" that there were many favourers of this most wicked con-
" juration in England, and induced by D'Alva and the car-
" dinal by money and promises, to take their part among
" the English as soon as they should see some armies in
" England. And that the said baron seemed to think this,
" when he told him, that when first the army should be
" transported into England, it should seize some place or
" town which might be fortified with a wall and a ditch, to
" be held so long, till men should come together from all
" parts of England, and join themselves with this army." 255
And then the paper concluded thus; " That these things
" were related to him, William Bromfield, by the lord De
" la Tour: present the nobleman Steven Bochart, lord Du
" Menillet, the 11th day of August, 1573. Signed,

" Will. Bromfield.
" S. Bochart.
" Bertrand de la Tour."

For church matters here at home, the queen saw it high Proclama-
time to provide for the security of the religion reformed, tions set
forth a-
and established in her realm. And therefore issued out gainst pa-
proclamations in favour of it, both against the papists and pists and
puritans.
the puritans also. September the 28th, a severe proclama-
tion went forth against traitors [namely, papists] that were
fled out of the realm, and against a great number of malicious libels printed against the government and the queen's
chief counsellors. Another proclamation was set forth, October the 20th, against the despisers and breakers of the orders prescribed in the Book of Common Prayer. The like
to another set forth June the 11th, before. Both which are Life of
set down in the Life of Archbishop Parker. These two last Archbishop
Parker,
looked chiefly towards the puritans. book iv. ch.
xxiv. xxxiii.

BOOK I.

Anno 1573.
The papists abroad called home.
Their pretence of going out of England.
The lord Windsor's letter, Sept. 5. Titus, B. 2.

And because all English papists, being the queen's sub-jects, now abroad, were commanded to come home, upon pain of treason, some pretended conscience for abiding abroad in catholic countries, that they might have the liberty of hearing mass, professing still their loyalty to the queen. One of these was Edward lord Windsor. Who for that purpose wrote earnest letters to the earl of Leicester, the earl of Sussex, and the lord admiral; shewing both the cause of his departure, and withal desiring the queen's leave, being come home, to enjoy his conscience. That to the earl of Sussex was writ in September: wherein he thus apologizeth for himself; " That he was constrained to make trial of his " good lords and friends, among whom he made account of " his good lordship; that he had written to the lord admi-" ral the causes at large that enforced him to take that hard " course and fortune, with desire to shew the same to him " and the earl of Leicester, as three of the noblest managers " in this our commonwealth; the rather to advertise his " lordship of the causes aforesaid, in that his sudden al-" teration of his present return home, not to be without " eminent danger to himself; although, as God knew, no " success in equity but his conscience. That his humble " suit now was, but to require his lordship, with the rest, to " be a mediator unto the queen's majesty, not to condemn " him, but to account of him as one of her loyal, faithful, " and loving subjects, in all matters, saving that was due " unto Almighty God; and with her majesty's favour, to " live there [abroad] or elsewhere: always shewing himself " an humble, careful, and obedient subject, touching her " majesty and the realm, *salva la conscientia.* And thus " humbly ending. From St. Thomas, the 5th of Sept. " 1573. Subscribing,

" Your lordship's poor friend,
" Edward Windsor."

256 Another of these fugitives, that went and tarried abroad for the sake of his religion, but professing also profound loyalty to the queen, was Tho. Coply, whom our historian

Tho. Coply, another fugitive, a

sheweth to have received much countenance and honour CHAP.
from two great neighbouring princes; viz. the king of XXVII.
Spain; who ennobled him, and gave him the title of *great* Anno 1573.
master of the Maes, and lord of Gatton, and set him forth pensioner
of Spain.
to sea, to make prize both of the English and Netherlanders in the year 1575. And he was recommended to the Camd. Eliz.
French king by Vaux, Don John's secretary; who honoured p. 208 and
220.
him with the dignity of knighthood, and title of baron,
about the year 1577.

A person of his character some may be inquisitive to His petition
know more of. Some further account of him I give from to the queen
for his
his own writings and letters. In this present year 1573, he lands.
sent a petition to the queen, for restoring to him his manor
of Gatton in Surrey: which came to the queen by his treason; as appears from the survey of the queen's manors. He
had been now, as the petition imported, five years abroad,
and had put himself in the king of Spain's service, and was
at that time there: urging, that it was the necessity he was
reduced to, by the queen's seizing upon his estate, that
made him do so. That he had a wife and seven children.
And concerning that service, he said plainly, that during
the time he was by his catholic majesty entertained, he
must and would serve with all fidelity and loyalty, as became him, both for the honour of himself and his nation.

His estate was seized for going beyond sea without spe- His plea for
cial licence. For which, he said, his learned counsel assured going beyond sea.
him not to be unlawful, by reason of his freedom in the
staple; which gave him liberty to pass and repass the seas
at his pleasure.

He urged likewise in his own behalf, that during his being beyond sea, he had behaved himself dutifully and quietly
every way: that no person living could charge him with any
disloyal or undutiful fact. He spake of the very hard dealings used to him at home, together with his friends and servants. And requested of the queen pardon for his departure to Antwerp without her leave; and for whatsoever
offence beside his enemies might have surmised against him,
for malice to his person, or love to his livings: and to afford

him her gracious licence to remain for so many years, as should please her majesty, in the parts beyond the sea, with-in such catholic state, as her majesty should best like of.

Conveys his lands before his going.

And as this gentleman requested the queen for his liberty of staying abroad upon protestation of his loyalty, so likewise for the restoring to him his estate on the same account. For this purpose he shewed, how he had conveyed his lands before his going away. And he thought it was so lawful a conveyance, that it could not be entered upon. And that he ought not by law to lose it. And then he prayed the queen to clear her virtuous conscience, (as he expressed it,) for the withholding of his living.

The next year, 1574, by the queen's ambassador, Dr. Wylson, then at Brussels, the lord treasurer Burghley (who was related to him, and his friend) sent an overture to him, that in case he would withdraw himself from thence, and live in Germany, there should an allowance be made him, and some good portion of his living.

257

Overtures sent to him by the queen's ambassador.

The English court seemed to expect some discoveries from him: who was in some repute in those parts. And in another of his letters he professed all duty to the queen: and he wished to God he had occasion offered to his affection and zeal to her, to testify it, with the shedding of his blood. And he seemed to comply with the lord treasurer's motion sent by Dr. Wylson, of departing from those parts. For in another letter, he desired him speedily to work his desired despatch. And the more frank and liberal his dealing should appear towards him, the more should be his bond; and the more his shame, if being so favourably restored to the service of his natural sovereign, he did not from thenceforth employ the best of his forces, to the yielding and answering all duties that might be expected of an honest man, both in respect of his allegiance and grateful acknowledgments.

Promiseth to make discovery.

His cause still hangs, the court yet dubious of him, notwithstanding all his fair words and protestations. For I find, in the year 1577, Dr. Wylson still tampering with him. To whom he promiseth now to shew himself the

queen's true subject, and to make discovery: who had re-   CHAP.
quired him to be plain and faithful in his dealings.   XXVII.

But this calling home of her subjects was necessary at Anno 1573.
this juncture, in respect of the foreign popish conspiracy
above mentioned. And the queen might justly refuse to
suffer them to remain in Spain, where this lord was, or in
Flanders, where her popish subjects commonly abode; because of those dangerous principles they sucked in there,
against the queen's government, especially in spirituals. As
in Lovain, (where a great many English retired for their
studies, as well as others,) these theses in the university
there were propounded some years before this; making it
unlawful for the civil magistrate to have any thing to do in
ecclesiastical matters. They were printed there, and were
as follow:

Quæstio theologica.

Num civilis magistratus, in his quæ fidem et religionem Theses pro-
concernunt, subsit potestati ecclesiasticæ, et eidem teneatur Lovain.
in his obedire.

Propos. { Sicut misit me Pater, et ego mitto vos. Joan. xx.
Amen, dico vobis, quæcunque alligaveritis super
terram, erunt ligata et in cœlo: et quæcunque
solveritis super terram, erunt, &c. Matt. xviii.
Obite præpositis vestris, et subjacete eis. Heb. xiii.
Reddite quæ sunt Cæsaris Cæsari, et quæ sunt
Dei Deo.

Conclusio 1.

Discrimen igitur est inter civilis et ecclesiastici magistratus
potestatem, in hoc constitutum; ut civilis magistratus habeat jus et authoritatem præcipiendi ea, quæ ad externam
morum justitiam, et temporalis vitæ quietem ac tranquillita-
tem pertinent. Sacer vero magistratus supremam habeat et
absolutam authoritatem præcipiendi ea quæ ad Dei justi-258
tiam et futuri sæculi felicitatem spectant. Qui ob id civili
est multo sublimior et præstantior. Et proinde civili nequa-
quam subditus.

Conclusio 2.

Quemadmodum igitur corpus subest et subservit animæ

BOOK I.

Anno 1573.

in hac mortali vita, ita et authoritas prophani magistratus subesse et subservire debet, in hac eadem mortali vita, potestati ecclesiasticæ in his quæ fidei, religionis et Dei sunt. Adeo ut quæcunque ad profectum religionis Christianæ a legitimis ecclesiæ præfectis rite decreta sunt et constituta, non tantum teneatur ipse magistratus civilis illis obedire, sed et co-operari, ut effectum sortiantur ; subditos authoritate sibi a Deo tributa ad eorum observationem compellando ; contumaces vero et inobedientes suo modo puniendo : nec alias leges ferre, aut aliter potestate uti, quam fidei et religioni expediat.

Conclusio 3.

Non est igitur potestatis civilis, constituere pastores, doctores, presbyteros, aliosque ecclesiæ ministros, aut præscribere eis leges ministrandi ; seu impedire, ne proprio fungantur officio. Unde recte patres in concilio Triden. statuerunt, nefas esse cuilibet seculari magistratui prohibere ecclesiastico judici, nequem excommunicet; aut mandare ut latam excommunicationem revocet; etiam sub prætextu, quod omnia quæ idem concilium præscribit in excommunicatione observanda, non essent observata ; cum non ad sæculares, sed ad ecclesiasticos hæc cognitio pertineat.

Conclusio 4.

Erant igitur qui dicunt, principum esse supplere negligentiam præsidum ecclesiæ, in purganda ea a falsa doctrina aut falso cultu. Cum potestatis civilis non sit judicare de scripturis et fidei dogmatibus, aut discernere veram doctrinam fidei a falsa; sed solius potestatis ecclesiasticæ. Cui indefectibilitas fidei a Christo permissa est.

The bishop of Durham's judgment of these conclusions.

These Lovanian conclusions were conveyed to the bishop of Durham, who thought fit to transmit them, enclosed in his letter, to sir William Cecil, secretary of state, with his judgment of them in these words : " I have sent your honour such conclusions as be disputed at Lovain, and sent " over hither. Wise men do mervail, that polity can suffer " such seed of sedition : although, for trial of the doctrine, " it were not amiss to hear the adversary, what he can say ; " yet that doctrine being received, and the contrary suffered

" to be spread abroad, to the troubling of the state, in my
" opinion, is dangerous. God turn all to the best. But
" surely evil men pike much evil out of such books, even
" against the polity."
Against any polity, indeed, but especially against the polity of England, where the laws of the land make the prince
supreme, as well in all causes spiritual as temporal : on
which foot the reformation of religion in this kingdom
stood. And these doctrines and opinions, vented and main- 259
tained in these countries, effectually tended to make the
queen's subjects there disloyal to their sovereign, turbulent
and seditious to the state; and therefore there was great
reason to call for them home.

As for the queen's subjects in Ireland, the pope took care An Irish
to continue them tight to his chair, by supplying that king- priest consecrated bi-
dom with Irishmen in orders, priests and bishops; who shop at
were to swear all duty and allegiance to him in the highest Rome.
degree, against all that should oppose the see of Rome.
And he appointed and nominated bishops for the sees there.
Some of them were consecrated at Rome. One of these,
whose name was Dermic O Clier, was consecrated there this
year, 1573, March 12, (the second year of pope Gregory
XIII.) bishop of Maion, in the province of Tuam. The
which consecration was performed by cardinal Sanctorius,
upon that pope's command, or oracle, as his word was
styled; vivæ vocis oraculo. The original instrument or bull
of this Irish bishop's consecration, by some means or other,
was taken, and sent over into the English court. Which I
have seen among the papers of the lord treasurer Burghley.
Wherein is certified, that before his consecration he solemnly swore obedience to the pope, according to the custom and manner of popish bishops, viz.

" That from that hour, as before, he would be faithful
" and obedient to blessed Peter, and the holy church of
" Rome, and to his lord, pope Gregory XIII. and to his
" successors; and that he should discover any practices that
" might be prejudicial to the rights, honours, privileges, &c.
" of the Roman church, and hinder them as much as he

" could.   That the decrees of the holy fathers, their rules,
" ordinances, reservations, &c. he should keep.   And that
" he should prosecute heretics, schismatics, and rebels to
" our lord the pope and his successors, &c.   And that if he
" should know any thing prejudicial to the rights and pri-
" vileges of the see of Rome to be attempted, he should hin-
" der them as much as he could ; and, as soon as he might,
" signify the same to the same his lord, or some other, by
" whom it might come to his knowledge," &c.   This whole
instrument, at length, will be found carefully transcribed in

the Appendix.   I only observe in this oath several obligations additional, which were not in the oaths imposed upon
other bishops formerly ; as may appear by the customary
oath taken by Cranmer.   See his Life.   Thus this clause is

added, which is not there : viz. " I shall not suffer any thing
" prejudicial to the rights and privileges of the Roman see;
" and if any such things shall be attempted, I shall hinder
" them as much as I can ; and, as soon as I can, shall
" signify the same to the same our lord, or to some other,
" by whom it may come to his knowledge.   The rules of
" the holy fathers, the decrees and ordinances, reservations
" or dispositions, promises and commands apostolical, with
" my whole power I shall observe, and cause them to be
" observed by others.   Heretics, schismatics, and rebels to
" the said our lord and his successors, I shall, according to
" my power, prosecute and impugn."   This, with other
clauses, are not in the oath taken by the said archbishop,
nor sworn to.

260
The council
to the com-
missioners
for uni-
formity,and
executing
laws for
that pur-
pose.
For the more effectual stopping of the variety used in the
public divine service of the church, and thereby to prevent
much strife and contention, a letter was written in November by the privy council, to certain chosen commissioners in
every shire, for the execution of a late proclamation for uni-
formity of religion and common prayer, by way of Oyer and
Terminer.   This met with papists as well as disaffected puritans.   It was penned by secretary Smith, as appears by
the hand in the minutes ; and was as follows :

" After our right hearty commendations. The queen's CHAP.
" majesty being much grieved to understand, that in divers XXVII.
" places of this realm there is much diversity, and there-Anno 1573.
" upon contentions and strifes risen, about the rites and ce-
" remonies of the sacraments and common prayer, hath of
" late set out an earnest proclamation, as you know, that
" speedy care should be had for the reformation of those
" abuses, and preventing of further danger that might
" ensue. The which to be done as carefully and seriously
" as may be, her highness hath made choice of you, as in
" whom her highness doth put special trust, that you will
" execute her gracious will and pleasure declared in that
" proclamation, according as in the act of parliament made
" in the first year of her majesty's reign : and yet ceaseth
" not still to call upon us, to have an eye to the repressing
" of those schisms, contentions, and diversities from the
" orders set forth in the Book of Common Prayer allowed
" by parliament, and thinketh every day too long until it
" be done.

" Wherefore we have thought good, by these our letters,
" to require you, so soon as conveniently you may, to meet
" and consult a convenient time and place ; and that being
" agreed upon, with all speed to inquire, and try the of-
" fenders according to the law.

" That her majesty's proclamation may not seem to be
" neglected and frustrate, nor the mischief suffered to pro-
" ceed any further. And what you shall have done herein,
" her majesty's will and pleasure is, that you shall, with all
" convenient speed as you may, certify her highness, or as
" is appointed in the commission, by your letters: and so from
" time to time, as occasion may serve, or that any thing shall
" be done by you by virtue of the said commission. Wherein
" we pray you not to fail : and so commit you to Almighty
" God. From Greenwich, the —— of November."

These commissions were made, under the great seal of The com-
England, to certain persons of trust in the several counties mission:
of the realm, whereof the archbishops and bishops were the queen's

BOOK I. principal, to inquire, hear, and determine especially of the of-fences committed against the orders for divine service. And

Anno 1573. the proclamation mentioned above was set forth in October:
proclama-tion for ob-serving or-ders of the church. whereby the queen would have the laws made in her time for the order of divine service observed, and the offenders duly punished. And that these her endeavours might the more effectually take place, divers things to this purpose, by her command, in the said month of November, were de-clared by the lord treasurer in the Star-chamber. Which

Life of Archbishop Parker, p. 456. are set down at large in the Life of Archbishop Parker.

But now see a little the success and issue of this commis-
261 sion in Norfolk. The justices in commission there, required
The bishop of Norwich writes to his chan-cellor for bringing in informa-tions to the commis-sioners. to look after the punishment of the despisers of the orders of the church, shewed themselves ready to execute the laws upon them, but expected information from the bishop and his officers. Hereupon the bishop of Norwich writ to his chancellor, " That for the better execution of the service " committed to them by the justices, touching the reform-" ing of such persons as should be found any way to dis-" obey the orders of the Book for the Form of Common-" Prayer and Administration of the Sacraments, it was " thought very necessary, that commandment be sent to his " archdeacons and their ministers, that they, and every of " them, in their several circuits, should give in charge to the " clergy and the questmen, to present before them, between " this and the first week in Lent, viz. before the first of " March next, the names and surnames of all such persons " as, dwelling within their several parishes, were negligent, " obstinate, or any otherwise enemies, or hinderers of her " majesty's proceedings, contrary to the said book, and the " statute provided in that behalf.

" He prayed and required him therefore, that upon sight " hereof, he should send forth his letters to every of the " said archdeacons and commissaries, charging them in his " [the bishop's] name, that they duly and with all diligence " execute the effect hereof; and to return such certificate " to the great inquest appointed to receive the same, he " being especially by them requested to have it so. And

" herein he prayed them to use their best diligence, and to CHAP.
" move the said commissaries to the like, as every of them XXVII.
" would answer the contrary at their perils." This was Anno 1573.
dated from Ludham, the 30th of January, 1573.

Many ministers in this diocese, being found unconform- Some sus-
able upon this inquisition, were suspended by the bishop pended are
permitted to
from reading the common-prayer and administering the sa- catechize
craments; as may be seen more particularly in Archbishop phesy.
and pro-
Parker's Life. But yet, thinking to make use of them still Life of
in the great want of preachers to instruct the people in that Parker,
Archbishop
great diocese, the bishop seemed to have permitted some of p. 457.
them to catechize the younger sort, and to *prophesy* in those
exercises set up in divers places, or winked thereat. But this
was thought to have been done amiss, by some in the commission aforesaid, as confirming these men in their want of
conformity. Therefore one of them, and he of some eminence, (but concealing his name,) sent his judgment and
advice to the bishop, in a letter, to this tenor; (which deserves to be set down at length, for giving more light in
this matter :)

" My duty unto your lordship humbly remembered. Epist. Joh.
" Whereas, sithence my last being with you at Norwich, I Norw.
Episc.
" have been advertised, that divers ministers within your dio- MSS. Joh.
Episc.
" cese in this county of Norfolk, for their disorderly usage Elien.
" in not observing the Book of Common-Prayer set forth by One of the
commission
" the queen's majesty, or for their contemptuous preaching writes to
" or speaking against it, contrary to the queen's highness' the bishop
against this
" laws, proclamations, and direct commandments given in permission.
" that behalf, are by your lordship and your officers se- 262
" questered, as well from saying the common-prayer or mi-
" nistering the sacraments, as also from preaching, until
" they will submit themselves, and live as it becometh good
" and obedient ministers and subjects in that function.
" Wherein, for that part, your lordship, in mine opinion,
" have done very well; if, as I am credibly given to un-
" derstand, your lordship, or your officers, had not given to
" divers of them toleration, or licence to catechize in their
c c 2

BOOK "parish churches, and to use the exercise of *prophesying*
I.
_____ "in the open congregation: which sufferance and permis-
Anno 1573. "sion is *ad appositum*, and greatly offensive. For whoso-
"ever should be admitted to instruct and teach in the mi-
"nistry ought to be modest, no quarrellers, first proved;
"and then to minister, if they be blameless. But these,
"being proved and tried, shew themselves stubborn and
"obstinate to the whole state, and disobedient ministers or
"subjects, crossing the prince's authority and laws; think-
"ing themselves wiser than the whole realm is besides, as it
"seemeth.

"Surely, my lord, such like are not to be tolerated, or
"suffered to teach, or use any exercise in the church, until
"they openly shew an humble submission, and conform
"themselves to the order prescribed by her majesty.
"Wherefore, your lordship shall do well to wink no longer
"at them, but presently to restrain them wholly, until they
"will reform themselves. Wherein your lordship shall shew
"yourself a good pastor, and avoid further inconveniences,
"that otherwise will, or are like to ensue, as is much to be
"feared. And if further complaint shall hereupon arise, it
"is not unlike but that your lordship's lenity and suffer-
"ance shall be imputed to be the whole or chief offence
"that may succeed thereof. And thus being bold, as your
"lordship's wellwisher, to inform you of that which I think
"is not fully or at all known unto you, I leave further to
"trouble you: beseeching God to send you your own good
"heart's desire. From ——, the 6th of March, '73.

"Your lordship's, to his little power,
"Joined in commission with you, N. N."

The bishop took well this seasonable and friendly admonition from this gentleman in the same commission with
himself; especially also understanding that complaints began to be made of this his sufferance. Whereupon, the
very next day, without further delay, he sent to his chancellor, to give order for the restraint of this liberty: signi-
The bishop fying to him, "That he heard, that some of those ministers
orders his

" that were suspended from the administration and serving CHAP.
" in their cures, were notwithstanding bold to preach in XXVII.
" *prophesies*, and to catechize, and therein dealt more libe- Anno 1573.
" rally than was convenient; whereby offence was taken, chancellor
" and he [the bishop] was advertised thereof. For remedy them.
" and restraint whereof, he required him, that in his name,
" either by his letter or otherwise, he should send forth-
" with unto his four commissaries, charging them, and
" every of them, that they call before them all such of the
" clergy in their several jurisdictions as had been suspended
" for causes aforesaid, or given over their livings, straightly 263
" charging such persons henceforth not to attempt either
" to preach, or prophesy, or to speak to the congregation
" by way of catechizing; unless such person or persons did
" first, before the said commissary, subscribe, or otherwise
" openly promise to submit himself to the order and con-
" formity appointed. And if any person should contemn
" their said charge, the same to be certified to him, [the
" bishop,] or other the said commissioners, to be otherwise
" entreated, as the cause should deserve. And herein he
" wished his chancellor, for his own part, and his other
" officers, to use all their best endeavours. And so he
" wished him well to fare. Dated from Ludham, March
" the 7th, '73."

And to prevent further addresses to the said bishop in His letter
behalf of these ministers, but the next day, upon some oc- to a gentle-
casion writing to Mr. Will. Heydon, a gentleman of good vourer of
quality in those parts, and a favourer of these preachers, nisters.
but in the said commission, the bishop shewed him how necessary it was now no longer to suffer them, or wink at their
preaching; hinting his own danger, and the notice that was
taken at it: viz. " That he thought good to let him under-
" stand, that he had received sundry letters, as well from
" some in authority as from some of the best worship there,
" signifying, that the suffering of such persons as were sus-
" pended, to preach, to prophesy, and to catechize, was
" cause of abuse and offence to some : and the same being
" spoken of, and misliked of some in authority, he [the bi-

" shop] heard of it hardly; and that he was constrained to
" restrain the same, unless he would willingly procure his
" own danger. That he had therefore sent out command-
" ment, that none such as were suspended, or had willingly
" given up their livings, should be suffered to speak in pro-
" phesy or otherwise, as is aforesaid, until such person do
" so conform himself to the ordinances of the church esta-
" blished by authority, and do, before the commissary of
" that circuit, promise the same by word or subscription."

And then addressing himself to Mr. Heydon : " Let not
" this seem strange to you, I pray you : for the matter is
" of importance, and toucheth me so near, as less than this
" I cannot do, if I will avoid extreme danger. And to pre-
" vent your purpose in writing or coming over in this case,
" I do by these most heartily pray you, as a commissioner
" put in trust, to assist me in this behalf, and not contrari-
" wise to persuade; since this purpose is necessary, and
" looked for at both our hands : and being a thing so rea-
" sonable, I cannot perform my duty if I shall neglect, or
" partially wink at such doings." And so leaving him to
Almighty God, with his hearty commendations, subscribed
himself his assured friend in Christ. Dated from Ludham,
March 8, 1573.

The queen's proclamation beforesaid, against despisers of
the orders of the church, and absenters from the public service of it, looked towards papists as well as others; and accordingly those in commission proceeded according to law
against them. At this time, a certain popish lady, the lady
Huddleston, inhabiting in the diocese of Ely, was one of
these, avoiding coming to church; and now, upon this inquisition, absenting herself from her house : and being
greatly suspected to contemn the order of religion settled,
the bishop of Ely, and commission there, being about to
send for her, she removed herself into another diocese, to a
place called Harling hall in Norfolk, a great harbour for
papists. This the said bishop signified to the bishop of
Norwich, and what a dangerous person she was, and that
he would do well to use his endeavour to take her. Ac-

The com-
missioners
call for a
popish lady.

264

cordingly, the bishop (in whose diocese she now was) framed .CHAP.
a letter to Ashfield, an active justice of peace in those parts, <u>XXVII.</u>
not knowing any more convenient. way to have her appre- Anno 1573.
hended, than to desire him to take the pains, either to travel
himself to Harling hall, where she was, or else to cause her
by his letters to come before him ; where she might lay in
good bonds with sureties of her appearance before the bishop
of Ely, or other the high commissioners, to answer such
matters as she might be charged withal : which perhaps
might fall out (as he wrote) worse than they knew of. For
surely, as the bishop added, there is a wicked nest of them
together, as he had been informed   He further excited the
said justice, by telling him, " that his travail herein would
" be acceptable to God, and profitable to the common-
" wealth." This was writ Feb. 18.

But he being justice of peace for Suffolk, and Harling
hall lying in Norfolk, he could not meddle therein ; desiring only sufficient warrant, and then, he said, he would be
ready, not only to fetch that lady, but any other papist
whatsoever within either of the two shires : praying his
lordship to follow this matter, which was so well begun.
The issue was, that the bishop (as he wrote to the bishop
of Ely) procured a warrant under three of their hands that
were commissioners, to call the lady Huddleston to answer
her disobedience. And the rather, because there was, as
he said, a wicked brood at that house, that ought to be
looked to.

CHAP. XXVIII.

*Chief puritans. Sampson and Dering checked. Their let-
ters and apologies: for a reformation of the church's government: and against the civil power and lordship of
bishops. Their solicitations of the lord treasurer to further their discipline. Sampson's intercession for his hospital: and for Mr. Heton. Dering brought into the
Star-chamber for words. His letter to the lord treasurer
thereupon. Articles required of him to subscribe. Other
articles of inquiry, for him to answer. Moor, of Norwich, confutes Dr. Pern's sermon. Mr. Cartwright. An
order from the commission ecclesiastical for seizing him.*

Sampson
writes to
the lord
treasurer
for a re-
formation
in church
govern-
ment.

BUT especially it was thought very necessary to provide
for the peace of the church, and due observation of the
worship of God, against the puritan faction, by reason of
the great opposition made by divers of their eminent men
this year, as well as of late, against it. Whereof Sampson,
master of an hospital in Leicester, was one. Who for that
cause was, several years before, deprived of the deanery of
Christ's Church, Oxon. This man made now an address for
mending the church's government, and to take directions
from Bucer's book, *De Regno Christi*, (whereof he sent him
an epitome,) for that purpose. He was now taken with the

March the
8th.

palsy, and nevertheless (in March) writ this earnest letter
(though by the hand of another) to the lord Burghley, as
one of the last (perhaps) he should write: prefacing the

His letter.
MSS.
Burghlian.

same, That it had pleased God to take from him *motum* of
half his limbs, though not *sensum;* which was the cause
why he then used the hand of another in writing to his
lordship. And that though this disease was to him *evangelium mortis;* and that he thanked God in Christ Jesus
he was ready at his call to depart in peace, and leave all
things in this world behind him; yet that he was constrained, ere he went, to trouble his lordship with two
things; which did so prick him forwards, that he could not
be satisfied but in moving his lordship in the same: because
in the one he might discharge his duty toward the church

of Christ, as in the other his duty towards a dear friend of CHAP.
his, (which being more private, I shall be silent of it here.) XXVIII.

Concerning the former, thus he expressed his zeal: "My Anno 1573.
" good lord, *pro Christo Domino dominantium rogo, ob-*
" *secro,* that there may be a consideration had of the state
" of the church of England.   The *doctrine* of the gospel is
" and may be purely preached in England.   Everlasting
" praise be to his Majesty for it.   But the *government* of
" the church appointed in the gospel yet wanteth here.
" The doctrine is good, the government by him appointed
" is good.   These are to be conjoined, and not separated.
" It is a deformity to see the church of Christ, professing
" his gospel, to be governed by such canons and customs 266
" as by which Antichrist did rule his synagogue.   I know
" there is now a great stir about this matter.   Much writ-
" ing, and little help.   Yea, of much writing ariseth much
" gall, and many other odd questions, frivolous and offen-
" sive.   *Nec erit finis quæstionum,* so long as these conten-
" tions are on foot.   An end there would be: a good end
" the Lord Jesus send.   My lord, this matter of reforming
" the state of the government of the church was in hand in
" the days of king Edward.   Yea, his father, after the
" abolishing of the pope's tyranny, thought it necessary to
" be considered of.   And therefore the law of the thirty
" commissioners was made; which was also renewed in king
" Edward's days.   And something was done then in con-
" cluding of canons for this purpose.

" In this time also, that learned Martin Bucer did write Bucer's
" a book of this matter to that godly king, entitling it *De* book, De
Regno
" *Regno Christi.*   I was so bold the last year, to write to Christi,
" your lordship of it, desiring you to read it.   There earnestly
recom-
" shall you see what wanteth of the full kingdom of mended.
" Christ in this church of England.   But because I know
" your many affairs do call you so diversely, that you can
" hardly find leisure to read any long tracts, therefore I
" have sent your lordship an epitome of it, drawn *fideliter*
" *et succincte.*   The long tract *De Matrimonio et Divortiis*
" I have on purpose left out; for his opinion in divorces I

" cannot approve. But otherwise, your lordship shall see
" him so well and so fully set forth the wants of the things
" of Christ's kingdom in this kingdom, that your lordship
" shall see what is wanting, and what is to be had and
" planted. He that concludes, that to have the church go-
" verned by meet pastors and ministers taketh away the au-
" thority of Christian magistrates, is by Bucer sufficiently
" confuted.

" My lord, I beseech you read it ; and I beseech you
" again, take the matter to heart. It is the cause of Christ
" Jesus, and of his church : it toucheth men's souls. My
" lord, if you consider deeply, how from time to time God
" hath dealt with you, surely I know you will confess, that
" you are bound to do the best to set Christ in his chair in
" this church of England ; that as he teacheth us, so he
" may rule and govern us. True and diligent ministers of
" the word, attending their flock, as Acts xx. are means to
" make to God a holy people, and to the queen's majesty
" good subjects. Help, my lord, this good work of the
" Lord your God. So shall you serve him that is *Rex*
" *regum:* and he will acknowledge that you have done him
" good service, when you, and all kings, and all lords shall
" appear before him, to be judged of that you have done in
" your office.

" Bucer wrote his book in England, being but a stranger;
" yet of England most aptly, touching the state of it, to
" the king of England : but by report of his familiars in
" Cambridge. And they were the same which are now
" archbishops of York[a] and Canterbury[b], bishop of Lon-
" don[c], Bradford, and such like. I know not what confer-
" ence they had with him when he made the book ; but I
" am sure, that since his death, in private talk, they have
" much approved his book. Let therefore this book of
" Bucer be called in question among them that *aliquid me-*
267 " *lius constituatur, et nequid in proxima synodo asperius*
" *constituatur.* Which I fear, unless your lordship do help,"
&c. Concluding, " Good my lord, use your authority for
" the glory of Christ, and the peace and good of the

a Grindal.
b Parker.
c Sandys.

" church. You cannot employ your authority in a better
" cause, nor in better service. And of the Lord Jesus you
" shall receive the reward of a faithful servant." Subscribing, " Your humble suppliant and poor orator *in et pro*
" *Christo Domino,*

" Tho. Sampson."

To this exhortation the lord treasurer gave a gentle and The lord
Christian answer, signifying, that he liked well of his mo- treasurer's
answer.
tion, but that he could not do that good which either Samp-
son would, or others thought he could. Which Sampson
followed with another more pressing one; and explaining
his meaning more plainly, to be for such a reformation of
the regiment of the church, as the wholly laying aside of all
doctors, proctors, chancellors, officials, and other ecclesiastical officers belonging to the bishops, that exercised *jus ca-
nonicum,* i. e. *papisticum.* This whole letter, in answer to
the lord treasurer's, may be read in the Appendix to the Book iv.
Life of Archbishop Parker. N°. 93.

If he meant, (as he seemeth to do,) that the regiment of
the church was to be reformed by laying aside bishops and
their superiority, and setting in the room thereof an equality
of ministers, Bucer is evidently against him; who, in the
said book, propounding to king Edward VI. that religion
might be restored, and the church of Christ be planted and
watered with fit ministers, writes thus: *Nunc ex perpetua* Bucer's
ecclesiarum observatione, ab ipsis jam apostolis, videmus, judgment
for bishops.
*visum et hoc esse Spiritui Sancto, ut inter presbyteros, qui-
bus ecclesiarum procuratio est commissa, unus ecclesiarum,
et totius sacri ministerii curam gerat singularem ; eaque
cura et solicitudine cunctis præeat aliis. Qua de causa*
episcopi *nomen, hujusmodi summis ecclesiarum curatoribus
est peculiariter attributum.* De Regno Christi, cap. 12.
pag. 98. " Now from the continual observation of the
" churches, and that even from the apostles themselves, we
" see that this hath also seemed good to the Holy Ghost,
" that among the priests, to whom the care of the churches
" most especially hath been committed, one of them take a

BOOK "singular care of the churches, and of the whole sacred mi-
I.   "nistry, and have the precedency of all the rest in the

Anno 1573. "same care and diligence. For which cause the name of
"*bishop* hath been peculiarly given to those highest super-
"visors of the churches." And again: *Hi enim, sicut dig-
nitate et demandata primaria ecclesiarum solicitudine, re-
liquos omnes sacri ministerii ordines antecedunt, ita debent
etiam voluntate et studio,* &c. Ubi supra, p. 99. "These,
"as in dignity and primary care of the churches intrusted
"to them, go before all the rest of the orders of the sacred
"ministry; so they ought also in will and application, in
"the right administration of the churches, excel all others."

268   He speaks also in the same chapter in approbation of the
three orders in the ministry, viz. of bishops, priests, and
deacons. Nor hath he a word of laying aside the episcopal
and ecclesiastical officers, viz. chancellors, officials, commissaries, proctors, &c. only advising, (that the bishops might
not be distracted with other business, but that they might
wholly give themselves to the promoting of religion,) that
they should have vicars and others of their clergy to assist
them, and to take care of other necessary affairs belonging
to them.

Sampson's   This Sampson, by reason of his incompliance with some
good deserts
towards the customs of this church in the public worship, was laid aside
hospital at from doing God service therein: yet was of use more pri-
Leicester.
vately, by governing of an hospital in Leicester; preferred
thereto by reason of his former figure in the church and
university, and suffering for the gospel by exile under queen
Mary. He was careful for the good estate of this hospital,
having been in great danger of sinking, by reason of the
concealers, but rescued by the good lord Burghley. Sampson now, having drawn up a book, in order to the better
establishment of it, came up in the month of July, and
brought it to that lord to read it over, and to consider it,
that it might take place. But now, having no leisure to
peruse it, being ready to attend the queen in her progress,
Sampson excited him to do it; praying him, that it might
for that purpose be carried along with him: adding, "That

" though this was but a trifle, and such as, in respect of his CHAP.
" continual and weighty affairs, he should not trouble his XXVIII.
" honour withal; yet to beggars, their trifle was great. Anno 1573.
" Neither was it, as his honour knew, accounted a trifle to
" hear and despatch the poor in their poor suits. As he
" had most favourably, not only undertaken, but finished
" the dangerous cause of his hospital, as he expressed his
" grateful sense of that good turn. And that for it all the
" poor there prayed for him, and he with them, that God
" would bless his honour. And so humbly beseeched him
" to continue his favour and aid, to the perfect ratifying
" that which had so well hitherto passed by his hands."
This was dated from London, July the 25th. Concluding
with his prayer, " That God Almighty would direct him in
" all his affairs, to do that which might be pleasing in his
" sight; so that his favour might be to his lordship's com-
" fort and life."

I cannot but add one thing more concerning Mr. Samp- Intercedes
son, which happened this year; namely, his compassion and a merchant,
gratitude also, towards a very good man and an English that had re-
merchant, who had been, in the time of the exile, a very exiles; now
bountiful benefactor unto Sampson, and the rest living reduced to
abroad in the time of queen Mary; which prompted him
now very earnestly to interpose with the lord treasurer in
his behalf, being now aged, and reduced to straits; giving
him this account, both of the person and of his request.
He called it, " A suit in most humble wise for himself; in-
" asmuch as it was for such a friend to him, as was *alter*
" *ego ;* and that *merito,* for that I have, said he, been long
" to him *alter ipse.* The man he meant, naming him, was
" that honest merchant, and in his company, a right mer-
" chant and worshipful, Mr. Heton. That in exile for the
" gospel, he relieved many *exules Christi,* and consumed
" himself greatly : and that piety planted in his heart had 269
" kept him from such courses as some had kept, to their
" enriching worldly. That his place of service his lord-
" ship knew. *At pius ille et bonus senex,* is to him so dear,
" and his state so much I pity, that if I had power to my

BOOK
I.

Anno 1573.

" will in this behalf, I would not be a petitioner for him to
" any body; for I know what I owe to him. And they
" which may, and are some ways bound, as I am, will not,
" or care not, though they know as much as I of him.
" *Hoc unum* I presume of your goodness to do; which is in
" most humble wise to beseech your lordship to be good to
" him. The queen's majesty, of her princely munificence,
" is bountiful to many. If it would please her majesty to
" give to this her good subject liberty to transport 3, 4, 5,
" or 6000 of English cloth, without paying of custom, his
" old age should be bountifully sustained by her princely
" liberality." He added, " that he did not, for he dared
" not, desire his lordship to be the means to move and ob-
" tain this for him; but only, that if his lordship could like
" of the suit to be moved by some other body to her ma-
" jesty, his lordship would give it his favour and further-
" ance. And if it should please him to like of the same,
" and to give his advice how it should be moved, he would
" follow his lordship's advice in the same: for he reposed,
" he said, all hopes of obtaining only in his good liking.
" In fine, he humbly beseeched his good lordship to pardon
" him. *Amici causam ago, viri probi, apud te, Domine præ-*
" *stantiss. sine apud quem nimium audeo.* But in this he
" humbly submitted his request to his wisdom and good-
" ness."

Dering, the
puritan, in
trouble, for
words in
his sermon.

Edward Dering (of whom something the last year) was
another of these principal puritan ministers; who being
reader of St. Paul's, had in his reading spoken some things
that were interpreted to reflect upon the magistrate, and
tending to the breach of the peace of the church. Whereupon he was forbid reading, by order of the privy council,
who were offended with him. He had a good talent in
preaching, and his congregation was very numerous: but his
judgment was well known for the bringing in a new model
of government in this church. On which account he was
watched by some: and some words that fell from him in
their hearing brought him to this trouble; though he denied them utterly, and that they were slanders raised of

him. And indeed, in one of his appearances before the attorney-general, the bishop of London did acknowledge he
could not accuse him thereof.

In the month of September he addressed himself to the
lord treasurer, (to whom he was well known,) desiring of
him not to come before their honours again, but that he was
contented to be judged by the bishops themselves, when
and where they should command him to appear; only that
it might not be deferred, that his place might be occupied
either by himself or some other; and that he might be
charged either with words or doings, wherein he had abused
himself: that upon knowledge thereof, his honour might
judge what he had deserved; a favour which he would
deny to none. And that if it were so appointed, that he
should read no more in Paul's, but faulty or faultless, all
should be one; then he could but pray to God, that he
would yet pardon his sins, who had deserved greater an- 270
ger. And withal, beseeched that lord to inquire after his
doings, till he could find but two witnesses that had heard
him speak evil. And if God should never give unto his
lordship so small a warrant of his evil behaviour, then he
prayed him to stand his good lord: and either to believe
his own judgment, who had heard him sometimes, or the report of a great number, who were daily present. And in
fine, that he might have that liberty, that in any other place
where he might be called, he might preach without blame,
as it was his duty.

Thus he insisted upon his innocency, and challenged any
to accuse him. But we shall not long hence find him charged
in divers articles in the Star-chamber, before the lords of the
council. And for a further vindication of himself, before
he should come to answer there, he took his pen, and wrote
a long letter; which he was minded to send to some one of
those lords, perhaps to the earl of Leicester; but after deliberation a day or two, he concluded to send it to the lord
Burghley. He chiefly laboured therein, to prove the lordship and civil government of the bishops to be unlawful, and

BOOK I.

Anno 1573.

His letter to the lord Burghley.

1 Tim. v. 19.

contrary to the scripture; as the main thing he thought that created him enemies. The letter, though long, I will faithfully set down from the original; wherein at large he sets forth his own case, and then afterwards his arguments from scripture against that government.

" Grace and peace from God the Father, &c. Bear with " me, I beseech your honour, though I trouble you, and " let the cause of my grief be the discharge of my boldness. " It behoveth me to discharge myself from the slanderer, " lest the gospel should be reproached in me.   And it be- " hoveth you to obey this commandment, *Receive no accu-* " *sation against a preacher* without good and sufficient " witness.   I know, my lord, you will not do it; and I " have good evidence of your equity in this behalf: but " yet I am bold to put you in mind of the word of· Christ, " which you cannot possibly remember too often.   I ask no " more than what is due unto me, even from her majesty's " seat of judgment and justice.   If I have done evil, let " me be punished; if not, let me be eased of undeserved " blame.   I crave no partiality, but I seek to answer, and " to make you [i. e. this lord, and the other of the lords of " the privy council] judges of my cause, before whose pre- " sence I ought to fear, and whose steps of their feet I do " humbly reverence.   And what, think you, have I done, " if I should be called, and before your honours be con- " vinced of these pretended crimes? With what shame " should I hide my face all the days of my life? Where " were the rejoicing that I have in God, in all things that " he hath wrought by me? Where were their comfort, that " have so desirously heard me? Where were the good opi- " nion of many, and all the good-will you have shewed me? " I am not so ignorant, that I see not this.   And therefore " persuade yourself that I am on a sure ground.   Trial " shall teach your eyes and ears a truth.   And to persuade " your heart, I give unto you my faith, I cannot accuse " myself either of any thought of mind, in which I have " not honoured the magistrate, and of word of my mouth,

" in which I have not regarded the peace of the church. CHAP.
" And I thank God of his unspeakable mercy, that hath XXVIII.
" kept for me this conscience against the day of trouble. Anno 1573.
    " If you muse now how these slanders have risen, you 271
" may easily know : the malice of Satan is great against the
" ministry of the gospel.   I know I have given no cause,
" more than I have confessed ; and with what words I have
" spoken it, I desire to be judged by the hearers.   And so
" much the bolder I speak now unto you, because my lord
" of London told me of late, before Mr. Attorney and Mr.
" Solicitor, that he could not accuse me of any such thing
" spoken in the pulpit.   Which discharge, as I was glad to
" hear, so I would have been much gladder, if upon so free
" a confession he would favourably have restored me to
" any lecture again.   But now it is that they know my
" mind, and long since they have had me in suspicion,
" therefore they would provide in time to take my lecture
" from me, lest I should speak any thing that would offend
" them hereafter.   This doing, though it be somewhat
" strange to punish a man before, lest hereafter he should
" offend ; yet I am contented with it, and leave it unto
" them, that should be as grieved to see so great a congre-
" gation so dispersed.
    " And because I will not appear to be led by fancy, Declares his
" wherein of a great many I am thought to be singular, I opinion
" will be bold with you, as the man whom, above others of bishops.
" your calling, I am bound to honour, to shew forth what is
" my opinion, and the reasons by which I am moved unto
" it.   Wherein, my good lord, I most heartily beseech
" you, break not, with any violence, the goodness of your
" nature, to make it favour falsehood ; but love the truth,
" whereunto you have well inclined, and which shall make
" you blessed in time to come.   I am thus persuaded :
    " *The lordship or civil government of bishops is utterly*
" *unlawful.*   My reason is this ; the kingdom of Christ is
" only a spiritual government : but the government of the
" church is a part of the kingdom of Christ : and therefore

" the government of the church is only a *spiritual* govern-
" ment.   What the kingdom is, and what government he
" hath established in it, learn not of me, but of God him-
" self.   The prophets do plentifully set it forth unto us.
" Esay saith, *He shall smite the earth with the rod of his*
" *mouth, and with the breath of his lips he shall kill the un-*
" *godly.*   And by what authority shall the ministers strike
" with a sword, or with a sentence from a civil judgment
" seat condemn the wicked?   The glory of the kingdom of
" Christ is thus described: *Ride upon the word of truth*
" *and of meekness and righteousness; and so thy right*
" *hand shall teach terrible things,* Psal. xlv. 4.   And again;
" *The Lord shall send the sceptre out of Sion,* (that is, his
" law,) *by which he shall be made ruler over all his enemies,*
" Psal. cx. 2.   And what can be plainer than the words of
" Christ himself; *My kingdom is not of this world,* John
" xviii. 36.   How plainly doth St. Paul say, *The weapons*
" *of our warfare, they are not carnal.*   Thus God hath ap-
" pointed it, to make his power known, that *by the foolish-*
" *ness of preaching he might confound the wisdom of the*
" *world,* and with the weak strength of the sound of words
" to overthrow the force of the hearts of men.   There are
" no chariots that go swift in victory, as the word of truth:
" no terror in the world that so shaketh the bowels, and
272 " maketh the thoughts to tremble, as the sword of the Spirit.
" There is no sceptre that reacheth so wide a dominion as
" the law of the majesty of God; which is written in the
" hearts of all the world, and condemneth all flesh before
" the majesty of God.   All other force is but little, and we
" may either withstand it, or fly from it.   But the power
" of the word is such as shall pass through all stops and
" hinderances.   *Every mountain shall be brought low, and*
" *every valley shall be filled: crooked things shall be made*
" *straight, and rough ways shall be made smooth,* that the
" *law may pass out of Sion, and the word of God from Je-*
" *rusalem.*   And so to whomsoever the Lord sendeth out
" his voice, it shall surely find him: for it is already in the

" conscience of man, whence he cannot fly. In his privy
" chamber it is nearest unto him, and when he is in his bed
" it presseth him most.

" Let him therefore that is King of kings have the pre-
" eminency of government, that is more glorious than
" princes. And let him, whose dominion is the kingdom
" of heaven, have the sword and the sceptre that is not
" fleshly. Let not a vile pope, in the name of Christ, erect
" a new kingdom, which Christ never knew; a kingdom of
" this world, which in the ministry the gospel hath con-
" demned. Which kind of rule hath set all out of order,
" and mingled together heaven and earth in confusion; so
" that God's ordinance cannot prevail, to deliver the sword
" into the hand of the magistrate, and take the word into
" the mouth of the minister. We have forgotten the voice,
" (which we might better remember,) *Put up thy sword*
" *into thy sheath.* And we know it not, that if God should
" fight for his gospel, he could send down many legions of
" angels to win the field. St. Paul saith, that *God hath*
" *chosen the weak things of the world to confound the*
" *mighty.* Which he had not done, if the strength of a
" kingdom should be in the ministry, or the arm of a prince
" in the hand of a preacher.

" And so I beseech you, my good lord, while God hath
" taken away a courage from princes, that they have suf-
" fered such a servant to sit in the monarchy of the world;
" hath not God recompensed the thraldom of their hearts
" upon their own heads, and made only a proud pope to
" tread them down all in dishonour? And in several reigns
" also, the popish prelacy hath shamed their princes, and
" sometimes raised up such rebellions, as have cost their
" kings both crown and life. Of these examples I find a
" great many. But I remember not one archbishop, or lord
" bishop, that ever saved a country, or brought peace unto it.
" Such have been God's judgments upon those that have
" put from themselves the honour of their crown, and taken
" justice from the unlawful minister that serveth in the com-
" monwealth, and made unto themselves new justices of the

" peace and quorum, new barons, new commissioners, new
" lord chancellors, which their fathers knew not, and taken
" out of the midst of pastors and bishops of the church;
" which before was not heard of.

" And now, as hitherto I have reasoned of the kingdom of
" Christ, in which and for which the ministry must serve;
" so now I beseech you also to consider the authority of
" the minister. Out of which I will reason thus. The
273 " king's minister or pastor hath his authority equal over
" king and subject: but the king's pastor must not execute
" civil punishment against his prince : therefore the king's
" pastor can be no civil magistrate. The truth of this rea-
" son is plain and evident. The Lord saith unto his mi-
" nister, *Behold, this day I have set thee over nations and*
" *over kingdoms, to pluck up, and to root out, to destroy,*
" *and to throw down, to build, and to plant,* Jer. i. 10. And
" St. Paul saith, *He was prepared to cast down every high*
" *thing that was exalted against the knowledge of God, and*
" *to bring into captivity every thought into the obedience of*
" *Christ.* St. James sharply reproveth it, if we have more
" regard unto a man with *a gold ring and goodly apparel,*
" than unto a poor man that is *in vile raiment.* He biddeth,
" *preach unto every creature: whose sins you forgive, they*
" *are forgiven ; and whose sins you retain, they are re-*
" *tained.* Here is no exception of one or other, but the
" sins of all are equally to be chastised; even as grace
" and mercy is equally preached. And let him persuade
" himself, whosoever will be exempted from this obedience,
" to be ruled in the church, God hath also exempted him
" from the grace that is dispensed by the church.

" And how can it possibly be otherwise, when the minister
" is but the mouth of God, in whose person Christ himself
" is either refused or received? Before whom to exalt a
" man, is to set up the clay above the potter; and to make
" a difference of persons, before whom there is neither Jew
" nor Gentile, bond nor free, prince nor subject.

" My lord, seeing all men are subject before the minister,
" even as himself also is subject to the words of his mouth,

" what power, what authority will you give unto him? Will
" you set him upon a seat of justice, and put a sword in his
" hand? Then bring the prince to plead her cause, Guilty,
" or not guilty? Fie upon the pope, that hath so dis-
" honoured God, and made the glory of his judgment seat
" to be spotted in the countenance of a faint-hearted king.
" We will be no proctors for such an untimely fruit, that
" hath made princes bondmen, nobility thraldom, and him-
" self a tyrant. Let us learn a better lesson of our Sa-
" viour Christ, *Date Cæsari quæ sunt Cæsaris, et quæ*
" *sunt Dei, Deo.* The prince alone is the person in the
" world, to whom God hath committed the seat of justice,
" and they only to execute the duty of it, to whom it is
" committed; at whose hands God will require it: how
" they have defended his church, given praise unto well-
" doing, and revenged the sins of all transgressors. For
" which end God hath given in subjection unto them the
" natural man, and hath heaped up unto the rulers all the
" glory of the world, which whosoever shall seek to spoil
" from them, he would change the counsels of the living
" God.
" The *minister* is appointed for another defence, where
" horsemen and chariots will do no good. They may hinder
" the minister, and make him forget his duty : they cannot
" profit him in his office and function. He must frame the
" heart, upon which you cannot set a crown ; and edify the
" soul, which flesh and blood cannot hurt. He sealeth unto
" the conscience God's mercies, which are sweeter than life,
" and maketh rich the thoughts with righteousness and 274
" peace, which shall abide for ever. To those that are dis-
" obedient he pronounceth the judgment that maketh the
" heart afraid; and to the poor in spirit he bringeth com-
" fort, which no tongue can express. And to these things,
" what availeth either sword or spear? God asketh but a
" tongue that is prepared to speak ; and he ministereth the
" power that is invisible. And cursed be the times that
" have bewitched to set up dumb dogs in so honourable a
" place.

" If this function were supplied with dutiful officers, the
" sword of the Spirit, which God hath given them, would
" vanquish Satan, and destroy the power of darkness,
" till the knowledge of God were plentiful upon earth,
" and all the joys of heart were sealed unto men in perfect
" beauty; till the eyes did see great happiness in the face
" of the heavens, and the ear did hear the sweet harmony
" of the forgiveness of the sins; till the meat tasted of that
" secret manna, of which he should eat for ever, and his
" drink were pure, of the water of life, which proceedeth
" out of the throne of God and of the Lamb; till his gar-
" ments did smell of the righteousness of Jesus Christ, and
" in life did shine the life of immortality. But I will not
" go about to express it in words, which the ear cannot
" hear, nor the tongue can speak. I beseech the Lord make
" you feel the pleasure of it within, till all the world be but
" dung, as St. Paul saith, in respect of Christ. For in him
" all honour is a glorious blessing, and without him but a
" covering of an after-woe. And when it shall fall in the
" dust, his sight of the sorrow that is behind shall make the
" man to mourn, when it is too late.

" If you will know this thoroughly and indeed, procure
" their liberty, which will tell you the truth: but if our
" sins shall procure, that instead of truth we shall hear flat-
" tering words, we shall prove it true, *Where no prophecy*
" *is, there the people perish,* Prov. xxix. 18. The days to
" come, which are the wisest witnesses, when they shall ask
" your opinion, you shall confess it is true.

" But now again to our purpose. And because I have
" spoken thus much, I will add the residue, that I may be
" known unto your honour, even as I am known unto my-
" self. As the minister hath nothing to do with the tem-
" poral sword, so much less it becometh him to be called
" *a lord.* The reason is plain in the scripture. They be
" called *fishers of men, labourers* in the harvest, *callers*
" unto the marriage, *servants* of the people, *workmen, mi-*
" *nisters, stewards, builders, planters,* &c. In all which
" they are removed from *a lordship* over the people. And

" again, they be called fellow-elders, fellow-helpers, fellow-
" workmen, fellow-soldiers, fellow-servants, fellow-travellers,
" &c. In which names they are forbidden lordship over
" their brethren. And surely, seeing we ought to have a
" religion in the words of the Holy Ghost, not lightly to
" change them, it cannot be but great rashness to refuse so
" many names of society, which God hath given us, and
" take another name, which is none of our own, and im-
" porteth a dominion over others.

  " And how can we yet doubt in the question of *lordship?* 275
" We appeal unto Christ, and the words of his mouth, to
" take up the controversy. The disciples had this conten-
" tion as well as we ; and they strove much who should be
" highest. Which strife, while our Saviour Christ will ap-
" pease, he pronounceth his sentence thus ; *He that will be*
" *greatest among you, let him be as the lowest : and he that*
" *will be highest, let him be the servant of all.* This is the
" brief definition of a superiority in the ministry : and this
" shall for ever determine the controversy, though all wis-
" dom in the world should reply against it. *My lord* and
" the *honour* both shall be judged by this. If he find his
" titles given him here, let him rejoice in his portion. If he
" have them not hence, he shall not have them of us. We
" will not so dishonour him that hath given the sentence.
" For besides that the words are plain, we have good ex-
" ample that this must be our trial. When St. Paul had a
" great controversy with many others, whose authority was
" most, by this rule he challenged all their preeminence to
" himself; because he was the least; he had laboured more
" than they all ; was more afflicted, more contemned, more
" despised; oftener whipped, scourged, stoned, imprisoned ;
" in more dangers by sea, by land, of thieves, of murder-
" ers, of kinsmen, of countrymen, and of all sorts ; in watch-
" ings, prayings, hunger, thirst, cold, nakedness, &c. and
" more exercised than any other, 2 Cor. xi. 23. Of this he
" was bold to set himself up, that no patriarch of the world
" had a lordship above him. And to the Galatians, against
" all pride and tyranny of false prophets, he maketh his

BOOK
I.

Anno 1573.

" challenge as greater than they all, because he carried the
" marks of the Lord Jesus in his body. Thus well had St.
" Paul learned, that the highest in the ministry must be the
" lowest. And he is the archbishop that hath suffered
" most. But as St. Paul is a good example, so let our Sa-
" viour Christ be his own interpreter, that by example and
" testimony we may be confirmed in truth.

" Will you know what this meaneth, *He that will be*
" *greatest, let him be the least; Non sic inter vos?* Luc.xxii.
" 26. That rule and lordship shall not be among you,
" which God hath given in the kingdoms of this world.
" You must be examples unto your flocks. You shall not
" exercise any lordships over *the heritage of God*, 1 Pet. v.
" 3. These words are plain witnesses in the mouths of
" two, our Saviour Christ and the apostle Peter. If you
" will have also an example of this, I will allege you one of
" great warrant. St. John reproveth one Diotrephes, who,
" not content with the dignity of συνεργὸς, or *fellow-work-*
" *man*, would needs be a lord, and rule over others; to ex-
" communicate and cast out of the church by his own au-
" thority.

" Now judge, my lord, by the spirit of wisdom which
" God hath given unto you, whether our lordships are of
" Christ or of Peter; or whether they more agree with
" Paul or with Diotrephes : and according as you think, so
" be a witness. And lest the subtilty of some should lead
" you from truth, as it is plainly proved, so I will plainly
" confute whatsoever the adversary can object against it.

276

Καταχυριεύ-
ειν, κατεξου-
σιάζειν : the
sense of
those words
in scripture.

" They will say, that in these places ambition and tyranny
" is only forbidden. And to persuade you the better of
" their learning, they will say, that the Greek word used in
" the scripture is καταχυριεύειν, which signifieth *to rule with*
" *severity and rigour.* The like is said of the other word,
" κατεξουσιάζειν. But proof of this they can possibly bring
" none : for the words in nature are indifferent, to signify
" well or ill. But for our proof, that in this place they sig-
" nify a lawful rule, St. Luke useth the simple verbs, κυρι-
" εύειν, and ἐξουσιάζειν : which by nature cannot signify an

" ambitious or tyrannical, but a lawful rule. And St. Mat-
" thew, as he is written in Hebrew, useth these words;
" which both signify a good government, and a maintenance
" of the inferior; as I have learned of those that under-
" stand the tongue. And therefore the nature of the word,
" which openly they preach of, it is all against them in this
" place. But let the word go, and see the matter. So the
" vanity of their answer shall the more appear.

" Christ doth forbid that which in the commonwealth is
" lawful; but ambition and tyranny is lawful no where.
" Christ forbiddeth that which was in the disciples; but to
" charge them with tyranny, it is to do them great wrong.
" Christ forbiddeth to be called in title of honour, εὐεργητὴς,
" a good and gracious lord; a name so far from ambition
" and tyranny, as the office of a bishop should be from a
" lordship. And Christ doth not bid them beware of am-
" bition, but bids them every one to be inferior to other:
" which is to beware of any lordship at all. And therefore
" this answer is but to strive against truth, and to shift it
" away under the name of tyranny; where our Saviour
" Christ condemneth all superiority.

" And therefore I beseech your honour, my very good
" lord, be a favourer of the truth, that will prevail. The
" scriptures that were alleged are no vain authorities, that
" are easily rejected, nor any dark speeches, that are hardly
" understood. The words are written by the apostles and
" prophets, and they have the strength of the Spirit of God.
" They shall sound far and near, and accomplish the work
" for which they were spoken, though all the world were
" in arms against them. In vain we cry, The state, the
" state, and the commonwealth; where indeed there is no
" state nor no commonwealth, but a subversion of both.
" For the lordship of a bishop hath ever been a plague-
" sore in the state of a kingdom, and is at this day a swell-
" ing wound, full of corruption in the body of a common-
" wealth; as appeareth in Scotland, France, Spain, Polonia,
" and otherwhere. And yet if the state did require it, the
" voice of the Lord must be obeyed, though all the king-

BOOK "doms in the earth did fall before it. God is not a man
I.   "that we may control his honour. He hath made both
Anno 1573. "heaven and earth; and when he shall appear, all the
"creatures of the world shall be moved at his presence;
"and the children of men shall throw down their crowns
"before him. Let us harden our hearts as the adamant
"stone, not to hear his counsel, yet when the force of his
"word shall knit together again our bones and ashes, that
"they may arise into eternal life, we shall say then, *Blessed*
"*is he that cometh in the name of the Lord.*

277   "For my part, I can but pray according as we are
"taught, *Thy kingdom come.* That his holy Spirit may
"make us now obedient, whose majesty, in the time ap-
"pointed, shall make his enemies afraid.

"And now to shut up this long discourse, (which yet I
"pray God it doth not make you weary,) to know better
"the *lordship* of a bishop, let us a little remember the ho-
"nour of our archbishop, which is Jesus Christ. He was
"born of a poor woman, in a strange place; and received
"into an inn, and put forth into a stable, wrapt in coarse
"clothes, and laid in a manger; persecuted from his swad-
"dling clothes, into strange countries, returning home in
"fear, and often hiding himself; brought up in the sweat
"of his brows, and the occupation of his father; mocked
"with his base parentage, and reproached with the name
"of *beggarly Nazareth:* not one of the nobility known to
"favour him, but a poor company, which were basely de-
"spised. In all his greatest glory he was laughed to scorn;
"and the title of his kingdom was set upon a cross of
"shame. And in this estate doth he not say unto his dis-
"ciples, *I have appointed you a kingdom, as my Father*
"*hath appointed unto me?* Luke xxii. 29. And how can
"you frame out of this pattern either pope's monarchy
"or the bishops' kingdoms; either a triple crown, so
"far above princes, or a sumptuous mitre, so unmeet for
"apostles?

"Surely, my lord, this gear it will not stand. It is a
"plant which our Father in heaven never planted; and it

" will be rooted out. It is of the pope, and it shall drink CHAP.
" of the same cup of confusion; of which the pope hath XXVIII.
" begun unto them. And doubt you not but it is of the Anno 1573.
" pope: for beside the plainness of the word of God, it is
" also printed before your eyes, that you might see the
" truth, though you would not hear it. For where is this
" lordship in the greatest honour, but where the pope's ho-
" liness is set highest? Where is it abated, but where the
" pope's head is broken? And where is it rejected, but
" where the pope is trodden under feet? It standeth with
" the pope; it reigneth with the pope; it falleth with the
" pope; it is shamed with the pope; and is it not of the
" pope?

    " And what, I beseech you, is the fruit it bringeth? Is Officials,
" it not the same that springeth out of the pope's breast? commissa-
                                                            ries, chan-
" What else are *officials, commissaries, chancellors, arch-* cellors, &c.
" *deacons,* &c. which rule and govern by the common Faculties.
" laws? Much worse than the statutes of Omri, and all the
" ordinances of the house of Achab: which uphold in the
" midst of us a court of Faculties; a place much worse
" than Sodom and Gomorrah. Bear with me, though I
" speak the truth. The great contrariety between the gos-
" pel and it hath printed in our hearts such a mortal ha-
" tred unto it, as never hereafter shall be reconciled. And
" in all that duty which I owe unto your honour in the
" Lord Jesu, I heartily wish that God may make you wor-
" thy to help his truth, which will prevail, whether you
" help it or no. For God is the father of it, and not man;
" and he hath taken the care of it, and not princes.

    " But now I have to answer many thoughts, which very 278
" easily will rise within you. You will muse first of the The state of
                                                            the primi-
" state of the primitive church; and think that Augustine, tive church
" Ambrose, &c. were all bishops. To this I answer, that as to bi-
                                                            shops, com-
" if they were, yet men must not prejudice the word of pared with
" God. True it is, they were bishops; but this is as true, ours.
" they were no lords, neither agreed with our bishops al-
" most in any thing, save only names. I. The bishops and
" ministers then were one in degree: now they are divers.

" II. There were many bishops in one town: now there
" is but one in a whole country. III. No bishop's autho-
" rity was more than in one city: now it is in many shires.
" IV. The bishops then used no bodily punishments: now
" they imprison, fine, &c. V. Those bishops could not ex-
" communicate or absolve of their own authority: now they
" may. VI. Then, without consent, they could make no
" ministers: now they do. VII. They could confirm no
" children in other parishes: they do now in many shires.
" VIII. Then they had no living of the church, but only in
" one congregation: now they have. IX. Then they had
" neither officials under them, nor commissaries, nor chan-
" cellors. X. Then they dealt in no civil government by
" any established authority. XI. Then they had no right in
" alienating any parsonage, to give it in lease. XII. Then
" they had the church where they served the cure, even as
" those whom we call now *parish priests*, although they
" were metropolitans or archbishops. These diversities they
" are very great; and if your honour doubt in any of them,
" when it shall please your honour, we will refuse no con-
" ference with whom you will.

What to be
said for
Cranmer,
Ridley, &c.
being bi-
shops.

" Again, you will think, if this be thus, how were Mr.
" Cranmer, Ridley, Latymer, Hooper, &c. all bishops and
" lords? To this we can say no more, but that the Lord
" had not yet revealed it unto them; but left them in
" that infirmity, as he left many of his saints before them
" in as great: and so leaveth yet a great many churches.
" Notwithstanding we reverence their memory, and love
" their ashes, which are buried in honour against the day of
" Christ.

The bishops
of these
times: what
to be
thought of
them.

" If you will object against us the bishops of our time,
" we may answer of them favourably, as before. We know
" their doings: and our hope is of them as of members of
" the church. We love them as brethren, and honour them
" as elders. And the Lord grant, that we have no cause to
" call back this praise, and dare not give it them. But this
" I must needs say, and freely confess, if I were in one of
" their places, I should not have been so soon persuaded.

" We are all men, and born in sin. If one speak against
" our belly, it hath no ears; or against our back, it hath
" no eyes. So that we will hardly see or hear a truth. But
" if the consent of men of our times may help the cause,
" then I trust it shall help us, that all reformed churches
" are of our side: and not one of them is governed by a
" lord bishop. But men are all men, and not meet to sit in
" judgment of the truth of God. If there were but one
" that built upon his word, he alone were on the rock
" which should never be removed.

" The which portion and inheritance of the truth, I be-
" seech the living God that it may be your lot. That in this
" great blessing, in which God hath blessed you, you may 279
" indeed be happy; and many years may heap up, unto the
" honour of all men, love of your brethren, favour of your
" prince, and (which is best of all) righteousness and peace,
" and joy of the Holy Ghost. That the necessity of death
" may more increase your hope, and the grave may be ac-
" ceptable, as to a child of God.

" You see how bold I have been with your honour; and
" I am not ignorant what portion of my life I have com-
" mitted into your hand. But I have done no more than I
" would have done to her majesty herself, if such occasion
" had been. For I cannot be persuaded to conceal any
" truth from such a magistrate as feareth God, and hath
" advanced his gospel. And if plain speech shall make you
" favour the cause, the Lord be praised that hath wrought
" his work in you. If you shall not yet believe, God hath
" a better time to work his will. And I beseech God, in
" these grievous times, to make me content with a good
" conscience; and enrich your honour with such grace, that
" when you shall think upon him in your bed, and remem-
" ber him in your night-watches, you may remember the
" nights of the prophet David, and feel his joy, that is, the
" God of glory. Amen. *Primo Novembris,* 1573.

" Your honour's bounden in the Lord Jesu,
" even as his own,

" Edward Dering."

I shall make no reflections upon this letter, but leave the reader to observe the zeal of these men against the constitu- tion of this church, and to weigh the strength of the argu- ments used against the English episcopacy. I shall only add, that Dering ushered in this his long letter, with an- other short one, dated two days after; importing the pri- vacy of his writing it.

" *Gratia et pax.* I meant not this letter to your honour.
" But if God have appointed it for the best, his name be
" praised. Read it, my good lord, I beseech you, and use
" it as you will. I never wrote it twice: neither can it pos-
" sibly be known to any but to your honour only. And so
" the Lord remember me in this trouble. I wish to do
" obediently unto you any duty, that you may know the
" truth."

To proceed then to his present trouble. It sprang from certain things said by him in the pulpit and elsewhere: for which he was brought before the lords of the council in the Star-chamber: and at a public dinner, where he read a chapter, and expounded it, (where Dr. Chaderton, Toy, the printer, and divers others were present,) " speaking " against godfathers and godmothers: and that the statute " of provision for the poor was no competent way devised " for it. And that he could provide for the poor two ways; " the one way by committing them to the rich, to be kept; " the other, *to what purpose is this superfluity?* and, *what* " *do we do with so much plate?* As though he were for a " community of things. That he put off his cap and said, " Now I will prophesy, Matthew Parker is the last arch- " bishop that ever shall sit in that seat. To which Mr. " Cartwright should say, *Accipio omen.*"

Dering's
words ut-
tered by
him : for
which he
was brought
into the
Star-cham-
ber.
MSS. Ceci-
lian.

280 For which expressions he wrote a paper to the lords in justification of himself, urging in the first place, that in mat- ters of accusation, not so much the words, as the manner of speaking ought to be witness of the truth. And then he proceeded to vindicate particularly what he had said: which are contained in the Appendix.

At this time I find, that in order to his restoration to his

ministry, these four articles were required of him by the
bishops, as it seems, (of whom he desired to be judged,) to
acknowledge and subscribe, viz. that the book of Articles Anno 1573.
agreed upon in the synod, 1563, was sound, and according Articles
to the word of God. 2. That the queen's majesty was the sent to him
chief governor, next under Christ, of this church of Eng- scribe.
land, as well in ecclesiastical as in civil causes. 3. That in Regist.
the Book of Common Prayer was nothing evil or repug-
nant to the word of God; but that it might be well used
in this our church of England. And 4. That the public
preaching of the word of God in this church was sound and
sincere; and the public order in the ministration of the sacraments was consonant to the word of God. To these he
sent in his answer, writ with his own hand, December 16.
That as he had promised to set down his mind, how far he
would yield in any thing he should be required, so accordingly he had done to those articles which were sent unto
him: not simply yielding to them, he said, in the very
words, as they were set down, nor yet so far declining from
them, as to give any a just offence of disagreement. Then
he lays down certain exceptions against all but the second
article. And then, in the conclusion, he declares, concerning
his conformable behaviour, viz. that while any law did bind His peace-
him to wear cap and surplice, he wore both. But that when conform-
he was at liberty, he would not wear them of devotion. And able beha-
that since, he never persuaded any man to refuse them.
That for the service book, he preached not against it. That
he came to church to hear the prayers; and according to
the book, he would, and willingly did, come to the Lord's
supper. But I refer the reader for these matters at large, to
a book called, *Part of a register of sundry memorable mat-* Page 81.
ters, &c.

There were also divers other articles ministered to him Other ar-
in this court of Star-chamber, to the number of twenty, for nistered to
more exact search and inquiry into his principles and opin- him in the
ions concerning the church, and its usages, practices, and ber.
clergy, and concerning the queen's authority. As, I. Whether the book entitled, The Book of Common Prayer, allowed by public authority in this realm, is to be allowed in

the church of God, by God's word, or no. II. Whether
the article set down by the clergy in a synod, and allowed
by authority, be according to God's word. III. Whether
we be tied by God's word to the order and use of the
apostles and primitive church in all things. IV. Whether
there be any right ministry or ecclesiastical government at
this time in the church of England. V. Whether nothing
may be in the church, either concerning ceremonies or regiment, but only that which the Lord himself in his word
commandeth. VI. Whether every particular church or parish in this realm of England, of necessity, and by the order of God's word, ought to have their pastors, elders, and
deacons, chosen by the people of that their parish ; and they
281 only to have the whole government of the church in matters
ecclesiastical. VII. Whether there is equality of all the ministers of this realm, as well concerning government and jurisdiction, as touching the ministration of the word and
sacraments. VIII. Whether the patrimony of ancient time
given to the church, for the maintaining of learning and
the service of God ; and to maintain the state ecclesiastical ; as bishops' lands, the lands pertaining to cathedral
churches, the glebe lands and tithes, by order of law, given
to parsons and vicars, are, by right and God's word, to
be taken from them. IX. Whether the ministers of this
realm, of what calling soever, now in place, allowed by the
laws and orders of this realm, be lawful ministers : and
whether their administration and ecclesiastical actions be
lawful and effectual. X. Whether, at a marriage, it is not
convenient to have a communion ; and convenient for the
new married persons to communicate : and at a funeral to
have a sermon. XI. Whether it be lawful for any man to
preach, but he that is a pastor ; and he only to preach to
his own flock ; or that that man may preach without a licence. XII. Whether it be better, and more agreeable to
God's word, and more convenient for the profit of God's
church, that a prescript order of common prayer be used ;
or that every minister pray publicly, as his own spirit shall
direct him. XIII. Whether children of such as be perfect
papists are to be baptized. And whether infants are within

the compass of God's covenant, and have faith. XIV. Whe- CHAP.
ther any ecclesiastical person may have more ecclesiastical XXVIII.
livings than one. XV. Whether one may be a minister Anno 1573.
that hath no peculiar flock assigned unto him; and whether an ecclesiastical person may exercise also a civil function. XVI. Whether all the commandments of God and of
the apostles are needful for salvation. XVII. Whether the
queen of England hath authority over the ecclesiastical
state, and in ecclesiastical matters, as well as over the civil
state. XVIII. Whether the queen of England be chief
governor, under Christ, over the whole church and state
ecclesiastical in this realm, or but a member of the same.
And whether the church of England may be established
without a magistrate. XIX. Whether the queen of England' be bound to observe the judicial laws of Moses concerning the punishing and remitting of criminal offences.
XX. Whether the queen of England may of herself, and
of her own authority, assign and appoint civil officers, or
no.

To all which Mr. Dering gave distinct and free answers
at large : which are also extant in the said register ; with
this preface to them: " That he humbly beseeched their ho-
" nours to remember his former protestation, That he never
" preached against this Book of [Common] Prayers; and
" that in his own book, extant in print, he had once spoken
" to the good allowance of it. Further, that he resorted to
" common prayers; and sometimes, being requested, he
" did, according as it was prescribed, say the prayers. If,
" notwithstanding, he should be urged now to speak what
" he thought, whereby he might seem to be called to a
" form of inquisition, as there was no law, by which God
" had tied him of duty to be his own accuser ; so he be-
" seeched their honours to let this his answer rather witness 282
" his obedience and humble duty, than be prejudicial, to his
" hurt and hinderance."

Mr. Moor, a puritan preacher in the city of Norwich, Moor con-
was of great vogue, and very popular in that city about Pern's ser-
this time : this man, upon a sermon Dr. Pern of Cambridge mon,
preached at
Norwich.

BOOK I. had preached in the cathedral, took upon him the next Sunday to confute the doctrine he had preached; not so

Anno 1573. agreeable undoubtedly to some puritan principles: and so intended to proceed in a further confutation thereof. This presently grew to some jars among the citizens, according as they stood affected. Which caused Dr. Gardiner, one of the prebendaries there, (of whom more hereafter,) prudently to inform the bishop (then at Ludham) hereof; and that he would write to Moor, and admonish him to go no further in the pulpit against Pern; which otherwise, he said, must breed some trouble. Which practice was very common in those times in the pulpits of the universities, and St. Paul's, and other churches.

Ecclesiastical commission send forth an order to seize Cartwright. Cartwright, another noted puritan, and obnoxious at this time, had given great offence by his public readings and writings against the constitution of the church, and was still unquiet after his discharge from the university; insomuch that the queen was very angry with him, and would have him brought to his trial, to answer for his dealings and misdemeanours. For whom there was now therefore issued out a strict order from the commissioners ecclesiastical to take him up, in pursuance, I suppose, of the proclamation against the Admonition to the parliament, and his vindication of it. The said order for the seizing of him was as followeth:

" *To all mayors, sheriffs, bailiffs, constables, headboroughs,*
" *and to all other of the queen's majesty's officers, unto*
" *whom this may come or appertain: to every one of*
" *them, as well within the liberties as without.*

MSS G. Petyt, arm. " We do require you, and therewith straitly command
" you, and every of you, in the queen's majesty's name,
" that you be aiding and assisting to the bearer and bearers
" hereof, with all the best means that you can devise, for
" the apprehension of one Thomas Cartwright, student in
" divinity, wheresoever he be, within liberties, or without,
" within the realm. And you having possession of his body
" by your good travail and diligence in this behalf, we do
" likewise charge you, (for so is her majesty's pleasure,)

" that he be brought up by you to London, with a suffi-
" cient number, for his safe appearance before us, and other
" her majesty's commissioners of Oyer and Terminer in
" causes ecclesiastical, for his unlawful dealings and de-
" meanours in matters touching religion and the state of
" this realm. And this fail you not to do, every one of
" you, with all diligence, as you will answer to the contrary
" upon your utmost perils. From London this 11th day of
" December, 1573.

" Edw. London.   John Rivers, mayor.   Wil. Cordel,
" [master of the rolls.]   Rob. Catlyn.   Gilb. Gerard,
" [attorney-general.]   Tho. Wylson, [master of re-
" quests.]   Leonel Ducket.   Alex. Nowel, [dean of
" St. Paul's.]   Gabriel Goodman, [dean of Westmin-
" ster.]   Tho. Seckford.   Tho. Bromley, [solicitor-
" general.]   Will. Fleetwood, [recorder.]"

CHAP. XXIX.

283

*The privy council warns those of the Dutch church against
receiving any puritans. That church's answer. Letters
between Rod. Gualter, an Helvetian divine, and the bishops of Ely and Norwich, concerning the puritans. The
papists grow confident. Fears and jealousies of them.
The high esteem had for the city of Zurick, and the divines of that city. A commission for executing of Birchet by martial law. The earl of Sussex to the lord treasurer to prevent it. The queen's order for his examination. A husbandman comes to the bishop of Norwich for
orders: refused. A gentleman hath words with the bishop about it : reconciled. A puritan stands to be schoolmaster at Aylsham : refused by the bishop : and why.*

At this time the lords of the privy council directed a letter in Latin, at good length, to the ministers and elders of
the Dutch church in London. The occasion was, a suspicion of seditious spirits, that might shroud themselves under that church, and enter themselves into their commu-

nion. The queen indeed had apprehensions, that those innovating persons that were now very busy, might cause those of that church to misuse the privileges, that she, out of compassion of their persecutions in their own countries, had granted them; they thinking to ingratiate themselves with the Dutch, because their devices seemed more conformable to their customs than our forms.

The lords
of the coun-
cil write
to that
church not
to receive
them.
Eccl. Belgic.
Lond. The lords put them in mind of the queen's pious commiseration of their condition, that had fled for the cause of religion into her kingdom, and of the protection she willingly had granted them; and that she therefore expected from them such returns of services and dutiful behaviour, as became thankful persons and good subjects. They spake favourably of the different practice of their public worship from ours; as all other churches had their various customs and usages. *Non ignoramus variis ecclesiis varios et diversos jam ab initio Christianæ religionis semper fuisse ritus ac ceremonias: dum hi stantes, illi in genua procidentes, alii proni procumbentes, adorant et precantur. Et tamen eadem pietas est ac religio, si vere, et ad verum Deum, oratio tendat, absitque impietas ac superstitio, &c.*
284 *Non contemnimus ritus vestros, neque vos ad nostros cogimus: probamusque ceremonias vestras, ut vobis et vestræ reip. unde orti estis, aptas et convenientes, &c.* " And that " they were not ignorant, that from the very beginning of " the Christian religion, various churches had their various " and divers rites and ceremonies. That in their service and " devotions, some stood, some kneeled, others prostrated " themselves. And yet the piety and religion the same, if " they truly, and to the true God, directed their prayers " without impiety and superstition." They added in their letter, " That they contemned not their rites, neither did " they compel them to those used in the English church. " And that they approved their ceremonies as fit and con- " venient for them, and that state whence they sprang. And " therefore they expected in like manner, that that congre- " gation should not despise those customs, that out of godly " principles, by the labour of wise and learned men, had

" been established in this church, and confirmed by the
" blood of many martyrs; and now a long time settled
" here.

" And therefore admonished them, that they should give
" no countenance to a sort of tumultuous and unquiet
" people, who would fain bring in a confusion into the
" church, nor approve of any of their doings. Nor would
" they suspect them to be guilty of such imprudence or in-
" constancy of wisdom. And that they should avoid any
" thing that might create a suspicion in them, of disturb-
" ing the peace of this estate and church. And that their
" wisdom would suggest to them, that such a behaviour
" might move the queen, who had upon the account of re-
" ligion received them into her kingdom, to banish them
" out of it. And so, in fine, they warned them against any
" such, whether English or of themselves, that endeavoured
" to blow up such sparks of discord, and to drive them from
" their flock. And particularly, not to receive into their
" communion any of this realm that offered to join with
" them, and leave the custom and practice of their native
" country."

And this, in conclusion, they wrote to them out of good-
will, to preven any cause of offence, or suspicion of ingratitude or disobedience towards her gracious majesty; and
in order to their living here in peace and security: and
they of the council would be ready to shew them all favour.

The said church prudently caused this letter to be publicly read in their congregation; and soon gave a very
humble and grateful answer, as it concerned them. First,
" Thanking the queen, and their honours, for their mani-
" fold favours, and the whole kingdom's civility towards
" them, a company of poor strangers; and that their in-
" habiting in the realm found such acceptance; nor that
" they were yet weary in shewing them their benevolence.
" And particularly, they mention the favour of allowing
" them their accustomed ceremonies in their religious wor-
" ship, in their own language, being united with the Eng-

The answer
of the
Dutch
church to
the coun-
cil's letter.

" lish in matters of doctrine. They hoped, that there
" should not be any occasion given by them to the queen
" or their lordships, to repent of these kindnesses vouch-
" safed them: adding, that it should appear, their honours
" had not been mistaken in their good opinion of them.
" They prayed, that it would please them not to believe or
" regard malicious reports to their prejudice: for that they
" countenanced no such tumultuous people, nor approved
" either of their words or actions. That they were none
" of those that despised the ceremonies of other churches;
285 " and that submission was due to what a pious magistracy
" had established, and what they judged was most fit for
" the people, and that tended to the promoting of god-
" liness.

" That they knew it became not them to be curious
" in other people's matters; much less to encourage any
" changes, or any persons in making them. And the care
" thereof they left to them whom God had ordained for
" the same; and who by experience best knew what was
" fittest for them who were committed to their charge.
" That for themselves, they promised that they would take
" all care not to do any thing that might give any suspi-
" cion or just offence to the queen or them. And that ac-
" cording to their commands, they would discharge out of
" their communion men of such tumultuous tempers, if
" there should be any: and that no English should be ad-
" mitted among them, who on such principles sought to se-
" parate themselves from the religious customs of their own
" country. That they had but four of the English nation
" in their church: and of each they gave account: two
" whereof had been exiles; and ever since their return had

N°. XXIX,
XXX.
" remained with them." This whole letter, with the former
from the council, remain yet in the archives of the same
Dutch church in Augustin friars, London. And as they
were translated from the Dutch, and communicated to me

a Mr. Daniel
Van Mil-
dert.
by one of the ancient elders thereof[a], I have thought worthy
to place in the Appendix.

Gualter of
Zuric writ-
This matter with the puritans (such, I mean, as withdrew

from our divine service, because of the ceremonies) was CHAP.
agitated hotly this year, as hath partly been shewed. And XXIX.
here I must mention a course that these disaffected men Anno 1573.
took: which was to appeal to the reformed churches eth to bi-
abroad; particularly that of Geneva and Helvetia; which concerning
they did some years ago, as may be seen at large in the the puri-
Annals of the Reformation. Whereof the divines of Hel- Vol. I.
vetia were of great esteem with ours; and that justly too,
who had so christianly and kindly received and entertained
them in the late popish reign; divers whereof were now bishops. Rodolphus Gualter, one of the chief ministers of
Zuric, in that country, had been prevailed withal to send
letters to some of these bishops in their behalf, for some favour to be shewn them. Which caused ours to write again
to him; to open to him the true state of the unhappy differences and divisions in this church; and to vindicate the
proceedings used by the government. Of which, Cox, bishop of Ely, had written at large to him; dilating upon the
unhappy condition of the English church, by reason of the
present contentions raised in it, by imposing the garments,
and some other ceremonies, indifferent in themselves; and
shewed him fully the state of the controversy. And then
excited him, according to his wisdom and learning, to write
a serious letter into England about it. Whereupon Gualter, in his answer to the said bishop, being more perfectly
instructed in these matters, shewed his utter dislike and dis-
allowance of those men, for making such contentions in the
English church, for such weak causes, as those indifferent
things required, were; and excusing himself for a former
letter in favour of them, as not truly understanding the
case: for this I refer the reader to archbishop Parker's Life of
Life, where this letter may be read.   Archbishop
                                                          Parker,
For this letter, and for another, written some years be- book iv.
fore, to another bishop, bishop Parkhurst, in a more mo- ch. 9.
derate style, this pious foreign divine was censured by Bishop
some here at home. Divers there were that disliked, that Parkhurst's
this foreigner should concern himself in these affairs of our Gualter.
church: and they were such as wished that such stress MSS. Joh.
                                                           D. Episc.
E e 4   Elien.

might not be laid upon ceremonies; but that in due time they might be wholly laid aside; and a reformation be made in this church more conformable to that of other churches; and especially that of Zuric. Gualter's great friend, the said bishop Parkhurst, seems to have been one of these. But these censures created a trouble to that modest, learned man; and made him wish, that he had wholly forborne writing his said letters, since they were no better interpreted. But Parkhurst comforted him, telling him, he should not repent his letter writ to him on that argument in the year 1566. Which was scarce sharp and vehement enough, as he said: " For that some of his brethren then " were esteemed too rigid and severe. And that now, this " year, 1573, some were esteemed too much addicted to ce- " remonies. But whatsoever it were, none as he knew, ac- " cused him [i. e. Gualter] of lenity: nor, as he judged, " ought any one, if he would weigh in an even balance " both letters, viz. that to him and that to the bishop of " Ely: and that for his part, (as the bishop proceeded,) he " did not disapprove of the ceremonies of our church: for " he thought them indifferent; but [speaking his mind more " freely in this his private letter to his intimate friend] he " could wish, he said, all were like to his church of Zuric."

Again, to the same, concerning Cox's letter. And in another letter to the said Gualter, dated February 4, speaking of the bishop of Ely's letter to him, he friendly gave him this advice: *Quid D. Eliensis ad te scripserit, vel quid potius per literas abs te extorserit, ignoro. Certe, mi Gualtere, nolui, ut te nimium hisce rebus frivolis immisceas. Non equidem nostras ceremonias, aut vestitum, improbo; sed res adiaphoras judico. At, o utinam, utinam, tandem aliquando omnes Angli ecclesiam Tigurinam, tanquam absolutissimum exemplar, imitandam, sibi serio, proponerent.* Int. Epist. D. Parkhurst. " That he " knew not what my lord of Ely had writ to him, or rather " what he had forced from him by his letters. But truly, " my Gualter, I would not have you too much mingle " yourself in these frivolous matters. Not that I disallow " of our ceremonies or habits; but I judge them to be

" things indifferent. But O! would to God, would to God, CHAP.
" once at last all the English people would in good earnest XXIX.
" propound to themselves to follow the church of Zuric, as Anno 1573.
" the most absolute pattern."

Dr. Whitgift was now busy in writing his Defence of his Whitgift
book against the Admonition ; and hearing that bishop Gualter's
Parkhurst had received letters from the said Gualter, and letters.
supposing he had wrote something in them of these present
controversies, prayed him that he would communicate to
him those letters ; or at least a copy of them. But the said
bishop thought fit to yield him neither. The reason, I suppose, was in favour of his friend, who cared no more to be
brought upon the stage. For this he mentioned to that divine ; and added, concerning the said Whitgift, that if any 287
thing made for the ceremonies, he presently clapped it into
his book, and printed it.

He gave Gualter also this further intelligence, as the ef-The papists
fect of these differences among the professors of the re-shew them-
formed religion in England. " That great dissensions were confidently
" now arisen between the protestants and papists here, and than before.
" daily did arise : [more boldly, it seems, shewing them-
" selves.] And that the papists lifted up their crests, and
" triumphed, as though they had gotten the victory against
" the protestants : while the protestants walked dejected
" and sorrowful. And that at this time there were not a
" few preachers that had laid down their cures of souls
" committed to them, and left them to wolves and idiots.
" And that if he asked him the cause, it was, in truth, be-
" cause they would not use the linen garment called a sur-
" plice. Which counsel of theirs," added the bishop, " I do
" not at all approve."

To which I will subjoin what the same bishop wrote in Fears from
the month of February to another of the ministers of that papists.
church of Zuric, namely, Bullinger, " That there were new to Bullin-
" and severe edicts or proclamations lately published against ger.
" such, who either contemned our ceremonies, or refused to
" observe them. And then prayed, God give it a good
" issue, and have mercy upon all the churches of Christ.
" *Faxit Deus, ne lateat anguis in herba.*"

Corre-
spondence
of the bi-
shop of
Norwich
with Bul-
linger.

All this shews the great respect our English divines, and many of the bishops, shewed to those of Helvetia; between whom there was a continual intercourse of letters. Bullinger, in a letter to bishop Parkhurst, had wrote, that he was that year in the seventieth year of his age: to which that bishop, in his next letter to that reverend father, answered, that he wished he might live to an hundred, for the church's sake.

His esteem
for the city
of Zuric.

Concerning this Bullinger, and that Gualter, before mentioned, with the other learned and godly men there at Tygur or Zuric, thus did Parkhurst, while he dwelt among them in his exile, describe them to Cole, a learned man of Oxford:

> *De Bullingero, Bibliandro, Martyre, Zancho,*
> *Et Gualthero, Gesnero, de Pelicano,*
> *Nostrum judicium si forsan, Cole, requiris;*
> *Hos ego doctrina eximios, pietate gravesque,*
> *Judico, queis similes perpaucos hic habet orbis.*

And of the city itself, this was the praise he gave of it, in a copy of verses to Harley, bishop of Hereford, while he sojourned there:

> *Urbs habet Helveticæ me nunc primaria gentis;*
> *Urbs plane armipotens, pacis amica tamen.*
> *Urbs fecunda piis verbi præconibus, atri*
> *Urbs expers odii, cædis, avaritiæ.*
> *Urbs, e qua pulsa est Venus, Ate, pulsus Iacchus.*
> *Urbs minime flagrans ambitione, dolo.*
> *Urbs, quæ blasphemos punit, litesque resolvit,*
> *Urbs, pietatis amans, justitiæque tenax.*

288

> *Urbs, evangelii quæ plantat dogmata sacri;*
> *Urbs, in quæ nulla est'fœda superstitio.*
> *O! si olim talis tellus Brittanna fuisset,*
> *Extera regna piis non adeunda forent, &c.*

Birchet's
bloody act
provokes
the queen
against the
puritans.

A great cause of these proclamations and strict charges, proceeding from the queen and her council, against the puritanical sect, was the horrible fact of Burchet, a great zealot this way; who thought it lawful to kill such as op-

posed them in their endeavours to bring in their model CHAP.
and discipline: and accordingly, in the heat of his zeal, as-   XXIX.
sassinated a courtier in the streets, thinking him to be Mr. Anno 1573.
Hatton; though it proved to be Hawkins, one of the captains of the queen's navy. Concerning which act, something hath been related by me elsewhere. This wicked Life of Bi-
principle of murdering for God's sake, the queen appre- ker, b. iv.
hended so much danger in, as that of her own life, as well chap. xxxiv.
as of others of chief rank about her, and so enraged her,
that at first she commanded this murderer to be immediately executed by martial law: and a commission for that
purpose was drawn up. And this she resolved to do, as her
sister queen Mary had done, in that severe reign, toward
Wyat: especially having heard it by report of the earl of
Leicester, and he from the admiral; yet not with any their
approbation of such rigorous doings.

So the queen, in her great closet, at service therein, gave She is
order to Mr. Secretary to bring to her the commission for execute him
execution of this man by the martial law, to be signed by by martial
her after dinner. But the earl of Sussex, lord chamberlain, law.
and the lord admiral, were much against it. And the lord
treasurer was not then at court, whose only advice was then
wanted to prevent it. The earl therefore, even while he
was at dinner, wrote to him, it being the 28th of October.
" First, praying God to put it into the queen's heart to do
" the best, and then acquainting him with particulars. As,
" that the lord admiral was greatly grieved with the speech,
" that he should devise it, when as he was directly against
" it: that indeed he had told my lord of Leicester of the
" execution done in London in the rebellion of Wyat, but
" he never told it to the queen: that the earl of Arundel
" was also very vehement against it in speech to him, [the
" lord chamberlain.] He added, That the queen asked for
" the lord treasurer, and seemed to look for his being at
" court, because it was holyday." At length, by the counsel, as it seems, of the lord treasurer, the queen set aside
that purpose of hers, of Birchet's speedy execution after that
manner; and he had time given him for divers days after.

BOOK I.

Anno 1573.

The queen orders that he be strict-lyexamined.

Who shewed at length some repentance of his villainous act; but afterwards repented of his repentance, and justified his doings. Which exceedingly provoked the queen: especially having, by prolonging of his life somewhat longer, given occasion to another horrible murder, committed by him; namely, killing his keeper. She had a mind more fully to sift the man, and to learn whence he had imbibed these wretched principles; therefore she would have him severely and accurately examined, both by lawyers and divines. And 289 this she shewed to the lord chamberlain to be her pleasure. And that in order thereunto, he should write unto the lord treasurer. Which he did the 11th of November, (the day before Birchet's execution,) to this tenor:

The lord chamber-lain's let-ter to the lord trea-surer about it.

" That the queen's majesty had commanded him to sig-
" nify unto him, [the said lord treasurer,] that all the
" means that might be, should be used to examine Birchet
" this night, and to-morrow in the morn before he was to
" be executed, of the matters ensuing: viz. Whether he
" did still continue in the detestable opinion which he did
" before recant ? Whom he knew to be of that opinion be-
" side himself ? Whether any person were privy to his in-
" tention to kill Mr. Hatton ? Whether he knew any per-
" son, beside himself, that had any such intention ? Whe-
" ther he thought, when he killed his keeper, that he had
" killed Mr. Hatton ; and what moved him to it ? What
" had moved him to alter from repenting of his former de-
" testable acts and opinion; for the which he had asked
" pardon of God, of the queen's majesty, of Mr. Hatton,
" and of Mr. Hawkins ? And, to the end the matter might
" be the more substantially handled, the lord chamber-
" lain added, That her highness would have Mr. Solicitor,
" and the recorder of London, with such other grave men
" as his lordship [the lord treasurer] should think fittest
" to examine him very diligently and exquisitely. And
" also the dean of Paul's, if he were in London, or the
" dean of Westminster, with such other godly preachers
" as his lordship should think fit, to persuade him, for
" the disburdening of his conscience, and the avoiding of

" damnation, to utter the truth in all these matters. Where-
" by her majesty conceived he might be brought to utter all
" the truth, and to discover all false practices, if such had
" been in this matter."

In this discourse, it is remarkable, the lord chamberlain
moved her majesty, that Dering or Sampson (if the other
could not get that which she desired to find) might deal
with him : to whom, perhaps, as the lord chamberlain suggested, for the credit and esteem he had of them, he would
upon their persuasion utter them sooner than to any other.
But her majesty would not allow of it.

As for the bishops of the church, they did what in them
lay, to take away any thing that might justly give offence :
as in the regulation of their courts, and in requiring competent learning, and study at one of the universities, in
those that hereafter were to be admitted into the ministry ;
as well as for their morals. For before these days, near the
beginning of queen Elizabeth's reign, and for some years after,
the bishops were fain sometimes to admit into holy orders
laymen, and such as formerly had followed trades or hus-
bandry, and that were but of little learning. Yet if they
were sober, and of honest lives, friends to the religion, and
could read well, they would ordain them readers or deacons, to supply small cures; very many in these times being
wholly vacant. This was the reason that many times unfit
men got into the church. But this was much complained
of ; and not without cause. And the bishops resolved, as
much as they could, to redress this abuse ; refusing henceforth to admit any such to orders, unless so qualified, as before. Some canons being made for that purpose, the bishop
of Norwich had a trial of this, this year ; as I find among
his letters.

290

Mr. Will. Heydon, a gentleman of good quality in Norfolk, an earnest professor of religion, and a dear friend of
that bishop, comes in June to Ludham, where the bishop
abode, and brings with him an old man, formerly an husbandman, past his labour, spent in the turmoils of the
world, that understood little or no Latin, to be made a mi-

Which oc-
casions
some quar-
rel with
the bishop
of Norwich.

nister. But whatever the solicitations of Mr. Heydon were
with his friend the bishop, his obligations to the good of his
diocese, and care of the church, were such, as he would not
admit this man into orders. Whereat the gentleman grew
angry, and the bishop, naturally somewhat hasty, was as
high; and very sharp words passed between them: and so
they parted. Which pleased the adversary: and it proved
a country talk. But such was the good and truly gospel
spirit both of the one and the other, that they were both
within a short time reconciled again: and Heydon, who
seemed to give the first cause, (being returned home to
Holt,) first made the offer of reconciliation; upon this pious
consideration of his, that the enemy might not blaspheme.
And the good bishop was as ready, with all joy and cheer-
fulness, to embrace the offer. Allow me therefore to recite
both their letters, containing in them so much of the true
Christian temper of brotherly love and condescension: I
have reposited them in the Appendix.

Number
XXXI.
[XXXI.]
Mr. Hey-
don's let-
ter, desir-
ing recon-
ciliation.

The short contents of Mr. Heydon's letter were, " That
" coming home, he met with some company that ripped up
" the bishop's circumstances from the top to the bottom,
" with no little joy; and that they were much pleased at
" the difference that had happened between them. He,
" upon this, considered the zeal of his lordship, and his own
" also, towards the gospel. And earnestly tendering his
" lordship's good estate, it put him upon the thoughts how
" meet and convenient it was that they should be reconciled.
" And that therefore, though perhaps he might have for-
" got the duty he owed to his lordship, and that his lord-
" ship also might have administered some cause for his
" choler; yet now considering his duty towards him, [the
" bishop,] and what credit his dealing ought to win towards
" the gospel, and to prevent the pleasure the common
" enemy, the papist, might take at these jarrings among
" the chief professors of it; he, for his part, for what sharp
" words he had spoken, acknowledged his own infirmity,
" and begged his lordship's pardon. And so prayed his
" lordship to acquit him with a line or two, to the satisfac-

CHAP.
XXIX.

Anno 1573.
The bi-
hop's
Christian
answer.

" tion and quieting of his mind ; he making as good ac-
" count of him, as the chiefest bishop in the land."

The bishop, within two or three days' space, gave him answer in a most obliging Christian manner: shewing him, "How
" glad he was, and thanked God for it, that he had moved
" that gentleman's heart so speedily, and, as it were, before
" the sun's going down, to forethink himself of something
" that had been lately done at his house.   And then vindi-
" cating himself in his refusal of that old man, prayed him
" to bear with him, though he agreed not with him in mat-
" ters that were in his judgment offensive to God and his own
" conscience, and slanderous to the church. And bid him re-
" member that saying, *Amicus, sed usque ad aras.*" And coming at length to argue with him about the matter, he asked
him, " Whether he ought to go clean contrary to that, to
" which he and all the bishops had subscribed. That his esti-
" mation would have been much impaired, if he should have
" granted that request of his. O! Mr. Heydon," added he,
" I and all other bishops have made too many such.   Ne-
" cessity drave us to do the same.   But to continue so to
" do, it were a fault too heinous.   And of late years he
" had taken great care in that behalf, and so he intended
" to continue, by God's grace.   And then, after some pe-
" riods, in conclusion he declared to him, that he forgat all,
" and forgave all unfeignedly : and that he did heartily re-
" joice to understand the same of him : and lastly, sub-
" scribed himself, his assured loving friend in Christ."

291

About this time something happened, (wherein the same
bishop was also concerned,) in which I cannot but observe
the care that was taken by some patrons in these times, that
is, such of them as looked upon it as a great trust, and so
used a conscience, what clerks they preferred to their benefices, that might be capable and fitly qualified to teach and
instruct, officiate and give good example to their flocks : and
so took greater and longer deliberation, before they made
their choice : or, perhaps, for the want of sufficient clerks in
those times, out of which to make a choice.   One of these
conscientious patrons I look upon the lord keeper Bacon to

A living
near laps-
ing in lord
keeper Ba-
con's gift,
for want of
a fit clerk.

be, who had kept the living of Stifkey, in the diocese of the
said bishop, in his hands, vacant now near six months, and
so ere long like to lapse to the bishop. To whom therefore
the lord keeper, in August, sent his letter, not to take that
advantage; and that, not having yet a fit clerk to present to
it, and being now ready to lapse, he would grant him some
longer time. The obliging answer the bishop gave that
lord was, " That he would grant him his own whole six
" months. And that as he was many ways most bounden
" unto his honour for many benefits, so he was most glad,
" when any ways he might shew himself thankful for the
" same : who neither had, nor was able to do it hitherto.
" That his honour should command his term of six months,
" for bestowing of his benefice. In which time, nothing, he
" said, should be attempted to the prejudice of his lord-
" ship's interest, or the hinderance of his honourable good
" purpose, in the placing of an able person : which the
" good bishop heartily wished, as well for the benefit of the
" inhabitants, as the neighbours adjoining." And so he was
persuaded Mr. Nathaniel Bacon [who was the said lord
keeper's son, and to whom he had sent a letter also] would
have a care thereof.

Such a conscientious care, I presume, was that also of the
learned and religious secretary of state, sir Tho. Smith, that
the schools should be supplied with able men, for the teaching and instructing the youth of the nation in learning and
Christian manners : who, in the same month, sent to the
same bishop, recommending one Johnson to the free-school
of Aylsham in Norfolk.

Secretary
Smith re-
commends
a school-
master for
Aylsham
school. The answer sent by the same person was to this tenor:
" That the order and foundation of that school was, for the
" bailiff and headboroughs to present, and the bishop to ad-
" mit. And that if the bearer should be named and elect-
" ed, as afore was said, he would be ready to further him.
292 " And would admit him, upon the trial of his ability; and
" the rather, in that it pleased his honour to commend him;
" being every way ready to gratify his honour."

But by what I have further to relate concerning the pro-

viding for this school, the bishop shewed his care of the CHAP.
schools in his diocese, and his caution, whom he admitted to XXIX.
the education of youth, as well as to be ministers, for the Anno 1573.
instruction and edification of the people.

Before Johnson's recommendation to the bishop for this The bishop
school of Aylsham, one Robert Harrison, M. A. living moved to
there, a man of some learning, but a puritan, had obtained admit a pu-
so much favour of several of the aldermen of Norwich, that ritan to it.
they recommended him to the bishop, to appoint and confirm him in that place. But this man had but a little before
shewed his disaffection to the liturgy of the church, by refusing to have some parts of the office of matrimony used at
his marriage: and thereupon declined to let the minister of
the parish perform the office. But, notwithstanding, when
he afterwards promised more conformity and obedience,
Tho. Peck, mayor, Drue Drury, Francis Roberts, John
Aldrich, aldermen, wrote a letter to the bishop, to grant his
consent for the placing of the said Harrison to be schoolmaster in the said school: whom they styled *an honest,
learned man*: adding, that they had lately conference with
Mr. Thexton, vicar of that parish, a learned man, as his
lordship well knew, and with divers others of the ancientest
and gravest of the town, about placing him in that school,
and found them well inclined thereto; notwithstanding he
had of late given some offence in the manner of his marriage. For which he had shewed some penitence, and had
likewise made a faithful promise before them, that he would
be neither author nor maintainer of any faction there This
letter was dated July the 22d.

To which the bishop the same month gave this grave an- The bishop
swer; " That he had been greatly laboured and dissuaded, refuseth
" both by some of the same town, as by other gentlemen of why. Ep.
" the country, who had their children to bring up, that he Episc. Park-
" should not admit this man. And surely, as he proceeded, hurst.
" there are great causes lead me thereto, if they, or any of
" them, be found true. First, he is a very young man; and
" though learned, yet, in respect of his age, and want of ex-
" perience, not so fit as many others. He is reported to

" condemn the reading of profane authors to children.
" Then dare I boldly say, he shall never bring up good
" scholars. And another great matter is, I have been cre-
" dibly informed, that he hath been troubled with a phrensy:
" which sickness, as it is thought incurable, so it is most
" dangerous to admit such a person to have rule over young
" ones; that besides his young years hath not power and
" rule over himself at all times. Touching his offence in
" the manner of his marriage, the same hath been doubled
" in him; that being overnight forewarned by one of his
" dearest friends, Mr. Greenwood, the schoolmaster there,
" (the new proclamation then newly set forth considered,)
" that he should admit Mr. Thexton the vicar, to marry
" him, and besides that, not to break the order of her ma-
" jesty's book in any part, yet notwithstanding he enter-
" prised, as you have heard; to the offence of divers, and to
" my great displeasure and discredit: being persuaded that
293 " fact of his is not unknown to my lord of Canterbury, and
" others of the best calling.

" And touching his penitence, it is far from that you
" write of, that, as I have been informed, he did rather
" confirm his disobedience, than any way submit himself for
" the same. And being for mine own part, in respect of my
" place, as also for duty and discharge of my conscience,
" bound to have a special care of the youth of the diocese,
" as the imps that by God's grace may succeed us, by good
" bringing up, and become worthy in the commonwealth;
" I cannot be easily persuaded to admit Mr. Harrison to
" any such charge over them. And thus I bid you heartily
" farewell. From Ludham."

Yet was the good bishop so yielding, that not long afterwards, upon other informations concerning this man, as
though he had been misrepresented, the bailiff and headboroughs presenting him, he admitted him to the school.
Which, (as the bishop concluded,) coming to the archbishop's
ear, caused him to write to the bishop, blaming him for it.
For in fine, the first report concerning Harrison's behaviour
and condition proving too true, together with some mis-

behaviour at the baptizing of a child, the bishop turned CHAP.
him out again; as hath been related more at large else- XXIX.
where.

Anno 1573.

William Hughes, D. D. was this year preferred to the Hughes, bi-
bishopric of St. Asaph. How this man afterwards behaved shop of St.
Asaph. His
himself, leased out the revenues of this see, converted many great mis-
benefices to his own use by *commendams*, and misgoverned government.
his diocese, out of a covetous disposition, came to light after
some years; informations of many great abuses being
brought to court against him. Which upon complaint seems Inquisition
to have brought on a visitation of that church; and in- made there-
into.
quisition to be made concerning the bishop's government,
and the state of the revenues of the see; what benefices the
bishop held in *commendam*, and what leases he had made,
and whether to the prejudice of his successors; of his visitations and his courts; what residence and hospitality among
his clergy were maintained. And a particular account thereof was sent up in the year 1587, being drawn up in writing; shewing the present state of that bishopric of St.
Asaph. Wherein was discovered, that most of the great
livings within the diocese, some with cure of souls, and
some without, were either holden by the bishop himself in
commendam, or else were in the possession of such men as
dwelt out of the country. That there were held by him sixteen livings, viz. nine cures, and seven *sine cures.* That
there was never a preacher within the diocese that kept ordinary hospitality, but only three. Whereby it came to pass,
that the former accustomed good and charitable housekeeping was quite decayed in the diocese. And particularly one,
that had two of the greatest livings in the diocese, was so
far from keeping hospitality, that he boarded himself in an
alehouse. That divers parcels of the bishopric were leased
out, and confirmed by him, to the hinderance of his successors: some whereof were lordships and manors, others
good rectories. That he had got all the keys of the chapter
seal within the keeping of his own chaplains; that he
might confirm what he would himself. That in his visitation, he caused the clergy of his diocese to pay for his diet,

and of the rest of his train, over and above the *procurations*, appointed by the law for that purpose. And lastly, that by his negligence there were so many recusants in that country, as then there were. This is a short abstract of that paper of information against that bishop, and was presented to the lord treasurer: and that I may not be thought to wrong the memory of a bishop long since deceased, and that the whole may be preserved, I have left it in the Appendix, faithfully transcribed from the original.

N°.XXXII.

Hughes un-
qualified to
be a bishop.
Of one Hughes, (in all probability the same with this bishop Hughes,) Davies, bishop of St. David's, gave notice to secretary Cecil, when in the year 1565 the said Hughes made an interest to obtain the bishopric of Landaff, then void. And prayed, " That a man of such deficiencies might " not fill such a weighty place in the church: for that he " was one that was utterly unlearned in divinity, nor was " able to render a reason of his faith. And what service " could such an one be able to do to God and the queen's " majesty in that place, that of all other places had of long " time most lacked good doctrine and true knowledge of " God?" But this bishop's whole letter, savouring of a right Christian and episcopal spirit, and containing some other remarks in it, and being but short, I have thought

[Number
XXXII.]
worthy to be read, and preserved in the Appendix: and also to store up as much as we can of the memory of our first protestant bishops; especially such as were exiles for the gospel, as this bishop of St. David's was one. To which I may add, that he was one of the bishops that assisted at the translation of the Bible in queen Elizabeth's reign; called therefore *the Bishops' Bible.*

CHAP. XXX.

Pilkington, bishop of Durham, desires the queen's leave to 295
come up this winter. Lands of the bishopric detained.
His letter thereof to the secretary Cecill. A contest be-
tween the bishop of Norwich, doctor Gardiner, and others,
about the archdeaconry of Norwich. The case. Gardiner
gets the deanery of Norwich. The bishop and he reconcil-
ed. Gardiner's good service to the church of Norwich. The
bishop of Ely visits St. John's college. Bingham, a great
soldier, recommended to the lord treasurer. Rafe Lane's
characters of Leicester, Burghley, Sussex, Hatton, and
other courtiers. A controversy in Bene't college, Cam-
bridge. Books now set forth. The queen's progress into
Sussex and Kent. The bishop of Norwich's letter to the
bailiff of Yarmouth, concerning the punishing of wicked-
ness there. The unseasonable weather this year.

I COME now to represent some particular persons, chiefly Remarks of
such as belonged to the church; and to gather up divers several per-
matters of remark concerning them; tending to retrieve
memorials of their piety, learning, or other concerns; happening within the compass of this year.

Pilkington, the grave and truly reverend bishop of Dur- Bishop of
ham, deserveth to have some notice taken of him here; be- Durham de-
ing one of the pious exiles, that at their return were the the queen to
first bishops settled in the newly reformed church of Eng- come up.
land. He was still alive, but by reason of his age very
much pinched by the winter's cold in that northern part of
the nation. The queen required residence of her bishops in
their dioceses; and would not permit them to come up to
London without special leave; that they might keep hospitality, and their presence might awe the papists, specially in
those parts. It was now September, in the declining of the
year, when this good bishop signified to the lord treasurer,
both his desire to come into these southern quarters, for
the avoiding the extremity of the winter-season, and also
his pious acquiescence in God's disposal of him, whatever
should happen. For these were his words to that lord;

" That the common griefs that he had suffered there for
" sundry winters past, made him to think what he should
" look for the winter that was then at hand. That it had
" begun so sharply with him already, that he feared the
" latter end would be worse. And therefore if his lordship
" thought good to move her majesty that he might come
" up this winter, he should desire him to let him under-
" stand her highness' pleasure. That if his wisdom thought
" the time served not for such a motion, he should content
" himself; and commit himself to his hand, that had both
296 " life and death, health and sickness at his commandment.
" There is," added he, " a highway to heaven, out of all
" countries. Of which free passage, I praise God, I doubt
" not."

And then to incline the queen to allow of his absence
from thence, he shewed, " That the country there (praising
" God for it) was outwardly quiet enough, and that more
" continuers than aforetime would abide there: as sir George
" Bowes and his brother there, [at Durham,] besides others
" of the council at York. He appointed nothing, but re-
" ferred him wholly to his lordship's discretion, to deal for
" him, as he saw cause. Only this he would crave of his
" goodness, to know, with such convenient speed as might
" be, what he might do with good leave, come or tarry;
" that he might prepare himself thereafter. For when the
" weather should be sharper, he should not be able to tra-
" vel, if he would, hereafter." And then he ended with a
prayer; " The great God long preserve you to serve him, to
" his glory, his lordship's honour, and the comfort of the
" people. 22d of September.

" Your lordship's to command,
" Ja. Duresme."

His letter to
Cecil con-
cerning the
lands of the
bishopric,
detained.
It may be added here, concerning this bishop, (because I
may not have occasion to say any thing more of him,) what
labour and care he took to preserve the revenues of his bishopric, (some parts whereof were unrighteously detained
till the year 1565,) and the endeavours he used for the re-

covery of them.   These were the detained lands, and their
values, as he wrote them down, and sent the paper thereof
to sir William Cecil, secretary.   The values were according
as the lord treasurer had rated them.

The detained lands.				Their value.		
Norham, and the shire	-	-		£120	0	0
Esington ward	-	-	-	323	13	4
Esington Coronator	-	-		72	9	0
Sadberg	-	-	-	23	0	11
Coton Mundivel	-	-	-	47	16	1
Middelham	-	-	-	19	6	11
Gateshed	-	-	-	24	11	7
Creik	-	-	-	-	39	7	$4\frac{1}{2}$
Allerton, and the shire	-	-		218	9	$1\frac{1}{4}$
A pension out of Howden	-		91	5	$8\frac{3}{4}$

All parcels of the county palatine.

The state of this business the bishop set down after this
manner, in a letter to the said Cecil, hoping to have some
order by his means:

" *Gratia et pax.*   I have sent your honour a note of such
" lands as be detained from me, with the *valor* of them, as
" the lord treasurer rated them.   Norham, and the shire, is
" exempted from Cumberland, and made part of the county
" palatine of Durham, and of as great liberties.   So is
" Creik in all things from Yorkshire.   And all suits and 297
" prisoners come to Durham.   Allerton has great liberties,
" but not fully so much.   All other parcels lie within the
" county of Durham.
     " The inconveniencies in detaining them, as the lawyers
" say, is such, that all such as hold any lands within these
" parcels of the bishop, cannot sell, nor aliene, nor make a
" good conveyance or state in law, to any person; not so
" much as a jointure to his wife, as hath been proved of
" late; nor sell any part after his office found.   Because the
" bishop cannot give him his *liberate* of them: as even now
" is in experience by one Claxton, that sold his land to Per-
" kinson.   Who procured divers of the council's letters, that

" I would grant him his *liverie :* which I cannot, being ex-
" empted from me.   Nor the queen's majesty nauther can
" graunt it him : for that she holdeth them contrary to law.
" And having not his liverie, say the lawyers, *nullum ei*
" *restat liberum tenementum.*   The like is judged to be in
" copyholders and leases also.   Which causeth great mur-
" murings among the people, and maketh many intruders
" and usurpers.   Whereof must needs issue infinite suits,
" brawlings, and quarrellings.   Which I am sorry should
" chance in the time, or by occasion of any that professes
" Christ's gospel.   And surely the people say, this is the
" fruit of our religion, to procure such mischiefs.

" I can wish the amendment of it, but God must work it.
" And for my own part, I will be no partaker of any such
" injuries to so many people, so farre as I may avoid it.

" Furthermore, it were time : the danger is great : the
" shire is small.   And yet if any of the wardens of the
" marches send for aid to the bishop on the sudden, he
" must give them help.   The shire is divided into four
" wards.   Of which is detained from me a ward and an half.
" There be seven lords within the shire, Northumberland,
" Cumberland, Westmorland, Dacres, Evers, Scrope, Lum-
" ley ; that have great lands and liberties ; where the bishop
" hath not to do.   Beside the dean and chapter, and the
" great liberty of the queen's majesty's lands in Bernard's
" castle, and other suppressed lands ; of which none be at
" the bishop's command.   All these being taken from the bi-
" shop, it is easy to see what aid the bishop shall be able to
" give in time of need.   For none of the others do sturre
" without special commandment from the prince : nor be at
" the warden's commandment.

" But this harm is not only in war, but in commissions,
" juries, carriages, &c.   None or few of these do serve the
" queen, save only the bishop's tenants, and few of the
" poorer freeholders.   The commodities, which be thought
" great for the wardship, marriages, and reliefs, I assure
" your honour, are very small.   For every man almost hath
" purchased suppressed lands, and so become wards to the

" queen. Truly, I have had only one poor relief these five
" years, of xxl. for all offices that were found. Cods, which
" is the great commodity of the country, there is none at all
" within these detained lands; nor wood, saving a little at
" Allerton: out of my woods, I give the tenants of these
" detained lands for their reparations. This commodity I
" have by it.. Besides, that I pay the queen's majesty her
" rent duly, although they pay me slowly.

    " God graunt, that these things may be duly considered;
" and then it will easily appear, whether I seek mine own
" profit, or the advancement of justice, and avoiding of in-
" juries and mischiefs to many people." And then, like a
holy bishop, he concludes with his prayer; " The Lord long
" preserve you to serve him, and his people, to his glory,
" their comfort, and your heart's ease.

" Yours wholly,
" Ja. Δύνωλμ."

    The bishop, who was thus diligent and conscientious in
soliciting the recovery of the lands and lordships aforesaid,
for the good of his church, was at last successful, and did
obtain the restoration of them again, by the good assistance
of Cecil: but still with the burden of a considerable rent-
charge to be paid to the queen, her heirs and successors, of
1020l. yearly; as appears by an authentic paper, expressive
of the same: that is, for the manors and lordships situate in
the county of York, and bishopric of Durham, 880l. For
those in Northumberland and Elandshire, in the county of
Northumberland, 140l. These lands were retained by virtue
of an act of parliament made in the first year of the queen.

    The foresaid paper (belonging to bishop Hutton's time)
bears this title: " A parcel of possessions late belonging to
" the bishopric of Durham, now retained in the hands of
" our sovereign lady Elizabeth, by virtue of an act of par-
" liament established in the first year of her reign. And
" then are set down the names of the lordships and manors
" situate in the counties of York and Durham. And then
" follows: *Quæ omnia præmissa concessa fuerunt Jacobo*

Those lands
restored to
the see by
the bishop's
means.

Paying a
yearly rent
to the
queen.MSS.
Burghlian.

BOOK
I.

Anno 1573.

"*nuper episcopo Dunelmensi; ac modo Matthæo episcopo* "*Dunelmensi: reddendo inde dominæ reginæ, hæredibus et* "*successoribus suis per annum* 880*l.*" And after this, there is a particular of the possessions in Northumberland; and the yearly payments for them, viz. 140*l.* And then, at the bottom thereof, is writ, "*Memorandum,* These two sums "above-mentioned have been yearly answered to her ma- "jesty, since the first retaining of the same hitherto."

These annuities, in the nature of a rent, were paid to the crown for those lands above specified, and seemed to be continued all along upon that bishopric, till the alienation of those very lands and estates long after, in the years of 1648 and 1649, &c. sacrilegiously sold away from it: (as the lands of the other bishoprics then were.) As an account thereof, together with their purchasers, and respective sums

Rev. T. Ba-
ker.

Number
XXXIII.

paid for them, was taken by the deputy register of that bishopric, which I have, for the reader's entertainment, reposited in the Appendix; as a copy thereof was communicated to me by a learned and worthy friend.

The bi-
shopric ex-
empted
from this
yearly pay-
ment; and
why.

But when the monarchy and episcopacy took place again at the happy restoration, this payment from that bishopric remained to the crown, until king Charles II. remitted it to that see on this account; viz. Upon his first coming in, there was an act made for taking away the *court of wards.* And

299

so the *court of wards,* that belonged to this county palatine of old, was also taken away by that act. Whereby the bishops of that see lost a good branch of their revenue. The king, in compensation for this, forgave the annuity of 880*l.* paid before to the queen dowager: making a grant to Cosins, that then was the learned and most worthy bishop of Durham, of an exemption from that annuity, belonging to the then queen-mother, in reversion after her death unto him, and then to his successors.

Life of Bi-
hop Co-
ns, p. 56.
n d 98.

This is mentioned in the Life of Bishop Cosins, by Dr. Basire; as a good deed to that bishopric, done and brought about by his means and interest. Which annuity had been a long time before accustomably paid to the queens of England.

But how these lands of this wealthy bishopric were looked
upon with an envious and greedy eye, even in queen Elizabeth's reign, may appear from the large and long leases
made by bishop Pilkington, but especially his next successor, bishop Barnes, to the queen, for the gratifying of some
gentlemen. Which may be seen from an original paper, belonging some time to the lord treasurer Burghley, now set
in the Appendix.
George Gardiner, D. D. a prebendary of the cathedral
church of Norwich, was this year nominated by the queen
to the deanery of the said church, as he had by her also,
about a year before, enjoyed the archdeaconry of Norwich,
by a lapse. Both which dignities were obtained for him by
the earl of Leicester's interest. He was a man of learning
and merit, and a hearty professor of the gospel; and of good
friendship and understanding with the bishop. But a difference now unhappily fell out between them. The cause
was a contention about the archdeaconry. The presentation
whereof had been granted before by the bishop to one Mr.
Roberts, an old and dear friend of his; who was at present
in possession. But nevertheless it was in contest between
the said Roberts and one Rugg. Who was also presented
to it by virtue of the next advowson of it, which the bishop
was said to have granted unto his false receiver, Thimelthorp. Who making over all his goods and chattels to one
Barnes, this advowson, being reckoned among them, came
hereby to the said Barnes: who, by virtue thereof, upon the
avoidance, presented Rugg. But while these two were at
law together, the right of presentation lapsed to the queen.
And Dr. Gardiner being now informed that the title of neither party was good, and that it was indeed lapsed, took
the opportunity, and got the grant thereof from the queen.
Hence a new lawsuit was ready to be commenced between
Roberts and Gardiner: and so hotly followed, that Roberts
told the other, he would not leave off to recover his right,
though it cost him 500l. Gardiner said, he had no such
substance, yet he would not give over so long as he had a
penny left.

BOOK
I.

Anno 1573.

The bishop
angry with
Gardiner.

300

But the bishop was exceedingly angry with Dr. Gardiner for this act of his : and there passed some angry letters from him to the other, telling him, " That he had done him " wrong two ways. First, in undermining his dear friend: " whom, as he knew, he [the bishop] loved and tendered " as himself. Next, in making him the cloak of that prac- " tice, [for Gardiner had reported, he had done it with the " bishop's consent,] that he was so far from granting, as he " had, and would withstand the same against any person, " that should offer so great wrong to his friend. That he " had hurt himself greatly herein, in confirming the opinion " that went of him, as ambitious, and seeking his own ad- " vancement, though his friends were hurt thereby. He " wished this rumour might cease, and spread no farther ; " and that he would give him none occasion of breach of " friendship or misliking ; who had ever been, since he " knew him, his trusty friend, in spite of all his enemies : " and he should find him still any ways ready to pleasure " him ; so that his [the bishop's] credit and the safety of " his other friends were not hurt thereby. He bade him be " judge himself, whether he ever granted any thing hurtful " to Roberts." The truth was, there were some overtures made to him by Gardiner, concerning his relinquishing of the archdeaconry upon some terms, which the bishop was privy to.

Gardiner
clears him-
self to the
bishop.

But Gardiner answered with words of all due respect and softness ; and in fine, he desired the bishop, that the case might be referred to lawyers and friends to judge of their right ; and that if the bishop would judge of any thing fitting for him to do about the award, he would be ready to do it.

Number
XXXV.

The bishop's angry letter to Gardiner caused him to write two letters, one to the bishop, and another to Roberts, which being so peaceably penned, and stating the matter, I have put into the Appendix.

In the mean time, Roberts, by the advice of the bishop, asked the judgment of two of the ablest lawyers, Mr. Gandy and Mr. Bell, (now speaker of the house of commons,) both afterwards judges.

The case was stated thus to Gandy. George Thimel- CHAP.
thorp, having right by advowson to the archdeaconry of XXX.
Norwich, conveyeth over his goods and chattels to certain Anno 1573.
trustees, and afterwards, in his own name, presenteth John The case
Rugg to the archdeaconry. My lord bishop making some Roberts and
exception, and commencing suit together with Mr. Roberts, Gardiner.
unto whom the said lord bishop had bestowed the advowson
in reversion, being patron thereof. While the said Mr.
Rugg and Mr. Roberts contend in law, and both installed,
and one year expired, one comes, supposing the queen's
majesty to have right by lapse, and begs the same of her
grace: whether may any such lapse fall to the prince, or
any person, *lite pendente, et ecclesia plena?* Mr. Gardiner
saith, Mr. Thimelthorp's advowson doth still remain good:
notwithstanding his conveyance can take no place now; but
the gift through Thimelthorp's negligence is fallen into
lapse.

This reason of Mr. Gardiner, that it should be in the The judg-
queen's gift by lapse, is utterly disliked of sergeant Gandy, ment of ser-
and some others that have been talked withal. And the dy and the
civil lawyers do generally disallow such kind of lapse. For civilians.
the while two persons do contend for a right of presentation
(which often happens) while the suit hangs, a third person
shall seek the lapse: which hath not been heard of before
this.

Then follow notes of Mr. Robert Bell, touching the matter above-written; viz.

" These instructions are in divers parts imperfect: how- 301
" beit, with conference with Mr. Gaiton and this bearer, I Mr. Bell
" take it, that I understand the cause; and, as I take it, his opinion.
" that Thimelthorp, by his deed of gift of his goods and Int. Epist.
" chattels to Barnes, hath given away his interest in the Ep. Parkh.
" advowson.

" *Item*, I think that Thimelthorp's interest, by both the
" several grants, was good in law.

" *Item*, I think, that Barnes his title is lost by lapse.

" *Item*, I think also, the prince cannot have any ad-
" vantage, because the promotion was full of an incumbent.

" And though it were by wrong, yet the title of the prince
" is not any way due, but by lapse.   And as this case is,
" there is no lapse.

" *Item*, Touching the draught of the act of parliament, it
" shall be considered of sufficiently, if the parliament doth
" hold.   And it is but lost labour to enter now into any
" further consideration, until the parliament begins; and
" then I will do the best I can."

[Bell, being speaker of the house of parliament, he was
desired to move the next sessions for an act to settle this
matter.   This refers, I suppose, to a bill, the late sessions of
parliament, 14 Eliz. touching *presentations by lapse*.   Which
was read twice, and ordered to be engrossed: but passed
not into an act.]

" *Item*, I think very clearly, that the parliament will not
" hold at this time, for divers causes and reasons, needless
" to be recited."

Some letters
between
Gardiner
and the bi-
shop about
this matter.
Gardiner, while this cause depended, was very uneasy,
and in a letter to the bishop told him, that he had lived so
much troubled and disquieted in mind about this matter,
that he could never rest, nor take his meat to his comfort.
And therefore concluded, that he would yield up his whole
right into his lordship's hands, to do withal as he should
think best.   Yet in a letter afterwards, he seemed to revoke
this, and insisted upon his own right.   For this the bishop
twitted him, and told him in a letter, he could expect no
favour at his hands, that had deserved none.   But Gardiner
again, in a more submissive manner, answered the bishop's
sharp letter, promising, " That if he would grant it was his
" right, then upon his letter he should have the sole inter-
" est, only considering his charges, as he should think good.
" So constant, said he, am I: adding, I had rather it be
" said, This man lost a good living to keep a friend, than
" lost a good friend to keep a living.   Finally, do with me
" (as he concluded) as you will; so as you deal after your
" old manner, like a friend.   All the world as yet shall not
" separate me from my lord the bishop of Norwich."   This
was writ the beginning of September.

The next month, the deanery of Norwich became void, by the decease of Salisbury the dean, who was also bishop of Man. The bishop of Norwich now thought to make use of this, as an opportunity to put an end to this troublesome business, by getting Gardiner placed in that dignity; and so to resign his pretences to the archdeaconry. This put him upon writing a letter to his good friend Dr. Wylson, at court; moving him to do his endeavour to procure Gardiner the deanery, but conditionally; and yet with respect to another divine that the said city laboured to procure the said deanery for. His letter was to this tenor: " That it was so " now, that my lord bishop of Man, being dean of Christ's 302 " Church, was departed this world, and great suit was made " for the same promotion. That the city of Norwich had " written up for one Mr. Bird, a very godly man, and well " learned. That he was also desired to write to him for one " Dr. Gardyner, who was also well learned, and a good " preacher. That he had given an archdeaconry to one " Mr. Roberts, (whom he called his dear friend,) whom the " said Gardyner, as he said, had endeavoured to supplant " of the foresaid promotion. And that when he came up to " London of late, he intended to pursue his purpose, as he " heard say. The bishop then requested Dr. Wylson, that " if he perceived that to be true, that he would do nothing " for him, being so ungrateful to him. But if he suffered " his friend Mr. Roberts to continue quiet in his living, " then he prayed him to do what he could either for Gar- " dyner or Bird: for to write against the whole city he " would not. And that either of them both was well able " to discharge that office."

But without this condition, hinted by the bishop, Gardiner, by the interest, not of Wylson, but a greater than he, viz. the earl of Leicester, obtained the deanery, and to be the queen's chaplain too. By which means he kept the contest still on foot; requiring terms before he would lay it down. Nay, and he had so much favour from the earl, that he got the earl to write an earnest and powerful letter to the bishop, to surcease, and permit him to enjoy his preferment quietly, in these words:

Anno 1573.

Earl of Lei-
cester's let-
ter to the
bishop of
Norwich, in
favour of
Gardiner.

" After my hearty commendations. Whereas it pleased the " queen's majesty, at my suit, to prefer Dr. Gardiner to the " archdeaconry of Norwich, for better encouragement and " recompence of his pains and travails in that diocese; I am " to desire you, that according to that her highness's grant, " he may have your favour and authority, for the present " possession thereof; not minding to prejudice any man's " right or title thereby: but desirous of his more easy and " speedy enjoying of that her majesty's benefit. And al- " though other means might have been made, either by her " highness's letters, or else the lords of the council, to con- " firm and establish him in his right; yet he and I are per- " suaded, my letter in his behalf will prevail and take effect " with you; under whom, and in whose diocese, he hath " bestowed the most part of his travail: being assured, that " for my cause he shall be rather furthered than hindered.

" And now for that it hath pleased her goodness to make " him her chaplain, and dean of Norwich, which are both of " considerable charge and countenance, I am persuaded of " your own consideration, you will seek his quiet herein, " for the better maintenance of them. The rather also, at " this my earnest letter and friendly request. And so I " bid you heartily farewell. From the court at Somerset- " house, the 4th of December, 1573.

" Your lordship's very loving friend,
" R. Leycester."

303
By this means, having the countenance of so great a courtier, Gardiner played his game, the better to obtain his terms of the bishop, in order to his laying down his pre- tences to the archdeaconry. And so at last, some while after, (that I may shorten this matter,) he offered to put the controversy wholly into the bishop's hands, either by himself, or with two others with him, indifferently chosen,

to end the same before the first of August next; which was CHAP.
the time of one whole year from his installation into the XXX.
archdeaconry: professing to the bishop, that if he would Anno 1578.
give him but one penny, he should hold himself contented.
Otherwise, [without this reference,] he offered but to take
his charges, which then were forty marks, and his advowson renewed, which his lordship gave him; whereby he
might quietly enjoy the same after Mr. Roberts's death.
And so he would faithfully and friendly join with Mr. Roberts in the maintenance of his possession.   Or else, if he
doubted of his interest, &c. that it could not be quietly enjoyed, [by the trouble that Rugg might give him,] he promised him assurance of 23*l.* 6*s.* 8*d.* by year, to be paid him
during his life; and would defend him against all men, for
the mean profits received since the death of the last incumbent, which was three hundred mark, toward his charges.

But the queen's letters, dated in June the next year, The queen
concluded the strife, commanding the bishop to suffer Dr. writes to
the bishop
Gardiner to execute the office of the archdeaconry; of of Norwich
which he had hitherto been hindered, (for what cause she in favour of
Gardiner.
knew not:) and to have and enjoy the commodities that
thereunto did in any respect belong, from the death of the
last incumbent, &c. " That he shall quietly enjoy our gift,
" until he be evicted by law out of the same."

But notwithstanding these differences and contentions Reconciled.
between these two good men, the bishop and the dean, all
ended in a very christian, charitable conclusion; and the
hearty friendship which was formerly between them was
perfectly restored.   And as a certain token thereof on the
dean's side, he set up a fair monument for the bishop, who
died the next year: at the foot whereof is engraven, (which
are the only words of the bishop's monument yet remaining,) *Viro bono, docto, et pio, Johanni Parkhursto, episcopo
vigilantissimo, Georgius Gardiner posuit hoc.*   And when
he died (which was many years after, viz. anno 1589) he
was buried near the bishop: which I suppose was by his
own order, in testimony of his esteem and love to him:
where his monument still remains by the bishop's.

It may be added here, for a grateful remembrance of Dr. Gardiner, the great pains and good service he did for

Anno 1573.
Dean Gar-
diner's good
service to
the church
of Norwich.
the church of Norwich, while he was dean; all the lands and revenues whereof being very near swallowed up by sir Thomas Shirley, and some others; who had obtained patents from the queen for concealed lands in these parts, that is, such as had been formerly given for superstitious uses, and so forfeited to the crown. And so far had these men proceeded and succeeded, to make the lands of that cathedral such, that about the year 1582, and after, divers parcels of that church's lands were sold away for ever, and money taken for them: others violently entered upon, with-

304 out payment of rent, or farm. Some tenants had paid no rent for some years. So that the church at last had not a parcel of land, no, not the houses within the cathedral church, but they had been offered to sale; or else money taken beforehand for long leases, hereafter to be granted. Now did Gardiner, the dean, bestir himself for several years, and made the best defence he could, partly by application to his powerful friends at court, particularly to the lord treasurer and the earl of Leicester: (to both whom I have his letters.) So that in the year 1588, after six or seven years' contest, he got her majesty's warrant, that the patentees should surrender their several interests, upon consideration, viz. The church to receive a new foundation and dotation from the queen; and they to have a new lease made from her, in such order, and with such conditions, and to such ends, as was in that warrant set down and expressed. And so I find, that Shirley, anno 1590, got a lease of ninety-nine years of the priory lands; Gardiner dying the year before.

Now something concerning university matters, wherein a bishop also was concerned. The fellows of St. John's college in Cambridge, weary, as it seems, of Mr. Shepherd their master, (whom but four years before they had chosen unanimously,) deprived him for the cause of discontinuance from the college longer than the statutes allowed, and chose Dr. Longworth master in his room. And of both these

acts done by them in the month of July, they sent intelligence to their patron the lord treasurer, with their names
subscribed : viz.

Stephen Cardinal,	John Duffielde,
Laurence Washington,	Edward Doughty,
John Langworth,	Maurice Faulkner,
Henry Hickman,	Thomas Randolph,
Francis Holt,	Thomas Leche,
James Mayor,	Abel Smith,
Robert Bolton,	Everard Digbye,
George Still,	John Palmer,
Thomas Smith,	Robert Booth,
Edward Ellis,	William Harrison,
Richard Some,	With others.

And for the better justifying of what they had done, they
drew up articles of divers accusations against him. The
first was, his unsatiable getting to his own use, from the
college and society thereof, by fraud and deceit. Secondly,
his sowing of contention, and maintaining of factions.
Thirdly, his tyranny, in taking all authority in elections to
himself, contrary to the order of their statutes; and in doing what him listed.

Under the second article, to make that good, they brought
these instances: 1. His choosing an unlearned and precise
president, out of his order and place, having six his seniors
to be preferred, and before, speaking openly against the
communion book.

Item, to another office, to wit, the deanship, he chose another, who for the like fantasies was in the town among
men of that profession, of most account. To him he committed the government of the youth. Who by his countenance were so corrupted, that there was almost never a boy
in the college which had not in his head a platform of a
church. Whereas also the same party did in open pulpit
pretend to confute Dr. Whitgift; and was rebuked by one
of his seniors. The master did not (as he was bound by
duty) take part with the senior, but rather justified the
other, in his inconsiderate and disorderly attempt. *Item*,

Articles of accusation against him.

305

G g 2

BOOK that he preferred Mr. Faucet; and that against the consent
I.   of six seniors, who not long before, in the presence of the
Anno 1573. master and all the seniors, did inveigh against the authority
Favours   of bishops. *Item*, that he punished one of the fellows in
faction.   the defending the estate, and suffered one other to confute
his defence without any manner of punishment. *Item*, that
he suffered one to proceed master of art, who before him
had been convinced of speaking against the communion
book, and master Whitgift his book. *Item*, whatsoever
hath been against the estate hath never been punished by
him, or confuted.

The bishop   Upon occasion of the distractions in this house of learn-
of Ely visits ing, the bishop of Ely (who was by the statutes appointed
the college. visitor) instituted a visitation; and had already entered
upon it, and adjourned it for some while. In the mean
time, the high chancellor of that university had sent to his
vice-chancellor, (who that year was Dr. Byng,) to be informed of these matters; and in his name, with other
heads, to take cognizance thereof, in order to decide and
put some end hereunto. The vice-chancellor informed the
said bishop of this message; but he insisted upon his right
of visiting that college. Yet, that his lordship might understand how he proceeded, he caused the vice-chancellor
to be present while he took the examination of these controversies; and what he himself, as visitor, did herein.
That so, from his vice-chancellor, his lordship might be
satisfied in the course he took, and what was actually done
by him. All which will be more perfectly known by the
vice-chancellor's letter to the said high chancellor: which
follows; viz.

The vice-   " That it might please his lordship, that upon the re-
chancellor's " ceipt of his letters concerning the quieting of certain
letter there-
upon.   " troubles, lately moved in St. John's college, he conferred
" with those heads of houses who were then at home. And
" that their opinion was, that forasmuch as among many
" other griefs and quarrels of that college, namely, that
" also concerning the vacation of the mastership was offered
" to the hearing and consideration of my lord of Ely: and

" that by consent of either party, as it seemed: and for
" that the said bishop had already begun his visitation
" there by ordinary authority granted him by the statutes
" of that house; he [the vice-chancellor] should do best to
" abstain from intermeddling in that cause, until he were
" fully advertised whether my lord of Ely's purpose was to
" proceed or desist from further dealing therein.

" Wherefore, as he went on, he gave his chaplain intelli-
" gence, expecting his answer, till the 19th of the then pre-
" sent September. At what time he understood that the
" bishop meant to be personally present the Monday fol-
" lowing, to go forward with his visitation in that college. 306
" That at his coming to town he declared to him the effect
" of his lordship's letters. That his answer was, that al-
" though, as he was persuaded, the deciding of that contro-
" versy pertained only unto him, as visitor, chiefly because
" they had attempted the new election, contrary to his in-
" hibition there published: wherein he had also summoned
" his said visitation: yet that he [the vice-chancellor] might
" certainly report unto his lordship upon what considera-
" tion he had stayed Mr. Shepherd in his room of the mas-
" tership, he caused in his [the vice-chancellor's] hearing
" the parties to object against the master, and him to an-
" swer for himself.

" That they charged him with divers points, but none What the
" tending to the amotion, saving one concerning his longer bishop did
in this vi-
" absence than statute permitted. To the which he an- sitation.
" swered, that where the statute granted him three months
" absence, they did him wrong to limit every month to
" twenty-eight days: seeing the common custom and use
" divideth the whole year but into twelve months. Se-
" condly, the statute dispenseth with him in these cases,
" to wit, sickness, the prince's service, affairs of the college.
" Of which, some he then proved, some he offered to prove
" within reasonable time. All which granted, he had to
" spare of his three months above twenty days. And lastly,
" he referred himself to their own reports, whether, accord-
" ing to the statute, they had granted him leave or no for

" six weeks longer, if need had been. To that it was re-
" plied, that where such leave cannot be granted but by
" consent of the more part of the seniors, some gave voice
" in that grant whom the statute did not license to be in
" place of seniors. Then the question was demanded, whe-
" ther any exception was made against them at the time of
" such voice giving. Which was denied.

" These things being thus, and more amply debated to
" and fro, my lord of Ely asked him [the vice-chancellor]
" what he thought in the case. Who shewed him, that in
" his opinion it were hard dealing to remove the master
" upon that statute of absence, without more substantial
" proofs than he had heard alleged. Touching other things
" there objected, both against the master and fellows, and
" also the scholars, after my lord of Ely had diversly, as
" he thought good, examined the particulars, calling the
" whole company into the chapel, he sharply and openly
" rebuked them all. And there, reserving the correction of
" the greater enormities to his further consideration, ex-
" horting and charging them to maintain unity, and to
" avoid contention, he continued his visitation till towards
" Easter next: the rather, (as he told the vice-chancellor,
" and other, the assistants,) that he might keep them the
" more in awe the mean time."

In conclusion, " that he had thus made relation of these
" matters the more largely, as well to advertise his honour
" of the certainty thereof, as also to excuse his long stay.
" And so resting always at his lordship's commandment, he
" humbly recommended the same to the tuition of God.
" Dated from Clare Hall, the 26th of September, 1573.
" Subscribing, Your lordship's unworthy deputy, ever at
" commandment, Thos. Byng."

307   This college's disturbances continued at least two years
longer, till the year 1575, when the queen sent down a special commission to certain heads, for the better and more
peaceable regulation of that house for the future, as may be
B. i. ch. 12. read afterwards: and in the Life of Archbishop Whitgift.

As I have made a few remarks concerning some bishops

and divines, by occasion of matters falling out towards them CHAP.
this year; so I will subjoin the mention of a great soldier, XXX.
of special note for his skill in military affairs, and his im- Anno 1573.
provement of the discipline of war, somewhat relating to Bingham, a brave sol-
him occurring this present year. His name was Bingham, dier, recom-
(probably the same with sir Richard Bingham, a noted com- mended to the lord
mander of the queen's in the wars of Ireland, of whom treasurer.
Camden gives a very good character.) This man had done Camd. Eliz.
good service in the late northern rebellion, anno 1569; p. 567.
but now in mean circumstances. Which occasioned Mr. Rafe Lane.
Rafe Lane (under whom he bore arms in that rebellion) to
recommend him very earnestly to the lord treasurer Burghley. Which Lane was a man of great knowledge for conduct in war, and of singular art and industry in many other
respects: which made him very dear to that nobleman;
who made use of him, and listened to many of his projects
and proposals. This gentleman now interceded with the May the
said treasurer for Bingham, giving this account of him, 19th.
(whose memory therefore deserveth to be preserved in
our records,) " That in the suppression of the rebels in the
" north, the queen had his painful and faithful service un-
" der Lane's conduct. Where, as he assured his lordship,
" he put in practice as rare points of warlike discipline, and
" as likely to have wrought, (if they had come to any ser-
" vice,) as at any time in these parts within our age had
" been seen.

" That his long experience, since the latter end of king
" Edward's reign; having been in France, where all queen
" Mary's reign he served, and until this latter expedition;
" joining to his practice and natural good capacity also
" *theoretic*, (a thing to old soldiers, as they were all for the
" most part utterly void of the same,) would, when occa-
" sion should serve, make him hereafter to appear as sin-
" gular to others, as he for his part, not without good
" proof, did already so esteem of him. And further, that
" of his life he was unto the world unspotted. And that
" which was the seal of all the rest, he was not only of
" sincere judgment in religion, but also, being void of

G g 4

BOOK
I.

Anno 1573.
" those ceremonial superstitions [of popery,] even deeply
" touched with the fear of God, as his modest conversation
" with all men did partly witness. In which principal
" respect he was bold, (as he proceeded,) the rather to re-
" commend him unto his lordship's special goodness; as in
" that he knew from what foundation his lordship fetched
" the beginning of wisdom: which is referred to all our
" actions, as well temporal as spiritual. And for that, to be
" plain (he said) with his lordship, he seldom had found
" any of his occupation [i. e. soldiers] (the more to be
" pitied) that way so singularly given."

This was a character given by Mr. Lane (in the foresaid
letter) of Bingham, which he himself was the bringer of:
" Knowing with how favourable an eye his lordship beheld
308 " virtue, though clothed in never so poor a weed, (as the
" preface of the letter ran,) and knowing withal how exact
" a judge his lordship was thereof, and how hard to be de-
" ceived with a shadow where the ground wanted. That he
" was therefore the rather bold, humbly and heartily to re-
" commend unto his goodness the humble suit of that poor
" gentleman."

I add one passage more of this writer, to excite the said
lord's good-will; " That he assured him, that his goodness,
" that should be bestowed on him for his sustenance, should
" be, towards God, charity; and to her majesty, the en-
" abling, for her highness's service, the most sufficient man
" for every kind of martial function, that of his calling
" this land now held."

Characters
of the
queen's
courtiers.
Now having given an account of some particular persons,
I shall give a brief character of queen Elizabeth's chief
courtiers at this time; as I read it in a private letter of one
that was now a courtier himself, the lord Gilbert Talbot,
eldest son of the earl of Shrewsbury; which he sent to his
father the earl, from the court, dated the 10th of May:
Lord Tal-
bot's letter
to the earl
his father.
Epist. Co-
mit. Salop.
In Offic.
Armor.
Which letter ran to this tenor: " That by the conveniency
" of the bearer, he thought good to advertise his lordship
" of the state of some there at the court, as near as he had
" learned by his daily experience. That the lord treasurer,

" even after the old manner, dealt with matters of the state
" only, and bore himself very uprightly. That my lord of
" Leicester was very much with her majesty; and that she
" shewed to him the same great good affection that she was
" wont. And that of late he had endeavoured to please her
" more than heretofore. That there were two sisters then
" in court, very far in love with him, as they had been
" long; viz. my lady Sheffield and Frances Haworth. That
" they, belike striving who should love him better, were at
" great wars together. And that the queen liked not well
" of them, nor the better of him. That by this means there
" were spies over him. That my lord of Sussex [lord high
" chamberlain] went with the tide, and helped to back
" others. But his own credit was sober, considering his
" estate. He was very diligent in his office, and took great
" pains. That my lord of Oxford was lately grown into
" great credit: for the queen's majesty delighted more in
" his personage, and his dancing, and his valiantness, than
" in any other. And he thought Sussex backed him all that
" he could. That were it not for his fickle head, he would
" surely pass any of them shortly. That my lady Burghley
" unwisely had declared herself, as it were, jealous: which
" came to the queen's ears: whereat she had been not a
" little offended with her. But now she was reconciled
" again. At all these love-matters my lord treasurer winked;
" and would not meddle any way.

" That Hatton [vice-chamberlain] was still sick; and it
" was thought he would very hardly recover of his disease;
" for it was doubted it was in his kidneys. That the queen
" went almost every day to see how he did. That now there
" were devices, chiefly by Leicester, and not without Burgh-
" ley his knowledge, how to make Mr. Edward Dier, as great
" as ever was Hatton. For now in this time of Hatton's sick-
" ness, the time was convenient. That it was brought thus
" to pass: Dier lately was sick of a consumption, in great 309
" danger; and, as his lordship well knew, he had been in
" displeasure for two years. It was made the queen to be-
" lieve, that his sickness came because of the continuance of

" her displeasure towards him: so that unless she would
" favour him, he was like not to recover. And hereupon
" her majesty had forgiven him; and sent unto him a very
" comfortable message. And he now was recovered again.
" And this, he added, was the beginning of this device.
" And these things, he said, he learned of such young fel-
" lows as himself. Further, that Mr. Walsingham was
" come that day [May the 10th] to the court, [being re-
" turned from his embassy,] and that it was thought he
" should be made secretary; sir Tho. Smith, and he, both
" together, to execute that office. That he had not yet
" told any news, having no time as yet to talk thereof, for
" his being welcomed home by his friends."

And now to return again to the university. A great
controversy there had been in Bene't college in Cambridge,
between Mr. Aldrich the master, and the fellows, about a
statute of that college, which the master had broken, and so
had forfeited his headship. It was, that the head of that
house must within so many years after his election take the
degree of bachelor of divinity: which he had not done, nor
intended to do; and that upon some principles he had imbibed (it seems) against taking university degrees. The business was at first referred by Aldrich and the fellows to
the archbishop, who had been master of that college heretofore, and so was well acquainted with the true state of it.
But Aldrich afterwards took other measures, and declined
the archbishop; whose judgment he knew was to displace
him, as guilty of an absolute breach of statute, and so of
perjury: and appealed to the chancellor of that university.
To whom the archbishop's advice was, that the cause might
be brought up before the commissioners ecclesiastical,
whereof himself was one: the heads of the university, excepting against that, as an infringement of their privilege;
which was, that all causes of any of their members should
be examined and determined within themselves, exclusively
to all others; the said chancellor then recommended the
cause to the vice-chancellor, and other chief heads, and
after full examination thereof, to inform him how they

found it, and give him their judgment. Which after ma- CHAP.
ture deliberation they did; and sent the same at length in XXX.
their letter. This affair is at large shewn in the Life of Anno 1573.
Archbishop Parker. Only this declaration to the chancel- Book iv.
lor, how the matter stood, and their thoughts thereof, was ch. 37.
there omitted: which bringing the cause to a conclusion, I
here supply.

The sum then of their said letter was, "That his grace The judg-
" the archbishop was the fittest man to end that matter, as ment of di-
vers heads
" the college had formerly addressed their letter to him, of the uni-
" finally to determine it. They shewed, that the like sta- versity.
" tutes were in other colleges, binding the collegiates to be
" qualified diversly: and that for the not accomplishing
" thereof, they have been put by from their rooms: that it
" were a dangerous thing to admit an example in one house
" contrary to the rest. And that the plain meaning of the
" statute was, that whoso had not the qualification required,
" was not to enjoy that place.

" That the party had heretofore consented to the arch- 310
" bishop's resolution of the said doubt. And that seeing
" his lordship [their chancellor] had before advised Al-
" drich to commit his cause to his grace; therefore they
" had addressed their letters to him, not doubting of his
" singular care for the good estate of that house; they not
" thinking it best for them to set down the definitive sen-
" tence." The whole letter is worth preserving, shewing a
decision of an university statute, and containing the result
of the judgment of divers wise and learned heads of that
university at that time, viz. Byng, Perne, Hawford, Kelk,
and Whitgift. See it at length in the Appendix. Number
[XXXVI.]

Some books I find this year published, wherein religion Horarium,
was concerned. Which were as followeth. A book of devo- i. e. Howrs
tions, called *Horarium,* or, the *Horary;* printed with privi- of Prayer;
a book now
lege at London, by William Seres; having been set forth printed.
first with the queen's authority, anno 1560, for the help and
direction of pious people in their devotions and prayers.
Dr. Cosins set forth in the year 1626, (a fifth edition Cosins's De-
votions.
whereof appeared in the year 1638,) *A collection of private*

devotion in the practice of the ancient church, called, The Hours of Prayer, as they were much after this manner published by authority of queen Elizabeth, 1560. In the preface to which, he saith, " That those his daily prayers " and devotions in that his book, for the most part, were " after the same manner and division of hours, as hereto- " fore they had been published among us by high and sa- " cred authority. And now were also renewed, and more " fully set forth again; and that for four reasons. I. To " continue and preserve the authority of the ancient laws " and old godly canons of the church. Which were made " and set forth for this purpose, that men, before they set " themselves to pray, may know what to say, and avoid, as " much as might be, all extemporal effusions, and irksome " and indigested prayers. II. To let the world understand, " that they who gave it out, and accused us here in Eng- " land, to have set up a new church and a new faith, to " have abandoned all the forms of prayer and devotion, to " have taken away all religious exercises and prayers of our " forefathers, to have despised all the ancient ceremonies, " and cast behind us the blessed sacraments of Christ's ca-
Sand. de Schism. Anglic. Calvin. Turcism. Brist. De- monstr.
" tholic church : that these men did little else than betray " their own infirmities, and had more violence and will than " reason or judgment for what they said, &c. As may also " appear by the public liturgy, and other divine offices of " our church, agreeable to them which the *ancients* used. " III. That they who are already religiously given, and " whom lets and impediments do often hinder from being " partakers of the public, might have here a daily and de- " vout order of private prayer, wherein to exercise them- " selves, and to spend some hours of the day at least in " God's holy worship and service. IV. That those who " perhaps are but coldly this way yet affected, might by " others' example be stirred up to the like heavenly duty of " performing their daily and Christian devotions to Al- " mighty God." This book had the approbation and li- cence of archbishop Abbot, Feb. 22, 1626. And as those were the causes of publishing the same so often then, so

no doubt, upon the same account, it was thought fit to be CHAP.
set forth twice in queen Elizabeth's reign. XXX.

In this year also came forth another little book of Latin Anno 1573.
prayers and lessons, for the use of schools, entitled, *Preces* 311
privatæ in studiosorum gratiam collectæ: et regia aucto- Preces pri-
ritate approbatæ: noviter impressæ. Printed by William tin Prayers
Seres. It contained, I. A calendar, together with various for Schools.
rules; as, concerning the year, with its parts: an economi-
cal table; wherein every one is admonished of his duty, in
whatsoever state of life he is. II. A catechism: which is
the same with our church catechism, but ending at the
Lord's prayer, expounded. III. Morning prayers. IV.
Evening prayers. V. Select prayers concerning the nativity of Christ, of his passion, of his resurrection, ascension,
and mission of the Holy Ghost, and of the holy Trinity.
VI. The Psalms; which they call the *penitential.* VII.
Other select psalms for the queen. VIII. *Flores Psalmo-*
rum. IX. To obtain remission of sins. X. Pious meditations of the frailty of life; the hope of the resurrection, &c.
XI. Prayers out of the Bible. XII. Prayers, or holy ejaculations. XIII. Other pious prayers. XIV. The blessings of the table, &c. XV. Other miscellaneous matters
added at the end. And lest any might make some objec-
tion against using prayers in Latin, as bordering upon the
popish Latin mass, the editor set forth a preface in this behalf; applying himself to the reader, that in setting forth
these Latin prayers, he intended not that such as were ignorant of the Roman tongue should repeat and use them,
when they were not by him understood: for that was very
far from his purpose. But that he caused them to be printed
for the sake only of such as were skilful and studious in the
Latin tongue, if they were minded to use them. But that
as for others that knew not that idiom, he exhorted and admonished them, that they should accustom themselves to
prayers written in the mother tongue, and be instant in
them, and make them familiar to them; lest, while they
willingly prayed in an unknown tongue, their minds, as St.
Paul said, in the mean time, be void of all fruit. And of

BOOK I.

Three sermons of Lever set forth.

Gualter's Homilies upon the First Epist. to the Corinthians.

The Works of Tyndal, Frith, and Barnes, set forth.

this he warned his reader again and again. And prayed the reader to take notice of this, that he might not misjudge what he had done.

This year also were set forth three sermons heretofore preached in great audiences by Tho. Lever, a very learned and pious professor of true religion, some time head of St. John's college, Cambridge, and an exile under queen Mary, now master of Sherborn hospital. The first preached in the shrouds at St. Paul's upon Rom. xiii. *Let every soul be subject to the higher powers.* The second before king Edward, upon St. John vi. 5. *When Jesus then lift up his eyes, and saw a great company come unto him, he saith unto Philip, Whence shall we buy bread, that these may eat?* The third at St. Paul's Cross, upon 1 Cor. iv. 1. *Let a man so esteem of us, as ministers of Christ, and disposers of the mysteries of God.*

Now also (or rather the end of the former year) did Rodolphus Gualter, a learned minister of Zuric, in Helvetia, and of great esteem with our bishops and divines, set forth his homilies in Latin, upon the First Epistle to the Corinthians; and dedicated his book to divers of the English bishops, namely, such as had been exiles at Zuric, and other cities in those parts; as Grindal, Sandes, Cox, Horne, Pilkington, Parkhurst, &c. To this last the book was delivered in December: and the next month, the said bishop, in a letter, shewed that learned man, how acceptable the present was to him, and professed in what part he took it, that he [Gualter] joined him with those other worthy and learned bishops in the dedication. In that prefatory epistle, (which was dated the calends of August, 1572,) that reverend author did learnedly treat of the dignity and unity of the church: wherein he shewed, that none ought rashly to depart from its society; and lamented those great and lamentable divisions in this church of England, by reason of those that scrupled the apparel appointed to ministers.

This year also came forth, printed by John Day, *The whole Works of William Tyndal, John Frith, and Dr. Barnes, three worthy martyrs, and principal teachers of this church of England. Collected and compiled in one* *tome, being before scattered, and now in print here exhi-* *bited to the church; to the praise of God, and profit of good* *Christian readers. Mortui resurgent.* It appears, by the subscription to the preface, to have been set forth by John Fox, the martyrologist. Which three he called there, *chief ringleaders in these latter times of the church of England:* and added, that we have reason to praise God for such good books left to the church. As for Tyndal, of him he saith, that he was commonly called, *the apostle of England:* " Such was his modesty, zeal, charity, and painful " travail; and that he never sought for any thing less than " for himself; for nothing more than for Christ's glory, " and the edification of others: for whose sake he bestowed " not only his labour, but his life and blood also. As the " apostles of the primitive age first planted the church in " truth of the gospel; so the same truth being again de- " faced and decayed, by enemies in this our latter time, " there was none that travailed more earnestly in restoring " of the same in this realm of England than did William " Tyndall."

To William Tyndall he joined John Frith and D. Barnes. " For that they, together with him, in one cause, and about " one time, sustained the brunt in this our latter age, and " gave the first onset against the enemies; and also for the " special gifts of fruitful erudition, and plentiful knowledge " wrought in them by God; and so by them left unto us in " their writings."

And he wished the like diligence had been used in search- ing after and collecting the works and writings of Wickliff, Purvey, Clark, Brute, Thorp, Huss, Hierom. But the art of printing being not yet invented, their worthy works were the sooner abolished. Such was then the wickedness of those days, and the practice of prelates then so crafty, that no good book could appear, though it were the scripture itself, in English, but it was restrained, and so consumed; as Fox judged.

He added, that in these works of Tyndal, Frith, and

Barnes, was to be found matter, not only of doctrine to inform thee, of comfort to delight thee, and of godly ensample to direct thee; but also of special admiration, to make thee wonder at the works of the Lord, so mightily working in these men, so opportunely in stirring them up, so graciously in assisting them.

313   And this gave occasion to this church historian, Mr. Fox, to subjoin, that the further he looked back into those former times of Tyndal, Frith, and other like, more simplicity, with true zeal and humble modesty, he saw, with less corruption of affection in them: and yet with these days of ours, I find, said he, no fault.

And then shewing his reason for publishing these works, that it was according to the promise that he had made in his Acts and Monuments, of spending some diligence in collecting and setting abroad the books of those martyrs (whereof he wrote) together, as many as could be found; to remain as perpetual lamps, shining in the churches, to give light to all posterity.

A Summary of Chronicles by John Stow.   John Stow, citizen of London, now set forth, in a small thick volume, *A summary of the Chronicles of England; from the first coming in of Brute into this land, until the year* 1573. Diligently collected, corrected, and enlarged by the author. It was dedicated by him to Robert earl of Leicester. And that partly, " because of his lordship's in-" clination to all sorts of knowledge; and especially the " great love he bore to the old records of deeds done by fa-" mous and noble worthies." In the same epistle dedicatory he shews the business and purpose of his book; viz. to be a " brief summary of the chiefest chances and acci-" dents that had happened in the realm to that age wherein " he lived." And that what he had done was " by confer-" ence of many ancient authors;" those he meant that were commonly called *chronicles*. Out of which he had gathered many notable things, as he said, most worthy of remembrance; which no man to that time had noted in our vulgar tongue.

Authors by him made use of.   The authors he made use of, both in Latin and English,

are set down by him in his said Summary, to a very great
number: which bespeak him a laborious antiquarian; besides his converse with many epistles, epitaphs, and other
pamphlets of antiquity for his purpose. There is moreover
in this his Summary, worthy our mention, another list of
many ancient writers of English history, with his account
and character of each of them, and their books, and times
wherein they lived; beginning with Asserus Menevensis.
Of whom, for a specimen, I will repeat what he writes.

"Asserus Menevensis. A man of great holiness and
"learning: who was sent for from St. David's, in Wales,
"by king Alfrede, and by him made bishop of Shirburne,
"now called Salisbury. It is said, that king Alfrede erected
"the school or university of Oxford. But this Asserus,
"writing purposely, diligently, and honourably, of king
"Alfred's noble acts, maketh no mention of it. Divers
"there be, and those ancient writers, which attribute all to
"the English school at Rome. Which the late, without
"consideration, do speak of Oxford." Asserus flourished
in the year after Christ's birth 890. In this Summary he
set down under each year the names of the mayors and
sheriffs; and throughout the book many remarkable passages of history relating to the city of London.

The queen's progress this summer was into Kent. She
set out from Greenwich the 14th of July. Thence to Croy-
don, to the archbishop's house; where she stayed seven
days. Thence to Orpington, the house of sir Percival Hart.
Thence to her own house, Knolle. Thence to Birlingham,
the lord Burgavennies. Thence to Eridge, another house 314
of that lord. Thence to Bedgbury, Mr. Culpepper's house.
Thence to Hempsted, Mr. Guilford's. Thence to Rye. So
to Sisingherst, Mr. Baker's, whom she knighted. Thence to
Bocton Malherb, to Mr. Tho. Wotton's there. Thence to
Mr. Tufton's at Hotherfield. Thence to her own house,
Westenhanger: the keeper whereof was the lord Buckhurst. And so to Dover. When she departed from thence,
at Folkston she was met with the archbishop of Canterbury
and the lord Cobham, and a great many knights and gen-

BOOK
I.

Anno 1573.

Some account of her journey.

Life of Abp. Parker, b. iv. ch. 30.

The French ambassador at Canterbury, the queen being there.

tlemen of that county, and so conducted to Canterbury, and lodged at the old palace of St. Augustine's: and treated by the archbishop, as we shall hear by and by. From Canterbury (where she tarried a fortnight) she passed to Sittingburn; and so to Rochester. Thence to her own house at Dartford. And at last came safely to Greenwich again.

From Mr. Gilford's house, (where she was August the 10th,) the lord Burghley, in a letter to the earl of Shrewsbury, gave this short account of their journey hitherto: " That the queen had a hard beginning of her progress in " the wild of Kent; and namely in some part of Sussex: " where surely were more dangerous rocks and valleys, as " he said, and much worse ground, than was in the Peak. " That they were bending to Rye; and so afterwards to " Dover; where, as he added, they should have amends." I will rehearse also the conclusion that lord made in his letter; wherein having mentioned the earl's noble seat of Chattesworth, that was then, as it seems, in building or adorning, " I must end with my most hearty commenda- " tions to your lordship, and my good lady, wishing myself " with her at Chattesworth; where I think I should see a " great alteration to my good liking. From the court at " Mr. Guilford's house."

In her passing, (I say,) she visited Canterbury. How magnificently she was received and entertained here by archbishop Parker, I have related elsewhere. This I only add, that while she was here, the French ambassador came to her. Who hearing the excellent music in the cathedral church, extolled it up to the sky, and brake out into these words: " O God! I think no prince beside, in all Europe, " ever heard the like; no, not our holy father, the pope " himself." A young gentleman that stood by, replied, " Ah! do you compare our queen to the knave of Rome; " or rather prefer him before her?" Whereat the ambassador was highly angered, and told it to some of the counsellors. They bade him be quiet, and take it patiently: for the boys, said they, with us do so call him, and the Roman Antichrist too. He departed with a sad countenance. This

passage, bishop Parkhurst wrote to Gualter of Zuric, in his CHAP.
correspondence with him. This French ambassador dined ——XXX.——
with the queen at the archbishop's palace : his title was *comes* Anno 1573.
Rhetius; with whom the queen after dinner had much discourse.

In the middle of the Latin Life of Archbishop Parker,
entitled *Matthæus*, there is a large blank left, as may be observed in the said Latin Life, printed in the Appendix to Nᵒ. XC.
the Life and Acts of that archbishop. In which blank P. 162.
place should have stood a particular description of the
queen's progress; and of her coming in her said progress to
Canterbury, and her most splendid entertainment by the 315
archbishop there. This undoubtedly was omitted by that
archbishop's order, to prevent any censures of him that
might be made thereupon. Yet the said description was
printed in that void place, in some few copies, rarely to be
(now especially) met withal. A worthy learned man, and a Rev. T. Ba-
great searcher after such curiosities, having obtained one of ker, Th. B.
these copies, communicated that material, omitted part of
the archbishop's history to me, which, on this occasion, I
have put into the Appendix as a great rarity: wherein the Number
queen's coming to that city, and reception both at the ca- XXXVII.
thedral and palace, is more largely related; and her departure thence, and the rest of her progress homeward.

It was sad to consider, that notwithstanding the restora- Wickedness
tion of the gospel under this queen, and that the bishops mouth.
and officers of the church did what they could in the exercise of discipline, for the restraint of sin and wickedness, as
adultery, fornication, profanation of the Lord's day, wrongs
done in matters testamentary, and the like; yet these transgressions did abound very much: as in other places, so I
find particularly in the town of Yarmouth, in the diocese
of Norwich. Notwithstanding the bishop had a commissary
there, on purpose to watch over and take care of those
parts; and as occasion served, to inform the bishop of any
irregularities and misdemeanours. But all little enough.
Insomuch, that two well-disposed persons, viz. Mr. Bacon
and Mr. Meek, bailiffs of Yarmouth, desired the bishop to

BOOK I.

Anno 1573.

The bishop of Norwich to the bailiffs there.

exercise his authority, and to punish wickedness. To which the bishop gravely and willingly condescended: " Commending their godly intent herein; adding, that all he " and they, with all his officers, could do, was too little; " sin did so much abound, and punishment thereof was so " slack. And that if he might perceive any default in his " officers, being thereof by them advertised, he would see " it amended. This notwithstanding he required of them, " that his commissary should not be interrupted in his of- " fice doing. And thus concluded, beseeching Almighty " God, that himself and they all might be earnestly bent, " that sin might be punished, to the example of the world, " whereby it might be left off." This letter was dated in November.

The unseasonable weather this year.

A dearth.

The season and weather this year I may be allowed to give a short hint of, since the abovesaid bishop thought fit to write of it as far as into Helvetia, to his learned friends, Gualter and Bullinger, there. That from November the last year, to Whitsuntide this, it was almost perpetual winter: for the cold winds, *eurus, aquilo, et septentrio*, that is, the east, north-east, and north, all that time only blew. The warm south and south-west never, or rarely. Yet there was scarcely snow or frost before candlemas. And then the country abounded with both. Which caused a very great dearth, not only of bread, but of all other things. Which the pious bishop attributed to this cause; because charity grew so cold. But in the latter end of June, notwithstanding, there appeared better hopes, and the standing corn every where very promising. But the harvest was not begun, especially in Norfolk, till Bartholomew-tide; and that a very moist and rainy season; scarce a fair day in the 316 whole harvest. So that no small part of the corn perished. However, the greatest part was saved by the unwearied pains and diligence of the harvest-men.

CHAP. XXXI.

Bullinger and Gualter, their judgments of the new dis-
cipline. The exercises : in what order and manner per-
formed in Hertfordshire ; by the direction of the bishop
of Lincoln. The exercises forbidden in the diocese of
Norwich. Some privy counsellors write to the bishop of
Norwich in favour of them : which occasions his letter to
the bishop of London for direction ; and to the bishop of
Rochester. Notice given to the archbishop of the sup-
pression of them. Not suppressed in other dioceses. The
book of the Troubles at Frankford printed. Reprinted,
1642. Some pretend to cast out devils. Account of two
persons afflicted with Satan, in a letter of the bishop
of Norwich to Bullinger. An innovation in the cathedral
church of Norwich. The bishop's letters thereupon. Ari-
anism and the family of love in Cambridgeshire.

AN argument of the correspondence held the year 1574, Anno 1574.
between some of the English bishops, and their old friends The judgment of the
of Zuric in Switzerland, was concerning those that laboured divines of
to bring in a ruling presbytery into this church, instead of Zuric concerning the
bishops; and for taking away their revenues, and putting innovators.
them to better uses. These were not approved of by those
divines. Bullinger, the chief of them, in a letter, dated May
the 10th, 1574, writ thus to one of our bishops concerning
these innovators. " They imitate, in mine opinion, those Bullinger's
" seditious tribunes of Rome, who, by virtue of the Agra- Surv. of
" rian law, bestowed the public goods, that they might en- the pretended holy
" rich themselves. That is, that you [the bishops] being discipl.
" overthrown, they might succeed in your places, &c. But Edit. 1593.
p. 452.
" they go about to erect a church, which they shall never
" advance as they desire ; neither if they should, can they
" ever be able to continue it." And after, in the same letter, " I would to God there were not in the authors of this
" presbytery *libido dominandi,* an ambitious desire of rule
" and principality. Nay, I think it ought especially to be
" provided for, that there be not any high authority given

BOOK   " to this presbytery. Whereof many things might be said;
I.   " but time will reveal many things which yet lie hid."

Anno 1574.   And Gualter, another divine at Zuric this same year, in
Gualter to   his letter to Sandys, bishop of London, delivered his mind
the bishop
of London.   thus concerning the discipline : " I understand that the strife
Ubi supra.   " among you, procured by certain turbulent innovators,
" doth wax hot ; and that they are gone so far, that under
317 " the plausible title of *good order and discipline,* they de-
" sire the whole government and policy of the church of
" England to be utterly overthrown. Surely I should
" mervaile at the immodesty and wilful desire of contention
" in these men, but that I see the same is practised else-
" where ; especially where the authority of the brethren of
" Geneva is so greatly esteemed, that Geneva is accounted
" the oracle of all Christendom. God hath indeed adorned
" that church with diverse excellent gifts, and the ministers
" thereof. Among whom, master Beza I have always re-
" verenced and loved ; and do so still. But yet I would
" wish them *modestius et humilius sapere :* and not seek
" to draw their shoe upon every man's foot, &c. What
" hath been done in the Palsgrave's country, as I writ unto
" you before." Which period of his former letter to the bishop of London, which Gualter here refers to, I will here
set down, for better clearing of the following part of his
letter.

" It was of late decreed by the minister of Heidelberg,
" that no man should be admitted to the Lord's supper,
" except he first offered himself to the pastor. For St.
" Paul's rule is not held sufficient there, viz. that every
" man should try himself. The elders did not agree to this
" decree. But yet notwithstanding it is urged in the name
" of the presbytery, nay, of the whole church, &c. There is
" there an Helvetian governor of the college of St. Denis,
" as innocent and godly a man as liveth. Howbeit Oliva-
" nus, the pastor, warned him by the crier of the presby-
" tery, in the name of all the elders, that he should not
" come to the Lord's supper. Adding this cause, that he
" could not admit him *absque animi sui offensione,* without

" the offence of his own mind. The party took this dealing CHAP.
" (as was reason) in ill part, and desired to know what he XXXI.
" had committed that deserved such a punishment. But they Anno 1574.
" answered him not otherwise, than that they continued in
" the same mind. Whereupon he offered a supplication to
" the prince elector, that he would compel them to shew
" the fault, if there were any, that he had committed. But
" to this day he could extort nothing else in effect from
" them. This is their goodly order; this their discipline."
And now I go on in Gualter's second letter, where I left off.

   " Surely the state there, [in the Palsgrave's country,] as
" touching discipline, and the government of the church, all
" men that come thence do say, it is worse than it was be-
" fore. And it is sure that many do repent that they ever
" admitted those men's counsel. But yet the Genevians do
" still endeavour to thrust their discipline upon all churches.
" And if they shall deny this, they may be sufficiently con-
" vinced by the books of theological examples that Beza
" published this other year. That they suggest their argu-
" ments and counsels, not only to you Englishmen, but in
" like sort to the Germans, Phrysians, Polonians, and Hun-
" garians. Whereby, among those that agreed well before,
" *rixæ et turbæ enascuntur,* brawlings and quarrels do
" arise, &c." And so having signified what troubles the innovators beyond the seas, as well as in England, did procure, he moved the bishop to do as he and Mr. Bullinger
did : that is, to moderate such busy wits (as they might)
for a time. " For (saith he) *spero, ædificium novæ disci-*
" *plinæ brevi propria mole ruiturum,* &c. I hope the frame 318
" of this new discipline will, in short time, fall of itself;
" considering that now it appears sufficiently, many are now
" become weary of it, that had it before in admiration."

   The same Helvetian divine wrote also this year to another Gualter to
bishop, his correspondent, namely, the bishop of Ely, upon the bishop
of Ely, p.
the same argument, two letters : which may be read in the 454.
Survey of the pretended holy discipline. In one whereof,
dated Aug. 20, are these words: " I shall not need to use
" many words, what I think of your *innovators,* sith I have

" done it in my last letters.   And surely I am greatly con-
" firmed in my former opinion, by the examples which such
" like innovators in Germany do bring forth.   *Video enim*
" *illis nominibus nihil ambitiosius, nihil insolentius, nihil*
" *ineptius fingi possit.*   For whereas there are many things
" most wickedly done by them daily, yet they are not
" ashamed to pretend the zeal of God, in excuse of those
" things, which, contrary to the word of God, they devise
" most wickedly and maliciously against the servants of
" Christ.   But as far as I can conjecture, many, by whose
" counsel and assistance the frame of this discipline was
" chiefly erected, are now ashamed of them."

Exercises among the ministers and curates of churches
(called *prophesyings*, from the apostle's word, 1 Cor. xiv.)
were now used in most dioceses.   The main end whereof
was for the inciting those that were in orders to apply themselves to the study and understanding of the holy scripture;
and to enable them to make profitable sermons, and to
preach in their several cures and parochial charges.   In
order to these exercises, the clergy were sorted into divers
competent companies or societies, by subscription of their
names; and particular churches and days appointed, and
the persons named to exercise and perform in their order:
and the rest, after the exercise was over, were to judge of
what had been spoken; and a moderator to be present, to
determine and conclude all.   That which was to be done at
these meetings was, that a certain portion of scripture given
should be handled by some of them assigned thereto, by
way of explication, and apt observations to be deduced from
thence.   The moderator was nominated by the bishop of
the diocese, as likewise the order of the whole allowed by
him.

This was practised, to the great benefit and improvement
of the clergy: many of whom, in those times, were ignorant, both in scripture and divinity.   In October this year,
the bishop of Lincoln settled orders and moderators for
these prophesyings in that part of Hertfordshire that lay in
his diocese, with his own hand subscribed to them; and the

like, no question, in the other parts of his see. It may be
worth recording the paper: which was in this tenor:

"First, It is thought meet, your exercises shall be kept
"every other week, upon the Thursdays, from nine of the
"clock in the forenoon until eleven, and not past. So that
"the first speaker exceed not three quarters of an hour, nor
"the two last half an hour between them both. The rem-
"nant of the time to be left for the moderator. If the
"Thursday shall fall out to be some holyday, then, &c."
[to be considered on what other day they were to be observed: as in the orders for these exercises in the diocese of 319
Chester. Some years after, I find they were ordered on the
Tuesday before by Chaderton the bishop.]

"A table of the names of the speakers being made, it
"may easily be known who should speak, whereof, at what
"time, and in what place, what course every man is bound
"to keep in his own person: except upon urgent occasion
"he be hindered. And then may he substitute a sufficient
"deputy: yet such an one as belongeth to our exercise:
"whose name shall be signified to the moderator before.
"So that the place be never destitute; and the brethren
"may know whom to look for.

"All the speakers ought carefully to keep them to the
"text; abstaining from heaping up of many testimonies,
"allegations of profane histories, exhortations, applications,
"common places, and divisions, not aptly grounded upon
"the text: not falling into controversies of our present
"time or state: neither glancing closely or openly at any
"persons, public or private; much less confuting one an-
"other. But contrariwise, all their care ought to be to rip
"up the text; to shew the sense of the Holy Ghost; and
"briefly, pithily, and plainly to observe such things as
"hereafter may well be applied in preaching, concerning
"either doctrine or manners.

"The text may be handled in this sort: if first, we shew,
"whether it depend of former words, or no. And how, and
"upon what occasion the words were spoken, the fact done,

" or the history rehearsed : so that this be soundly gathered
" out of the scriptures: the drift and scope of the words,
" and the plain meaning of that place of scripture, is to be
" opened : the property of the words to be noted, whether a
" figure, or no: the use of the like phrase of scripture in
" other places: reconciling such places as seem to repugn :
" lay forth the arguments used in the text: shew the vir-
" tues and vices contained or mentioned therein ; and to the
" fulfilling or breach of which commandment they belong.
" How the present text hath been wrested by the adversa-
" ries : and how and wherein they have been deceived.
" What points observed that may serve for confirmation of
" faith, and exhortation to sanctification of life, against oc-
" casion shall be offered of preaching.

" After the first speaker hath ended, the second is to
" speak of the same text, and in the same order: having a
" careful respect to add, and not to repeat; to beware, as
" much as in him lieth, that he utter no contradiction to
" the former speaker. If it fall out the former shall give
" out any false doctrine, the public confutation and qualify-
" ing of the words is to be left to the moderator: and the
" matter itself further to be handled privately, by the
" brethren. The same order in the same text hath the
" third speaker to keep. And both of them, as the rest, are
" bound not to exceed the time.

" Prayers ought to be made by the first speaker for the
" whole state of the church, at the beginning of the exercise
" shortly; and at the end by the moderator: namely, for
" the queen's majesty: by whose good means God hath
" granted us liberty to proceed cheerfully in such exercises.
" Especially, we have to pray for the grace of God's holy
320 " Spirit, for truth, unity, reverence, discretion, and dili-
" gence in our ministry. The form of prayer is further to
" be prescribed.

" Our exercise shall be had only and wholly in the Eng-
" lish tongue ; avoiding allegation of scripture, fathers, pro-
" fane authors, &c. in the Latin, for spending of time : un-

" less the force of some Latin or Greek word, for further
" instruction, be shewed as a thing most necessarily to be
" noted, where ability will serve.

" The exercise ended, the brethren coming together, [the
" assembly being dismissed,] and the first speaker for that
" time put apart, and all, so many as have not given their
" names to our exercise, secluded; the moderator shall re-
" quire of the brethren, by order, their judgments concern-
" ing the first speaker, for whose cause chiefly the day's
" meeting and assembly hath been. First, how sound his
" doctrine; how he kept his text, or wherein he swerved;
" how truly scripture expounded, and testimonies alleged;
" how he hath observed our order of prophesy; how plain
" or obscure his words; how modest his speech or gesture;
" how seemly, reverend, and sober his whole action in the
" exercise hath been; and wherein he failed. Withal is to
" be considered, how some of his words doubtfully spoken
" may be charitably expounded and construed in the better
" part. This done, the first speaker must be contented to
" be admonished by the moderator, and the rest of the
" brethren, of such things as shall seem to the company
" worthy admonition. The same inquiry is to be made of
" the life of the speakers in their course. That we may all
" be reformed both in doctrine and in life.

" In this consultation, and after this admonition to the
" speakers, shall be moved, by any of the brethren, any
" doubt that justly might rise of the text, and not yet an-
" swered by any of the speakers. Wherein he is to be re-
" solved by the speakers and moderator: but if he seem not
" yet so fully satisfied, and the question of importance, by
" consent of the brethren, it shall be deferred, until the next
" exercise, for the first speaker for that time to handle, in
" the entrance of that day's prophesy. Further, none of
" the speakers shall take upon him publicly to make an-
" swer, unless he be able presently, pithily, and plainly to
" answer the same.

" No man shall willingly shun the exercise, or fail in his
" course; neither shew himself disordered, or refuse, or

" stomach such brotherly admonition as is to be used; nei-
" ther speak publicly or privately against any good order
" taken by the brethren, and ratified by our ordinary. And
" if any shall so do, and be found therein incorrigible, we
" have leave to put out his name in the table, till he be re-
" formed. And in the mean while we are to signify his
" fault unto the bishop.

" The appointing of the ministers to our exercises be-
" longeth unto our ordinary. Neither are we to place any
" to the same, but such as shall be admitted by him, and
" those whosoever shall first yield to the observation of
" these orders, and testify the same by their subscription."

321

The bishop's allowance.

The bi-
shop's al-
lowance.

" These orders of exercise offered to me by the learned
" of the clergy of Hertfordshire, I think good and godly,
" and greatly making to the furtherance of true doctrine,
" and the increase of godly knowledge in them that are not
" as yet able to preach: specially, if the same rules be so-
" berly, with wisdom and discretion, observed. Therefore
" I earnestly exhort and require all such, as will not shew
" themselves to be backward in religion, and hinderers of
" the truth, diligently to observe the same, and resort unto
" the exercise. Or if they will not presently, upon the
" warning of the moderators, to appear before me, to yield
" an account, why they will not submit themselves to so
" godly and profitable an exercise.

" Nevertheless, I require, that you admit not any to be
" president or moderator in that exercise, but such as I have
" allowed by this present subscription, before that I, upon
" particular trial, shall accept and allow the same. Nor
" shall you permit any stranger to speak among you, but
" such as you know will stay himself within the compass of
" these orders, and not break them, to the defaming of the
" present state of the church of England. Or if any shall
" so do, be he stranger or other, that presently one of the
" moderators stay him, that he proceed not therein. This
" 26th of October, anno 1574.

" Thomas Lincoln."

" For this present time, until I have further trial of
" others, I appoint the chief moderators, these whose names
" are subscribed, one at least of which I require always to
" be at the exercise: Mr. Horn of Hempsted, Mr. Mount-
" ford of Tuynge, Mr. Hammond of Leachwould, Mr. Pot-
" kin of Lilly.

" All which I require to have diligent care of the ob-
" servation of the former orders, as they will answer to the
" contrary."

These exercises or prophesyings were practised at Holt,
and other places in the diocese of Norwich, by the countenance and encouragement of that bishop, till in the very
beginning of this year, 1574, when the archbishop of Canterbury had received a command from the queen (who had
heard they were abused) to send to all the bishops of his
province, to put them down. The bishop of Norwich was
surprised, when the archbishop sent this order to him; and
being willing to suppose he meant only the regulation of
the abuses thereof, shewed the archbishop, how these exercises daily brought singular benefit to the church of God,
as well to the clergy as laity; and that it was a right necessary exercise to be continued, if it were not abused.
Which he acknowledged had been once or twice by busy
speakers against conformity in religion. But that they had
been silenced, until they should subscribe the articles, &c.

In this very time (which was the beginning of May)
Grindal, bishop of London, and three others of the privy
council, sir Francis Knowles, sir Walter Mildmay, and sir
Tho. Smith, secretary of state, wrote to the bishop of Norwich, commending much those exercises used in his diocese;
and advised that they might not be hindered or stayed, but
might proceed and go forward, to God's glory, and edifying
of the people. This was writ May the 6th. Of this letter
the bishop soon acquainted the archbishop; whose order
from the queen seemed contrary to this of the queen's counsellors. Wherefore the archbishop desired to know what
those privy counsellors' warrant was for their so writing
unto him. This caused the said bishop of Norwich to de-

Marginal notes:
CHAP. XXXI.

Anno 1574.
The mode-
rators ap-
pointed.

Exercises in
the diocese
of Norwich
forbidden.

322
Some privy
counsellors
write to the
bishop of
Norwich in
favour of
the exer-
cises.

BOOK
I.

Anno 1574.

His letter
to the bi-
shop of
London
about this
matter.

spatch a letter to the bishop of London (who was known to
favour the exercises) for instructions what answer to make
to the archbishop: importing, " That he had received from
" him, and the said three privy counsellors, letters to this
" effect, that whereas certain godly exercises of *prophesying*
" were used in these parts, and some not well disposed to-
" wards true religion, did speak evil, and slander the same,
" that he should notwithstanding proceed and go forward
" in the same; so as no seditious, hypocritical, or schisma-
" tical doctrines were taught or maintained in the same, &c.
" And that not long before the receipt of their letters, he
" had word sent him by a chaplain of my lord of Canter-
" bury's grace, that the queen's commandment was, that
" these exercises should be suppressed: and that now lately
" his grace, understanding that he [the bishop of Norwich]
" had received these letters from his lordship and the rest,
" willed him to let him understand what their warrant was;
" since her majesty, as his grace wrote, had commanded
" him to write to all his brethren of this province to the
" contrary. That therefore, before he should do any thing
" in answer to his grace, he thought good to signify thus
" much to his lordship: praying him of his friendly advice
" herein. That neither his duty might be neglected, in an-
" swering his grace's request; nor the same answer to be
" such as might offend his lordship and the rest of the
" honourable, that had written for the continuance of that
" godly exercise of expounding the scriptures: which un-
" doubtedly had brought singular benefit to the church of
" God. This was dated May 28, from Ludham."

And as he wrote the former letter to the bishop of London, so, being loath to be an instrument of forbidding a
matter of such excellent use to the church, as he esteemed
it, he wrote to another bishop, Freke, bishop of Rochester,
the queen's great almoner, for his thoughts and advice
about the same matter. The answer, it seems, given him
by both these right reverend bishops, however they approved the exercises, at this juncture, was, to comply.

And as the bishop had consulted with these two court

prelates concerning this weighty matter, so for his own satis- CHAP.
faction he thought fit to communicate it to some of his XXXI.
learned and discreet brethren of the clergy, to confer with Anno 1574.
them about it. One Matchet also, a chaplain of the arch- gusted at
bishop's, coming down into those parts, had reported it to his letter in
divers. Whereby the archbishop's letter of stopping the ex- the diocese.
ercises got wind in that diocese, and gave great occasion of
talk there : which, coming to his grace's ears, gave him
some disgust. For which the bishop of Norwich thus vin- 323
dicated himself ; " That whereas his grace seemed to mislike,
" that he should communicate with his friends concerning
" such matters as he [the archbishop] wrote in his letters,
" that if the cause were weighty, he could not but think it
" needful to take advice. And yet," he added, " that he im-
" parted not such matter to many, or to talkative persons.
" And that concerning such public commandments as could
" hardly be kept close, others in such matters were to be
" suspected, rather than himself, for opening them to their
" ears and handling ; to whom they came before he heard
" or received them : as particularly that commandment
" which his grace sent for the suppressing of prophesies,
" written in a letter to Matchet his chaplain : and the same
" uttered to sundry persons, after he had an understanding
" thereof."

But our bishop obeyed, and sent to his chancellor, that These exer-
being commanded by the archbishop, in the queen's name, cises suppressed.
that the prophesying throughout his diocese should be suppressed ; therefore, that he should give notice to every one
of his commissaries, that in their several circuits they should
suppress the same.

And so the bishop signified to the archbishop, concerning Signified by
his conformity to the queen's commandment, together with the bishop
to the arch-
some account of the letter late written to him from the privy bishop.
counsellors : " That it might like his grace to understand,
" that certain, of good place and great credit, had writ unto
" him not long since, not by the way of any warrant, but as
" giving advice ; that, so as nothing was brought in ques-
" tion, tending to controversy and frivolous contention, or

BOOK "contrary to her majesty's commandment, or laws esta-
I.   "blished, the exercise of prophesying might well be con-
Anno 1574. "tinued. But notwithstanding, knowing from his grace,
"that her majesty's commandment was, that the same
"should be suppressed through his grace's province, he
"had already stayed them himself in some places, and had
"commanded his officers to suppress the same throughout
"his diocese. This was dated June the 7th."

The conten-   The ministers of this diocese indeed seemed to be more
tion among contentious about orders and usages of the church prescrib-
the minis-
ters. The ed, as, what bread was to be used in the Lord's supper,
occasion
thereof.   whether wafer or common loaf bread, as well as other ob-
servances: and these controversies brought unseasonably
into their exercises; thus disputing upon things established.
The report whereof came up (as it is like) to the ears of the
court: which might give occasion to the staying of them in
Not-yet   this diocese particularly. For the archbishop had not sent
forbidden
in other   the like order to other dioceses; as appears by the bishop of
dioceses.   Rochester's answer to the bishop of Norwich's letter, above
mentioned: which was to this purpose, (after he had observed that the bishop had liked and allowed of his advice;) "That whereas his lordship would understand, whe-
"ther the like commandment were generally given through-
"out this province, I must tell your lordship, answered
"he, that I hear of no such commandment, neither in Lon-
"don diocese, neither yet in mine, nor elsewhere. But
"then he added, that the bishop of London himself, and
"others, had taken such order, that no man within any of
"their dioceses, in any matter of controversy, shall have
324 "any thing to do. And so, by this means, the exercise is
"continued, to the comfort of God's church, increase of
"knowledge in the ministry, without offence. And so he
"doubted nothing but so it should do within his diocese
"[of Norwich,] if his lordship would observe the like order.
"And so resting, and taking his leave of his lordship.
"Dated from the court the 13th of June."

How these exercises came afterwards more peremptorily
to be put down, and what displeasure the queen conceived

against archbishop Grindal for his refusal to do it, may be CHAP.
seen at large in that archbishop's Life, with his plain and XXXI.
excellent letter to the queen, in favour of the same, and in Anno 1574.
excuse of himself.   Book ii.
                                                           ch. 8.
But notwithstanding some stops put to these exercises, The exer-
they were generally so approved, in regard of the benefit of cises in the
them, in bringing in the knowledge of the scriptures among Chester.
both ministers and people, the better to confirm all against
the errors and superstitions of popery, that it was not long
ere they revived again. Thus I find in the year 1585 there
was a regulation, rather than a beginning of them, in the
diocese of Chester, Dr. William Chaderton (sometime master of Queen's college in Cambridge) now being bishop of
that see. There were directions set down for that ecclesiastical exercise, and the manner of proceeding therein; the
office of the moderators; rules to be observed by the speakers and writers; the times of meeting; the towns where;
viz. Prescot, Burie, Padian, and Preston. And this in pursuance of letters from the privy council. All the people had
liberty to resort to the sermon; but none to the exercise
that followed, but parsons, vicars, curates, and schoolmas-
ters. And them always personally to appear, upon pain of
forfeitures, and sometimes suspension. Notice also was to
be then taken of the clergy's behaviour. All to be begun
and ended with prayer. The whole paper is worth perusing, which I have put in the Appendix, friendly com- Numbers
municated to me by the learned and curious Ralph Tho- XXXVIII.
resby of Leeds, esquire.   XXXIX.
As conformity now unto the orders of the church was The dili-
more strictly required, and refusal thereof, or variation disaffected
from the same, more narrowly looked unto; so those that to the
were disaffected thereto continued very stirring and dili- church.
gent, as well in finding fault therewith, as in commending
their own platforms, in books by them published. In one Troubles at
whereof, that came forth this year, they thought fit thus to Frankfort,
represent or bespatter the church, in respect of the igno- p. 169.
rance or inability of some ministers that served in it: "That
" in most part of the realm, preachers there were none, nor

VOL. II.   I i

" any that could or would preach, very few excepted; sav-
" ing certain wanderers. Among whom, and especially in
" some shires, were such ruffianly rakehells and common
" cozeners permitted and suffered. By whose preaching
" the word of truth was become odious in the eyes of the
" people, &c. And that in most places the ministry did
" stand and consist of old popish priests, tolerated readers,
" and many now made ministers: whose readings were such,
" that the people could not be edified: especially where one
" was tolerated to serve two or three churches; and turning
" their backs to the people." [That is, I suppose, standing
at the table with their faces eastward; and so reading the
office.]

325   The said book, out of which this citation is taken, and
which came forth this year, must have a remark or two.
Now it was thought fit by the puritan faction, (thinking it
to tend to their purpose,) to publish some history of the
troubles that arose in the English congregations of exiles,
fled to Frankford in Germany, which began anno 1554.
Where some of them laboured to have the English service
laid aside, and another form of divine service used, more
agreeable to that of the church of Geneva: which occasioned
at last a separation. The blame of the contention was endeavoured to be laid upon those that would not admit of
any alteration in the English book. The author of the account of those troubles (who seems himself to have been then
there) foresaw, that some would take offence at his publishing thereof at this time: but he, on the contrary, thought
it might serve to a good purpose: namely, that the reading
thereof might mollify the present proceedings against the
puritans, and open to them a way for more favour and liberty, when every one might see, what occasion of bitter
strife and unhappy division the Common Prayer Book and
ceremonies had given before. Thus writing; " That against
" the offence that some might take at these his trifles, he
" set the great profit that this might bring to God's church
" and to posterity: who being taught by other men's harms,
" might learn to beware, if they would be happy. The

" hope whereof had greater force to push his pen forward
" to the finishing of the work, than the displeasure of some
" could be, to withdraw him from the same, &c. Protesting
" before God, that in writing this discourse he had respect
" to God's glory, the defence of his sacred truth, and the
" clearing, as far as he might, of so many excellent, learned
" persons, on whose necks these stirs were laid, as authors
" of the same. Yet he did this with some unwillingness :
" saying, that God knew how the keeping of these things
" almost for the space of twenty years in secret did suffice
" to witness with him, that he had no great pleasure to utter
" them. And that he went upon his work after great
" strivings and strugglings with himself, till he could no
" longer conceal it :" [that is, because of the severe methods
now taken with men of the same principles with those dissenting brethren at Frankford.]

It is remarkable, that this book was thought fit by some The same
to be reprinted, anno 1642, as tending to favour the courses reprinted,
anno 1642.
that were at that time in hand, to throw off the Common
Prayer Book, and to blacken, as much as they could, the
church and churchmen. As is hinted by these words added
in the title-page of that edition ; " In which discourse, the
" gentle reader may see the very original and beginning of
" all the contention that hath been there, and what was the
" cause of the same. And is humbly dedicated to the view
" and consideration of the honourable and high court of
" parliament, and of the reverend divines of the intended
" ensuing assembly." But yet the book itself must be acknowledged to be of good use, for the accounts given therein of the names of such English persons as were exiles for
religion, and the several places in Germany and Helvetia,
where they seated themselves, and for divers original letters,
and other papers, to let in knowledge of their affairs.

It was a practice of some ministers in these times, espe-326
cially such as were puritans, (to reconcile to themselves the Some pretend to cast
greater opinion of the common people,) to take upon them out devils.
Discov. of
to dispossess evil spirits out of the bodies of people, but counterf.
chiefly of boys and young women. Such a thing happened Pract. by
Dr. Hars-
ner.

this year: one Mildred, base daughter of Alice Norrington, at Westwel in Kent, was pretended to be troubled with a devil. In the dispossessing of whom, two ministers, viz. Roger Newman and John Brainford, were employed; and were said to have effected the business. But notwithstanding all the specious pretences, it was confessed in the end to be but a mere cozenage. And but two years before, at Maidstone in the same county, was such a counterfeit possession of a Dutch fellow of twenty-three years old, said to be possessed with ten devils, pretended to be dispossessed by the mighty providence of God, Jan. 27. And a book was writ to that purpose; where it was styled a very wonderful and strange miracle. To which book, the mayor of Maidstone, Nicasius Vander Scheure, minister of the Dutch church there, and John Stikelbom, the instrument, forsooth, that cast out the said devils, with divers others, subscribed their names.

A girl in
Norwich
possessed.
The bishop
relates it to
Bullinger. Yet ought we not to be altogether obstinate against the belief of all diabolical possessions. For what shall we think of the relation of the bishop of Norwich, concerning two possessed in that city, this very year; and who thought fit to write it unto Bullinger in Switzerland: That a Dutch girl, about seventeen or eighteen years of age, a servant to a preacher of that church, was for a whole year miserably vexed by Satan. Which maid, in all her temptations and dilacerations, [torments,] remained firm in the faith, and did very valiantly resist the adversary. That at last, by God's help, the Devil, being overcome, left her. And, as it were, the same moment, invaded the son of a certain senator; whom, for some weeks together, he did vex incredibly. And that by his [the bishop's] command, public prayers were made in the city, with fasting, till even. The Lord had mercy also upon the boy, and overcame the enemy. The boy was thirteen or fourteen, and well versed in the scriptures, according to his years. And being firm in faith, made use of the same scriptures against the enemy. And then the said bishop concludes with these words: *Vivit Dominus, per quem pueri et puellæ, imbecillis alioqui naturæ,*

tantum et tam immanem adversarium vincere possunt. Deo CHAP.
sit laus.   XXXI.

Innovation in the divine service was suddenly brought Anno 1574.
into the cathedral church in Norwich, at evening service, in Innovation,
one of the Christmas holydays, by Limbert, Chapman, and order of ser-
Roberts, three of this church.   These, in the time of read- vice intrud-
ing the lessons, had inveighed against the manner of the cathedral of
singing there, and termed it *disordered;* and wished it ut- Norwich.
terly thence to be banished.   And one of these starting up
at that time, took upon him to use another, and a new form
of service, contrary to that ordered by her majesty and the
book.   When Dr. Gardiner, the dean, stood up, and confuted the reasons the others had brought; and put some remedy for the future against such attempts, by causing this
last to be committed to prison.   Yet some reflection the dean
now made upon the bishop.

The bishop, who was now at Ludham, soon understood 3 2 7
all this, and declared himself very much displeased at these
surprising innovations; approving also what was done for
the punishments of these men, in order to the restraining of
such practices hereafter; signifying his mind thus to the
dean: " How those ministers had done very indiscreetly, The bishop
" and that which was contrary to her majesty's godly pro- to the dean
" ceedings; and how he liked, that he, [the dean,] as he Int. epist.D.
" heard, had very pithily confuted certain of their reasons; Parkhurst.
" and that he had otherwise taken order with those men, episc.Norv.
" for preventing their attempting the like.   And that if he
" thought he of himself could not bring it to pass with
" effect, if he advertised him [the bishop] thereof, he should
" have (he added) his best aid and advice, both against
" those, or any other enterprising the like.   But whereas
" the dean had then in open speech touched him [the bi-
" shop] and his officers, that admitted such as they were,
" this the bishop shortly shewed him that he misliked, since
" that he [the dean] knew he had not been made privy to it;
" but that they were, in that reading, appointed by himself,
" [the dean,] as he thought.   The bishop subjoined, that
" he liked well of committing to prison that one busy fel-

i i 3

" low, that starting up, had appointed another order of ser-
" vice than was allowed, and was therefore worthily com-
" mitted, both for example to others, and for avoiding of
" further inconvenience that might have happened. And so
" praying for the peace and godly quietness of the church
" of God, with hearty commendations to himself, he took
" his leave of him." Dated January 3, 1574.

In a letter of the same date, he wrote to his chancellor,
" That he wished these men had not attempted thus against
" the practice of this church, allowed by the prince's con-
" sent and authority, both there and in all other cathedral
" churches that he could hear of. And misliking, for his
" own part, those sudden innovations against authority, he
" would do his endeavour to reform such persons. And
" that in committing that person who took upon him a new
" order of service, contrary to her majesty's order and book,
" and to be an example to others, surely you have done her
" majesty (said he) good service. And that if at any time
" the like troubles should arise, he prayed him to proceed
" in the reformation thereof in any of his clergy ; wherein
" he [the bishop] would assist him, if need should require;
" and think himself also much bound unto him." And in
answer to his chancellor's letter, which now the same day
(it seems) came to hand, " he thanked him for it, thougn
" the matter was not pleasant ; desiring him to be helpful,
" to the uttermost of his power, to withstand and avoid these
" innovations : which, for my part, said he, I do in no case
" like of. And fearing lest these doings might grow to
" greater inconveniencies, he thought good to advertise him
" of his meaning and disliking ; as before he had written."

An Arian
in Cam-
bridgeshire.

Confutat.
of certain
articles by
Wil. Wil-
kins, 1579.

And in the very next diocese, that of Ely, there were
some heresies and dangerous opinions sprung up already,
and maintained. One Wilkinson, of that diocese, (who
wrote a book against the *family of love*,) mentioned one
in Cambridgeshire, that was a flat Arian ; and that under
his own hand, and before some men of worship, anno 1574,
March 24, in Cambridge, he denied Christ to be God equal
with his Father. Moreover, that he asserted children were

not by nature sinful, neither ought to be baptized, till years
of discretion.   And further affirmed, that the regenerate ____
sin not: and that Paul's epistles were not to be more ac- Anno 1574.
counted of than the letters of private men.   This man once
recanted his errors; but since fell into the same again.   His
name was W. H. of B. i. e. Balsham, I suppose.

At this man's house lodged sometimes Vitells, a Dutchman, the great spreader of the sect of the *family of love* in
these parts: and he used to confer with him, and those of
that family, concerning their opinions.

This Arian would seem, in the company of simple men, to
be very learned.   But they that had talked with him affirmed, that he had many words, but small wisdom, and was but
small in wit, and might have been better occupied to learn
the first principles of God's fear, and to get himself instructed, before he taught that to others, that he had no
skill of.   Here in Cambridgeshire also did that sect very
much increase, and united themselves into a kind of church,
with officers.   And the chief elders of the *lovely fraternity*, The sect of
some of them were weavers, some basket-makers, some musi- the family
cians, some bottle-makers, and such other like; which by spread here.
travelling from place to place did get their livings.   They
which among them bore the greatest countenance were
such as, having by their smooth behaviour and glozing talk
deceived some justices of peace, and other worshipful of the
country where they dwelt, had gotten licences to trade for
corn up and down the country; and using such a running
kind of traffick, kept not commonly any one certain abiding
place; but running and frisking from place to place, stayed
not for the most part any where long, save where they light
upon some simple husbandman, whose wealth was greater
than his wit.   His house, if it were far from company, and
stood out of the common walk, was a fit nest, wherein all
the birds of that feather used to meet together.   This account we have of one that lived in those times and in those
parts, and made his observations of them.   And from whom
we shall have a fuller account of them and their doctrines
under the year 1579.

CHAP. XXXII.

*Many papists set at liberty upon sureties. Dr. Yong moves
the lord treasurer to go out of the Marshalsea for his
health. Sampson writes a smart letter to the treasurer
on this occasion. Pensioners of the king of Spain, the
queen's subjects; and their particular pensions. Practice
to poison the lord treasurer. Mass said in London in
divers places. A token sent from the Scottish queen to
queen Elizabeth. Her majesty melancholy. Her progress. The queen checks the young earl of Oxford: re-
sented by him. The bishop of Ely's revenues aimed at.
Slandered. He refuseth to lend his house at Holborn.
Story, bishop of Hereford, sues to the lord treasurer in
behalf of some of his clergy; vexed by pretence of the
statute of suppression of colleges. The trouble the town
of Wells gave the bishop thereof. The death of Parkhurst, bishop of Norwich. His character.*

Fecken-
ham and
other priests
set at li-
berty.

WE come now to look upon those dangerous enemies,
both of the church and kingdom, the papists.

The state was so unwilling to inflict the rigour of the laws
against them, (so I will say, rather than indeed favourable
to them,) that it set at liberty this year divers of them, as
yet detained in prison. The like whereof was done at divers other times afterwards; as particularly in the year 1583,
by the clemency of the queen and council, seventy papists
were dismissed, and sent beyond sea; some whereof had
been condemned to die. This year, 1574, Feckenham,
Watson, and divers others in the Tower, or some other
prisons, had their liberty; but under some bonds of appearance, and to keep within certain bounds allotted them.

Popish
priests in
the north
expect the
like liberty.

The papists that were imprisoned in the north, upon this
indulgence, expected also their liberty; and petitioned accordingly to the council in the north, and namely to the
lord president, and the archbishop of York, requiring it as
it were of right. But it was not thought convenient by the
said president and archbishop, that the example should be

followed in those parts. "For if such a general jubilee CHAP.
" should be put in use there, (as the archbishop of York XXXII.
" writ in a letter to the lord treasurer,) a great relapse Anno 1574.
" would soon follow after in those parts." And he prayed
their lordships of the council to consider of it, if any such
suits should be made.   I find Dr. John Yong (who was, I Dr. Yong.
think, formerly of St. John's college in Cambridge, and a
great antagonist to Martin Bucer) this year desiring his
liberty for some time, upon sureties, to go out of prison to
recover his health, in a letter to the lord treasurer, from the
Marshalsea, dated in June, being then, as he wrote, sixty 330
years of age.   The letter being but short, from so memorable a man of that party, I will set down.

" Miraris fortasse, inclytissime vir, quid sit, quod me mi- Dr. Yonge's
" sellum moveat, has tandem ad tuam dignitatem, maximis liberty.
" et gravissimis negotiis occupatam, supplices literas scri-
" bere : profecto, ut uno verbo expediam, non aliud quam be-
" nignitatis tuæ et clementiæ fiducia, ac mearum miseriarum
" atque infirmitatum incrudescens sæpius acerbitas, &c. Hoc
" a præstantia tua, si modo digneris placabiliter hominem
" tenuem audire, obnixe peto et rogo, ut per tuam authori-
" tatem potestas mihi fiat, ad tempus aliquod exeundi e car-
" cere, ut medicos ob corporis valetudinem consulere, et
" quæ ad salutem sunt, exercere valeam.   De mea pacifica
" ac tranquilla interea temporis, moderatione ac vivendi or-
" dine, atque de reditu in carcerem tempore constituto ac
" præfinito, fidejussores idoneos interponam, &c.   Kalend.
" Junii.

          " Tuæ sublimitatis in precibus non immemor,
                    " Johannes Yonge, jam sexagenarius."

This favour he requested was promised, but, it seems, not
performed.   Therefore the next year he solicits the same
noble person to permit him the next summer to go to the
Bath, according to the advice of his physicians; addressing
himself thus to him :

" Iterum cogor, illustrissime vir, et mihi tuo merito sem-
" per observantissime domine, tuam pietatem implorare,

" &c.   Sicut priora tua in me collata beneficia nunquam ex
" animo meo excidere possunt, (pro quibus id unum quod
" possum, pro te scilicet, et tua selecta conjuge ac sobole,
" Deo supplices preces reddo,) ita nunc supplex ad tuam
" singularem clementiam confugio, &c.   Digneris concedere
" mihi hoc verno ac æstivo tempore facultatem balneas vi-
" sendi.   Id superiori anno promissum, sed non præstitum :
" et tunc et nunc per medicos valetudinis causa consultum.
" Quod sive concesserit tua illustris magnificentia, sive non
" concesserit, tuæ prudentiæ ac pietati committens, (cui me
" devinctum agnosco,) perpetuo apud Deum pro te tuisque
" deprecator ero, &c.   E sede Mareschallica, 1575, decimo
" Martii.   Tibi deditissimus, siquid esset in quo tuo honori
" servire, aut gratificari possit.

" Johannes Yonge."

This liberty
granted to
papists dis-
liked.

But the setting these men at liberty gave great disgust to
many, as being judged a matter of very dangerous consequence ; their very principles leading them into practice
against religion and the queen's life.   And it was reported
commonly, that the lord treasurer's gentleness had been the
cause of this counsel.   Hence Dr. Sampson, (of whom before,) from Leicester, sends him his mind and thoughts of
this, in a plain letter wrote in December.   First, excusing
himself in writing to him upon a report.   And then, supposing the report true, expostulating with him concerning
this clemency, after this manner :

Sampson's
thoughts
thereof to
the lord
treasurer.

" That if he could drive that rumour that came on him
" [the lord treasurer] to such a certain head, as St. Paul
" did that of the Corinthians, that he [Sampson] might say,
" *Significatum est mihi a familiaribus Chloæ,* then would
" he write more determinately than he did.   But since he
" could not do so, and yet that he still heard the rumour, he
" thought it much better to write to him what he did hear
" of him, than either to keep silence in hearing the rumour,
" or to report it himself to others."   And then he proceeded
to tell him, " That it was reported of him, that his lordship
" had been the means of the late delivery of the imprisoned

331

" papists. And that he did purge himself to them of the
" cause of their imprisonment.

" That touching the first, he was not, he said, so full of
" hatred, that he did envy their liberty. And that he was
" so far from envying their good, that he wished to them
" that liberty, of which he feared they did make.but small
" account. The same, he meant, of which Christ Jesus
" spake, Joann. viii. *Si filius vos liberos reddiderit, vere li-*
" *beri eritis.* And again, to his disciples, *Si vos manseritis*
" *in sermone meo, vere discipuli mei estis, et cognoscetis*
" *veritatem, et veritas liberos reddet vos.* That he was not
" so envious, but that he wished them this liberty. He
" would they were so well learned, that they would become
" the disciples of Christ. So should they taste of this happy
" liberty. And if, by getting unto them bodily liberty, he
" [the lord treasurer] could procure them this also, he
" should do a deed of godly charity. But that to attain
" this, they must become learners, hearers, and believers of
" Christ's word preached. So long as they were imprisoned,
" they would say, they could not come to hear the sermons :
" but now that they were at liberty, and might hear, they
" should by authority be compelled to hear. Faith, he
" added, comes not by compulsion, but *fides ex auditu.*
" And Augustin praised this in the rulers of his time, that
" they did by authority compel the Donatists to come to the
" congregations of the Christians, to hear the sermon. On
" which hearing, in some of them followed faith ; and the
" fruitful conversion from heresy to truth was wrought in
" some of them."

He added further, " That he did not require the enforc-
" ing of them at the first to receive the holy sacrament, but
" to hear the word preached. For it was the seed which is
" cast into all sorts of grounds, and that which, being rightly
" received, would frame them to be meet receivers of the
" holy sacrament. That haply by hearing, God would
" catch some of them to life. Wherefore, as they had li-
" berty, so he advised to let them have their liberty recom-
" mended to them, with charge and condition, that they do

" resort to sermons, and to have conference with godly,
" learned men: that all means might be used for their con-
" version, as Christian charity required: else their liberty
" would serve to confirm themselves and others in popish
" obstinacy, and to turn yet more from hearing, and coming
" to the congregation of Christ. That they shall wander
" and rove about as the pope's reconcilers, to the great hurt
332 " of many, and hinder the course of Christ's gospel." And
then he asketh, " Who shall be guilty of this fact before the
" Lord? Even with them, you, by whose means they are
" helped to this hurtful liberty."

And then he comes to write to the said lord, " touching
" the rest of the report; that if he received them as men to
" be pitied and helped by him, for the cause of their im-
" prisonment, and therefore worthy of his favour and
" friendship, view well, said he, what you do. You do
" justify their wicked cause. You cannot be friendly to
" them, but you must become a friend to popery. In
" which doing, what is it that you can promise yourself? Is
" it heaven? Is it God's favour? Nay, truly: for they are all
" the enemies of God; enemies to his truth and gospel. For
" the matter in controversy between us, which profess the
" gospel, and them, resteth not, as some have thought, only
" in certain ceremonies, but in points of doctrine, faith, and
" salvation. To the truth of these points they are enemies.
" Against them they do hold heresy, and speak blasphemy.
" To be the lover of this, and friend, favourer, and helper
" of it, is to go headlong to hell, whereinto they do lead.
" As it is said of their like and forefathers, Matt. xxiii. *Fa-*
" *ciunt filios gehennæ.* At their hands, therefore, (as he
" went on,) you cannot look to be helped to heaven. What
" is it then that you may hope for of them? the upholding
" of your worldly honour? This thing extended, hath so
" many pinching points in it, that I may of purpose pass it
" over: two things only I will shortly say, it is a concluded
" ἀξίωμα among papists, confirmed by practice, and shewed
" to be an article of their unchangeable faith, *Fides non est*
" *servanda hæreticis.* Cant and recant; do what you will,

" when they by flattering have allured you, and you by be-
" lieving of them are seduced, you shall drink of that cup
" that Northumberland did, *jubente Maria;* and as all
" other noblemen seduced by popish flattery have drunk,
" both in France and Flanders, as you do know. Trust to
" it, they will never state any sure contract with you, but
" in your own blood. And so they will make of you and
" other English, examples to the world of their faithless
" fidelity, if they catch but you.

" My second thing is, consider, my lord, what you are,
" and how God hath dealt with you. You know how you
" did fall in queen Mary's days: you know what you sought
" then, and how God, which knoweth all your doings much
" better than yourself doth, did contrary your purposes
" and desires. For you offended him ; you did not serve
" him well. If you have repented that rightly, God hath
" forgiven you truly. And in professing of the gospel, God
" hath so advanced you, that I think you could never hope
" for more than he hath given you in the world. And ought
" this now to be the recompence which you make to God
" for his goodness, thus to strike hands with the enemies,
" and in them, *quasi bellum Deo indicere,* to hinder the
" gospel, to hurt and wound the church, his children, to
" pleasure his enemies? Ought it, my lord, ought it to be
" so ? It ought not truly. I trust it be not so evil with
" you, as one doubting, notwithstanding the report I write.
" But if it be so, or hereafter shall be so, know you, that
" God will not leave it unrevenged in you. Only he is *bea-*
" *tus, qui perseveraverit in finem.* Which in God I do 333
" heartily wish to you.

" Good my lord, do not say, as one great man said,
" Isa. x. *Manus mihi fecit mihi hæc omnia :* but confess
" God and his goodness, and give to him due glory. Be
" zealous in and for the Lord. And as I did once write to
" you, be now as Eliachim was in the reign of Ezechias, and
" you shall find at the hand of God as he did, Isai. xxii.
" For God's sake put your policy to school to God. Say
" not of yourself as he did, Esa. x. *I am wise ;* but *consule*

BOOK
I.

Anno 1574.

" *Dominum,* and do nothing *inconsulto Domino.* Then the
" promise is made to Jehosuah, *Prudenter ages in omnibus*
" *ad quæ perges.* Whatsoever in old time hath past, the
" Lord Jesus teach you, and work in you that which St.
" Paul writeth, Eph. iv. *Deponere juxta priorem conversa-*
" *tionem veterem hominem, qui corrumpitur juxta concu-*
" *piscentias, &c. Renovari vero spiritu mentis ; et induere*
" *novum hominem, qui juxta Deum conditus est, per justi-*
" *tiam et sanctitatem veritatis.* This is to be in Christ, a
" sound Christian ; 2 Cor. v. *Si quis est in Christo nova*
" *creatura est.* In him I do wish you a good new year. If I
" did not find myself bound in conscience to wish your good,
" I would not thus write. *Ego animam meam libero* to-
" wards you. The rudeness of my evil writing, your lord-
" ship will impute to my lameness. Your lordship's at com-
" mand, Lame Tho. Sampson." Dated from Leicester, 31st
December, 1574.

Pensioners
in Spain.
Their
names and
pensions.

Thus disliked by the queen's protestant subjects were the
favours shewn to papists and popish priests, and those of
the court blamed that moved the same. Further jealousies
arose in the minds of the good people of the land, of the
safety of the church and nation at this time, in respect of
those numbers of pensioners then in Spain, the queen's subjects ; harboured there and in Flanders, and encouraged to
take pensions, to become traitors, and to do mischief both to
the queen, and the religion and good estate of their country. The following list will shew this, giving an account of
the names of the pensioners, (many whereof had been in the
rebellion in the north,) and their several pensions. The
authentickness whereof will appear, in that the paper thereof
is endorsed thus by the lord Burghley's own hand ; *Pensioners in Spain, Sept.* —, 1574. *Sent from sir Francis Englefield to the duke of Feria.* The figures set to each name, I
suppose, are ducats.

Persons provided for here.

Countess of Northumber-		Lord Dacre - - - - - -	200
land - - - - - - - -	200	Lady Hungerford - -	100
Earl of Westmoreland	200	Sir Francis Englefield -	84

Mr. Christopher Nevyl	60	Mr. Hugh Owen - - -	40	CHAP.
Sir John Nevyl - - - -	60	Mr. Nolworth - - - - -	40	XXXII.
Mr. Dr. Parker - - - -	50	Mr. George Tyrrel - -	30	Anno 1574.
Mr. Richard Norton -	56	Mr. Jenney - - - - - -	30	334
Mr. Copley - - - - - -	60	Mr. Tichburn - - - - -	30	
Mr. Markenfeld - - - -	36	Mr. George Smith - -	30	
Mr. Tempest - - - - -	40	Mr. Bath - - - - - - -	30	
Mr. Bulmer - - - - - -	30	Mr. Robert Owen - - -	30	
Mr. Danby - - - - - -	30	*Not yet granted.*		
Mr. Francis Norton - -	36	Mr. Powel, priest - - -	16	
Mr. Thwing - - - - -	30	Mrs. Story, widow - -	16 *di.*	
Mr. Chamberlain - - -	60	Mr. Olyver - - - - - -	8	
Mr. Lygons - - - - - -	40	Tho. Kinred - - - -	16 *di.*	
Mr. Standen - - - - -	50	Mr. James Hamiltown -	80	
Mr. Mocket - - - - - -	30	Mr. John Hamiltown -	60	

Persons gone towards Spain, to serve for pensions.

My lord Edward Seymor.	Mr. Blackstone.
Mr. Southwel.	Mr. Prideaux.
Mr. Carew.	Mr. George Moor.
Mr. Harecourt.	———— Williams.
Mr. Francis Moor.	John Story.

There is another more particular account of such English Littleston's gentlemen as came into Spain for entertainment at Madrid, intelligence and their gifts and pensions, made by one Littleston, (perhaps tlemen in a spy in Spain,) and given in to the lord treasurer Burgh-Spain. ley this year. The paper is superscribed by the same, *To the right honourable, his singular good lord, the lord high treasurer of England.* And that it is authentic, it was thus endorsed by the said treasurer's own hand, *Littleston's declaration, November* 1574, *of certain English gentlemen that have entertainment of the king of Spain.* This paper contains some other pensions besides those above named. It deserves a place in the Appendix : where it appears, that the N°. XL. whole sum of the pensions granted to the queen's rebels in Flanders, by the king of Spain yearly, amounted to two hundred thirty-one thousand ducats.

BOOK
I.
Anno 1574.
A practice
in Italy to
poison the
lord trea-
surer. MSS.
Burghley.

And how busy the papists now were, appeared by a particular practice of theirs this year; which was, to poison the
queen's great and able statesman, viz. the lord treasurer;
namely, to do it by a letter to be sent to him.   There was
one in Italy that would do it for 6000 crowns.   One at Antwerp took it in hand.   And the Italian was to come thither
to teach him to do it; and was therefore to have a suitable
reward, yet with some abatement of the former sum.   A
private letter to this purport came, by God's good providence, into the hand of an English merchant abroad, who
discovered it secretly to some person of honour, (perhaps
secretary Walsingham,) and so it came to the knowledge of
that lord.   And likewise a second letter, thus endorsed by
the hand of the lord treasurer himself, *ult. Novembris* 1574.
A copy of a letter, found in Bridges, [Bruges, in Flanders,]
by one Allyn, a merchant, [written to some honourable person,] *concerning a practice to poison the lord Burghley.*
The letter follows :

" Whereas I wrote to your honour of a practice in Italy
" against my lord treasurer for 6000 crowns; the matter
" came in question, when sir F. [probably sir Francis Engle-
" field] came to Brussels: and the conclusion was, that for
" 5000 crowns one would have taken in hand to have poi-
" soned him with a letter.   Or else, if any would take upon
" him to put it in execution, he would come to Antwerp, and
335 " teach it to him that would take it in hand for 3000 crowns.
" And if the party that should do it would come into Italy,
" where he is, he would teach him for 2000 crowns.   And
" he should have proof of it by a dog, which he should have
" in his own keeping: whereby he should not be deceived.

" This news being brought, it was considered, that the
" best way, for that the thing was great, was to get one to
" learn it, and to put it in execution; and the matter was
" proffered to me, for that it was thought I had a great
" quarrel to my lord, for that he was my heavy lord in the
" time of my wrongful troubles.   Howbeit, the matter was
" never broken to me for that end : the cause, for that they

" would first provide the money; and depending chiefly
" upon sir F. So when two came, whose names I cannot
" decipher, that earnestly required his aid, with his counsel
" and money towards a good deed," &c.

Mass was usually said in many places in London. And Persons
(some information being given of this) a privy search was taken at
mass in se-
appointed to be made at the same time, being Palm-Sunday, veral places.
the 4th of April: when were apprehended divers persons in
the lady Morley's chamber, by Algate; namely, the lady
Morley, sir Edward Stanley, knt. the lady Jarman, Dolman
the Jesuit, and divers others, both men and women, to the
number of twenty-three. At the lady Guilford's, in Trinity-
lane, beside Queenhithe, were likewise taken at mass, the
same time, the said lady, and her daughter and her son,
Olyver Heywode, priest, and a gentlewoman to the countess
of Darby, and others, to the number of eleven. Also at
Mr. Carus his house, beside Lymehouse, near London, were
found the same day, by Mr. Recorder of the city of London,
(not at mass, but all things prepared for the saying of mass,)
Tho. Carus, esq. and his wife, ———— Thornborow, esq. and
the lady Browne, and others.

A further account of the seizing these persons at mass in Further in-
London, we have in a letter written four days after from formation
of it from
court, from Dr. Gardiner, dean of Norwich, to the bishop court.
there. Therein also shewing, from some of the priests' own Int. epist.
D. P. Park-
confessions, that there were five hundred masses said on hurst. ep.
Norw.
that day in England; and then advising the bishop to look
to his own diocese, where not a few priests and professed
papists were connived at, he feared, even by some of his own
officers. He shewed the apprehensions justly arising from
these numerous popish adversaries, to the queen and state;
and what blame she herself laid upon the bishops for the
same. The letter (which is worthy the preserving) ran to
this purport:

" That there was on Palm-Sunday last, at one hour, at Fifty-three
" four sundry masses, in four sundry places, and out corners persons
taken at
" of the city of London, fifty-three persons taken; whereof mass.
" the most part were ladies, gentlewomen, and gentlemen.

" Two and twenty of them stood stoutly to the matter;
" whereof the lady Morley and the lady Browne (who had
" paid before an 100 marks for her offence) were the
" chief. The priests gloried in their doings, and affirmed,
" that there were five hundred masses in England said that
" day. That the queen's majesty did say openly, it was the
336 " negligence of the bishops, and their chancellors, arch-
" deacons, and commissaries, that was the cause of all this."
Whereupon the dean added, " That it stood his lordship
" [the bishop] in hand, to look about, that the tenth part
" of these masses were said in his diocese, (if there were so
" many masses said,) good conjectors said so. And then
" he prayed God none of his officers were culpable in con-
" senting to them." And adding, " The days be danger-
" ous; the Devil is busy to lull men asleep in security, and
" to be negligent in their offices, that require vigilant pas-
" tors, to such time as he may by policy plant ignorance and
" idolatry, to be commended with cruelty. The greatest
" diligence is too little, and the least spark of careless neg-
" ligence is too much. Dated from court, April 8, 1574,
" subscribing,

" Your lordship's to use in Christ,

" George Gardiner."

Bristow's
Motives set
forth.
About this year, R. Bristow, of the English college at
Doway, set forth his *Motives* unto the Catholic faith, to the
number of forty-eight : a book of great vogue with the
papists : which Dr. Fulk, of Cambridge, now answered, in a
treatise called *The Retentive.* In the year 1599, it was
printed again at Antwerp. And again, the next year, 1600,
one Dr. Hil put it forth at Antwerp, entitled then, *Reasons
for the Catholic Religion,* in number twenty-five, as a new
book of his own; but containing much of the form and
manner, and all the matter for the ground thereof, taken
out of Bristow : which was fully and learnedly answered by
George Abbot, D. D. master of University college, Oxon,
afterwards archbishop of Canterbury. And in our time
came out Bristow's *Motives* again, with a new name, viz.

The touchstone of the new gospel: which Dr. Simon Patrick, CHAP.
afterwards bishop of Ely, briefly and effectually answered. XXXII.
Thus had this book been made use of by those of that reli- Anno 1574.
gion, even to our days, as a doughty piece, to persuade to
the Roman Catholic religion.

Notwithstanding the Scottish queen remained the stay of A present
the papists' hopes, and the dread of the queen's good sub- to the queen from
jects, yet her majesty shewed still a respect towards her. the Scot-
There were now presents passed between them.   A messen- tish queen.
ger from queen Mary brought some tokens to queen Elizabeth; which she kindly accepted of, and shewed it to her
ambassador residing here; and withal told him, that she
would requite her with some like token from herself: which
also she bade him acquaint his mistress with. Of which
passage the earl of Leicester soon informed the earl of
Shrewsbury, that so he might be the first bringer of that
news to that queen, being in his custody.

But the queen was now melancholy, and so had been for The queen
many days, occasioned by some weighty causes of state; melan-
and how to interpret the same was uncertain, as the same choly.
Leicester, then near her majesty, shewed that lord at the
same time.

Now for more private, domestic, and personal matters.
The queen still remained sad and pensive in the month of
June; and so the earl of Shrewsbury's son, then at court,
wrote to his father, as Leicester also had done; and that it
should seem she was so troubled for some important matters 337
then before her. But notwithstanding, that month she be- The queen
gan her progress; which might perhaps divert her. It was progress.
thought she would go to Bristow. The gests were making
in order thereto. Mr. Hatton (not well in health) took this
opportunity to get leave to go to the Spaw, and Dr. Julio (a
great court physician) with him; whereat the queen shewed
herself very pensive, and very unwilling to grant him leave,
for he was a favourite. These are some of the contents of
a private letter of the lord Talbot, to the earl his father.
As also, that the lord treasurer, intending to wait upon the
queen when she came to Woodstock, as she had appointed

him, secretary Walsingham signified to him, that the queen now had a disposition, that he, with the lord keeper, and sir Ralph Sadler, chancellor of the exchequer, should tarry at London. The cause wherefore was unknown to the lord treasurer, but seemed to be a surprise to him: but he said, he would do as he was commanded. The queen seemed to be apprehensive of some dangers in her absence, (which might give occasion to her melancholy,) and therefore thought it advisable for those staid counsellors to remain behind.

The earl of
Oxford dis-
contented
about some
suit to the
queen.

The young earl of Oxford, of that ancient and Very family of the Veres, had a cause or suit that now came before the queen: which she did not answer so favourably as was expected; checking him, it seems, for his unthriftiness. And hereupon his behaviour before her gave her some offence. This was advertised from the lord chamberlain to the lord treasurer; who, being master of the wards, had this earl under his care, and whom he afterwards matched his daughter Anne unto. The news of this troubled that lord: saying, " He was sorry her majesty had made such " haste; and had answered him so, that he feared the se- " quel might breed offence, if he were ill counselled: that " is, in case he should, upon this, yield to such heads as " himself, which he was apt enough to do." And then gave

this favourable character of the said young earl: " that " howsoever he might be, for his own private matters, of " thrift unconsiderate, he dared avow him to be resolute in " dutifulness to the queen and his country. And then " prayed God, that the usage of that poor young earl " might not hazard him to the profit of others."

What the troubles and disturbances of the bishops, given them by some of the laity, especially of the disaffected, hath been occasionally shewed from time to time. One of the clamours against them was, that they were rich and covetous; hoping thereby to shorten their revenues, and get some shares thereof among themselves. Cox, the good bishop of Ely, had a deep portion of envy and disquiet on this account, by particular informations given to the lord treasurer how

rich he was. A wealthy bishopric indeed his was. But these
men considered not the necessary and continual charges and
expenses in repairs, hospitality, charity, duties, taxes, that
went out of it. This report (which that lord also partly
believed) coming to the pious bishop's ears, he thought fit
to declare his mind to the said lord, and to open what in
truth his own circumstances were: that so he might stop
any danger of that nature that might happen, by imposing
upon the queen, or otherwise. And therefore after this 338
manner did he write, in the month of April, to the lord
treasurer, both in behalf of himself and other his fellow-
bishops.

" That he trusted it was not true, that his lordship should
" conceive of him that he was rich, and had great heaps of
" money lying by him. For that he accounted that state
" [and niggardly disposition] to be miserable and sinful,
" especially in that needy and beggarly time; and also their
" fens, loods, dikes, and banks, [belonging to that bi-
" shopric,] almost then in all places so sore decayed. That
" he meant not to trouble his lordship with discoursing of
" his estate : which partly he had done to the archbishop
" of Canterbury ; *qui nuper erat in simili seductione.*
" That he was loath to utter his bare condition : but I dare
" protest, as he added, *coram Domino in conscientia bona,*
" that my sum is well under a thousand pounds ; as he was
" able, he said, to declare. And then, on occasion of these
" slanderous reports, he used these words ; *Ora obloquentia*
" *Deus veritatis vindex obstruere dignetur.* That he wished
" rather an hundred others to talk their pleasures, than his
" lordship should conceive any thing amiss of him, and
" otherwise than truth would bear. And therefore he
" thought good at this time to signify thus much unto his
" good lordship, as to his dearest friend on earth. *Dominus*
" *Jesus te nobis diutissime servet incolumem.* Written from
" his house at Downham, April 28, 1574."

Such reports of this bishop, and his wealth, might have
been made at court, to incline the queen the more to command him to part with his city house, in Holborn, to sir

Christopher Hatton; who was very intent upon it, as well as
several other noblemen, to strip it from the bishopric. Letters therefore were procured to be written to the bishop of
Ely for that purpose, by the lord treasurer : or at least to
lend the house to a nobleman, a friend of his. But, to the
lasting commendation of this bishop, knowing he could not
with any conscience diminish the revenues of that which he
was but intrusted with as a steward, he gave this wise and
stout answer to that lord, after his very hearty commendations to him :

His answer,
refusing to
lend it.
"That he had considered his suit which he made so
" friendly for a nobleman, for his house in Holborn. But
" that his request and suit unto his lordship, as to his
" dearest friend, was to stay the suit, whereunto he could
" not conveniently yield without some just displeasure and
" misliking of divers nobles of this realm, and they his dear
" friends ; who, in like request, at his [the bishop's] reason-
" able desire, had been quietly and friendly stayed. And
" yet, he added, he had had some experience what inconve-
" nience had fallen by lending of an house.

" Again, when her majesty appointed him to that office,
" he had, he said, free access and entry into all his houses :
" and truly, I would, as he added, be very loath to leave my
" house possessed and inhabited ; that, when God should
" call me, my successor shall be driven to make suit for
" his own house. That the state of the world at this day
" being, as his lordship knew,

" *Turpius ejicitur quam non admittitur hospes.*

339 " Further, that his sundry suits and causes there [at
" London and Westminster] were such, that he looked
" every term, when he should be forced to repair thither
" himself. At what time he meant not to be destitute of
" his house. That, moreover, his house had at that present
" some furniture in a readiness ; which, if another man
" should enter in, he should be forced troublesomely to
" convey away, or to thrust it on heaps in some corner.
" Wherefore he most heartily desired his good lordship to

" stand his friend and good lord in this case, as heretofore CHAP.
XXXII.
" he had been accustomed; so as he might enjoy his own
" to his own use and commodity. And then concluded with Anno 1574.
" something in Latin, as of more privacy, and touching
" that lord himself: viz. *Atque hic aurem tibi vellico. Hoc*
" *facies alteri, quod tibi vis fieri. Neque tibi unquam ex-*
" *cidat, te adeo huc esse evectum, ut verbi ministris in me-*
" *dio nationis pravæ degentibus, unicum sis fere asylum.*
" Thus the Lord have you in his blessed keeping. From
" my house in Downham, the 3d of February, 1574."

Story, bishop of Hereford, also, the only bishop in king Some parishes in the diocese of Hereford in danger by the statute of suppression of colleges.
Edward's reign then alive, and one of those bishops that
assisted at the consecration of archbishop Parker, did this
year intercede with the same lord for some of the clergy of
his diocese that were vexed, and like to be thrown out of
their livings, (and many more after them, if this matter
were not stopped,) by an unjust pretence to a statute against
superstitious foundations. The actors in this business were
some clerks of the exchequer: who endeavoured, in hopes
of gain to themselves, to bring some of the parish churches
of that diocese under the statute of *suppression*, as though
they were colleges; namely, such churches as were divided
into portions, where there were two or three parsons belonging thereto. The church of Bromyard particularly had
been long in suit: and the parsons thereof by this means
greatly impoverished; being from time to time delayed. And
two or three other great churches besides, in the same diocese, in present suit; and more were threatened to come in
shortly. Of these practices this good bishop had carefully
informed the lord treasurer before, hoping thereby to stop
the further proceedings of these (whom he called) *lewd
clerks*. But, it seems, they had some secret favour in the
office, or other maintenance; insomuch that they continued
to vex and molest the poor incumbents. Of this the bishop The bishop writes to the lord treasurer in their behalf.
put the lord treasurer in mind again; as by whose wisdom
the church of England had been defended, even from the
beginning hitherto.

He used arguments earnestly with this lord: as, of the

great inconvenience of allowing such things; and what a dishonour and blemish it would cast upon the protestant religion, and expose it to the contempt of papists; and would be to the church of England a great slander, if her parish churches should be thus destroyed. And that it would make the reproaches of Dorman and others true; that our churches now, some of them, were turned into houses for private men to live in, and some others were made stables, and others demolished flat to the ground. For that, indeed, by giving way to these evil men's practices, not only many parish churches in his diocese, but many others also throughout the whole realm, both parsonages and vicarages, would 340 be overthrown. And therefore he desired, that those persons of his diocese now prosecuted might have speedy trial, and be heard according to order of law, without further delay, with this favour. This letter, containing matter of so weighty a concern, and wrote by so venerable a bishop, must have a place in the Appendix.

Nº. XLI.

The town of Wells endeavour to get a grant for a corpora- tion.

Trouble also was created to another bishop this year, namely, Barklay, bishop of Bath and Wells, by the townsmen. Which made him apply himself to the same common *asylum* of the bishops and clergy, viz. the lord treasurer. The case was this. Those of the town of Wells, thinking themselves too much under the bishop's jurisdiction, and hoping to make themselves more free and independent upon him and his successors, and for some other worldly considerations in some of them, namely, their own private ends, had solicited the queen to grant the renewing of their ancient but decayed corporation; pretending to have had it ever since king Edward the Third's reign. The bishop, esteeming himself bound to preserve the privileges of his bishopric, and to prevent any encroachments upon it and its benefits, did his endeavour to stop their proceedings, and hinder the grant. And in order to that, in the month of February,

The bishop of Bath and Wells op- poseth it: and why.

17 Eliz. advertised the treasurer by letter, " That if the " townsmen should enjoy their corporation, as they called " it, grounded upon an old charter, (as they would blind " the eyes of the world, but utterly defaced, as it appeared,

" by king Edward III.) they should work in the end their
" own destruction; and should covertly carry away the
" commodity belonging to the queen's majesty and her suc-
" cessors, and spoil the bishop that then was, and those that
" should follow after him for ever." He informed further,
" That the town had no trade whereby to maintain a
" mayor, a recorder of the same town, a justice, and two
" other justices within the same town; which they had then
" gotten by their corporation. That the mayor that then
" was, was not able to give his sergeants meat; but they
" were constrained, notwithstanding their attendance, to
" seek their meat at home, or elsewhere. That the next
" year, they must either have a shoemaker or a baker to
" be their mayor; and so a justice of peace. That the town
" was poor, and stood by handicraftsmen: which, if the bi-
" shop were not present, and the masters of the cathedral
" church, (for which causes there was great resort to the
" town,) they were not able to get their bread, much less to
" feed others."

He informed the lord treasurer moreover, " That there
" were three or four lately gotten up, that were very de-
" sirous to have the stock and land of the town into their
" own hands; thinking by dominion (if they could get the
" bishop's liberties) to bring the commonalty of the town and
" country, that resort thither the two market-days, viz. Wed-
" nesday and Saturday, into such bondage, that thereby they
" would not seem only to be rulers, but also to get great gain.
" And that even so they did in the said king Edward's days.
" Whereupon he was moved to deface, before their faces,
" (*propter melius et majus commodum*,) the grant that he
" had made them. I use, added the bishop, the terms of
" the book case, well known to the learned in the law.
" That it might therefore please his good lordship to con-
" sider thereof: and, for the better quiet and commodity 341
" of the town, to take such order as should be for further-
" ance of the same. That they should be bound in duty
" to pray for his lordship's prosperity; and he himself
" should not fail, during life, so to do. Dated from Wells,

" the vii. of Febr. *anno R. reginæ* xvii. Subscribed, Your
" lordship's daily orator,

" Gilbert, Bath and Wells."

The towns-
men ex-
claim a-
gainst the
bishop, and
accuse him.
The bishop did also employ his lawyers to impeach this
attempt of the townsmen; and was so successful at length,
that they, finding they could not prevail by law, sought by
all sinister means to molest him, and now took this course
to obtain their purpose: to put up a supplication to the
queen, for the having a new corporation, only to maintain
the name of the mayor, recorder, and two justices; so that
they might have four justices of the peace within the town.
Febr. 28. Which thing, as the said bishop in another letter to the
same lord informed, was never heard of in that town before.
They also intended by a multitude (or, as we now say, a
mob) to make an exclamation against the bishop, and to
suborn such matter in malice as they possibly could, to discredit him. Whereupon he addressed again to that lord:
to whom his humble suit was, that he might not be ill
thought of, till he came to his answer; and then he doubted
not, but, by the grace of God, he should so answer them to
every point, that they should have small joy, as he said, of
their evil doings. And then he should not fail of his
bounden duty, to pray for his lordship's prosperity.

These men still prosecuted their suit; and seemed at
length in effect to have obtained a new grant, as they desired: and likewise pursued their complaints against the bishop, as though, by virtue of his power, he had laid heavy
burdens unjustly upon them. Which occasioned a third
letter from him to the said nobleman: herein urging the
injury hereby done to the bishopric, by infringing the liberties that the queen had before granted to him and his
successors, when she made him bishop; as also the wrong
done to herself and crown. For to this tenor he wrote in
The bi-
shop's ur-
gent letter
against this
grant.
April: "advertising him, that the townsmen of Wells had
" gotten a corporation lately; whereby, if they should en-
" joy the same, they did not only imbecile her majesty's
" grants, and the grants of her highness' progenitors, but

" also take away her own commodities for ever. And should
" thereby take away the liberties belonging to the bishopric,
" confirmed by her majesty to him and his successors. For
" the which he did, and they should, pay a yearly portion,
" and should receive nothing for the same."

He added, " That he was desirous to answer their untrue
" suggestions. And that he would be reported by town and
" country, worshipful and others, in whatsoever the said town
" of Wells had been governed, since he had been bishop.
" He desired his lordship to consider further, how many
" towns of new corporations were come to decay. Whereof
" they had good experience, both within that shire, and not
" far off without it, in sundry and divers places. And that if
" his lordship would command the bearer of his letter to
" attend him at his leisure, he would give his lordship fur- 342
" ther to understand, that it was his [the bishop's] duty to
" the queen constrained him to complain; and the pity he
" bore to the town, which was like to come to decay, that
" moved him to be thus an humble suitor to his lordship."
And so desired his good lordship to be his friend. This
was dated from Wells, the 25th of April, 1574.

This year ended the life of another worthy bishop and
confessor, Parkhurst, bishop of Norwich; of whom several
notices have been given before. He died in the latter end
of the year after his great climacteric. He had been greatly
afflicted with the stone (which he called his *familiar tor-
mentor*) in the winter before, being at London, and made
bloody urine for two days together sometimes, in the
months of October, November, and December, and voided
seven stones in January. This was joined with a fever. Insomuch that he had three physicians; an Englishman, a
Fleming, and an Hungarian. By whose help at last he recovered. But after that, he lived physically, that is, *miserably;* as he wrote himself to one of his friends at Tigur.
He had been domestic chaplain to Katharine duchess of
Suffolk, and queen Katharine Parr; and tutor at Oxford to
the most learned, and ever highly deserving of this church,
bishop Jewel; and was rector of the rich parsonage of

Clive. Which, together with his country and all that he
had, he voluntarily forsook, for the sake of Christ and his
gospel, in the reign of queen Mary. And was an exile at
Zuric in Switzerland. Where, when once one coming to the
door of the house where he sojourned, and asked him if his
master were at home, it stirred him a little, and gave him
occasion to meditate some verses. Whereof this was a part:

> *Vah! nequeo esse servus;*
> *Multorum qui fuerim dominus.*

And ever after, he had a great sense of the favour and
protection he received in Helvetia, especially of the learned
men of Zuric, one of the protestant cantons there; where
he lived with his wife safely: and received such civilities
then from them, Bullinger, Lavater, Wolphius, Simler, and
especially Gualter, that he could never forget as long as he
lived; and always held a fraternal and dear correspondence
with them. And so delighted was he with the discipline
and doctrine of that church, that he often wished that our
church were modelled exactly according to that. And in
gratitude to Rodolph Gualter, (in whose house he and his
wife seem to have been harboured,) he maintained his son,
young Rodulph, first at Cambridge, and then at Oxford,
and in other places while he was in England, at his sole expense, though he were somewhat a prodigal youth; and
gave him a *viaticum*, to bear his charges when he returned
home. He used to give sixty liveries twice a year to his
servants and retainers. Afterwards, by reason of the queen's
debts that fell upon him by the wrongs of his collector
Thimelthorp, (failing of his payment of the tenths of the
clergy for the 12th and 13th years of the queen,) he was
forced to retrench, being then bound to pay to the queen
400*l.* in one year; that is, 100*l.* each term; and so fell to
forty liveries, and after to thirty.

He kept twenty-six men-servants in his house: among
whom were, besides his secretary and gentleman, a cook, a
middle cook, a brewer, a cater, a baker, a yeoman of the
horse, a bailiff, two carters, and divers other inferior ser-

vants; besides six maids, six retainers, four poor aged folks CHAP.
maintained in the house, and three scholars found by him, XXXII.
one at Oxford, another at Norwich, and a third at Ips- Anno 1574.
wich.

This bishop was supposed to be inclinable to the puritans, He was
and to wink at them. But how he did indeed stand affected favour the
in that behalf, take his own words once to his chancellor in puritans.
this year: " That he must needs allow the diligence of such
" as endeavoured to preserve the godly ordinances of the
" realm, to the maintenance of the peace, and her majesty's
" quiet government: thanking and commending him for his
" travail and care: and praying him to spare no person; as
" well such as, being too forward, needed a sharp bit and
" rein to restrain their haste, as such also as, being too slow,
" did wilfully and stubbornly, like resty jades, draw back-
" wards, and therefore deserved sharp spurring." The archbishop of Canterbury also thought him a man of too much
lenity: and hereupon gave him once, in a letter, some favourable advertisements; hinting, how even a friend of his
disliked his government.

Upon which admonition of the archbishop, the bishop re- His plea for
turned him this answer: " What I am, and what my doings in his letter
" are, cannot be hidden; and therefore do I refer myself to to the arch-
" the reports, not of any one, but of all severally. This I bishop.
" find, by good proof, that the rough and austere manner
" of ruling doth the least good; and, on the other part, the
" contrary hath and doth daily reclaim and win divers.
" And therefore do I choose rather to continue my accus-
" tomed and natural form and manner, which I know how
" it hath and doth work, than with others by rigour and
" extremity to overrule," &c.   And so well was he beloved
in his diocese, that it was but a year before his death, that
he occasionally signified unto the same archbishop, that he
had not an ill-willer of countenance in all the shire but one,
and that was Mr. Drury: yet even he also outwardly bore
him a friendly countenance.

He was naturally somewhat hasty, but soon appeased His temper
again. He would speak his mind freely, and fear none in a tian disposi-
                                                          tion.

BOOK I.

Anno 1574.

good cause. A true friend, and easily reconciled to any against whom he had taken a displeasure. He appointed in his diocese, (that was large,) for the better oversight thereof, ten commissaries; to whom he, as occasion served, sent instructions for the regulation and order of his see. He could have been willing to allow a liberty of officiating in the church to such as could not conform to some of the ceremonies of it; looking upon them as indifferent matters: but, upon command from above, he readily obeyed his prince's and metropolitan's authority. He was a friend to *prophecies;* that is, to the meetings of the ministers in several appointed parish churches in his diocese, as in St. Edmund's-bury, &c. to confer together about the interpretation and sense of the scriptures. But the queen forbidding it, upon some abuses thereof, the archbishop signified to him her will; and he, in obedience, sent to his archdeacons and commissaries, to have them forborne for the future.

344

His friends at court.

His great and cordial friends at court, among others, were sir William Cecil, sir Walter Mildmay, Dr. Tho. Wylson. Whom he made use of, by frequent letters to them, upon occasion.

His housekeeping and hospitality.

For some years before his death he retired from Norwich, and lived at his house at Ludham: where latewardly he retrenched his family for his debt to the queen; yet lived in some port still. But before that misfortune, his hospitality was so notable, that though the proportion of his yearly revenues was much inferior to others, it gave place to none of his profession and degree. He was not contented to feed the poor at his gate with fragments and scraps, but he had a table set for them; bringing them into his house, and having all necessaries ministered unto them, for the relief of their needs. He was ready to do good to all men, but especially to the household of faith. As for his life and conversation, it was such as might be counted a mirror of virtue, wherein appeared nothing but what was good and godly: an example to the flock in righteousness, in faith, in love, in peace, in word, in purity. He preached diligently, and exhorted the people that came to him. He was a learned man,

as well in respect of human learning as divine, well seen in CHAP. XXXII.
the sacred scriptures; an earnest protestant, and lover of
sincere religion; an excellent bishop, a faithful pastor, and Anno 1574.
a worthy example to all spiritual ministers in his diocese,
both for doctrine, life, and hospitality. This is the cha- Pref. to
Relics of
Rome.
racter given him by one that well knew him, and was a native of Norfolk, Thomas Becon, his contemporary, and of
known eminency in those days.

CHAP. XXXIII.   345

*Bishop Parkhurst's regulation of abuses in his registers.
About wills and testaments. Dr. Toby Matthew hath a
prebend in Wells: some account of him. The ill condition
of Manchester college. Rafe Lane offers to go against
the Turk, in the king of Spain's service. A corporation
for turning iron into copper. Dee's offer to discover
treasure hid. Proclamation against excess in apparel.
Sir William Pickering, an accomplished gentleman, dies.
Wolf, the printer, dies: his cosmography. Message of
the protestant princes of Germany to the queen.*

AND here, that I may gather up and preserve all that is Bishop
Parkhurst's
regulation
of his
courts and
officers.
worthy the recording of this pious bishop of Norwich, I
have found among his writings and letters the regulation
of his ecclesiastical court and officers, especially registers,
with their fees; set down either by himself or his special
order: viz. as follows:

*Abuses in my diocese concerning my registers, and other
officers.*

First, if any man depart, and make his testament. And Abuses
about last
wills and
testaments.
Int. MSS.
D. Joh.
nup. episc.
Elien.
in the same, name two or three executors, one of them
being more subtle than the other, getteth the testament,
and straightway, yea, sometimes before the testator be buried, cometh to the register, and proveth the testament
alone, without the consent of the rest. Whereunto the seal

is clapped in all haste. By means whereof he taketh so much
of the goods as he listeth.   So that the goods are not
equally divided among them according to the testator's mind.
Whereupon groweth much suit and trouble : and the rest of
the executors are without remedy.   By means whereof the
testament be not performed ; and many poor widows and
infants deceived of their right.

Therefore no testament shall be proved hereafter, but in
the presence of the judge, who ought to foresee this inconvenience.   And the judge only shall keep the seal.

Item, Whereas lawful testaments be made, divers times
there be obtained letters of administration, alleging, that
the testator died intestate.   Which letters be granted by and
by for filthy lucre sake.   For this the register taketh two
fees for one thing.   And by this means ariseth much suit :
and trouble: and manytimes the executors, for the avoiding
of suits, are compelled to renounce the testaments.   And so
they be not performed: to the undoing of many widows and
fatherless children.

Therefore hereafter no administration shall be granted,
without sufficient testimony that the party died intestate.

346   *Item,* It is reported, that the registers take two or three
fees for the administration of one man's goods.   For if a man
die intestate, divers times the administration of the goods is
granted in all haste to such as by law ought not to have the
same.   Whereupon riseth great suit.   So that before the
same be called in again, and an order granted to such as by
law ought to have it, a great part of the goods are spent
and wasted, to the great hinderance and undoing of many
widows and fatherless children.

Therefore no administration shall be granted hereafter,
without sufficient testimony, that the party who desireth the
same be the wife, or next of blood.

Item, It is reported, that letters of *colligendum* be granted
to such as have no right thereunto ; either executorship or
kindred.   Which have caused much suit and trouble.

Therefore no letters of *colligendum* shall be granted

hereafter, but where there is a testament. And then to be granted to the executors only, *sub spe testamenti appro-* bandi.

Item, It hath been reported, that there hath been an ungodly practice used in my diocese of late time. Which is, that when a testament hath been proved twenty or thirty years, more or less, at the request of any party pretending a title to the lands or goods, the executors are compelled to prove the same by witness. Which if they cannot do, either for that the witnesses be departed; or else so long agone, that the contents thereof be out of mind and remembrance, the same shall be disproved. And such as hold lands or goods by the testaments, are clean discharged thereof, to the great undoing of many.

Therefore hereafter no executors shall be compelled to prove a testament or will by witness, after that they have them under the seal of office. But if any party intend to disprove the same, let them do it by what ways and means they can otherwise.

Item, If any come to the register for a citation for any cause, the scribe maketh it before the party have declared the cause to the judge; who, upon hearing thereof, might and ought to move the parties to quietness: and manytimes there go forth citations: and when the cause cometh to the hearing of the judge, it is mere temporal.

Therefore hereafter no citation or other process shall be made, without the decree and commandment of the judge. And the judge only shall keep the seal.

Item, I have been informed, that there is more taken for fees, and writings of testaments and administrations, than should be taken by law; and for citations, institutions and inductions, and other things, more of late days, and even in my time, than hath been taken heretofore.

Therefore you shall cease from such exactions hereafter. And I will know how you be able to answer for that you have done already. And then follows a true certificate and note of fees and duties paid heretofore, and at present for citations and all other ecclesiastical instruments concerning

BOOK I.

Anno 1574.

Nº. XLII.

347

Allowance to this bishop's successor for dilapidations.

Dr. Matthews hath a prebend in Wells.

his consistory court; and what innovated. Which may be found in the Appendix.

His successor, bishop Freak, found some of the houses of the bishopric out of repair, and the abbey of St. Benedict especially. The house at Norwich, and that at Ludham, he repaired: and by law obtained allowance out of Parkhurst's estate for dilapidations. And that, it seems, in so large a measure, that the former bishop's servants were cut off from the legacies by his will bequeathed them. But to make some amends, the present bishop (whether voluntarily, or by order of the court) allowed something unto them. But as for the said abbey, the bishop did labour to be excused from putting that into any repairs; applying to the lord Burghley to obtain the queen's favour to be discharged from repairing or rebuilding rather (as he said) that abbey. And that because it was so utterly decayed; and likewise because he had bestowed so much upon putting the other houses into good repair. And since the house of St. Benedict was quite down; and the scite so unwholesome, that he neither would inhabit the same himself, nor could think that any of his successors would be resident there. And no prejudice would hereby come to any of them. He added, that his lordship would greatly pleasure him in compassing this suit for him. And thus we take our leave of good bishop Parkhurst.

Toby Matthews, S. T. P. (bred up at St. John's college, Oxon, afterwards of Christ Church,) was August 13, this year, presented to Comb 9th, a prebend in the church of Wells. Whom I mention now, because he was afterwards a great light in this church of England, namely, dean of Christ Church, Oxon. Then dean, then bishop of Durham, and archbishop of York, successively. A great preacher, and a pious, holy man. This venerable prelate first entered into orders by the motion and counsel of Dr. Calfhill, a learned dignitary of the church in those times, and his cousin: though his father and mother, persons of good quality, (who seemed to be disaffected to religion,) were not inclinable thereto; as I have seen in a letter to

the said Calfhill, soon after written to sir William Cecil,
" That he was bound by all honest means to prefer his
" cousin, as well in respect of his rare abilities, as also for Anno 1574.
" that he had followed his advice in entering into the mi-
" nistry, against the good-will of father and mother, and
" other his able friends." Matthews was soon sent for to
court by the earl of Leicester, having been recommended to
him by his said kinsman; as also to the said secretary
Cecil, who, by soliciting the queen, obtained for him the
deanery of Durham divers years after[a]; though she stuck ·Ann.1582.
a good while, because of his youth and his marriage.

When he departed from court to Durham, Cecil, (now When made
lord Burghley,) according to his grave and godly way, gave Durham,
him much good counsel for his wise and good behaviour of his answer
himself, and discharging of his duty in that place; and the Burghley's
next year sent him a letter of the same import by Mr. Ton- advice.
stal going down thither. The dean, who was of a good,
mild, as well as well-advised disposition, returned that lord
this answer; " That he trusted the grace of God should
" enable him to follow his counsel, to the discharge of his
" calling, as it had persuaded him to like thereof to the
" contentation of his mind. Wherein if any defect should
" at any time appear, especially coming to his lordship's 348
" ears, he would most humbly beseech his lordship to make
" him know it; and he did promise and desire to be re-
" formed by his authority, and directed by his wisdom
" therein, and in all things else; even as by the Socrates or
" Solomon of our age."

Ill was the state of Manchester college now, that noble The ill
and useful foundation for learning, and propagation of re- Manchester
ligion in those northern parts. Their plate and ornaments college.
detained, their lands entered upon, by pretence of concealment; and the same persons had taken away their evidences. Add to the rest, their preacher was assaulted and
wounded, as he was going to preach in one of the chapels
belonging thereto. Of all this Herle, the warden of Manchester, thought fit to acquaint the lord treasurer with, the
common patron of religion and learning. By whose letter it

appeared, that all this violence was done after the archbishop of York and other the queen's commissioners had
made a new establishment of that college, and placed learned
men there, and settled the lands of it anew : all confirmed by
virtue of the queen's letters patents. The letter was as followeth :

The warden
of the col-
lege gives
an account
thereof to
the lord
treasurer.

" Almightie God preserve your good lordship in myche
" felicitie. Pleasith your honorable lordship to understond,
" that where of late my lord's grace of York, and the com-
" missioners there, at the queen's majesty's commandment,
" have stablished an order for the college of Manchester,
" and placed both honest and learned men there : and the
" lands and revenues they have so ordered as is most ne-
" cessary for the hospitality and relieving the poor there.
" Which doing of theirs of likelihood has displeased some
" men : for on Midlent Sunday last, as our preacher (who
" is a batchelor of divinity) was riding to preche at one of
" the chapels of the parish, being distant from the parish
" church four miles, one William Smyth of the parish of
" Manchester met him by the way, and taking his horse
" by the bridle, drew his dagger, and beat and wounded
" him with three wounds. And if his horse had not broke
" out of the hand of the said Smyth, of likelihood he had
" slain him. Desiring therefore your lordship to help us,
" that quietly we may there do our function and office : or
" else if we shal be thus beaten, as before this time, and now
" our preacher is, we shal never be able to live with them ;
" except they may be punished, to the terrour of others.

" They have also caused one Thomas Stawnton, attour-
" ney of the dutchy of Lancaster, to enter into certain
" lands of the said college, called *obyte lands ;* and would
" have it conceled lands. And yet it is conteined within
" our letters patents of our foundation. And if the lands
" be taken from us, we be not able to maintain the com-
" pany. They have also taken away al our evidences and
" letters patents ; and of ornaments and plate, as much
" as the worth of 500 marks. Which plate is the queen's
" majesty's. And altho' we have proof, to whose hands

" it came after the deprivation of my predecessor, yet it is
" kept from us. Wherefore we request your honour to
" help our poor college, as before this time you have holpen
" us, (Almighty God reward you for hyt,) or else our col-
" lege had been utterly destroyed and spoiled. Whereas
" it would be able to maintain learned men to the help of
" that country. And this ye bind us to be your daily ora-
" tors; and also of al those that help to the ayd therof.
" This leaving your honour to Almighty God.

" By your lordship's ever to command,
" Thomas Herle, warden of Manchester."

This intercession in behalf of the college was very commendable in the warden. Yet not long after, did this very
warden (if I mistake not) contribute to the undoing of the
college, for the enriching of himself, as we shall read under
the year 1576.

Rafe Lane, a great soldier in these times, and that had
served the queen against the rebels in the north, and of
considerable abilities otherwise, and of reputation with the
lord treasurer and earl of Leicester, was now going to the
Spanish army that was raised against the Turks. This
man had earnestly affected the Levant service against that
enemy of Christendom: and for that purpose to gather a
regiment of his own, amounting to a thousand or two thousand men; and to head them by allowance of the king of
Spain, and to be in his pay, with letters from the queen.
Whereupon he caused somebody to ask Anthony Guerasse,
that king's agent here, his opinion, If any bulk of Englishmen, being of service, either for sea or land, or both, were
offered unto the king his master, from hence, whether the
same would be accepted with pay or not? To which question, being asked the said Anthony, his answer was directly,
" That if the same might be with her majesty's favour, he
" knew assuredly, that they should not only be largely en-
" tertained in respect of their pays; but also otherwise
" most honourably used, and most heartily welcomed by the
" king. Yea, and that it would open a great deal of kind-

Rafe Lane,
a great sol-
dier, is go-
ing to serve
against the
Turk.

The Spa-
niard will-
ing to en-
tertain him
against the
Turk.

L l 3

BOOK
I.

Hath the
queen's
leave.

The earl of
Leicester's
advice to
Lane.

The earl of
Leicester to
Dr. Wylson,
to further
Lane's bu-
siness.

" ness between those two great princes, her majesty and the
" Spaniard."

Hereupon Lane entered his suit unto her majesty for
two years leave to seek his own adventure by service. Which
in the end he obtained by honourable friends; obtaining
her majesty's letters, dated the 15th of January, 1574, unto
the commendator in Flanders; testifying her majesty's liking unto the said service intended. Upon this, he made his
conditions to the said commendator: which were, exemption of his regiment from inquisition: authority from the
king of absolute punishment of all offences committed
within the regiment: authority also to banish all our English rebels or fugitives out of the fellowship of his regiment:
also, for pay and impress. Lastly, for return in security of
the same.

In the mean time the earl of Leicester, Lane's friend, advised him to take heed he were not deceived in his reckoning; grounding himself to furnish up any sufficient numbers of men, to discharge his offers, upon the bare promises
of such [disbanded men, serving sometime under the prince
of Orange.] As, if they should break touch with him, he
350 would not only himself be ashamed, but also thereby even
her majesty in a sort touched; and all his honourable
friends in like manner dishonoured. That earl alleged himself for example; who in queen Mary's time, upon faithful
promise of forty gentlemen unto him, the said king of Spain,
sold an 100 mark land, to prepare himself for the service.
And in the end, not five kept any touch with him. He
gave him warning also of the fault, ordinary to this nation;
which was, in a strange country still to contend.

The queen had been persuaded by the said earl (who favoured this English gentleman's design) to write to the commendator. And so he signified to Dr. Wylson at that court,
that the queen's majesty, at suit of his very friend Rafe
Lane, her servant, was purposed to grant him licence, with
certain English soldiers under his conduct, to serve the
king of Spain against the Turk this next summer, and had
at this present written to signify the same to his commen-

dator; meaning shortly to write to the king, his master, to CHAP.
declare unto him as well her good meaning in the journey, XXXIII.
as also the great care she had to favour her servant in so Anno 1574.
godly and honourable an enterprise. That Mr. Digby, the
bearer of his letter, was sent on purpose to deliver her majesty's letters to the commendator; and further to deal with
him concerning certain articles, to be agreed upon for the
regiment in the voyage. All which, and the whole plot and
state of the matter, he should more particularly and at large
declare unto him. The earl prayed Wylson to hear him,
and upon his information, to take occasion to deal effectually with the commendator, in such sort as he should think
most convenient and behoveful for the furtherance of this
intent. Adding, that though the matter itself moved him
to like well hereof, yet the person also made him earnest for
him. And so much the rather, for that being an equerry,
he was (as Wylson knew) of his band. He very heartily desired him, what favour he could, to shew effectually herein;
and would heartily thank him for it. Written the 19th of
January, 1574.

This matter was so nice, and so suspicious, to have any Another re-
thing to do with the Spaniard, that another of Lane's port of this
friends, viz. Atye, the said earl's secretary, gave him another caution; advertising him, at the bottom of the same
letter, that it was told him, that the rumour was spread in
divers places, that his power that he levied for the journey
was meant to do service against the prince of Orange. That
he knew the truth to be otherwise; but that it was said to
be rumoured by Guarez himself, [the agent,] as though the
queen's majesty and his master were now upon such condition agreed. That it might perhaps serve him for some
purpose. What it might hinder or further him, [Mr. Lane,]
he could not tell; but because it was credibly told, he
thought it not amiss, with occasion of writing, to signify unto
him.

What I have further to shew of this offered exploit, is
from Mr. Lane's own pen, in some sheets of paper, with

this title, *A view of my proceedings in my intended service,
by the favour of God, and gracious leave of the queen's
most excellent majesty, from my first entry into the secret
thereof, unto the 21st of January,* 1574, *with the copies of
my letters written unto the commendator: the articles of
my offered service; and also of my letters written to Mr.
Dr. Wylson concerning the premises.* Which I refer to be
read in the Appendix.

He moves for a despatch, having the queen's leave.

Whether any thing came of this offer, I know not: it
hung for six months: for I find in June, that Lane moved
it to the lord treasurer; putting him in mind, that upon
her majesty's late good pleasure, made known unto him by
herself, touching her gracious liking and determination, for
a trial of the amendment of his hard past fortune, he
should, according to his long suit, with her majesty's good
leave, employ himself for two years, in his desired foreign
service against the common enemy of Christendom, under
don John d'Austria. And that he had requested a friend with
earnest speeches to break his matter to Antonio Guarasso:
therewith assuring him of her majesty's good liking of the
same from her majesty's own mouth; and so reminding the
treasurer of what had been transacted in that business before, in order, as it seems, to the bringing it to effect.

A project of turning iron into copper now in hand.

A great project had been carrying on now for two or
three years, of alchymy, William Medley being the great
undertaker, to turn iron into copper. Sir Thomas Smith,
secretary of state, had, by some experiments made before
him, a great opinion of it. And for the better carrying it
on, and bearing the expenses, it was thought fit to be done
by a corporation: into which, by Smith's encouragement,
the lord Burghley and the earl of Leicester entered themselves, with others: each member laying down an 100*l.* to
go on with it; as hath been shewn in the Life of Sir Thomas Smith. But the thing underwent delay, till in December this year, that lord, according as Smith advised him,
for his better satisfaction, to send some able person to Medley, to see his method, and by discourse to understand his

Life of Sir T. Smith, p. 133, &c.

ability, sent William Humfrey, assay-master of the Tower CHAP.
mint, and a chymist, with some other learned in that science, XXXIII.
to see what Medley could do, or pretend to.

Accordingly, one night there was a meeting of him, and Some, sent
Mr. Topcliff, and Medley, before sir John Ebots. Then by the lord
they entered into discourse of the bounds of metals in force Burghley,
of nature. Humfrey disliked of Medley's undertakings; discourse
thereof.
because it overreached the course of nature in metals.
Which by great and mystical experiences hath been found,
and is to be shewed wonderful [I do but transcribe from a
paper sent in to the lord Burghley] in any man's sight, as
well by calcination as by distillation, and namely by corro-
sive waters of distillation. In which the proper natures of
metal may be truly judged of, so far as is limited within
the compass of reason. As for example, gold dissolved
into water cannot be brought to the chief part of his body
again, but by the help of silver and quicksilver; and that
part which the salts hold up, and do keep in oil, will not
settle, nor separate, but by the help of blood; so that it be
not of man or sheep. *Item*, Silver dissolved into water, is
only called to his body by copper, saving a small part,
which is fixed with the spirit of salles or sea-water. In like
manner, copper dissolved into water is to be called to his
body by iron. Nay, iron dissolved into water is to be called
to his body by wood, chiefly of oak. And if any of these
should be put to the contrary office, as gold to call down 352
silver, &c. they can do nothing.

Considering these limits of nature, which God hath ordained in metals, it may appear whether this be beyond all
judgment in nature or not: for the said Mr. Medley affirmed, that there was no copper in the earth before it be
transmuted. In which his opinion, I, [the abovesaid assay-
master,] to give God the glory of his creation, affirmed unto
him, that I durst undertake before your honour, [the lord
treasurer Burghley,] to draw all spirits from the earthly
substance; and of the corps remaining, to deliver to your
lordship the copper that it containeth, without the help of
iron, or any other metal: which is to be done by the very

natural means for the separation of spirits. He nevertheless denieth that by that means copper should be gotten.
But if any might so be gotten, it would be a very small proportion, to the substance of that which by many degrees may
be transmuted by the water drawn from that earth: for he
saith, that of an hundred weight of earth oftentimes imbibed, he will convert more iron into copper than an hundred weight cometh to. Which to be done with rain water,
and not with water of the property of the earth, were wonderful, to surmount the principal in weight: and so far beyond my poor knowledge and aim, as one thing may be from
another.

For to this day I have neither read, nor proved of any
feasible knowledge, that ever any thing would deliver a
greater weight than himself. And yet I have some apert
arts of metals and salles [salts] not common to the world.
Whereof sundry have been left to posterity by some of my
kindred for many years together. But this matter is beyond
the reason of all. Nevertheless, the copper which is brought
into this *crocum*, in the sight of that right worshipful gentleman, sir John Ebots, being simply done, as by his report
appeareth, is so rich a thing, as if the earth, whereof their
transmuting water is drawn, would yield but half his own
weight in metal of copper, considering the speedy means of
bringing it to metal, it is the richest matter that in all mine-
ral causes hath been yet revealed to this state. And truly
from this earth, if the property be as it is reported, any
young man of good entrance to metalline actions might
learn lessons from the same all his life long.

Mr. Medley promised sir John Ebots to have a furnace
ready by Saturday; wherein he will melt simply *crocum* of
itself. Yet that will so fall out then with additament of
great work it may be done better. But he seemed to be ill-
willing to let me see it; and complained to sir John Ebots,
as though some went about to deprive him of his art and
labours. Whereof I am sure it is not your lordship's mind:
neither by my good-will would I be made an instrument to
such a purpose, though your honour may command me, so

far as life reacheth, &c.   As for other matters, which mine CHAP.
ears have heard of this earth, rather miraculous than com- XXXIII.
prehensible by any course of nature in metal causes, I do Anno 1574.
doubt.

But March was now come; and yet little or nothing was It is de-
done in this pretendedly advantageous project.   But the pre- layed; and
tence of the delay was the great expense required for lead, 353
iron, cask, workmen, vessels, housing, building, casting up
of earth, and other necessaries; which the undertaker of
himself could not bear.   Therefore the said earl and the secretary, (who were earnest in it,) and, by their persuasion,
the lord treasurer, did assist with round sums of money.
And Smith determined to send down his servant with Medley, ready to go down to the works; who might make a calculation, whether it would turn to account.   Which however
they themselves were in some doubt of, yet were resolved,
upon some probabilities, to make the trial.   Wherein how
busy and diligent sir Tho. Smith was, (who had a head that
way,) may be read in two letters; which I have placed in
the Appendix; not only to give some light into this project, N°. XLIII,
but also to preserve what memorials may be retrieved of that XLIV.
great, learned, and good man; not falling under my hands
when I writ his life.

This leadeth me to say something that occurreth this Dee the
year, of another way to the acquisition of vast treasure, un- astronomer
dertaken by John Dee.   This is the first time I meet with discover
the mention of that great and famous English mathemati- treasure.
cian and astronomer; noted throughout the world for his
deep knowledge in those sciences.   He was the son of Roland Dee, a servant to king Henry VIII.   Which Roland
had received some hard dealing; and was so disabled from
leaving his son due maintenance.   This year I find the said
John Dee offering to the lord treasurer Burghley, by his
art, to discover to the queen where treasure was concealed
in the bowels of the earth.   The treasurer, valuing the man
for his learning, had vouchsafed, in the midst of his weighty
business of state, to admit him to conversation with him.
Which in a letter he thankfully took notice of.   Which let-

ter I choose to set down, because it will declare much, both
of the man, his learning, and of his offer : and will preserve
some notable memorial of him.   See it exemplified in the
Appendix.

The sum whereof was, " That for the suit he would
" gladly have opened to the lord treasurer by word of
" mouth, he desired him to view in this letter a pattern of
" some part of it, viz. so much of his intent and studious
" doings, as was well known unto his honour, and the
" most part of all the universities in Christendom, (and
" further,) that for twenty years past, and longer, it might
" truly be avouched, that he had a marvellous zeal, en-
" dured great travail and toil, both of mind and body,
" spent many hundred pounds, only for the attaining some
" good and certain knowledge in the best and rarest mat-
" ters, mathematical and philosophical.   And that by due
" conference with all persons that ever he yet met with
" in Europe, the poor English Briton [meaning himself]
" had carried away the bell : for which he gave God the
" glory.   That the same zeal remained, yea rather, was
" grown greater; but that his ability, in respect of charges,
" was far less.   And that somewhat occasioned his suit, (for
" procuring speedy means of good knowledge,) upon no
" small hopes that some needful support would be for him
" devised, through the good favour the queen bore to him,
" or through the procurement of some of the right honour-
" able counsellors; who by some hard dealing, his father,
354 " servant to her majesty's father, was disabled from leaving
" him due maintenance, &c.   That in zeal to the best learn-
" ing and knowledge, and incredible toil in body and mind
" for many years, therefore only endured, he knew most
" assuredly that the learned never bred any man whose
" account therein could be greater than his, &c.   That he
" had, for twenty years space, sundry matters [about trea-
" sure hid in the ground] detected to him in sundry lands.
" That he had been sued unto by sundry sorts of people;
" who, some of them by vehement dreams reiterated ; some
" by visions; others by speech formed to their imaginations

" in the night, had been informed of certain places where CHAP.
" treasure lay hid. And these would not deal further in XXXIII.
" search, for some reasons, till he should encourage or Anno 1574.
" counsel them to proceed. But that he would never in-
" termeddle, &c. That he made it always his chief reckon-
" ing to do nothing but what might stand with the profes-
" sion of a true Christian and of a faithful subject.

" But that if, besides all books, dreams, visions, reports,
" and the *virgula divina*, by any other natural means, and
" likely demonstrations of *sympathia et antipathia rerum*,
" or by attraction or repulsion, the places might be descried
" or discovered, where gold, silver, or better matter did lie
" hid within certain distance ; how great a commodity should
" it be for the queen, and the common wealth of this king-
" dom, if by such a secret it might be deciphered in precise
" place. And also where in this land any mines or veins of
" silver and gold ore are naturally planted. And he pro-
" mised to discover such a certain mine in some place of her
" majesty's kingdom, for her only use: upon this con-
" sideration, that she would give him, by her letters pa-
" tents, her right and propriety in all *treasure trouvé*, by
" digging in any of her kingdoms." The rest I refer to the
letter.

And being a man studious of antiquities, he had dis-Dee disco-
covered another sort of treasure, viz. of many ancient re-vers ancient
records in
cords, in an old chapel in or near Wigmore castle, and for-Wigmore
merly belonging to the abbot ; which had lain there rotting castle cha-
pel.
and tossed about unregarded. In the perusal of these pa-
pers he was desirous to bestow some of his leisure time, by
way of recreation, expecting to collect thence some historical matters, either of chronicle or pedigree. And therefore Mr. Harly,
requested a letter from the lord treasurer to Mr. Harly, keeper of
the records
keeper of the records of that castle, to permit him to resort there.
thither ; promising the said lord to give him account of
whatsoever he should find there worthy his knowledge, and
particularly any thing relating to his lordship's family. Dee writes
This John Dee, (that I may bring more of his story to-instructions
gether,) in May, anno 1580, wrote instructions for the north-for the
north-east
passage.

east passage to China, delivered to the two masters, Charles Jackman and Arthur Pett, at the court day, May 17, holden at the Moscovy house in London. With which instructions a new chart, made by his hand, was given also to each of them, expressing their Cathay voyage more exactly than any yet published.

Dee's discourse of reforming the vulgar calendar: read over by the lord treasurer.

355

He did also soon after write a very learned discourse about the reformation of the calendar. And asserted therein eleven days to be added to the calendar rather than ten, according to the Gregorian reformation of it. This discourse did the lord Burghley in his retirement read over in the year 1583, and gave the following account thereof in writing, (being absent from court,) to his son Robert Cecil; and to be by him, as it seems, imparted to the queen; with the effect of his discourse with the author himself.

His judgment thereof.

" I have perused Mr. Dee's book concerning his opinion
" for the reformation of the old Roman calendar. And I
" have conferred also by speech with him at good length
" thereon. And I find his judgment resolute for the error
" and inconvenience, to have it continual, [that is, to keep
" to our old way of reckoning the year.] But he differeth
" in the quantity of the error : for he hath many proofs by
" demonstration astronomical, that the superfluous number
" of days to be abridged are eleven, where the Gregorian
" judgment makes them to be but ten. I am not skilful in
" the theoricks, to discern the points and minutes; but yet
" I am inclined to think him in the right line : for I find he
" maketh his root from the very point of the nativity of
" Christ, in the meridian of Bethlehem. And the Romans
" have made their root from the time of the council of
" Nice. And according to that, they may make their opinion.
" But by Mr. Dee it appeareth, the error in computation
" grew between the *radix* of Christ's nativity and the cele-
" bration of the Nicene council. Which he proveth by a
" great number of good authorities; such as I think the
" Romanists cannot deny.

" It were good, in mine opinion, (whereunto he also con-
" senteth,) that by her majesty's order some skilful men in

" this science, as Mr. Diggs, and others, to be called out of CHAP.
XXXIII.
" the universities, might peruse his work, and confer the
" thing by speech. And though he discovereth the ten days Anno 1574.
" to be insufficient, yet he yieldeth, for conformity, with
" the rest of the world, to assent to the reformation of our
" English calendar, with the abridgment of ten days only;
" so as the truth be denounced to the world, that it ought
" to be eleven days. Hoping that the truth will draw the
" Romanists, and the other parts of Christendom, to take
" out of their calendar hereafter the same odd day. There
" appeareth great cause to have this conference accelerated.
" For that it is requisite for a secret matter to be reformed
" before November. So as either every month, from March
" to November, may bear equal defalcation, or else some
" one month bear the whole. Thus much I thought good
" briefly to deliver you mine opinion."

A few contents of this famous book may be collected from Four asser-
certain notes, Mr. Cecil, the lord treasurer's son, took out tions in that
book, noted
of it. Setting down (as I take it from his MS.) four strange by Mr. Rob.
points therein laid down. I. The great declination of the Cecil.
sun is yearly changeable. Which was in Christ's time more
northerly and southerly, than now it is, by twenty-four
prime minutes of a degree. II. The prick in the heaven,
where the sun is the highest, called *apogæum*, hath varied.
For in Christ's time, it was about the fifth degree of Ge-
mini. And so twenty-five degrees before the beginning of
Cancer. And now it is past the 8th degree of Cancer,
about fifty-five minutes. III. The third is the alteration of
the sun's distance from the centre of the earth. For the 356
eccentricicle of the sun is less than it was in Christ's time by
106 parts. And now the sun being in the ninth degree of
Cancer, he is nearer the earth than he was in Christ's time
by 1199 of our miles. IV. The fourth point is, the alteration of the fixed stars, declining to the east more than in
former times, although they keep their own mutual distance. This for Dee.

There came forth this year a proclamation for regulating The queen
issueth a

BOOK
I.

Anno 1574.
proclama-
tion against
excess in
apparel.

apparel: which by this time grew to be so excessive and costly, that the queen thought fit now (as she had done two or three times before) to retrench it; and to oblige her subjects to more thrift in their clothes. It hath this preamble, (shewing the evil of wearing sumptuous apparel;) " That " excess of apparel, and the superfluity of unnecessary fo- " reign wares thereto belonging, now of late years was " grown by sufferance to such an extremity, that the mani- " fest decay not only of a great part of the wealth of the " whole realm generally was like to follow, by bringing the " realm such superfluity of silks, cloths of gold, silver, and " other most vain devices, of so great cost for the quantity " thereof, as of necessity the money and treasure of the " realm is and must be yearly conveyed out of the same, " to answer the said excess; but also particularly the wast- " ing and undoing of a great number of young gentlemen; " men otherwise serviceable; and others, seeking by show " of apparel to be esteemed as gentlemen: who, allured by " the vain show of those things, did not only consume " themselves, their goods and lands, which their parents " had left unto them, but also ran into such debts and " shifts, as they could not live out of danger of laws, with- " out attempting of unlawful actions: whereby they were " not any ways serviceable unto their country, as otherwise " they might have been. Which great abuses turning both " to so manifest a decay of the wealth of the realm, and to " the ruin of a multitude of serviceable young men, and " gentlemen, and of many good families:

" The queen therefore had, of her own princely wisdom, " so considered these inconveniencies and evils, that she had " of late, with great charge to her council, commanded the " same to be presently and speedily remedied, both in her " own court, and in all other places of her realm, according " to sundry good laws heretofore provided." At the end of this proclamation are set down the brief contents of certain clauses of the statutes of king Henry VIII. and queen Mary, about apparel, with some moderation thereof, to be

observed, according to a former proclamation in the first CHAP.
year of her reign. For which the reader may have recourse <u>XXXIII.</u>
to the Appendix.

The realm was so apt to transgress in this point, and so N°. XLVI.
much affected gayety in apparel, that before this, in the eighth proclama-
year of the queen's reign, dated at Greenwich, February 12, tion for ap-
1565, she set forth a proclamation for apparel. And here parel.
the preamble was, " That she considered the extremities
" that a great number of her subjects was grown to by ex-
" cess in apparel, both contrary to the laws of the realm,
" and to the disorder and confusion of the degrees of all
" states; wherein all diversity of apparel hath taken place;
" and finally, to the subversion of all good order, by reason 3 5 7
" of remissness and impunity."

To which I may add another proclamation to the same And others
intent, anno 1577, with certain additions of exceptions; and intent.
another, anno 1579, 22 Eliz. entitled, *A proclamation with
certain clauses of divers statutes, and other necessary additions; first published in the* 19*th year of the queen, and
now revived by her highness's commandment, to be put
in execution upon the penalties in the same contained.* And
yet another in the 30th year of her reign, anno 1588, or rather a *declaration* of her will and command, to have certain
laws and orders put in execution against excess of apparel;
notified by her commandment, in the Star-chamber, Feb.
12. It is called there, *An intolerable abuse, grown to an
unmeasurable disorder.*

Sir William Pickring, knt. died this year: whom I men- Sir William
tion, as being one of the finest gentlemen of this age, for his Pickring
worth in learning, arts, and warfare; and who was once in
nomination to marry queen Elizabeth. His father was sir
William Pickering, knt. marshal to king Henry VIII.
" This his son was a person nobly endowed in body and
" mind. *Literis excultus, et religione sincerus. Linguas
" exacte percalluit.* He served four princes, viz. Henry
" VIII. Edward VI. queen Mary, and queen Elizabeth.
" To the first he served in the wars; to the second he was
" ambassador to the court of France; to the third, viz. to

" queen Mary, he served in an embassy into Germany; and
" to queen Elizabeth *summis officiis devotissimus*." This
was written on his tombstone in the church of St. Helen's,
London.   In which parish Pickring-house was: where he
lived, and was buried thence: age 58.   His executors
were sir Thomas Heneage, knt. treasurer of the queen's
chamber; John Asteley, esq. master of the queen's jewels;
Druc Drury, and Tho. Wotton, esqrs. who set up a goodly
monument for him.

Wolf, the
printer,
dies.
To which I join Reginald Wolf, a German by birth, a
very famous and skilful printer for many years in London;
who died in November this year.   A learned and a good
man.   He was employed in printing several of archbishop
Cranmer's books, and most of the public orders and books
for religion in the times of Henry VIII. king Edward, and
queen Elizabeth.   Bishop Parkhurst, in a letter to Gualter,
concerning the death of this Wolf, calleth him, *bibliopola-
rum Londinensium flos*.   He lived in St. Paul's church-yard,
at the sign of the Brasen Serpent.   He was printer to the
queen, and a citizen of great esteem and reputation.   Sir
William Cecil took particular notice of him, and favoured
him; and so did Parker, archbishop of Canterbury.   For
twenty-five years he laboured in compiling and preparing,
His Cosmo-
graphy.
in order to the publishing, an *Universal Cosmography;*
and therewith certain particular histories of every known
nation.   And he had several learned men to assist him in
Epist.dedi-
cat. to Ho-
linshed's
Chronic.
this work, and to peruse the collections that he made.   Ra-
phael Holinshed was one of them.   And so far did the
said Wolf proceed in this nobly designed work, that little
wanted of the accomplishment thereof, when he died.   By
his decease no hope remained to see that performed, which
he had so long travailed in.   Those he put in trust to dispose of his concerns after his departure, willed the said
358 Holinshed to continue his endeavour for the furtherance
of the aforesaid work.   And Wolf himself left it to his care
to see it brought to some perfection.   But the volume grew
so great, that the executors were afraid to defray the charges
of the impression.   And so Holinshed did retrench and

contract his designs, to the history of England, Scotland,
and Ireland, only.

The histories that he gathered for this end, he conferred,
as he tells his reader, the greatest part with Wolf, in his life-
time, to his liking: who had procured him so many helps to
the furtherance thereof, that he was loath to omit any thing
that might increase the reader's knowledge; which was the
cause of the largeness of the book. In his chronology he
followed Functius, according to the advice and direction also
of the said Wolf.

I shall conclude this year with the mention of a message,
sent to the queen in the month of December, from some
protestant princes in Germany, by their agent Petrus Dathenus: offering her certain propositions, for the common
safety of them and their religion, and (as those princes
added) highly necessary for the Christian state. It seems
to have been concerning entering into an alliance, to which
they invited the queen. The lord treasurer being now laid
up with the gout, the messenger sent the same propositions
to him by Mr. H. Killegrew, with their letter. By which
letter those princes exhorted him to move the queen in the
said matters; and that it would be an office most grateful to
God and the Christian world, and most useful to this kingdom especially, and worthy of immortal glory to posterity.
And by another letter written to that lord by Dathenus, in
the same month, he prayeth him, that he would advise her
majesty that which might be favourable to the protestant
princes; which would also be advantageous to the interest of
religion.

CHAP. XXXIV.

A parliament: and convocation. The troubles of the bi-
shop of Ely, for the preserving of the revenues of his see.
His excellent letter to the queen thereupon; and to Dr.
Masters; and to the lord treasurer, upon articles of ac-
cusation preferred against him to the queen and council.
The malice and slanders of them. His satisfactory an-
swers. Comes up to answer before the council. The
lord treasurer his friend. Reconciles him to the queen.
The case of Downham park; claimed by the lord North,
from the bishop, upon account of an old lease.

A parlia-
ment.
A bill about
religion.

THE parliament was now sitting in the months of February and March, 18 Elizabeth. What was done there of
political matters, I refer the reader to the other historians,
and especially to D'Ewes' Complete Journal of that queen's
parliaments. But some particulars relating thereunto may
deserve to be mentioned, as I gather them from some private letters to the earl of Shrewsbury from his two sons,
Gilbert and Francis, then members of the lower house;
shewing, " how there was at this time a great resort from
" all places thither, [to the court,] and that notwithstand-
" ing, all things were in such quiet, that, besides matters of
" parliament, they knew nothing worth advertising him of."
That there was a bill in the higher house to this import;
" That whosoever would not receive the communion, and
" come to church, should pay yearly a certain sum of money.

Febr. 20.

" But that it was not yet come down to their house. That
" as for the rest of the bills, except that of the subsidy,
" they were matters of no great moment, though they were
" for the reformation of abuses." This parliament was
prorogued on the 15th of March to the 5th of November.
" Where, after the lord keeper's answer to Bell the speaker's
" oration, [the import whereof was an earnest motion to her

Epist. Com.
Salopien. in
Offic. Ar-
mor.

" majesty to marry,] she herself made a very eloquent and
" grave oration, which (as those gentlemen expressed it to
" the earl in their letter) was as well uttered and pro-
" nounced as it was possible for any creature to do." And

therefore pity it is, that it remains not on record, as some of her speeches do, either in the Journal of parliament, or in _____ D'Ewes' supplies of many deficiencies there, by the neg- Anno 1575. lects of the clerks of both houses in that queen's reign. Nor doth he himself so much as make any mention of this notable speech.

The convocation at this time of parliament, sitting, framed The convo-
cation
articles, fifteen in number, touching the admission of apt frame arti-
persons to the ministry, and for the establishing of good cles.
 orders in the church : which were published by the queen's authority. And though they are not in bishop Sparrow's Collection of Articles, Injunctions, &c. yet they may be found in the Life of Archbishop Grindal. Life of Bi-
shop Grin-
It will in part shew the state of the church in these times, dal, p. 194. to observe the labours used by many great men, to get some 360 of the manors and revenues of the sees from the bishops; The bishop
of Ely's
by applying themselves to the queen, requiring them either troubles for
preserving
to make exchanges, or to grant long leases, or else to make his reve-
them grant away some parts thereof ; and so to impoverish nues.
their sees. This year the ancient good bishop of Ely (who had deserved passing well of learning and of the church, both in the days of king Henry and king Edward) met with great trouble on this occasion from the lord North, and Mr. Christopher Hatton, vice-chamberlain to the queen, and her favourite.

This gentleman had lately desired the bishop's house in Mr. Hatton
endeavours
Holborn by lease. And it seems had also got a letter to to get a
the bishop in favour thereof : but the bishop excused it, and lease of his
house in
urged, in all the best terms he could, that he could not be London.
without his house when he should come up to London. Nor could he be so injurious to his successors, as it might prove after his decease ; which could not be long. Yet offering to do for him whatsoever he conveniently might, and would gladly tender it to him ; especially, because the queen had made so good choice of him to attend her person.

But when nothing afterwards would serve, but that the The bishop
refuseth to
whole seat of the bishops of Ely, in Holborn, must be alien- alienate
ated and passed away by him to the said Hatton, (who, by Ely-house
to him.

BOOK
I.

Anno 1575.

His letter
to the
queen.

his favour with the queen, had obtained her letter for that purpose,) this created him a new trouble; nor herein could he comply. And by a Latin letter, in an elegant style, mixed with cogent reasons, from that trust that was committed to him, when he was made bishop, and the wrong he should do to the see, and his successors, he humbly suggested to the queen his refusal; importing, " That her ma-" jesty's letter did not a little disturb and terrify him. For " that which he at first feared, when he granted a part of " his house for some years to Mr. Hatton, was now plainly " come to pass. And confessing, that his predecessors were " more constant than he. For her royal father, king Henry " VIII. obtained not Ely-house for Wriothesly, his chan-" cellor, only for a time. Nor could the mighty duke " of Northumberland drive the bishop from his house in " that time; nor had he (the present bishop) yielded his " said house to her servant, Parris, however she had for-" merly requested it. But at last, wearied with prayers, he " had let a part of it for twenty-one years unto her servant " Hatton, lest he might seem to be guilty of ingratitude " towards her majesty. But that since now it was required, " that he should grant it away for ever, and other things " likewise appendant to it, to these it was hard for him " to yield." He added, " He sailed between Scylla and " Charybdis: that he could have wished rather to die, (God " he called to witness,) than deservedly to offend her ma-" jesty; but if we rashly offend our God, a second death " were to be feared." And so the bishop went on at large, excusing himself to her in this demand. But I leave the

No. XLVII.

whole letter in the Appendix; which cannot be read but with much pleasure and satisfaction: concluding, that to a perpetual alienation of that his house, his fearful conscience could never yield. It was dated from Ely-house.

361

And the
lord North
other ma-
nors.

Again, some noblemen, and, among the rest, the chief was the lord North, endeavoured to fleece this bishopric. The last named got letters from the queen, dated in May 1575, to the bishop, to part with the manor and lands of Somersham, one of the best manors of the bishopric. And by

getting a lease of one of the bishop's tenants, claimed Down- CHAP.
ham-park, another part of his revenues; and was like vio- XXXIV.
lently to enter into possession of it.   And because the bi- Anno 1575.
shop would not yield, and professed that he could not in
conscience betray that which was intrusted to him, and
wrong the church of God, the angry and fierce lord endeavoured to draw the queen's indignation upon him, for his
humble letter of refusal to her, and other sinister informations; which we shall hear of by and by.   Nor did this attempt against him pacify him; but further, he caused a
great number of articles to be drawn up against him, the
bishop, as some great criminal, for him to answer before the
privy council.   When these articles of accusation were He accuses
brought to the lord treasurer Burghley, he communicated the bishop
them to secretary Walsingham: who both were of this articles.
judgment, that if the articles were personal, as about his
covetousness, ill housekeeping, &c. the fault was rather to
light upon him, than that the see should suffer for it, as the
secretary wrote well in his letter to that lord, when he sent
him the principal matters wherewith the bishop was to be
charged, and by whom.   " I am," said he, " of your lord-
" ship's opinion, that if he [the bishop] be found guilty, the
" penalty must light upon him, and not upon the see."

But let us see the process of this business.   First, the The bi-
wronged bishop having received her majesty's letter above ter to the
said, (wrote in May, not received by him till the 18th of queen.
June,) returned a very earnest, wise, and godly answer on
the same day, penned with all submission; and yet shewing
plainly to her the danger of sacrilege, and cautioning her of
drawing sin upon herself by such fleecing of the church.
In which letter (which was written in Latin) he thus addressed to her; " That her majesty had seriously requested
" him to make a demise of the lands in Somersham.   This
" he acknowledged put him into fear and doubt what to do.
" That if he should not answer the desire of so great a
" prince and queen, that had so many ways merited of him,
" he might be esteemed ungrateful, and draw on himself an
" indignation heavier than death itself.   And again, if he

" should deny their request and desire, who with so much
" solicitation had obtained these letters from her majesty,
" they would take it very grievously, and accuse him of in-
" gratitude and stubbornness, and would not cease to draw
" him into her highness's hatred.   And on the other side, if
" he should grant that which they desired, he should greatly
" injure and wrong both himself and his successors ; and so
" he should be esteemed unjust, if he should yield to their
" unjust desires.   That in this matter some noblemen had
" of late tried him, both by entreaty, money, and friends,
" to overcome him ; but hitherto he had held out uncon-
" quered.

"   But that now, when they came to try their last effort,
" he was forced to fly to his last refuge ; that is, to his hum-
" ble prayers. *Wherefore,* (as he then proceeded to address
362 " the queen,) *for equity and for justice sake, and by that*
" *compassion born with you, I pray and beseech you, let*
" *not your high prudence take it amiss, if I produce rea-*
" *sons which move me, not to answer this demand.*   That
" he knew that tributes and taxes, and also tenths, first-
" fruits, and subsidies, were due to the higher powers ; yea,
" that whatsoever came into their use, came into the public
" good : but that the condition of subjects was far different.
" For they that gaped after, and laid snares for other men's
" profits, were not to be yielded to, but rather resisted ;
" especially, if they went so far as to fly upon the goods of
" the church.   For if pious kings and queens, and truly
" noble men, yea, if the common people also, inflamed with
Gal. vi.   " the zeal of propagating the gospel, had communicated to
" them of all their goods, who had instructed them in the
" word of God, how godless and ignoble were they to be
" judged, who did not only not communicate to their in-
" structors in any good things, but endeavoured to diminish
" and take away the goods of the instructors, and wickedly
" to convert them to their own uses.   That he certainly
" sinned against the law of nations, who violated and an-
" nulled the testament and last will of a testator.   That St.
Gal. ii.   " Paul writ, that *when a man's testament stands proved, no*

" *man rejecteth, or addeth any thing to it.* Besides, when
" God in his law had abundantly supplied his priests and
" Levites for their subsistence ; and when nature itself de-
" dicated the same ; and that St. Paul writ, that *we must*
" *live of the gospel.* Lastly, if the Spirit of God had so
" warmed the breasts of Christians with a zeal of godliness,
" that they had most devoutly placed out their goods, their
" farms, and fields, unto pious uses, to wit, for the propa-
" gation of the gospel, and to keep hospitality, (he asked,)
" who was he that dared to destroy this divine provision?
" That God was very angry with the people, that his mi-
" nisters were miserably spoiled; *yea, are cursed with a*
" *curse,* said he.

" That it were to be wished from the Lord God, that the
" rule of nature, nay, that the rule of Jesus Christ, rested in
" the breasts of those that catched at other men's goods,
" *viz. Do that to another, which ye would another should do*
" *to you.* Further he asked, whether it was not trouble-
" some enough, that her majesty's priests every where were
" despised and trodden upon, and were esteemed as the off-
" scourings of the world, unless the commodities which they
" possessed were thus licked and scraped away from them?
" Praying God to grant better things. That it would be
" notable ingratitude, if their [the bishops'] labours and
" dangers, or rather God by them, had driven the pope and
" all papistry out of England ; if they had placed a king
" and a queen in their most just thrones ; if, lastly, by
" them the houses and the lands of monks, without number,
" had rescued abundance of the English from beggary, and
" enriched others with wealth, and others advanced to ho-
" nours : was this their reward in the end, to be recom-
" pensed with ingratitude? That they should be deprived
" of their profits, and should fill up the bottomless pit of
" evil concupiscence. In a word, that it was greatly to be
" lamented, that they who attempted these things were not
" afraid to contemn the manifest command of the great
" God, and dared also to ensnare her majesty in the like 363
" danger. It was commanded, *Thou shalt not covet any*

" *one's house*, &c.   That it was not lawful to violate the
" command of God ; nor was it lawful to yield help or fa-
" vour to those that violated a command."

And then he concluded his letter to her in this affection-
ate manner : " These weights of the justest arguments do
" so press and terrify my mind, that I dare by no means to
" assent to such votes.   And furthermore, by all that is sa-
" cred, I most humbly pray and beseech you, that we may
" prevail upon your piety to give us leave to use and enjoy
" those things, which your benignity hath heretofore con-
" ferred upon us, ministers of the word, so long as we shall
" not seem unworthy of this our function.   For Christ Jesus
" sake, be ye a most pious nurse, favourer, and defender of
" your clergy, in this wicked and atheistical age.   And let
" your most prudent piety vouchsafe candidly to interpret
" this my confidence, proceeding from a pious heart, possess-
" ed with a fear of God.   The Lord Jesus Christ preserve
" your majesty through many ages safe, to the glory of his
" name, and the prosperity of his holy church.

" Your majesty's chaplain, and most humble bishop."

This courageous letter, and yet accompanied with a decency suitable to majesty, written in very elegant Latin,
(whereof this is but the imperfect translation,) deserveth,
both for the style and matter, to be preserved among our
records, where I have accordingly placed it.

The holy bishop observed well the malice of the foresaid
lord ; and it concerned him to make all the friends he could
against this *northern* blast.   And therefore soon after his
letter to the queen, he wrote both to the lord treasurer, relating to him the whole matter ; and urging his ancient
friendship, to interpose for him to the queen.   And he wrote
also to Dr. Masters, the queen's physician, who was often
about her person ; and so might take his opportunity to
speak in the bishop's cause.

In his private letter to the queen's physician, he told him,
how the lord North, and others, urged the queen to get the
manor of Somersham from the bishopric ; and how they

Nº. XLVII.

The bishop
makes
friends at
court.

Writes to
the queen's
physician ;

had at length cunningly brought her (he would not say, seduced her) to it.   And that all this evil, as he heard, came from the north.   The letter being short, I will set it down.   *Olim principes, nobilesque, zelo evangelii propagandi accensi, sua bona terrasque contulerunt.   Hodie qui curios simulant et bacchanalia vivunt, tanquam harpyiæ rapacissimæ, evangelium spoliant.   Ager meus Somershamensis plures habet competitores, quam unquam habuit formosissima Helena, contra manifestum Dei mandatum, Non concupisces, &c.   Adeo ut regiam majestatem eo callide adegerint, nolo dicere seduxerint, ut ipsa in suum usum dimissionem Somershamiæ, a me petat.   Ab aquilone, (ut auditum habeo,) panditur hoc malum.   Majestatis suæ petitioni non consensi.   Siquid vel verbulo me juvare poteris, spero te mihi non defuturum esse.   Dominus Jesus tibi benedicat.*   In which letter he subjoined, that the lord North stormed that he was dishonoured, and that her majesty must not put up such an answer.

By some words in this letter wrested by the bishop's ene- 364 mies, the queen hearing thereof, conceived a displeasure against him, as we shall see by and by.

To the lord treasurer Burghley, some months after, viz. in November, he applied himself also, being under great concern for certain articles that were in much spite and rancour to be laid against him.   He was now at his manor of Downham; there, it seems, to keep possession against his foresaid enemy, that pretended to his park there, as was said before.   In his letter, the bishop shewed at large to that lord the condition in which he was like to be brought by the implacable malice of the person aforesaid: all the actions of his years ripped up, and grievous crimes, even of *premunire*, to be laid to his charge; the queen to be provoked against him; and a commission to be taken out for a strict examination of all his doings.   For thus did the afflicted bishop pour out his complaint into his friend the treasurer's bosom.

" Right honourable sir. I have heretofore troubled you " with the understanding of my matters. The truth is, I

" considered how ye were overwhelmed with the multitude
" of causes, &c. But now, sir, because I am driven *tan-*
" *quam ad sacram anchoram,* do crave your friendly aid.
" For that *amicus certus in re incerta cernitur.* It is too
" manifest, that a great many are very desirous, and gape
" greedily, *ad deplumandum graculum Æsopicum, quem*
" *indignum putant alienis ornari plumis.* Such are their
" judgments. If we had no lordships nor manors, we
" should never be troubled. But if we have them by need-
" ful, godly, and charitable order, and just laws, *Væ! illis,*
" *qui nobis negotium facessunt.* They look and contend
" vehemently for a more pure reformation. But if the
" church's lands were dispersed, their reformation would
" soon be at an end.

" I understand that the lord North is in high displeasure
" against me for Somersham. He stirreth coals strongly.
" He hath a commission, as he saith, to search and ransack
" all my doings, since my first entry. He saith, he hath
" found already plentiful matter against me ; which, if it be
" true, I shall not be turned out of my living only, but shall
" be brought *ad extremam mendicitatem.* For, as he re-
" porteth, there are found five *premunires* against me, and
" two against Dr. Ithel, my chancellor. Indeed, two were
" enough to undo us both. Again, he blazeth abroad, that
" I pass little upon her majesty's letters, and take them and
" count them but a blast of wind. Whereby her majesty's
" indignation is greatly stirred against me ; and that she
" should say, she hath borne with me, and put up many
" complaints against me, in consideration of my age, and for
" that I was her father's and brother's servant ; and that
" she perceived now, there was no good nature in me.

" *Hæc sunt tela mortalia, ægrum pectus ad mortem us-*
" *que torquentia et vexantia.* How false and untrue it is,
" that I should so little pass of her highness' letters, I cer-
" tainly know, *et Christus Jesus et testis et judex est,* I
" never thought any such thing.

365   " Furthermore, sir, if this commission of examination go
" forward, in this dangerous world, so sore bent against men

" of our religion, ye know full well, *quam facile sit baculum*
" *invenire, ut canem cædas*. I cannot think that this hurly-
" burly should rise of Mr. Hatton, for the first denial of his
" suit.   For as he wrote to me to have my house by lease, I
" could not grant it without the injury of my successors;
" whereunto in conscience I cannot yield. I would gladly
" do for Mr. Hatton what I might conveniently do ; and I
" gladly tender him, for that her majesty hath so good choice
" of him.

  " In the end, let me entreat you, my good lord, to be a
" means, that the commission may be stayed. For *etsi nihil*
" *mihi conscius sum, non tamen in hoc justificatus sum*.   I
" will not dissemble my doing *coram Domino et Christo ejus*.
" I am doing, in laying forth Christ through his grace, and
" the plain way to heaven, in teaching the true obedience,
" and charitable dealings ; rebuking of sin, and reforming of
" errors, (which some little regard, and some cannot bear ;)
" in severe correcting and punishing of vices. *Et hinc illæ*
" *lachrymæ*. Now then, in the end, thus to be recom-
" pensed, shall be a comfort to the wicked, and a grief to
" the godly.   I acknowledge her majesty's great goodness
" and tender affection towards me, since the beginning of
" her majesty's reign.   I have felt of that, and do acknow-
" ledge that printed in heart, expressed in words, and de-
" clared in deeds. Whatsoever I can or may do, shall be at
" her majesty's commandment ; matters of conscience, and
" matters of God, touching the edifying his church, only
" excepted.   For herein, *magis obediendum est Deo quam*
" *hominibus;* not doubting, but that the holy gospel will so
" stay her majesty's heart, that she will never devise nor
" desire any thing that is against God ; but if she be charita-
" bly admonished, she will make a godly stay.

  " I intend, God willing, to repair to London with conve-
" nient speed.   I would be very loath to be sent for as a
" notorious offender. Which thing would minister too much
" fond talk among the fond heads in the world. The whole
" matter I commit to your prudent device, as to my most
" dear and assured friend. *Dominus Jesus diu te servet in-*

"*columem regno, reginæ et reip.* From my house at Down-
" ham, 21st November, 1575.

" Your lordship's assured, Rich. Ely."

It was but the next month the good bishop received some
comfortable intelligence from the said lord, (on whom he so
entirely depended in this difficulty,) with expressions of his
real friendship and good-will, promising him therein, undoubtedly, what assistance lay in his power. For which the
bishop, in another letter writ towards the latter end of December, expressed a grateful sense; and withal shewed him
how ungrateful that lord was to him, who had done many a
good turn for him, and particularly had made him his high
steward; and how he was now labouring by a wile, to get
his park from him. He sent withal enclosed a copy of some
of the articles against him, (as many as he could procure,)
366 for the said lord treasurer to peruse, with his answer to
them; and another paper containing reasons, by the bishop
drawn up, against alienating the goods of the church. And
so again recommending himself and his cause unto his
friendly and godly judgment. The tenor of which letter
was, " That he daily felt his friendly zeal and good-will
" towards him. That he found it true, *amicus certus in re*
" *incerta cernitur.* That he doubted not, but that his lord-
" ship weighed thoroughly how uncharitably he was handled,
" for that he would not yield to the ungodly request of him,
" who, professing entire friendship, was fallen away to be an
" open adversary, to onerate him [the bishop] with a num-
" ber of injuries done by him, and with her majesty's griev-
" ous indignation against him. The bishop added, that he
" had done more for him than for any nobleman in Eng-
" land: and because he could not wring from him the prin-
" cipal member of his living, he pretended he was now dis-
" honoured, and sought revengement."

And one instance more of lord North's injustice he mentioned to that lord, to whom he was now writing; " That
" he had lately bought a title of one Austen Styward; and
" on that pretence had made entry upon his park at Down-

" ham, by colour of a lease; and that if he were not by and
" by, by some means, stayed, he feared he would enter *im-*
" *petuose.*"

He added, " That he, the bishop, had gotten as many
" accusations as he could come by, and made answer unto
" them; whereof he had sent secretly a copy to his lord-
" ship; to the intent that at his convenient leisure he might
" peruse it, and judge of it according to his wisdom: and
" that he had made suit to the honourable council for a copy
" of matters exhibited against him, that he might not be ut-
" terly to seek when he should be called to answer."

And then he made this melancholy observation of the
poor church's condition; " That when he considered the
" far-fetch of the papist, the dangerous drift of the preci_
" sian, the greedy gaping of the atheists, he was marvel-
" lously moved to suspect the worst; and to cry to God to
" preserve his church."

The bishop acquainted the treasurer further with another
particular of the lord North's resolution: " That he wrote
" to some of his friends, that he would try what he could do
" by law, by the council, and by the parliament. What
" lurked under that, the bishop said, he should much fear,
" but that he was persuaded, that her majesty, himself, [the
" lord treasurer,] and a few other, *statis in fide, et viriliter*
" *agitis,* [stood fast in the faith, and would quit themselves
" like men.]"

And withal he sent the treasurer a few reasons, which
ought, he said, to move good Christians to tender the state
of the ministers of God's sincere religion. For which reasons I refer the reader to the Appendix.

Numb.
XLVIII.

The next month, the malice continuing, the bishop again
applied himself to his friend, the lord treasurer. The occasion was this: the private letter that he wrote to Dr. Masters,
mentioned above, some way or other, was intercepted; and
fell into the hands of his enemy, the lord North: who
thought he had now gotten an effectual advantage against
him, by rendering him odious to the queen, for some ex-

Slandered
to have re-
flected on
the queen.

367

BOOK
I.

Anno 1575.

pressions in that letter; as though he had called her majesty
an harpy and plunderer of the church. This coming at
length to the bishop's ears, he was glad again to use all his
endeavours with the lord treasurer, to set him right with
the queen. He was now come up to London, to be ready
to answer those articles before mentioned against him. And
from his house in Holborn he thus writ to that lord, his
friend, on this present occasion.

Which oc-
casioned'
him to write
again to the
lord trea-
surer.

" My very good lord, I trust I shall be able to answer to
" all mine accusations before indifferent judges : which I
" doubt not God will send me. Only one thing, which is
" not yet put in, (otherwise taken than I meant,) may
" breed some disliking : which is this : at what time I sent
" mine answer to her majesty for Somersham, I wrote a
" private letter to Dr. Masters, being stirred by an earnest
" zeal against such as, without the fear of God, seek their
" own gain with the spoil of God's ministers. This letter
" the lord North, before it was delivered, hath perused,
" whether by opening thereof, or otherwise, God knoweth.
" He chargeth me, that I term her majesty *harpyiam et lu-*
" *pum :* for that I writ against such harpies and wolves, *qui*
" *inhiant ecclesiasticis bonis.* And that there I did add
" these words, *Etiam ipsa in idem crimen delapsa.*

" *Siquid hic peccaverim, non recuso temeritatis et stulti-*
" *tiæ crimen agnoscere, et ad innatam regiæ celsitudinis*
" *clementiam confugere.* Truly I wrote in this sort to Dr.
" Masters purposely for that I knew him to be a man zeal-
" ous towards the word of God and the ministers thereof,
" and faithfully tendering her majesty's honour. And I
" knew, that he, having convenient occasion, would humbly
" and prudently admonish her majesty of such greedy men,
" which would abuse her honourable letters. Whose godly
" mind was never to force any man to his hinderance. For
" in maintaining and aiding such manner of men, her ma-
" jesty should seem to be partaker of their crimes. *Quod*
" *absit :* in the height and zeal against the lord North his

" uncharitable dealing, I was stirred up to write much
" after the example of the prophets, of Christ himself, his
" apostles, and other godly fathers heretofore.

" I pray you, my good lord, to open this matter, as you
" shall have opportunity, that I may feel some taste of her
" godly clemency. *Dom. Jesus te nobis diutissime servet in-*
" *columem.* From my house in Holbourn, this 18th day of
" February, 1575.

" Your lordship's assured,

" Richard Ely."

Thus was the aged bishop fain to come up even in the cold,
sharp, winter weather, in the month of January, to answer
what articles of pretended crimes and misdemeanours were
laid against him: but not doubting to make his innocence
appear as manifest as their malice. But first he laboured to
get access to her majesty's presence. In order to which he
addresseth a message to his friend the lord treasurer after
this manner; " That importunate beggars, where they find
" most relief, there most often they resort. That his lord-
" ship's friendship being so ready towards him, made him
" still to be bold upon him. And that he was very desir-
" ous to give his dutiful attendance upon her majesty. But
" that unless he might know it to be her highness's good
" contentation, *non libenter me ingero;* [i. e. he would not
" willingly intrude himself.] And therefore heartily prayed
" him, as his opportunity should serve, to understand her
" majesty's pleasure therein.

The bishop
comes up to
answer the
articles laid
against him.

368

" That he had perused all the accusations against him
" [whereof there were divers sheets] and would gladly an-
" swer them, when and where the honourable council should
" appoint him." Adding these modest words; " *Non me*
" *per omnia justificabo. Certe nihil mihi conscius sum.*
" *Sed non in hoc justificatus sum.* I will not dissemble
" mine infirmities and faults; but surely the accusations are
" frivolous, untrue, slanderous, malicious, &c. A sore cause
" in a commonwealth, for a man to be so ransacked upon
" mere malice and displeasure. *Exemplum in rep. bene in-*

BOOK I.

" *stituta non ferendum.*" This was dated from his house in Holborn, January the 18th, 1575.

Anno 1575.
The lord North's charges upon the bishop in a letter to him.

Now to look more particularly into these heavy charges laid against the bishop, I shall first set down the contents of a letter sent from the lord North to the bishop: to which the bishop gave distinct answers in another to that lord. That lord wrote, " That what he had done, he was urged " thereto by such commandment as he dared not disobey. " That he wished from the bottom of his heart, that the " bishop would shake off his stubbornness. That to the " queen as yet he had done no special service, [as he, the " lord North, had by an embassy.] That he [the bishop] " lived wretchedly, both within and without his house. " That he was extremely covetous: a mervailous dairy man, " a rich farmer, &c." To these, and the like personal accusations and complaints, the full and satisfactory answers that he made, being somewhat large, I lay in the Appen-

No. XLIX. dix: a copy of which he sent to the lord treasurer, for the making him the better acquainted with the controversy on both sides.

More objections and blames laid upon the bishop. With his answer.

These complaints were drawn up in a letter from the lord North to the bishop, November 20. Again, divers objections more he made, in another letter to the said bishop, December 11. As, how the bishop commonly granted the *good abearing*, and made it a common bond in the isle of Ely. That when the bishop of Ely should forgive any man, [it was so seldom or never done,] that he would say, *Nunc dimittis;* and divers such like: which, with the bishop's an-

Numb. L. swers, are also put in the Appendix.

More complaints still.

These were not all, but there was also drawn up a large book of sundry complaints of divers persons against the bishop; many of them false, and all of them misrepresented. Which he answered article by article. Which, for the vindication of the memory of an excellent bishop, and that had a great hand in our first reformation, and one of king Edward's instructors, I have likewise thought fit to preserve

Numb. LI. in the Appendix. Wherein will be seen many remarks of that bishop's life, condition, and actions. The aforesaid

lord, the bishop's great adversary, had got together a large
list of supposed injuries done by him to his tenants, who
came to him (on pretence as high steward) with their complaints : which he received, in order to the doing them jus- 369
tice against the bishop.   But the bishop, as he said, had
made him his high steward, to be his friend and defender, The lord
not to hear every light and untrue tale to his infamy and high stew-
prejudice. Nor was he such an high steward, to hear causes ard, exceed-
and complaints, as he told him, and to redress them at his
pleasure. For that appertained partly to himself, and partly
to the chief justice of the isle, with the rest of the justices,
according to ancient grants to that bishopric.   But by the
perusing of that book of accusations, and the bishop's plain
answers to them, it will appear how falsely and undeservedly he was charged ; and with how much spite the accusers' minds were filled ; and governed by that Machiavel-
lian maxim, *Fortiter calumniare, aliquid adhærebit*. The
complainants were for the most part his tenants ; and their
complaints depending upon personal and private peaks
against the bishop, of supposed wrongs done them, and
brought in under the countenance of this lord. Which in
effect did but the more betray them and their evil doings,
which the bishop checked and punished : as may evidently
appear by the bishop's distinct answers, giving a true account of each matter.

After the matters for accusation of him were brought The lord
near to a ripeness, in order to the calling him into question, the bishop's
and good progress made therein, the lord treasurer plainly side. And
saw through it, and the malice thereof : and appeared to be some.
on the bishop's side. For which some of the adverse party
had not spared to blame that lord ; as siding with one who
was to be called into question by the queen's order and
commandment. For so the lord North gave it out, to palliate these his doings, that what he had done was by order
of a person that he dared not to disobey. This matter gave
occasion to his writing another letter to the said lord trea- Which oc-
surer, dated Jan. ult. importing, " How it added to the casions an-
" heap of his griefs, that the lord treasurer should be from the bi-

" charged for dealing for him. That it was true, the lord
" North had writ to him, [i. e. the bishop,] that what he
" had done, he was urged thereto by such commandment
" as he durst not disobey. Whereupon the bishop said, he
" knew and felt, *quod indignatio principiis mors est.* Yet
" considering her majesty's equity and constant benevolence
" towards her old and faithful friend, he could hardly be
" persuaded, that her highness should give order to him,
" who upon displeasure went about to seek his discredit
" and undoing. That as to his accusers, it was his desire to
" answer to them all. And that if he had injured any man,
" he would fully satisfy him. If otherwise, he had dealt
" hardly with any, he was to amend the offence. And then
" he used St. Paul's words, *Nihil mihi conscius sum, sed
" non in hoc justificatus sum.*" And then added, " That
" here he must appeal to her highness's clemency, and to
" the mercy of our heavenly Father. And that as for the
" false and slanderous accusations, [whereof there were
" good store heaped up against him,] those he referred to
" the judgment of her majesty and her honourable council.
" And so praying the Lord Jesus to preserve his lordship
370 " very long in safety to the church, [which had now so
" many enemies,] the queen, and the kingdom."

Makes his
submission
to the
queen.

At length, according to his abovesaid ingenuous offer to
the lord treasurer, he made his submission to the queen:
which he called *a satisfaction;* and which she graciously
accepted of. And so by little and little this storm blew
pretty well over. But the poor bishop was, notwithstanding, engaged with the lord North in a long suit: that lord
having gotten into his hands a lease made long before, viz.
14 Hen. VIII. Whereby all the manor of Downham was
demised by a long lease to one Meggs: whereby he pretended also to the park. The question was, whether the
park was also a part of the demise: which though it had
been hitherto enjoyed by the succeeding bishops of that
see, yet by virtue of that lease this lord claimed it.

The case be-
tween the
bishop and

The case was drawn up, and signed by both their hands,
as the true state of that controversy. And it was this:

" Whether the soil of the park passeth by the words of the CHAP.
XXXIV.
" lease, or no?" The words were : " Nicholas, bishop of Ely
" 14 Hen. VIII. made a demise to Tho. Meggs, by these Anno 1575.
" words : *Omnes terras dominicales, prat. pascua, et pastu-* the lord
North, for
" *ras, cum eorum pertinent. et commoditat. quibuscunque,* Downham
" *manerio de Downham, rectoria cum libertat. unius felde,* park.
" *advocat. ecclesiæ ibid. reddit. tenent. ibid. feod. milit.*
" *wardis. maritgagiis, relev. esceat. forisfact. perquisit. et*
" *cur. prefat. epo. et successorib. suis except. et omnin. re-*
" *servatis, habend. pro termin. octoginta annorum.* Before
" this time upon issue joined, whether Goodric, the bishop,
" had entered into part of the premises, letten, or not, evi-
" dence was given that he had entered into parcel of his
" park. And no other evidence given to prove any entry
" into any other of the demised premises. The jury
" found, that the bishop had entered into part of the de-
" mised premises.

" Richard Ely.   Richard North."

What the success and end of this lawsuit was, I know
not.

These troubles raised against the aged bishop by papists, Dr. Whit-
gift to the
bishop con-
cerning his
troubles.
puritans, and atheists, (as the bishop himself suggested,)
were of three sorts, violence, slander, and fraud ; the two
last especially. But they could not but stir up sober and
godly men to compassion and fellow-feeling with him. Thus
Dr. Whitgift, dean of Lincoln, and a prebendary of his
church, in the midst of these his disturbances, (in a letter to
him in December 1575,) prayed God " to make him strong,
" and to give him the spirit of boldness and fortitude in
" that time of his personal persecution ; for so, he said, he
" must call it, seeing, as St. Augustine saith, that the ene-
" mies of the church persecuted it after three sorts, *gladio,*
" *lingua, dolo :* and that notwithstanding the persecution
" of the sword, God be thanked, was not yet, how fierce
" the other two were, could not be unknown to any ; espe-
" cially to his lordship, who tasted of them. And that
" touching the papists in his diocese, there would not be

BOOK
I.

Anno 1575.
Dr. Ken-
net's Case of
Impropriat.
Append. p.
21.

" much done, unless his lordship called earnestly on the
" matter. For certainly, as he added, the lord North will
" bolster out that notorious papist, Mr. Perrie, as he hath
" done hitherto. Such is his zeal, &c. meaning his *pre-*
" *tended zeal* for pure religion."

———————◆———————

371   CHAP. XXXV.

> *St. John's college in Cambridge in disorder. The bishop of*
> *Ely visitor thereof: concerned therein. His advice for*
> *new statutes for that house. His letters to the lord trea-*
> *surer in that behalf. A case between Westminster school,*
> *and Christ's Church, Oxon. A sect called the family of*
> *love. Their Apology set forth. Their confession. A prin-*
> *ciple or two of theirs. The family of the Mount. The*
> *family of the Essentialists. Etchard one of this sect: his*
> *letter. Anabaptists: some recant. Two burnt: and why.*
> *Cartwright's second Reply. Sampson to the lord treasur-*
> *er, in behalf of his hospital at Leicester. Bishop Pilking-*
> *ton refuseth to grant a lease of Norham waters. Peter*
> *Baro is made lady Margaret professor in Cambridge.*

The bishop
of Ely con-
cerned in
St. John's
college, as
visitor.

OUR said bishop of Ely had other business this year,
that employed him, a little before those troubles befell him :
both as he was visitor of a college in Cambridge ; and also
as he was inspector into the regular conformity and sound
doctrine of those in his diocese. St. John's college, a great
society, was often divided into factions. And a great cause
thereof was partly the principles that many among them
embraced, thwarting the practice of divine worship used in
this church, and partly in affecting different men for their
heads, upon election. The statutes of the college also were
here and there blotted out, and interpolated. The good bishop, who, as bishop of Ely, was nominated in their statutes for the care of that house, found it past his skill and
power to settle the controversies, and confirm peace and
quiet there. And therefore thought it advisable that some
learned men of the university should be employed by public

authority, to make new statutes, and abolish the old. And CHAP.
for this purpose he recommended this needful business to XXXV.
the lord treasurer; both as he was now that university's Anno 1575.
high chancellor, and as he had been formerly a member of
that college. To him therefore, in the month of June, from June 29.
Dodington, he wrote his thoughts in a letter.

Of this business of St. John's college, some account hath Life of
been given elsewhere: to the further understanding of which Whitgift,
affair, this letter of the bishop's, as also another that follows, book i. ch.
will contribute.

" The great zeal you bear for the queen's government of Recom-
" the university of Cambridge, whereof you are high chan-matter to
" cellor, and the love you have towards St. John's college, the chancel-
" (where you sucked much good learning,) do move you, I university.
" doubt not, to be careful for the preservation of both. I
" also, being put in trust by the statutes of that college, 372
" think myself bound to conserve, as much as in me lieth,
" the quiet state of that house; and especially, having been
" somewhat disquieted now and then in pacifying of con-
" tentions and troubles; which have grown, partly through
" the folly and stoutness of unbridled youth, and partly by
" the imperfection of their statutes: which, through altera-
" tion of time, have been altered and changed, by adding
" to and taking away, by putting out and interlining.
" That in some points, their statutes, being doubtful, breed
" quarrelling and contention. For remedy whereof, if the
" statutes of St. John's might be diligently perused, ex-
" amined, and perfectly compiled into one body, certainly,
" great quietness, unity, and concord should increase, and
" continue in that college, to the glory of God, and further-
" ance of good learning.

" Sir, I am not to teach you in this matter; but if it
" please you to hear my poor advice, if ye require, or her
" majesty command, three or four doctors of the uni-
" versity, men zealous, learned, and acquainted with sta-
" tutes, to bring the said statutes into good order, and
" into a perfect volume, I doubt not, they will diligently,
" readily, and faithfully perform it. Which done, I mean

" to confer with them, and to peruse them over again.
" Then, in case your lordship hath no leisure to peruse
" them, ye might entreat her majesty, (whose godly zeal is
" always ready for the furtherance of good order,) to send
" down these statutes, by her majesty's full authority, all
" former statutes being repealed. My zeal and duty to-
" wards St. John's have moved me thus much to signify to
" your good lordship at this present, *ut sopiatur tandem*
" *contentionis malum.*"

Another
letter from
the bishop,
upon new
troubles
arising in
the college. But however new statutes were not, upon this good motion of the bishop, as yet obtained, things, by his care and
labour, were pretty well pacified in the college; and a worthy and learned master [Dr. Still] was placed. But within
five or six months, ferments began to arise again there.
Which caused another motion from the bishop to the lord
treasurer for new statutes. For in the month of December,
being then at Downham, he put that lord in mind, " That
" it was not unknown to him, in what trust the bishop of
" Ely for the time being was put by the statutes of that
" college, to visit and redress things amiss, and stay the
" house in peaceable quietness, to the intent the scholars
" there might the more diligently apply their learning, and
" use themselves in the true service of God, to his glory.
" Further, that it was not unknown to him, how painfully
" and carefully he [the bishop] had travailed at sundry times,
" to appease such controversies and unseemly contentions,
" which Satan had stirred up very dangerously in that col-
" lege. That lately, by God's grace, all things were quieted :
" a new master was well and quietly placed, a worthy,
" learned, and a zealous man. The unclean spirit was dri-
" ven out. But alas!" added he, " he beginneth to enter
" again with seven spirits worse than himself. For even at
" this present there was," he said, " a new broil like to be
" broached, unless it were met with in time. That he had
" [before this] wrote to his lordship, to lay to his helping
373 " hand : and that therein he had declared himself to be
" ready and willing : only there lacked a man to prosecute
" the cause."

He subjoined, " That the greatest cause of jars and con-
" tentions appeared to be, for that their statutes were un-
" certain and imperfect: being in some places razed, and
" some lines stricken through with a pen, as it seemed good
" to the commissioners in king Edward's time and in queen
" Mary's: who in judgment, as he knew, were diverse.
" That now sure, if it might please him to move her ma-
" jesty's gracious goodness, for a commission to certain of
" the most wise and discreet of the university: that they,
" by her majesty's authority, might stay presently all mat-
" ters of contention, and cause good order to be kept in all
" things, till such time, as by her highness' commandment,
" the statutes might be fully perused, and brought to per-
" fection: and so confirmed and ratified: and delivered unto
" the said college, from thenceforth invariably to be ob-
" served and kept. He trusted, that by such means all
" things should be stayed quietly and godly: as her gra-
" cious majesty, so tendering learning and godliness, would
" be easily inclined to such a good work.

" And that as for him, [the lord treasurer,] so endued
" with zeal towards learning, and so fatherly tendering the
" college of St. John's, he doubted not, but he would set
" forward this necessary matter, what he could. And he
" sent withal the names of those that were thought most
" meet for the commission: adding, that none of the house
" might travail in this matter, because of their oath. And
" so in the conclusion, praying the Lord Jesus to have him
" in his blessed keeping."

Those persons, which the bishop nominated to that lord, New sta-
for the inspecting the old statutes, and settling new ones, tutes made
for St.
were Dr. Pern, Dr. Harvy, Dr. Ithel, and Dr. Whitgift, all John's col-
ancient heads of colleges, and civilians also, except the last. lege.
The issue was, that by the pains and diligence of these
grave and experienced men, besides the high chancellor and
the bishop, a new set of statutes was at last framed and
established for that house.

Another college's affair occurs this year in the other uni- A case be-
versity, namely, that of Christ's Church, Oxon: which will tween
Westmin-

BOOK I.

Anno 1575.

ster school and Christ Church, Oxon.

not be out of place here to adjoin. The case was this: Tho. Ravis and Edward Carow, both educated at Westminster school, were sent this year thence to that college to be elected students. But were refused, a letter from the queen requiring or recommending another person to be received by the dean and canons. Whereupon they both wrote their letters of complaint against the college to the lord treasurer Burghley: especially that lord having sent a recommendatory letter with Ravis, when he repaired to Oxford. But Ravis finding no admission, signified to that lord his ill success, in a well-penned Latin epistle: which is dated in January. I shall give the contents of it, the rather, because he was that Ravis that was afterwards bishop of London; viz.

Ravis, a Westminster scholar, refused by the college.

"That he went with his lordship's letters to Oxford, and "delivered them, and that he had tarried there for some "time, expecting the accustomed benefit, [of Westminster "scholars,] but was forced to come back without it; *omni* 374 "*spe derelictus;* when nothing was done that the lord "treasurer required. And that the reason, when Ravis in- "quired, he found to be; that it was a matter in doubt, "whether they should prefer the statute of Westminster "school before certain letters of the queen: [who had sent "her letters to them, to elect some other person; and both "they could not do:] the resolution of which, they left to "be determined by his judgment. Ravis urged that lord "to determine in behalf of that statute of Westminster. "And that he having now a power of deciding this matter "in the behalf of poor scholars, inflamed towards the study "of learning, would do that good work to determine, *utrum* "*illa Westmonasterii schola, tua semper bonitate munita,* "*pristino eoque legitimo emolumento spolietur, ac jamdiu* "*rerum injuria, et temporum iniquitate vexata, aliquando* "*per te tuamque mansuetudinem recreetur.*"

This letter came backed the same day with another from the other scholar, Edw. Carow: telling that lord, "how "both his own hope, *et quanta omnium illius gymnasii* "*salus in te sita, et allocata sit. Non mea solum, sed totius* "*Westmonasterii jam res agitur.* And that this matter

" now in doubt was the pillar of that shop of eloquence: CHAP.
" [as he called that school.] And that if that were broken XXXV.
" or weakened, the whole house would inevitably fall, and Anno 1575.
" come flat to the ground."

The lord treasurer seemed to be on the scholars' side. Lord trea-
For in a letter that he had writ to the college, he blamed surer's letter to
them for their neglect in electing Westminster scholars : Christ's
Church
and that the year before, they admitted but one of three about the
scholars from Westminster, though they had room for more. scholars.
The dean of Westminster seemed also to have put the said
lord on to write this.

But in this reproof, the dean and chapter of Christ's
Church were concerned to vindicate themselves. And for
that purpose they sent their letters, and Mr. Dorset, one of
their canons, up to the said lord treasurer, to inform and
satisfy him, that these were false suggestions, and that his
lordship was abused with such false reports. And they desire, that master dean of Westminster, and the said Dorset,
might both appear before him; and that he would hear
both of them. The sum of their letter was:

" That the last year, 1574, they had then but one place Their letter
" indeed void : and so but one this year. And that their in answer,
in their own
" case was but ill for the most part. Because several scholars vindication.
" used to get letters from the queen, and others got them-
" selves elected. And all crowded into the college with ex-
" pectation to be admitted: and would cry out loudly
" against the college, if they were not all received; whereas
" there wanted other places and rooms for them. And then
" it may be, they, one or two of three or four that came,
" were elected. Thus at this time there were four came to
" them : two brought letters from the queen for places : and
" two others chosen at Westminster, last St. Peter's day.
" Now, what to do they consulted : and not knowing what,
" they now beseeched him, that he would direct them (see-
" ing they could place but one) which to take, and which
" to refuse. That so they might neither give cause of of-
" fence to the queen, nor seem to break the orders set down
" for Westminster."

And whereas it was also suggested to that lord, that the college could have no better choice of scholars to admit, than out of Westminster school; to this they answered, " That if they were free, they might make choice of a great " many, both poor and towardly: who were not only gram- " marians, as Westminster scholars were, but logicians of " two or three years standing: and yet could attain no bene- " fit nor standing in their college. And so in fine they " commended the whole cause between them and West- " minster to his lordship."

The sect of the family of love taken notice of.

About this time, or somewhat before, a sect that went by the name of *the family of love* began to be taken notice of. It was derived from Holland; where one H. N. [i. e. Henry Nicolas] was the founder of it. A company of these were discovered in the parish of Balsham in Cambridge-shire, the bishop of Ely's diocese. In this society was one Robert Sharp, parson of Strethal in Essex, and divers other persons of good reputation. These were taken up: but when they came to be examined before Dr. Perne, the rec-tor of that parish, they were found to be none of that sect, but suspected only: because they used to meet together on certain holydays after supper. And there they read the scriptures, and sung psalms, and conferred together upon matters of religion, and propounded questions, for the edi-fying themselves in godliness. And this these well-disposed persons did, instead of the common custom on holydays of carding and dicing, and spending the time at alehouses. And accordingly, they made a declaration and confession of this, and of their sober opinions and doctrines; and sub-

Life of Archbishop Parker, book iv. ch. 40.

mitted to authority. All which was certified, and given in by Dr. Pern, Decemb. anno 1574. The said confession and declaration we have set down at large elsewhere.

Apology of the family of love set forth this year.

But certain it is, that these that went by the name of the *family of love* did spread themselves: and about this year they set forth a book in behalf of themselves: written by one of the queen's menial servants, as the title-page pre-tended. It was entitled, *An Apology*, and presented by the author to the parliament that then was. This book was re-

printed in the times of libertinism, anno 1656, by Giles
Calvert.   It bare this title, *An apology for the service of
love, and the people that own it, commonly called,* the family of love.   *Being a plain but groundly discourse about
the right and true Christian religion.* " Set forth dialogue-
" wise, between the citizen, the countryman, and an exile.
" As the same was presented to the high court of par-
" liament in the time of queen Elizabeth: and penned by
" one of her majesty's menial servants: who was in no
" small esteem with her, for his known wisdom and godli-
" ness."   There was also set at the end of the Apology an
account of their faith, entitled, *A brief rehearsal of the belief of the good-willing in England, which are named the*
family of love; *with the confession of their upright Christian religion, against the false accusation of their against-
speakers.*   Set forth likewise anno 1575.

Herein they profess to believe the apostles' creed, as it is
used and repeated by us.   Then there follows an orthodox
confession of the Trinity, Father, Son, and Holy Ghost.
Then the confession of their religion: viz. " That consider-
" ing the great love of God towards us and all mankind: in
" that he hath created the man, like unto his own image; and
" also set him in the fulness of life ; and how that he hath
" moreover (when we were become his enemies, through
" the transgressing of his word, and children of death) yet
" further extended his love towards us, and sent his only
" Son Jesus Christ into this world.   Which hath to our
" atonement suffered the death of the cross, we ourselves
" being guilty.   When we consider all this great love ex-
" tended on us, so are we moved to love him again : stand-
" ing even so *religati,* or bound again (and so *religious*) to
" love the same God of life, with all our heart, soul, and
" might, and our neighbour as ourselves.   And for that
" cause, to the end that we might uprightly shew forth the
" same, both in the deed and truth, we read the holy scrip-
" tures of the prophets and apostles of Christ ; and all other
" books which exhort us unto such an upright life and love
" of God and our neighbours: not using any other cere-

*Their con-
fession of
their faith.*

376

" monies, laws, statutes, neither sacraments of baptism and
" supper of the Lord, than such as are ministered in the
" church of England.   And to that end, obey we also our
" sovereign lady the queen ; and the magistrates, our fore-
" goers, both spiritual and temporal.   And, that of God's
" behalf, and even for our conscience and the peace's cause.
" Paying all tribute unto these said magistrates ; living
" obediently and subject-like, even as it is meet and right,
" under their laws.   And also, dealing with all men up-
" rightly, faithfully, and charitably ; even as we ourselves
" would gladly be dealt withal at their hands; keeping like-
" wise peace with all men, so far as is possible for us.   And
" that, being told to be the fulfilling both of the law and
" the prophets, and likewise the doctrine of Christ and his
" apostles, (as is said,) contained in the Old and New Testa-
" ment.   And our conscience beareth us record, that all
" such single-minded ones ought to be defended by the go-
" vernors from injustice and tyrannical oppression.   This
" same is finally the contents of our belief, and the ground
" of our religion."

The reason
of their set-
ting forth
the same.
They assign also the reason of their setting forth this
their belief in these words, " Forasmuch as we are bruited
" and defamed with many manner of false reports and lies
" by certain malicious and slanderous persons, that never
" yet communed with us of any such thing, as they crimi-
" nate and charge us withal ; to the great defacing and
" hindering of us and our good name and fame among
" such to whom we rest as yet unknown.   For that they
" might thereby bring us into contempt and obloquy.   And
" so make us detestable and monstrous before the eyes
" of the common people.   As also have moved, with their
" slanderous reports, the spiritual rulers and magistrates, to
" cast some of us into prison; and drive us therethrough
" to great trouble and charges.   Whereas men have not
" justly to blame, accuse, detect, or burden us, as trans-
" gressors of the law: be it against any of the queen's ma-
" jesty's proceedings in causes ecclesiastical, or else in her
" political laws of government, in causes temporal.   But

" have always shewed ourselves (like as become liege sub-
" jects to do) to live and walk in all dutiful obedience loy-
" ally towards the same."

This was the fair profession and protestation they made; 377
but how they were represented in these times by others, and Represent-
who chiefly were their accusers, and what the great crimes detestable
laid to their charge were, may be learned from their said sectaries.
Apology: viz. " That they were bruited forth (and that
" chiefly by the preachers) for the most detestable sectaries
" or heretics that ever reigned on the earth; yea, and as
" people not worthy to live in a commonwealth. That they
" denied Christ, the Trinity, and the Lord's Prayer. That
" they were *libertines,* and laid with one another's wives.
" That they desired to have all men's goods in common.
" That they would have no magistrates. That they ac-
" counted whoredom, murder, poisoning, &c. to be no sin.
" That they denied the resurrection of the flesh, and the
" immortality of the soul. That they justified themselves
" by their works without Christ: and that they confounded
" the scriptures, and would not have them used; and said,
" that they lived without sin. That they were against the
" state: and that they would obey Turk, pope, or any
" other, of what religion soever, under whom they dwelt.
" And that when they were commanded of a magistrate to
" render an account of their faith, or religion, they used to
" dissemble, and meant not the same that they said."

Whether this sect of the *service of love* were of such pro- Persons of
fligate principles and practices may be doubted; but that ciples
anabaptists and libertines (of whom those crimes were too shroud
true) shrouded themselves under those of this denomination, under this
may be justly suspected.   sect.

And when this writer comes to point out who their great Their
enemies, and such as exposed them to suffering and impri- torted upon
sonment, were, he sheweth, that they were such as taught their ac-
men disobedience to magistrates and laws, and usually cited
that place of scripture, *It is better to obey God than man:*
such as drew the people's hearts from obedience to fantasies: and who, of all, were the most dangerous, and whose

own company were, by the higher powers, dealt withal for
those very things which their teachers say concerning them.
For they, indeed, were the persons that would have no governors, &c. And while they set all men to wonder at
them, [of the *family of love,*] they themselves were guilty.
And then the same apologist descendeth more particularly
to describe those that persecuted them, insomuch that they
were cast into dungeons and prisons: that they were a certain sort, that, besides other lawful officers and spiritual governors, were crept in amongst them, scattered almost the
land through; which also had gotten great stipends out of
men's benevolence; and they preached without either order
from her majesty, or any public authority; yea, and were
supposed to be to the number of four or five thousand.
And (which was further to be noted) they paid no tenths
nor subsidies. Also, they cried out against all spiritual
offices and officers, although they were found meet for that
function by learned men, and thereto had authority, by
laws and statutes confirmed; whom notwithstanding they
called, and taught others to call them, *dumb dogs,* and
sleeping hounds, with such like names. Whom to redress,
her majesty had granted commissions [ecclesiastical.] " But
" wot you what?" added he. " Those for whose reformation
378 " the same was granted have so prettily handled the mat-
" ter, that they, either by substitution of commission, or
" else by some other trick, have now to deal in the com-
" mission themselves by their own hands: and so compel
" men to yield to their dangerous attempts. By whom also
" they [of the *family*] were thus strangely handled. A
" strange metamorphosis! when the offenders against all
" laws are made judges over the true observers of all good
" laws, and reverencers of all authority."

Their opi-
nion of pre-
destination.
I will mention a principle or two which they owned, and
so leave them. The one was their judgment of *predestination.* There are two, (as they write in their Apology,) with
their members, that are predestinated, or preordained; the
one unto preservation, and the other unto condemnation,
from the beginning. The one is Christ, the man of God,

predestinated unto preservation; and with him all his in- CHAP.
corporated members.   The other is the man of sin, Anti- XXXV.
christ, predestinated unto condemnation; and in him all his Anno 1575.
incorporated members. As for any other predestination than
this, (come it out of Turkey or elsewhere,) I know not of
it.

     They allowed of going to mass.   For when the *country-* They allow-
man, one of the speakers in the dialogue, had told the *exile,* ed going to
                                                              mass.
the other speaker, that they were suspected to be superstitious papists, and that this administration, called *the service of love,* was published to the end to maintain all superstition and abuse in the Roman religion; he answered,
that in truth, so far forth as he could perceive, the author
of those books, [viz. H. N.] in the ministration of love, did
neither maintain nor allow of any manner of superstition
frequented in the Roman or popish church: but indeed he
seemed so to open and disclose the first ground of the same
religion, and the signification of every thing, [i. e. by favourable allegories,] as well their sacraments as ceremonies;
as willing that every one that should happen to dwell where
the same were by the laws of the land allowed, and being
commanded to obey their rulers and their laws, and for
obedience sake not to rebel in any case, that they rather
should go to church where the same were administered;
and there to make mark only upon the signification of the
same, and what a Christian life and obedience to God and
governors, the same, in their right signification, do ask and
require of them.   And yet he acknowledged them no otherwise but as sacraments, ceremonies, signs, images, figures,
or shadows of good and holy things.   But, however, he put
the countryman out of doubt, that they utterly detested
[notwithstanding this compliance] all superstitious papistry.
By these passages and hints, we may understand what sort
of men and principles this *family,* or *service of love,* in these
days consisted of.   And which appeared again openly in
the time of the anarchy in the last age: now, I think, extinct.   For I remember, a gentleman, a great admirer of
that sect, within less than twenty years ago, told me, that

BOOK I.

there was then but one of the *family of love* alive, and he an old man.

Anno 1575.
Some of the family recant.
Stow's Annals.

But notwithstanding the above fair representation of themselves, their practices and opinions were found so erroneous and dangerous, that five of them recanted at Paul's Cross in the month of June.

379

Other sects by the name of families.

Divers other odd sects, about these times, bearing pretty fantastical names, had their proselytes: as the family of the *mount*, the family of the *essentialists*, &c. All which seemed to be no other than some subdivision and slips of the family of *love*. And of these, some were ministers. Of these was one John Etchard, minister of Darsham in Suffolk; and another was John Eaton. I shall give the reader some strictures of a letter of the former, without date, but, as it seems, near this time, with some mention of the latter. I met with it in the Paper Office at Whitehall. On the backside whereof was endorsed, *Pseudapostolical.* It beginneth thus:

Etchard, one of this sect, his letter.
Paper-Office.

" To all you faithful in Christ Jesus; saints by calling; " justified by his blood and righteousness, and sanctified " by faith in him; that take the Lord Jesus to be your " wisdom, righteousness, sanctification, and redemption: " grace, mercy, and peace to you from God our Father, " and from the Lord Jesus Christ. When the apostle Paul " foresaw that he was ready to be offered up, and the time " of his departure was at hand, he said, *I have fought a* " *good fight,* &c. So likewise the faithful servant of Jesus " Christ, Mr. John Eaton, that planter with Paul, and fa- " ther of many children, &c. For to your knowledge he " begat many in the faith, and the Lord blessed his la- " bours," &c. In the margin of this letter is added this note: *John Eaton was divers years questioned and cen- sured by the high commission, for maintaining, that God cannot see sin in the justified.* And then, applying those words of St. Paul to himself, speaking to Timothy, " *Thou* " *hast fully known my doctrine, manner of living, purpose,* " *faith, long-suffering, love, patience, persecutions, afflic-* " *tions, which came upon me at London, Norwich, and*

" *Wickham.   Which persecutions I suffered.   But from*
" *them all the Lord delivered me,* &c.   You, believers, are
" dead to sin before God, and buried also, as you are bu-
" ried with him in baptism.   And as men do not use to
" mortify him that is dead and buried already, so believers
" do not take away their sins out of God's sight by morti-
" fication ; because they are dead and buried unto sin be-
" fore God in Christ already, by God in baptism.   So that
" though we, by virtue of the Spirit, do mortify our mem-
" bers upon earth, yet the Spirit of God doth know that
" their sin is pardoned, washed away, and put out of God's
" sight ; covered, and not imputed.   Which all signify the
" same thing ; that is, perfect remission of sin."   By which
words he seemed to hold no sin in God's people.

The sectaries of the *family of the mount* held all things The family
common, and lived in contemplation altogether ; denying of the
all prayers, and the resurrection of the body.   They ques- Mount.
tioned, whether there were an heaven or an hell, but what is Paper-
in this life.   And they said, that what the scriptures spake Office.
of, was begun and ended in men's bodies here, as they do
live.   As heaven was, when they do laugh and are merry ;
and hell, when they are in sorrow, grief, or pain.   And
lastly, they believed that all things came by nature.   This
was acknowledged by one that had been of their society, to
be held by them when he kept them company ; and many
other things as bad, or worse.

The *family of the essentialists* had their opinions from 380
one Mrs. Dunbar, a Scotch woman.   These held there was The family
no sin at all : but what is done, God doth all, in what kind of the Es-
soever it be.   One Lockley, a tailor, one of these, used to sentialists.
say, *Sin? What sin, man? There is no man sinneth at all.*
He said further, in contempt of the holy altar in the church,
where the Lord's supper is celebrated, that the altar did
stand like a cook's dresser-board.   This man had many
meetings up and down, and would spend 20*l.* or 30*l.* at a
sitting.

These, and the like, were the spawn and improvements H. Nicolas's
of this *family of love;* of the which, Henry Nicolas, of Hol- books, the
ground of
o o 2   these sects.

BOOK land, was the founder: whose books and writings were
I. brought over hither, and translated; and secretly dispersed
Anno 1575. and sold, as wonderful discoveries. One of them was his
Rules of Perfection; especially his book called *Theologe
Germane.* There were of them in Latin MSS. And one
Fisher, a barber, wrote them out, and sold them, after (as
it is likely) they were translated into English. In these
papers, whence I extract these things, there were also set
down the names of those of the sects, and the places where
they dwelt. Which were undoubted the confessions of some
of them brought before the commissioners ecclesiastical.

Anabaptists   The anabaptistical sect, that sprang from Germany, was
condemned,
submit.   now not uncommon here, especially such as were of the
Dutch nation. This year, five of them, condemned for heresy, submitted themselves; namely, Hendric Ter Woort,
Gerard Van Byler, Jan Peters, Hans Vanderstrate, ——
Hemels. Confessing now to believe Christ's incarnation,
the baptizing of children, the office of magistrates, to be necessary, and owning the lawfulness of swearing. The form
of their recantation and penance at Paul's Cross is set down
Stow's   by John Stow, under this year; being performed by them
Annals.   there on Easter-day. Yet I find two anabaptists were burnt
Two are
burnt : and   in Smithfield not long after, viz. July 22; namely, John
why.   Wielmacker and Hendrick Ter Woort, (who it seems had
recanted before, if it were the same,) after that they had
been sixteen weeks in prison. The privy council would not
spare them, notwithstanding the earnest intercession of the
Dutch MSS. Dutch congregation, for divers weighty reasons laid before
them. But the chief causes of their executions were, because they would not own them for Christian magistrates,
and had been banished a year before.

Cart-   But the sectaries of most account, and that created the
wright's
Second Re-   state most trouble, were those that followed Tho. Cart-
ply comes   wright, and others of that sort, who, condemning the episco-
forth.   pal government of the church, laboured the overthrow of
the bishops and their revenues, and much of the form of
the liturgy established and used. Some account hath been
given elsewhere of his writings in behalf of the *Admonition*

to the parliament, and against the learned books of Dr. CHAP.
Whitgift, confuting that Admonition, and in vindication of ____XXXV.____
this church.   The said Cartwright's last book, wherein he Anno 1575.
had the last word, (called his *second Reply to Dr. Whitgift,*) Life of
came out this year, printed (as it seems by the letter) in Whitgift.
Holland.   This hath been sufficiently taken notice of in
Archbishop Whitgift's Life.   I shall only here observe the Book i.
haughty and abusive spirit of the man, by two or three 381
passages in the said *second Reply.*   Whereof this was one:
" Because the answerer [i. e. Whitgift] will yield no obe-
" dience unto the truth, unless she take him by the collar,
" and have her hand upon his throat, the fondness of the
" collection shall thus appear unto him."   This was his expression against a period of Dr. Whitgift's, who, disliking an
inference of Mr. Cartwright's, had called it a *pretty and
fond collection.*

Again ; " I doubt whether, for the vanity of his accusa-
" tion, I should vouchsafe it of answer, which, for his strong
" and bitter words, might seem to require a large defence."
Again ; " If I had met with the vainest trifler and hawker
" after syllables which can possibly be, yet the sentence I
" set down is sufficiently fenced against all his greediness of
" snapping at it."

Once more; " Mr. Doctor, seeking busily to hide his naked-
" ness, findeth not so much as a fig-leaf to cover his shame
" withal ; nay, in seeking a hole to hide it, hath met with a
" hill, to shew it further off."   This is a specimen of Cartwright's way of writing, and treating his adversary : who
thought not fit to give that Reply any answer, when it was
come thus to words.

It was the favour of the times towards Cartwright, and Sampson,
others of that sort, who could not (or would not) come in the hospital
to serve in the church of God as public ministers, to permit at Leicester,
them to enjoy places of another nature than parochial cures ; well of it.
as hospitals endowed; and they dispensed with therein. Thus
as the aforesaid Mr. Cartwright was master of an hospital in
Warwick, and Lever another near Durham, so Dr. Sampson
had the hospital in Leicester, wherein, to his commendation,

he was very useful in respect of his care of it: and twice
did good service to it, for its good estate, and the preservation of its revenues.   Which he did by his interest with, and
application to, the good lord treasurer.   It was a few years
before in danger of ruin by the decays of it, which was remedied by the favour and interposing of that lord.   And
now, certain tithes granted to it for the maintenance of hospitality there, by a long lease from the abbey of Leicester,
had been begged by some, after the expiration thereof;
which would have sunk the rents of the hospital much.
Whereupon Sampson, in the month of October, thus applied himself in a letter to the treasurer, by the hand of
another, himself being lame of the palsy ; (wherein the state
and case of the hospital will appear.)

His letter
in behalf
of it.
Paper-
Office.
" That the experience which he had of his favour towards
" that hospital in a great matter (as himself knew) truly
" tried, did encourage him in another matter of less mo-
" ment, by humble suit to assay his favour again for it.
" The case was this: the founders of that hospital had by
" testament at their deaths bequeathed unto it one lease of
" a tuyth [tith] of one field, lying by Leicester, called *the*
" *south field ;* which they had taken of the abbey of Leicester
" standing.   The yearly rent of which tuyth was 5*l.* 6*s.* 8*d.*
" which was from time to time received there [at the hos-
" pital] by one Mr. Hunt; who, as he understood, was an
" accountant in the exchequer.   That the founders had in
" this wise left the same for a necessary maintenance of hos-
382 " pitality unto this poor hospital.   And that so it had been
" continued unto that day.   In which said lease, granted by
" the abbot, this house had yet nigh thirty years to come, to
" enjoy: but that such was the unsatiableness of some minds,
" that (as he was credibly informed) one which was toward
" an office, made an assured account among his friends, that
" he had already gotten this tuyth by lease in reversion,
" and thinketh in short space to make an entry into the
" same.

" Indeed, my good lord, (as he proceeded in his letter,)
" for my own part, I need not to be greatly careful here,

" considering the length of the term, which is yet to come,
" to the use of this hospital; as, if it pleased his honour, he
" might see by the lease itself, which he had committed to
" the keeping of the bearer thereof, Mr. Frauncis Hastings;
" whom he had, he said, also desired, in his defect, to be
" their procurator in this behalf, to his honour. That as
" the founders had both carefully and charitably conveyed
" that lease by testament to this hospital, for maintenance of
" relief and hospitality therein, so would he [Sampson] be
" right glad to procure, by such means as he could, that
" this same their charitable devise might still continue ac-
" cordingly. And loath would he be, to have the same cut
" off in his time.

    " And therefore he was in this behalf humbly to make
" two suits to his honour; the granting of one of which
" should suffice: either that this hospital might have this
" lease, which now it enjoyed, confirmed, and the term of
" years augmented by her majesty, under her great seal of
" the exchequer; or else, that it might please her highness,
" by his lordship's favourable procurement, to grant this
" same tuyth to this hospital for ever, paying to her high-
" ness, her heirs and successors, the annual rent of 5l. 6s. 8d.
" And that if either of these might through his goodness
" be procured to this hospital, he would bind it to pray for
" him, as for a singular benefactor; not only for repairing
" of it, when it was in danger of ruin and decay, but also
" for this recovering of this poor maintenance; without
" which it must needs decay. And thus hoping for his
" favourable answer by Mr. Francis Hastings, the bearer
" hereof, he humbly took his leave, recommending him to
" the grace of God. Dated from Leicester, October the
" 28th, 1575."

    And it appeared how ready the lord treasurer was to do
this good thus moved: for an act was procured, (undoubtedly by this means,) the parliament now sitting, for confirmation of this hospital. And the bill being brought down
from the upper house, was the next day read the first, second, and third time, and passed. So quick a despatch it

Act for the
hospital at
Leicester.

D'Ewes'
Journal,
p. 252.

BOOK I.   had, that the publisher of the journal of that parliament set this note at it, *Quod nota.*

Anno 1575.   As Dr. Sampson had thus betaken himself to the lord

Bishop Pilkington applies to the treasurer for a favour to his see.   treasurer for his hospital, so, for some other favours, did Pilkington, the good old bishop of Durham, do, (the last year of his life, and the last time we shall hear of him,) to this common patron of the clergy and their causes. The one was relating to his office as treasurer, viz. that he, [the bi-

383   shop,] for preventing the trouble of his sending the clergy's tenths, and the danger of robbery by the way, might pay them in at Berwic, as the other bishops in those parts did. The other matter which he desired of his lordship was, to know how his answer for the lease that was required of him, for the fishing in the bishop's waters at Norham, was taken; to be made, it seems, for the benefit of some courtier: which he would not yield to, to the injury of the bishopric. Tho. Barnes, his next successor, did. Surely, added he, the state of that place is miserable, and would be looked to without delay. And so concluded, praying the Lord of hosts to strengthen the weak body of his lordship, long to serve him, to the comfort of his people. I add this the rather, it being the last I find of this pious, apostolical bishop and confessor.

Peter Baro, a foreigner, made Margaret professor.   By the means of this kindly affectioned nobleman, Peter Baro, a French protestant, of good learning, fled from his own country, for avoiding the persecution, was made this year the lady Margaret's professor of divinity at Cambridge: and held the said lecture to the year 1596; when he resigned it, foreseeing, that, for maintaining some doctrines about *universal grace,* he could not hold it much longer. His cause, and Barret's of Caius college, may be seen at large in a MS. sometime belonging to archbishop Whitgift, now lodged in Trinity college, Cambridge.

CHAP. XXXVI.

The lord treasurer suspected by the queen to favour the
queen of Scots.   His thoughts thereof in a private letter
to the earl of Shrewsbury.   News at court.   The prince
of Orange offers the queen the Low Countries.   Addresses
to her from France and Spain.   Divers fly hither from
the Low Countries.   New privy counsellors.   A project
for translating of bishops.   The state of Ireland.   The
good service of the earl of Essex there.   Nic. Morton,
the pope's great factor : his family.   Their treasons and
conspiracies.   A deappropriation.   Knights' fees, and re-
lief, due from the earl of Salop.   The queen's progress.

THIS good lord Burghley, the great patron and asylum Anno 1575.
of learned and pious men, met himself with great difficulty The queen suspects the
at this time by means of the queen's jealousy, as though he treasurer's
secretly favoured the Scottish queen against her; which favour to-
some of his back-friends at court had buzzed in her majesty's Scottish
ears in his absence at Buxton well, where, with the queen's queen: and why.
leave, he was gone for his health sake.   This some had busily
persuaded the queen was but a pretence, that he might
thereby meet the Scottish queen, and privately confer with
her.   By the likelihood whereof, it took its effect with the 384
queen.   But when he perceived this by her behaviour towards him, it created him great anxiety.   And in truth he
was in danger of her frowns, and consequently thereupon of
more and greater harms.   This he wrote very privately,
upon a particular occasion, to the earl of Shrewsbury, who
now had made an offer of marrying his son to that lord's
daughter: which he therefore declined at that juncture,
lest it might more confirm the queen in her suspicion, since
this earl was that queen's keeper at this time.   And therefore, that he might not seem to slight so honourable a favour offered him by the earl, and so draw on him his displeasure, and yet decline the motion at present, he, with his
own hand, gave him to understand his present circumstances, to this purport :

BOOK
I.

Anno 1575.

His letter
to the earl
of Shrews-
bury there-
upon.

" That he could not sufficiently express in words his in-
" ward, hearty affection, that he conceived by his lordship's
" friendly offer of the marriage of his younger son; and
" that in such a friendly sort, by his own letter, and pro-
" ceeding from himself. Now, as he thought himself much
" beholden to him for this his lordship's kindness, and ma-
" nifest argument of a faithful good-will, so must he pray
" his lordship to accept his answer, with his assured con-
" tinuance in the same towards him. That there were espe-
" cially two causes, why he did not in plain terms consent
" by way of conclusion hereto. The one, for that his
" daughter was but young in years; and upon some rea-
" sonable respect he had determined (notwithstanding he
" had been very honourably offered matches) not to treat of
" marrying of her, (if he might live so long,) until she should
" be above fifteen or sixteen. And that if he were of more
" likelihood himself to live longer than he looked to do, she
" should not, with his liking, be married before she were
" eighteen or twenty. But the second cause why he de-
" ferred to yield to conclude with his lordship, was grounded
" upon such a consideration, as, if it were not truly to satisfy
" his lordship, and to avoid a just offence which his lord-
" ship might conceive of his forbearing, he would not by
" writing or message utter, but only by speech to himself."
And then he proceeded to the cause in these words :

" My lord, it is over true, and over much against reason,
" that upon my being at Buckston's last, advantage was
" sought by some that loved me not, to confirm in her ma-
" jesty a former conceit, which had been laboured to be
" put into her head, that I was of late time become friendly
" to the queen of Scots, and that I had no disposition to
" encounter her practices. And now, at my being at Bux-
" ton's, her majesty did directly conceive, that my being
" there was, by means of your lordship and my lady, to enter
" into intelligence with the queen of Scots. And hereof, at
" my return to her majesty's presence, I had very sharp re-
" proofs for my going to Buxton's, with plain charging of
" me for favouring the queen of Scots; and that in so

" earnest a sort, as I never looked for, knowing my inte-
" grity to her majesty; but especially, knowing how contra-
" rious the queen of Scots conceived of me, for many things
" past, to the offence of the queen of Scots. But it was
" true, as he continued, that he never indeed gave just cause
" by any private affection of his own, or for himself to
" offend the queen of Scots; but that whatsoever he did, 385
" was for the service of his own sovereign lady and queen:
" which, if it were yet again to be done, he would do, he
" said. And that though he knew himself subject to con-
" trary workings of displeasure, yet would he not, for re-
" medy of any of them, both decline from the duty he owed
" to God, and his sovereign queen. For he knew, and did
" understand, that he was in this contrary sort maliciously
" depraved; and yet in secret sort on the one part, and that
" of long time, that he was the most dangerous enemy and
" ill-willer to the queen of Scots! on the other side, that he
" was also a secret well-willer to her and her title, and that
" he had made his party good with her."

Whereupon he makes this reflection: " Now, my lord,
" no man can make both these true together. But it suf-
" ficeth for such as like not me in doing my duty, to de-
" prave me; and yet in such sort it is done in darkness, as
" I cannot get opportunity to convince them in light. In
" all these crossings, my good lord, I appeal to God, who
" knoweth, yea, I thank him infinitely, who directeth my
" thoughts to intend principally the service and honour of
" God, and jointly with it the surety and quietness of my
" sovereign lady the queen's majesty. And for any other
" respects, but that may tend to these two, I appeal to God
" to punish me, if I have any. As for the queen of Scots,
" truly I have no spot of evil meaning to her; neither do I
" mean to deal with any titles to the crown. If she shall
" intend any evil to the queen's majesty, my sovereign, for
" her sake, I must and will mean to impeach her; and
" therein I may be her unfriend, or worse."

And then turning to the private matter between them,
that gave occasion to all his discourse above, he subjoined:

" Well, now, my good lord, your lordship seeth I have
" made a long digression from my answer.   But I trust
" your lordship can consider what moveth me thus to di-
" gress.   Surely, it behoveth me not only to live uprightly,
" but to avoid all probable arguments that may be gathered,
" to render me suspected of her majesty, whom I serve
" with all dutifulness and sincerity.   And therefore he ga-
" thered this, that if it were understood that there were a
" communication, or a purpose of a marriage between the
" earl's son and his daughter, he was sure there would soon
" some advantage be sought to increase these sinister sus-
" picions.   For which purpose, considering the young years
" of their two children, and supposing the matter were fully
" agreed between them, the parents, yet, since at present
" the marriage could not take effect, he thought it best to
" reserve and keep this motion in silence.   And yet so to
" order it with themselves, that when time should hereafter
" be more convenient, they might, and then also with less
" cause of vain suspicion, renew it.   And in the mean time
" he must confess himself much bounden to his lordship for
" his goodness ; wishing his son all the good education that
" might be meet to teach him to fear God, to love his lord-
" ship, his natural father, and to know his friends without
" any curiosity of human learning ; which, without the fear
386 " of God, he saw did great hurt to all youth in that time
" and age."   And so this wise and wary nobleman concluded, praying him to bear with his scribble, which he
thought his lordship would hardly read ; and yet he would
not, he said, use his man's hand in such a matter as this
was.   Dated from Hampton-court, the 24th of December,
1575.

News at
court.
Epist. D.
Com. Salop.
    The news at court now was, (as I take it from a letter of
Francis Talbot, then at Hampton-court, to the abovesaid
earl of Shrewsbury, his father,) " That the matter of
" choosing counsellors remained doubtful, but daily it was
" looked for, that some new ones should be chosen, [several
" of the old ones being by this time dead.]   That there
" were ambassadors now at court from France, both from

" the king and monsieur, [duke d'Alançon, who joined him-
" self with the-protestants in those civil wars and confu-
" sions then in that kingdom.] That there was a bruit that
" monsieur was poisoned ; but no advertisements were come
" to the contrary. That he had referred his cause to be
" dealt in by her majesty, between him and his brother the
" king. How her majesty would please to deal in it was
" not yet known : but the ambassadors made show of desire
" to be despatched. That sir Henry Cobham was there,
" returned out of Spain, with answer of his message."
[Which was to persuade that king to make peace with the
Netherlanders, shewing him how dangerous their revolt
would be, especially the French being solicited to assist
them ; which the queen herself was jealous of.]

He went on with his news; " That there was come one
" from the prince of Orange, out of the Low Countries,
" with a couple of chief merchants of Flanders, to make
" offer of the country, to be defended, into her majesty's
" hands. And that if it would please her to keep it, they
" would betake themselves to merchandry, and pay her ma-
" jesty such tribute as before they paid to the king of Spain.
" And that they also required speedy answer. That the
" council were all at the court. That the city daily, and
" the ambassadors, came to them : and the ambassadors had
" had audience twice. That her majesty was troubled with
" these causes; which made her very melancholy, and
" seemed greatly to be disquieted. And what should be
" done in these matters, as yet it was unknown. But she
" heard the ambassadors on all sides ; who laboured greatly
" one against another. And that her majesty had it put
" unto her, to deal both between the king of Spain and the
" Low Countries, and the king of France and his brother.
" And that her majesty might deal as it pleased her: for
" he thought they were both weary of the wars, especially
" Flanders ; which, as the report went, was utterly wanting
" of money, munition, and powder: and therefore had of-
" fered their country to the queen's majesty." This was
dated from Hampton-court the 4th of February, 1575; and

BOOK
1.

Anno 1575.

Foreigners
fly hither
from Flan-
ders : desire
to be mem-
bers of the
Dutch
church.

387

Ruytinck's
Journal.
Librar.
Dutch Ch.

New per-
sons ad-
mitted to
the privy-
council.

subscribed, *Your lordship's loving and most obedient son,*
Frauncis Talbot.

And such, indeed, was the sad condition of the people of
the Low Countries at this time, that great numbers of them
had fled over hither, and desired to join with the Dutch
church in London, and to become members thereof. Yet
so tender was the queen of breaking with that proud and
powerful prince, the king of Spain, that she would not admit
of this, nor give countenance to such as fled away out of
these countries under his subjection. For it is remarkable
what is set down and recorded in a journal of the Dutch
church in London, written by Simeon Ruytinck, one of
their ministers in those times, and yet preserved in their
church : " That when divers foreigners had come hither on
" account of religion, and desired to be admitted in com-
" munion with the rest of the Dutch church, the queen
" hearing of it, commanded the lord mayor to disperse them
" from London. Whereupon they applied to the bishop of
" London, to represent their case to the queen and coun-
" cil." Who did so. And the council sent a letter in answer to the said church, June 29, 1574, in favour, that that
church should advise those new members to depart from
London, [where they were more obvious to be taken notice
of by king Philip's spies,] and to go to other parts of the
kingdom ; [where there were also churches of protestant
professors.] Which that church did accordingly.

Whereas mention was made above in Mr. Talbot's letter
concerning the discourse at the queen's court of some new
privy-counsellors ; the reason thereof was, because by this
time a great many of the old ones were dead, and likewise
of the old nobility. I find among the lord Burghley's MSS. a
paper of his own handwriting, containing the names of such
as were dead, and such as still remained alive, and also of
such as were thought fit, by reason of their great possessions,
to be received into the rank of the nobility : which I make
no doubt was to be laid before the queen. First, there be
set down the names of noblemen and knights, and other
gentlemen, counsellors in the time of king Edward, from

the first of that king, that were dead, forty in number. And only four in this year, 1575, remained alive; viz. Henry earl of Arundel, Edward earl of Lincoln, William lord Burghley, and sir Ralph Sadler. And of the catalogue of queen Mary's council, which were twenty-one, two only remained then alive, viz. archbishop Hethe and sir Francis Englefield. Likewise of queen Elizabeth's counsellors, six were dead; viz. Thomas duke of Norfolk, sir Edward Rogers, sir Tho. Parry, sir Ambrose Cave, sir Richard Sackvile, and Dr. Wotton. Remaining alive, lord keeper Bacon, lord treasurer Burghley, Thomas earl of Sussex, lord chamberlain, Edward lord Clinton, lord admiral, Henry earl of Arundel, Ambrose earl of Warwick, George earl of Salop. So that there were but seven old privy-counsellors, of the nobility, alive.

There was now also, upon the death of Matthew Parker, archbishop of Canterbury, deliberation had about the translation of the bishops, for the advancing them to better sees. The reason whereof, whether for their encouragement, or with an eye rather to the benefit arising to the treasury by first-fruits, I do not determine. Some respect, it seems, was had to the latter, because in the catalogue drawn up, the first-fruits of each bishopric is noted. And it seems probable to have been propounded to the treasurer. I shall here give a transcript of this paper, entitled, *A note, how the bishoprics in England may be transferred without any just cause of much offence to the bishops. November* 1575.

A project for translating the bishops to other sees.

York to Canterbury - - per annum.	3093 18	9
London to York - - - - - - -	1609 19	2
Durham to Ely - - - - - - - -	2134 18	8
Ely to Winchester - - - - - - -	2491 9	8
Winchester to Durham - - - - -	1821 0	6
Norwich to London - - - - - -	1109 8	4
Sarisbury to Norwich - - - - - -	899 8	7
Worcester to Sarisbury - - - - -	1367 11	8
Lincoln to Worcester - - - - -	1049 17	3
Bath to Lincoln - - - - - - -	894 18	1

388

Gloucester to Bath - - - - - - -	533	1	3
Exeter to Gloucester - - - - - -	315	7	3
Litchfield to Exeter - - - - - -	500	0	0
Hereford to Litchfield - - - - - -	703	5	2
Chichester to Hereford - - - - -	768	10	10
Carlisle to Chichester - - - - - -	677	1	3
Peterborough to Carlisle - - - - -	531	4	11
Chester to Peterborough - - - - -	414	19	11
Chester; to be never placed, being void,	420	1	8
Rochester; to be never placed, being void	358	3	7

Bangor
St. Asaph's   } to stand still, because they be but poor,
St. David's   } and in Wales.

This was the device of somebody, unknown, (surely,) to raise money out of the church and churchmen, for the queen, or rather for themselves; and for that end, to swallow up the revenues of two bishoprics wholly.

The state of Ireland; in a letter from the master of the rolls there. Oct. 27.

For the present state of affairs in Ireland, I shall relate them from a letter of sir Nicholas White, master of the rolls there, to the lord Burghley; written from Waterford in the month of October. " And now to follow my promise of " advertisement to your honour, I will briefly touch some " things of the matters of this state; and that freely without " mistrust: because I know to whom I write, and have also " determined to write of certainties that I know: and in " the rest to utter but mine opinion. And first, touching

Earl of Essex.

" the earl of Essex, [general of the queen's forces in Ire- " land,] I find, that he hath brought the north of Ireland " to a manifest appearance of reformation; when the great- " est there were contented to accept some small portions, to " yield both rent and duty for the same: and, I doubt not, " with the expenses of a little more time and charges, would " have reduced that province [of Ulster] to perpetual obe- " dience." [The queen, it seems, had now, in the middle of his successes, sent for him home. It was by the instiga- tion of the earl of Leicester; who afterwards had him sent over again, and got him poisoned.]

" But (as White went on) what good thing can be hoped

" for here, when a prince's determination, touching so great
" an enterprise, in the hands of so sufficient and so honour-
" able a subject to perform it, shall be so suddenly re-
" voked. And if I might with all humility say it to her
" highness, there are two things of great moment that seem
" strange to us here, if they be true. The one is, the
" letting of the realm [of Ireland] to farm; wherein so
" many hearts may be alienated from the landlord to the
" farmer. And the other is, the casting up of the earl's en-
" terprise betwixt the fallow and the seed : which will make
" Ulster desperate, and all the rest doubtful. And truly, if 389
" she look not back where she began, and revey both the
" man and the matter, she shall puff up the Irish into in-
" corrigible pride, and pull down the hearts of all good
" English subjects, to a perpetual diffidence of any settled
" government in this realm." And he addeth, to the honour of that earl, " There cannot go out of this land a
" man with greater fame of honour, nor can come in, whose
" bounty hath deserved more. And if that noble mind of
" his, desirous of honour, and so careless of gain, were em-
" ployed, with the association of grave council, I believe,
" God hath ordained him to do great things. But here I
" leave him, and the success of all his causes, to God's holy
" will. I told sir William Fitz-Williams mine opinion
" touching the earl of Kildare, who deserveth well to be
" corrected, but hardly to be cut off for any traitorous in-
" tent against the prince, howsoever covetousness might
" move him to envy the gain of captains here."

About this year I meet with some account of the family
of Nicolas Morton, priest, a notable busy factor for the pope
in England in these times : who stirred up the rebellion in
the north, anno 1569. headed by the earls of Northumberland and Westmorland; and who was sent from Rome, to
pronounce queen Elizabeth an heretic, and thereby to have
forfeited her crown and kingdom. One Afferton, in the
north, was apprehended about this time, and so closely examined by Topcliff, (a great instrument of the queen's for
discovering of popish traitors and treasons,) that he was

Nic. Mor-
ton, a priest,
his rela-
tions; and
their con-
spiracies.

Topcliff
bringeth
Afferton to

brought to reveal strange conspiracies. He was servant to
Sampson Morton, nephew to the said Nicolas : which Nicolas, and Robert his brother, were the sons of Charles
Morton, of Bautree, esq. that married the daughter of
Dalyson ; whose race was universally papists, descended as
well by the man as woman. This Charles married three
wives : the first was Plumpton, of Plumpton, esq. ; the second was a daughter of Norton, sister to the two rebels of
that name, Richard and Thomas, and sister to the mother
of Thomas Markamvil, the rebel ; his third wife was Olive,
first wife to Thurland, another great papist. One of which
family was Thurland, master of the Savoy, discovered to be
a priest, and outed. Sampson and Daniel, sons of the said
Robert, and nephews to Nicolas, this year, or the next, fled
over to their uncle, upon the apprehending of the said
Afferton : who revealed the desperate conspiracies, as well
of that priest's resorting into England, as of his sending
and receiving intelligence to and from the north, and other
matters of weight ; and that these were notorious lewd papists,
and ready to execute any act of mischief.

The said Robert had also, beside Sampson and Daniel,
another son elder to them, a fugitive too, and married to a
sister of Edmund Thurland : which Edmund was described
to be a man altogether Hispaniolized, being brought up in
Spain, and living an obscure life, as did his brother Robert
Morton. He also was a good space with his uncle Nicolas,
a fugitive at Rome ; and brought over from thence strange
intelligence, and continually hath done. His resort was to
Bautree, and lived obscurely there at that town of danger, being open to all parts of England and Scotland, being within
390 half a mile of the highway. He used to ride secret and suspect journeys to the sea-coast, and to and from the north, as
Plumpton, Cleveland, &c. It was situate within fifteen or
sixteen miles of Sheffield-castle, where the queen of Scots
was kept ; [and so conveniently placed to take an opportunity of favouring her escape, or otherwise for carrying intelligence.]

This was a dangerous nest in the north. And those of

the gang were under the guidance of this notorious bi- CHAP.
gotted priest, Nicolas Morton, who fled to Rome presently XXXVI.
after her majesty's coronation; and still both resorted into Anno 1575.
England, and sent messages hither, as he used to do before
the rebellion. His arrival and taking ship was at Grimesby,
a port fit for his purpose, and at Boston. And his place of
stay was Bautree aforesaid, a dangerous place, where he was
born, and where his nephews also harboured.

I shall insert into this history one particular matter, which The church
how little soever it may be thought, yet because of the of Staplegrove deap-
strangeness and rarity of it may deserve to be recorded. propriated.
It was the *deappropriation* of an impropriation in the dio- Regist.Bath
and Wells.
cese of Bath and Wells; which was restored back to the
church by Dier, lord chief justice in the reign of king Philip
and queen Mary; and by James Dier and his heirs for ever
made presentative, or presentable lawfully, and by royal
authority. It was the church of Staplegrove juxta Taunton. And James Dier, knt. and capital justiciar of the
bench, presented Chr. Dyrling thereunto, Sept. 17, void by
the death of Walter Gardiner.

The earl of Shrewsbury was called upon this year, by the Knights'
fees, due
chancellor of the duchy of Lancaster, for certain knights' from the
fees, due from him to the queen, and likewise for his relief, earl of Salop.
upon the death of the earl his father; which were behind- Ex Offic.
hand unpaid for some years. And to shew the manner of Armor.
these payments to the crown in these times, I will set down
a letter sent in March to the said earl, by the said chancellor
Sadleir, and G. Bromley, attorney-general, viz. " That it
" would like his lordship to understand, that whereas he did
" hold of her majesty, as of her castle and honour of Tick-
" hil, parcel of her duchy of Lancaster, in the county of
" Nottingham, the manor of Wirkson, with the members of
" the same, by the service of five knights' fees and the
" fourth part of a knight's fee; for the which his lordship
" was to pay yearly unto her majesty, for his respect of
" homage of and for the same, the sum of thirty-five shil-
" lings, after the rate of 6s. 8d. for every knight's fee: and

" also where his lordship was to pay more unto her majesty,
" for his relief, due after the death of my lord his father,
" the sum of 26*l.* 5*s.* after the rate of an hundred shillings
" for every of the said knight's fees. Which said several
" sums, as they did understand, were not yet satisfied, nor
" paid by his lordship to the feodary of the said castle, ac-
" cording to an extract to him delivered, for the collection
" thereof, among others, under the seal of the said duchy.

" These were therefore to desire his good lordship to give
" order for the payment of the said several sums unto the
" hand of Thomas Bulbak, her majesty's feodary there; or
" else, if by the search of his evidence he should find any
" good matter for the discharge thereof, or of any part or
" parcel thereof, it might please his lordship to send some
391 " one, the next term, sufficiently instructed, to satisfy the
" court of the duchy in that behalf. From the duchy
" house at the Savoy, the 1st of March, 1575." Subscribed
by R. Sadleir and G. Bromley.

The queen's progress this summer was towards Warwick-
shire; of which, and of her most splendid reception by the
earl of Leicester at Kenelworth-castle, I find not a word
in our historians, except a short mention of it in the additions to the late edition of Camden's Britannia; an account
whereof may well deserve a place here. There is a particular relation of it, which I have seen; writ at that time by
way of letter, from an officer, attendant then at court, to a
friend of his, a citizen of London, printed upon thin vellum.
The writer was Rob. Lanham, gent. clerk of the council-
chamber door; the person written to was Humfrey Martin,
mercer. The purport whereof was as followeth :

The queen's
progress.
" That the entertainment was so great and noble, that for
" person, place, time, cost, devices, strangeness, and abun-
" dance of all that ever he saw, and wherever he had been,
" in France and Flanders, long, and many a day, he never
" saw anywhere so memorable as this.

Her recep-
tion at Ke-
nelworth-
" The 9th of July, (being Saturday,) at Ichingham, a
" town and lordship of the earl of Leicester's, within three

" miles of Killingworth, [Kenelworth,] he, the said earl, CHAP.
" made the queen a great cheer at dinner, and gave her XXXVI.
" pleasant pastime, in hunting by the way after dinner: so Anno 1575.
" that it was eight o'clock before she came to Killingworth; castle, by
" where, in the park, about a flight shot from the brays, and Leicester.
" first gate of the castle, one of the ten sibyls, comely clad A sibyl.
" in a pall of white silk, pronounced a proper poesy in Eng-
" lish rhyme and metre, in effect, how great gladness her
" gracious presence brought into every steed, [i. e. place,]
" where it pleased her to come; and especially now into
" that place, that had so long longed for the same.   Ended
" with prophecy certain, [as the sibyls were *fatidicæ*,] of
" much and long prosperity, health, and felicity. This the
" queen graciously accepting, passed by the next gate of
" the brays, which they called *the tiltyard*, for the length,
" largeness, and use.

    " Here a porter, tall of person, big of limbs, stark of The porter.
" countenance, wrapt all in silk, with club, and keys of
" quantity according, in a rough speech, full of passion in
" metre, while the queen came within his ward, burst out in
" a great pang of impatience, to see such uncouth trudging
" to and fro, such riding in and out, with such din and noise
" of talk, within his charge; whereof he never saw the like,
" nor had any warning once, ne yet could make to himself
" any cause of the matter: at last, upon better view and ad-
" visement, as he pressed to come nearer, confessed anon,
" that he found himself pierced at the presence of a person-
" age, so evident expressing an heroical sovereignty over all
" the whole estate.   This calmed his storms, proclaims open
" gates and free passage to all; yields over his club, his
" keys, his office, and all; and on his knees humbly prays
" pardon of his ignorance and impatience. Which her high-
" ness graciously granting, he caused the trumpeters, that 392
" stood upon the walls of the gate there, to sound up a tune
" of welcome.

    " These trumpeters, six in number, every one eight foot Trumpet-
" high, and in due proportion of person beside, all in long ers.

" garments of silk suitably, each with his silver trumpet, of
" a five foot long, formed taper-wise, and strait from the
" upper part unto the nether end ; where the diameter was a
" sixteen inches over, and yet so tempered by art, that being
" very easy to the blast, they cast forth no greater noise,
" nor a more unpleasant sound for time and tune, than any
" other common trumpet, be it never so artificially framed.
" These harmonious blasters began from the foreside of the
" gate, at her highness' entrance, and walked upon the
" walls, unto the inner, making their music ; while her high-
" ness, all along this tiltyard, rode unto the inner gate, next
" the base court of the castle.

" And here the *lady of the lake*, famous in king Ar-
" thur's book, [for there was a fine lake near this castle,]
" with two nymphs waiting upon her, arrayed in silk, at-
" tended her highness' coming, fleets to land, from the
" midst of the pool, upon a moveable island, blazing with
" torches ; meeteth the queen with a well penned metre,
" consisting of the auntienty of the castle ; who had been
" owners of the same even till this day, and were for the
" most part earls of Leicester : how she had kept this lake
" since king Arthur's days ; and now, understanding of her
" highness' coming hither, thought it her office in humble-
" wise to discover herself, and her estate, offering up to the
" same her lake and power therein, with promise of repair
" unto the court. The queen thanked this lady ; and to
" add withal, We had thought, indeed, the lake had been
" ours. And do you call it yours now ? Well, we will
" herein common more with you hereafter.

" This pageant was closed up with a delightful harmony
" of hautboys, shalms, cornets, and such other loud music,
" that held on whilst she passed from thence toward the
" castle-gate. Whereunto, from the base court, over a dry
" valley, cast into a green form, was framed a fair bridge of
" a twenty foot wide, and a seventy foot long, gravelled for
" treading, railed on either part, with seven posts on a side,
" that stood a twelve foot asunder, thickened between with

" well proportioned pillars, turned. Upon the first pair of
" foot long, two foot wide, and high ———. In them live
" bitterns, curlieus, shovelards, hernshaws, godwits, and
" such dainty birds, of the brats of Sylvanus, the god of
" fowls. On the second pair, two great silver bowls, fitted
" for the purpose, full of apples, pears, cherries, filberts,
" walnuts, fresh upon their branches; and with oranges,
" pomegranates, lemons, and pippins; all the gifts of Po-
" mona, the goddess of fruit. The third pair of posts, in
" two such silver bowls, had all in ears, green and old,
" wheat, barley, oats, beans, and pease, as the gifts of Ceres.
" The fourth post on the left hand, on a like silver bowl,
" had grapes in clusters, white and red, graced with their
" vine leaves. The match post against it had a pair of
" great white silver livery-pots, for wine; and before them
" two glasses, of good capacity, filled full, the one with white 393
" wine, and the other with claret; so fresh of colour, and of
" look so lovely smiling to the eyes of many, that by their
" leering they could have found in their hearts, as the even-
" ing was hot, to have kissed them sweetly: and these the
" presents of Bacchus, the god of wine. The fifth pair had
" each a fair large tree, strawed a little with fresh grass;
" and in them conger, burt, mullet, fresh herring, oysters,
" salmon, crevis, and such like, from Neptune, the god of
" the sea. On the sixth pair of posts were set two ragged
" staves of silver, as my lord [earl of Leicester] gives them
" in arms, beautifully glistering, with armour thereupon de-
" pending, brass arrows, spear, shield, head-piece, gorget,
" corslets, swords, targets, and such like, for Mars his gifts,
" the god of war: importing the protection of her highness'
" person, that was so kindly pleased here to take her har-
" bour. On the seventh posts, the last, and next to the cas-
" tle, were pight two fair bay branches, of a four foot high,
" adorned on all sides with lutes, viols, shalms, cornets,
" flutes, recorders, and harps, as the presents of Phœbus,
" the god of mirth, for rejoicing the mind; and also of phy-
" sic, for health to the body.

BOOK I.

Anno 1575.

" Over the castle gate was fastened a table, beautifully
" garnished above with her majesty's arms, and set with ivy
" wreaths, bordered about, of a ten foot square: the ground
" black: whereupon, in large white capital Roman, fair
" written, was a poem, mentioning these gods and their gifts,
" presented unto her highness, and was as followeth :

Verses over
the castle
gate.
The capitals
here were
inscribed in
gold.

Ad majestatem regiam.

Jupiter huc certos cernens TE *tendere gressus,*
Cælicolas, PRINCEPS, *actutum convocat omnes.*
Obsequium præstare jubet, TIBI, *quemque benignum :*
Unde suas Sylvanus aves, Pomonaque fructus :
Alma Ceres fruges, hilarantia vina Lyæus :
Neptunus pisces, tela et tantantia Mavors :
Suave melos Phœbus, solidam longamque salutem :
Dii TIBI, REGINA, *hæc, cum sis* DIGNISSIMA, *præbent*
Hæc TIBI, *cum Domino dedit se et Werda Kenelmi.*

The poet's
habit.

" These verses were pronounced by a poet, in a long ce-
" rulacious garment, with side and wide sleeves, Venetian-
" wise, drawn up to the elbows. His doublet sleeves, under
" that, crimson; nothing but silk: a bay garland on his
" head, and a scroll in his hand; making first an humble
" obeisance at her highness' coming, and pointing unto
" every present, as he spake.

The queen
lights.

" And so she was received with a fresh delicate harmony
" of flutes. And so she passed into the inner court; and
" there she lighted down from her palfrey, and was con-
" veyed up to her chamber. After followed a great peal of

Fireworks.

" guns, and lightning by fireworks, a long space together ;
" as though Jupiter would shew himself to be no further
" behind with his welcome than the rest of the gods; and

394 " that he would have all the country know. For in-
" deed the noise and flame was heard and seen twenty
" miles off.

Sunday
kept.

" On Sunday, the forenoon was occupied (as the sab-
" bath-day) in quiet and vacation from work, and in di-
" vine service, and preaching at the parish church. The

" afternoon, in excellent music of sundry sweet instru- CHAP.
" ments, and in dancing of lords and ladies, and other wor- XXXVI.
" shipful degrees, uttered with lively agility and commend- Anno 1575.
" able grace.

" At night, late, after a warning piece or two, [as Ju-
" piter's respects to the queen,] were blazes of burning
" darts, flying to and fro; beams of stars coruscant; streams
" and hail of fiery sparks; lightning of wildfire in water
" and land; flight and shot of thunderbolts; all with con-
" tinuance, terror, and vehemency, as though the heavens
" thundered, the water scourged, and the earth shook. This
" lasted till after midnight.

" On Monday, being hot, she kept in till five a clock even- She hunts
" ing; and then went forth in the chase, to hunt the hart, in the
chase.
" &c. And so from Monday to Tuesday, and all the other
" days, was entertained with variety of sports and pleasure,
" till Sunday, when they went to church, and heard prayers
" and a sermon. And in the afternoon sports again.——
" That afternoon, [as the relater expresseth it,] in ho-
" nour of this Kenelworth-castle, and of God and St.
" Kenelme, (whose day by the kalendar this was,) was a
" solemn country bridal, with running at quintin. The
" queen stayed here nineteen days, entertained all the while
" with recreations, speeches, plays, &c. till July 27."

While she was here at Kenelworth, she knighted Thomas Knights
Cecill, the lord treasurer's son; Henry Cobham, the lord made.
Cobham's brother; Thomas Stanhope, Arthur Basset, and
Thomas Tresham, men of great worship all.

And she also touched nine of the king's evil. Which is Toucheth
thus expressed by this writer: " That of her mercy and for the
king's evil.
" charity, nine were cured of a painful and dangerous dis-
" ease, called *the king's evil*. For the kings and queens of
" this realm, without other medicine, (save only by handling
" and prayer,) only do cure it."

Concerning Kenelworth-castle, and some of the prepara- Ammu-
tions made by the earl against the queen's coming thither, nition
brought
one in those times writes; " That in this castle there was to Kenel-
worth-
castle.

" sufficient to furnish ten thousand soldiers, of all things
" necessary for horse and man; besides all munition and
" artillery, brought thither when her majesty was there,
" never carried back again."

THE END OF VOL. II. PART I.

Lightning Source UK Ltd.
Milton Keynes UK
28 March 2011

169985UK00001B/65/P